HIDDEN®
Coast of California

HIDDEN®

Coast of California

Ray Riegert

SEVENTH EDITION

Ulysses Press®
BERKELEY, CALIFORNIA

Published by: ULYSSES PRESS
              P.O. Box 3440
              Berkeley, CA 94703-3440

ISSN 1523-5769
ISBN 1-56975-170-6

Printed in Canada by Transcontinental Printing

20 19 18 17 16 15 14 13 12 11 10

UPDATE AUTHOR: Stephen Dolainski
EDITORIAL DIRECTOR: Leslie Henriques
MANAGING EDITOR: Claire Chun
PROJECT DIRECTOR: Natasha Lay
COPY EDITOR: Steven Schwartz
EDITORIAL ASSOCIATES: Lily Chou, Marguerite Clipper,
   Jen Anderson, Tom Hinds
TYPESETTER: David Wells
CARTOGRAPHY: Claire Chun, Phil Gardner, Rob Harper
INDEXER: Sayre Van Young
COVER PHOTOGRAPHY:
   FRONT: Robert Holmes (Lost Coast,
   Humboldt County)
   CIRCLE: Chuck Place (Malibu Pier)
   BACK: Larry Ulrich (Little Harbor Campground,
   Catalina Island)
ILLUSTRATOR: Victor Ichioka

Distributed in the United States by Publishers
Group West, in Canada by Raincoast Books,
and in Great Britain and Europe by World
Leisure Marketing

For Keith and Alice

Acknowledgments

Despite all the road trips and research, writing represents only a fraction of the effort that went into this book. It's the people back home who carried it through to completion. My wife and co-publisher Leslie worked on every phase of the project—planning, designing, coordinating, correcting, overseeing, and polishing the prose. The volume is a testimonial to her talents. I owe her a world of gratitude for her diligence and devotion.

Claire Chun did a brilliant job in coordinating the production.

I also want to thank Natasha Lay, Lily Chou, Steven Schwartz, Marguerite Clipper, Jen Anderson, and Tom Hinds for their editorial assistance; David Wells for the typesetting; and Sayre Van Young for her comprehensive but accessible index.

*

Ulysses Press would like to thank the following readers who took the time to write in with suggestions that were incorporated into this new edition of *Hidden Coast of California*:

Dolores Austin of Escondido, CA; Barry and Dolores Bell of British Columbia, Canada; Brenda J. Chapel of San Francisco, CA; Carol Craddock of Foothill Ranch, CA; Giles Kirk Davis; Betsy & Jim Driebeek of Hamden, CT; Adam Gileski and Jon Rosky; Robert M. Hausman of Washington, DC; Henry K Kawamoto, Jr.; Gilbert W. Keech of Chevy Chase, MD; Juli Kelen of Olympia, WA; Angela Lepito; Mrs. Monica T. Livingston of Tucson, AZ; Chris Miller of Los Gatos, CA; Taylor Morris of Scottsdale, AZ; Rob Perelli-Minetti; Donna Sample of San Jose, CA; Geri Snyder of Ann Arbor, MI; Dr. Richard J. Stone of Great Britain; Michelle Stuckey of Los Angeles, CA; Gregory Stephen Taylor; David Williams of Carlsbad, CA.

What's Hidden?

At different points throughout this book, you'll find special listings marked with a hidden symbol:

◄ HIDDEN

This means that you have come upon a place off the beaten tourist track, a spot that will carry you a step closer to the local people and natural environment of the Coast of California.

The goal of this guide is to lead you beyond the realm of everyday tourist facilities. While we include traditional sightseeing listings and popular attractions, we also offer alternative sights and adventure activities. Instead of filling this guide with reviews of standard hotels and chain restaurants, we concentrate on one-of-a-kind places and locally owned establishments.

Our authors seek out locales that are popular with residents but usually overlooked by visitors. Some are more hidden than others (and are marked accordingly), but all the listings in this book are intended to help you discover the true nature of the Coast of California and put you on the path of adventure.

Write to us!

If in your travels you discover a spot that captures the spirit of the Coast of California, or if you live in the region and have a favorite place to share, or if you just feel like expressing your views, write to us and we'll pass your note along to the author.

We can't guarantee that the author will add your personal find to the next edition, but if the writer does use the suggestion, we'll acknowledge you in the credits and send you a free copy of the new edition.

ULYSSES PRESS
3286 Adeline Street, Suite 1
Berkeley, CA 94703
E-mail: readermail@ulyssespress.com

Contents

Maps

OUTDOOR ADVENTURE SYMBOLS

The following symbols accompany national, state and regional park listings, as well as beach descriptions throughout the text.

▲	Camping		Waterskiing
	Hiking		Windsurfing
	Biking		Canoeing or Kayaking
	Horseback Riding		Boating
	Swimming		Boat Ramps
	Snorkeling or Scuba Diving		Fishing
	Surfing		

ONE

The Coast of California

California. The word comes from an old Spanish novel about a mythic island populated by Amazons and filled with gold. It was, according to the author, "very near to the terrestrial paradise." The first part of this magical land to be explored, and the area which still symbolizes the California dream, is the coast.

Stretching 1100 miles along the rim of the Pacific, it is a wildly varied region with sharp mountains and velvet beaches, barren sand dunes and rich estuaries. Los Angeles, San Francisco, and San Diego, three of the nation's largest cities, are here, together with the old mission centers of Santa Barbara and Monterey. There are small fishing towns and international shipping ports, Victorian neighborhoods and oceanfront mansions.

Powerfully influenced by early Spanish culture, the coast today is responding to a fresh influx of Mexican immigrants as well as a growing Asian population. It is a region both at the edge of the continent and at the cutting edge of the global shift toward Asia and the Pacific Rim.

The California shore is also one of the most popular travel destinations in the world. Tens of millions of visitors explore its byways and beaches every year. *Hidden Coast of California*, the only guidebook to deal exclusively with this amazing territory, is an attempt to make the entire area accessible to everyone.

For those seeking the good life, each chapter describes the hotels, restaurants, shopping places, and night-owl roosts that dot every town along the coast. There is information on transportation, bicycling, and water sports. Then, when the spirit of adventure takes hold, there are descriptions of secluded beaches, remote hiking trails, and sightseeing spots both famous and unknown.

Beginning in San Francisco, *Hidden Coast of California* explores Northern California first and then moves on to Los Angeles and the southern coast. San Francisco is described as a port city, with special emphasis on its Pacific shoreline and magnificent bay. The North Coast chapter, extending from Marin County all the way to the Oregon border, ranges through redwood forest, along twisting country roads, and high above sharp ocean cliffs.

Then, venturing south from San Francisco, the North Central Coast and South Central Coast chapters contain a string of oceanfront mission towns—Santa Cruz, Monterey, San Luis Obispo, Santa Barbara and Ventura—as well as the magnificent coastline of Big Sur.

The many faces of Los Angeles are uncovered to reveal Long Beach with its island neighborhood and industrial complex, the tumbling Palos Verdes Peninsula, the blond-haired surf cultures of the South Bay, bohemian Venice, and ultra-chic Malibu. Moving south into Orange County, the book scopes out the surfing scene at Huntington Beach, then sweeps through Newport Beach and Laguna Beach. Finally, it takes in the sparkling bays and historic neighborhoods of San Diego.

The entire coastline is a land of rare opportunity, where visitors can stay in art deco hotels or quaint country inns, bivouac on the beach or dine on fresh California cuisine. A multicultural extravaganza as well as a region of extraordinary beauty, the California Coast is a place for creative travelers, those anxious to combine the easy life of cities with the challenges of the open ocean in a place very near indeed to "the terrestrial paradise."

▼▼▼▼▼▼▼▼▼▼▼▼▼▼▼▼

The Story of the Coast

GEOLOGY

Things are never what they seem. Trite though that adage might be, it perfectly fits the California Coast. Lined with softly rolling hills and bounded by a pacific sea, the shoreline is actually a head-on collision between the edge of the ocean and the rim of North America.

Two tectonic plates, those rafts of land that float upon the earth's core, meet in California. Here the North American Plate and the Pacific Plate push against each other in a kind of international arm wrestle. Between them, under colossal pressure from both sides, subject at any moment to catastrophic forces, lies the San Andreas fault, villain of the 1906 San Francisco earthquake.

Things were not always as they are. About 150 million years ago, the coast rested where the Sierra Nevada mountains reside today. Then the North American Plate shifted west, riding roughshod over the Pacific Plate, compressing and folding the earth upward to create the Coast Ranges, and moving the continent 100 miles westward.

Just 25 million years ago, a blink of the eye in geologic time, the Pacific Plate shifted north along the San Andreas fault, creating the Central Coast from what had been part of Baja. This northerly movement continued, building pressures of unimaginable magnitude, and formed the Transverse Range five million years ago.

As a result of this continental shoving match, modern-day California comprises three distinct regions. In the south, the Peninsular Range, built of granite, runs from the tip of Baja to the Los Angeles basin.

After a journey of a thousand miles along the Pacific coast, the chain is broken by the Transverse Ranges, those unusual mountain formations which run east and west rather than north to south. Formed of 1.7 billion year old gneiss, among the oldest rock in North America, the mountains reach to Point Conception, the geographic dividing point between Northern and Southern California.

To the north rise the Coast Ranges, a series of sharp mountains which resume the march from south to north. Built of shale, sandstone, and other sedimentary rocks, the Coast Ranges extend all the way up the San Francisco peninsula, through Northern California to Oregon.

Today the San Andreas fault reaches the coast just south of San Francisco, then cuts north through Stinson Beach, Bodega Bay, and Point Arena, before heading seaward from Shelter Cove. Meanwhile the Pacific Plate, carrying Los Angeles, is shifting north along the North American Plate, which holds San Francisco, at a pace that should position the rival cities next to each other in about ten million years. Anyone planning to hitch a ride north should pack extra sandwiches and prepare for a long wait at the side of the road.

AMERICAN INDIANS

Before the advent of European settlers as many as 300,000 American Indians inhabited California. Of the 50 groups present, 16 lived along the coast and on offshore islands. Far to the south were the Diegueño; the Chumash occupied the South Central Coast while Costanoan Indians dominated the North Central Coast. North of San Francisco the coast Miwok, Pomo, and Athabascan language groups held sway. In the northwest corner of the state the Wiyot, Yurok, and Tolowa fished offshore waters.

They were hunter-gatherers, exploiting the boundless resources of the ocean, picking wild plants, and stalking indigenous animals. Primitive by comparison with the agricultural tribes of the American Southwest, coastal tribes chipped obsidian points for arrows, fished with hooks and nets, and used harpoons to spear migrating salmon.

Dwellings were basic, dome-shaped, and fashioned from woven grasses and wooden poles. Each village included storehouses, a ceremonial lodge, burial grounds, and individual quarters, as well as a *temescal*, or sweat lodge, that served as a kind of American Indian men's club.

Men did the hunting, women gathered and cooked, and everywhere village life centered around the family. Polygamy was practiced and wives were purchased. The religious life of the community was conducted by shamans, who "cured" diseases by sucking out the illness. In some places jimsonweed was used to induce visions and became the basis of a cult.

Richer and more sophisticated than inland tribes, the coastal Indians themselves varied greatly. Language barriers were all but insurmountable. There were 21 different language families in California, further divided into dialects, often mutually unintelligible. Natives of San Diego could not understand Indians a few miles away in San Luis Rey.

Yet they fought less than American Indians elsewhere on the continent and went to battle for revenge rather than plunder. When they did war—fighting with clubs, bows, and rocks—they were known to torture enemies and slaughter women and children.

Among the more advanced coastal tribes were the Chumash, who established an elaborate system of trade. Sailing in wood-planked canoes called *tomols*, they commuted to the Channel Islands and bartered with neighbor tribes. Other Indians used tule balsa canoes built from rushes; and along the open, rocky coast around Humboldt Bay, the northwestern California tribes hollowed canoes from redwood trunks.

These northerly tribes, greatly influenced by the rich cultures of the Pacific Northwest, hunted sea lions, spearing them with harpoons that carried barbed points of bone and antler. They also developed social classes and, like the Chumash, established a more elaborate social system.

Otherwise they were much like the tribes all along the California Coast, weaving beautiful baskets, making ceramics, and fashioning jewelry from shell and coral. They gambled, smoked tobacco, and used beads as currency. And everywhere they looked to the sea as provider and destroyer, drawing their livelihoods from its waters. They fished, canoed, dove, and gathered shellfish —rich, plentiful quantities of shellfish, which archaeologists later found in refuse mounds 30 feet deep, mounds that represented thousands of years of simple life along the California Coast.

HISTORY   **DISCOVERY AND EXPLORATION**   If the story of the world starts at the creation, the history of California begins with Juan Rodriguez Cabrillo. The year was 1542 and Cabrillo, a Portuguese navigator in the employ of the Spanish crown, sailed north from

KILL THE CARTOGRAPHER!

Sebastian Vizcaíno, who charted and named much of the California coast, so grossly exaggerated the harbor of Monterey that his mapmaker was eventually hanged. Vizcaíno's 1602 story of this perfect port proved so distorted that when Juan Gaspar de Portolá, exploring California by land in 1769, saw Monterey, he failed entirely to recognize it.

Mexico, pressing forward the boundaries of empire. Seeking the elusive Northwest Passage, he tacked up the coast of Baja, landing in San Diego, then pushed on to Santa Catalina Island, Point Conception, Monterey, and Point Reyes.

For years Spanish conquistadors in Mexico had pursued El Dorado, a mythic land ruled by a king whose people covered him in gold dust. Francisco Vasquez de Coronado trekked off seeking the Seven Cities of Cibola while from his base in Mexico City Hernan Cortes sent expeditions north from Mexico City in pursuit of untold wealth. Though they found neither fabulous kings nor gilded cities, Cabrillo had discovered a new land, Alta California, which he promptly claimed for the Spanish crown.

To world powers, even unpromising land is a prize to be coveted. The British, determined to thwart Spanish conquests in the New World, harried the Spanish and encouraged privateers to plunder their galleons. Sir Francis Drake, the most famous of these adventurers, happened upon the coast in 1579, possibly landing at Point Reyes and, naturally, claiming the territory for England.

This outpost of empire, known to the British as Nova Albion, proved more significant to the Spanish. Since their ships, laden with luxurious goods from the Philippines, passed California en route to Mexico, they began seeking ports of call. In 1587 Pedro de Unamuno anchored at Morro Bay. Eight years later Sebastian Rodriguez Cermeño, a daring seaman, swept down the coast past Cape Mendocino, lost his ship to a ferocious storm in Drake's Bay, then pressed on with 70 men in an open launch.

THE MISSIONS To the early explorers, all California was one grand disappointment. It was a region that promised rich gold discoveries, but delivered none, was rumored to contain a Northwest Passage, but did not, and which was desolate, dangerous, and difficult to reach. The British virtually ignored it and the Spanish took more than two centuries to even begin colonizing the place.

Then in 1769, as Portolá and Padre Junípero Serra ventured north to establish the first mission in San Diego, the California dream began. Portolá continued on to Los Angeles, and following a route which would become the fabled El Camino Real, reached San Francisco Bay, perhaps the first explorer to discover the site. Later Captain Juan Bautista de Anza opened the territory farther north.

But it was Father Serra, the hard-driving Franciscan missionary, who penned the early chapter in the history of the coast. Between 1769 and 1823, he and his successor, Padre Fermin Francisco de Lasuen, established a chain of 21 missions from San Diego to Sonoma. Fortified with presidios, they became the backbone of Spain's Colonial empire.

Serra's dream of a New World became a nightmare for American Indians. Devastated by European diseases, they were forcibly converted to Catholicism and pressed into laboring on the missions. While their slaves were dying in terrible numbers, the Spanish, dangerously overextended, were beleaguered with other problems throughout the empire. In 1821 Mexico declared its independence and Alta California, still numbering only 3000 settlers, was lost.

MANIFEST DESTINY   Abandoned and ignored for centuries, the California Coast was becoming an increasingly vital area. British ships had re-entered the Pacific in force and by 1812 the Russians, lured by the region's rich fur trade, built Fort Ross on the Sonoma coast. More important, the United States, asserting itself as a commercial power, was dispatching New England harpooners in pursuit of California gray whales. Whaling stations were built in San Diego, Palos Verdes, and farther north along the coast in Monterey and Bolinas.

Meanwhile the Mexican government secularized the missions in 1833, distributed the land to early settlers and American Indians, and ushered in the era of the *ranchos*. These generous land grants, often measuring 75 square miles and lining the narrow coastal strip once occupied by the missions, became huge cattle ranches. Merchants from New England traded pewter, copper, and jewels for animal skins as a lucrative trade developed. Hides came to be known as "California banknotes," and Richard Henry Dana, sailing along the coast in 1834, immortalized the industry in *Two Years Before the Mast*.

Gazing round him at the rich ocean and undeveloped shore, Dana remarked that "In the hands of an enterprising people, what a country this might be!" The thought was occurring increasingly among Americans, who tried unsuccessfully to buy California from Mexico. Manifest Destiny was on the march, wagon trains were crossing the Sierra Nevada with pioneers, and even the interior valleys were filling with Americans.

Finally in 1846 American settlers, with assistance from the United States government, fomented the Bear Flag Revolt. Colonel John Charles Fremont seized San Francisco while Commodore John D. Sloat took Monterey. Just two years before precious metal was finally found in Spain's fabled land of gold, the stars and stripes flew over California.

THE GOLD RUSH   On January 28, 1848, a hired hand by the name of James Marshall discovered gold in the Sierra foothills, revealing how near the Spanish had come to their vision. But the yellow metal that lured and eluded the conquistadors proved to be located not along the coast they had settled but far to the interior.

The California Dream was realized. For anyone with courage and ambition, it represented a chance to blaze trails and become rich in the flash of a fortuitous find. Gold became the currency of Manifest Destiny, drawing 100,000 people across an implacable land and creating a civilization on the fringes of a continent.

San Francisco became the capital of that civilization. The town's population exploded with prospectors and a wild Barbary Coast ghetto grew along the Bay. Over 500 businesses sold liquor; gambling, drugs, and prostitution were rampant; gangs roamed the boom town and iron-fisted vigilance committees enforced law and order. Sailors were shanghaied and failed prospectors committed suicide at the rate of 1000 per year.

The North Coast, filled with lumber needed in the gold mines, also flourished. Mills and settlements by the hundreds were established and every cove became a shipping port. Mendocino, Fort Bragg, Eureka, and other timber towns soon dominated the area.

> By 1850, about 500 ships, whose fickle crews had deserted for the gold fields, lay abandoned in San Francisco Bay.

The Gold Rush not only brought prospectors and loggers to Northern California: many of America's finest writers were soon mining literary material. Mark Twain arrived during the 1860s, as did local colorist Bret Harte. Ambrose Bierce excoriated everyone and everything in his column for William Randolph Hearst's *Examiner*. In 1879, Henry George published a book in San Francisco called *Progress and Poverty*, which propounded a revolutionary system of taxation. Robert Louis Stevenson explored the Bay Area a few years later, and Jack London used it as a setting for his adventure tales.

THE INDUSTRIAL AGE   By the time the continental railroad connected the California Coast with the rest of the country in 1869, Southern California trailed far behind its northern counterpart. Los Angeles, the largest town in the region, numbered 6000 people. During the 1870s the south began to rise. The Southern Pacific railroad linked San Pedro and Santa Monica with the interior valleys where citrus cultivation was flourishing. Southern California's rich agriculture and salubrious climate led to a "health rush." Magazines and newspapers romanticized the region's history and beauty, leading one writer to proclaim that "if the Pilgrim fathers had landed on the Pacific Coast instead of the Atlantic, little old New York wouldn't be on the map."

San Diego, Santa Monica, and Santa Barbara became fashionable resort towns, and the port of San Pedro expanded exponentially, making Los Angeles a major shipping point. Around the turn of the century Henry Huntington, nephew of railroad baron Collis P. Huntington, established the Pacific Electric Railway Company. Within a few years this ruthless and creative businessman revolutionized the beach towns of Los Angeles. Buying tracts along the coast, then extending his red trolley line to one coastal town after another, Huntington became wealthier than even his uncle, creating in the process a land boom and population explosion up and down the coast.

The fishing industry, developed by the Chinese between 1860 and 1880, proved as lucrative as tourism and shipping. While Huntington was wresting control of the coast, local Portuguese, Japanese, Italians, and Yugoslavs were forcing the Chinese from the offshore fishing grounds.

When oil was discovered early in the 20th century, Southern California also became a prime drilling region. Oil wells sprang up along Huntington Beach, Long Beach, and San Pedro, adding to coastal coffers while destroying the aesthetics of the shore. The Signal Hill field in Long Beach, tapped by Shell Oil in the 1920s, became the richest oil deposit in the world and Los Angeles became the largest oil port. Little wonder that by 1925, flush with petroleum just as the age of the automobile shifted into gear, Los Angeles also became the most motor-conscious city in the world. The Pacific Coast Highway was completed during the 1930s, "auto camps" and "tourist cabins" mushroomed, and motorists began exploring the California Coast in unprecedented numbers.

MODERN TIMES   Meanwhile San Francisco, long since recovered from the horrific 1906 earthquake that shattered the San Andreas fault and rocked the coast, was becoming a strategic military area. During World War II the Navy also developed port facilities in San Diego. Coastal defense bases grew at Camp Pendleton, Vandenberg, Point Mugu, Fort Ord and in Marin County.

This rush to protect the coast turned into a kind of social mania in 1942 when the United States government, in one of the most racist acts in its history, ordered the "relocation" of 93,000 Japanese Americans. Stripped of their rights, they were removed from coastal regions where, it was charged, they could aid the Japanese Empire. In fact the only attack on the coast occurred when a lone submarine lobbed a few shells at an oil field near Santa Barbara, doing minor damage to a wooden pier.

After the war, development of another sort became the order of the day. Homes and businesses sprouted up along the entire coastline. Los Angeles became the nation's second largest metropolis, and California, 80 percent of whose residents live within 30 miles of the coast, became the most populous state.

This unbridled development, combined with the 1969 Santa Barbara oil spill and plans for a controversial nuclear power plant in Diablo Canyon, led to the creation of the California Coastal Commission. Established by California voters in 1972, this watchdog agency has succeeded in slowing development and preserving the natural beauty of the shoreline.

Also in 1972, Congress established the Golden Gate National Recreation Area in and around San Francisco. Then, just six years later, it created the Santa Monica Mountains National Recreation Area in Southern California.

The years from the 1970s to the early 1990s were marked by both natural disasters and cultural accomplishments. On nature's side of the balance, drought conditions prevailed all along the coast during the mid-'70s and for a five-year span beginning in the 1980s. El Niño, a warm ocean current, disrupted weather patterns during this period and forced southern marine life species to migrate north. Then in 1989 a monstrous earthquake struck the San Francisco Bay Area, followed by other destructive temblors on the North Coast in 1992 and in the Los Angeles region in 1994.

Culturally, the era saw the 1984 Olympics come to Los Angeles and the state-of-the-art Monterey Bay Aquarium open along the Central Coast. The California Conservation Corps began its crucial environmental work in 1976, and during the next decade Congress provided legislation for Channel Islands National Park and a marine sanctuary around the Farallon Islands. Then, during the 1990s, the U.S. Army moved out of the Presidio, a spectacular 1400-acre park in San Francisco. This entire complex, with its historic structures and forested hills, became part of the Golden Gate National Recreation Area.

By the time the conservation movement began to flex its muscle, however, California had already demonstrated—through its tourism, ports, oil deposits, aircraft industry, construction trade, and fishing fleet—that the gold sought centuries before by Spanish explorers did not lie in the hills, but along the state's extraordinary coastline.

The Life of the Coast

FISH & FISHING

The poet William Butler Yeats wrote of "the mackerel-crowded seas," oceans filled with a single species. Along California's lengthy coastline, in the shallow waters alone, over 250 kinds of fish thrive. Most are small, exotically colored creatures, which in an entire lifetime barely venture from their birthplace. Others, like the king salmon and steelhead trout, live off the Northern California coast until summer and fall, then run upstream for miles to spawn in freshwater.

Among California's other well-known species are halibut, surf perch, and rockfish, found along the entire coast, and game-fish like barracuda, yellowtail, and bonito, which inhabit the kelp beds of Southern California. There are also bluefin tuna, albacore, and Yeats' fabled mackerel.

Most famous of all is the shark, 30 species of which prowl California's coastal waters and bays. While none particularly savor human flesh, all but a few are carnivores, and do periodically leave their teeth in divers and surfers. The great white shark, a fearful beast which grows to 25 feet in length, is now a common resident along the coast, where it feeds on sea lions, seals, and sea otters.

Methods for catching these different species are about as numerous as the fish themselves. There's surf casting, rock fishing, poke-pole fishing in tidepools, trolling and deep-sea fishing from party boats. Fishing licenses are required of everyone over 16 years old, except people fishing from public piers. Regulations and information can be obtained from the Department of Fish and Game. ~ 1416 9th Street, 12th floor, Sacramento, CA 95814; 916-653-7664.

SHELLFISH   Crustaceans and mollusks, those hard-shelled characters we usually encounter only in biology class and later in life on the dinner table, abound along the California coast. Among the crustaceans are lobsters, crabs, prawns, and shrimps, while the local mollusks include mussels, oysters, squid, clams, and abalone.

California spiny lobsters live on the coast of Southern California, inhabiting rock crevices by day and foraging at night for mollusks and fellow crustaceans. Rock crabs, another crusty crustacean, dine in turn on abalone, picking apart their shells. In the endless chain of carnivorous consumption, rock crabs, particularly the large Dungeness variety, end up in local restaurants.

Most common among the mollusks is the mussel, a black-shelled creature that grows in clumps along rocks and pilings. Several species of oyster inhabit the area, the most common being the Pacific oyster, introduced from Japan. Then there are the squid, considered shellfish because of their small internal shells. Caught at night with the help of floodlights, they are among the region's most important commercial catches.

Several species of clams proliferate along the coast, such as soft-shell, gaper, geoduck, bent-nosed, and Washington clams, which inhabit the mud flats of bays and lagoons. Along the gravel areas of the bays are little-neck clams, also known as rock cockles. And on the beaches of Humboldt and Del Norte counties re-

GRUNION RUNS

Grunion actually climb onto land to lay their eggs. These small silvery fish come ashore between March and August after particularly high tides. The females anchor themselves in the sand and lay as many as 3000 eggs, which are hatched by surf action. During these grunion runs, popular from Morro Bay south, the fish are so plentiful they can be caught by hand.

side razor clams, known for their delicious flavor and frustrating ability to rapidly bury themselves beneath the sand.

One of the state's best known shellfish is the Pismo clam, a species characterized by a thick, gray-white shell marked with annual bands. Living as long as 35 years and growing up to seven inches in diameter, they flourish along the San Luis Obispo coast, favoring cold, turbulent water rich in nutrients and oxygen.

Beds of these bivalves once lined the shore, serving as a staple in the diet of coastal Indians. In 1914 bag limits were 200 per person, but by 1947 commercial clamming was outlawed. Today sport clamming is still permitted though heavy storms have seriously diminished the beds. Easily located, Pismo clams reside no more than six inches beneath the sand in water about three feet deep at low tide. To catch them, clammers work parallel to the shore, probing the sand every two inches with a clam fork.

Favorite food among the sea otters, and at gourmet restaurants, is red abalone. Of some 100 abalone species worldwide, only Pacific varieties grow to significant size; the red abalone, reaching 13 inches in length, is the largest. Marked by jet-black tentacles and a red fringe along the shell, they hold tenaciously to offshore rocks, many clinging to the same stone their entire lives.

Back in the 1930s abalone were harvested commercially in Northern California and great piles of their shells lined the road between Monterey and Castroville. In those days three million a year were taken, many processed in factories along Cannery Row. Today commercial harvesting occurs only in Southern California, but amateur divers still gather them everywhere along the coast.

Prized for their delicious meat, abalone also have beautiful shells with mother-of-pearl interiors that cast iridescent colors. Coastal Indians used abalone shells for barter and one tribe, the Ohlone, or abalone people, took their name from this valuable shellfish.

TIDEPOOLS

It's a climactic scene in that Hollywood classic, Chinatown. Jack Nicholson, portraying a 1930s-era private eye, is about to accuse John Huston of murdering his own partner. But Huston, a deceitful and powerful businessman playing the innocent, waxes sentimental about the dead friend. His partner, Hollis Mulwrey, had been water commissioner, a great man who early in the century brought water to the Los Angeles basin, transforming a dusty town into a metropolis. Yet Hollis was a simple man, sensitive to nature, and loved the sea.

"Hollis was always fascinated by tidepools," Huston intones. "Do you know what he used to say? 'That's where life begins—sloughs, tidepools.'" As Huston knows, tidepools are also where life ends: he murdered Mulwrey by drowning him in one.

Poor Hollis' fascination with tidepools is shared by everyone. These rocky pockets, exposed to view at low tide, are microcosms of the world. Delicately poised between land and sea, they are a frontier dividing two wildly varied environments.

Life flourishes here, but living is not easy. Denizens of tidepools are exposed to air twice a day during low tide. They must adapt to dehydration, the heat of the sun, and the effects of the atmosphere. Rain brings fresh water to a saline environment, disturbing the precious equilibrium. Waves, particularly during severe storms, wreak havoc with reefs. Exceptionally high or low tides upset the rhythm of air and water exposure.

It is this balance between time in the air and water that differentiates the tidal life forms. Tidepools, or intertidal areas, are divided into four zones, which parallel the beach and vary in their distance from shore.

The splash zone, dampened by mist and occasional large waves, rests far up along the beach and is inhabited by green algae and small snails. Below it lies the upper intertidal zone, an area covered only during high tide. Here barnacles, chitons, and limpets cling to rocks, closing tight during low tide to preserve moisture.

Covered by water twice a day, the middle intertidal zone is home to mussels and rock weed. Since mussels grow in clumps, they form a biological community in themselves, sheltering varieties of plants and animals, some of which spend their entire lives in a single clump.

Starfish, which generally inhabit the low intertidal zone, feed on these mussels, prying open the stubborn shells with their powerful suctioned tentacles. This fourth region, uncovered only when the ocean deeply recedes during minus tides, supports the most diverse life forms. Sea urchins, abalone, and anemones flourish here, as do crabs, octopus, and chitons, those oval-shaped mollusks that date back to before the age of dinosaurs.

COASTAL PLANT LIFE

From the rim of the sea to the peaks of surrounding mountains, the coastline is coated with a complex variety of plant life. Several plant communities flourish along the shore, each clinging to a particular niche in the environment. Blessed with a cooler, more moderate climate near the ocean, they are continually misted by sea spray and must contend with more salt in their veins.

On the beaches and along the dunes are the herbs, vines, and low shrubs of the coastal strand community. Among their numbers are beach primrose, sand verbena, beach morning-glory, and sea figs, those tenacious succulents that run along the ground sprouting magenta flowers and literally carpeting the coast. Characterized by leathery leaves that retain large quantities of water, they are the plant world's answer to the camel.

Ocean
Safety

For swimming, surfing, and skindiving, few places match the California Coast. With endless miles of white sand beach, it attracts aquatic enthusiasts from all over the world. Many water lovers, however, never realize how awesome the sea can be. Particularly in California, where waves can reach significant heights and currents often flow unobstructed, the ocean is sometimes as treacherous as it is spectacular. People drown every year on California beaches, others are dragged from the surf with serious injuries, and countless numbers sustain minor cuts and bruises.

These accidents can be entirely avoided if you relate to the ocean with a respect for its power as well as an appreciation of its beauty. All you have to do is heed a few simple guidelines. First, never turn your back on the sea. Waves come in sets: one group may be small and quite harmless, but the next set could be large enough to sweep you out to sea. Never swim alone.

Don't try to surf, or bodysurf, until you're familiar with the sports' techniques and precautionary measures. Be very careful when the surf's high.

If you do get caught in a rip current, do not swim *against* it: swim *across* it, parallel to the shore. These currents, running from the shoreline out to sea, can often be spotted by noting their ragged-looking surface water and foamy edges.

When stung by a jellyfish, mix unseasoned meat tenderizer with alcohol, leave it on the sting for ten or twenty minutes, then rinse it off with alcohol. Old Hawaiian remedies, which are reputedly quite effective, involve applying urine or green papaya. If you step on the sharp, painful spines of a sea urchin, soak the affected area in very hot water for 15 to 90 minutes. Another remedy calls for applying urine or undiluted vinegar. If any of these preliminary treatments do not work, consult a doctor.

Oh, one last thing. The chances of encountering a shark are about as likely as sighting a UFO. But should you meet one of these ominous creatures, stay calm. He'll be no happier to see you than you are to confront him. Simply swim quietly to shore. By the time you make it back to terra firma, you'll have one hell of a story to tell.

Around the mud flats and river mouths grow rushes, pickle-weed, tules, cord grass, and other members of the salt marsh community. Low, shrubby plants growing in clumps, these hearty fellows are inundated by tides and able to withstand tremendous concentrations of salt.

Coastal sage scrub inhabits a broad swath from above the water line to about 3000 feet elevation. White and black sage, wild buckwheat, and California sagebrush belong to this community of short, tough plants.

The chaparral community grows in thick, often impenetrable stands along the hillsides and mountains. These scrub oak, manzanita, and Christmas holly bushes lend a distinct character to the fabled rolling hills of California. Down along the rivers and creeks resides the riparian community whose members range from willow, alder, and big-leaf maple to redwood and Douglas fir.

There are wildflowers everywhere—violets, lilies, irises, azaleas, wild roses, and of course California poppies, the state flower. Buttercups, with their shiny yellow petals, are abundant. Growing from the coast right out to the desert are the lupines, silky bushes with whorled flowers that stand straight as bottlebrushes.

The cactus family is represented by the prickly pear with its sharp spines and yellow blossoms; and there are nasty thickets of gorse, poison hemlock, and tenacious thistles. Several species of fern occupy coastal bluffs, descending to the very edge of the beach. In addition to serrated sword ferns and giant horsetails, these include California lace ferns and Saint Catherine's lace, with petals like finely woven textiles.

Then there are the trees—lofty Monterey pine; the rare Torrey pine that grows only in San Diego County and on an offshore island; oak, laurel, maple, and alder; fir, spruce, and cedar. The fabled Monterey cypress inhabits a picturesque region along the Monterey coast, the only place in the world it is found. Giant redwoods, the tallest trees on earth, grow in awesome groves along the coastal fog belt, living for centuries and reaching 350 foot heights.

And don't forget the tree that has no branches and sheds little shade, but is the foremost symbol of California—the palm tree. There are Pindo palms from Paraguay, European hair palms, plume palms from Brazil, blue palms, Washington palms, and the Erythea. Among the most common are the California palm, largest native palm in the continental United States, and the date palm, which lines many California streets and is nicknamed "pineapple palm" for its trunk's resemblance to the tropical fruit.

SEABIRDS   Somehow the mud flats of San Francisco Bay are the last place to go sightseeing, particularly at high tide, after the flood has stirred the ooze. But it is at such times that birdwatchers gather to view flocks of as many as 60,000 birds.

The California shore is one of the richest bird habitats anywhere in North America. Over 500 species are found across the state, many along the coast and its offshore islands.

Coastal species fall into three general categories—near-shore birds like loons, grebes, cormorants, and scoters, that inhabit the shallow waters of bays and beaches; offshore birds, such as shearwaters, which feed several miles off the coast; and pelagic or open-ocean species like albatross and Arctic terns, that fly miles from land and live for up to 20 or 30 years.

A kind of streamlined hawk, the peregrine falcon is one of the fastest birds alive, capable of diving at 200 miles an hour to prey on ducks, coots, and terns.

Joining the shore birds along California's beaches are ducks, geese, and other waterfowl. While waterfowl dive for fish and feed on submerged vegetation, near-shore birds use their sharp, pointed beaks to ferret out inter-tidal animals. Both groups flee the scene each year, flying north in spring to Canada and Alaska or south in autumn to Mexico and Central America, along the Pacific flyway, that great migratory route spanning the western United States.

Some birds, like canvasback ducks, loons, and Arctic terns, fly a route entirely along the coast. Others finish wintering in California and make a beeline due east. The short-tailed shearwater, one of the world's smallest but greatest travelers, leaves everything far behind. Breeding off the coast of Australia, this incredible bird flies a figure eight around the Pacific, skirting California and covering 20,000 miles.

Ospreys inhabit large nests which can often be seen high in shoreline trees. Also known as fish hawks, these are handsome birds with brown head crowns and six-foot wingspans. Ever the gentle creature, ospreys nab fish by circling over the ocean, then diving talons first into the water.

Whistling swans, white birds with black bills and yellow eye-spots, arrive in California from the Arctic every November. Residing until March, they build nests and breed cygnets before returning to colder climes.

Among the most beautiful birds are the egrets and herons. Tall, slender, elegant birds, they live from January until July in Bolinas and other coastal towns, engaging in elaborate courtship rituals. Together with more common species like sea gulls, sandpipers, and pelicans, they turn travelers into birders and make inconvenient times, like the edge of dawn, and unusual places, like swamps, among the most intriguing possibilities California has to offer.

MARINE MAMMALS

Few animals inspire the sense of myth and magic associated with the marine mammals of California. Foremost are the ocean-going animals like whales, dolphins, and porpoises, members of the unique Cetacean order that left the land 30 million years ago for the alien world of the sea. Six species of seals and sea lions also inhabit the coast, together with sea otters, those playful creatures that delight visitors and bedevil fishermen.

While dolphins and porpoises range far offshore, the region's most common whale is a regular coastal visitor. Migrating 12,000 miles every year between the Bering Sea and Baja Peninsula, the California gray whale cruises the shoreline each winter (see "Whale Watching" in Chapter Eight). Measuring 50 feet and weighing 40 tons, these distinguished animals can live to 50 years of age and communicate with sophisticated signaling systems.

The seals and sea lions that seem to loll about the shoreline are characterized by small ears and short flippers equipped for land travel. Fat and sassy, they have layers of blubber to keep them warm and loud barks to inform tourists who's king of the rookery.

Even people who never venture to the ocean have seen California sea lions, those talented circus performers. Occupying the entire coast, particularly around Santa Barbara, they stay offshore for months at a time, landing only during breeding season.

Harbor seals differ from these showmen in an inability to use their hind flippers for land travel. Not to be upstaged, they sport beautiful dark coats with silver and white spots from which they borrow their second name, leopard seals. Like other pinnipeds, harbor seals feed on fish, shellfish, and squid. Largest of all the pinnipeds are the Northern elephant seals, those ugly but lovable creatures that grow to 16 feet and weigh three tons. Characterized by a huge snout, they come ashore only to molt, mate, and give birth. Breeding season, beginning in December, is the best time to watch these waddling characters. The males wage fierce battles to establish who will be cock of the walk. A few weeks after the males finish their tournament the females arrive.

"Sentence first," said the Queen of Hearts in *Alice's Adventures in Wonderland*, "verdict afterwards." In the upside-down world of the elephant seal, birth comes first, then breeding. Within days of arriving onshore, the females give birth to 75-pound pups.

LOOK, BUT DON'T TOUCH

When you go searching for tidepool creatures remember, even out here in the wild, there are a few rules of the road. Collecting plants and animals, including dead ones, is strongly discouraged and in some places entirely illegal. Follow the old adage and look but don't touch. If you do turn over a rock or move a shell, replace it in the original position; it may be someone's home. Also watch out for big waves and exercise caution—it can be dangerous out there.

Three weeks later the mothers breed with their mates, conceiving pups that will be born eight months later.

Every California visitor's favorite animal is the sea otter. A kind of ocean-going teddy bear, they are actually members of the weasel family, weighing up to 85 pounds, measuring about four feet in length, and characterized by thick fur, short paws used for feeding and grooming, and webbed hind feet that serve as flippers. Intelligent critters, sea otters are quite capable of using tools—rocks with which they pry tenacious shellfish from the ocean bottom and hammer open shells. Voracious eaters, sea otters feed on abalone, sea urchins, and crabs, consuming as much as 25 percent of their body weight daily.

Like many other California marine mammals, sea otters were hunted to near extinction by 19th-century fur traders. Today the animals have made a remarkable recovery, populating the coast from the Channel Islands to Monterey. Inhabiting kelp beds where they are often difficult to spot, these sleek animals can best be seen during feeding their time in early morning and late afternoon. Watch carefully for the hungry sea gulls that patiently circle kelp beds in search of sea otter scraps. Then look for a reddish-black animal, relaxing on his back, tapping a rhythm with a rock and abalone shell, his mouth curved in a cunning smile.

▼▼▼▼▼▼▼▼▼▼▼▼▼▼

Traveling the Coast

SEASONS

The California Coast extends all the way from Mexico to Oregon. Along this entire expanse the weather corresponds to a Mediterranean climate with mild temperatures year-round. Since the coastal fog creates a natural form of air conditioning and insulation, the mercury rarely drops below 40° or rises above 70°. September and October are the hottest months, and December and January the coolest.

Spring and particularly autumn are the ideal times to make a visit. During winter, the rainy season brings overcast days and frequent showers. Summer is the peak tourist season, when voluminous crowds can present problems. Like spring, summer is also a period of frequent fog; during the morning and evening, fog banks from offshore blanket the coast, burning off around midday.

Since most winter storms sweep in from the north, rainfall averages and the length of the rainy season diminish as you head southward. Crescent City receives 70 inches of rain annually, San Francisco averages about 20 inches, and San Diego receives only 10 inches of rain a year. Inversely, temperatures vary widely from north to south: Eureka ranges from an average temperature of 47° in January to 57° during August, while down south, San Diego rises from 55° to 70° during the same months. The ocean air also creates a significant amount of moisture, keeping the state's average humidity in the neighborhood of 65 percent and making some areas, particularly Northern California, seem somewhat colder than the thermometer would indicate.

CALENDAR OF EVENTS

JANUARY   **San Francisco**   During the end of January or early February, the Chinese New Year features an extravagant parade with colorful dragons, dancers, and fireworks.
North Central Coast   The AT&T Pebble Beach National Pro-Am, an annual golf tournament, swings into action along the Monterey Peninsula.
South Central Coast   The Hang Gliding Festival in Santa Barbara features contests and demonstrations by local pilots.

FEBRUARY   **North Coast**   The Crustacean Festival and World Champion Crab Races takes place in Crescent City; if you forget to bring your own, you can rent a racing crab. Who said California lacks culture?
South Central Coast   New Orleans–style jazz accompanies a parade and costume ball at the San Luis Obispo **Mardi Gras**.
Orange Coast   In Laguna Beach, arts and crafts displays highlight the **Laguna Beach Winter Fest**. Meanwhile along the coast, crowds gather for seasonal **grunion runs**. In Dana Point the Festival of the Whales features a concert series, sporting competitions, and a film fest, as well as a street fair.

MARCH   **San Francisco**   Bands, politicians, and assorted revelers parade through the city on the Sunday closest to March 17, marking **St. Patrick's Day**.
North Coast   Mendocino and Fort Bragg celebrate a **Whale Festival** with whale-watching cruises, lighthouse tours, art shows, and winetasting.
South Central Coast   Stars and stargazers gather for **Santa Barbara's International Film Festival**.
Orange Coast   The **Fiesta de las Golondrinas** commemorates the return of the swallows to Mission San Juan Capistrano.
San Diego Coast   The **Ocean Beach Kite Festival**, with contests for flying and decorating kites, takes place at Ocean Beach.

APRIL   **San Francisco**   Japantown's **Cherry Blossom Festival** features parades, tea ceremonies, theatrical performances, and martial arts displays. **Opening Day on the Bay** launches the yachting season with a blessing of the fleet and a parade of decorated boats. The **San Francisco International Film Festival** offers a wide selection of cinematic events at participating theaters throughout the city.
North Coast   The two-day **Fisherman's Festival** in Bodega Bay is host to a decorated fishing-boat parade as well as bathtub races, face painting, a multi-media art show, and more.
South Central Coast   Enjoy amazing ocean views as you jog along Highway 1 in the **Big Star International Marathon**, featuring a fun run and relay race so everyone can participate.

Los Angeles Coast   Race car buffs head to the **Long Beach Grand Prix**.

San Diego Coast   The **Santa Fe Market** in Old Town features Southwestern and American Indian arts, crafts, demonstrations, and food.

San Francisco   Over 100,000 hearty souls (soles?) run the **Bay to Breakers Foot Race**, many covering the 7.5-mile course in elaborate costumes.

MAY

North Central Coast   An annual Portuguese fete in Ferndale since 1871, the **Chamarita/Holy Ghost Festival** falls on the seventh Sunday after Easter and commemorates the end of an Old Country famine with free food and wine, a parade, and dances.

South Central Coast   Food, exhibits, and dancing highlight the Italian celebration, **I Madonnari**, held in Santa Barbara.

San Diego Coast   Carlsbad hosts the spring observance of the semi-annual **Village Faire**, with hundreds of exhibits, an elephant ride, petting zoo, and countless food stands. In Old Town, the **Cinco de Mayo** celebration is highlighted by mariachis, traditional Mexican folk dancers, food, and displays.

San Francisco   The **Gay Pride Parade**, with its colorful floats and imaginative costumes, marches to the Civic Center. June launches the performances of the two-month-long **Stern Grove Midsummer Music Festival**, which showcases international music and dance, vocal ensembles, opera, and jazz.

JUNE

South Central Coast   A parade and many other festivities highlight Santa Barbara's **Summer Solstice Celebration**.

San Diego Coast   The **Old Globe Theater Festival** starts its summer run in Balboa Park with Shakespeare's classics.

San Francisco   Here, at Crissy Field, and throughout Northern California, firework displays commemorate the **Fourth of July**. The **San Francisco Marathon** begins in Golden Gate Park, then winds for 26.2 miles through the streets of San Francisco to the Civic Center.

JULY

North Central Coast   The **Carmel Bach Festival** includes recitals, weekend matinees, and evening concerts of classical and baroque music. Monterey is busy with its popular **Greek Festival**.

Los Angeles Coast   Every Thursday evening during July and August the **Santa Monica Pier Twilight Dance Series** features a variety of live music from reggae to western swing. Surfers hang ten at the **International Surf Festival** on Hermosa, Manhattan, Torrance, and Redondo beaches.

Orange Coast   The **Arts Festival and Pageant of the Masters**, one of Southern California's most notable events, occurs in Laguna Beach.

San Diego Coast   The **San Diego Symphony's Summer Pops** begins its series of evening concerts.

AUGUST   **San Francisco**   The **County Fair Flower Show**, at the Hall of Flowers in Golden Gate Park, displays thousands of blooms.
North Central Coast   Monterey hosts the **Great Squid Festival**, Salinas celebrates its **Steinbeck Festival**, and Pebble Beach sponsors the **Concours d'Élégance**, a classic auto show.
South Central Coast   Santa Barbara rounds up everyone for a rodeo, open-air food markets, a children's parade, and live entertainment at the five-day-long **Old Spanish Days**. Polo players from around the world gather in Santa Barbara for the prestigious **Pacific Coast Open Polo Tournament**.

SEPTEMBER   **San Francisco**   This month for music is marked by the opening of the **San Francisco Opera** and the **San Francisco Symphony**, as well as the annual **Blues Festival** and **Opera in the Park**.
North Central Coast   It's also the magic month for the internationally renowned **Monterey Jazz Festival**. Over in Castroville, they stage an **Artichoke Festival**, complete with the Artichoke Queen coronation and an artichoke-eating contest.
South Central Coast   Thousands flock to Ventura's **California Beach Party** for fun in the sun with food, arts and crafts booths, live entertainment and sporting events.
San Diego Coast   The **Cabrillo Festival** in Point Loma commemorates the discovery of the California coast.

OCTOBER   **San Francisco**   **Columbus Day** is marked by a parade, bocce ball tournament, and the annual blessing of the fishing fleet. Cowboys celebrate at the **Grand National Rodeo, Horse, and Stock Show** in Daly City. The **San Francisco Jazz Festival** kicks off in late October to present two week's worth of concerts, dance, performances, and tributes to the masters.
North Central Coast   The fun-filled **Art and Pumpkin Festival** in Half Moon Bay features pie-eating contests, food booths, and crafts exhibits.
South Central Coast   Pismo Beach, the "clam capital of the world," presents its annual **Pismo Beach Clam Festival** with feasting, live entertainment, and arts and crafts booths.

NOVEMBER   **San Francisco**   The **San Francisco Bay Area Book Festival** is the place to go to meet local publishers and hear author readings. Several fairs and festivals kick off the holiday season. One notable event is the **Harvest Festival & Christmas Crafts Market**.
North Coast   Mendocino hosts a **Thanksgiving Festival** complete with musical performances and crafts exhibits.

South Central Coast The annual **World Music Festival** takes place in Santa Barbara, highlighting music and dance from such places as Africa, Spain, and the Caribbean.

San Diego Carlsbad hosts the year's second **Village Faire** (see May listing).

San Francisco Celebrate the holiday season at the **Sing-It-Yourself Messiah**. There are also **Christmas Parades** in many towns throughout Northern California.

DECEMBER

Southern California During the holidays several coastal communities, including San Diego, Huntington Beach, Naples, and Marina del Rey, mark the season with **Christmas Boat Parades**. San Diego, San Luis Obispo, and other Southland cities celebrate the Mexican yuletide with **Las Posadas**.

Several agencies provide free information to travelers. The **California Office of Tourism** will help guide you to areas throughout the state. ~ P.O. Box 1499, Department TIH, Sacramento, CA 95812; 800-862-2543, 916-322-2881; www.gocalif.ca.gov. The **San Francisco Visitors Information Center** is an excellent resource for San Francisco. ~ Hallidie Plaza, Lower Level, Powell and Market streets, San Francisco, CA 94101; 415-391-2000; www.sfvisitor.org. For information on the North Coast counties between San Francisco and Oregon, you should contact the **Redwood Empire Association**. ~ 2801 Leavenworth, San Francisco, CA 94133; 415-394-5991, 800-200-8334. Also consult local chambers of commerce and information centers, which are mentioned in the various area chapters. For the Los Angeles area, the **Los Angeles Visitors and Convention Bureau** can help. ~ 633 West 5th Street, Suite 6000, Los Angeles, CA 90071; 213-624-7300, 800-366-6116. The **San Diego International Visitors Information Center** can provide information on the San Diego area. ~ 401 B Street, Suite 1400, San Diego, CA 92101; 619-236-1212.

▼▼▼▼▼▼▼▼▼▼
Before You Go

VISITORS CENTERS

There are two important guidelines when deciding what to take on a trip. The first is as true for the California Coast as anywhere in the world—pack light. Dress styles here are relatively informal and laundromats and dry cleaners are frequent. The airlines allow two suitcases and a carry-on bag; try to take one suitcase and perhaps a small accessory case.

PACKING

The second rule is to prepare for cool weather, even if the closest you'll come to the mountains are the bluffs above the beach. While the coastal climate is temperate, temperatures sometimes descend below 50°. Even that might not seem chilly until the fog rolls in and the ocean breeze picks up. A warm sweater and jacket are absolute necessities. In addition to everyday garments, pack shorts year-round for Southern California, and remember, everywhere along the coast requires a raincoat between November and March.

LODGING   Overnight accommodations along the California Coast are as varied as the region itself. They range from highrise hotels and neon motels to hostels and bed-and-breakfast inns. One guideline to follow with all of them is to reserve well in advance.

Check through each chapter and you're bound to find something to fit your budget and personal taste. Neon motels offer bland facilities at low prices and are great if you're economizing or don't plan to spend much time in the room. Larger hotels often lack intimacy, but provide such conveniences as restaurants and shops in the lobby. My personal preference is for historic hotels, those slightly faded classics that offer charm and tradition at moderate cost. Bed-and-breakfast inns present an opportunity to stay in a homelike setting. Like hostels, they are an excellent way to meet fellow travelers; unlike hostels, California's country inns are quite expensive.

> Book reservations in advance: the California coast is an extremely popular area, particularly in summer, and facilities fill up quickly.

To help you decide on a place to stay, I've organized the accommodations not only by area but also according to price. *Budget* hotels are generally less than $60 per night for two people; the rooms are clean and comfortable, but not luxurious. The *moderate* price hotels run $60 to $120, and provide larger rooms, plusher furniture, and more attractive surroundings. At deluxe-priced accommodations, you can expect to spend between $120 and $175 for a homey bed and breakfast or double in a hotel or resort. You'll usually find spacious rooms, a fashionable lobby, a restaurant, and a group of shops. If you want to spend your time (and money) at the very finest hotels, try an *ultra-deluxe* facility, which will include all the amenities and cost more than $175. Contact **Bed & Breakfast International** to give you a hand in finding a cozy place to stay. ~ P.O. Box 282910, San Francisco, CA 94128; 800-872-4500; www.bbintl.com.

DINING   It seems as if the California Coast has more restaurants than people. To establish a pattern for this parade of dining places, I've organized them according to location and cost.

Within a particular chapter, the restaurants are categorized geographically and each individual restaurant entry describes the establishment as budget, moderate, deluxe, or ultra-deluxe in price.

Dinner entrées at *budget* restaurants usually cost $9 or less. The ambience is informal café-style and the crowd is often a local one. *Moderate* price restaurants range between $9 and $18 at dinner and offer pleasant surroundings, a more varied menu, and a slower pace. *Deluxe* establishments tab their entrées from $18 to $25, featuring sophisticated cuisines, plush decor, and more personalized service. *Ultra-deluxe* dining rooms, where $25 will only get you started, are gourmet gathering places where cooking (one hopes) is a fine art form and service a way of life.

Breakfast and lunch menus vary less in price from restaurant to restaurant. Even deluxe kitchens usually offer light breakfasts and lunch sandwiches, placing them within a few dollars of their budget-minded competitors. These early meals can be a good time to test expensive restaurants.

TRAVELING WITH CHILDREN

Visiting California with kids can be a real adventure, and if properly planned, a truly enjoyable one. To ensure that your trip will feature the joy, rather than the strain of parenthood, remember a few important guidelines.

Children under age five or under 40 pounds must be in approved child restraints while riding in cars/vans. The back seat is safest.

Use a travel agent to help with arrangements; they can reserve spacious bulkhead seats on airlines and determine which flights are least crowded. Bring everything you need on board—diapers, food, toys, and extra clothes for kids and parents alike. If the trip to California involves a long journey, plan to relax and do very little during the first few days.

Always allow extra time for getting places. Book reservations well in advance and make sure the hotel has the extra crib, cot, or bed you require. It's smart to ask for a room at the end of the hall to cut down on noise. Be aware that many bed-and-breakfast inns do not allow children.

Even small towns have stores that carry diapers, food, and other essentials; in larger towns and cities, convenience stores are often open all night (check the yellow pages for addresses).

Hotels often provide access to babysitters. Also check the yellow pages for state licensed and bonded babysitting agencies.

A first-aid kit is always a good idea. Ask your pediatrician for special medicines and dosages for colds and diarrhea.

DISABLED TRAVELERS

California stands at the forefront of social reform for the disabled. During the past decade, the state has responded with a series of progressive legislative measures addressing the needs of the blind, wheelchair-bound, and others.

The **Department of Motor Vehicles** provides special parking permits for the disabled. Many local bus lines and other public transit facilities are wheelchair-accessible.

There are also agencies in California assisting persons with disabilities. For tips and information about the San Francisco Bay area, contact the **Center for Independent Living**, a self-help group that has led the way in reforming access laws in California. ~ 2539 Telegraph Avenue, Berkeley, CA 94704; 510-841-4776. Other organizations on the coast include the **Westside Center for Independent Living**. ~ 12901 Venice Boulevard, Los Angeles, CA 90066; 310-390-3611. In San Diego, contact **The Access Center of San Diego**. ~ 1295 University Avenue, Suite 10, San Diego, CA 92103; 619-293-3500; www.primenet.com/~lathrop/acsd.

The **Society for the Advancement of Travel for the Handicapped** (SATH) is an organization that can provide information. ~ 347 5th Avenue, #610, New York, NY 10016; 212-447-7284; www.sath.org. Or try **Flying Wheels Travel**. ~ P.O. Box 382, Owatonna, MN 55060; 800-535-6790; www.flyingwheels.com. **Travelin' Talk**, a networking organization, also provides information. ~ P.O. Box 3534, Clarksville, TN 37043; 931-552-6670.

Be sure to check in advance when making room reservations. Many hotels and motels feature facilities for those in wheelchairs.

SENIOR TRAVELERS

The California Coast is an ideal spot for older vacationers. The mild climate makes traveling in the off-season possible, helping to cut down on expenses. Many museums, theaters, restaurants, and hotels offer senior discounts (requiring a driver's license, Medicare card, or other age-identifying card). Be sure to ask your travel agent when booking reservations.

AARP offers membership to anyone over 50. AARP's benefits include travel discounts with a number of firms. ~ 601 E Street NW, Washington, DC 20049; 800-424-3410; www.aarp.com. For those over 60, **Elderhostel** offers numerous educational programs in California. ~ 75 Federal Street, Boston, MA 02110; 617-426-7788; www.elderhostel.org.

Be extra careful about health matters. Bring any medications you use, along with the prescriptions. Consider carrying a medical record with you—including your current medical status, and medical history, as well as your doctor's name, phone number and address. Also be sure to confirm that your insurance covers you away from home.

WOMEN TRAVELING ALONE

Traveling solo grants an independence and freedom different from that of traveling with a partner, but single travelers are more vulnerable to crime and must take additional precautions.

It's unwise to hitchhike and probably best to avoid inexpensive accommodations on the outskirts of town; the money saved does not outweigh the risk. Bed and breakfasts, youth hostels and YWCAs are generally your safest bet for lodging, and they also foster an environment ideal for bonding with fellow travelers. Feminist bookstores are also good sources of information.

Keep all valuables well-hidden and clutch cameras and purses tightly. Avoid late-night treks or strolls through undesirable parts of town, but if you find yourself in this situation, continue walking with a confident air until you reach a safe haven. A fierce scowl never hurts.

These hints should by no means deter you from seeking out adventure. Wherever you go, stay alert, use your common sense and trust your instincts. If you are hassled or threatened in some way, never be afraid to scream for assistance. It's a good idea to carry change for a phone call and to know the number to call in case of emergency. For more hints, get a copy of *Safety and Security for Women Who Travel* (Travelers Tales, 1998).

Most areas have 24-hour hotlines for victims of rape and violent crime. **Bay Area Women Against Rape** operates a 24-hour crisis line in San Francisco. ~ 415-647-7273, 510-845-7273. Several Southern California communities offer women's resource centers, referral numbers, and health centers. In the Los Angeles and Ventura County area consult the **Women's Yellow Pages**. ~ 818-995-6646.

GAY & LESBIAN TRAVELERS

The California Coast offers countless opportunities for gay and lesbian travelers to unwind, or wind up, in an atmosphere of tolerance. Without doubt, San Francisco is one of the premier gay and lesbian vacation spots in the country. The Castro Street and Polk Street neighborhoods, as well as the South of Market district, are all major gay areas. Each offers gay-owned and gay-friendly lodging, restaurants, and nightspots. (See the "Gay Neighborhoods" and "South of Market" sections in Chapter Two, and "Gay and lesbian travelers" in the index.) In many ways, the entire city is a gay-friendly enclave. Gays and lesbians constitute a powerful voting block in local politics, and some gay supervisors currently serve on the Board of Supervisors.

For weekly updates on the gay community, pick up a *Bay Area Reporter*, which focuses on local news, arts, and entertainment. ~ 415-861-5019. *Odyssey* hits the stands twice a month and gives the lowdown on happening nightspots for gays and lesbians. ~ 415-621-6514. *Frontiers* is biweekly, publishing articles of interest to the gay community. ~ 415-487-6000; www.frontiers web.com. The bi-monthly *San Francisco Bay Times* deals with gay issues and doubles as a resource guide. ~ 415-227-0800. *Icon*, a monthly lesbian newspaper, features interviews and news articles. ~ 415-863-9536; e-mail iconlesmag@aol.com.

If you find yourself in need of medical or legal help there are several resources available. **California AIDS Hotline** is the area's very best resource for counseling and referrals. ~ 415-863-2437. The AIDS/HIV **Nightline** staffs operators from 5 p.m. to 5 a.m. ~ 415-434-2437. **Community United Against Violence Hotline** is available 24 hours a day to assist gay, lesbian, and bisexual people who have been physically assaulted. ~ 415-333-4357.

Despite its name, **The Women's Building** is a community center with bulletin boards loaded with information for gays, lesbians, and bisexuals. ~ 3543 18th Street, San Francisco; 415-431-1180. Medical attention for lesbian and transgender women can be had (by appointment only) at the **Lyon-Martin Women's Clinic**. ~ 1748 Market Street, Suite 201, San Francisco; 415-565-7667.

Although Southern California is often known for its social and political conservatism, the tolerance that accompanies the booming entertainment industry makes certain areas inviting and exciting for gay and lesbian travelers. For more information on hotels, shops, restaurants, and nightclubs catering to gay and lesbian travelers, see the "Long Beach" section in Chapter Six, the "Laguna Beach" section in Chapter Seven, and "Gay and lesbian travelers" in the index.

If you're a fan of cozy lodgings, you can arrange book a room ahead of time by calling **Caritas Bed & Breakfast Network**, a national reservation service that works exclusively with gay- and lesbian-owned bed and breakfasts. ~ 75 East Wacker Drive, Chicago, IL 60601; 312-857-0801, 800-227-4827, fax 312-857-0805. After arriving in town, visitors may want to make their first stop the **Los Angeles Gay & Lesbian Center**, a resource center with informative bulletin boards, brochures, counseling, and, for the long-term visitor, job placement services. Should you get slapped with one of L.A.'s famous jaywalking tickets, they also offer legal services. ~ 1625 North Schrader Boulevard; 213-993-7400, www.gay-lesbian-center.org. Pick up a copy of the *Edge*, which comes out twice a month—almost as often as the average Sunset Strip pedestrian—and covers the goings-on in L.A. County. ~ 6434 Santa Monica Boulevard, West Hollywood; 213-962-6994; e-mail edgemag@earthlink.net. Also look for the bimonthly *Nightlife Entertainment Magazine*; it's full of movie, theater, and club reviews that cover the area between Santa Barbara and San Diego. ~ 6255 Sunset Boulevard, Suite 2000, Hollywood; 213-462-5400; e-mail nlmagazine.com@aol.com. Women may consult *Female FYI*, a monthly publication based in L.A. that covers the statewide entertainment scene. Along with reviews, interviews, health, and travel, the magazine has a comprehensive club guide and calendar of events. ~ 8033 Sunset Boulevard, Suite 2013, Los Angeles; 213-460-7025, 888-460-7001.

Farther south, San Diego's Hillcrest district is the focus of that city's gay scene, with guesthouses, stores, and cafés. (See "San Diego Gay Scene" in Chapter Eight.)

In San Diego, get a copy of *Gay & Lesbian Times*, a weekly publication with local and world news, business, sports, weather, and arts sections. It also contains a calendar of events, and a directory of gay-friendly businesses and establishments. ~ 3911 Normal Street, San Diego; 619-299-6397; www.members.aol.com/

uptownpub/glt. *Update* is another weekly that covers gay and lesbian news, and gives you a feel of San Diego and Southern California. ~ 2801 4th Avenue, San Diego; 619-299-4104. **The Lesbian and Gay Men's Community Center** is open for drop-in counseling, mental health services, or support groups—or stop by on Thursday nights for bingo. Closed Sunday. ~ 3916 Normal Street, San Diego; 619-692-2077. The Center also runs a **phone line** that provides information around the clock about upcoming events, community resources and visitor information. ~ 619-294-4636.

Passports and Visas Most foreign visitors need a passport and tourist visa to enter the United States. Contact your nearest U.S. Embassy or Consulate well in advance to obtain a visa and to check on any other entry requirements.

FOREIGN TRAVELERS

Customs Requirements Foreign travelers are allowed to carry in the following: 200 cigarettes (1 carton), 50 cigars, or 2 kilograms (4.4 pounds) of smoking tobacco; one liter of alcohol for personal use only (you must be 21 years of age to bring in alcohol); and US$100 worth of duty-free gifts that can include an additional quantity of 100 cigars. You may bring in any amount of currency, but must fill out a form if you bring in over US$10,000. Carry any prescription drugs in clearly marked containers. (You may have to produce a written prescription or doctor's statement for the custom's officer.) Meat or meat products, seeds, plants, fruits and narcotics are not allowed to be brought into the United States. Contact the **United States Customs Service** for further information. ~ 1300 Pennsylvania Avenue NW, Washington, DC 20229; 202-927-6724.

Driving If you plan to rent a car, an international driver's license should be obtained before arriving in the United States. Some car rental agencies require both a foreign license and an international driver's license. Many also require a lessee to be at least 25 years of age; all require a major credit card. Seat belts are mandatory for the driver and all passengers. Children under the age of five or under 40 pounds should be in the back seat in approved child-safety restraints.

Currency United States money is based on the dollar. Bills generally come in denominations of $1, $5, $10, $20, $50 and $100. Every dollar is divided into 100 cents. Coins are the penny (1 cent), nickel (5 cents), dime (10 cents) and quarter (25 cents). Half-dollar and dollar coins are rarely used. You may not use foreign currency to purchase goods and services in the United States. Consider buying traveler's checks in dollar amounts. You may also use credit cards affiliated with an American company such as Interbank, Barclay Card, VISA and American Express.

Electricity and Electronics Electric outlets use currents of 110 volts, 60 cycles. To operate appliances made for other electrical systems, you need a transformer or other adapter. Travelers who use laptop computers for telecommunication should be aware that modem configurations for U.S. telephone systems may be different from their European counterparts. Similarly, the U.S. format for videotapes is different from that in Europe; National Park Service visitors centers and other stores that sell souvenir videos often have them available in European format on request.

Weights and Measures   The United States uses the English system of weights and measures. American units and their metric equivalents are: 1 inch = 2.5 centimeters; 1 foot (12 inches) = 0.3 meter; 1 yard (3 feet) = 0.9 meter; 1 mile (5280 feet) = 1.6 kilometers; 1 ounce = 28 grams; 1 pound (16 ounces) = 0.45 kilogram; 1 quart (liquid) = 0.9 liter.

▼▼▼▼▼▼▼▼▼▼▼▼▼▼▼
Outdoor Adventures

CAMPING

The state oversees 265 camping facilities. Amenities at each campground vary. There is a day-use fee of $3–$6 per vehicle. Campsites range from about $10 up to $30 (a little less in off season). For a complete listing of all state-run campgrounds, send $2 for the *Official Guide to California State Parks* to the **California Department of Parks and Recreation**. ~ P.O. Box 942896, Sacramento, CA 94296; 916-653-6995; www.ceres.ca.gov/parks. Reservations for campgrounds can be made by calling 800-444-7275.

For general information on National Park campgrounds, contact the **National Park Service**. ~ Western Region Information Center, Fort Mason, Building 201, San Francisco, CA 94123; 415-556-4122; www.nps.gov/goga. To reserve a National Park campsite call the park directly or call 800-365-2267.

In addition to state and national campgrounds, the California Coast offers numerous municipal, county, and private facilities. See the "Beaches and Parks" sections in each area chapter for the locations of these campgrounds.

PERMITS

WILDERNESS PERMITS   For camping and hiking in the wilderness and primitive areas of national forests, a wilderness permit is required. Permits are free and are issued for a specific period of time, which varies according to the wilderness area. You can obtain permits from ranger stations and regional information centers, as described in the "Beaches & Parks" sections in each chapter. Information is available through the U.S. Forest Service. ~ 630 Sansome Street, San Francisco, CA 94111; 415-705-2874; www.r5.pswfs.gov.

FISHING LICENSES   For current information on the fishing season and state license fees, contact the **Department of Fish and Game**. ~ 3211 S Street, Sacramento, CA 95816; 916-227-2244; www.dfg.ca.gov.

TWO

San Francisco

 It is a city poised at the end of the continent, civilization's last fling before the land plunges into the Pacific. Perhaps this is why visitors demand something memorable from San Francisco. People expect the city to resonate along a personal wavelength, speak to them, fulfill some ineffable desire at the center of the soul.

There is a terrible beauty at the edge of America: the dream begins here, or ends. The Golden Gate Bridge, that arching portal to infinite horizons, is also a suicide gangplank for hundreds of ill-starred dreamers. Throughout American history, those who crossed the country in search of destiny ultimately found it here or turned back to the continent and their own past.

Yet San Francisco is only a city, a steel-and-glass metropolis mounted on a series of hills. With a population of about 778,000, it covers 47 square miles at the tip of a peninsula bounded by the Pacific Ocean and San Francisco Bay. An international port and gateway to Asia, San Francisco supports a multicultural population with large concentrations of Chinese, Hispanics, Blacks, Italians, Filipinos, and Japanese. Adding to the cosmopolitan atmosphere is a gay population constituting perhaps 20 percent of the city's residents.

The myth of San Francisco originates not only from its geography, but its history as well. If, as early Christians believed, the world was created in 4004 B.C., then the history of San Francisco began on January 28, 1848. That day a hired hand named James Marshall discovered gold in California. Year One is 1849, a time etched in the psyche of an entire nation. The people swept along by the mania of that momentous time have been known forever since as "'49ers." They crossed the Rockies in covered wagons, trekked the jungles of Panama, and challenged the treacherous seas around Cape Horn, all because of a shiny yellow metal.

During the Gold Rush, a Barbary Coast ghetto grew along the Bay. Over 500 businesses sold liquor; gambling, drug sales, and prostitution were rampant; gangs roamed the boomtown and iron-fisted vigilance committees enforced law and order. Sailors were shanghaied and failed prospectors committed suicide at the rate of 1000 per year.

Gold in California was the quintessence of the American Dream. San Francisco became the center of that dream. The peaceful hamlet was transmogrified into a hellbent city, a place to make the Wild West look tame. Its population exploded from 900 to 25,000 in two years; by 1890 it numbered 300,000.

Amid all the chaos, San Francisco grew into an international city. Because of its multicultural population, and in spite of periodic racial problems, San Francisco developed a strong liberal tradition, an openness to the unusual and unexpected, which prevails today.

Of course San Francisco's most famous encounter with the unexpected occurred on April 18, 1906. Dream turned to nightmare at 5:12 that morning as a horrendous earthquake, 8.3 on the Richter scale, rocked and buckled the land. Actually, the infamous San Francisco earthquake owed its destructive ferocity more to the subsequent fires than the seismic disturbance. One of the few people killed by the earthquake itself was the city's fire chief. Gas mains across the city broke and water pipes lay shattered. Within hours, 50 separate fires ignited, merged, and by nightfall created firestorms that tore across the city. Three-quarters of San Francisco's houses were destroyed in the three-day holocaust, 452 people died, and 250,000 were left homeless.

The funeral of "Emperor Norton," a Gold Rush–era character, drew about 10,000 mourners.

The city whose municipal symbol is a phoenix rising from the ashes quickly rebuilt. City Hall and the Civic Center became part of a resurrected San Francisco. The Golden Gate and Bay bridges were completed in the 1930s, and during World War II the port became a major embarkation point for men and material. A city of international importance, San Francisco was the site for the signing of the United Nations charter in June 1945.

It entered the post–World War II era at the vanguard of American society. San Francisco's hallmark is cultural innovation. This city at continent's edge boasts a society at the edge of thought. During the 1950s it became the Beat capital of the world. Allen Ginsberg, Jack Kerouac, Gary Snyder, and other Beat poets began haunting places like Caffe Trieste and the Co-Existence Bagel Shop. The Beats blew cool jazz, intoned free-form poems, and extolled the virtues of nothingness.

Not even Kerouac and his colleagues were prepared for San Francisco's next wave of cultural immigrants. During the late 1960s this mecca for the misplaced became a mystical gathering place for myriads of hippies. The Haight–Ashbury neighborhood was the staging area for a movement intent on revolutionizing American consciousness.

By the 1970s San Francisco was becoming home to a vital and creative minority, gay men and women. The city's gay population had increased steadily for decades; then, suddenly, San Francisco's open society and free-wheeling lifestyle brought an amazing influx of gays. In 1977, Supervisor Harvey Milk became the nation's first outfront gay to be elected to a major municipal post. That same year the city passed a landmark gay rights ordinance. With an advancing population that today numbers more than 200,000, gays became a powerful social and political force.

Throughout the 1980s and 1990s, San Francisco has retained a gay supervisor whose constituency represents an integral part of the city's life. Today the gay population leads the fight against the AIDS epidemic that has devastated its ranks.

A multicultural society from its early days, San Francisco remains a city at the edge, open to experiment and experience. The city does sometimes seem to contain as many cults as people, but it also boasts more than its share of artists and activists.

There are also problems: during the last few decades, San Francisco's skyline has been Manhattanized, crowded with clusters of dark skyscrapers, and the city has allowed its port to decline. Most cargo ships travel across the Bay to Oakland, while San Francisco's once great waterfront is being converted into gourmet restaurants and chic shopping malls. It is a city in love with itself, trading the mundane business of shipping for the glamorous, profitable tourist industry.

In October 1989 San Francisco once again demonstrated its unsettling ability to combine good fortune with tragedy. As the nation's television viewers settled in to see the third game of the World Series, being played in Candlestick Park between the San Francisco Giants and neighboring Oakland Athletics, they found themselves watching a 7.1 level earthquake. The trembler rocked the stadium and rolled through Northern California, leaving 67 dead, and causing more than $10 billion in damage. After the dust cleared and weeks of startling media reports, U-Haul trucks became harder and harder to come by as people frantically left the state. Now it's turned around, with very low unemployment and few rental vacancies in San Francisco.

Perhaps Rudyard Kipling was right. He once called the place "a mad city—inhabited for the most part by perfectly insane people." William Saroyan saw it as "a city that invites the heart to come to life . . . an experiment in living." The two thoughts do not contradict: San Francisco is madly beautiful, a marvelous and zany place. Its contribution to the world is its lifestyle.

The people who gravitate here become models—some exemplary, others tragic—for their entire generation. Every decade San Francisco moves farther out along the edge, maintaining a tradition for the avant-garde and iconoclastic that dates back to the '49ers. The city is a jigsaw puzzle that will never be completed. Its residents, and those who come to love the place, are parts from that puzzle, pieces which never quite fit, but rather stand out, unique edges exposed, from all the rest.

Downtown

Visit any city in the world and the sightseeing tour will begin in a vital but nebulous area called "Downtown." San Francisco is no different. Here, Downtown is spelled Union Square (Geary and Stockton streets), a tree-dotted plot in the heart of the city's hotel and shopping district. Lofty buildings bordering the area house major department stores while the network of surrounding streets features many of the city's poshest shops and plushest hotels.

Text continued on page 34.

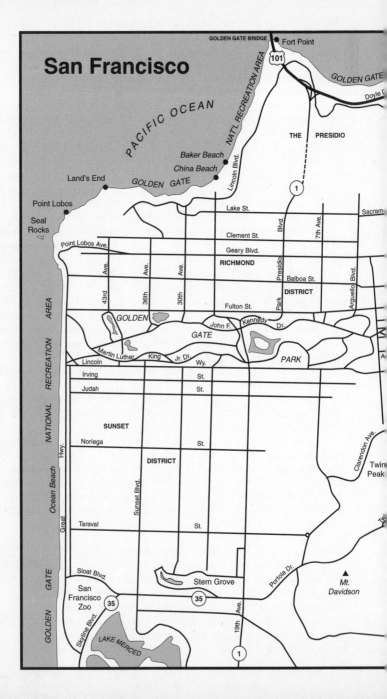

San Francisco

GOLDEN GATE BRIDGE   Fort Point

101

GOLDEN GATE

Doyle

NAT'L RECREATION AREA

PACIFIC OCEAN

THE   PRESIDIO

Baker Beach

China Beach

Lincoln Blvd.

Land's End   GOLDEN   GATE

1

Point Lobos

Lake St.

Sacram.

Seal
Rocks

Blvd.

7th Ave.

Point Lobos Ave.

Clement St.

Geary Blvd.

Presidio

RICHMOND

Ave.

Ave.

Ave.

Balboa St.

Arguello Blvd.

DISTRICT

43rd

36th

30th

Fulton St.

Park

GOLDEN

John F.   Kennedy   Dr.

GATE

Martin Luther   King   Jr. Dr.

PARK

A

Lincoln   Wy.

NATIONAL   RECREATION   AREA

Irving   St.

Judah   St.

SUNSET

Clarendon Ave.

Noriega   St.

Twin
Peak

DISTRICT

Sunset Blvd.

Ocean Beach

Taraval   St.

Tw

Sloat Blvd.

Portola Dr.

Stern Grove

Mt.
Davidson

San
Francisco
Zoo   35

35

19th Ave.

GOLDEN   GATE

Great   Hwy.

Skyline Blvd.

LAKE MERCED

1

SIGHTS   Union Square's most intriguing role is as San Francisco's freeform entertainment center. On any day you may see a brass band high-stepping through, a school choir singing the world's praises, or a gathering of motley but talented musicians passing the hat for bus fare home.

Cable cars from the nearby turnaround station at Powell and Market streets clang past en route to Nob Hill and Fisherman's Wharf. So pull up a patch of lawn and watch the world work through its paces, or just browse the Square's hedgerows and flower gardens. While you're here, you'd be wise to stop by the San Francisco Visitors Information Center for some handy brochures. ~ Hallidie Plaza, Lower Level, Powell and Market streets; 415-391-2000.

Then you can head off toward the city's high voltage Financial District. Appropriately enough, the route to this pinstriped realm leads down Maiden Lane, headiest of the city's high-heeled shopping areas. Back in Barbary Coast days, when San Francisco was a dirty word, this two-block-long alleyway was wall-to-wall with bawdy houses. But today it's been transformed from red light district to ultra-chic mall. Of particular interest among the galleries and boutiques lining this pedestrian-only thoroughfare is the building at 140 Maiden Lane. Designed by Frank Lloyd Wright in 1948, its circular interior stairway and other unique elements foreshadow the motifs he later used for the famous Guggenheim Museum.

LODGING   **BUDGET LODGING**   The cheapest accommodations in town are found in the city's Tenderloin district. Situated between Union Square and the Civic Center, this area is an easy walk from restaurants and points of cultural interest. The Tenderloin is a sometimes dangerous, sleazy neighborhood filled with interesting if menacing characters, the kind of place you stay because of the low rents rather than the inherent charm. Still, if the spirit is willing, the purse will certainly be appreciative. Just don't flaunt the purse—or the camera for that matter.

Rooms at the Youth Hostel Centrale are very basic. Although they lack any decorations or private baths, the rooms are clean and feature wall-to-wall carpeting and televisions. You get, as they say, what you pay for. In this case, you pay very very little and get a tidy, immaculate environment. With its 18 rooms, the hostel is a wayfarer's oasis. ~ 116 Turk Street; 415-346-7835.

There are two sister hotels within two blocks of one another. The James Court features 36 beige-colored rooms, 10 with private baths. ~ 1353 Bush Street; phone/fax 415-771-2409.

The American Youth Hostel—Union Square is *the* place if you are looking for budget accommodations in the heart of the city.

Rooms are shared (two to six bunks per room) and a kitchen is available for guests to use. ~ 312 Mason Street; 415-788-5604, fax 415-788-3023.

For native funk at rock bottom rates consider the **Adelaide Inn**. Billed as "San Francisco's unique European pensione," it is an 18-room, family-operated establishment. There is a small lobby plus a coffee room and kitchen for the guests. The room prices, with continental breakfast included, are friendly to the pocketbook. Rooms are small, tidy, and plainly furnished; each is equipped with a sink and television; bathrooms are shared. Most important, the inn is located in a prime downtown location, not in the Tenderloin. ~ 5 Isadora Duncan Place; 415-441-2261, fax 415-441-0161.

> Union Square is a scene—where the rich and powerful come to view the merely talented, where panhandlers sometimes seem as plentiful as pigeons.

Another budgeter's resting place is **Temple Hotel**. Located near the Financial District, it features a small, stylish lobby highlighted with one of those old-time iron elevators. For a budget price you can stay in a well-kept room with shag carpeting and a shared bath. Or you can rent a room with a private bath in this colorful hotel. ~ 469 Pine Street; 415-781-2565; e-mail romsdahl@earthlink.net.

MODERATE LODGING   In my opinion the best hotel buys in San Francisco are the middle range accommodations. These usually offer good locations, comfortable surroundings, and reasonable service at a cost that does not leave your pocketbook empty. Happily, the city possesses a substantial number of these facilities, the best of which are listed below.

Somehow the **Commodore International Hotel** does not quite live up to its baronial name. The place does feature a spacious lobby with bas-relief work along the walls, and there is a coffee shop and a cocktail lounge attached. But the rooms are undistinguished. Unambitiously decorated with sketches of San Francisco, they include wall-to-wall carpeting, televisions, shower-tub combos, and the usual creature comforts. Rooms vary in price, depending on "newness" and location. Recommended as a backup hotel, the Commodore International is a fair buy, but does not match other hotels in its class. ~ 825 Sutter Street; 415-923-6800, 800-338-6848, fax 415-923-6804; www.joiedevivre-sf.com.

The **Sheehan Hotel** was once the YWCA, which means it offers facilities not usually found in a moderately priced hotel, like a swimming pool and exercise rooms. But it's definitely not the Y anymore. The rooms have been nicely decorated with prints on the walls and antique-looking lamps, and the bathrooms are large. Guests can enjoy a complimentary continental breakfast in the lobby tearoom. ~ 620 Sutter Street; 415-775-6500, 800-848-1529, fax 415-775-3271; www.citysearch.com/sfo/sheehanhotel.

DELUXE LODGING   European elegance at reasonable cost: that's
what the **Beresford Hotel** has offered its clientele for years. You'll
sense a touch of class immediately upon treading the lobby's red
carpet and settling into a plump armchair. There's a historical flair
about the place, highpointed by the adjoining White Horse Tavern
and Restaurant, with its Olde England ambience. Upstairs the
rooms are outstanding—shag carpets, wooden headboards, original paintings, comfortable furnishings, small refrigerators, and
a marble-top vanity in the bathroom. All this, just two blocks
from Union Square. If you can beat it, let me know how. Complimentary continental buffet. ~ 635 Sutter Street; 415-673-9900,
800-533-6533, fax 415-474-0449; www.beresford.com.

The **Beresford Arms** is a sister hotel to the Beresford. Featuring
a similar antique lobby, the Beresford Arms has gracefully decorated its public area with a crystal chandelier, leather-tooled tables, stuffed armchairs, and an old grandfather clock. Casting
that same European aura, rooms often feature mahogany dressers
and headboards as well as the expected amenities like wall-to-wall
carpeting, tile tubs, spacious closets and VCRs with movie rentals
at the desk. All at the same moderate prices as the Beresford. The
Arms has suites with jacuzzis, kitchenettes, and wet bars. ~ 701
Post Street; 415-673-2600, 800-533-6533, fax 415-474-0449.

The **Hotel Carlton** features a rich lobby with marble floors,
brass wall sconces, and a fireplace. The rooms have been decorated subtly and with great care and are reasonably priced. Complimentary wine is served from 6 to 7 p.m. in the lobby. Though
located about a quarter-mile from Union Square, the Carlton is
highly recommended. ~ 1075 Sutter Street; 415-673-0242, 800-
922-7586, fax 415-673-4904; carltonhotel.com.

The brilliant polished wood facade of the **Savoy Hotel** provides only a hint of its luxurious interior. The lobby is the first
word in elegance with black and white marble floors, brass fixtures, and dark woods. The rooms at this lavish but affordable hotel second the invitation of the lobby. Sporting a French-country

NOTHING STAID IN THIS HOTEL

From the wild and crazy lobby with its dervish chairs to the sapphire
theater curtains in all 140 rooms, the **Hotel Triton** is a place with a sense
of humor. If you are seeking a hotel with a fantasy mural, furniture
that appears to undulate, iridescent throw pillows, starburst light
fixtures, and room service from several trendy restaurants, look
no further. An added plus is its proximity to Chinatown. ~ 342
Grant Avenue; 415-394-0500, 800-433-6611, fax 415-394-0555;
www.hotel-tritonsf.com. DELUXE TO ULTRA-DELUXE.

motif, they blend floral prints with attractive wood furniture. An afternoon tea-and-sherry hour is included. Add a tile bath-shower, goosedown featherbeds, color television, plus plenty of space, and you have one very noteworthy hotel. ~ 580 Geary Street; 415-441-2700, 800-227-4223, fax 415-441-0124.

The upscale **Nob Hill Hotel** boasts rooms and suites decorated in Italian Renaissance style, appointed with antiques and marble bathrooms. In addition, suites are equipped with wet bars and hot tubs. Continental breakfast included. ~ 835 Hyde Street; 415-885-2987, fax 415-921-1648; www.nobhillhotel.com.

Hotel David sits smack-dab in the center of the theater district, but even more important, it is located over David's Delicatessen, one of the best delis in town. The lobby is nearly nonexistent, but the rooms are attractively done in modern deco style, with warm woods, red bedspreads, and a print of a cobbler over each bed bringing a smile to those who enter the room. This hotel is immaculately clean, and anyone would be hard-pressed to find a speck of dust anywhere. The room rate includes an all-you-can-eat breakfast from the deli menu. This place is a true original. ~ 480 Geary Street; 415-771-1600, 800-524-1888, fax 415-931-5442.

Another upscale establishment is the **Hotel Union Square**. Built early in the century to accommodate visitors to the Panama–Pacific International Exposition, this 131-plus room hotel has been exquisitely decorated. Mystery writer Dashiell Hammett and playwright Lillian Hellman, who reportedly once frequented the place, might recognize it even today. The lobby possesses a contemporary ambience with its mosaic murals. The old speakeasy is reputed to have included a secret "chute entrance" from Ellis Street. Walls upstairs have been sandblasted to expose original brick and the rooms are decorated in quiet hues and floral prints. ~ 114 Powell Street; 415-397-3000, 800-553-1900, fax 415-885-3268; www.hotelunionsquare.com.

Up on Cathedral Hill, a mile or two from the Downtown district, stands **The Majestic**. As a hotel this five-story structure dates from 1902 when The Majestic opened as one of the city's first grand hotels. It underwent several incarnations before finally being reincarnated as The Majestic. The current 57-room establishment features a restaurant, bar, and attractive lobby. Some rooms are strikingly appointed with canopied beds, European antiques, and marble bathrooms. Rates start in the deluxe range. ~ 1500 Sutter Street; 415-441-1100, 800-869-8966, fax 415-673-7331; www.expedia.com.

ULTRA-DELUXE LODGING   Elegance and style? That would be the **White Swan Inn**. A six-story, English-style building with curved bay windows, the White Swan was originally built in 1908 as a small hotel. Today it is a fashionable bed and breakfast with a living room, library, solarium, and small courtyard. The decorative theme, reflected in the garden, wallpapers, and art prints, is English. Each room contains a fireplace, television, telephone, wet bar, coffee maker and private bath. Like the public rooms, they are all beautifully appointed. ~ 845 Bush Street; 415-775-1755, 800-999-9570, fax 415-775-5717; www.foursisters.com.

The **Hotel Rex** is one of those quirky kinds of places that sets itself apart from more ordinary hostelries. The lobby looks like a library, where you long to spend the evening curled up in front of the fireplace, with a glass of sherry and an antique book chosen from the hundreds on shelves around the room. The rooms are decorated in an eclectic mix and match of stripes and plaids, and the beds have teak headboards. ~ 562 Sutter Street; 415-433-4434, 800-433-4434, fax 415-433-3695.

Accommodations at the 25-story **Hotel Nikko** exude *shibui*, a Japanese word that expresses elegant simplicity. Smooth-edged contemporary furnishings and natural colors. Some rates include access to business services and fitness facilities, including a glass-enclosed rooftop swimming pool. ~ 222 Mason Street; 415-394-1111, 800-645-5687, fax 415-394-1106; www.nikkohotels.com.

Once inside the 21-story **Pan Pacific San Francisco**, some guests simply cannot believe there are 329 rooms and suites here; the ambience is more like that of an intimate small hotel. Guest rooms have fine furnishings, custom cabinetry, and distinctive arched windows. Despite their size, they feel cozy, almost too much so. Oversized marble baths and attentive valet service are extra indulgences at this ultra-deluxe-priced hotel a block west of Union Square. ~ 500 Post Street; 415-771-8600, 800-533-6465, fax 415-398-0267; www.panpac.com.

DINING

HIDDEN ▶

What can you say about a cozy restaurant that's always packed with diners? In the case of **Nhu's Vietnamese Cuisine**, you can say it passes the ultimate test of authenticity: not only Vietnamese are drawn to this unassuming café; the menu offers something for everyone. There are steamed rice dishes with spicy chicken, Vietnamese pork kebab, or lemon-grass beef, plus beefball soup, sautéed vegetables, imperial rolls, prawns, and chicken salad. Closed Sunday. ~ 581 Eddy Street; 415-474-6487. BUDGET.

Whoever coined the slogan "Eat at Joe's" surely had San Francisco in mind. The city sports a dizzying number of restaurants named after the omnipresent Joseph. But down along Taylor Street rests the **Original Joe's**. It's one of those cafés where the waiters don tuxes and the prices never compete with the quality of the food. A San Francisco institution, Original Joe's is in its third generation of operation by the same family. At least one waiter has been there over 50 years. The menu features a steak-and-chop

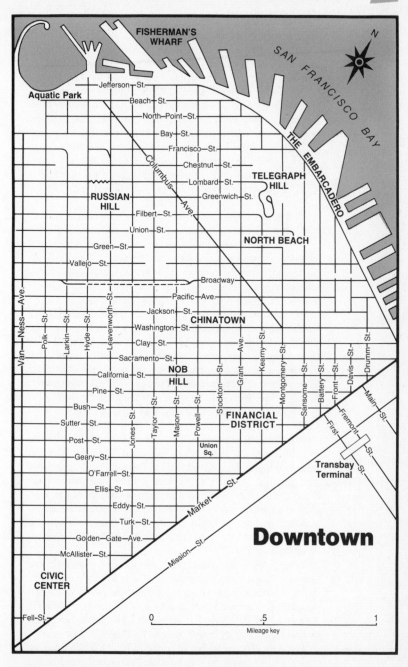

Downtown

menu which also includes Italian and fresh seafood dinners. Open for any meal. ~ 144 Taylor Street; 415-775-4877. MODERATE.

Whether they are hungry or not, Dashiell Hammett fans always track down **John's Grill**. It's the restaurant that detective Sam Spade popped into during a tense scene in *The Maltese Falcon*. Today the wood-paneled walls, adorned with memorabilia and old photos, still breathe of bygone eras. Waiters dress formally, the bartender gossips about local politicians, and the customers sink onto bar stools. The menu features broiler and seafood dishes as well as a nostalgic platter of chops, baked potato, and sliced tomato (what Spade wolfed down on that fateful day). No lunch on Sunday. ~ 63 Ellis Street; 415-986-3274. MODERATE TO DELUXE.

Stuck for a place to dine? There are more than 3000 restaurants in this city of 778,000.

Sushi Man is a matchbox sushi bar with matchless style. If that's not evident from the plastic sushi displays in the window, then step inside. The tiny wooden bar is decorated with serene silk screens and fresh flowers. Owner Ryo Yoshioka has earned a deserved reputation for his sushi creations. There's *sake* (smoked salmon), *mirugai* (clam), as well as sashimi. Dinner only. ~ 731 Bush Street; 415-981-1313. MODERATE.

Maiden Lane used to be a perfect spot for slumming; today it's a fashionable shopping district. But there's one place along the high-priced strip that brings back the easy days. **Bistro 69** is an unassuming deli serving a good array of sandwiches, salads, and mouth-watering pastries. Dine alfresco at one of the little tables out front or pull up a chair inside this brick-walled establishment. At lunch there will likely be a line extending out the door. Also open for breakfast. Closed Sunday. ~ 69 Maiden Lane; 415-398-3557. BUDGET.

It is the rare restaurateur who can please both Los Angeles and San Francisco, but that's exactly what Wolfgang Puck has done in bringing his talents north to **Postrio**. Puck's innovative food pairings, such as Chinese duck with braised endive, spicy cashews and green peppercorn sauce, and sautéed salmon with plum glaze and wasabi mashed potatoes, compete for attention with an absolutely stunning dining room. Brunch on Sunday. Reserve far in advance. ~ 545 Post Street; 415-776-7825. DELUXE TO ULTRA-DELUXE.

After dining at **Tempura House,** you will understand why the Financial District crowd goes out of its way to eat there. What's delivered to your table looks exactly like the plastic meals displayed in the front window, and everything's delicious. Tempura is the specialty of the house, but the grilled fish, sukiyaki, and sushi also rate highly. ~ 529 Powell Street; 415-393-9911. MODERATE.

HIDDEN ►

Indonesia Restaurant has developed a loyal following among the many San Franciscans who have lived or traveled in Indonesia.

And for good reason. The complex and diverse flavors in this tiny, crowded hole-in-the-wall establishment tantalize the taste buds. Such favorite dishes as *gado-gado*, *soto ayam*, beef curry, *mie goreng*, *rendang*, and *sate* are included on the menu, as well as many others. ~ 678 Post Street; 415-474-4026. BUDGET.

SHOPPING

Union Square quite simply is *the* center for shopping in San Francisco. First of all, this grass-and-hedgerow park (located between Post and Geary, Stockton and Powell streets) is surrounded by department stores. **Macy's** is along one border. ~ 170 O'Farrell Street; 415-397-3333. **Saks Fifth Avenue** guards another. ~ 384 Post Street; 415-986-4300. **Neiman-Marcus**, the Texas-bred emporium, claims one corner. ~ 150 Stockton Street; 415-362-3900. An elite men's clothing shop named **Bullock & Jones** is also situated in this well-heeled neighborhood. ~ 340 Post Street; 415-392-4243. Once the haven of myriad European specialty boutiques, Union Square is becoming a hot address for sport-shoes shops, entertainment-company merchandising centers, and mass-appeal clothing stores.

Of course, that's just on the square. Beyond the plaza are scads of stores. Along Stockton, one of the streets radiating out from the square, you'll find a number of prestigious shops.

Then if you follow Post, another bordering street, there is **Gump's**, which features fine imported decorations for the home. If you get bored looking through the antiques, china pieces, and oriental art, you can always adjourn to the Crystal Room. ~ 135 Post Street; 415-982-1616.

The streets all around host a further array of stores. You will encounter jewelers, clothing designers, boutiques, furniture stores, tailor shops, and more. So take a gander—there's everything out there from the unexpected to the bizarre.

Braunstein/Quay Gallery is an outstanding place to view the work of local artists. As the catalog claims, owner Ruth Braunstein "embodies the brash, irreverent, and irrepressible energy of the San Francisco art world." This contemporary gallery also exhibits works from other parts of the world. ~ 250 Sutter Street; 415-392-5532.

Tillman Place Bookshop is a postage stamp–sized store tucked into an alleyway. Within, however, you'll find a tasteful collection of coffee-table books, paperback classics and travel guides, all contained in a Victorian setting. ~ 8 Tillman Place; 415-392-4668.

When looking for maps and travel guides, try **Thomas Brothers Maps**. This company actually produces many of the maps it sells and has gained renown for its excellent city maps. ~ 550 Jackson Street; 415-981-7520.

Also consider the **Rand McNally Map & Travel Store**. Here is everything the wanderer could conceivably desire: guidebooks, maps, globes, language tapes, and geography games for kids. ~ 595 Market Street; 415-777-3131.

Harold's Hometown News is a shop specializing in "hometown newspapers." There are dailies from all over the world. For homesick travelers, or those just interested in a little local news, it's a godsend. ~ 524 Geary Street; 415-441-2665.

American Indian Contemporary Arts is the place to go for traditional and contemporary works. Squash blossom jewelry, mask art, and moccasins are exhibited alongside mixed media and acrylic paintings. You'll also find books, posters, and videos focusing on American Indians. ~ 23 Grant Avenue; 415-989-7003.

The Galleria, a glass-domed promenade lined with fashionable shops, attracts a well-heeled crowd—showcasing designer fashions and elegant gifts. ~ 50 Post Street; 415-956-2846.

A nine-story vertical mall, the **San Francisco Shopping Centre** sports six stacked spiral escalators that ascend through an oval-shaped, marble-and-granite atrium toward the retractable skylight. The mall includes nearly 90 upscale shops selling everything from men's and women's sportswear to jewelry and unique gifts. The center is all crowned by a five-floor **Nordstrom**, the high-quality fashion department store. ~ 5th and Market Streets; 415-243-8500.

One notable Maiden Lane shop is **Folk Art International**, offering antique Guatemalan woven shirts, folk sculptures, baskets, pottery, coconut masks, and other folk crafts from Latin America. Europe and Asia are also represented with antique jewelry from India and gem-quality Baltic amber from Poland and Denmark. ~ FLW building, 140 Maiden Lane; 415-392-9999.

NIGHTLIFE   Since its rowdy Gold Rush days, San Francisco has been renowned as a wide-open town, hard-drinking and easygoing. Today there are over 2000 places around the city to order a drink, including saloons, restaurants, cabarets, boats, private clubs, and even a couple hospitals. There's a bar for every mood and each occasion.

When looking for nightlife, it is advisable to consult the *SF Bay Guardian* or the "Datebook," commonly called the "pink section," in the Sunday *San Francisco Examiner and Chronicle* for current shows and performers. However you decide to spend the evening, you'll find plenty of possibilities in this city by the Bay.

San Francisco's answer to a Scottish pub is **Edinburgh Castle**, a cavernous bar complete with dart board. There's a beamed ceiling, heavy wooden furniture, and convivial crowd—Scotland incarnate. ~ 950 Geary Street; 415-885-4074.

Then, if you like key-plunking saloon music, there's **Lefty O'Doul's**. Friendly, informal, and filled with baseball memorabilia, the place is named for an old-time local ballplayer. ~ 333 Geary Street; 415-982-8900.

The **Warfield Theatre**, owned by the late rock impresario Bill Graham's company, brings in top groups from around the country. Bill Graham Presents produces other shows regularly throughout the Bay Area. ~ 982 Market Street; 415-775-7722.

The **Plush Room** in the York Hotel caters to an upscale clientele and draws big-name cabaret acts. It's a lovely setting. Cover. ~ 940 Sutter Street; 415-885-2800.

The "On Broadway" theater scene in San Francisco is on Geary Street, near Union Square; while the "Off Broadway," or avant-garde drama, is scattered around the city.

Built in 1910, the Beaux Arts–style **Geary Theater** reopened in 1996 after extensive repair and renovation, and now features a sky lobby. This state historic landmark is home of the **American Conservatory Theater**, or ACT, the biggest show in town. It's also one of the nation's largest resident companies. The season runs from September to July, and the repertory is traditional, ranging from Shakespeare to French comedy to 20th-century drama. ~ Geary Theater, 415 Geary Street; 415-749-2228.

The **Curran Theatre** brings Broadway musicals to town. ~ 445 Geary Street; 415-551-2000. **Golden Gate Theatre** also attracts major shows and national companies. Built in 1922, the theater is a grand affair with marble floors and rococo ceilings. ~ 1 Taylor Street, at the corner of 6th and Market streets; 415-551-2000. Among the city's other playhouses is the **Marine's Memorial Theatre**. ~ 609 Sutter Street; 415-771-6900. **Theatre on the Square** is right on Union Square. ~ 450 Post Street; 415-433-9500. Close to the Civic Center is the **Orpheum Theatre**. ~ 1192 Market Street; 415-551-2000. Experimental theater is the specialty of **Cable Car Theatre**. ~ 430 Mason Street; 415-956-8497.

Many local radio stations sponsor event hotlines. There's the KKSF **Bayline**, with information on concerts, traffic, and weather. ~ 415-357-1037. Live 105's **The What Line** provides details on concerts, movies, and the dance club scene. ~ 415-357-9428. Or check KFOG's **Digital Switchboard** for local goings-on. ~ 415-777-1045.

▼▼▼▼▼▼▼▼▼

Civic Center

On the other side of the Downtown district, to the southwest, rises the Civic Center, architectural pride of the city. The prettiest path through this municipal meeting ground begins in United Nations Plaza at Fulton and Market streets.

SIGHTS

Every Wednesday and Sunday this promenade is home to the **Heart of the City Farmers' Market**, an open-air produce fair that draws farmers from all over Northern California.

◄ HIDDEN

To experience one of the country's most modern information centers, saunter on over to the main branch of the **San Francisco**

Public Library in its $104.5 million headquarters that opened in the spring of 1996. Exemplifying the fact that libraries are not just about books anymore (in fact, critics charge that the architectural splendor and special features have resulted in a lack of shelf space), the main branch's facilities include 400 electronic workstations with free connection to the Internet. Among the library's 11 special-interest research centers are the San Francisco History Center, the Gay and Lesbian Center, and the Art and Music Center. ~ 100 Larkin Street; 415-557-4400.

With its bird-whitened statues and gray-columned buildings, the Civic Center is the domain of powerbrokers and political leaders; ironically, its grassy plots and park benches also make it the haunt of the city's homeless. As you pass the reflecting pool and then ascend the steps of **City Hall,** you'll see how both halves live.

Modeled after the national capitol, this granite and marble edifice sports a gold-leaf dome that is actually higher than the one in Washington. Recently renovated and retrofitted, the rotunda is a dizzying sandstone and marble affair encrusted with statuary and encircled by a wrought-iron balcony. French Renaissance in style, City Hall is the centerpiece of the Civic Center, which in turn is the ultimate expression of the "City Beautiful" philosophy that inspired the rebuilders of post-earthquake San Francisco to design one of the country's most splendid civic centers. ~ Polk and Grove streets.

If you go around City Hall on to Van Ness Avenue, you'll be standing face to facade with the center of San Francisco culture. To the right rises the Veterans' Building, which formerly housed the San Francisco Museum of Modern Art. ~ 401 Van Ness Avenue. Centerstage is the **War Memorial Opera House,** home of

✔ **CHECK THESE OUT—UNIQUE SIGHTS**

- Stroll along **Herb Caen Way** for expansive views of Treasure Island and the Bay Bridge. *page 49*
- Wander Chinatown's **Waverly Place,** an alley-like street where mystery writer Dashiell Hammett led readers in *Dead Yellow Women.* *page 55*
- Step back to days of yore as you board one of the **Historic Ships** docked at the Hyde Street Pier. *page 66*
- Don headphones for the **Alcatraz** audio tour and experience this former prison through the voices of its former guards and inmates. *page 67*

one of the world's finest opera companies as well as the San Francisco Ballet Company. ~ 301 Van Ness Avenue at Grove Street.

To the left, that ultramodern glass-and-granite building is the **Louise M. Davies Symphony Hall**, home of the San Francisco Symphony. Through the semi-circle of green-tinted glass, you can peer into one of the city's most glamorous buildings. Or if you'd prefer to be on the inside gazing out, there are tours of the hall and its cultural cousins next door. Admission. ~ Van Ness Avenue and Grove Street; information, 415-552-8338.

One of the best places in town to appreciate the city's rich cultural tradition is the **San Francisco Performing Arts Library and Museum**. The collection covers San Francisco's musical and theatrical heritage with photos, programs, books, and costumes. The exhibits cover everything from Jean Cocteau to the local symphony association. Closed Sunday through Tuesday. ~ 401 Van Ness Avenue; 415-255-4800.

Guided tours of the Civic Center begin at the **San Francisco Public Library** (call 415-557-4266 for information on tours).

A two-story motor court flanking a pool courtyard, spacious rooms and suites with a soft tropical motif, a Caribbean-style restaurant . . . can this be the heart of San Francisco? It is, and it's the **Phoenix Hotel**, just a long block from Civic Center. Concierge services and the patronage of music-business mavens may make the Phoenix the hippest inn in town. ~ 601 Eddy Street; 415-776-1380, 800-248-9466, fax 415-885-3109; www.joiede vivre-sf.com. DELUXE.

LODGING

◄ HIDDEN

Located on the border between the city's stately Civic Center and unwashed Tenderloin district, **San Francisco Central** YMCA has singles and doubles with shared baths. In traditional Y-style, the rooms are as clean as they are sterile; they are scantily furnished and tend to be cramped. But for those prices—which include a continental breakfast and free use of the sunroof, pool, sauna, steam room, weight room, laundry, aerobics area, and basketball and racquetball courts—who's complaining? ~ 220 Golden Gate Avenue; 415-885-0460, fax 415-885-5439; e-mail rdenoia @ymca.org.inter.net. BUDGET.

Right on the edge of the Civic Center, the **Hotel Renoir** is one of the more economical accommodations. The lobby is lined with Renoir prints and decorated in gold and soft peach colors. There's a lounge and a friendly ambience about the place. The only detraction is its location on busy Market Street and proximity to the city's Tenderloin district; but the moderate room tabs make it worth the price. Rooms are small but reasonably well furnished. The accommodations I saw featured wall-to-wall carpeting, color television, steam heat, plush furniture, and a tile bathroom with shower-tub combination. ~ 45 McAllister Street; 415-626-5200, 800-576-3388, fax 415-626-0916; www.renoir hotel.com. DELUXE.

DINING   This area spotlights several outstanding dining rooms. One of the best in my opinion is **Hayes Street Grill**, a chic establishment situated within strolling distance of the opera and symphony. Specializing in mesquite-grilled entrées, it features fresh fish dishes, dry-aged steak, and chicken breast. Excellent food. No lunch on the weekend. ~ 320 Hayes Street; 415-863-5545. MODERATE TO DELUXE.

No place is a better example of the eccentric establishments for which San Francisco is famous than **Mad Magda's Russian Tea Room & Café**. You can enjoy a cup of smoked Russian tea or a bowl of homemade borsch, while getting tarot cards, tea leaves, or your palm read by the resident psychic. The sandwiches are named after famous Russians. Catherine the Great is tuna with cheese; Tolstoy, a long sandwich with ham, turkey, and several cheeses; Faberge, baked eggplant, mozzarella, and balsamic vinaigrette on a baguette. Open for three meals a day. ~ 579 Hayes Street; 415-864-7654. BUDGET.

HIDDEN ►   **Vicolo Pizzeria** may be a bit hard to find, but the reward is gourmet pizza different than any you may have tasted before. The restaurant's decor, marked by corrugated steel hanging from the walls, is a reminder that the building was formerly an auto mechanic's shop. Served primarily by the slice, Vicolo's pizza is characterized by its distinctive cornmeal crust. Sausage, four cheese, and two vegetarian varieties are the standards, with other choices changing regularly. ~ 201 Ivy Street; 415-863-2382. BUDGET.

Stars earned its stripes from day one with the stylish cuisine of Jeremiah Tower, a highly celebrated chef in the New American cuisine constellation. Seafood, warm salads and French-inspired chicken entrées shine especially bright here. No lunch on the weekend. ~ 555 Golden Gate Avenue; 415-861-7827. DELUXE TO ULTRA-DELUXE.

Max's Opera Café serves a variety of fare ranging from smoked barbecued ribs to California cuisine, but the standouts are the thick pastrami, corned beef, and turkey breast sandwiches accompanied by tangy coleslaw and potato salad. A lively bar area features occasional impromptu entertainment by the staff, some of whom are budding tenors and sopranos. ~ 601 Van Ness Avenue; 415-771-7301. MODERATE.

A café setting that features brass fixtures, pastel walls, bentwood furniture, and Asian artwork make **Thepin** an inviting Thai establishment. The fare, ranging from red curry duck to marinated prawns and chicken breast, is also a winner. Specialties include sliced chicken and shrimp with spinach in peanut sauce, marinated filet of salmon in curry sauce, and sliced green papaya salad with tomatoes and chili pepper. No lunch on the weekend. ~ 298 Gough Street; 415-863-9335. MODERATE.

Hayes Valley lies directly west of the Civic Center and has as its focus the block bounded by Hayes, Franklin, Grove, and Gough streets. Of particular importance here is the **Vorpal Gallery**. One of the city's finest galleries, it features works by Jesse Allen, Ken Matsumoto, and other contemporary artists. There are also paintings and prints by such 20th-century masters as Pablo Picasso and M. C. Escher, as well as by Yozo Hamaguchi, the master of mezzotint. ~ 393 Grove Street; 415-397-9200.

SHOPPING

The **San Francisco Women Artists Gallery** across the street features artworks mostly by Bay Area women. The variety of arts and crafts is impressive and the pieces are quite good. Several other galleries are located in the immediate neighborhood, making the Hayes Street corridor an artists' enclave. ~ 370 Hayes Street; 415-552-7392.

F. Dorian specializes in crafts from all over the world including ethnic and contemporary items. The company also sells antique furniture from the Philippines, Indian oil lamps, Indonesian diary boxes, and exotic jewelry. ~ 388 Hayes Street; 415-861-3191.

Just a few blocks away lies **Opera Plaza** (Van Ness and Golden Gate avenues), an atrium mall with shops, restaurants, and a movie theater collected around a courtyard and fountain. It's a pretty place to sit and enjoy the day. For booklovers there's an excellent bookstore here: **A Clean Well-Lighted Place For Books**. ~ 601 Van Ness Avenue; 415-441-6670.

San Francisco is rich culturally in its opera, symphony, and ballet, located in the Civic Center area. Since tickets to major theatrical and other cultural events are expensive, consider buying day-of-performance tickets from **San Francisco Ticket Box Office Service** (TIX) on Stockton Street between Post and Geary streets. Open from 11 a.m. until just before showtime, they sell tickets at half-price on the day of the show and full price for future events. Closed Sunday and Monday. ~ 415-433-7827; www.theatrebayarea.org.

NIGHTLIFE

San Francisco takes nothing quite so seriously as its opera. The **San Francisco Opera** is world class in stature and invites operatic greats from around the world to perform. As a result, tickets can be very difficult to obtain. The international season begins in mid-September and runs 'til mid-January. ~ 301 Van Ness Avenue; 415-864-3330.

The **San Francisco Symphony** stands nearly as tall on the world stage. The season extends from September until June, with a series of special concerts through July. Michael Tilson Thomas conducts, and guest soloists have included the likes of Jessye Norman and Itzhak Perlman. ~ Davies Hall, Van Ness Avenue and Grove Street; 415-864-6000.

The **San Francisco Ballet**, performing for more than a half-century, is the nation's oldest permanent ballet, and one of the finest. Featuring *The Nutcracker* during Christmas, the company's official season runs at the Opera House from February until May. In addition to original works, they perform classic ballets. ~ 301 Van Ness Avenue; 415-865-2000.

Over at the **Great American Music Hall**, a vintage 1907 building has been splendidly converted to a nightclub featuring a variety of entertainers. Included in the lineup are musical greats like Hoyt Axton, Etta James, and Queen Ida, as well as contemporary rock-and-roll acts like the Dave Matthews Band. ~ 859 O'Farrell Street; 415-885-0750.

▼▼▼▼▼▼▼▼▼▼
Embarcadero

Where the city's skyscrapers meet the Bay is the Embarcadero. This waterfront promenade has become increasingly appealing since the 1989 earthquake, which resulted in the dismantling of a freeway that once ran along the bayfront. Today the vistas are unobstructed and the strip is wide open for leisurely wandering.

Back in Gold Rush days, before the pernicious advent of landfill, the entire area sat beneath fathoms of water and went by the name of Yerba Buena Cove. Matter of fact, the hundreds of tall-masted ships abandoned here by crews deserting for the gold fields eventually became part of the landfill.

Nature is rarely a match for the shovel. The Bay was pressed back from around Montgomery Street to its present perimeter. As you head down from the Financial District, walk softly; the world may be four billion years old, but the earth you're treading has been around little more than a century.

SIGHTS

Fittingly enough, the first place encountered is **Embarcadero Center**, a skein of five skyscrapers rising sharp and slender along Sacramento Street to the foot of Market Street. This $645 million complex, oft tagged "Rockefeller Center West," features a three-tiered pedestrian mall that links the buildings together in a labyrinth of shops, restaurants, fountains, and gardens.

Embarcadero Five is the **Hyatt Regency**. It's one of the few hotels you'll ever find detailed as a sightseeing feature. The reason is the lobby, a towering atrium that rises 170 feet. It's a triangular affair lined with a succession of interior balconies that rise to a skylighted roof. Along one side, plants cascade in a 20-story hanging garden, while another wall is designed in a zigzag shape which gives the sensation of being inside a 21st-century pyramid. ~ Corner of Market and California streets.

Speaking of the future, that blocky complex of cement pipes from which water pours in every direction is not an erector set run amok. It's **Vaillancourt Fountain**, situated smack in the Hyatt's front yard. The patchwork of grass and pavement surrounding is **Justin Herman Plaza**, a perfect place for a promenade or picnic. Craft vendors with engraved brass belt buckles, silver jewelry, and beanbag chairs have made the plaza their storefront and skaters have made it their playground. It's also the starting point for the monthly roving bicycle protest known as Critical Mass.

Just across the road, where Market Street encounters the Embarcadero, rises San Francisco's answer to the Statue of Liberty. Or what was the city's answer at the turn of the century, when the clock tower of the **Ferry Building** was as well-known a landmark as the Golden Gate Bridge is today. Back then there were no bridges, and 100,000 ferryboat commuters a day poured through the portals of the world's second busiest passenger terminal. Built in 1896, the landmark is making a comeback. Sleek, jet-powered ferries stream into refashioned slips, and plans are afloat to space age the entire complex with the help of noted architect I. M. Pei.

You might want to walk the ramp that leads up to the **World Trade Center**, on Embarcadero at the foot of Market Street. It's lined with Covarrubias' murals that were preserved from the 1939 Golden Gate International Exposition. They look like those maps in your old sixth grade social studies book; one vividly depicts "the people of the Pacific" with aborigines sprouting up from the Australian land mass and seraped Indians guarding the South American coast. Another pictorial geography lesson features the Pacific economy with salmon swimming off the North American shore and rice bowls growing in China.

One positive result of the horrendous 1989 Loma Prieta earthquake was the demolition of the Embarcadero Freeway, a long-time eyesore that ran like a concrete scar through the waterfront area. Now that the freeway is gone, there is a lighter and brighter look to the area, with palm trees planted along the Embarcadero and more expansive views of the Bay Bridge and Treasure Island. In 1996, the city named the pedestrian promenade that parallels the boulevard **Herb Caen Way**, in honor of San Francisco's famous gossip columnist, who died in 1997. At the same time, a new neighborhood is fast growing up around and to the south of lower Market Street with apartments, restaurants, nightspots, and a Saturday morning farmers' market.

The Rincon Annex is a restored 1930s post office with magnificent WPA murals glorifying science and technology. It is connected to the **Rincon Center**, a popular gathering spot for locals, especially at noontime. The center features a cluster of eateries offering everything from Korean noodles to Indian curries. The eateries surround a central indoor courtyard dining area and spectacular, rainfall-like fountain. ~ 101 Spear Street; 415-777-4100.

Stretching from either side of the Ferry Building are the rows of **shipping piers** that once made San Francisco a fabulous harbor. Today much of the commerce has sailed across the Bay to the Port of Oakland. To recapture San Francisco's maritime era, head north on Embarcadero from the Ferry Building along the odd-numbered piers. The city looms to your left and the Bay heaves and glistens before you. This is a world of seaweed and fog horns where proverbial old salts still ply their trade. Blunt-nosed tugboats tie up next to rusting relics from Guadalcanal. There are modern jet ferries, displaying the latest aeronautical curves and appearing ready at any moment to depart from the water for open sky. The old, big-girthed ferries have been stripped of barnacles, painted nursery colors, and leased out as office space; they are floating condominiums.

Along this parade of piers you'll see a number of cavernous concrete wharves astir with forklifts and dockhands. Locomotives shunt with a clatter, trucks jockey for an inside post, and container cranes sweep the air. Other piers have fallen into desuetude, rust-caked wharves propped on water-rotted pilings. The only common denominators in this odd arithmetic progression of piers are the seagulls and pelicans whitening the pylons.

Across from Pier 23, **Levi's Plaza** features a grassy park ideal for picnicking; just beyond Pier 35 there's a waterfront park with a wonderful vantage for spying on the ships that sail the Bay. ~ 1155 Battery Street.

LODGING Just one block from the Embarcadero and convenient to the Financial District, the **Hotel Griffon** offers 62 attractive rooms appointed with modern art, window seats, oversized mirrors, and, in a few cases, bay views. A cozy lobby features a library and fireplace, and there's an adjacent fitness center. ~ 155 Steuart Street; 415-495-2100, 800-321-2201, fax 415-495-3522. ULTRA-DELUXE.

On the same block is **Harbor Court Hotel** where some of the 131 rooms and suites also offer marine views. Guest rooms are small but attractively appointed with nautical prints, big mirrors, canopied beds, and brass sconces. The lobby is large, comfortable, and ideal for leisurely afternoons. You can also relax at the health club and indoor pool next to the hotel. ~ 165 Steuart Street; 415-882-1300, 800-346-0555, fax 415-777-5457; www.harbor-courthotel.com. ULTRA-DELUXE.

San Francisco's modern version of camp is **Fog City Diner**. It is the most upscale diner you've ever seen. Check out the exterior with its art deco curves, neon lights, and checkerboard tile. Then step into a wood-and-brass paneled restaurant that has the feel of a club car on the Orient Express. Featuring California cuisine, the menu changes frequently, though on a given day it will be the same for both lunch and dinner. Everything is à la carte, including the Fog City T-shirts. What can I tell you except to book a reservation in advance. ~ 1300 Battery Street; 415-982-2000. MODERATE.

DINING

One of San Francisco's finest and most authentic Hong Kong–style restaurants is not located in Chinatown, but is tucked into a corner of the Embarcadero Center. **Harbor Village** serves exquisite Cantonese dishes such as crisp, juicy roast chicken, steamed catfish, and shark's fin soup in an elegant setting of Chinese antiques and teak furnishings. At lunchtime, its dim sum selections are among the best in the city. ~ 4 Embarcadero Center; 415-781-8833. MODERATE TO DELUXE.

◄ HIDDEN

Head on down to **Pier 23 Cafe**, a little shack between Fisherman's Wharf and downtown, for unique waterfront dining. The place is funky but nice, with white tablecloths and linen napkins on the tables. Dine inside or on the huge back patio overlooking the bay. This restaurant specializes in seafood and offers six or seven fish specials daily. The deep-fried calamari appetizer and the oven-roasted crab with garlic, parsley, and butter dipping sauce are two of the most popular items on the menu. ~ Pier 23; 415-362-5125. MODERATE.

◄ HIDDEN

Shoppers along the Embarcadero head for the **Embarcadero Center**, located on Sacramento Street near the foot of Market Street. At publication time, it was under re-construction, slated for completion sometime in 1999.

SHOPPING

The Holding Company is crowded with young professionals on the make. Closed Saturday and Sunday. ~ 2 Embarcadero Center; 415-986-0797.

NIGHTLIFE

◆◆

CLASSROOM CUISINE

With two restaurants, the **California Culinary Academy** offers everything from a green salad to a classical European buffet. Here students under faculty supervision hone their talents. Located in a skylit Neo-classic hall, the Careme Room serves three-course lunches and seven-course dinners as well as weekend buffets. Downstairs, the Academy Grill serves à la carte specialties such as eggplant parmigiana and calamari *fritti*. ~ 625 Polk Street; 415-771-3500, ext. 229. MODERATE TO ULTRA-DELUXE.

Over at the Hyatt Regency, there's a revolving rooftop bar, **The Equinox**. A glass-encased elevator whisks you to this aerie, where you can pull up a window seat and watch the world spin. ~ 5 Embarcadero Center; 415-788-1234.

Pier 23 is a funky roadhouse that happens to sit next to the San Francisco waterfront. The sounds emanating from this saloon are live jazz, reggae, salsa, and blues. Highly recommended to those searching for the simple rhythms of life. There's music every day, sometimes in the afternoon, sometimes at night. Cover. ~ Embarcadero and Pier 23; 415-362-5125.

Funk bands get the everyday groove going at **Harry Denton's Bar & Grill**. In the back room late in the week, deejays spin disco and funk to young, well-dressed professionals. Cover. ~ 161 Steuart Street; 415-882-1333.

▼▼▼▼▼▼▼▼▼▼
Chinatown

It's the largest Chinatown outside Asia, a spot that older Chinese know as *dai fao*, Big City. San Francisco's Chinatown also ranks as the city's most densely populated neighborhood. Home to about 40,000 of the city's 150,000 Chinese, this enclave has been an Asian stronghold since the 1850s. Originally a ghetto where Chinese people were segregated from San Francisco society, the neighborhood today opens its arms to burgeoning numbers of immigrants from a host of Asian nations.

On the surface, this pulsing, noisy, chaotically colorful 70-square-block stretch projects the aura of a tourist's dream—gold and crimson pagodas, stores brimming with exquisite silks and multicolored dragons, more restaurants per square foot than could be imagined, roast ducks strung up in shop windows next door to Buddhist temples and fortune cookie factories.

But Chinatown is far more than a tourist mecca. This crowded neighborhood is peopled with families, powerful political groups, small merchants, poor working immigrants and rising entrepreneurs molding a more prosperous future. Although the "city within a city" that Chinatown once symbolized now encompasses only a quarter of San Francisco's Chinese people, it's still a center of Chinese history, culture, arts, and traditions that have lived for thousands of years.

In dramatic fashion, you enter Chinatown through an arching gateway bedecked with dragons. Stone lions guard either side of this portal at Grant Avenue and Bush Street.

SIGHTS

To stroll the eight-block length of Chinatown's **Grant Avenue** is to walk along San Francisco's oldest street. Today it's an ultramodern thoroughfare lined with Chinese arts-and-crafts shops, restaurants, and Asian markets. It's also one of the most crowded streets you'll ever squeeze your way through. Immortalized in a song from the musical *Flower Drum Song*, Grant Avenue, San Francisco, California, U.S.A., is a commotion, clatter, a clash of cultures. At any moment, a rickety truck may pull up beside you, heave open its doors, and reveal its contents—a cargo of chinaware, fresh produce, or perhaps flattened pig carcasses. Elderly Chinese men lean along doorways smoking fat cigars, and Chinatown's younger generation sets off down the street clad in leather jackets.

Known to local folks as the "Pyramid building," the Transamerica Building is a 48-story structure that rises 853 feet above the city pavement.

At the corner of California Street, where cable cars clang across Grant Avenue, rises the lovely brick structure of **Old St. Mary's Church**. Dating to 1854, this splendid cathedral was originally built of stone quarried in China. Just across the way in **St. Mary's Square**, there's a statue of the father of the Chinese Republic, Dr. Sun Yat Sen, crafted by San Francisco's foremost sculptor, Beniamino Bufano. You might take a hint from the crowds of businesspeople from the nearby financial center who bring their picnic lunches to this tree-shaded plaza.

Next you'll encounter **Mam Kue School**. With an iron fence, mullioned doors, and pagoda-like facade, it's an architectural beauty ironically backdropped by a glass-and-concrete skyscraper. ~ 755 Sacramento Street.

As you walk along Grant Avenue, with its swirling roof lines and flashing signs, take a peek down **Commercial Street**. This curious brick-paved street permits a glimpse into "hidden" Chinatown. Lined with everything from a noodle company to a ginseng shop, this tightly packed street also houses the **Mow Lee Company**, Chinatown's second oldest establishment. ~ 774 Commercial Street.

After you've immersed yourself in Chinese history, head down to **Portsmouth Square** (Kearny and Washington streets) for a lesson in the history of all San Francisco. Formerly the city's central plaza, it was here in 1846 that Yankees first raised the Stars and Stripes. Two years later, the California gold discovery was announced to the world from this square. Rudyard Kipling, Jack London, and Robert Louis Stevenson once wandered the grounds. At one corner of the park you'll find the bronze statue of a galleon celebrating the ocean-going Stevenson. Today this gracious park is a gathering place for old Chinese men playing mah jongg and practicing tai chi. From the center of the plaza, a walkway arches directly into the **Chinese Culture Center**, with its displays of Asian art. Located on the third floor of the Holiday Inn Hotel, it's closed Monday. ~ 750 Kearny Street; 415-986-1822.

Now that you've experienced the traditional tour, you might want to explore the hidden heart of Chinatown. First take a stroll along **Stockton Street**, which runs parallel to, and one block above, Grant Avenue. It is here, not along touristy Grant Avenue, that the Chinese shop.

The street vibrates with the crazy commotion of Chinatown. Open stalls tumbling with vegetables cover the sidewalk, and crates of fresh fish are stacked along the curb. Through this maze of merchandise, shoppers press past one another. In store windows hang Peking ducks, and on the counters are displayed pigs' heads and snapping turtles. Rare herbs, healing teas, and chrysanthemum crystals crowd the shelves.

The local community's artwork is displayed in a fantastic **mural** that covers a half-block between Pacific and Jackson streets.

To further explore the interior life of Chinatown, turn down Sacramento Street from Stockton Street, then take a quick left into Hang Ah Street. This is the first in a series of alleyways leading for three blocks from Sacramento Street to Jackson Street. When you get to the end of each block, simply jog over to the next alley.

HIDDEN ▶   A universe unto themselves, these **alleyways of Chinatown** are where the secret business of the community goes on, as it has for over a century. Each door is a barrier beyond which you can hear the rattle of mah jongg tiles and the sounds of women bent to their tasks in laundries and sewing factories.

Along Hang Ah Street, timeworn buildings are draped with fire escapes and colored with the images of fading signs. As you cross Clay Street, at the end of Hang Ah Street, be sure to press your nose against the glass at **Grand Century Enterprise**. Here the ginseng and other precious roots sell for hundreds of dollars a pound. ~ 858 Clay Street; 415-392-4060.

The next alley, **Spofford Lane**, is a corridor of painted doorways and brick facades humming with the strains of Chinese melodies. It ends at Washington Street where you can zigzag over to

◆◆◆

CHINATOWN—A DIFFERENT PERSPECTIVE

Just off the notorious Columbus/Broadway intersection lies a museum that will open wide your perspective on Chinatown's history. The **Chinese Historical Society of America** graphically presents the history of San Francisco's Chinese population. In the museum is a magnificent collection of photos and artifacts re-creating the Chinese experience from the days of pig-tailed "coolies" to the recent advent of ethnic consciousness. Moderate in size but wide in scope, the museum is a treasure house with a helpful and congenial staff. Open Tuesday through Friday, 10 a.m. until 4 p.m. or by appointment. ~ 644 Broadway, #402; 415-391-1188.

Ross Alley. This is the home of the **Golden Gate Fortune Cookie Factory**. At this small family establishment you can watch your fortune being made. ~ 56 Ross Alley; 415-781-3956.

The last segment in this intriguing tour will take you back to **Waverly Place**, a two-block stretch leading from Washington Street to Sacramento Street. Readers of Dashiell Hammett's mystery story, *Dead Yellow Women*, will recall this spot. It's an enchanting thoroughfare, more alley than street. At first glance, the wrought-iron balconies draped along either side of Waverly evoke images of New Orleans. But not even the French Quarter can boast the beauty contained in those Chinese cornices and pagoda swirl roof lines.

Prize jewel in this architectural crown is **Tian Hou Temple**. Here Buddhists and Taoists worship in a tiny temple overhung with fiery red lanterns. There are statues portraying battlefields and country landscapes; incense smolders from several altars. From the pictures along the wall, Buddha smiles out upon the believers. They in turn gaze down from the balcony onto Chinatown's most magical street. ~ 125 Waverly Place.

Just uphill from Chinatown stands the **Cable Car Museum**, a brick goliath which houses the city's cable cars. The museum here provides a great opportunity to see how these wood-and-steel masterpieces operate. The system's powerhouse, repair, and storage facilities are here, as are the 14-foot diameter sheaves that neatly wind the cable into figure-eight patterns. The museum also has on display three antique cable cars, including the first one ever built. ~ 1201 Mason Street; 415-474-1887.

DINING

Vegetarians favor **Lotus Garden**, a lovely restaurant that includes a Taoist temple on its upper floor. With Asian murals and ornamented altars, the temple provides a calming retreat from bustling Chinatown. The restaurant itself is equally mellow. In addition to standard Chinese vegetarian fare, it serves up exotic dishes like sweet corn and snow fungus soup, plus bitter melon with sliced gluten puff. ~ 532 Grant Avenue; 415-397-0707. BUDGET.

Among budget restaurants, **Sam Wo** is a San Francisco classic. Dining in this jook house is a rare adventure. The entrance is also the kitchen, and the kitchen is just a corridor filled with pots, stovepipes, cooks, and steamy smells. Sam Wo's menu is extensive and the food is quite good for the price. ~ 813 Washington Street; 415-982-0596. BUDGET.

For luxurious dining in the heart of Chinatown, no place matches the **Empress of China**. Set on the top floor of the China Trade Center, with nothing between you and heaven, it is a culinary temple. Dining rooms are adorned with carved antiques and the maitre'd dons a tuxedo. Lunch at this roof garden restaurant begins with appetizers like Shanghai dumplings and barbecued quail, then graduates to lichee chicken and Manchurian beef. Dinner is the true extravagance. The menu includes a royal variety of chicken, duck, lamb, shellfish, pork, and beef dishes. ~ 838 Grant Avenue; 415-434-1345. DELUXE TO ULTRA-DELUXE.

Of course, the ultimate Chinatown experience is to dine dim sum style. Rather than choosing from a menu, you select dishes from trundle carts laden with steaming delicacies. A never-ending convoy of waitresses wheels past your table, offering plates piled with won tons, pork tidbits, and Chinese meatballs. It's up to you to create a meal (traditionally breakfast or lunch) from this succession of finger-size morsels.

HIDDEN ▶ My favorite dim sum restaurant is tucked away in an alley above Grant Avenue. Personalized but unpretentious, more cozy than cavernous, **Hang Ah Tea House** is a rare find. Enter the dining room with its Chinese wood carvings and fiberglass tables. Serving a full Mandarin cuisine as well as dim sum portions, it warrants an exploratory mission into the alleys of Chinatown. No dinner Monday. ~ 1 Hang Ah Street; 415-982-5686. BUDGET.

The brightly lit yellow sign outside **Gold Mountain Restaurant** attracts its share of tourists and passersby. Nonetheless, this clean and modern dining room serves trusty claypot specialties, traditional seafood and noodles, and dim sum at lunch. Try the three treasures in black bean sauce, a colorful dish with red bell peppers, eggplant and stuffed tofu. ~ 644 Broadway near Powell Street; 415-296-7733. BUDGET TO MODERATE.

Overlooking Portsmouth Square on the second story of a nondescript building, the **Oriental Pearl** serves sophisticated, gourmet dim sum, a step above the usual Chinatown teahouse. Here dim sum is ordered from a menu, allowing diners to concentrate on conversation and cuisine, rather than being distracted by the contents of passing carts. Such treats as shrimp and scallop dumplings, pork buns, and chicken meatballs emerge hot and fresh from the kitchen. White tablecloths, mahogany chairs, and classical Chinese music make this a quiet oasis from the busy streets of Chinatown below. ~ 760–778 Clay Street; 415-433-1817. BUDGET.

SHOPPING   Shopping in Chinatown brings you into immediate contact with both the common and the unique. If you can slip past the souvenir shops, many of which specialize in American-made "Chinese products," you'll eventually discover the real thing—Chinese arts and crafts as well as Asian antiques.

Grant Avenue is the neighborhood's shopping center, but local Chinese favor Stockton Street. My advice is to browse both streets

as well as the side streets between. Some of the city's best bargains
are right here in Chinatown.

The best bar in Chinatown, **Li Po**, is complete with incense, lan-   **NIGHTLIFE**
terns, and carved statuary, plus an incongruous jukebox featur-
ing Caucasian favorites. The potions they mix here are powerful
and exotic; the place has an air of intimacy. ~ 916 Grant Avenue;
415-982-0072.

It's a region of contrasts, a neighborhood in transition.
North Beach combines the sex scene of neon-lit Broadway   **North Beach**
with the brooding intellect and Beat heritage of Grant
Avenue and Columbus Street. Traditionally an Italian stronghold,
North Beach still retains its fabulous pasta palaces and bocce ball
courts, but it's now giving way to a growing influx of Chinese
residents.

Introductions to places should be made gradually, so the visitor comes slowly but certainly to know and love the area. In touring North Beach, that is no longer possible, because the logical
spot to begin a tour is the corner of Broadway and Montgomery
streets, at night when the neon arabesque of Broadway is in full
glare.

Broadway, you see, has long been San Francisco's answer to Times   **SIGHTS**
Square, a tawdry avenue that traffics in sex. While the neighborhood is steadily changing, it still features strip joints, peekaramas,
and X, Y, Z-rated theaters—a modern-day Barbary Coast.

After you've dispensed with North Beach's sex scene, your
love affair with the neighborhood can begin. Start at **City Lights
Bookstore**. Established in 1953 by poet Lawrence Ferlinghetti,
City Lights is the old hangout of the Beat poets. Back in the heady
days of the '50s, a host of "angels"—Allen Ginsberg, Jack Kerouac, Gary Snyder, and Neal Cassady among them—haunted its
book-lined rooms and creaking staircase. Today the place remains
a vital cultural scene and gathering point. It's a people's bookstore
where you're invited to browse, carouse, or even plop into a chair
and read awhile. You might also check out the paintings and old
photos, or perhaps the window display. Forty years after the Beats,
the inventory here still represents a "who's who" in avant-garde
literature. ~ 261 Columbus Avenue; 415-362-8193.

Vesuvio Café, just next door, was another hallowed Bohemian
retreat. ~ 355 Columbus Avenue; 415-362-3370. Then head up
nearby Grant Avenue to the **Caffe Trieste**, at the corner of Vallejo
Street. With its water-spotted photos and funky espresso bar, the
place has changed little since the days when bearded bards dis-

cussed cool jazz and Eisenhower politics. ~ 601 Vallejo Street; 415-392-6739.

You're on "upper Grant," heart of the old Beat stomping grounds and still a major artery in the city's Italian enclave. Chinatown is at your back now, several blocks behind, but you'll see from the Oriental script adorning many shops that the Asian neighborhood is sprawling into the Italian. Still remaining, however, are the cafés and delicatessens that have lent this area its Mediterranean flair since the Italians moved in during the late 19th-century.

Beyond Filbert Street, as Grant Avenue continues along the side of Telegraph Hill, the shops give way to Italian residences and Victorian houses. When you arrive at Lombard Street, look to your left and you'll see the sinuous reason why Lombard is labeled "The Crookedest Street in the World." Then turn right as Lombard carries you up to the breeze-battered vistas of Telegraph Hill.

Some of the nation's most outstanding WPA murals decorate Coit Tower's interior. Done as frescoes by New Deal artists, they sensitively depict the lives of California laborers.

Named for the semaphore station located on its height during the 1850s, **Telegraph Hill** was a Bohemian haunt during the 1920s and 1930s. Money moved the artists out; today, this hillside real estate is among the most desirable, and most expensive, in the city.

Poking through the top of Telegraph Hill is the 180-foot-high **Coit Tower** (admission for elevator to observation platform). Built in 1934, this fluted structure was named for Lillie Hitchcock Coit, a bizarre character who chased fire engines and became a fire company mascot during the 1850s. Lillie's love for firemen gave rise to stories that the phallic tower was modeled after a fire hose nozzle. Architectural critics scoff at the notion.

Upstaging these marvelous artworks is the view from the summit. All San Francisco spreads before you. That sinewy structure to the right is the **Bay Bridge**, which stretches for eight and one-quarter miles, the world's longest steel bridge. It is interrupted in its arching course by **Yerba Buena Island** and its manmade extension, **Treasure Island**, which was created for the 1939 Golden Gate International Exposition. The Bay Bridge's gilded companion to the left is the **Golden Gate Bridge**. Between them lies San Francisco Bay. Tugs and freighters slide past in search of mooring. Fog horns groan. From this aerie the distant sloops and ketches look like children's toys blown astray in a pond puffed with wind.

The island moored directly offshore is **Alcatraz**, named for the pelicans which still inhabit it, but mostly known for the notorious prisoners who have long since departed its rocky terrain. Looming behind America's own Devil's Island is **Angel Island**.

That high point on the horizon, between the Golden Gate and Angel Island, is serene **Mt. Tamalpais**, crown jewel in Marin County's tiara. Across the water, where the Bay Bridge meets terra firma, are the East Bay cities of Berkeley and Oakland. Behind you, past the highrise cityscape, the hills and streets of San Francisco gracefully sweep out toward the sea.

Now that all San Francisco has been spread before you like a tableau, it's time to descend into the hidden crannies of the city. Unlike Coit Tower, there will be no elevator to assist on the way down, but then again there won't be any tourists either.

After exiting Coit Tower, turn right, cross the street, and make your way down the brick-lined staircase. In the middle of San Francisco, with wharves and factories far below, you have just entered a countrified environment. Ferns and ivy riot on either side of the **Greenwich Steps**, while vines and conifers climb overhead.

◄ *HIDDEN*

At the bottom of the steps, turn right, walk a short distance along Montgomery Street, then head left down the **Filbert Steps**.

◄ *HIDDEN*

Festooned with flowers and sprinkled with baby tears, the steps carry you into a fantasy realm inhabited by stray cats and framed with clapboard houses. Among the older homes are several that date to the 1870s; if you follow the Napier Lane Boardwalk that extends from the steps, there are falsefront buildings from which sailors reportedly once were shanghaied.

Retracing your tracks back up the steps, then descending the other side of Filbert Street, you'll arrive at **Washington Square**, between Filbert and Stockton streets in the heart of North Beach. It's hard to imagine that Washington Square was a tent city back in 1906. The great earthquake and fire totally devastated North Beach, and the park became a refuge for hundreds of homeless. Nestled between Russian and Telegraph hills, this is the gathering place for San Francisco's "Little Italy." In the square, old Italian men and women seek out wooden benches where they can watch the "young people" carrying on. From the surrounding delis and cafés you might put together a picnic lunch, plant yourself on the lawn, and catch this daily parade. But if you come early in the morning, you will see evidence of the slow transition North Beach is undergoing: fifty or more Chinese and Westerners practice tai chi in the square.

St. Peter & Paul Catholic Church anchors one side of the square. Its twin steeples dominate the North Beach skyline. The facade is unforgettable, an ornate affair upon which eagles rest in the company of angels. The interior is a wilderness of vaulting arches hung with lamps and decorated in gilt bas-relief. Tourists proclaim its beauty. For my taste, the place is overdone; it drips with architectural jewelry. Everything is decoration, an artistic happening; there is no tranquility, no silent spot for the eye to rest. ~ Filbert Street, between Powell and Stockton streets; 415-421-0809.

North Beach Museum, housed inside Bay View Bank, presents a history in black-and-white. There are sepia photos of Sicilian fishermen, pictures of the terrible quake, and other images of the folks who make North Beach such an intriguing place to visit. Boat reproductions and some Chinatown items are among the artifacts. Closed Saturday and Sunday. ~ 1435 Stockton Street; 415-626-7070.

LODGING

As a nighttime visit to North Beach will clearly indicate, this neighborhood was not made for sleeping. The "love acts" and encounter parlors along Broadway draw rude, boisterous crowds until the wee hours.

But if noise and neon have a soporific effect upon you, or if you have some bizarre and arcane need to know what sleeping on the old Barbary Coast was like, check out **Europa Hotel**. The price is certainly right, and you get a clean, carpeted room and shared bath. ~ 310 Columbus Avenue; 415-391-5779. BUDGET.

HIDDEN ▶

Or better yet, retreat a little farther from Broadway to the **Hotel Bohème** and take a step back into North Beach history. This European pensione–style hotel has been decorated to reflect the beat-generation era, complete with a black-and-white photo retrospective. Poet Allen Ginsberg even stayed here. Rooms feature antique wardrobes, tile bathrooms, and black iron beds. Ask for one of the rooms in the back, which are quieter than those along Columbus Avenue. ~ 444 Columbus Avenue; 415-433-9111, fax 415-362-6292; www.hotelboheme.com. MODERATE TO DELUXE.

DINING

Dining at **Helmand** is like visiting the home of an upper-class Afghani family. Lush handmade Afghan carpets, beautiful chandeliers, and paintings add a touch of elegance, and the food is

✔ CHECK THESE OUT—UNIQUE LODGING

- *Budget:* Check into downtown's **Adelaide Inn**, San Francisco's funky but tidy "unique European pensione." *page 35*
- *Moderate:* Slip away from the city noise and cozy up to a warm fireplace at **Seal Rock Inn**. *page 82*
- *Deluxe:* Unpack your bags at one of the hippest spots in town, the **Phoenix Hotel**, a block from Civic Center. *page 45*
- *Ultra-deluxe:* Settle down and indulge yourself at the **White Swan Inn**, where elegance and style are the trademarks of this 1908 hotel cum bed and breakfast. *page 37*

Budget: under $60   Moderate: $60–$120   Deluxe: $120–$175   Ultra-deluxe: over $175

first-rate. You can feast on grilled rack of lamb, roasted chicken, and many vegetarian dishes in this dinner-only establishment. *Aushak*, Afghan ravioli stuffed with leeks and topped with ground beef marinated in yogurt, can be habitforming. A true find among the sleazy strip joints of Broadway. ~ 430 Broadway; 415-362-0641. MODERATE.

At **Little Joe's and Baby Joe's** the food is outstanding and it's prepared before your eyes by some of the city's great showmen. Working a row of oversized frying pans, these jugglers rarely touch a spatula. Rather, with a snap of the wrist, they flip sizzling veal, steak, or calamari skyward, then nonchalantly catch it on the way down. This restaurant also serves delicious fish, roast chicken, and sausage dishes, each accompanied by pasta and sautéed vegetables. Very crowded, especially on weekends. ~ 523 Broadway; 415-433-4343. MODERATE.

Some of the best pizza in town is served at **Tommaso's Neapolitan Restaurant**, where the chefs bake in an oak-fired oven. The creations they prepare have resulted in this tiny restaurant being written up in national magazines. As soon as you walk in you'll realize it's the food, not the surroundings, that draws the attention. Entering the place is like stepping down into a grotto. The walls are lined with booths and covered with murals; it's dark, steamy, and filled with inviting smells. Director Francis Ford Coppola drops by occasionally, as should every pizza and pasta lover. Dinner only. Closed Monday. ~ 1042 Kearny Street; 415-398-9696. MODERATE.

At least once during a North Beach visit, you should dine at a family-style Italian restaurant. Dotted all around the neighborhood, these establishments have a local flavor unmatched by the area's chic new restaurants. A good choice is **Capp's Corner**, a local landmark adorned with celebrity photos, more celebrity photos, and a few photos of celebrities. The prix-fixe dinner includes soup, salad, pasta, entrée, and dessert—more food than anyone could consume in a day, much less a sitting. Some of the entrées are fettuccine with rock shrimp, chicken cacciatore, osso buco, lamb shanks and other choices. No lunch on the weekend. ~ 1600 Powell Street; 415-989-2589. MODERATE.

Why anyone would want to dine in a place frequented by writers is beyond me, but if the spirit moves you, and your stomach agrees, head over to the **Washington Square Bar & Grill**. This literary gathering spot is often elbow-to-elbow with such questionable characters as local novelists, newspaper journalists, and aspiring word merchants. They come to gossip and to engage in that vaunted avocation of scribblers everywhere, the imbibing of spirits. Occasionally they wander from the brass-rail bar to the dining area, where the lunch and dinner menu changes daily. It's actually an excellent restaurant, and an even better place to drink. ~ 1707 Powell Street; 415-982-8123. MODERATE TO DELUXE.

For traditional Basque cuisine, consider **Des Alpes Restaurant**. An oilcloth restaurant with a small bar out front, it serves full-course dinners. Selections are limited to a few entrées each night, so call ahead for the day's menu. On a typical evening, they'll be serving chicken with rice, roast lamb, roast beef, or New York steak; dinner also includes soup, salad, coffee, and dessert. A good spot for a family-style meal. Closed Monday. ~ 732 Broadway; 415-391-4249. MODERATE.

The heart of North Beach beats in its cafés. Gathering places for local Italians, the neighborhood's coffee houses are also literary scenes. Step into any of the numerous cafés dotting the district and you're liable to hear an elderly Italian singing opera or see an aspiring writer with notebook in one hand and espresso cup in the other.

The best North Beach breakfasts are the Continental-style meals served in these cafés. But any time of day or night, you can order a croissant and cappuccino, lean back, and take in the human scenery. Foremost among these people-watching posts is **Caffe Trieste**, the old Beatnik rendezvous. ~ 601 Vallejo Street; 415-392-6739. Another prime location is **Caffe Puccini** with heavenly homemade *tiramisu*. ~ 411 Columbus Avenue; 415-989-7033. **Mario's Bohemian Cigar Store**, right on Washington Square, is also popular. ~ 556 Columbus Avenue; 415-362-0536.

The *New Yorker* once called **Hunan Restaurant** "the best Chinese restaurant in the world." Those are pretty big words, hard to prove this side of Peking. But it's certainly one of the best San Francisco has to offer. Understand now, we're talking cuisine, not ambience. The atmosphere at Hunan is characterized by noise and crowds; there's a bar and a contemporary dining room adorned with color photographs. But the food will transport you to another land entirely. It's hot, spicy, and delicious. From the dining room you can watch masterful chefs working the woks, preparing pungent sauces, and serving up bean curds with meat sauce, Hunan scallops, and a host of other delectables. A culinary experience well worth the price. ~ 924 Sansome Street; 415-956-7727. MODERATE.

SHOPPING   Shopping in North Beach is a grand escapade. As you browse the storefronts here, do like the Sicilians and keep an eye out for Italian treasures. Like the hand-painted ceramics and colorful wall-hangings still brightening many a home in old Italia.

For the mod mob, there are slick boutiques and avant-garde novelty shops. To start, why not choose a place that stocks both the traditional and the avant-garde: **City Lights Bookstore**. Within the hallowed confines of this oddly shaped store is a treasure trove of magazines on arts and politics, plus lots of books on everything from nirvana to the here and now. ~ 261 Columbus Avenue; 415-362-8193.

Biordi Art Imports provides the Italian answer to gourmet living. Specializing in Italian ceramics, the place is loaded with Italian imports. There are hand-painted pitchers from Florence and De Simone folk art from Palermo, noodle makers, and hand-painted dinner ware. To decorate the home, Biordi's has wall mirrors framed in ceramic fruit, hand-painted umbrella stands, and other high-kitsch items. Walking through this singular shop is like browsing an Italian crafts fair. ~ 412 Columbus Avenue; 415-392-8096.

Gone With the Wind meets *American Graffiti* at **Show Biz**, a shop stuffed full of movie and theater memorabilia—old posters, cartoon character figurines, magazines, and rock-and-roll relics. ~ 1318 Grant Avenue; 415-989-6744.

No North Beach shopping spree would be complete without a visit to **A. Cavalli & Company**. Operating since 1880, this family business caters to all sorts of local needs. They offer an assortment of Italian cookbooks as well as records and tapes ranging from Pavarotti to Italian new wave. Cavalli's also stocks Italian travel posters, Puccini opera prints, Italian movies on cassette, and magazines from Rome. ~ 1441 Stockton Street; 415-421-4219.

North Beach, the old Beatnik quarter, is the area for slumming. It's door-to-door with local bars and nightclubs, not to mention the few topless and bottomless joints that still remain along Broadway. **NIGHTLIFE**

Vesuvio Café hasn't changed much since the Beat poets haunted the place during the days of Eisenhower. Kerouac, Ginsberg, Corso, and the crew spent their nights here and their days next door at City Lights Books. It's still a major North Beach scene, rich in soul and history. ~ 355 Columbus Avenue; 415-362-3370.

Across the street is **Spec's Museum Café**, another bohemian haunt. There's nary a bare spot on the walls of this literary hangout; they're covered with all manner of mementos from bumperstickers to a "walrus' penis bone." A great place to get metaphysical. ~ 12 Saroyan Place; 415-421-4112.

To step uptown, just walk down the hill to the **San Francisco Brewing Company**. Built the year after the 1906 earthquake, it's a mahogany-paneled beauty with glass lamps and punkah wallah fans. Legend tells that Jack Dempsey once worked here as a bouncer. It's also the first pub in San Francisco to brew its own beer on the premises. ~ 155 Columbus Avenue; 415-434-3344.

There are two theater clubs worthy of note. **Finocchio's** features a succession of screamingly outrageous female impersonators. The costuming is colorful and the acts very bitchy. But the best performance of all is by the audience: the place draws busloads of tourists who figure these wild displays are just another part of the city's notorious lifestyle. Closed Sunday through Wednesday. Cover. ~ 506 Broadway; 415-982-9388.

Club Fugazi has an equally outlandish musical revue, *Beach Blanket Babylon*, which has been running for over 20 years. The scores and choreography are good, but the costumes are great. The hats—elaborate, multilayered confections—make Carmen Miranda's adornments look like Easter bonnets. Shows run Wednesday through Sunday. Cover. ~ 678 Beach Blanket Babylon Boulevard (Green Street); 415-421-4222.

Bimbo's 365 Club showcases an eclectic mix of live music from jazz and rock to French pop stars. Check out the live mermaid that frequently frolics in the oversize aquarium. Call for list of events. Cover. ~ 1025 Columbus Avenue; 415-474-0365.

▼▼▼▼▼▼▼▼▼▼▼▼▼
Fisherman's Wharf

Places have a way of becoming parodies of themselves—particularly if they possess a personal resonance and beauty or have some unique feature to lend the landscape. People, it seems, have an unquenchable need to change them.

Such is the fate of Fisherman's Wharf. Back in the 19th century, a proud fishing fleet berthed in these waters—the shoreline was a quiltwork of brick factories, metal canning sheds, and woodframe warehouses. Genoese fishermen with rope-muscled arms set out in triangular-sailed *feluccas*—a joke to the west wind. They'd captured the waterfront from the Chinese and would be supplanted in turn by Sicilians. They caught sand dabs, sea bass, rock cod, bay shrimp, king salmon, and Dungeness crab. Salt caked their hands, wind and sun gullied their faces.

Today the woodplanked waterfront is hardly a place for fishermen. It has evolved into "Tourist's Wharf," a bizarre assemblage of shopping malls and penny arcades that make Disneyland look like the real world. The old waterfront is an amusement park with a wax gallery, a Ripley's museum, and numerous trinket shops. The architecture subscribes to that modern school which makes everything look like what it's not—there's pseudo-Mission, ready-made antique Victorian, and simulated falsefront.

But salt still stirs the air here and fog fingers through the Bay. There are sights to visit along "the Wharf." It's a matter of recapturing the past while avoiding the plastic-coated present. To do that you need to follow a basic law of the sea—hug the shoreline.

SIGHTS   On the corner of Embarcadero and Beach Street, **Pier 39** itself is an elaborately laid-out shopping mall catering primarily to tourists who spill over from neighboring Fisherman's Wharf. In addition to a plethora of waterfront shops and restaurants, Pier 39 features jugglers, yo-yo champs, and other entertainers who delight the crowd with their sleight of hand.

The central attraction at Pier 39 is the colony of **sea lions** that has taken up residence on the nearby docks. Numbering 400 at times, these thousand-pound pinnipeds are a cross between sea slugs and sumo wrestlers. They began arriving in 1989, taking over a marina, causing a ruckus, and creating the greatest stench this side of a sardine factory. But when Pier 39 attracted over 10 million people the next year, placing it behind Orlando's Disney World and Anaheim's Disneyland as the most popular tourist spot in the country, the local merchants decided to welcome the smelly squatters as permanent residents.

On a given day there might be jugglers, clowns, or other entertainers performing free at Pier 39.

For an up-close look at other residents of the San Francisco Bay, including sharks and fish, go to **Underwater World**. Put on headphones for a 40-minute narrated journey along moving walkways through a 400-foot-long transparent tunnel into two giant two-story tanks. These tanks contain rays, salmon, crabs, jellyfish, eels, and more than 150 examples of the six shark species found in surrounding waters. The only other aquarium like it in the United States is at the Mall of America in Minneapolis. Admission. ~ Pier 39; 415-623-5300.

Pier 45 is a working wharf, bleached with bird dung and frequented by fishing boats. From here it's a short jog to the docks on Jefferson Street, located between Jones and Taylor streets. The remnants of San Francisco's fishing fleet lies gunnel to gunnel here. The *Nicky-D*, *Ocean Star*, *Daydream*, *Phu Quy*, *Hai Tai Loc*, and an admiralty of others cast off every morning around 4 a.m. to return in late afternoon. With their brightly painted hulls, Christmas tree rigging, and roughhewn crews, they carry the odor and clamor of the sea.

Docked at Pier 45 at the Embarcadero is the **S.S. Jeremiah O'Brien**, the only one of 2751 World War II Liberty Ships to remain in original condition. A beamy hulk, the *Jeremiah O'Brien* numbers among its combat ribbons the D-Day invasion of Normandy. Visitors may walk the decks of the old tub, explore the sailors' quarters, and descend into the depths of the engine room. Call ahead for tour information. Admission. ~ 415-441-3101.

Fish Alley is another nostalgic nook. Just duck into the narrow corridor next to Castagnola's Restaurant on Jefferson Street and walk out towards Scoma's Restaurant. Those corrugated metal sheds lining the docks are fish-packing operations. The fleet deposits its daily catch here to be processed for delivery to restaurants and markets. This is an area of piers and pilings, hooks and hawsers, flotsam and fish scales, where you pay a price to recapture the past: as you work further into this network of docks, ap-

◄ HIDDEN

proaching nearer and nearer the old salty truths, you'll also be overwhelmed by the putrefying stench of the sea.

For a breather, it's not far to the Hyde Street Pier, where history is less offensive to the nose. Docked along the length of this wharf are the **Historic Ships**. Part of the San Francisco Maritime National Historical Park, they include a wood-hulled, three-masted schooner, *C. A. Thayer*, that once toted lumber along the California coast. You can also board the *Eureka*, an 1890 paddle-wheeler which ferried commuters between San Francisco and Sausalito for almost 30 years. Currently the largest floating wooden structure on earth, it served as police headquarters for the crime-fighting crew on TV's *Nash Bridges*. To walk this pier is to stride back to San Francisco's waterfront at the turn of the century. Salt-bitten lifeboats, corroded anchors, and old coal engines are scattered hither-thither. The *Eppleton Hall* is an old paddlewheeler and the *Alma* a "scow schooner" with a flat bottom and square beam. A three-masted merchant ship built in Scotland in 1886, the *Balclutha* measures 301 feet. This steel-hulled craft sailed around Cape Horn 17 times in her youth. She loaded rice in Rangoon, guano in Callao, and wool in New Zealand. Today the old ship's cargo consists of a below-deck maritime museum and a hold full of memories. Admission. ~ 415-556-3002.

Together with the nearby **National Maritime Museum**, it's enough to make a sailor of you. The museum, in case you mistook it for a ferryboat run aground, is actually an art deco building designed to resemble the bridge of a passenger liner. Onboard there's a weird collection of body parts from old ships plus models, scrimshaw displays, and a magnificent photo collection. ~ Beach and Polk streets; 415-556-2904.

All these nautical showpieces are anchored in **Aquatic Park**, which sports a lovely lawn that rolls down to one of the Bay's few sandy beaches. A mélange of sounds and spectacles, the park has a bocce ball court where you'll encounter old Italian men exchanging stories and curiously eyeing the tourists. There are street vendors galore. If that's not enough, you can watch the Powell and Hyde Street cable cars being turned around for their steep climb back up Nob Hill. Or catch an eye-boggling glimpse of San Francisco Bay. Alcatraz lies anchored offshore, backdropped by one of the prettiest panoramas in this part of the world.

Since you're in earthquake country why not stop by **The Museum of the City of San Francisco**. Historic photographs, paintings, and artifacts tell the story of that fateful day in 1906 and shed new light on the story of California's greatest natural disaster. Among the notable exhibits is the Goddess of Liberty statue from the old city hall. Closed Monday and Tuesday. ~ In the Cannery, Beach and Leavenworth streets; 415-928-0289.

Cruising the Bay

Pier 41 is the departure point for the Blue and Gold Fleet, which sponsors Bay cruises, Alcatraz tours, and ferry service to Angel Island, Sausalito, and Tiburon. ~ 415-773-1188.

The trip to **Alcatraz** is highlighted with a National Park Service tour of the infamous prison. Originally a fort and later a military prison, Alcatraz gained renown as "The Rock" when it became a maximum security prison in 1934. Al Capone, "Machine Gun" Kelly, and Robert "Birdman of Alcatraz" Stroud were among its notorious inmates. On the tour, you'll enter the bowels of the prison, walk the dank corridors, and experience the cage-like cells in which America's most desperate criminals were kept. You can listen to an audio cassette of former guards and prisoners remembering their time at The Rock.

The prison closed in 1963; then in 1969 a group of American Indians occupied the island for almost two years, claiming it as Indian territory. Today Alcatraz is part of the Golden Gate National Recreation Area.

A cruise to **Angel Island State Park** is a different adventure entirely. Unlike "The Rock," this star-shaped island is covered with forest and rolling hills. During previous incarnations it has served as a military installation, quarantine station, immigration center, and prisoner of war camp. Today, the largest true island in San Francisco Bay is a lacework of hiking and biking trails and flowering meadows. For an overview visit the visitors center at Ayala Cove. Here you'll find a diorama and map of the island, historical exhibits, a self-starting 20-minute video that reviews the history of the island, and the light fixture from an old lighthouse. You can trek five miles around the island or climb to the top for 360° views of the Bay Area.

Deer graze throughout the area and there are picnic areas galore. It's a perfect spot for a day in the sun. Along the way you can visit the small Immigration Station Museum, which is dedicated to the history of the island's early immigration station. Touching photographs document the story of this "West Coast Ellis Island." Except for the visitors center, which is open year-round, the buildings on Angel Island are open weekends only April through October. A tram operates on weekends in summer. (The day-use fee is included in the ferry price; however, there is a $5 day-use fee if you bring your own boat.) ~ 415-435-1915.

LODGING   Fisherman's Wharf contains more hotels than fishermen. Most facilities here are overpriced and undernourished. I'm only going to mention a few, since I think you'll do much better financially and experience San Francisco more fully in a downtown or neighborhood hotel.

The first is **The Wharf Inn,** a place best described as nondescript. This 51-room motel is a squat four-story affair with purple doors and beige trim. The moderate-size rooms have contemporary though unimaginative decor. The ambience is one of naugahyde and simulated wood; the place is clean and bright, offering the same type of facility you could have downtown for moderate cost. In an area of pricey hotels, The Wharf Inn has the best rates around. ~ 2601 Mason Street; 415-673-7411, 800-548-9918, fax 415-776-2181; www.wharfinn.com. DELUXE.

Lodging in the **Sheraton at Fisherman's Wharf,** a sprawling 524-room facility, feature spacious rooms tastefully furnished in Sheraton fashion, plus room service and nightly turndown service. The hotel has other alluring features like a brick-paved entranceway, liveried doormen, swimming pool, and attractive gift shops. ~ 2500 Mason Street; 415-362-5500, 800-325-3535, fax 415-956-5275; www.sheraton.com. ULTRA-DELUXE.

The **Hyatt at Fisherman's Wharf** is a 313-room luxury retreat that is faced in antique brick and illuminated through skylights. It comes complete with pool, spa, and fitness center. ~ 555 North Point Street; 415-563-1234, 800-233-1234, fax 415-749-6122; www.hyatt.com. ULTRA-DELUXE.

Smaller in scale than the Hyatt, the 200-room **Tuscan Inn Best Western** is richly decorated and more intimate. This Italian-style boutique hotel features a garden court and an Italianate lobby complete with fireplace. ~ 425 North Point Street; 415-561-1100, 800-648-4626, fax 415-561-1199; www.tuscaninn.com. DELUXE TO ULTRA-DELUXE.

DINING   Dining at Fisherman's Wharf usually means spending money at Fisherman's Wharf. The neighborhood's restaurants are overpriced and over-touristed. If you look hard enough, however, it's possible to find a good meal at a fair price in a fashionable restaurant. Of course, the easiest way to dine is right on the street, at one of the **seafood cocktail stands** along Jefferson Street. An old wharf tradition, these curbside vendors began years ago feeding bay fishermen. Today they provide visitors an opportunity to sample local catches like crab, shrimp, and calamari. ~ BUDGET.

Situated between the Wharf and North Beach, **Café Francisco** enjoys the best of both worlds—it's strolling distance from the water and possesses a bohemian flair. A great place for light and inexpensive meals, this trendy café serves salads and sandwiches for lunch. Breakfast at the espresso bar ranges from a continental repast to bacon and eggs. Decorated with changing exhibits by local artists, it attracts a local crowd. ~ 2161 Powell Street; 415-397-2602. BUDGET.

The **Eagle Café** is another old-timer. It's so much a part of San Francisco that plans to tear the place down years ago occasioned a public outcry. Instead of flattening the old woodframe building, they lifted it—lock, stock, and memories—and moved it to the second floor of the Pier 39 shopping mall. Today it looks like an ostrich at a beauty pageant, a plain all-American café surrounded by glittering tourist shops. The walls are covered with faded black-and-white photos, Eagle baseball caps, and other memorabilia. Actually, the bar is more popular than the restaurant. Who wants to eat when they can drink to old San Francisco? The bar is open all day and into the night. ~ Pier 39; 415-433-3689. BUDGET TO MODERATE.

Would you believe a hidden restaurant in tourist-mobbed Fisherman's Wharf? **Scoma's** is the place. Seafood is the password to   ◄ HIDDEN
this chummy restaurant. There's *cioppino alla pescatore*, a Sicilian-style broth; *calamone alla anna*, squid prepared "in a totally different manner"; or just plain old sole, snapper, shrimp, or scallops. There's lobster tail, too, and Dungeness crab. ~ Pier 47 near the foot of Jones Street; 415-771-4383. MODERATE TO DELUXE.

For the sights, sounds, and seafood of the San Francisco waterfront, Scoma's is the catch of the day. For spicy food from the subcontinent, everyone's choice is **Gaylord India Restaurant**. From its third floor corner roost in Ghirardelli Square, this fashionable dining emporium enjoys a startling view of San Francisco Bay. It also hosts an extensive menu that varies from tandoori chicken and spiced lamb to meatless entrées such as eggplant baked in a clay oven, creamed lentils, or spiced cauliflower and potatoes.

✔ CHECK THESE OUT—UNIQUE DINING

- *Budget:* Have your palm read by the resident psychic at **Mad Magda's Russian Tea Room & Café** after enjoying a flavorful bowl of homemade borscht. *page 46*
- *Moderate:* Travel to Afghanistan at the **Helmand**, where the food will tantalize your taste buds and the ambience will please as well. *page 60*
- *Moderate to deluxe:* Plunge into **Harbor Village** for excellent dim sum in an authentic Hong Hong–style eatery outside Chinatown. *page 51*
- *Deluxe to ultra-deluxe:* Make reservations far in advance for a tempting meal at Wolfgang Puck's **Postrio**. *page 40*

Budget: under $9   Moderate: $9–$18   Deluxe: $18–$25   Ultra-deluxe: over $25

Gaylord creates a warm ambience into which it introduces a deliciously tangy cuisine. ~ 900 North Point Street; 415-771-8822. MODERATE.

Albona Ristorante Istriano is a high-heeled hole-in-the-wall, a small but fashionable restaurant serving Venetian and Central European dishes. The interior is a mélange of beveled mirrors, white linen tablecloths, burgundy banquettes, and fresh flowers. The menu, not to be upstaged, includes sauerkraut braised with prosciutto, pan-fried gnocchi, and exotic entrées like braised rabbit with juniper berries and *brodetto alla Veniziana* (fish stew or soup). Dinner only. Closed Sunday and Monday. ~ 545 Francisco Street; 415-441-1040. MODERATE.

SHOPPING   Fisherman's Wharf is a shopper's paradise . . . if you know what you're doing. If not, it's a fool's paradise. This heavily touristed district houses a mazelike collection of shops, malls, arcades, and galleries. Most of them specialize in high-priced junk. How someone can arrive in the world's most splendid city and carry away some trashy trinket to commemorate their visit is beyond me. But they do. Since you're certainly not the type searching out an "I Got Crabs at Fisherman's Wharf" T-shirt, the best course is to go where the natives shop.

Though its wooden boardwalks and clapboard buildings look promising, **Pier 39** proves hardly the place for bargains or antiques. It's a haven for tourists and features gift stores that range from cutesy card shops to places selling ceramic unicorns. There are restaurants and stores galore, plus an amusement arcade. Kids usually enjoy the carnival atmosphere here. ~ Embarcadero and Beach Street; 415-981-7437.

One noteworthy exception to Pier 39's tourist-oriented selection of shops is **The National Park Store**, the only bookshop I know that comes with a view of sea lions basking in the sun. It offers a complete selection of travel, hiking, and wildlife books and also sells educational toys, American Indian arts and crafts, and other gifts. ~ Pier 39; 415-433-7221.

For locally crafted goods, be sure to watch for the **street vendor stalls**. Located along Beach Street between Hyde and Larkin,

THE SAN FRANCISCO "STAFF OF LIFE"

Another San Francisco favorite, sourdough bread, can be tasted at **Boudin Bakery**. A pungent French bread particularly popular in seafood restaurants, sourdough is the staff of life in these parts. Boudin Bakery, founded in 1849, has had plenty of time to fit its recipe perfectly to the local palate. ~ 156 Jefferson Street; 415-928-1849. BUDGET.

and on side streets throughout the area, they offer hand-fashioned wares with homemade price tags. You'll find jewelry, leather belts, statuary, framed photos of the bay city, tie-dye shirts, kites, and anything else the local imagination can conjure.

Before people buy anything in the City, they go to **Cost Plus World Market** and see if it's there. If so, it's cheaper; if not, maybe they don't really need it. You'll find jewelry, ceramics, wallhangings, and a host of other items. There are temple rubbings from Thailand, amber jewelry from Egypt, Indian mirrorcloths, scenic San Francisco posters, brassware, household furnishings, clothes, gourmet foods, wine, etc. Everything under the sun, at prices to brighten your day. ~ 2552 Taylor Street; 415-928-6200.

Another popular spot among San Franciscans is the old brick canning factory on Jefferson and Leavenworth streets. Thanks to innovative architects, **The Cannery** has been transformed into a tri-level mall dotted with interesting shops. The central plaza, with its olive trees and potted flowers, contains picnic tables, several cafés, and snack kiosks. Among the dozens of shops are many selling handcrafted originals. ~ 415-771-3112.

The chocoholics who don't know will be delighted to discover that the home of Ghirardelli chocolate, **Ghirardelli Square**, has been converted into yet another shopping complex. This early-20th-century factory is yet another example of old industrial architecture being turned to contemporary uses. Around the factory's antique chocolate making machines is located a myriad of shops varying from designer outlets to sundry stores. You'll also find import stores, boutiques, and so on. ~ 900 North Point Street; 415-775-5500.

NIGHTLIFE

The **Eagle Café**, perched beside Fisherman's Wharf, appears like some strange bird that has landed in the wrong roost. All around lies touristville, polished and preening, while the Eagle remains old and crusty, filled with waterfront characters. Old photos and baseball caps adorn the walls, and in the air hang memories more than 50 years old. ~ Pier 39; 415-433-3689.

Don't know any local people, but still like to party? Head for **Lou's Pier 47**, have a meal, and dance the afternoon and night away. For eats, there are sandwiches, burgers, pastas, and fried, grilled, or sautéed fish and seafood. The 16 bands that play each week in the glass-enclosed nightclub upstairs range from rhythm-and-blues and Motown to light rock. The music begins at 4 p.m. daily and at noon on the weekends. Cover. ~ 300 Jefferson Street; 415-771-0377.

Buena Vista Café, situated near Fisherman's Wharf, is popular with local folks and tourists alike. There's a fine old bar and a friendly atmosphere, and the place claims to have introduced America to Irish coffee. ~ 2765 Hyde Street; 415-474-5044.

▼▼▼▼▼▼▼▼▼▼
The Presidio

What was previously the oldest active military base in the country is now part of the country's largest urban national park. The Presidio is also a National Historic Landmark. It was established by the Spanish in 1776 and taken over by the United States in 1846. Civil War troops trained here, and the Sixth Army established the base as its headquarters. Even when it was a military base, the Presidio had the feel of a country retreat. Hiking trails snake through the 1400 acres of undulating hills sprinkled with acacia, madrone, pine, and redwood trees, and there are expansive bay views. Although still under development, there are plans for new hiking trails, museums, education centers, and conference facilities.

SIGHTS

The best way to explore the Presidio is by stopping first at the **William Penn Mott, Jr. Visitor Information Center**. The folks here are very knowledgeable; they will provide you with a map and they can also arrange guided tours with a park ranger. ~ Building 102, Montgomery Street; 415-561-4323.

Make your next stop the **Presidio Army Museum**. This three-story museum was originally a hospital, built in 1857. Faced with pillars and protected by a collection of antique cannons, it's still an imposing sight. The displays inside consist primarily of Presidio history, military uniforms, and weapons. Closed Monday and Tuesday. ~ Funston Avenue near Lincoln Boulevard.

The nearby **Officers' Club**, a tile-roof, Spanish-style structure, includes part of the original 1776 Presidio, one of the first buildings ever constructed in San Francisco. ~ Moraga Avenue.

The **National Cemetery**, with rows of tombstones on a grassy knoll overlooking the Golden Gate Bridge, is San Francisco's salute to the nation's war dead. ~ Lincoln Boulevard.

HIDDEN ►

The remainder of our Presidio tour is of a more natural bent. There's **El Polin Spring** where, as the brass plaque proclaims, "the early Spanish garrison attained its water supply." History has rarely been made in a more beautiful spot. The spring is set in a

◆◆◆

THE LAST STAND

The battle lines are drawn at **Lover's Lane**. March, or even stroll, along this narrow pathway, and review these armies of nature. On one side, standing sentinel straight, out-thrust arms shading the lane, are the eucalyptus. Mustered along the other front, clad in darker uniforms, seeming to retreat before the wind, are the conifer trees. Forgetting for a moment these silly games soldiers play, look around. You are standing in an awesome and spectacular spot, one of the last forests in San Francisco. ~ In the southeast corner of the Presidio.

lovely park surrounded by hills upon which eucalyptus trees battle with conifers for strategic ground. Hiking trails lead down and outward from this enchanted glade. ~ Located at the end of MacArthur Avenue.

Mountain Lake Park, stationed along the Presidio's southern flank, is another idyllic locale. With grassy meadows and wooded walkways, it's a great place to picnic or stroll. The lake itself, a favorite watering hole among ducks visiting from out of town, is skirted with tule reeds and overhung with willows. ~ Lake Street between 8th and Funston avenues.

The park's prettiest walk is along the **Presidio Wall** bordering Lyon Street. Starting at the Lombard Street Gate, where two cannons guard the eastern entrance, walk uphill along Lyon Street. That wall of urbanity to the left is the city's chic Union Street district, breeding place for fern bars and antique stores. To the right, beyond the Presidio's stone enclosure, are the tumbling hills and towering trees of the old garrison.

After several blocks, Lyon ceases to be a street and becomes a staircase. The most arduous and rewarding part of the trek begins; you can follow this stairway to heaven, which happens to be Broadway, two heart-pounding blocks above you. Ascend and the city falls away—the Palace of Fine Arts, Alcatraz, the Marina, all become landing points for your vision. Closer to hand are the houses of San Francisco's posh Pacific Heights district, stately structures looming several stories and sprawling across the landscape. When you reach the stone steps at the top of Broadway, they will still rise above, potent and pretentious, hard contrast to the Presidio's leafy acres.

Golden Gate Park

It is the Central Park of the West. Or perhaps we should say that Central Park is New York's answer to Golden Gate Park. It extends from the Haight-Ashbury neighborhood, across nearly half the width of the city, all the way to the ocean. With its folded hills and sloping meadows, its lakes and museums, Golden Gate is everyone's favorite park.

Once an undeveloped region of sand dunes, the park today encompasses over 1000 acres of gardens, lawns, and forests. The transformation from wasteland to wonderland came about during the late-19th and early-20th centuries through the efforts of a mastermind named John McLaren. A gardener by trade, this Scotsman could rightly be called an architect of the earth. Within his lifetime he oversaw the creation of the world's largest human-made park.

What he wrought was a place that has something to suit everyone: there are tennis courts; lawn bowling greens; hiking trails; byways for bicyclers, rollerskaters, skateboarders, even unicyclers;

a nine-hole golf course; archery field; flycasting pools; fields for soccer and football; playgrounds; riding stables; even checker pavilions. Facilities for renting bicycles and skates are located just outside the park along Haight and Stanyan streets.

Or, if you'd prefer not to lift a finger, you can always pull up a shade tree and watch the parade. The best day to visit Golden Gate Park is Sunday when many of the roads in the eastern end of the park are closed to cars but open to skaters, jugglers, bicyclers, troubadours, mimes, skateboarders, impromptu theater groups, sun worshippers, and anyone else who feels inspired.

Touring the park should be done on another day, when you can drive freely through the grounds. There are two roads spanning the length of the park. Each begins near Stanyan Street on the east side of Golden Gate Park and runs about four miles westward to the Pacific. The best way to see this area is to travel out along John F. Kennedy Drive and back by Martin Luther King, Jr. Drive, detouring down the side roads that lead into the heart of the park.

SIGHTS

The first stop along John F. Kennedy Drive lies immediately after the entrance. That red-tile building overgrown in ivy is **McLaren Lodge**, park headquarters and home base for maps, brochures, pamphlets, and information. (McLaren Lodge is closed on weekends, but maps are available at the kiosk near the carousel.) ~ Stanyan and Fell streets; 415-831-2700.

The startling glass palace nearby is the **Conservatory**. Built in 1879 and Victorian in style, it's being restored after sustaining severe damage in a 1995 winter storm. Although it's not open to the public, the Conservatory still makes for a stunning photo-op.

Just down the street is **Rhododendron Dell**. A lace-work of trails threads through this 20-acre garden; if you're visiting in early spring, when the rose-hued bushes are blooming, the dell is a concert of colors.

Just beyond this garden beats the cultural heart of Golden Gate Park. Located around a tree-studded concourse are the De Young Museum, Academy of Sciences, and Japanese Tea Garden. The **M. H. De Young Memorial Museum** houses an impressive collection. Exhibits trace the course of American art from colonial times to the mid-20th century, including an important collection of colonial-era art donated by the Rockefellers. The Art of the Americas gallery features ancient art from Central and South America as well as North American art of the past four hundred years. There's also an intriguing display of works from Africa and Oceania, as well as Classic Greek art. The De Young has one of the largest collections in the nation. Closed Monday and Tuesday. Admission. ~ 415-750-3600.

Debatably, the *pièce de résistance* of this entire complex is the **Asian Art Museum** adjacent to the De Young. Featuring major pieces from China, Tibet, Japan, Korea, Iran, Syria, and throughout the continent, this superlative facility is the largest museum in the country devoted exclusively to Asian art. Some of the pieces date back 6000 years. Closed Monday. Admission. ~ 415-668-8921.

It takes a facility like the **California Academy of Sciences**, called the "Smithsonian of the West," to even compete with a place like the De Young Museum. Here you'll find a planetarium where the stars rise all day, an array of African animals grouped in jungle settings, and a "roundabout" aquarium in which you stand at the center of a circular glass tank while creatures of the deep swim around you. A tremendous place for kids, this natural history museum also features numerous "hands-on" exhibits. Admission. ~ 415-750-7145.

If you're like me, it won't be more than an hour or two before museum fatigue sets in and dinosaur vertebrae start looking like rock formations. It's time for the **Japanese Tea Garden**. Here you can rest your heavy eyes on carp-filled ponds and hand-wrought gateways. There are arch footbridges, cherry trees, bonsai gardens, and, of course, a tea house where Japanese women serve jasmine tea and cookies. Admission.

All these cultural gathering places cluster around a **Music Concourse**.

You can get back on John F. Kennedy Drive and resume your self-guided tour by continuing to **Stow Lake**. This is a donut-shaped body of water with an island as the hole in the middle. From the island's crest you can gaze across San Francisco from Bay to ocean. Or, if an uphill is not in your day's itinerary, there's a footpath around the island perimeter that passes an ornate Chinese pagoda. There are also rowboats, pedalboats, and electric motorboats for rent, and a small snack bar.

Next along John F. Kennedy Drive you'll pass **Rainbow Falls**. That monument at the top, from which this cascade appears to spill, is **Prayerbook Cross**, modeled after an old Celtic cross.

This is followed close on by a chain of meadows, a kind of rolling green counterpoint to the chain of lakes which lie ahead. **Speedway Meadow** and **Lindley Meadow** offer barbecue pits and picnic tables; both are fabulous areas for sunbathing.

Spreckels Lake is home to ducks, seagulls, and model sailboats. Across the road are the **Golden Gate Park Stables**, where you can take riding lessons. ~ John F. Kennedy Drive and 36th Avenue; 415-668-7360.

Immediately beyond is the **Chain of Lakes**, a string of three reservoirs stretching the width of the park, perpendicular to John

F. Kennedy Drive. Framed by eucalyptus trees, they offer hiking paths around each shoreline. As you circumnavigate these baby lakes, you'll notice they are freckled with miniature islands. Each lake possesses a singular personality: North Lake is remarkable for its hip-deep swamp cypress; Middle Lake features an island tufted with willows; and South Lake, tiniest of the triplets, sprouts bamboo along its shore.

If these ponds be babies, the great mother of them all rests nearby. Where the road meets the Pacific you'll come upon the **Dutch Windmill**, a regal structure built in 1903. With its wooden struts and scale-like shingles, it braves the sea's inevitable west winds. The Dutchman's cousin, **Murphy Windmill**, an orphan with broken arms, lives several hundred yards down the coast.

From here at continent's edge, it's a four-mile trip back through the park along Martin Luther King Jr. Drive. After picking it up at Murphy Windmill, you will find that this softly curving road passes lakes and forests, meadows and playgrounds. More important, it borders **Strybing Arboretum**, a place specially made for garden lovers. Strybing is a world within itself, a 70-acre flower quilt stitched together by pathways. Over 5000 species peacefully coexist here—dwarf conifers and sprawling magnolias, as well as plants from Asia, the Andes, Australia, and America. There is a "redwood trail" devoted to native California plants, a "garden of fragrance" redolent of flowers, and a Japanese strolling garden. It's a kind of park within a park, a glorious finale for your visit to this park within a city. ~ 415-661-1316.

▼▼▼▼▼▼▼▼▼▼▼▼▼▼▼▼

Golden Gate National Recreation Area

One of the City's most spectacular regions belongs to us all. The Golden Gate National Recreation Area, a 74,000-acre metropolitan park, draws about 20 million visitors annually. A place of natural beauty and historic importance, this magnificent park stretches north from San Francisco throughout much of the Bay Area. In the city itself, the Golden Gate National Recreation Area forms a narrow band around the waterfront. It follows the shoreline of the Bay from Aquatic Park to Fort Mason to the Golden Gate Bridge. On the ocean side it encompasses Land's End, an exotic and untouched preserve, as well as San Francisco's finest beaches.

SIGHTS   The most serene way to begin exploring the Golden Gate National Recreation Area is via the **Golden Gate Promenade**. This three-and-a-half-mile walk will carry you across a swath of heaven that extends from Aquatic Park to the shadows of the Golden Gate Bridge.

Just start in the park and make the short jaunt to the **Municipal Pier**. This hook-shaped cement walkway curls several hun-

dred yards into the Bay. As you follow its curving length a 360°
view unfolds—from the Golden Gate to the Bay Bridge, from
Mt. Tamalpais to Alcatraz to downtown San Francisco. The pier
harbors fisherfolk and seagulls, crabnetters and joggers; few tourists seem to make it out here.

From the pier it's uphill and downstairs to **Fort Mason Center**, a complex of old wharves and tile-roof warehouses that was
once a major military embarkation point. Fort Mason today is
the cultural heart of avant-garde San Francisco. During the 1970s
the warehouses were recycled into offices; over 50 nonprofit organizations subsequently set up shop. ~ Marina Boulevard and
Buchanan Street; 415-979-3010.

Nearly all the arts and crafts are represented—several theater
groups are home here; there is an on-going series of workshops in
dance, creative writing, painting, fabric weaving, printing, sculpture, music, and so on. A number of environmental organizations
also have offices in the center. As one brochure describes, "You
can see a play, stroll through a museum or gallery, learn how to
make poetry films, study yoga, attend a computer seminar, or find
out about the rich maritime lore of San Francisco."

At the **San Francisco Craft and Folk Art Museum** exhibitions
range from Cook Island quilts to San Simeon architect Julia Morgan's craftware. You'll also want to visit the gift shop where they
sell native and tribal goods, as well as a wide variety of jewelry
and contemporary craft. Closed Monday. Admission. ~ Fort
Mason, Building A; 415-775-0990.

Museo Italo Americano presents samplings of Italian artistry.
The museum is dedicated to displaying the works of Italian and
Italian-American artists and culture. The permanent collection
features the work of several artists, some of whom have made
San Francisco their home for years. There are also temporary ex-

IT'S HANDS-ON TIME HERE

If education is on your mind, note that the Palace of Fine Arts houses the
Exploratorium. A great place to bring children, this "hands-on" museum, with imaginative exhibits demonstrating the principles of optics,
sound, animal behavior, etc., was once deemed "the best science museum in the world" by *Scientific American*. It's an intriguing place
with constantly changing temporary exhibits and permanent displays
that include a "distorted room"lacking right angles and an illusion-
ary mirror into which you seemingly pass. Also check out the
Tactile Dome (reservations required), an enclosed crawl-space of
textural adventures. Closed Monday. Admission. ~ Marina
Boulevard and Lyon Street; 415-561-0360.

hibits ranging from 1930s photos of Italy to a pictorial display of contemporary Italian cinematographers like Francis Ford Coppola, Dino deLaurentiis, Michael Cimino, and Martin Scorcese. Closed Monday and Tuesday. Admission. ~ Fort Mason, Building C; 415-673-2200.

For a look at the rich culture of our neighbor to the south, visit the **Mexican Museum**. There are rotating exhibits of pre-Columbian art, Mexican Colonial art, and Mexican-American contemporary art. Exhibits in the galleries change every several months. Closed Monday and Tuesday. Admission. ~ Fort Mason, Building D; 415-441-0404.

Now that you're fully versed in the arts, continue on the shoreline to the **Marina**, along Marina Boulevard. (The remainder of the tour can be completed by car, though walking is definitely the aesthete's and athlete's way.) Some of this sailor-city's spiffiest yachts are docked along the esplanade.

Nearby **Marina Green**, a stretch of park paralleling the Bay, is a landlubber's haven. Bicyclers, joggers, jugglers, sunbathers, and a world of others inhabit it. The park's most interesting denizens are the kitefliers who fill the blue with a rainbow of soaring colors.

Continue on past a line-up of luxury toys—boats with names like *Haiku*, *Sea Lover*, *Valhalla*, and *Windfall*. When you arrive at the far end of that small green rectangle of park, you'll have to pay special attention to your navigator; you're on Marina Boulevard at the corner of Yacht Road; if going by car, proceed directly ahead through the U.S. Army gate and follow Mason Street, Crissy Field Avenue, and Lincoln Boulevard, paralleling the water, to Fort Point; if on foot, turn right onto Yacht Road, then left at the waterfront, and follow the shoreline toward the Golden Gate Bridge.

Before doing either, you have an alluring detour in store. Turn left at Yacht Road, cross Marina Boulevard, and proceed to that magnificent Beaux-Arts monument looming before you. It's the **Palace of Fine Arts**, a domed edifice built of arches and shadows. Adorned with molded urns and bas-relief figures, it represents the only surviving structure from the 1915 Panama–Pacific International Exposition. Happily, it borders on a sun-shivered pond. The pond in its turn is peopled by mallards and swans, as well as pintails and canvasbacks from out of town. Together, the pool, the pillars, and surrounding park make this one of the city's loveliest spots for sitting and sunning.

But enough for detours; we were embarked on a long march to the bridge. If you cheated and drove, you're already at Fort Point, and we'll catch up with you later; otherwise you're on foot, with the Bay at your side and the Golden Gate dead ahead. This is a land where big freighters talk to foghorns, and sloops scud along soundlessly. The waterfront is a sandy beach, a rockpile in seeming upheaval, then beach again, sand dunes, and occasional shade trees. That wooded grove rising to your left is the Presidio; those bald-domed hills across the Bay to the right are the Marin Headlands, and the sharp-rising buildings poking at your back are part of the San Francisco skyline. You'll pass a Coast Guard Station and a fishing pier before arriving at the red brick fort that snuggles in the arch of the Golden Gate Bridge.

Modeled on Fort Sumter and completed around the time Confederate forces opened fire on that hapless garrison, the **Fort Point National Historic Site** represents the only brick fort west of the Mississippi. With its collection of cannons and Civil War–era exhibits, it's of interest to history buffs. Call for information on guided tours and special programs. Closed Monday and Tuesday. ~ End of Marine Drive; 415-556-1693.

> At Fort Point, if you follow the spiral granite staircase to the roof, you'll stand directly beneath the Golden Gate Bridge and command a sentinel's view out into the Pacific.

From Fort Point, a footpath leads up to the observation area astride the **Golden Gate Bridge**; if driving, take Lincoln Boulevard to the vista point. By whichever route, you'll arrive at "The Bridge at the End of the Continent." Aesthetically, it is considered one of the world's most beautiful spans, a medley of splayed cable and steel struts. Statistically, it represents one of the longest suspension bridges anywhere—6450 feet of suspended concrete and steel, with twin towers the height of 65-story buildings, and cables that support 200 million pounds. It is San Francisco's emblem, an engineering wonder that has come to symbolize an entire metropolis.

If you're game, you can walk across, venturing along a dizzying sidewalk out to one of the most magnificent views you'll ever experience. The Bay from this height is a toy model built to scale; beyond the bridge, San Francisco and Marin, slender arms of land, open onto the boundless Pacific.

The Golden Gate Promenade ends at the bridge, but Lincoln Boulevard continues along the cliffs that mark the ocean side of San Francisco. There are **vista points** overlooking the Pacific and affording startling views back toward the bridge. After about a mile you'll reach **Baker Beach**, a wide corridor of white sand. Ideal for picnicking and sunbathing, this lovely beach is a favorite among San Franciscans. ~ Off Lincoln Boulevard on Gibson Road. Adventurers can follow this strand, and the other smaller beaches with which it connects, on a fascinating walk back almost all the way to the Golden Gate Bridge. With the sea unfolding on one side and rocky crags rising along the other, it's definitely

HIDDEN ► worth a little sand in the shoes. As a final reward, there's a **nude beach** on the northern end, just outside the bridge.

Lincoln Boulevard transforms into El Camino del Mar which winds through Sea Cliff, one of San Francisco's most affluent residential neighborhoods. This exclusive area has something to offer the visitor in addition to its scenic residences—namely **China Beach** (formerly known as James Phelan Beach). A bit more secluded than Baker Beach, this pocket beach is backdropped by a rocky bluff atop which stand the luxurious plate-window homes of Sea Cliff. Named for the Chinese fishermen who camped here in the 19th century, the beach has a dilapidated beach house and restroom facilities. (To get there, turn right on 25th Avenue, left on Sea Cliff Avenue, then follow until it dead ends.)

Continuing on El Camino del Mar as it sweeps above the ocean, you'll come upon San Francisco's prettiest museum. With its colonnaded courtyard and arching entranceway, the **California Palace of the Legion of Honor** is modeled after a gallery in Paris. In fact, a mini pyramid mirroring the one at the Louvre sits in the courtyard, letting light into the gallery below. Appropriately, it specializes in European art and culture. The exhibits trace European aesthetic achievements from the religious art of the Middle Ages to Renaissance painting, the Baroque and Rococo periods, and the Impressionists of the 19th and 20th centuries. Closed Monday. Admission. ~ 34th Avenue and Clement Street, in Lincoln Park; 415-750-3600.

After you've drunk in the splendid view of city and Bay from the museum grounds, head downhill on 34th Avenue past the golf course, turn right on Geary Boulevard, which becomes Point Lobos Avenue, then turn right on to El Camino del Mar and follow it to the end. (Yes, this is the same street you were on earlier; no, I'm not leading you in circles. It seems that years ago landslides collapsed the midriff of this highway, leaving among the survivors two dead-end streets known forever by the same name.)

HIDDEN ► This is **Land's End**, a thumb-like appendage of real estate which San Francisco seems to have stolen from the sea. It is the

LAKE MERCED

At the intersection of Skyline and Lake Merced boulevards lies **Lake Merced**, a U-shaped reservoir which has the unusual distinction of once having been salt water. Bounded by the Harding Park golf links and hiking trails, it provides a pretty spot to picnic. If you decide to pass up the hang gliding at Fort Funston, you might rent a rowboat or canoe at the clubhouse here and try a less nerve-jangling sport. The lake is stocked with catfish and trout. ~ 415-753-1101.

nearest you will ever approach to experiencing San Francisco as the Costanoan Indians knew it. Hike the trails which honeycomb the hillsides hereabout and you'll enter a wild, tumbling region where winds twist cypress trees into the contours of the earth. The rocks offshore are inhabited by slithering sea creatures. The air is loud with the unceasing lash of wave against shoreline. Land's End is San Francisco's grand finale—a line of cliffs poised at the sea's edge and threatening imminently to slide into eternity.

From the parking lot located at the end of El Camino del Mar, walk down the steps that begin at the USS *San Francisco* Memorial Flagpole, and head east on the trail to the water. That dirty blonde swath of sand is a popular **nude beach**, perfectly situated ◀ HIDDEN here in San Francisco's most natural region.

(**Note:** while hiking the footpaths in the region, beware! Land's End is plagued by landslides and foolish hikers. Remain on the trails. Exercise caution and this exotic area will reward you with eye-boggling views of Marin's wind-chiseled coast.)

Continuing down Point Lobos Avenue, at the corner where the road turns to parallel the Pacific Ocean, rest the ruins of the **Sutro Baths**. From the configuration of the stones, it's a simple trick to envision the foundation of Adolf Sutro's folly; more difficult for the mind's eye is to picture the multitiered confection that the San Francisco philanthropist built upon it back in 1896. Sprawling across three oceanfront acres, Sutro's baths could have washed the entire city. There were actually six baths total, Olympian in size, as well as three restaurants and 500 dressing rooms —all somehow contained beneath a stained-glass dome.

Towering above them was the Cliff House, a Gothic castle which survived the earthquake only to be consumed by fire the very next year. Following several reincarnations, the **Cliff House** is a rather bland structure housing several restaurants and tourist shops. Also here is the National Park Service information office (415-556-8642) and a great view. From this crow's nest you can gaze out over a sweeping expanse of ocean. ~ 1090 Point Lobos Avenue. Just offshore the **Seal Rocks** lie anchored. Don't look for the seals, though. They have all moved to Pier 39.

Below the Cliff House, extending to the very end of vision, is the Great Highway. The salt-and-pepper beach beside it is **Ocean Beach**, a slender ribbon of sand that decorates three miles of San Francisco's western perimeter. Remember, this is San Francisco— land of fog, mist, and west winds—beachwear here more often consists of sweaters than swimsuits. The water, sweeping down from the Arctic, is too cold for mere mortals; only surfers and polar bear swimmers brave it. Nevertheless, to walk this strand is to trek the border of eternity. American Indians called San Francisco's ocean the "sundown sea." If you'll take the time some late afternoon, you'll see that the fiery orb still settles nightly just offshore.

Located on Skyline Boulevard at the far end of Ocean Beach, **Fort Funston** is the prettiest stretch to stroll. The fort itself is little more than a sequence of rusting gun emplacements, but there is an environmental education center and a half-mile nature trail here that winds along cliffs overlooking the sea. It's a windblown region of dune grass and leathery succulent plants, with views that span San Francisco and alight on the shore of Marin. Hang gliders dust the cliffs of Fort Funston, adding another dramatic element to this spectacle of sun and wind.

Heading back along the Great Highway, you'll encounter the **San Francisco Zoo**. Housing over 50 endangered species, plus an excellent gorilla habitat and Primate Discovery Center, it's a great place to visit. Admission. ~ 45th Avenue and Sloat Boulevard; 415-753-7061.

LODGING   Say the word "hostel" and the first pictures to come to mind are spartan accommodations and shabby surroundings. At **Hostelling International—San Francisco—Fort Mason** that simply is not the case. Set in Fort Mason, an old military base that is now part of a magnificent national park, the hostel overlooks San Francisco Bay. In addition to eye-boggling views, the facility is within walking distance of the Marina district and Fisherman's Wharf. The hostel itself is contained in a World War II–era infirmary and features a living room, kitchen, and laundry, as well as a café that offers stunning views of the bay. The rooms, carpeted and quite clean, are dorm-style with 4 to 12 bunk beds in each. No smoking or alcohol-imbibing; strict noise curfew at midnight. Reservations recommended. ~ Fort Mason, Building 240, Bay and Franklin Streets; 415-771-7277, fax 415-771-1468. BUDGET.

If you're seeking a hotel near the ocean, removed from the hubbub of downtown San Francisco, consider **Seal Rock Inn**. Perched on a bluff overlooking the Pacific, it's located just outside the Golden Gate National Recreation Area, a stone-skip away from Ocean Beach and Golden Gate Park. The 27 guest rooms are spacious, easily sleeping four people. Furnishings and decor are unimaginative but quite comfortable; the rooms are carpeted wall-to-wall and equipped with televisions and telephones. Also, a godsend in this region of frequent fog, some rooms have fireplaces. These are a little extra, as are rooms featuring mini-kitchenettes and panoramic ocean views. ~ 545 Point Lobos Avenue; 415-752-8000, fax 415-752-6034; www.sealrockinn.com. MODERATE.

San Francisco's first motel is a 24-room art deco beauty. Built in 1936, the same year as the Golden Gate Bridge, the **Ocean Park Motel** combines modern furnishings, cedar paneling, and floral wallpapers. In addition to attractive rooms (some with kitchens) and large family suites, there are an outdoor hot tub, courtyard,

and small playground. ~ 2690 46th Avenue; 415-566-7020, fax
415-665-8959; e-mail ocnprk36@aol.com. MODERATE TO DELUXE.

One of San Francisco's most popular vegetarian restaurants is incongruously situated in an old waterfront warehouse. With pipes
exposed and a metal superstructure supporting the roof, **Greens
at Fort Mason** possesses the aura of an upscale airplane hangar.
But this eatery, run by the Zen Center, has been deftly furnished
with burlwood tables, and there's a view of the Golden Gate out
of the warehouse windows. Lunch brings mesquite-grilled vegetable brochettes, pita bread stuffed with hummus, and daily
specials. Dinner is pre-set on Saturday. The menu changes daily,
but may include fougasse with red onions, spinach linguine,
Tunisian salad, and eggplant soup. Reservations recommended.
No lunch Monday; brunch only on Sunday. ~ Fort Mason, Building A; 415-771-6222. MODERATE TO ULTRA-DELUXE.

DINING

Try as you might to escape the trodden paths, some places in
the world are simply inevitable. Such a one is the Cliff House, a
historic structure at the edge of the sea which is positively inundated with tourists. Since there's little else out on the city's ocean
side, you may find yourself at one of the three dining areas here.
Downstairs at the **Seafood & Beverage Co.** you'll find a trim
restaurant overlooking Seal Rocks and serving lunches and dinners of steak, poultry, and seafood; also Sunday brunch. ~ 1090
Point Lobos Avenue; 415-386-3330. MODERATE TO DELUXE.

Upstairs at the Cliff House offers the same view in a café-cum-
formal setting. The breakfast and lunch menu boasts 30 kinds of
omelettes as well as soups and sandwiches. At dinner the wait staff
changes into nicer clothes, the linen goes on the tables, and the
café changes into a formal dining room. There's pasta, several seafood selections, and a few chicken, steak, or veal entrées. ~ 1090
Point Lobos Avenue; 415-386-3330. MODERATE TO DELUXE.

For a tad less expensive meal, head uphill a few steps to **Louis'**,
a cliffside café that's been family-owned since 1937. The dinners,
served with soup or salad, include New York steak, prawns, scallops, and hamburger steak. The café's breakfast and lunch are
similar all-American affairs. Add a postcard view of the Sutro
Baths and Seal Rocks and you have one hell of a bargain. ~ 902
Point Lobos Avenue; 415-387-6330. MODERATE.

Seafood lovers start lining up early at the popular **Pacific
Café** in the outer Richmond District where the wait for a table
is soothed by a complimentary glass of wine and convivial talk.
Then it's time to sink into a high-backed wooden booth and ponder the daily specials, which always include a wide assortment of
grilled fresh fish and frequently ahi tuna garnished with wasabe
butter, spicy crab cakes, and garlic-infused steamed mussels. Din-

ner only. ~ 7000 Geary Boulevard; 415-387-7091. MODERATE TO
DELUXE.

Out in San Francisco's southwest corner, in Harding Park on
the shores of Lake Merced, you'll discover a spiffy dining room,
The Boathouse Sports Bar and Restaurant. With pretty views, it
offers a lunch and dinner menu of steak, seafood, sandwiches, and
salad. They take their sports themes seriously. Corridor walls are
lined with photos of local athletes and every corner (as in all four)
has a television to keep you posted on the latest scores. If you're
out here to begin with, it's probably to go golfing, boating, hiking, or hang gliding, so the athletic ambience shouldn't bother you.
Saturday and Sunday brunch. ~ 1 Harding Park Road; 415-681-
2727. MODERATE.

NIGHTLIFE   Where San Francisco meets the Pacific, there's **Phineas T. Barna-
cle**. Set in the Cliff House, it's heavily touristed and rather pricey,
but the views are unmatched: Seal Rocks stand sentinel offshore.
~ 1090 Point Lobos Avenue; 415-386-3330.

The **Magic Theatre** has premiered several plays by the Pulitzer
Prize–winning dramatist Sam Shepard, who was playwright-in-
residence here for several years. Plays by new playwrights are performed nearly year-round. ~ Located at Fort Mason, Building D;
415-441-8822.

The **Palace of Fine Arts Theatre** hosts international performances featuring virtuoso musicians from India, Africa, the Middle East, and other points near and far, as well as ethnic dance
and film festivals. ~ Bay and Lyon streets; 415-567-6642.

▼▼▼▼▼▼▼▼▼▼▼▼▼▼▼
Gay Neighborhoods

San Francisco's gay neighborhoods center
around Castro Street, Polk Street, and in the
South of Market area. The city's lesbian com-
munity focuses along Valencia Street in the Mission District. With
a population that today numbers perhaps 200,000, the community has become a powerful social and political force. In 1977,
Supervisor Harvey Milk became the nation's first outfront gay
elected to a major municipal post. Since then, despite the AIDS
epidemic, San Francisco has retained gay supervisors and the gay
community has remained an integral part of the city's life.

LODGING   Throughout the Castro and Polk districts are numerous hotels
catering primarily to gay travelers. Others in these areas serve a
wide-ranging clientele, including many gay guests.

There are two hotels located in the center of the action. The
first is the **Inn on Castro**, an eight-room bed and breakfast housed
in an old Victorian. A class establishment all the way, the inn adds
subtle touches like fresh flowers. Each room is decorated in a different fashion, and the house atmosphere is comfortable and per-

sonal. The rooms all have private baths. Because of its popularity, the hotel recommends advance reservations. ~ 321 Castro Street; 415-861-0321; www.innoncastro.com. DELUXE.

Several blocks from Castro Street is **The Willows Bed and Breakfast Inn,** a beautiful 12-room facility that attracts both gay and straight guests. Each room has been furnished with antique wooden pieces and adorned with French art prints. The trademark of this cozy hostelry, however, is the willow-branch furniture designed expressly for the Inn. It's personal touches like this, as well as breakfast and turndown service with a glass of sherry included, that make it a special place. Shared bath. ~ 710 14th Street; 415-431-4770, fax 415-431-5295; www.willowsSF.com. MODERATE TO DELUXE.

Nancy's Inn is a friendly, private lesbian home offering sleeping accommodations to women travelers. Located in a quiet residential neighborhood near Twin Peaks, the house is full of women's energy and decorated with women's art. There are two bedrooms, and a sliding glass door leads from one bedroom to a deck in the back. The bathroom is shared. Close to public transit. ~ 415-239-5692; e-mail nancysbed@aol.com. BUDGET.

The **Inn San Francisco** resides in a 19th-century world. Set in a grand four-story Victorian, this splendid mansion has been furnished entirely with period pieces. There are gilded mirrors and beveled glass in the parlors, wall sconces and marble sinks in many rooms, as well as other antique flourishes. There is a rooftop sundeck, which provides a great view of the city, and an English garden in the back with a gazebo and hot tub. Room prices in this elegant establishment all include a full buffet breakfast; the moderate prices are for rooms with shared baths; deluxe to ultra-deluxe have private facilities; ultra-deluxe come with hot tubs or jacuzzis. The clientele is both gay and straight. ~ 943 South Van Ness Avenue; 415-641-0188, 800-359-0913, fax 415-641-1701. MODERATE TO ULTRA-DELUXE.

Midway between Castro Street and the Haight-Ashbury neighborhood is the **Metro Hotel**. Appealing to a mixed clientele, there are 23 rooms, a small lobby, an adjoining café downstairs, and an English garden. The guests rooms are carpeted wall-to-wall, furnished with oak pieces, and decorated with wallhangings. Each has a private bath (shower only) and color television with cable. Set in a white stucco building, it is clean and comfortable. While the location is not ideal, it is close enough to key neighborhoods to make the hotel worth the cost of admission. ~ 319 Divisadero Street; 415-861-5364, fax 415-863-1970; www.citysearch.com. BUDGET TO MODERATE.

The **Alamo Square Inn** offers not one but two Victorian mansions, a Queen Anne and a Tudor Revival, both predating the 1906 earthquake by a decade. The bed-and-breakfast hostelry, which welcomes both gays and straights, is just a ten-minute walk from Castro Street and offers a choice of nine individually decorated rooms, a self-contained apartment and three suites, including one with a sunken jacuzzi and private deck. ~ 719 Scott Street; 415-922-2055, 800-345-9888, fax 415-931-1304; www.alamo inn.com. MODERATE TO ULTRA-DELUXE.

Those in search of the quintessential "Painted Lady" Victorian will not want to miss **Chateau Tivoli**, a dazzling three-story 1892 mansion resplendent with gold leaf, stained-glass windows, and elaborate iron grillwork. There are even antique pieces that belonged to Sally Stanford, a real painted lady and madam in San Francisco. Accommodations include five rooms, three suites, and one efficiency unit, most with private marble bathrooms and some with canopy beds, fireplaces, and decks. The clientele is both straight and gay. Wine and cheese are served in the afternoon, and a Sunday champagne brunch is included in the rates. No smoking. ~ 1057 Steiner Street; 415-776-5462, 800-228-1647, fax 415-776-0505; www.chateautivoli.com. MODERATE TO ULTRA-DELUXE.

A European-style boutique hotel, the **Leland Hotel** offers 108 rooms, most with private baths and sunny bay windows, and 16 studio apartments. Most guests are gay men, but women are also welcome. In the midst of the Polk Street bar-and-restaurant scene, the hotel bar is a popular gay gathering spot. ~ 1315 Polk Street; 415-441-5141, 800-258-4458, fax 415-441-1449. MODERATE.

DINING

Over in the Castro Street neighborhood, **Caffe Luna Piena** is a good choice for a casual meal. You can dine indoors or outside on a tree-studded patio. They feature a breakfast menu that includes poached eggs, omelettes, and eggs Benedict. Lunch consists of hamburgers, sandwiches, salads, and pasta. The restaurant serves dinner as well. No dinner on Monday. ~ 558 Castro Street; 415-621-2566. MODERATE.

Anchor Oyster Bar is a hole-in-the-wall café which happens to serve delicious shellfish. There are oysters on the half shell, steamed clams and mussels, seafood cocktails, and various daily specials. Recommended for lunch or dinner. No lunch on Sunday. ~ 579 Castro Street; 415-431-3990. MODERATE.

Hot 'N' Hunky, an impeccably designed burger joint, appeals to both gays and lesbians and packs them in from 11 a.m. to midnight (1 a.m. Friday and Saturday). The decor is classic diner with blue-and-white tiled floor, formica-topped tables, a jukebox in the center, and pictures of Marilyn Monroe on the walls. Hot 'N' Hunky serves 17 kinds of burgers, as well as hot dogs and other sandwiches. ~ 4039 18th Street; 415-621-6365. BUDGET.

A good place after a late movie at the Castro Theater is **Orphan Andy's**, one of the few San Francisco restaurants open 24 hours. Decorated with a colorful 1950s diner theme with a counter and leatherette booths, Orphan Andy's serves up good burgers, sandwiches, omelettes, and other classic coffee-shop fare. ~ 3991 17th Street; 415-864-9795. BUDGET.

Exceptionally popular with the locals, **Cafe Flore** has a partially enclosed outside patio, where diners can watch life in the Castro go by. Inside, the floor is tiled, the atmosphere casual and relaxed. You order at the window from a blackboard menu listing soups, pastas, sandwiches, and burgers. There's also an espresso bar. ~ 2298 Market Street; 415-621-8579. BUDGET.

Open for breakfast and lunch, catering to a mixed clientele, and particularly popular with women, is **Just For You**. This diner in the Potrero Hill district has counter service and tables and is decorated with photographs and artwork by local artists. The cuisine is a mix of American and Cajun, with cornmeal pancakes and grits for breakfast, hamburgers and crabcake sandwiches at lunch. ~ 1453 18th Street; 415-647-3033. BUDGET.

A gathering spot for casual meals and entertainment is **Red Dora's Bearded Lady Women's Café**. Open from morning to early evening, the café offers breakfast specials, salads, and hearty soups. Live music and spoken-word entertainment is often presented on weekends. ~ 485 14th Street; 415-626-2805. BUDGET.

Located south of Market, the women-owned-and-operated **Chat House** serves up caffeinated brews and inventive dishes to a mixed clientele in a relaxed café setting. For lunch or dinner, sample the fried oyster BLT, vegetable garden burger, or chicken salpicon. Breakfast, lunch, and dinner are served weekdays and Saturdays; breakfast only on Sunday. ~ 139 8th Street; 415-255-8783. BUDGET.

Open until the wee hours, **Hamburger Mary's** draws gays and straights alike. When the crowd is not drinking famous daiquiris in Cissy's Saloon, it's gorging on hamburgers, sandwiches, omelettes, and vegetarian food. ~ 1582 Folsom Street; 415-626-1985. MODERATE.

Dollar for dollar, the best dining spot along Polk Street is **Swan Oyster Depot**. It's a short-order place serving fresh prawns, crabs, lobster, shrimp, and oysters, all displayed in trays out front. The place consists simply of a counter lined with stools and is always packed. The depot opens at 8 a.m. and closes at 5:30 p.m. Closed Sunday. ~ 1517 Polk Street; 415-673-1101. MODERATE.

There are about a thousand restaurants in San Francisco named Hunan, and the second most popular name seems to be Cordon Bleu. The place claiming to be the original **Cordon Bleu Vietnamese Restaurant** is a simple café-style establishment serving a wide array of Southeast Asian dishes. They serve imperial rolls, shishkabobs, beef dishes, and tasty five-spice roast chicken. No lunch on Sunday. Closed Monday. ~ 1574 California Street; 415-673-5637. BUDGET.

◄ HIDDEN

SHOPPING   The Castro Street shopping district stretches along Castro from 19th Street to Market Street, then continues for several blocks on "Upper Market"; there are also several interesting stores along 18th Street. The entire area is surprisingly compact, but features a variety of shops. Together with Polk Street, it represents the major gay shopping area in San Francisco.

Headlines is San Francisco's answer to a gay department store. Each of these sprawling shops features sections devoted to clothing, knickknacks, housewares, greeting cards, jewelry, and novelty buttons. To shop the Castro Street corridor and bypass Headlines is like window browsing New York and ignoring Bloomingdales. ~ 2301 Chestnut Street, 549 and 557 Castro Street, and 838 Market Street; 415-956-4872.

Along "Upper Market," there's **Image Leather** for black leather. ~ 2199 Market Street; 415-621-7551.

Good Vibrations, a popular sex toy, book, and video emporium designed in the late 1970s especially for women, has become a San Francisco institution. The store sells erotic literature, self-help sex books, feminist erotica, videos and sex education films, and an unbeatable array of vibrators and electric massagers. A highlight of the store is an antique vibrator museum with some rather unusual items like a cranked version that looks like a rolling pin. ~ 1210 Valencia Street; 415-974-8980.

Polk Street is wall-to-wall with designer fashion shops, boutiques, and all manner of clothing outlets. The central gay area stretches from Post Street to Washington Street, but savvy shoppers will continue on to Union Street, since several intriguing stores lie on the outskirts of the neighborhood.

At the **Tibet Shop** are *sili* bangles, painted lanterns, Buddha figurines, prayer beads, and monastic incense. This wonderful little shop also has vests, skirts, dresses, shirts, and jackets made in Nepal by Tibetans. ~ 1807 Polk Street; 415-982-0326.

NIGHTLIFE   One example of San Francisco's wide-open tradition is the presence of almost 200 gay bars in the city. There's everything here from rock clubs to piano bars to stylish cabarets. Some are strictly gay, others mix their customers, and some have become so popular that straights have begun to take them over from gays.

There are a dozen or so bars in the Castro Street area, many open from early morning until the wee hours. Among the nicest is **Twin Peaks Tavern** with its overhead fans and mirrored bar. ~ 401 Castro Street; 415-864-9470.

Across the street and down a few doors is the disco-blasting **Castro Station**. ~ 456-B Castro Street; 415-626-7220.

A foot-stompin' gay country-and-western dance club in the South of Market area, **Rawhide 2** features deejay music every night. Country-and-western dance classes are offered on week nights for a fee. Weekend cover. ~ 280 7th Street; 415-621-1197.

Nearby, you'll find **The Stud**, everybody's favorite gay bar. Everybody in this case includes aging hippies, multihued punks, curious straights, and even a gay or two, all packed elbow to armpit into this pulsing club. Cover on most nights. ~ 399 9th Street; 415-863-6623.

The scene is different down the street at the **San Francisco Eagle**, a leather bar. ~ 398 12th Street; 415-626-0880.

San Francisco's lesbian hangouts are located around Valencia Street, but in other parts of the city as well. Catering primarily to women, **The Café** is a mirrored club with lots of neon, pool tables, pinball machines, and two full bars. There's DJ music nightly in the lounge. ~ 2369 Market Street; 415-861-3846.

A cabaret offering comedy, theater, and music, **Josie's Cabaret and Juice Joint** produces everything from standup routines to plays on the tragedy of AIDS. Each month the walls of this renovated warehouse are graced with a new art show. Cover for some shows. ~ 3583 16th Street; 415-861-7933.

For women who are ready to relax there's **Osento Bath House**, a quiet and comfortable Japanese-style bath for women. The blue-tiled bath accommodates seven comfortably; there are also massage and sauna facilities and a sun deck for lounging. Open from 1 p.m. to 1 a.m. ~ 955 Valencia Street; 415-282-6333.

Universe is the hottest gay dance club on Saturday nights. Deejays spin a mix of techno, house, and disco dance music. Cover. ~ 177 Townsend Street; 415-974-6020.

Plays with gay and lesbian themes are the focus of **Theatre Rhinoceros**, an acclaimed company that presents performances at two theaters, Rhino's Mainstage and Rhino's Studio. ~ 2926 16th Street; 415-861-5079.

San Francisco's answer to off-off-Broadway is **The Marsh Theater**, a small, informal theater billed as a "breeding ground for new performers," which offers plays and spoken-word entertainment frequently, but not exclusively, on women's topics. Monday nights are reserved for performers trying out new work. ~ 1062 Valencia Street; 415-641-0235.

▲▲

SHOPPING FOR A GOOD CAUSE

Shopping at **Under One Roof** is like giving to a good cause. This store is underwritten by individuals and corporations, so 100 percent of the profits are donated to more than 60 northern California AIDS service organizations. It sells a wide selection of items, including candles, soaps, lotions, coffee, candy, T-shirts, jewelry, and gay and lesbian books. ~ 2362-B Market Street; 415-252-9430.

Over in the Polk Street neighborhood, the **Eleven-Hundred Club** starts at noon and parties late. With its raw-wood interior the place has an open air about it. ~ 1100 Polk Street; 415-771-2022. Nicest of all the neighborhood bars, however, is **Kimo's**. With mirrors and potted palms all around, it's a comfy atmosphere. ~ 1351 Polk Street; 415-885-4535. Another attractively appointed rendezvous is the oak-and-brass **Giraffe**. ~ 1131 Polk Street; 415-474-1702.

The **N'Touch** has a disco dancefloor plus video monitors. There is always a lively crowd here. With flashing lights and ample sound, it's a good spot for dancing and carousing. Most nights have shows or other entertainment. Cover some nights. ~ 1548 Polk Street; 415-441-8413.

For live entertainment, check out **The Q. T.** Open seven nights a week, it has live music Saturday, featuring local bands as well as hot sounds from out of town. ~ 1312 Polk Street; 415-885-1114.

▼▼▼▼▼▼▼▼▼▼▼▼
South of Market

Just over 20 years ago, South of Market, popularly known as SOMA, had the reputation as one of the most unattractive and unsafe neighborhoods in the city. Filled with residential hotels, vacant warehouses, and seedy bars, it was ignored by many of the city's residents. This neglect presented an opportunity for those who wanted to be isolated, and in the '70s SOMA became a hub for the gay-bathhouse crowd and the gay-leather crowd.

During the '80s SOMA metamorphosed again. Gay bathhouses were closed in a sweep by government officials and replaced by trendy nightclubs; gay-leather bars with names like "The Arena" became popular dance clubs with names like the "DNA Lounge."

The underused warehouses then brought in a different countercultural crowd—artists. Modeling themselves after the residents of New York City's SOHO (South of Houston) district, Bay Area artists converted SOMA warehouses into combination live/work spaces featuring art galleries, performance spaces, and music studios. Many of San Francisco's most creative people still live and display (or perform) in small galleries and theaters throughout SOMA. (A new controversy, however, centers on the yuppie influx into the warehouse district. The artists complain about rising rents and the scarcity of space; yuppies complain about the club noise.) Independent retailers also took advantage of the cheap warehouse space by opening large factory outlets and discount stores. These were followed in the '90s by national superstores.

Catering to this modern urban crowd are many restaurants and cafés that offer a true SOMA twist to their atmosphere and menu. Don't be surprised if your café table has a computer hooked up to the Internet or the restaurant you're dining at has decor created during the slow hours before lunch.

Named for George Moscone, the San Francisco mayor assassi-
nated in 1978, **Moscone Center** is a mammoth convention center that extends across 1.2 million square feet. With restaurants,
hotels, apartments, and stores encircling it like satellites, the center is the dominant feature in San Francisco's fastest-changing
district. ~ Howard Street between 3rd and 4th streets.

An important addition to the area is **Yerba Buena Gardens**,
a project that was 30 years in the making but is proving to be
worth the wait by providing a forum for the visual and performing arts as well as some much needed green space.

One component of the ten-acre complex located on top of the
underground Moscone Convention Center is the **Center for the
Arts at Yerba Buena Gardens** with two buildings, one designed
by the acclaimed Japanese architect, Fumihiko Maki. It includes
three galleries devoted to visual arts and high-
tech installations. It includes a screening room
for video and film. (Open Tuesday through Sunday from 11 a.m. to 6 p.m.) A large multipurpose
room called "The Forum" hosts special events. In
addition, a 750-seat theater offering a diverse lineup
of music, dance, and performance art. Softening the
contemporary hard edges of Yerba Buena is a five-and-
a-half-acre esplanade of gardens and outdoor public art.
Admission for the galleries. ~ 415-978-2787.

> A focal point of Yerba
> Buena Gardens is the
> Martin Luther King Jr.
> Memorial, a graceful
> waterfall spilling
> over Sierra granite.

The **San Francisco Museum of Modern Art**'s popularity
soared after it moved to its South of Market location in 1995,
and it is now one of the top-ten most visited museums in the
United States. The building, designed by Swiss architect Mario
Botta, is a Modernist work of art in itself, distinguished by a
tower finished in alternating bands of black and white stone.
Inside are three large galleries and more than 20 smaller ones, to-
taling 50,000 square feet. The second floor displays selections
from the museum's permanent collection. The third-floor gallery
features photographs and works on paper. The top two gallery
floors accommodate special exhibitions and large-scale art from
the museum's collection. Closed Wednesday. Admission. ~ 151
3rd Street; 415-357-4000.

One of SOMA's more prominent galleries, **The Ansel Adams
Center** features four galleries of fine art photography. All of them
have changing exhibits that range from 19th century to contemporary. Closed Monday. Admission. ~ 250 4th Street; 415-495-
7000.

The **Cartoon Art Museum** is also located in the Yerba Buena
neighborhood. The museum features rotating exhibits of cartoon
art in all its various incarnations: newspaper strips, political car-
toons, comic books, and animation are amply represented. Highlights include a children's gallery and a bookstore. One of only

◀ HIDDEN

three museums of its kind in the United States, this rare treat should not be missed. Closed Monday and Tuesday. Admission. ~ 814 Mission Street; 415-227-8666.

DINING

Among several trendy restaurants here is the **Cadillac Bar**, a raucous Mexican eatery that may be the noisiest place you've ever entered. The bar itself is *muy grande*, a massive wood structure adorned with sombreros and a wall-length mirror. Cooking is by mesquite grill (what else?), but the menu ain't your standard south-of-the-border inventory. We're talking prawns with *aguacate* sauce, red snapper with sautéed chiles, marinated skirt steak, and chicken stuffed with jalapeños and bacon. Warehouse chic. ~ 1 Holland Court; 415-543-8226. MODERATE.

It's not every day you can enjoy a dry martini while seated at a curved pink leatherette bar right out of the '50s and then be treated to a postmodern nouvelle American dinner, but that's the case at **Julie's Supper Club**. Despite the loud music, insist on a table in the front room, to enjoy the passing array of trendy SOMA club-goers. Stick with the imaginative salads for starters, followed by outstanding chicken, lamb, or fish dishes. Dinner only. ~ 1123 Folsom Street; 415-861-4084. MODERATE.

A hotspot not far from the Yerba Buena Gardens complex is **Restaurant Lulu**, a noisy warehouse-sized restaurant that draws in crowds at lunch and dinner for superb meats and chicken prepared on a brick rotisserie. Also noteworthy are the shellfish selections such as iron skillet–roasted mussels and Dungeness crab with garlic. ~ 816 Folsom Street; 415-495-5775. MODERATE.

In the morning **South Park Café** is a casual coffee-and-croissant place for folks who live and work in the area. At lunch and dinner the café, which has only a long bar and a few tables, is a popular gourmet dining spot known for imaginative salads and daily meat and fish specials. In the early evening there's a special tapas menu. Closed Sunday and dinner only on Saturday. ~ 108 South Park; 415-495-7275. MODERATE.

NIGHTLIFE

If you find SF's nightlife options overwhelming, **3 Babes and a Bus** allows you a 45-minute taste of different scenes, from '70s disco and Top-40 to salsa and R&B. For a flat fee, this nightclub-touring company takes care of the driving and cover charges while ensuring priority entry to a number of clubs on this four-hour tour. Reservations recommended. ~ 415-552-2582.

The newest addition to the ultra-hip turn-of-the-century retro-Jetsons style is the **Mercury**. With a mirror bubble-bar, waitresses attired in Audrey Hepburn dresses or ostrich plumes, and a restaurant serving French cuisine with a Pacific-rim infusion, this is not a place for sensory deprivation. The outside is only marked by big silver gates. No jeans, no tennies—they will turn you away. ~ 540 Howard Street, between 1st and 2nd streets; 415-777-1419.

For some live acoustic sounds from local bands or deejay-spun jazz, check out **Brain Wash**. There's always something happening at this hip café which also doubles as a . . . laundromat! ~ 1126 Folsom Street; 415-431-9274.

There is only one thing in the world better than a rocking nightclub: three rocking nightclubs. That's what you get over at 3rd and Harrison streets where **The X** (415-339-8686) features modern rock on Friday night. On Saturday **City Nights** (415-339-8686) jumps to the sound of Top-40 hip-hop in the same location. On Thursday, it's gay and lesbian night at **The Box** (415-206-1652). Cover. ~ 715 Harrison Street.

The San Francisco Mime Troupe has performed musical political satires in the city's parks for a quarter of a century. ~ 855 Treat Avenue; 415-285-1717.

Voted Best Brewpub in a local newspaper poll (*Bay Guardian*) two years in a row, **Twenty Tank Brewery** packs in those who prefer a pub to a South of Market club. Formerly a sheet metal shop, this brewery sports 1930s industrial decor and houses brewers who are truly creative, producing such brews as Pollywanna Porter and Kinnikinick Old Scout Stout. While enjoying a beer, you can also throw a few darts or play shuffleboard. ~ 316 11th Street; 415-255-9455.

The DNA **Lounge** has lasted much longer than most trendy clubs. The scene is high-decibel with a mixed crowd clearly born to dance. And dance they do, on all sides of an oval bar in the middle of a bare-wood floor. At a quieter upstairs bar you can discreetly observe the goings-on. Cover. ~ 375 11th Street; 415-626-1409.

Some of the classic Bay Area rock and blues performers appear at **Slim's**, possibly because entertainer Boz Scaggs is an owner. But there is also a hefty line-up of alternative rock bands, so the crowd could be grey- or green-haired at this all-ages club. Usually a cover. ~ 333 11th Street; 415-522-0333.

With more than 800 bands performing each year, the **Paradise Lounge** is one of the busiest clubs on the West Coast. Three stages offer as many as five acts nightly. The early-bohemian Above Paradise Room leans toward acoustic performances. In the pumped-up Downstairs Lounge, a kind of 1974 downtown Reno venue, you'll enjoy hard rock and R&B. The Blue Room's main stage is a straight ahead performance space. There's also an elegant turn-of-the-century pool room with walnut wainscotting. Occasional cover. ~ 1501 Folsom Street; 415-861-6906.

Club TownSend, opened in 1989 in a veritable cavern, that, despite its size, is SRO on weekends. Like the 3rd and Harrison venue, TownSend is occupied with different clubs on different days. **Cue** is all-women, sponsored by Page Hodel Productions. **Universe** is a house club, packed with the gay muscle crowd. The

Pleasure Dome is a gay disco. Cover. ~ 177 Townsend Street at 3rd Street; 415-974-6020. The **King Street Garage** is the back of the block-wide building, and has a similar smorgasborg of clubs. ~ 174 King Street; 415-974-6020.

With over 40 tables, **The Great Entertainer** is one of the largest poolhalls on the West Coast. Located in a former warehouse, this vast establishment also offers snooker tables, shuffleboard, Ping Pong, darts, video games, and a full bar. ~ 975 Bryant Street; 415-861-8833.

Project Artaud, which occupies a city block south of Market at the edge of the Mission district, presents a dizzying array of SF theater and dance performances ranging from the traditional (Odissi from India, for example) to the absurd. Theater Yugen Noh Space (415-621-7978) and A Traveling Jewish Theatre (415-399-1809) are among the companies in permanent residence. ~ 450 Florida Street; 415-621-7797.

▼▼▼▼▼▼▼▼▼▼▼▼▼▼ Outdoor Adventures

If you hanker to spend a day deep-sea fishing for rock cod, bass, salmon, and other gamefish, check out **Hot Pursuit Sport Fishing**. The

SPORT-FISHING

large party boat takes you past the Golden Gate Bridge. ~ Fisherman's Wharf, corner of Jefferson and Jones; 650-965-3474. **Wacky Jacky** takes you out on her 50-foot *Delta*, often heading out to the Farallon Islands in search of salmon. ~ Fisherman's Wharf, Pier 45; 415-586-9800. Bring a lunch and dress warmly.

SAILING & NATURE CRUISES

Some of the world's most challenging sailing can be found on San Francisco Bay. To charter motor- and sailboats and captains, contact **A Day on the Bay**. ~ San Francisco Marina; 415-922-0227. Spend an afternoon cruising the Bay on a motorized yacht with **Pacific Marine Yacht Charters**. They offer a two-hour brunch excursion around the Bay on Sunday. ~ Pier 39; 415-788-9100.

For tours of the Farallon Islands contact the **Oceanic Society**. From the deck of their 63-foot vessel you'll observe harbor seals and sea lions. Puffins, porpoises, and humpback, blue, and gray whales also frequent the waters. Tours of the Farallon Islands are offered June through November; whale-watching tours go from December until April. Reservations required. ~ Fort Mason Center, Building E; 415-474-3385.

KITE FLYING

San Francisco has been called the "city of kites." Ocean breezes, mild weather, and lots of open space create perfect conditions for kite flying. Nearly every day, brightly colored streamers litter the sky, swooping and soaring. Popular kite-flying spots include the Marina Green, Golden Gate Park's Polo Field, Lake Merced, and Fort Funston.

Local kite stores sell exotic designs ranging from traditional box kites to tandems, octagons, hexagons, and silk dragons. Try **Kite Flite** for your flyer. ~ Pier 39; 415-956-3181.

HANG GLIDING & PARA-SAILING

If you'd prefer to soar the skies yourself, you should try hang gliding. For lessons in paragliding, contact **Airtime of San Francisco**. Flights offer views of the coastline. ~ 3620 Wawona Street; 415-759-1177. For those interested in hang gliding, there are great sites at Fort Funston (Skyline Boulevard at the far end of Ocean Beach) and Westlake (just south of Fort Funston). If you're not ready to test those wings, you'll find it's fun just watching.

INLINE SKATING

When Sunday rolls around, several hundred folks are apt to don inline skates and roller skates and careen along the sidewalks and streets of Golden Gate Park. John F. Kennedy Drive, on the east side of the park, is closed to cars on Sundays and holidays. It's great exercise, and a lot of fun, to boot. Skate rentals are available outside of the park at **Skates on Haight**. ~ 1818 Haight Street; 415-752-8376. You can also rent on the park's north side from **Golden Gate Park Skates and Bikes**. ~ 3038 Fulton Street at 6th Avenue; 415-668-1117.

Or, if you want to get downright serious about it, roll over to the **Bladium**. Billed as "inline hockey's premier facility," this popular sports center features a full-size roller-hockey rink as well as an equipment shop, changing rooms, and snack shop. With open rink times and pick-up games every day, it's a great place to enjoy indoor roller hockey. ~ 1050 3rd Street; 415-442-5060.

JOGGING

In a city of steep hills, where walking provides more than enough exercise, jogging is nevertheless a favorite pastime. There are actually places to run where the terrain is fairly level and the scenery spectacular. Most popular are the Golden Gate Bridge, the Presidio Highlands, Ocean Beach, Golden Gate Park, and Angel Island.

✔ **CHECK THESE OUT—UNIQUE OUTDOOR ADVENTURES**

- Spy on the mighty humpback as it travels the Pacific, or observe porpoises, puffins and sea lions on a nature cruise. *page 94*
- Go fly a kite, or watch as others circle and swoop their adult toys high above the Marina Green. *page 94*
- Soar through the air on a multicolored hang glider as you skirt sand dunes and the Pacific Ocean. *page 95*
- Roll along through Golden Gate Park, where they close the streets on Sundays and holidays and everyone is on wheels— skates or bikes, that is. *page 95*

Parcourses, combining aerobic exercises with short jogs, are located at Justin Herman Park (the foot of Market Street near the Ferry Building; half course only), Marina Green (along Marina Boulevard near the foot of Fillmore Street), Mountain Lake Park (Lake Street between 8th and Funston avenues), and the Polo Field in Golden Gate Park.

SWIMMING   Although the air temperature remains moderate all year, the ocean and bay around San Francisco stay cold. If you're ready to brave the Arctic current, join the hearty swimmers who make the plunge regularly at Aquatic Park. Many of these brave souls belong to either the **Dolphin Club** or the **South End Rowing Club**. Both clubs are open to the public (on alternating weekdays) and provide saunas and showers for a small fee. ~ Dolphin Club: 502 Jefferson Street; 415-441-9329. South End Rowing Club: 500 Jefferson Street; 415-776-7372.

SURFING   West of Golden Gate Park there are several spots along San Francisco's wide, sandy **Ocean Beach**; however the conditions vary seasonally and because of strong rip currents, this is not a place for beginners. **Fort Point**, located on the bay side of the Golden Gate Bridge's south tower, is another surf break in the city. Fast-flowing currents moving out the Gate make this another spot for expert surfers only.

GOLF   For the earthbound, golf can be a heavenly sport in San Francisco. Several courses are worth checking out. With two separate tee boxes, the **Glen Eagles International Golf Club** features a nine-hole course that's hilly and narrow. This public course rents power carts, but has no pro shop. ~ 2100 Sunnydale Avenue; 415-587-2425. **Golden Gate Park Golf Course** is a short but tricky nine-hole course close to the ocean. They rent pull carts and clubs at this public course. ~ 47th Avenue and Fulton Street; 415-751-8987. **Harding Park Golf Course** is considered to be one of the finest public courses in the country. There is an 18-hole course and a 9-hole course. Power and pull cart are available to rent, as well as golf clubs. ~ Harding Park Road and Skyline Boulevard; 415-664-4690.

TENNIS   With over 150 free public courts, San Francisco could easily be called The City of Nets. **Golden Gate Park** (John F. Kennedy and Middle drives; fee) has 21 courts. In the Marina try the four courts at **George Moscone Playground** (Chestnut and Buchanan streets; lighted). A popular spot in the Mission is **Mission Dolores Park**, with six lighted courts (18th and Dolores streets). On Nob Hill the three courts at **Alice Marble Memorial Playground** (Greenwich and Hyde streets) are recommended. In Chinatown try the one court at the **Chinese Playground** (Sacramento Street and Waverly Plaza; lighted). Over in North Beach try the **North Beach Playground**, where there are three lighted courts (Lombard and Mason streets). For more information on all city courts call the San Francisco Parks and Recreation Department. ~ 415-753-7032.

San Francisco is not a city designed for cyclers. Some of the hills are almost too steep to walk and downtown traffic can be gruelling. There are places, however, that are easy to ride and beautiful as well. **Golden Gate Park**, the **Golden Gate Promenade**, and **Lake Merced** all have excellent bike routes. **BIKING**

Among the city's most dramatic rides is the bicyclists' sidewalk on the **Golden Gate Bridge**. Or, if you're less adventurous, the **Sunset Bikeway** begins at Lake Merced Boulevard, then carries through a residential area and past views of the ocean to the Polo Field in Golden Gate Park.

Bike Rentals   To rent a mountain bike or hybrid in the city, contact **Lincoln Cyclery**, adjacent to Golden Gate Park. They also sell bikes and gear. ~ 772 Stanyan Street; 415-221-2415. Right around the corner, you can rent from **Park Cyclery**. They have mountain bikes, road bikes, and tandems. ~ 1749 Waller Street at Stanyan Street; 415-221-3777. The **Angel Island Company** rents 21-speed mountain bikes, tandems, junior bikes, and child trailers to explore that state park's paved paths. ~ Angel Island; 415-897-0715.

The major highways leading into San Francisco are **Route 1**, the picturesque coastal road, **Route 101**, California's coastal north–south thoroughfare, and **Route 80**, the transcontinental highway that originates on the East Coast.

Transportation

CAR

San Francisco International Airport, better known as SFO, sits 15 miles south of downtown San Francisco off Routes 101 and 280. A major destination from all points of the globe, the airport is always bustling. **AIR**

Most domestic airlines fly into SFO, including Alaska Airlines, American Airlines, Continental Airlines, Delta Airlines, Hawaiian Airlines, Southwest Airlines, Trans World Airlines, United Airlines, and USAir.

International carriers are also prominent here: Aeroflot, Air Canada, British Airways, China Airlines, Canadian Airlines International, Japan Airlines, Lufthansa German Airlines, Mexicana Airlines, Philippine Airlines, Qantas Airways, Singapore Airlines, TACA International Airlines, and Virgin Atlantic Airways have regular flights into San Francisco's airport.

The SFO **Ground Transportation Information Service** is a free service that will help you plan your way to and from the airport via buses, shuttles, taxis, limousines, and more. ~ There's an information booth in the baggage claim area of each SFO terminal; 800-736-2008.

To travel from the airport to downtown San Francisco, call **San Francisco Airporter**, which runs frequently. ~ 415-495-8404. **Supershuttle** provides door-to-door service. ~ 415-558-8500. Or catch a **San Mateo County Transit**, or **SamTrans**, bus (800-660-4287) to the Transbay Terminal (425 Mission Street) or transfer in Colma or Daly City to BART (415-992-2278). Taxi and limo service are also available, or try **Lorrie's Airport Service.** ~ 415-334-9000.

BUS

Greyhound Bus Lines (800-231-2222) services San Francisco from around the country. ~ Buses arrive and depart from the Transbay Terminal. ~ 425 Mission Street; 415-495-1575.

Also consider the **Green Tortoise**, a New Age company with a fleet of funky buses. Each is equipped with sleeping platforms allowing travelers to rest as they cross the country. The buses stop at interesting sightseeing points en route. The venerable Green Tortoise, an endangered species from the '60s, travels to and from the East Coast, Seattle, Los Angeles, and elsewhere. It provides a mode of transportation as well as an experience in group living. ~ 494 Broadway, San Francisco, CA 94133; 415-821-0803.

TRAIN

For those who prefer to travel by rail, **Amtrak** provides train service via the "Coast Starlight," "California Zephyr," and "San Joaquin." These trains arrive at and depart from the Emeryville train station, with connecting bus service to San Francisco's Ferry Building, where Market Street meets the Embarcadero. ~ 800-872-7245.

CAR RENTALS

The easiest way to explore San Francisco is by foot or public transit. Driving in San Francisco can be a nightmare. Parking spaces are rare, parking lots expensive. Then there are the hills, which require you to navigate along dizzying inclines while dodging cable cars, trollies, pedestrians, and double-parked vehicles. The streets of San Francisco make Mr. Toad's wild ride look tame.

If you do decide to rent a car, most of the major rental agencies have franchises right at the airport. These include **Avis Rent A Car** (800-331-1212), **Budget Rent A Car** (800-527-0700), **Dollar Rent A Car** (800-800-4000), **Hertz Rent A Car** (800-654-3131), and **National Interrent** (408-777-9207).

For less expensive but also less convenient service, try the rental agencies that are located outside of the airport and provide pick-up service: **Ace Rent A Car** (415-771-7711), **California**

Compacts Rent A Car (408-777-9207), and **Flat Rate Rent A Car** (408-777-9207).

San Francisco is a city where public transit works. To get anywhere in the city, call **San Francisco Muni** and a friendly operator will direct you to the appropriate mode of public transportation. ~ 415-673-6864.

PUBLIC TRANSIT

Over 90 bus lines travel around, about, and through the city. Trolley buses, street cars, light-rail subways, and cable cars also crisscross San Francisco. Most lines operate daily (with a modified schedule on weekends and holidays). Free transfers allow a 90-minute stopover or connection to two more lines. Exact fares are required. For complete information on the Muni system, purchase a copy of the "Muni Street and Transit Map" from the Visitor Information Center (900 Market Street; 415-391-2000), the Information Desk at City Hall, or local bookstores and corner groceries.

Unlike San Francisco's classic cable cars, the **Bay Area Rapid Transit System**, or BART, operates silver streamlined cars that zip beneath the city's streets. This space-age transit system travels from Downtown to the Mission District, Glen Park, and Colma. It also runs under the San Francisco Bay to the cities of Oakland, Berkeley, and outlying parts of the East Bay. Trains run about every 8 or 20 minutes depending on the time of day. BART opens at 4 a.m. (6 a.m. on Saturday and 8 a.m. on Sunday) and closes at midnight every night. ~ 650-992-2278.

Many surrounding communities feature transportation services to and from San Francisco. To the north, **Golden Gate Transit** provides both bus and ferryboat service. ~ 415-923-2000. South of San Francisco, **San Mateo County Transit**, or **SamTrans**, offers bus service as far south as Palo Alto. ~ 800-660-4287. In addition, **Caltrain** provides daily commuter service from San Jose to San Francisco with stops along the way. ~ Fourth and Townsend Streets; 800-660-4287.

Across the Bay, **Alameda–Contra Costa Transit**, or AC Transit, carries passengers from Oakland, Berkeley, and other East Bay cities to the Transbay Terminal in downtown San Francisco. ~ 510-839-2882.

Cable cars, those clanging symbols of San Francisco, are *the* way to see this city of perpendicular hills. This venerable system covers a ten-mile section of downtown San Francisco.

CABLE CARS

The cable car was invented in 1873 by Andrew Hallidie and works via an underground cable that travels continuously at a speed of nine and a half miles per hour. Three of the system's original twelve lines still operate year-round. The Powell–Mason and Powell–Hyde cars travel from the Downtown district to Fisherman's Wharf; the California Street line runs east to west and passes through Chinatown and Nob Hill.

Built partially of wood and furnished with old-style running boards, these open-air vehicles are slow and stylish. Edging up the city's steep heights, then descending toboggan-run hills to the Bay, they provide many of San Francisco's finest views. Half the joy of riding, however, comes from watching the operators of these antique machines. Each has developed a personal style of gripping, braking, and bell-ringing. In addition to the breathtaking ride, they'll often treat you to a clanging street symphony.

TAXIS

Cabs are plentiful, but flagging them down is a trick—it's best to call by phone. The main companies are **DeSoto Cab Company** (415-673-1414), **Luxor Cabs** (415-282-4141), **Veteran's Taxi Cab Company** (415-552-1300), and **Yellow Cab** (415-626-2345).

WALKING TOURS

San Francisco is a city made for walkers. Appropriately, it offers a number of walking tours which explore various neighborhoods and historical spots.

Chinese Heritage Walks, conducted every Saturday and Sunday at 2 p.m. by the Chinese Culture Center, reveals the true Chinatown. Weekday tours except Monday at 10:30 a.m. They also offer a **Culinary Walk**, which visits markets and herb shops, then stops for lunch in a dim sum restaurant. Every day but Monday at 10:30 a.m. Reservations required. Fee. ~ Holiday Inn at the corner of Kearny and Washington streets; 415-986-1822.

Wok Wiz Walking Tours, led by cookbook author Shirley Fong-Torres and staff, features local markets, pastry shops, tea tasting or ceremonies, herbal pharmacies, temples or other attractions. A dim sum lunch is optional. This two and a half hour walk is a convenient way to get acquainted with Chinatown's culinary culture. Fee. ~ 654 Commercial Street; 415-981-8989.

City Guides, a volunteer organization sponsored by the Friends of the San Francisco Public Library, offers free tours of various locations throughout the city. They include separate tours of Pacific Heights Victorians, Historic Market Street, North Beach, Nob Hill, Coit Tower, and other points of interest. For information on times and starting places, call 415-557-4266.

Experience San Francisco's gay community by **Cruisin' the Castro** with host Trevor Hailey. Approximately four hours long, this easy, educational walking tour includes a visit to the Names Project Museum for a look at the AIDS Memorial Quilt, and a brunch stop at a neighborhood eatery. Reservations required. Fee. ~ 415-550-8110.

THREE

North Coast

When visitors to San Francisco seek a rural retreat, paradise is never far away. It sits just across the Golden Gate Bridge along a coastline stretching almost 400 miles to the Oregon border. Scenically, the North Coast compares in beauty with any spot on earth.

There are the folded hills and curving beaches of Point Reyes, Sonoma's craggy coast and old Russian fort, plus Mendocino with its vintage towns and spuming shoreline. To the far north lies Redwood Country, silent domain of the world's tallest living things.

Along the entire seaboard, civilization appears in the form of fishing villages and logging towns. Matter of fact, a lot of the prime real estate is saved forever from developers' heavy hands. California's Coastal Commission serves as a watchdog agency protecting the environment.

Much of the coast is also preserved in public playgrounds. Strung like pearls along the Pacific are a series of federal parks—Golden Gate National Recreation Area, Point Reyes National Seashore, and Redwood National Park.

The main highway through this idyllic domain is Route 1. A sinuous road, it snakes along the waterfront, providing the slowest, most scenic route. Paralleling this road and following an inland course is Route 101. This superhighway streaks from San Francisco to Oregon. It is fast, efficient, and at times boring. In the town of Leggett, Route 1 merges into Route 101, which continues north through Redwood Country.

Route 1 runs through San Francisco into Marin County, passing Sausalito before it branches from Route 101. While the eastern sector of Marin, along San Francisco Bay, is a suburban sprawl, the western region consists of rolling ranch land. Muir Woods is here, featuring 1000-year-old redwoods growing within commuting distance of the city. There is Mt. Tamalpais, a 2571-foot "sleeping maiden" whose recumbent figure has been the subject of numerous poems.

According to some historians, Sir Francis Drake, the Renaissance explorer, landed along the Marin shore in 1579, building a fort and claiming the wild region for dear old England. The Portuguese had first sighted the North Coast in 1543 when they espied Cape Mendocino. Back then Coastal Miwok Indians inhabited Marin, enjoying undisputed possession of the place until the Spanish settled the interior valleys during the early 1800s.

To the north, in Sonoma County, the Miwok shared their domain with the Pomo Indians. After 1812 they were also dividing it with the Russians. The Czar's forces arrived in California from their hunting grounds in Alaska and began taking large numbers of otters from local waters. The Russians built Fort Ross and soon proclaimed the region open only to their shipping. Of course, these imperial designs made the Spanish very nervous. The American response was to proclaim the Monroe Doctrine, warning foreign powers off the continent.

By the 1830s the Russians had decimated the otter population, reducing it from 150,000 to less than 100. They soon lost interest in the area and sold their fort and other holdings to John Sutter, whose name two decades hence would become synonymous with the Gold Rush.

Many of the early towns along the coast were born during the days of the '49ers. Established to serve as pack stations for the mines, the villages soon turned to lumbering and fishing. Today these are still important industries. About seven percent of California's land consists of commercial forest, much of it along the coastal redwood belt. Environmentalists continue to battle with the timber interests as they have since 1918 when the Save-the-Redwoods League was formed.

The natural heritage they protect includes trees which have been growing in California's forests since before the birth of Christ. Elk herds roam these groves, while trout and steelhead swim the nearby rivers. At one time the forest stretched in a 30-mile-wide swath for 450 miles along the coast. But in little more than a century the lumber industry has cut down over 90 percent of the original redwoods. Presently, 87,000 acres of ancient trees remain, over 90 percent of which are protected in parks. The fate of one unprotected grove, the Headwaters Forest in Humboldt County, which contains the world's largest privately owned stand of old-growth redwoods, has been an emotional issue, resulting in the arrest of scores of protesters during the past several years. The federal government is currently negotiating to purchase 7500 acres of old-growth and second-growth redwoods in the forest from the Pacific Lumber Company.

Another, much younger, cash crop is marijuana. During the '60s and early '70s, Mendocino and Humboldt counties became meccas for counterculturalists intent on getting "back to the land." They established communes, built original-design houses, and plunged into local politics. Some also became green-thumb outlaws, perfecting potent and exotic strains of sinsemilla for personal use and black-market sale. They made Northern California marijuana famous and helped boom the local economy. In November 1996, California voters passed Proposition 215, an initiative legalizing the use of marijuana for medical purposes. Although 38 states had also passed similar bills prior to this occasion, California was the first to actually enact the proposition as law.

The North Coast has become home to the country inn as well. All along the Pacific shoreline, bed and breakfasts serve travelers seeking informal and relaxing accommodations. Local artisans have also proliferated, while small shops have opened to sell their crafts.

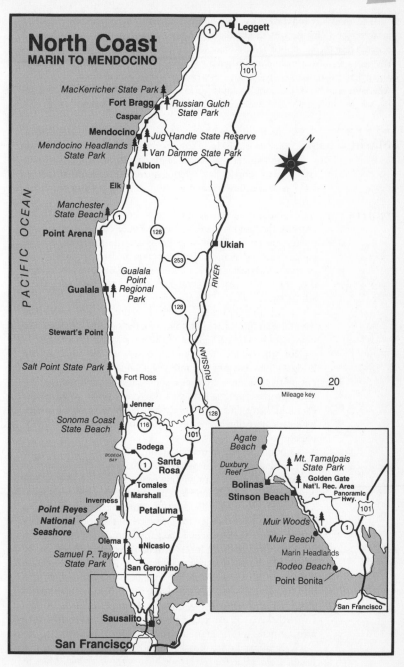

North Coast
MARIN TO MENDOCINO

Leggett

MacKerricher State Park
Fort Bragg
Caspar
Russian Gulch
State Park
Mendocino
Jug Handle State Reserve
Mendocino Headlands
State Park
Van Damme State Park
Albion

Elk

PACIFIC OCEAN

Manchester
State Beach
Point Arena

Ukiah

Gualala
Point
Regional
Park
Gualala

RUSSIAN RIVER

Stewart's Point

Salt Point State Park

Fort Ross

Jenner

Sonoma Coast
State Beach

Bodega

BODEGA
BAY

Santa
Rosa

Tomales
Marshall

Inverness

Point Reyes
National
Seashore

Petaluma

Olema
Nicasio
Samuel P. Taylor
State Park
San Geronimo

Sausalito

San Francisco

0   20
Mileage key

Agate
Beach

Duxbury
Reef

Mt. Tamalpais
State Park
Golden Gate
Nat'l. Rec. Area

Bolinas
Stinson Beach

Panoramic
Hwy.

Muir Woods

Muir Beach

Marin Headlands

Rodeo Beach
Point Bonita

San Francisco

The great lure for travelers is still the environment. This coastal shelf, tucked between the Coast Ranges and the Pacific, has mountains and rivers, forests and ocean. Once the habitat of Yuki, Athabascan, Wiyot, Yurok, and Tolowa Indians, it remains an adventureland for imaginative travelers. Winters are damp, mornings and evenings sometimes foggy, but the weather overall is temperate. It's a place where you can fish for Chinook salmon, go crabbing, and scan the sea for migrating whales. Or simply ease back and enjoy scenery that never stops.

Marin Coast

As frequently photographed as the Golden Gate Bridge, the coast of Marin County consists of rolling ranch lands and spectacular ocean bluffs. It extends from San Francisco Bay to Tomales Bay, offering groves of redwoods, meadows filled with wildflowers, and miles of winding country roads.

SIGHTS   An exploration of this vaunted region begins immediately upon crossing the Golden Gate Bridge on Route 101. There's a **vista point** at the far north end of the bridge affording marvelous views back toward San Francisco and out upon the Bay. (If some of your party want to start off with an exhilarating walk across the bridge, drop them at the vista point on the city side and pick them up here a little later.)

Once across the bridge, take the first exit, Alexander Avenue; then take an immediate left, following the sign back toward San Francisco. Next, bear right at the sign for Marin Headlands.

For what is literally a **bird's-eye view** of the Golden Gate Bridge, go three-tenths of a mile uphill and stop at the first turnout on the left. From here it's a short stroll out and up, past deserted battery fortifications, to a 360° view point sweeping the Pacific and Bay alike. You'll practically be standing on the bridge, with cars careening below and the tops of the twin towers vaulting above you.

Continue along Conzelman Road and you will pass a series of increasingly spectacular views of San Francisco. Ahead the road will fall away to reveal a tumbling peninsula, furrowed with hills and marked at its distant tip by a lighthouse. That is **Point Bonita**, a salient far outside the Golden Gate. After heading to the point, you can peer back through the interstices of the bridge to the city or turn away from civilization and gaze out on a wind-tousled sea.

Nature writes in big letters around these parts. You're in the **Marin Headlands** section of **Golden Gate National Recreation Area**, an otherworldly realm of spuming surf, knife-edge cliffs, and chaparral-coated hillsides. From Point Bonita, follow Field Road, taking a left at the sign for the **Marin Headlands Visitors Center**, where you can pick up maps and information about the area, or make a camping reservation. ~ 415-331-1540.

Walk along **Rodeo Beach**, a sandy corridor separating the Pacific from a tule-fringed lagoon alive with waterfowl. Miles of hiking trails lace up into the hills (see the "Hiking" section at the end of this chapter). At the far end of the beach you can trek along the cliffs and watch the sea batter the continent.

At the nearby **California Marine Mammal Center** are seals, sea lions, and other marine mammals who have been found injured or orphaned in the ocean and brought here to recuperate. Center workers conduct rescue operations along 1000 miles of coastline, returning the animals to the wild after they have gained sufficient strength. ~ From Alexander Avenue take Conzelman Road, follow the signs; 415-289-7325.

SAUSALITO Sausalito is a shopper's town: galleries, boutiques, and antique stores line Bridgeway, and in several cases have begun creeping uphill along side streets. **Plaza Vina del Mar** (Bridgeway and El Portal), with its elephant statues and dramatic fountain, is a grassy oasis in the midst of the commerce. Several strides seaward of this tree-thatched spot lies **Gabrielson Park**, where you can settle on a bench or plot of grass at water's edge.

Continue along the piers past chic yachts, delicate sloops, and rows of millionaires' motorboats. To get an idea of the inland pond where the rich sail these toys, check out the U.S. Army Corps of Engineers **San Francisco Bay Model**. Built to scale and housed in a two-acre warehouse, this hydraulic model of San Francisco Bay is used to simulate currents and tidal flows. An audiotape guided tour leads you around the mini-Bay. When the model actually runs, you can watch the tide surge through the Golden Gate, swirl around Alcatraz, and rise steadily along the Berkeley shore. The tidal cycle of an entire day takes 14 minutes as you witness the natural process from a simulated height of 12,000 feet. Also part of the permanent exhibit is a display portraying Sausalito during World War II, when it was converted into a mammoth shipyard that produced almost 100 vessels in three years. Closed Sunday and Monday; call ahead to make sure the model will be operating. ~ 2100 Bridgeway, Sausalito; 415-332-3870.

✔ **CHECK THESE OUT—UNIQUE SIGHTS**

- Go tidepooling at **Duxbury Reef**, and spot starfish, periwinkles, limpets, and other clinging critters in a remarkable marine preserve. *page 108*
- Stop in at Point Reyes National Seashore's **Miwok Indian Village**, featuring replicas of round-domed shelters. *page 109*
- Hop on board the **Skunk train**, a logging train dating back to 1885 that takes you through 40 miles of redwood forests. *page 127*
- Step back to the Victorian era when you visit **Ferndale**, a perfectly refurbished town featuring Gothic Revival, Queen Anne, and other "painted ladies." *page 143*

Imagine a cluster of seven buildings and more than 100 hands-on activities all devoted to children ages one through ten. Throw in a multimedia center and a miniature model of the ports of San Francisco and what you have is a place called the **Bay Area Discovery Museum**. Closed Monday. Admission. ~ 557 East Fort Baker, Sausalito; 415-487-4398.

I heartily recommend the quarter-mile self-guided tour through the **Richardson Bay Audubon Center and Sanctuary**. It will provide an inkling of what Marin was like before the invention of cars and condominiums. During the winter months harbor seals can be seen in sanctuary waters. You can wander through dells and woodlands, past salt marshes and tidepools. Also contained on the property is **Lyford House**, a magnificent Victorian which commands a strategic spot on the shore of Richardson Bay. On Sunday afternoon from October through April, tours are given of the interior. The sanctuary is closed on Monday and Tuesday. Admission. ~ 376 Greenwood Beach Road, Tiburon; 415-388-2524.

> Contrary to rumor, on a clear day you cannot see forever from Mt. Tam, but you can see north toward Redwood Country and east to the Sierras.

SAUSALITO TO POINT REYES   From Sausalito follow Route 101 north a few miles, then pick up Route 1. You'll be on the northern leg of one of the most beautiful roads in America. With its wooded sanctuaries and ocean vistas, Route 1 is for many people synonymous with California.

When Route 1 forks after several miles, turn right on Panoramic Highway toward Muir Woods and Mt. Tamalpais; the left fork leads to Stinson Beach, but that comes later. It's uphill and then down to **Muir Woods National Monument**, a 560-acre park inhabited by *Sequoia sempervirens*, the coast redwood. Though these forest giants have been known to live over two millennia, most enjoy a mere four-to-eight-century existence. In Muir Woods they reach 240 feet, while further up the coast they top 350 feet (with roots that go no deeper than six feet!). ~ 415-388-2596.

Facts can't convey the feelings inspired by these trees. You have to move among them, walk through Muir's Cathedral Grove where redwoods form a lofty arcade above the narrow trail. It's a forest primeval, casting the deepest, most restful shade imaginable. Muir Woods has the double-edged quality of being the redwood forest nearest to San Francisco. It can be horribly crowded. Since silence and solitude are vital to experiencing a redwood forest, plan to visit early or late in the day, and allow time to hike the more remote of the park's six miles of trails.

Back up on Panoramic Highway, the road continues through Mt. Tamalpais State Park en route to **Mt. Tamalpais'** 2571-foot peak. Mt. Tam, as it is affectionately known, represents one of

the Bay Area's most prominent landmarks. Rising dramatically between the Pacific and the Bay, the site was sacred to Indians. Even
today some people see in the sloping silhouette of the mountain
the sleeping figure of an Indian maiden. So tread lightly up the
short trail that leads to the summit. You'll be rewarded with a
full-circle view that sweeps across the Bay, along San Francisco's
miniature skyline, and out across the Pacific.

Continue on Panoramic Highway as it corkscrews down to
Stinson Beach. Better yet, take the longer but more spectacular
route to Stinson: backtrack along Panoramic to where the fork
originally separated from Route 1 (Shoreline Highway). Turn right
and head north on Route 1.

Shortly, a turnoff will lead down to **Green Gulch Farm**, a 115-
acre Zen retreat tucked serenely in a coastal valley. Residents here
follow a rigorous program of work and meditation. There is a
temple on the grounds and guests are welcome to tour the organic
farm. Sunday is the best day to visit since a special meditation program and speaker is offered then. ~ 1601 Shoreline Highway, near
Muir Beach; 415-383-3134.

It's not far to **Muir Beach** where you'll find a crescent-shaped
cove with sandy beach. Though swimming is not advised, this is
a good spot for picnicking. About a mile further up the road, follow the "vista point" sign to **Muir Beach Overlook**. Here you
can walk out along a narrow ridge for a view extending from
Bolinas to the coastline south of San Francisco. It's an outstanding place for whale watching in winter. Matter of fact, this lookout is so well placed it became a site for World War II gun batteries, whose rusty skeletons remain.

You have entered a realm that might well be called the Land
of a Thousand Views. Until the road descends to the flat expanse
of Stinson Beach, it follows a tortuous route poised on the edge
of oblivion. Below, precipitous cliffs dive to the sea, while above
the road, rock walls edge upward toward Mt. Tamalpais. Around
every curve another scene opens to view. Before you, Bolinas is
a sweep of land, an arm extended seaward. Behind, the San Francisco skyline falls away into the past. If God built highways, they'd
look like this.

Stinson Beach, that broad sandy hook at the bottom of the
mountain, is one of Northern California's finest strands. Anglers
haunt the rocks along one end in pursuit of blenny and ling cod,
while birdwatchers are on the lookout for sandpipers, shearwaters, and swallows. Everyone else comes for sand, surf, and sun.

Birdwatchers also flock to **Audubon Canyon Ranch**, located
astride Route 1 on Bolinas Lagoon. Open on weekends and holidays from mid-March to July (or by appointment), the ranch includes four canyons, one of which is famed as a rookery for egrets

and herons. From the hiking trails here you can see up to 90 bird species as well as gray fox, deer, badgers, and bobcats. ~ Route 1; 415-868-9244.

Bolinas Lagoon is also a bird sanctuary. Great egrets, ducks, and great blue herons make this one of their migratory stops. A colony of harbor seals lives here permanently and is joined in summer by migrating seals from San Francisco.

To reach the next point of interest you'll have to pay close attention. That's because you're approaching **Bolinas**. To get there from Route 1, watch for the crossroad at the foot of the lagoon; go left, then quickly left again and follow the road along the other side of the lagoon; take another left at the end of the road.

There should be signs to direct you. But there probably won't be. Not because the state neglected them or highway workers forgot to put them up. It seems that local residents subscribe to the self-serving philosophy that since Bolinas is beautiful and they got there first, they should keep everyone else out. They tear down road signs and discourage visitors. The rest of Northern California is fair game, they seem to say, as long as Bolinas is left as some sort of human preserve.

The place they are attempting to hide is a delightful little town which rises from an S-shaped beach to form a lofty mesa. There are country roads along the bluff that overhangs the beach.

Whether you stroll the beach or hike the highlands, you'll discover in the houses here a wild architectural array. There are domes, glass boxes, curved-roof creations, huts, ranch houses, and stately brown-shingle designs.

Bolinas, abutting on the Point Reyes National Seashore, is also a gateway to the natural world. Follow Mesa Road for several miles outside town and you'll encounter the **Point Reyes Bird Observatory**, where scientists at a research station study a bird population of over 200 species.

HIDDEN ►

On the way back to town take a right on Overlook Drive, then a right on Elm Road; follow it to the parking lot at road's end. Hiking trails lead down a sharp 160-foot cliff to **Duxbury Reef**, a mile-long shale reef. Tidepool-watching is great sport here at low tide: starfish, periwinkles, abalone, limpets, and a host of other clinging creatures inhabit the marine preserve. Back in 1971 a huge oil spill endangered this spectacular area, but volunteers from all around the state worked day and night to save the reef and its tenacious inhabitants. Just north of this rocky preserve is **Agate Beach**, an ideal spot to find agates, driftwood, and glass balls (however, no collecting is permitted).

Back on Route 1, continue north through the Olema Valley, a peaceful region of horse ranches fringed by forest. Peaceful, that is, until you realize that the **San Andreas Fault**, the global suture that shook San Francisco back in 1906, cuts through the valley.

As a matter of fact, the highway you are traveling parallels the fault line. During the great quake, houses collapsed, trees were uprooted, and fences decided to mark new boundaries.

As you turn off Route 1 onto Sir Francis Drake Boulevard headed for the Point Reyes Peninsula, you'll be passing from the North American Plate, one of the six tectonic plates on which the entire earth's surface rides, to the Pacific Plate, which extends across the ocean. It is the pressure formed by the collision of these two great land masses that causes earthquakes. No sign will notify you as you cross this troubled geologic border, no guide will direct you along the rift zone. If you're like the people who live hereabouts, within 15 minutes of crossing over you'll have forgotten the fault exists. Especially when you see what is served on the Pacific Plate.

POINT REYES NATIONAL SEASHORE   Point Reyes National Seashore is without doubt one of the finest seaside parks on any of the world's six plates. It is a realm of sand dunes and endless beaches, Scottish moors and grassy hillsides, salt marshes and pine forests. Bobcats, mountain lions, fox, and elk inhabit its wrinkled terrain, while harbor seals and gray whales cruise its ragged shoreline. More than 45 percent of North American bird species have been spotted here. The Seashore also supports dairies and cattle ranches. In October of 1995, fire ripped through Point Reyes, burning 12,000 acres. All areas have since been cleared and await your exploration. All trails listed here and in the "Hiking" section are open and additional trails lead through the charred area, giving you a close-up look at the awesome healing power of nature.

The first stage in exploring this multifeatured preserve involves a stop at the **Bear Valley Visitors Center**. Here you can obtain maps, information, and camping permits. ~ Bear Valley Road; 415-663-1092. A short hike from the center will lead visitors to a **Miwok Indian Village**, where the round-domed shelters and other structures of the area's early inhabitants have been re-created.

Most points of interest lie along Sir Francis Drake Boulevard, which rolls for miles through the park. It will carry you past the tiny town of **Inverness**, with its country inns and ridgetop houses, then out along **Tomales Bay**. Like the Golden Gate, this finger-shaped inlet is a drowned river valley.

Deeper in the park, a side road twists up to Mount Vision Overlook, where vista points sweep the peninsula. At **Johnson's Oyster Company**, along another side road, workers harvest the rich beds of an estuary. The farm is a conglomeration of slapdash buildings, house trailers, and rusty machines. The shoreline is heaped over with oyster shells and the air is filled with pungent odors. Raw oysters are for sale. Even if you don't care for them, you might want to visit anyway. After all, when was the last time

you saw an oyster farm? Closed Monday. ~ 17171 Sir Francis
Drake Boulevard, Inverness; 415-669-1149.

The main road continues over folded hills that fall away to
reveal sharp bluffs. Farm animals graze through fields smothered
in wildflowers. There are ocean vistas stretching along miles of
headland.

On **Drake's Beach** you can picnic and beachcomb. Or gaze at
the surrounding cliffs and wonder whether they truly resemble the
White Cliffs of Dover. That question has raised a debate that has
continued for decades. It seems that in 1579 the English explorer
Sir Francis Drake anchored somewhere along the Northern California coast. But where? Everyone seems to have a theory about
where the Englishman set ashore, but the
U.S. Coast and Geodetic Survey and other
authoritative sources claim it was right here
at Drake's Bay. Find out more at the **Ken
Patrick Visitor Center**, which also features an
aquarium and interactive computer displays.
Saturday and Sunday only.

A brass plate, purportedly left
by Drake, was discovered near
San Francisco Bay in 1936;
later it was believed that the
plate had been first located
near Drake's Bay and
then moved; finally the
plate was deemed a
counterfeit.

Point Reyes Beach (also known as "North
Beach" and "South Beach"), a windy ten-mile-
long strip, is an ideal place for beachcombers and
whale-watchers. From there, it's not far to the end
of Point Reyes' hammerhead peninsula. At one tip is
Chimney Rock, a sea stack formed when the ocean eroded away
the intervening land mass, leaving this islet just offshore. On the
way to Chimney Rock you'll pass an **overlook** that's ideal for
watching sea lions; then from Chimney Rock, if the day is clear,
you'll see all the way to San Francisco.

At the other tip is **Point Reyes Lighthouse**, an 1870-era beacon located at the foggiest point on the entire Pacific coast. The
treacherous waters offshore have witnessed numerous shipwrecks,
the first occurring way back in 1595. The original lighthouse, constructed to prevent these calamities, incorporated over a thousand
pieces of crystal in its intricate lens. A modern beacon eventually
replaced this multifaceted instrument, but the old lighthouse and
an accompanying information center are still open to the public
Thursday through Monday. ~ 415-669-1534.

HIDDEN ▶   From Olema you can continue north on Route 1 or follow a
looping 25-mile detour through the region's **pastoral interior**. On
the latter, Sir Francis Drake Boulevard leads east past bald-domed
hills and isolated farms. Livestock graze at the roadside while overhead hawks work the range. Grassland gives way to dense forest
as you enter the realms of **Samuel P. Taylor State Park**. Then the
road opens again to reveal a succession of tiny, woodframe towns.

At San Geronimo, turn left on Nicasio Valley Road. This carries you further into the pastoral region of west Marin, which

varies so dramatically from the county's eastern suburban enclaves. Indeed, the inland valleys are reminiscent more of the Old
West than the busy Bay Area. At the Nicasio Reservoir, turn left
onto Point Reyes–Petaluma Road and follow it to Sir Francis
Drake Boulevard, closing the circle of this rural tour.

From Olema, Route 1 continues north along Tomales Bay,
the lovely fjord-shaped inlet. Salt marshes stretch along one side
of the road; on the other are rumpled hills tufted with grass. The
waterfront village of Marshall consists of fishing boats moored
offshore and woodframe houses anchored firmly onshore. Then
the road turns inland to Tomales, another falsefront town with
clapboard church and country homes. It continues past paint-
peeled barns and open pastureland before turning seaward at
Bodega Bay.

LODGING

Casa Madrona Hotel features a New England–style complex of
rooms attached to a 19th-century landmark house. You'll find
this two-part structure on a Sausalito hillside overlooking San
Francisco Bay. The guest rooms have a personal feel and individual names. The "Artist's Loft" is decorated with antique
artists' supplies and enjoys a bay view from its large deck, while
the "La Posada" is styled after an old Portuguese inn. There are
also five private cottages available at this 35-room bed and breakfast. Breakfast, afternoon wine and cheese included. ~ 801 Bridgeway, Sausalito; 415-332-0502, 800-567-9524, fax 415-332-
2537; www.casam.com. DELUXE TO ULTRA-DELUXE.

Calling the accommodations at **East Brother Light Station**
unusual is a slight understatement. Where else can you find a bed
and breakfast inn located within a lighthouse on an offshore island? The old beacon was built back in 1873 and operated for
almost a century. Today the two-story house and light station feature four bedrooms furnished with period pieces. Guests travel
out to this one-acre hideaway by motorboat and enjoy a multicourse dinner as well as breakfast the next morning. Of course,
there's a premium on such seclusion: rates run in the ultra-deluxe
range and reservations must be made far in advance. Shared and
private bathrooms are available. Open Thursday through Sunday,
this San Pablo Bay retreat is a unique opportunity to trade the
trappings of civilization for your own private island. ~ 117 Park
Place, Point Richmond; 510-233-2385, fax 510-235-5234; www.
ebls.org. ULTRA-DELUXE.

Marin Headlands Hostel, also known as Golden Gate Hostel,
is ideally located in the spectacular Marin Headlands section of
the Golden Gate National Recreation Area. Housed in a historic
woodframe building, this hostel's 103 dormitory-style accommodations go for low prices. There are kitchen facilities available,
laundry, a game room, a living room and a few private rooms.

Like most hostels it is closed during the day; you're permitted access only at night and in the morning. Reservations are advised during the summer. ~ Fort Barry, Building 941; 415-331-2777. BUDGET.

HIDDEN ►   **Green Gulch Farm**, a Zen retreat and organic farm, offers a guest residence program. Located on a 115-acre spread in a lovely valley, it's a restful and enchanting stop. Enroll in the Buddhist Practice Retreat Program, stay three days or longer, and you will pay moderate rates. The schedule involves meditation, chanting and bowing, as well as manual labor and includes all meals. Or you can simply rent a room by the night (at deluxe prices including meals). With nearby hiking trails and beaches, it's a unique place. ~ 1601 Shoreline Boulevard near Muir Beach; 415-383-3134; www.zendo.com/~sfzc/index.html. MODERATE TO DELUXE.

Most folks grumble when the fog sits heavy along the coast. At **The Pelican Inn**, guests consider fog part of the ambience. Damp air and chill winds add a final element to the Old English atmosphere at this seven-chamber bed and breakfast. Set in a Tudor-style building near Muir Beach, The Pelican Inn re-creates 16th-century England. There's a pub downstairs with a dart board on one wall and a fox hunting scene facing on another. The dining room serves country fare like meat pies, prime rib, and bangers. Upstairs the bedrooms complete the theme. The room I saw contained time-honored furnishings, a wooden chest that looked to have barely survived its Atlantic crossing, and a few other antiques. The bed was canopied and the walls adorned with period prints. Highly recommended; reserve well in advance. ~ Route 1, Muir Beach; 415-383-6000, fax 415-383-3424; www.pelicaninn. com. ULTRA-DELUXE.

The Sandpiper is ideally located just a short stroll away from Stinson Beach, close enough to hear the surf wash the sand. Once

----

✔ CHECK THESE OUT—UNIQUE LODGING

- *Budget:* Come to **Marin Headlands Hostel** for cheap sleep, stay for the fabulous scenery of the Golden Gate National Recreation Area. *page 111*
- *Moderate:* Make yourself at home at **Mar Vista Cottages at Anchor Bay,** with 12 private woodframe cottages boasting ocean views. *page 129*
- *Deluxe to ultra-deluxe:* Please your senses with an amazing blufftop view and a good night's sleep at **Elk Cove Inn.** *page 131*
- *Ultra-deluxe:* Bed down in the Tudor-style **Pelican Inn** after enveloping yourself with English ambience in its downstairs pub. *page 112*

Budget: under $60   Moderate: $60–$120   Deluxe: $120–$175   Ultra-deluxe: over $175

rundown, the motel's rooms and cottages have been thoroughly upgraded and redecorated with country-style furnishings, cable TV, VCRs, and fireplaces. A backyard area with barbecues, tables, and umbrellas is available to guests. ~ 1 Marine Way, Stinson Beach; 415-868-1632. MODERATE TO DELUXE.

High on a hill above Stinson Beach is **Casa del Mar**, a lovely peach-colored stucco Mediterranean-style bed-and-breakfast inn surrounded by terraced gardens brimming with succulents, flowers, herbs, and vegetables. Four upstairs guest rooms have French doors opening onto private verandas and are adorned with such touches as paintings by West Marin artists and soft down comforters. ~ 37 Belvedere Avenue, Stinson Beach; 415-868-2124, 800-552-2124, fax 415-868-2305. DELUXE TO ULTRA-DELUXE.

Smiley's Schooner Saloon and Hotel is one of the cheapest deals around. This modest facility, located in the rustic town of Bolinas, has easy access to the beach. Accommodations are clean and nicely appointed. The rooms are done in a rose color with antiques and have no radio, TV, phones, or other newfangled inventions. Light sleepers be forewarned, however: the bar downstairs is a favorite haunt of late-night revelers. ~ 41 Wharf Road, Bolinas; 415-868-1311, fax 415-868-0502. MODERATE.

There's also **Grand Hotel**, a tiny business where the two units share a bath and a kitchen. The proprietor also serves as a referral service for other places in town, so check with him about local accommodations. ~ 15 Brighton Avenue, Bolinas; 415-868-1757. BUDGET.

As country living goes, it's darn near impossible to find a place as pretty and restful as Point Reyes. People with wander in their hearts and wonder in their minds have been drawn here for years. Not surprisingly, country inns sprang up to cater to star-struck explorers and imaginative travelers. Seven of these small bed and breakfasts, dotted in towns around Point Reyes National Seashore, have joined together to form an information service, **The Inns of Point Reyes**. Contact them for a descriptive brochure. ~ P.O. Box 176, Point Reyes, CA 94956; 415-663-1420. Another good source is **Point Reyes Lodging**, which offers 24-hour information on 22 inns and cottages in coastal Marin. ~ 415-663-1872, 800-539-1872; www.ptreyes.com.

Coastal Lodging of West Marin is a telephone service providing information on local accommodations. Specializing in cottages, guest homes, and inns, they can help visitors find lodging all around the Point Reyes area. ~ 415-663-1351.

Within Point Reyes National Seashore, consider the **Point Reyes Hostel**, providing low-rent lodging. In addition to 44 dorm-style accommodations, the hostel has a patio, a ranch-style kitchen, a living room with a wood-burning stove, and private room. Perfect for explorers, it is situated two miles from the ocean near several hiking trails. The hostel is closed from 9:30 a.m. to 4:30 p.m. Reservations recommended. ~ On Limantour Road, Point Reyes National Seashore; Box 247, Point Reyes Station, CA 94956; 415-663-8811; www.hiayh.org/ushotel/pnwreg/pointr. BUDGET.

Nearby in Inverness there's **Motel Inverness**, commanding a location along Tomales Bay that would be the envy of many well-heeled hostelries. Unfortunately, the architect who designed it faced the rooms toward the road, not the water. You can, however, enjoy views of the bay in the motel's common room, which features a billiards table, stereo and pinball machine. The guest rooms come equipped with color televisions and cable. The entire hotel is a nonsmoking establishment. ~ 12718 Sir Francis Drake Boulevard, Inverness; 415-669-1081. MODERATE.

In a secluded setting on four acres bordering Tomales Bay is **Sandy Cove Inn**, which offers a private world shared with horses, sheep, deer, osprey, egrets, hawks and quail. The Cape Cod–style house is bordered by cottages with three guest rooms, each with a fireplace, private deck and entrance, Turkish kilim rugs, and antique-finished pine furniture. A country breakfast prepared with home-grown ingredients is served in the privacy of your own room. No smoking is permitted anywhere. ~ 12990 Sir Francis Drake Boulevard, Inverness; 415-669-2683, 800-759-2683, fax 415-669-7511; www.sandycove.com. ULTRA-DELUXE.

Another favorite bed and breakfast lies along the flagstone path at **Ten Inverness Way**. The place is filled with pleasant surprises, like fruit trees and flowers in the yard, a hot tub, a library and a warm living room with stone fireplace. The five bedrooms are small but cozy, carpeted wall-to-wall, and imaginatively decorated with hand-fashioned quilts; all have private baths. It's a short stroll from the house to the shops and restaurants of Inverness. ~ 10 Inverness Way, Inverness; 415-669-1648, fax 415-669-7403, www.teninvernessway.com. DELUXE TO ULTRA-DELUXE.

DINING

From the Marin Headlands region, the nearest restaurants are in the bayside town of Sausalito. Then, progressing north, you'll find dining spots scattered throughout the towns and villages along the coast.

You'll know the bill of fare by the name—**Hamburgers**; and you can tell the quality of the food by the line outside. Local folks and out-of-towners alike jam this postage stamp–sized eatery. They come not only for charcoal-broiled burgers, but bratwurst, Italian sausage, foot-long hot dogs, barbequed chicken, and steak sandwiches as well. It's tough securing a table, but you can always pull up a bench in the park across the street. ~ 737 Bridgeway, Sausalito; 415-332-9471. BUDGET.

Sausalito sports many seafood restaurants, most of which are overpriced and few of which are good. So it's best to steer a course for **Seven Seas**. It lacks the view of the splashy establishments, but does feature an open-air patio in back. The menu includes scallops, bouillabaisse, and salmon. Landlubbers can choose from several meat platters; at lunch sandwiches are served; open for breakfast on Sunday. ~ 682 Bridgeway, Sausalito; 415-332-1304. MODERATE.

If you long for a sea vista and an eyeful of San Francisco skyline, try **Horizons**. Housed in the turn-of-the-century San Francisco Yacht Club, this spiffy seafood restaurant has a wall of windows for those inside looking out, and a porch for those who want to be outside looking further. Then, of course, there's the food: shellfish and other aquatic fare, with chicken, pasta, and steak dishes added for good measure. Some beautiful carpentry went into the design of this place. There's also a popular bar here, making it a choice spot to drink as well as eat. Open for brunch, lunch, and dinner every day. ~ 558 Bridgeway, Sausalito; 415-331-3232. MODERATE TO DELUXE.

If the tide doesn't carry you, current trends may very well deliver you to the door at **Guaymas** in Tiburon. This upscale Mexican restaurant prepares fresh tortillas and tamales daily. Pork, steak, and shrimp dishes are prepared on a mesquite grill; or try the duck with pumpkin seed sauce or the red snapper sautéed with jalapeños and onions. Located next door to the ferry dock, Guaymas rounds out the bill of fare with a bay view. ~ 5 Main Street, Tiburon; 415-435-6300. MODERATE.

Stinson Beach sports several restaurants; my favorite is the **Sand Dollar Restaurant**, with facilities for dining indoors or on the patio. At lunch this informal eatery serves hamburgers and sandwiches. At dinner there are fried prawns, scallops, fresh fish dishes and pastas; they also serve meat dishes like chicken parmesan and steaks. Soup or salad is included and so is homemade garlic bread. With a fireplace and random artwork on the wall, it is a cozy local gathering point. ~ 3458 Route 1, Stinson Beach; 415-868-0434. MODERATE.

In Bolinas, consider **The Shop**, where you can pull up a table or counter space and order from a soup, salad, and sandwich menu. With its dark pine walls and rustic decor, this café has a singular air. A good spot for a light meal. Closed Monday and Tuesday. ~ 46 Wharf Road, Bolinas; 415-868-9984. BUDGET TO MODERATE.

The Station House Café comes highly recommended by several local residents. There is a down-home feel to this wood-paneled restaurant. Maybe it's the artwork along the walls or the garden patio. Regardless, it's really the food that draws folks from the sur-

◄ HIDDEN

rounding countryside. The dinner menu includes fresh oysters, plus chicken, steak, and fish dishes. There are also daily chef's specials, such as salmon topped with a dill-smoked salmon sauce. Dinners are served with soup or salad, and a basket of cornbread and piping hot popovers. The Station House also features a complete breakfast menu; at lunch time there are light crêpe, pasta, and seafood dishes, plus sandwiches and salads. ~ 11180 Main Street, Point Reyes Station; 415-663-1515. MODERATE.

The Grey Whale, a woodframe café in the center of tiny Inverness, serves delicious pizza and bakery goods as well as soups and salads. The place has a touch of city style in a country setting; there are overhead fans and an espresso machine. ~ 12781 Sir Francis Drake Boulevard, Inverness; 415-669-1244. BUDGET TO MODERATE.

Manka's Inverness Lodge is set in a 1917 hunting lodge with open fireplace and American arts and crafts. This white-tablecloth dining room prepares American regional cuisine. Diners can feast on poached salmon, grilled venison, boar, or duck. Dinner only. Closed Tuesday and Wednesday. ~ 30 Callendar Way, Inverness; 415-669-1034. DELUXE TO ULTRA-DELUXE.

SHOPPING   The best shopping spot in Marin is the town of Sausalito. Here you can stroll the waterfront along Bridgeway and its side streets, visiting gourmet shops, boutiques, and antique stores. One of the Bay Area's wealthiest towns, Sausalito sports few bargains, but it does host an assortment of elegant shops.

A standout among the art galleries lining Sausalito's streets is **Louis Aronow Gallery.** Two floors exhibit an extensive collection of original paintings and limited-edition prints, and glass and bronze sculptures. ~ 686 Bridgeway, Sausalito; 415-331-4000.

The downtown facility most crowded with shops and shoppers is **Village Fair,** a multilevel mall boasting 37 stores. Here are leather shops, jewelers, clothing stores, confectioners, notion shops, crafts galleries, ceramic shops, and so on. ~ 777 Bridgeway, Sausalito; 415-332-1902.

Past Sausalito, the shopping scene along the North Coast is concentrated in a few towns. There are small shops scattered

HANDCRAFTED HAVEN

During the '60s and '70s many talented people, caught up in the "back to the land" movement, migrated to the state's northern counties. Here they developed their skills and further refined their art. As a result, crafts like pottery, woodworking, weaving, stained-glass manufacturing, jewelry, and fashion designing have flourished.

about in rural areas, but the best selection of arts and crafts is located around Point Reyes.

Stinson Beach Books may be located in a small town, but it handles a large variety of books. Compressed within the confines of the place is an array of travel books, field guides, bestsellers, novels, how-to handbooks, etc. It's a great place to stop before that long, languorous day at the beach. ~ 3455 Shoreline Highway, Stinson Beach; 415-868-0700.

For an idea of the local art scene, you should certainly stop by **Bolinas Gallery**. Judy Molyneux has stocked it with an impressive selection of her work. Closed weekdays. ~ 52 Wharf Road, Bolinas; 415-868-0782.

Gallery Route One spotlights sculptures, photographs, and paintings by contemporary regional artists. Closed Tuesday through Thursday. ~ 11101 Route 1, Point Reyes Station; 415-663-1347.

Shaker Shops West is a marvelous store specializing in reproductions of Shaker crafts, particularly furniture. In addition to rag rugs, candlesticks, and woven baskets, there are beautifully handcrafted boxes. The Early American household items range from cross-stitch needlepoint to wall clocks. Touring the store is like visiting a mini-museum dedicated to this rare American community. Closed Monday. ~ 5 Inverness Way, Inverness; 415-669-7256.

There are small bars and local gathering places along the coast, but few sophisticated nightspots. To give you a general idea of the scene, such as it is, I've listed several suggestions. It's also a good idea to ask around town about special events and locally favored hangouts. **NIGHTLIFE**

The window simply reads "Bar"; the address is 757 Bridgeway in Sausalito; and the place is famous. Famous for its name, the **no name**, and because it's a favored hangout among young swingers and old salts alike. With an antique bar, piano, and open-air patio, it's a congenial spot to bend an elbow. You'll hear live music Tuesday through Sunday nights. Featuring mostly jazz, the bands also play blues, rock, and some oldies. ~ 415-332-1392.

When the sun goes down in Bolinas, you are left with several options. Sleep, read, curl up with a loved one, fade into unrelieved boredom, or head for **Smiley's Schooner Saloon**. Since local folks often follow the latter course, you're liable to find them parka-to-parka along the bar. They come to shoot a few rounds of pool, listen to weekend live music, and admire the lavish wood-panel bar. Smiley's, after all, is the only show in town. Occasional cover. ~ 41 Wharf Road, Bolinas; 415-868-1311.

Local folks in Point Reyes Station ease up to a similar wooden bar at **Old Western Saloon** practically every night of the week. But on Friday and Saturday, when the place features dancing 'til the wee hours, the biggest crowds of all arrive. Occasional cover. ~ 11201 Route 1, Point Reyes Station; 415-663-1661.

BEACHES & PARKS

KIRBY COVE 🚶 🚴 🐎 ⛺ 🚣 This pocket beach, located at the end of a one-mile trail, nestles in the shadow of the Golden Gate Bridge. The views from beachside are unreal: gaze up at the bridge's steel lacework or out across the gaping mouth of the Gate. When the fog's away, it's a sunbather's paradise; regardless of the weather, this cove is favored by those who like to fish. Facilities include a picnic area and toilets. ~ The beach is located in the Marin Headlands section of the Golden Gate National Recreation Area. Take the first exit, Alexander Avenue, after crossing the Golden Gate Bridge. Then take an immediate left, following the sign back toward San Francisco. Next, bear right at the sign for Marin Headlands. Follow Conzelman Road three-tenths of a mile to a turnout where a sign will mark the trailhead; 415-331-1540.

▲ There are four sites for tents only; $20 per night. Reservations are required; call special park uses at 415-561-4304.

HIDDEN ►

UPPER FISHERMAN'S BEACH 🚴 🐎 ⛺ 🚣 This is a long, narrow corridor of sand tucked under the Marin Headlands. With steep hills behind and a grand view of the Golden Gate in front, it's a perfect place for naturists and nature lovers alike. It is a popular beach for nudists, although not officially recognized as such. It cannot be found on maps or atlases, but local folks and savvy travelers know it well (some call it "Black Sands"). There are no facilities here. ~ Located in the Marin Headlands section of the Golden Gate National Recreation Area. Follow the directions to the Kirby Cove trailhead (see listing above). Continue on Conzelman Road for two and a third miles. Shortly after passing the steep downhill section of this road, you'll see a parking lot on the left with a trailhead. Follow the trail to the beach.

RODEO BEACH 🚶 🚴 🐎 🏄 🚣 A broad sandy beach, this place is magnificent not only for the surrounding hillsides and nearby cliffs, but also for the quiescent lagoon at its back. It boasts a miniature island offshore, named appropriately for the creatures that turned its surface white—Bird Rock. Given its proximity to San Francisco, Rodeo Beach is a favorite among the natives. The beach has restrooms. Beware of the strong undercurrents and rip tides. ~ Located in the Marin Headlands section of the Golden Gate National Recreation Area. After crossing Golden Gate Bridge on Route 101, take the first exit, Alexander Avenue. Then take an immediate left, following the sign back toward San Francisco. Next, bear right at the sign for Marin Headlands. Follow this road to Rodeo Beach; 415-331-1540.

▲ Though not permitted on the beach, camping is available at three campgrounds in the area. They are hike-in campgrounds, ranging from 100 yards to 3 miles. There are five sites at Haypress, three sites at Hawkcamp, and three sites at Bicentennial; no water; fires are not permitted. These campgrounds are for tents only, all are free, and permits are required. Call the information number above for more details.

MUIR WOODS NATIONAL MONUMENT 🚶 If it weren't for the crowds, this redwood preserve would rank little short of majestic. Designated a national treasure by President Theodore Roosevelt in 1908, it features stately groves of tall timber. There are six miles of hiking trails, a snack bar, a gift shop, and restrooms. Day-use fee, $2. ~ Located off Route 1 on Panoramic Highway about 17 miles north of San Francisco; 415-388-2596.

MT. TAMALPAIS STATE PARK 🚶🚴🐎 Spectacularly situated between Mt. Tamalpais and the ocean, this 6300-acre park offers everything from mountaintop views to a rocky coastline. More than 50 miles of hiking trails wind past stands of cypress, Douglas fir, Monterey pine, and California laurel. Wildlife abounds. The countryside attracts nature lovers and sightseers alike. Facilities include picnic areas, restrooms, a refreshment stand, and a visitors center (open weekends only); ranger stations are located in various parts of the park. Every year since 1913 a mountain play has been staged in the amphitheater. Parking fee, $5. ~ Follow Route 1 north through Mill Valley; turn right on Panoramic Highway, which runs along the park border.

▲ There are 16 sites at Pantoll Park Headquarters (415-388-2070); facilities in this well-shaded spot include picnic areas, restrooms, running water; $15 to $16 per night. There's also camping at Frank Valley Horsecamp (good for people on horseback), located near Muir Beach in the southwest end of the Park. Picnic tables, pit toilet, running water; reservations are required and can be obtained at park headquarters. For information on Steep Ravine Environmental Camp see the listing below.

MUIR BEACH 🚶🚴🐎 ⛵🏊🚣 Because of its proximity to San Francisco, this spot is a favorite among local people. Located at the foot of a coastal valley, Muir forms a semicircular cove. There's a sandy beach and ample opportunity for picnicking. Other than picnic tables the facilities are limited to toilets. ~ Located on Route 1, about 16 miles north of San Francisco; 415-388-2596.

STEEP RAVINE ENVIRONMENTAL CAMP Set on a shelf above the ocean, this outstanding site is bounded on the other side by sharp slopes. Contained within Mt. Tamalpais State Park, it features a small beach and dramatic sea vista. This is a good place for nature study. ~ Located along a paved road off Route 1 about one mile south of Stinson Beach. Turn at the sign; 415-388-2070.

▲ There are six walk-in tent sites ($10 per night) and ten rustic cabins ($30 per night). Reservations are required; call PARKNET at 800-444-7275.

HIDDEN ► **RED ROCK BEACH** 🚶 🏖 🚣 One of the area's most popular nude beaches, this pocket beach is wall-to-wall with local folks on sunny weekends. Well protected along its flank by steep hillsides, Red Rock is an ideal sunbathers' retreat. There are no facilities here. ~ Part of Mt. Tamalpais State Park, Red Rock is located off Route 1 about one mile south of Stinson Beach. Watch for a large (often crowded) parking area on the seaward side of the highway. Follow the steep trail down to the beach.

STINSON BEACH PARK 🚶 🎣 🏄 🏖 🚣 One of Northern California's finest beaches, this broad, sandy corridor curves for three miles. Backdropped by rolling hills, Stinson also borders beautiful Bolinas Lagoon. Besides being a sunbather's haven, it's a great place for beachcombers and birdwatchers. To escape the crowds congregating here weekends, stroll up to the north end of the beach. You'll find a narrow sand spit looking out on Bolinas. You still won't have the beach entirely to yourself, but a place this beautiful is worth sharing. There are picnic areas, a snack bar, and restrooms; lifeguards in summer. Because of currents from Bolinas Lagoon, the water here is a little warmer than elsewhere along the Northern California Coast (but it's still brisk by Atlantic coast standards). If you dare swim anywhere along the North Coast, it might as well be here. ~ Located along Route 1 in the town of Stinson Beach, 23 miles north of San Francisco; 415-868-0942.

BOLINAS BEACH 🏃 🚴 🚶 🎣 🏖 🚣 Beginning near Bolinas Lagoon and curving around the town perimeter, this salt-and-pepper beach provides ample opportunity for walking. A steep bluff borders the beach. In the narrow mouth of the lagoon you can often see harbor seals and waterfowl. There are no facilities but the town of Bolinas is within walking distance. ~ Located at the end of Wharf Road in Bolinas.

AGATE BEACH AND DUXBURY REEF A prime area for beachcombers, Agate Beach is rich in found objects and objects waiting to be found—(however, collecting is not permitted). At low tide, Duxbury Reef to the south is equally outstanding for tidepool gazing. Both are highly recommended for adventurers, daydreamers, and amateur biologists. There are no facilities. ~ From Olema–Bolinas Road in Bolinas, go up the hill on Mesa Road, left on Overlook Drive, and right on Elm Road. Follow Elm Road to the parking lot at the end; take the path down to the ocean.

HIDDEN ► **HAGMAIER POND** 🏊 Favored by swimmers and nude sunbathers, this miniature lake offers a variation from nearby ocean beaches. It's fringed with grassland and bounded by forest, mak-

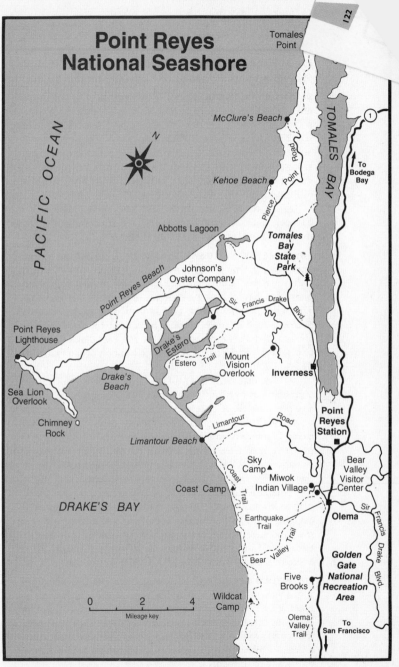

Point Reyes National Seashore

Tomales
Point

PACIFIC OCEAN

McClure's Beach

TOMALES BAY

① 1

To Bodega Bay

Kehoe Beach

Pierce Point Road

Abbotts Lagoon

Point Reyes Beach

Johnson's Oyster Company

Tomales Bay State Park

Sir Francis Drake

Drake's Estero

Sir Francis Drake Blvd

Point Reyes Lighthouse

Estero Trail

Mount Vision Overlook

Inverness

Sea Lion Overlook

Drake's Beach

Point Reyes Station

Chimney Rock

Limantour Road

Bear Valley Visitor Center

Limantour Beach

Sky Camp

Coast Trail

Miwok Indian Village

Olema

Sir Francis Drake Blvd

Coast Camp

DRAKE'S BAY

Earthquake Trail

Golden Gate National Recreation Area

Bear Valley Trail

Five Brooks

To San Francisco

Olema Valley Trail

Wildcat Camp

0   2   4
Mileage key

ing it an idyllic spot within easy reach of the highway. There are no facilities. ~ On Route 1 go three-and-a-half miles north of the Bolinas turnoff (at the foot of Bolinas Lagoon). You'll see a shallow parking lot on the right side of the highway. A dirt road leads uphill several hundred yards to the lake; take the first left fork.

SAMUEL P. TAYLOR STATE PARK Located several miles inland, this redwood facility provides an opportunity to experience the coastal interior. The place is heavily wooded and offers 2700 acres to roam. Wildflowers adorn the park entrance and gentle hiking trails. In addition to the trails, there are campgrounds and a creek. The park has picnic areas, restrooms, and showers. Day-use fee, $5. ~ On Sir Francis Drake Boulevard, east of Route 1 and six miles from Olema; 415-488-9897.

▲ There are 60 sites, 25 for tents only, no hookups; $12 to $16 per night. Reservations are required from Memorial Day through Labor Day; call PARKNET at 800-444-7275.

POINT REYES NATIONAL SEASHORE One of the great natural features of Northern California, this 72,000-acre park contains everything from windblown beaches to dense pine forests. No traveler should miss it. The park's facilities include an information center, picnic areas, restrooms, and 140 miles of hiking trails; restaurants and groceries are located in the nearby towns of Inverness and Point Reyes Station. ~ Located off Route 1 about 40 miles north of San Francisco; 415-663-1092.

▲ You may camp in any of four campgrounds, which are all accessible only by hiking trails or bikes. Each campground charges $10 per night. Sky Camp, with 12 primitive sites, sits on the side of Mt. Wittenberg, commanding stunning views of Drake's Bay. Coast Camp rests on a bluff above a pretty beach; there are 14 primitive sites. Glen Camp lies in a forested valley and has 12 primitive sites. Wildcat Camp nestles in a meadow near the beach; there are 7 primitive sites. Each camp is equipped with toilets, non-potable water, and picnic areas. Wood fires are not allowed; plan to bring alternate campfire materials. Permits are required; camping fee is $10 per night. You are limited to four nights in the park. Reservations are strongly recommended. For reservations call 415-663-8054. Permits can be obtained at Bear Valley Visitors Center. ~ Point Reyes, CA 94956; 415-663-8054.

LIMANTOUR BEACH This white sand beach is actually a spit, a narrow peninsula pressed between Drake's Bay and an estuary. It's an exotic area of sand dunes and sea breezes. Ideal for exploring, the region shelters over 350 bird species. There's good (but cold) swimming and fishing seaside. The only facilities are toilets. ~ Once in Point Reyes National Seashore, follow Limantour Road to the end.

▲ None, but the Point Reyes Youth Hostel is located on the road to Limantour.

TOMALES BAY STATE PARK 🏃 ⛵ 🐟 🚣 ⚓ This delightful park, which abuts on Point Reyes National Seashore, provides a warm, sunny alternative to Point Reyes' frequent fog. The water, too, is warmer here in Tomales Bay, making it a great place for swimming, as well as fishing and boating. Or check out the self-guided nature trail for a description of the relationship between American Indians and local plants. The virgin grove of Bishop pine is a special treat. Rimming the park are several sandy coves; most accessible of these is Heart's Desire Beach, flanked by bluffs and featuring nearby picnic areas. From Heart's Desire a self-guided nature trail goes northwest to Indian Beach, a long stretch of white sand fringed by trees. Hiking trails around the park lead to other secluded beaches, excellent for picnics and day hikes. No dogs allowed. The park has picnic areas and restrooms. Day-use fee, $5. ~ From Route 1 in Olema take Sir Francis Drake Boulevard to Inverness. From Inverness it's another eight miles. When Sir Francis Drake forks, take the right fork, which becomes Pierce Point Road. Then follow Pierce Point Road to the park; 415-669-1140.

▲ There are six sites for tents only; $3 per night per person. Campsites are hike-in or bike-in only.

SHELL BEACH ⛵ 🐟 🚣 ⚓ Actually part of Tomales Bay State Park, this pocket beach is several miles from the park entrance. As a result, it is often uncrowded. A patch of white sand bordered by steep hills, Shell Beach is ideal for swimming and picnicking. No dogs allowed. The only facilities are toilets. ~ Once in Point Reyes National Seashore, take Sir Francis Drake Boulevard one mile past Inverness, then turn right at Camino del Mar. The trailhead is located at the end of this street; follow the trail three-tenths of a mile down to the beach.

MARSHALL BEACH 🏃 ⛵ 🐟 🎣 🎿 🚣 ⚓ This secluded ◄ HIDDEN beach on Tomales Bay is a wonderful place to swim and sunbathe, often in complete privacy. The beach is a lengthy strip of white sand fringed by cypress trees. ~ Once in Point Reyes National Seashore, take Pierce Point Road. Immediately after passing the entrance to Tomales Bay State Park, turn right onto the paved road. This road travels uphill, turns to gravel and goes two-and-six-tenths miles to a gate. From the gate you hike one-and-a-half miles along the road/trail to the beach.

▲ Camping is allowed on the beach; be sure to pack out everything you packed in. For information, call 415-663-8054.

ABBOTTS LAGOON 🏃 Because of its rich waterfowl population and beautiful surrounding dunes, this is a favorite place among hikers. From the lagoon it's an easy jaunt over the dunes to Point

Reyes Beach. The only facilities are toilets. ~ Once in Point Reyes National Seashore, take Pierce Point Road. The trailhead is located along the roadside, two miles past the turnoff for Tomales Bay State Park; follow the trail one mile to the lagoon.

KEHOE BEACH 🚶 🏊 Bounded by cliffs, this strand is actually the northern end of ten-mile-long Point Reyes Beach. It's a lovely place, covered with wildflowers in spring and boasting a seasonal lagoon. The isolation makes it a great spot for explorers. The only facilities are toilets (at the trailhead). ~ Once in Point Reyes National Seashore, take Pierce Point Road. The trailhead is along the roadside four miles past the turnoff for Tomales Bay State Park; follow the trail a half-mile to the beach.

MCCLURE'S BEACH 🚶 🏊 Of the many beautiful beaches in Point Reyes National Seashore, this is by far my favorite. It is a white sand beach protected by granite cliffs which stand like bookends on either flank. Tidepool watching is a great sport here; if you arrive during low tide it's possible to skirt the cliffs along the south end and explore a pocket beach next door. But don't let a waxing tide catch you sleeping! Swimming is dangerous here; surf fishing, birdwatching, and driftwood gathering more than make up for it. Quite simply, places like this are the reason folks visit Northern California. The only facilities are toilets (at the trailhead). ~ Located in Point Reyes National Seashore at the end of Pierce Point Road. A steep trail leads a half-mile down to the beach.

POINT REYES BEACH 🏊 It will become wonderfully evident why this is nicknamed "Ten Mile Beach" when you cast eyes on this endless sand swath. A great place for whale watching, beachcombing, and fishing, this is not the spot for swimming. Sharks, riptides, and unusual wave patterns make even wading inadvisable. Also the heavy winds along this coastline would chill any swimmer's plans. But that does not detract from the wild beauty of the place, or the fact you can jog for miles along this strand (also referred to as North Beach and South Beach). Restrooms are the park's only facilities. ~ Located off Sir Francis Drake Boulevard about 14 miles from park headquarters.

DRAKE'S BEACH 🏄 🏊 Edged by cliffs, this crescent beach looks out upon the tip of Point Reyes. Since it's well protected by Drake's Bay, this is a good swimming spot. It also provides interesting hikes along the base of the cliffs to the inlet at Drake's Estero. Facilities include picnic areas, restrooms, a visitors center, and a snack bar. ~ Off Sir Francis Drake Boulevard, 15 miles from park headquarters.

OLEMA RANCH CAMPGROUND This roadside camping park has facilities for trailers and tent campers. The price however, ain't

cheap—$18 for a tent and two people. That will buy a pl◌
ground in a grassy area. Creekside sites are available for ◌
You won't have a sense of wilderness amid the Winnebagos ◌
but the place is strategically situated along Route 1 near the ◌
off for Point Reyes National Seashore. There are picnic areas, ◌◌◌
rooms, showers, a playground, and a laundromat. ~ 10155 Route
1 in Olema; 415-663-8001.

▲ There are 230 sites for tents and RVs (full hookups available); $18 to $25 per night.

▼▼▼▼▼▼▼▼▼▼▼▼

Sonoma & Mendocino Coast

Just north of Marin County lie the coastlines of Sonoma and Mendocino, beautiful and still lightly developed areas. Placid rangeland extends inward while along the shoreline, surf boils against angular cliffs. Far below are pocket beaches and coves; offshore rise dozens of tiny rock islands, or sea stacks. The entire coast teems with fish —salmon and steelhead—as well as crabs, clams, and abalone. Rip currents, sneaker waves, and the coldest waters this side of the Arctic make swimming inadvisable. But the landscape is wide open for exploration, enchanting and exotic.

SIGHTS

Jenner, Mendocino, and Fort Bragg are among the small towns along this endless coastline, but the first place you'll come to is a somewhat different type community. In fact the fishing village of **Bodega Bay** might look vaguely familiar, for it was the setting of Alfred Hitchcock's eerie film *The Birds*. It's questionable whether any cast members remain among the population of snowy egrets, but the Bay still supports a variety of winged creatures—conservation efforts have encouraged a comeback among the endangered brown pelicans and blue herons.

Here, at **Lucas Wharf**, and elsewhere along this working waterfront, you can watch fishermen setting off into the fog every morning and hauling in their catch later in the day. ~ At Route 1 and Smith Brothers Lane, Bodega Bay.

For a rustic detour, you can follow Coleman Valley Road when it departs from Route 1 north of Bodega Bay. A rolling country road, it weaves through farmland and offers great views of ocean and mountains. About ten miles out it leads to the forest-rimmed village of **Occidental**.

When Route 1 winds down to the woodframe town of **Jenner** (population 200, elevation 19), where the broad Russian River meets the ocean, you can take Route 116 up the river valley to the fabled Russian River resort area and the town of Guerneville.

The Russians for whom the river is named were explorers and trappers sailing down the Pacific coast from Russian outposts in Alaska. They came in search of sea otters and in hope of opening trade routes with the early Spanish settlers. In 1812 these bold outlanders went so far as to build **Fort Ross**, a wooden fortress overlooking the sea. The old Russian stronghold, located about 13 miles north of Jenner, is today a state historic park. Touring the reconstructed fort you'll encounter a museum, an old Russian Orthodox chapel, a stockade built of hand-tooled redwood, barracks and officers' houses, and a couple of seven-sided blockhouses. Together they provide an insight into an unusual chapter in California history. Admission. ~ 707-847-3286.

From Jenner north through Fort Ross and beyond, Route 1 winds high above the coast. Every curve exposes another awesome view of adze-like cliffs slicing into the sea. Driving this corkscrew route can jangle the nerves, but the vistas are soothing to the soul. With the exception of scattered villages, the coastline remains undeveloped. You'll pass sunbleached wooden buildings in the old town of Stewart Point. Then the road courses through **Sea Ranch**, a development bitterly opposed by environmentalists, which nevertheless displays some imaginative contemporary-design houses set against a stark sea.

Just north of Point Arena, a side road from Route 1 leads out to **Point Arena Lighthouse**. The original lighthouse, built in 1870, was destroyed in the 1906 San Francisco earthquake, which struck Point Arena even more fiercely than the bay city. The present beacon, rebuilt shortly afterwards, rises 115 feet from a narrow peninsula. The lighthouse is open for tours. The views, by definition, are simply outstanding. Open from 11 a.m. to 3:30 p.m. during the week and from 10 a.m. to 3:30 p.m. on weekends. Admission. ~ 707-882-2777.

In Mendocino County, the highway passes through tiny seaside villages. Elk, Albion, and Little River gaze down on the ocean from rocky heights. The coastline is an intaglio of river valleys, pocket beaches, and narrow coves. Forested ridges, soft and green in appearance, fall away into dizzying cliffs.

The houses which stand amid this continental turmoil resemble Maine saltboxes and Cape Cod cottages. In the town of **Mendocino**, which sits on a headland above the sea, you'll discover New England incarnate. Settled in 1852, the town was built largely by Yankees who decorated their village with wooden towers, Victorian homes, and a Gothic Revival Presbyterian church. The town, originally a vital lumber port, has become an artists' colony. With a shoreline honeycombed by beaches and a villagescape capped with a white church steeple, Mendocino is a mighty pretty corner of the continent.

Mendocino Headlands State Park, located atop a sea cliff, offers unmatched views of the town's tumultuous shoreline. From the bluffs you can gaze down at placid tidepools and wave-carved grottoes.

Adjacent to the park is the historic **Ford House,** an 1854 home with a small museum, which also serves as a visitors center for the park. ~ Main Street, Mendocino; 707-937-5397.

The best way to experience this antique town is by stopping at the **Kelly House Museum.** Set in a vintage home dating from 1861, the museum serves as an historical research center and unofficial chamber of commerce. Open daily from 1 to 4 p.m. from June 1 through November 1; open Friday through Monday from December through May. Admission. ~ 45007 Albion Street, Mendocino; 707-937-5791.

Among Mendocino's intriguing locales are the **Chinese Temple,** a 19th-century religious shrine located on Albion Street (open by appointment only); the **Presbyterian Church,** a national historic landmark on Main Street; and the **MacCallum House,** a Gingerbread Victorian on Albion Street, which has been reborn as an inn and restaurant. Another building of note is the **Masonic Hall,** an 1865 structure adorned with a hand-carved redwood statue on the roof. ~ Ukiah Street.

Then after meandering the side streets, stop at the **Mendocino Art Center.** Here exhibits by painters, potters, photographers, textile workers, and others will give an idea of the tremendous talent contained in tiny Mendocino. ~ 45200 Little Lake Street, Mendocino; 707-937-5818.

North of town, on the way to Fort Bragg, stop at **Jug Handle State Reserve.** Here you can climb an ecological stairway which ascends a series of marine terraces. On the various levels you'll encounter the varied coast, dune, and ridge environments that form the area's diverse ecosystem. ~ Along Route 1 about one mile north of Caspar; 707-937-5804.

Near the center of Fort Bragg you can board the **Skunk train** for a half- or full-day ride aboard a steam engine or a diesel-powered railcar. Dating from 1885, the Skunk was originally a logging train; today it also carries passengers along a 40-mile

THE GARDEN BY THE SEA

For a thoroughly delightful stroll to the sea, meander through the **Mendocino Coast Botanical Gardens.** This coastal preserve, with three miles of luxuriant pathways, is "a garden for all seasons" with something always in bloom. The unique Northern California coastal climate is conducive to heathers, perennials, succulents, and rhododendrons, which grow in colorful profusion here. Trails lead past gardens of ivy, ferns, and dwarf conifers to a coastal bluff with vistas up and down the rugged shoreline. Admission. ~ 18220 North Route 1, Fort Bragg; 707-964-4352.

route through mountains and redwoods inland to Willits and back. For information, contact California Western Railroad. Reservations recommended. ~ Fort Bragg; 707-964-6371.

North of Fort Bragg, Route 1 runs past miles of sand dunes and traverses several small towns. Then, after having followed the coast all the way from Southern California, it abruptly turns inland. The reason is the mysterious Lost Coast of California. Due north, where no highway could possibly run, the King Range vaults out of the sea, rising over 4000 feet in less than three miles. It is a wilderness inhabited by black bears and bald eagles, with an abandoned lighthouse and a solitary beach piled with ancient Indian shellmounds.

LODGING   Located a few miles east of Bodega Bay, the **Inn at Occidental** is a charming Victorian homestead encircled by a wide porch bedecked with pots of pink geraniums and white wicker rockers. The eight guest rooms are furnished with antique mahogany, pine beds, down comforters, and display cases of antique glass and pottery from the owner's private collection. A full breakfast is included, as is access to the garden jacuzzi. ~ 3657 Church Street, Occidental; 707-874-1047, 800-522-6324, fax 707-874-1078. DELUXE TO ULTRA-DELUXE.

A prime Jenner resting spot is **Jenner Inn and Cottages,** a bed and breakfast overlooking the river. Several buildings comprise the spread: you can rent a room, a suite, even a house. One of the less expensive accommodations, the personalized "Gull Room," features a quilted bed, old oak wardrobe, and a deck overlooking the river. The "Captain Will's Room," a higher-priced suite, adds features like a hand-carved headboard, living room with a wood stove and antique rocker, and a loft for extra guests. ~ 10400 Route 1, Jenner; 707-865-2377, 800-732-2377, fax 707-865-0829. MODERATE TO ULTRA-DELUXE.

A fair bargain can be found along the coast at **Fort Ross Lodge,** two miles north of the old Russian fort. Overlooking the ocean, this 22-unit establishment consists of a cluster of wood-frame buildings. The rooms have ocean views; the ceilings are knotty pine, floors are carpeted wall-to-wall, and the varied decor includes everything from wicker to antique furniture. There are TVs, VCRs, and private baths in all rooms, plus a community sauna and hot tub. ~ 20705 Route 1, Jenner; 707-847-3333, 800-988-4537. MODERATE TO DELUXE.

Several lodges along the California coast reflect in their architecture the raw energy of the surrounding sea. Such a one is **Timber Cove Inn.** Elemental in style, it is a labyrinth of unfinished woods and bald rocks. The heavy timber lobby is dominated by a walk-in stone fireplace and sits astride a Japanese pond. The 51 guest rooms are finished in redwood with beams and columns exposed. Many are decorated with Ansel Adams prints. Furniture is fashioned from oak and a Japanese motif is reflected in the hot tubs. A bit too stark and unfinished for my taste, the guest rooms are also looking a bit old and dated, although they do afford marvelous views of the mountains and open sea. Many have decks, fireplaces, and hot tubs. All have TVs and phones. Timber Cove, fittingly, rests on a cliff directly above the ocean. Restaurant and lounge. Ask about winter rates. ~ 21780 North Route 1, 15 miles north of Jenner; 707-847-3231, 800-987-8319, fax 707-847-3704. MODERATE TO ULTRA-DELUXE.

Set on a plateau above the ocean, **Stillwater Cove Ranch** is set on lovely grounds and populated with peacocks. Formerly a boys' school, this complex of buildings has been transformed into a restful retreat. Accommodations are varied, from single rooms to a cottage with a fireplace. Even the dairy barn can house guests: it's been converted to a bunkhouse with kitchen. Stillwater Cove is certainly worth checking into. Closed for one week before Christmas. ~ 22555 Route 1, 16 miles north of Jenner; 707-847-3227. BUDGET TO MODERATE.

Accessible via a scenic country lane, **Timberhill Ranch** is as serene and simple a resort as you'll find anywhere in California. Fifteen handmade cedar cottages dot the forested hillside property, each with cozy quilts, fireplaces, and decks where you can enjoy breakfast . . . or share it with the resident ducks. Tennis courts, a pool, and a jacuzzi with a view may be enough to keep guests ranch-bound for days. Rates include breakfast and dinner, the latter a multicourse gourmet affair in the main lodge. ~ 35755 Hauser Bridge Road, Cazadero; 707-847-3258, 800-847-3470, fax 707-847-3342; www.timberhillranch.com. ULTRA-DELUXE.

Sea Ranch Lodge is the ultimate Sonoma coast retreat. Miles of secluded beaches and hiking trails, fields of wildflowers and beautiful bluffs make this resort a perennial favorite. The lodge, faced with weathered wood siding, offers 20 rooms, most with views. Recent redecoration emphasizes earth tones that blend in with the natural surroundings; there are phones and new furniture. But the biggest draw is the array of contemporary-style homes, spaced far apart and set amid fields of windblown grasses. Offering sea and mountain views, they constitute the heart and soul of this unique North Coast colony. There is a restaurant, a store and nearby hiking and biking trails. ~ 60 Sea Walk Drive, Sea Ranch; 707-785-2371, 800-732-7262, fax 707-785-2124. DELUXE TO ULTRA-DELUXE.

Mar Vista Cottages at Anchor Bay is a community of 12 separate cottages scattered around eight acres of oceanview property. Each is an old woodframe affair with a sitting room and kitchen as well as a bedroom. Several are equipped with decks, fireplaces, or wood stoves. A soaking tub and barbecue facility on the property are surrounded by trees; a short path leads across Route 1 to the beach. ~ 35101 South Route 1, Gualala; 707-884-3522. MODERATE.

HIDDEN ►   Built in 1903, the **Gualala Hotel** is a massive two-story structure. It's an old clapboard affair, fully refurbished, that includes a bar and dining room. The 19 rooms upstairs are small, but the wallpaper, decor, and old-time flourishes give the place a comfy traditional feel, making it a rare find on the North Coast. Because of the downstairs restaurant/bar, it can get noisy at times. ~ 39301 Route 1, Gualala; 707-884-3441. BUDGET.

A short distance north of the Gualala Hotel, but a long step up in price, is the **Old Milano Hotel**. Dating from 1905, it is one of those very special places that people return to year after year. The two-story shiplap house rises between a delicately tended garden and the sea. Anchored just offshore is Castle Rock, a dramatic sea stack. But this pales in comparison to the interior. Each of the six bedrooms upstairs has been furnished and decorated with luxurious Victorian antiques: oil paintings, brass lamps, quilts, oak headboards, and plump armchairs. There are two shared baths, and the downstairs master suite has its own bathroom. The "wine parlor" downstairs features a stone fireplace and the music room is decorated with William Morris designs. Little wonder the house is registered as a historic place. There are six cottages available, as well as an old caboose converted into living quarters. ~ 38300 Route 1, Gualala; 707-884-3256. MODERATE TO ULTRA-DELUXE.

For a rustic detour, follow Coleman Valley Road when it veers away from Route 1 north of Bodega Bay. It winds through farmland and offers great views of ocean and mountains, and leads to the forest-rimmed village of Occidental.

Every one of the sixteen rooms at **Seacliff** stares straight at the Pacific Ocean, and some days you can see whales rubbing their bellies on the sandbar. Accommodations are simple but entirely comfortable, with everything you need for an atmospheric retreat: fireplaces, two-person whirlpool tubs with ocean views, downy kingsize beds and plush comforters, coffee makers and refrigerators stocked with complimentary champagne. The staff treats you like family. ~ Route 1, Gualala; 707-884-1213, 800-400-5053. MODERATE TO DELUXE.

Country inns of this genre are quite abundant farther north. Near the town of Mendocino there are numerous bed and breakfasts, some outstanding. The seaside towns of Elk, Albion, Little River, Mendocino, and Fort Bragg each house several. Prices are generally high, but for intimacy and personal care, Northern California's inns are unparalleled.

Among the more renowned is **Harbor House Inn**. Set on a rise overlooking the ocean, the house is built entirely of redwood. The living room alone, with its fireplace and exposed-beam ceiling, is

an architectural feat. The house was modeled on a design exhibited at San Francisco's 1915 Panama–Pacific Exposition. Of the
ten bedrooms and cottages, most have fireplaces and patterned
wallpaper as well as antique appointments. Rates include breakfast and dinner. ~ 5600 South Route 1, Elk; 707-877-3203. ULTRA-
DELUXE.

A message in a guest room diary at **Elk Cove Inn** reads: "A
view, with a room." The view is of knobby coast and simmering
surf of ice blue and shaggy dunes falling away. The room is perfect for watching it all: a comfortable cabin with dramatic beamed
ceiling, gas fireplace at the foot of your featherbed, carafe of port
waiting on the nightstand. In the morning, proprietor Elaine Bryant lays out an elaborate buffet—baked pears stuffed with almonds
and cream cheese, egg and cheese soufflés—in the main 1883 Victorian house, a short walk from the four bluff-top cabins. There
are six guest rooms in the main house, some with dormer windows overlooking ocean, others with French doors opening onto
riotous gardens. ~ 6300 South Route 1, Elk; 707-877-3321, 800-
275-2967, fax 707-877-1808. DELUXE TO ULTRA-DELUXE.

Heritage House was constructed in 1877 and reflects the New
England architecture popular then in Northern California. Baby
Face Nelson is reputed to have hidden in the old farmhouse which
today serves as the inn's reception and dining area. Most guests
are housed in nearby cottages which, like the hideout itself, overlook a rocky cove. Some rooms have jacuzzis and private decks.
Closed from the end of November to early February (except for
the week of Christmas and New Year's Eve). ~ 5200 North Route
1, Little River; 707-937-5885, 800-235-5885, fax 707-937-0318.
MODERATE TO ULTRA-DELUXE.

The New England–style farmhouse that has become **Glendeven** dates even farther back, to 1867. The theme is country living, with a meadow out back and dramatic headlands nearby.
The sitting room is an intimate affair with a baby grand piano and
comfortable armchairs set before a brick fireplace. In the rooms
you're apt to find a bed with wooden headboard, an antique wardrobe, and perhaps ferns hanging from the ceiling. Glendeven is
as charming and intimate as a country inn can be. A full breakfast is brought to your room on a tray. ~ 8221 North Route 1,
Little River; 707-937-0083, 800-822-4536, fax 707-937-6108.
MODERATE TO ULTRA-DELUXE.

The **Little River Inn**, centered in a quaint 1850s-era house,
has expanded into a mini-resort with 64 units, a restaurant, tennis courts, a lounge, and a nine-hole golf course. Intimacy was
lost along the way, but a host of facilities were added. Rooms at
the inn proper, decorated in early-California fashion, are deluxe
priced. There is also a tastefully done motel wing as well as a series of cottages. The cottages are paneled in wood, furnished in

hardwood, and decorated with watercolors. Like most of the other accommodations, they afford grand ocean views. ~ 7751 North Route 1, Little River; 707-937-5942, 888-466-5683; www.little riverinn.com. MODERATE TO ULTRA-DELUXE.

Rachel's Inn overlooks Van Damme State Park, with trails that deliver you instantly to rocky coast and the shiny bald heads of grey seals. Nine rooms, spread between two buildings, are extra spacious and decorated with walls of warm white, folded linen draperies, antique dressers and woodburning hearths. Bach streams through the living room, where a Matisse hangs on one wall. Rachel serves breakfast in the elegant dining room, plying plates with baked apples and cranberry pancakes and herbed cheese omelettes with black beans. ~ 8200 North Route 1, two miles south of Mendocino; 707-937-0088, 800-347-9252. DELUXE TO ULTRA-DELUXE.

A minute from downtown Mendocino, set right where Big River meets the ocean, **Stanford Inn** is both woodsy and New Agey. The rambling lobby is paneled in Ponderosa pine and looks across to Pacific headlands; llamas and geese roam terraced lawns; and "biodynamic" nurseries provide fare for the inn's outstanding vegetarian menus. Families love it here; kids can play with the inn's three dogs. There's kayaking and redwood outrigger canoeing down Big River, and mountain biking along Pacific cliff trails. Couples go for the handsome, intimate rooms with Lexington furnishings, woodburning fireplaces, and VCRs (the inn stocks 900 videos). You'll also find a wonderful greenhouse pool with gardens of palms and bougainvillea, and water that's bathtub-warm year-round. ~ Route 1 and Comptche Ukiah Road, Mendocino; 707-937-5025, 800-331-8884, fax 707-937-0305; www.stanfordinn. com. ULTRA-DELUXE.

Set in a falsefront building which dates to 1878, the 51-room **Mendocino Hotel** is a wonderful place, larger than other nearby country inns, with a wood-paneled lobby, full dining room, and living quarters adorned with antiques. There are rooms in the hotel with both private and shared baths as well as quarters in the garden cottages out back. ~ 45080 Main Street, Mendocino; 707-937-0511, 800-548-0513, fax 707-937-0513. MODERATE TO ULTRA-DELUXE.

The queen of Mendocino is the **MacCallum House Inn**, a gingerbread Victorian built in 1882. The place is a treasure trove of antique furnishings, knickknacks, and other memorabilia. Many of the rooms are individually decorated with rocking chairs, quilts, and wood stoves. Positively everything—the carriage house, barn, greenhouse, gazebo, even the water tower—has been converted into a guest room. ~ 45020 Albion Street, Mendocino; 707-937-0289, 800-609-0492. MODERATE TO ULTRA-DELUXE.

Also consider **Mendocino Village Inn Bed and Breakfast,** a vintage 1882 house that has two attic rooms, one with a sea view. A blue-and-white clapboard building with mansard roof, the place offers more spacious accommodations with private baths at higher prices. Full breakfast and afternoon hors d'oeuvres included. No credit cards. ~ 44860 Main Street, Mendocino; 707-937-0246, 800-882-7029; www.bestinns.net/usa/ca/ mendo.html. MODERATE TO DELUXE.

The nearby **Sea Gull Inn** has nine rooms, some with ocean views. In a land of pricey hotels, this bed-and-breakfast establishment is a rare discovery. Choose to stay in the main house or in the cottage set in the garden. ~ 44960 Albion Street, Mendocino; 707-937-5204, 888-937-5204, fax 707-937-3550. BUDGET TO DELUXE.

Set on two landscaped acres overlooking Mendocino village and the coast, the **Joshua Grindle Inn** is a 19th-century New England–style farmhouse with ten spacious rooms, all with sitting areas, and some with wood-burning fireplaces and ocean views. An inviting gathering spot during evening hours, the parlor offers a cheerful fire and an antique pump organ. Full breakfast included. ~ 44800 Little Lake Road, Mendocino; 707-937-4143, 800-474-6353; www.joshgrin.com. DELUXE TO ULTRA-DELUXE.

For women guests only, **Sallie & Eileen's Place** offers a studio A-frame cottage and a spacious cabin three miles from Mendocino. The studio has a fireplace, rockers, and a sunken tub, while the cabin, which can sleep up to six, has a loft bedroom, a woodstove, a deck, and a private backyard. ~ Box 409, Mendocino, CA 95460; 707-937-2028. MODERATE.

Tucked away in a quiet residential neighborhood, the **Avalon House,** a 1905 craftsman dwelling, has been lovingly converted into a B&B inn. Each room is individually appointed with handmade willow furniture and antiques. Gardens surround the house. A real gem. ~ 561 Stewart Street, Fort Bragg; 707-964-5555, 800-964-5556; www.theavalonhouse.com. MODERATE TO DELUXE.

The **Bowen's Pelican Lodge & Inn** is an 1890-vintage bordello that has been converted into a country inn with six guest rooms (two with shared baths). The place sits across the street from the ocean with a path that leads down to a sandy beach. ~ 38921 North Route 1, Westport; 707-964-5588. BUDGET TO MODERATE.

DINING

For the best meal hereabouts (or for that matter, anywhere about), head for **River's End Restaurant**. Situated at that momentous crossroad of the Russian River and Pacific Ocean (and commanding a view of both), this outstanding little place is a restaurant with imagination. How else do you explain a dinner menu that ranges from *médallions* of venison to crisped duckling to coconut-fried shrimp; or a Sunday brunch that includes German glazed apple pancakes and *gravlax* with shrimp and capers? Not to mention good service and a selection of apéritifs. River's End is a great place for ocean lovers and culinary adventurers. Closed Monday through Thursday from October through May. ~ 1048 Route 1, Jenner; 707-865-2484. MODERATE TO ULTRA-DELUXE.

The **Salt Point Bar and Grill** features a small restaurant serving breakfast, lunch, and dinner. The menu relies on seafood—halibut, oysters, prawns, scallops—but also includes chicken, steak, and other dishes. At lunch, enjoy a variety of salads, sandwiches, or seafood selections. ~ 23255 North Route 1, 17 miles north of Jenner; 707-847-3234. MODERATE TO DELUXE.

Built in 1903, the **Gualala Hotel** has an attractive dining room with a menu that varies from country fried chicken to breaded oysters. Stops along the way include snapper, ravioli, and rib-eye steak. Lunch is served and you can also stop for a hearty breakfast featuring omelettes. What makes dining here really special is the old hotel with its big front porch and antique decor. ~ 39301 Route 1, Gualala; 707-884-3441. MODERATE.

Okay, so **St. Orres** is yet another California cuisine restaurant. But it's the only one you'll see that looks as if it should be in Russia rather than along the California coast. With its dizzying spires, this elegant structure evokes images of Moscow and old St. Petersburg. Serving dinner only, the kitchen provides an ever-changing menu of fresh game and fish dishes. The fixed-price menu will include hot and chilled soups, poached salmon, rabbit, rack of lamb, stuffed wild boar, and several seasonal specialties. Even if you're not interested in dining, it might be worth a stop to view this architectural extravaganza. Dinner only. Closed Tuesday and Wednesday from January through May. Cash or check only. ~ 36601 Route 1, Gualala; 707-884-3303. ULTRA-DELUXE.

The **Galley at Arena Cove** looks out on a pier as well as a series of ocean bluffs. With a hand-carved bar and wood-plank dining room, it's a local seafood restaurant serving fresh red snapper, sautéed prawns, oysters, and broiled swordfish. If an oyster bar and homemade clam chowder don't interest you, there are steaks and chops at this good ol' style eating place. Open for breakfast, lunch, and dinner. ~ 790 Port Road, Point Arena; 707-882-2189. MODERATE.

Although the dining room at **Harbor House Inn** mainly serves guests at this bed-and-breakfast, there are at least two extra tables for two people each evening. A fire in the fireplace will keep you warm and cozy on a cold coastal night, and in the summer you can watch the sunset over the ocean out of the huge windows. The chef prepares a set menu, served at 7 p.m., with entrées such as salmon, pork tenderloin, or halibut. A vegetarian meal can also be prepared upon request. Reservations are required. ~ 5600 South Route 1, Elk; 707-877-3203. ULTRA-DELUXE.

The **Albion River Inn**, set high on a hillside above the Albion River and the ocean, is a plate-glass dining spot serving California cuisine, and specializing in otherworldly ocean views. The pasta, seafood, vegetables, and herbs are all fresh. You can also dine on steaks and pasta. Dinner only. ~ 3790 North Route 1, Albion; 707-937-4044. MODERATE TO DELUXE.

I'm told that the **Little River Restaurant** is an absolute must. In the summer it's open Friday through Tuesday, just for dinner, and has but a half-dozen tables. The California cuisine includes appetizers of escargot and steamed clams. For entrées there are roast duck with apricot-vermouth sauce, quail in a hazelnut-port sauce, and filet mignon stuffed with prosciutto. ~ 7750 North Route 1, Little River; 707-937-4945. DELUXE.

◄ HIDDEN

A morning ritual for locals and visitors alike is to climb the rough-hewn stairs to the loft-like **Bay View Café** for coffee, French toast, or fluffy omelettes. On sunny afternoons, the deck overlooking Main Street and the coastal headlands makes an ideal lunch spot, especially for fish and chips or a jalapeño chile burger. ~ 45040 Main Street, Mendocino; 707-937-4197. BUDGET.

At the **Mendocino Hotel** you can enjoy California-style cuisine in the main dining room or out in the "garden room." The menu represents a mix of meat and seafood entrées such as filet mignon, smoked duck ragoût, and oysters in puff pastry. The ambience in this 19th-century building evokes Mendocino's early days. ~ 45080 Main Street, Mendocino; 707-937-0511. MODERATE TO DELUXE.

Situated in a cozy little house, the **Moosse Café** offers imaginative seasonal dishes. There's wild mushroom lasagna, smoked salmon, and braised lamb shank. For dessert of course you have

●●●

✔ **CHECK THESE OUT—UNIQUE DINING**

- *Budget:* Meet Mendocino "society" at **Bay View Café** and savor the fluffy omelettes or spicy burgers. *page 135*
- *Moderate:* Enjoy fresh oysters or piping hot popovers at **The Station House Café**, a local Point Reyes Station hangout. *page 115*
- *Moderate to deluxe:* Imagine yourself a guest at a stately dinner party while you dine at the majestic **Benbow Inn**. *page 151*
- *Ultra-deluxe:* Make believe you're in Russia at **St. Orres**, an exceptional eatery where the architecture summons an image of St. Petersburg. *page 134*

Budget: under $9   Moderate: $9–$18   Deluxe: $18–$25   Ultra-deluxe: over $25

to sample the moosse puff. ~ 390 Kasten Street, Mendocino; 707-937-4323. BUDGET TO MODERATE.

For French and California cuisine, **955 Ukiah Street** is an address worth noting. Candles, fresh flowers, and impressionist prints set the tone here. Serving dinner only, it prepares brandied prawns, red snapper in phyllo pastry, roast duck, and calamari. For the diet-conscious, they also offer lighter dishes. Closed Monday and Tuesday from July through October, and Monday through Wednesday from November through June. ~ 955 Ukiah Street, Mendocino; 707-937-1955. MODERATE.

Mendocino's best-known dining room is well deserving of its renown. **Café Beaujolais**, situated in a small antique house on the edge of town, serves designer dishes. Dinner, served seven nights a week, is ever changing. Perhaps they'll be serving warm duck salad and Thai rock shrimp salad with entrées like *poulet verjus*, chicken braised with Navarro vineyards Verjus, leg of lamb stuffed with garlic, and steamed salmon with chervil *sabayon* sauce. Excellent cuisine. Closed from the day after Thanksgiving until December 26. ~ 961 Ukiah Street, Mendocino; 707-937-5614. DELUXE.

The dining rooms of the 1882 **MacCallum House Restaurant** are beautiful, the walls and ceilings covered with carved redwood and fir, the tables glittering with firelight and candlelight. Everything on the menu is excellent. Start with an Alexander's Antidote aperitif (champagne with puréed blackberries and schnapps) and an appetizer of Pacific Rim oysters with gazpacho relish. Then try the pan-seared ahi with tomatoes, capers, and mushrooms, or the sautéed chicken with a honey-rosemary glaze, or the caramelized scallops with vanilla-saffron sauce. There's a lighter café menu served in the bar. ~ 45020 Albion Street, Mendocino; 707-937-5763. MODERATE TO DELUXE.

Fort Bragg's favorite dining spot is easy to remember—**The Restaurant**. Despite the name, this is no generic eating place but a creative kitchen serving excellent dinners. The walls are hung with dozens of paintings by local contemporary artists, lending a sense of the avant garde to this informal establishment. The Restaurant's menu offers seasonal entrées like sautéed prawns, salmon, rockfish, and vegetarian selections. Choose from a selection of house-made desserts, including ice creams and sorbets. Open for Sunday brunch, lunch Thursday and Friday, and dinner every day except Wednesday. ~ 418 North Main Street, Fort Bragg; 707-964-9800. MODERATE TO DELUXE.

SHOPPING   In the New England–style town of Mendocino you'll discover a shopper's paradise. Prices are quite dear, but the window browsing is unparalleled. Housed in the town's old Victorians and Cape Cod cottages is a plethora of shops. There are stores specializing in soap, seashells, candles, and T-shirts; not to mention bookstores, potters, jewelers, art galleries, and antique shops galore. Most are located along the woodframe Main Street, but also search out the side streets and passageways in this vintage town.

One particularly noteworthy gallery is the **William Zimmer Gallery**, which houses an eclectic collection of contemporary and traditional arts and crafts. ~ Kasten and Ukiah streets, Mendocino; 707-937-5121. Be sure to also check out **Highlight Gallery**, featuring displays of handmade furniture, contemporary art, jewelry, and woodwork. ~ 45052 Main Street, Mendocino; 707-937-3132. The **Mendocino Art Center** houses numerous crafts studios as well as two art galleries. ~ 45200 Little Lake Street, Mendocino; 707-937-5818.

Books are the order of the day at the **Gallery Bookshop and Bookwinkle's Children's Books**. ~ Main and Kasten streets, Mendocino; 707-937-2665.

There's music four nights a week at the **Caspar Inn**. This down-home bar room spotlights local bands as well as groups from outside the area. Hit it on the right night and the joint will be rocking. If you've overdone your partying by the end of the night, ask management about the rooms they have available. Cover. ~ 14961 Caspar Road, Caspar; 707-964-5565. **NIGHTLIFE**

For a night on the town, enjoy a quiet drink at the **Mendocino Hotel**. You can relax at a Victorian-style lounge or in an enclosed garden patio. ~ 45080 Main Street, Mendocino; 707-937-0511.

For a pint of Guinness and a game of backgammon, slip into **Patterson's Pub**. The pub is small, in keeping with its Irish persona, and furnished in dark wood and brass. There's no live entertainment, but the local characters and friendly chit chat should more than make up for the absence of loud music. ~ 10485 Lansing Street, Mendocino; 707-937-4782.

The Restaurant has live jazz on Friday and Saturday nights, and Sunday brunch. ~ 418 North Main Street, Fort Bragg; 707-964-9800.

DILLON BEACH Located at the mouth of Tomales Bay, this beach is popular with boaters and clammers. The surrounding hills are covered with resort cottages, but there are open areas and dunes to explore. There are picnic areas and restrooms, groceries, boat rentals, and fishing charters. Day-use fee, $5. ~ From Route 1 in Tomales take Dillon Beach Road west for four miles; 707-878-2204. **BEACHES & PARKS**

▲ Located nearby, Lawson's Landing (707-878-2443) has open meadow camping for tents and RVs (no hookups); $12 per night. Take note: this campground hosts hundreds of trailers.

DORAN REGIONAL PARK

This peninsular park is situated on a sand spit between Bodega Harbor and Bodega Bay. With a broad sand beach and good facilities, it's an excellent spot for daytrippers and campers alike. You can explore the tidal flats or fish up on the jetty. There are picnic areas, restrooms, and showers. Day-use fee, $3. ~ Located off Route 1, a half mile south of Bodega Bay; 707-875-3540.

▲ There are 134 sites for tents and RVs (no hookups); $13 per night for Sonoma County residents and $15 for nonresidents.

BODEGA HEAD

There are pocket beaches here dramatically backdropped by granite cliffs. A good place to picnic and explore, this is also a favored whale-watching site. There are restrooms and showers located in nearby Westside Park (707-875-3540). ~ Off Route 1 in Bodega Bay along Bay Flat Road.

▲ Westside Park has 47 tent/RV sites (no hookups); $15 a night; $13 a night for Sonoma County residents.

SONOMA COAST STATE BEACH

This magnificent park extends for 13 miles between Bodega Head and the Vista Trail. It consists of a number of beaches separated by steep headlands; all are within easy hiking distance of Route 1. The beaches range from sweeping strands to pocket coves and abound with waterfowl and shorebirds, clams, and abalone. The park headquarters and information center is at Salmon Creek Beach, where endless sand dunes backdrop a broad beach. Schoolhouse Beach is a particularly pretty pocket cove bounded by rocky cliffs; Portuguese Beach boasts a wide swath of sand; Blind Beach is rather secluded with a sea arch offshore; and Goat Rock Beach faces the town of Jenner and is decorated with offshore rocks. Pick your poison—hiking, tidepooling, birdwatching, whale watching, camping, picnicking, fishing—and you'll find it waiting along this rugged and hauntingly beautiful coastline. Bodega Dunes, Salmon Creek Beach, Schoolhouse Beach, Goat Rock, Wrights Beach and Portuguese Beach have restrooms; Bodega Dunes and Wrights Beach also feature picnic areas. Day-use fee for developed campgrounds, $5. ~ Located along Route 1 between Bodega Bay and Jenner; 707-865-2391.

▲ At Bodega Dunes, there are 98 tent/RV sites (no hookups); $16 a night. At Wrights Beach, there are 30 tent/RV sites (no hookups); $20 a night. Reservations are required; call PARKNET at 800-444-7275. At Pono Canyon and Willow Creek there are 31 walk-in primitive sites; $10 per night.

FORT ROSS REEF CAMPGROUND

Set in a canyon surrounded by bluffs, this facility is beautifully located and features a redwood grove. At one time it was a private park, but the state took it over. The result is a public facility with spectacular surroundings and gorgeous views. There are picnic areas and restrooms. Day-use fee, $6. ~ Located at 19005 Route 1, 12 miles north of Jenner; watch for a cluster of white barns on the west side of the highway; 707-847-3286.

▲ There are 20 tent/RV sites (no hookups); $12 per night. Open April to November. Depending on the weather, fires may not be allowed.

STILLWATER COVE REGIONAL PARK 🚶 🛶 ⚓ Situated amid pine trees on a hillside above the ocean, this is a small park with access to a beach. The canyon trail leads up to the restored (but closed) Fort Ross Schoolhouse. There are picnic areas, restrooms, and showers. Day-use fee, $3. ~ Located on Route 1, about 16 miles north of Jenner; 707-847-3245.

▲ There are 23 tent/RV sites (no hookups); $15 a night.

OCEAN COVE STORE AND CAMPGROUND 🚶 🚴 🏊 🛶 ⚓ This privately owned campground has sites on a bluff above a rocky shoreline. Anglers catch everything from salmon to rockfish. The scenery is mighty attractive, and the campsites are well removed from the road. There are hot showers and primitive toilets. ~ Located on Route 1 about 17 miles north of Jenner; 707-847-3422.

▲ There are 150 tent/RV sites (no hookups); $12 per night, $1 extra for dogs. Closed from November through March.

SALT POINT STATE PARK 🚶 🚴 🏊 🛶 ⚓ Extending from the ocean to over 1000 feet elevation, this 6000-acre spread includes coastline, forests, and open range land. Along the shore are weird honeycomb formations called *tafoni*, caused by sea erosion on coastal sandstone. Up amid the stands of Douglas fir and Bishop pine there's a pygmy forest, where unfavorable soil conditions have caused fully mature redwoods to reach only a few feet in height. Blacktail deer, black bear, mountain lions, and bobcats roam the area. Miles of hiking trails lace the park, including one through a rhododendron reserve. There are picnic areas and restrooms. Day-use fee, $5. ~ Located on Route 1 about 20 miles north of Jenner; 707-847-3221.

▲ There are three campgrounds here with sites for tents and RVs (no hookups); $14 to $16 per night. Reservations are required on weekends and from April to October; call PARKNET at 800-444-7275.

GUALALA POINT REGIONAL PARK 🚶 🛶 🛶 ⚓ Located where the Gualala River meets the ocean, this charming place has everything from a sandy beach to redwood groves. Across the river, there are kayak and canoe rentals. There are picnic areas, restrooms, and an information center. Day-use fee, $3. ~ Located along Route 1 due south of Gualala; 707-785-2377.

▲ There are 19 tent/RV sites (no hookups) and 6 walk-in sites; $15 per night.

MANCHESTER STATE BEACH 🕴 🏃 ⛵ This wild, windswept beach extends for miles along the Mendocino coast. Piled deep with driftwood, it's excellent for beachcombing and hiking. There are picnic areas, restrooms, and an information center. ~ Located along Route 1 about eight miles north of Point Arena; 707-937-5804.

▲ There are 46 tent/RV sites (no hookups) and 10 primitive, hike-in environmental sites; $12 per night; first-come, first-served.

VAN DAMME STATE PARK 🕴 🚲 ⚓ ⛵ Extending from the beach to an interior forest, this 2069-acre park has several interesting features: a "pygmy forest" where poor soil results in fully mature pine trees reaching heights of only six inches to eight feet; a "fern canyon" smothered in different species of ferns; and a "cabbage patch" filled with that fetid critter with elephant ear leaves —skunk cabbage. This park is also laced with hiking trails and offers excellent beachcombing opportunities. Facilities include a visitors center, picnic areas, restrooms, and showers. Day-use fee, $5 for the fern canyon. ~ On Route 1 about 30 miles north of Point Arena, or three miles south of Mendocino; 707-937-5804.

▲ There are 74 tent/RV sites (no hookups); $16 per night. For reservations call PARKNET at 800-444-7275.

MENDOCINO HEADLANDS AND BIG RIVER BEACH STATE PARKS 🕴 🏃 ⚓ ⛵ These adjoining parks form the seaside border of the town of Mendocino. And quite a border it is. The white sand beaches are only part of the natural splendor. There are also wave tunnels, tidepools, sea arches, lagoons, and 360° vistas that sweep from the surf-trimmed shore to the prim village-scape of Mendocino. The only facilities are restrooms; private canoe rental nearby. ~ Located in the town of Mendocino.

RUSSIAN GULCH STATE PARK 🕴 🚲 🏇 ⚓ ⛵ Set in a narrow valley with a well-protected beach, this park has numerous features. There are marvelous views from the craggy headlands, a waterfall, and a blowhole that rarely blows. Rainbow and steelhead trout inhabit the creek while hawks and ravens circle the forest. There are picnic areas, restrooms, and showers. Day-use fee, $5. ~ Located along Route 1 two miles north of Mendocino; 707-937-5804.

▲ There are 30 sites for tents and RVs (no hookups); $16 per night. For reservations call PARKNET at 800-444-7275.

MACKERRICHER STATE PARK 🕴 🚲 🏇 🏃 ⚓ 🚤 ⛵ Another of the region's outstanding parks, this facility features a crescent of sandy beach, dunes, headlands, a lake, a forest, and wetlands. Harbor seals inhabit the rocks offshore and over 90 bird species frequent the area. The park has picnic areas, restrooms, and showers. ~ Along Route 1 about three miles north of Fort Bragg; 707-937-5804.

▲ There are 142 sites for tents and RVs (no hookups), 10 walk-in sites, and 3 hike-and-bike sites ($3 per night, per person) $16 per night. For reservations call PARKNET at 800-444-7275.

Near the nondescript town of Leggett, Route 1 joins Route 101. Logging trucks, those belching beasts that bear down upon you without mercy, become more frequent. You are entering Redwood Country.

▼▼▼▼▼▼▼▼▼▼▼▼
Redwood Country

This is the habitat of *Sequoia sempervirens*, the coastal redwood, a tree whose ancestors date to the age of dinosaurs and which happens to be the world's tallest living thing. These "ambassadors from another time," as John Steinbeck called them, inhabit a 30-mile-wide coastal fog belt stretching 450 miles from the Monterey area north to Oregon. Redwoods live five to eight centuries, though some have survived over two millennia, while reaching heights over 350 feet and diameters greater than 20 feet.

There is a sense of solitude here uncapturable anywhere else. The trees form a cathedral overhead, casting a deep shade across the forest floor. Solitary sun shafts, almost palpable, cut through the grove; along the roof of the forest, pieces of light jump across the treetops, poised to fall like rain. Ferns and a few small animals are all that survive here. The silence and stillness are either transcendent or terrifying. It's like being at sea in a small boat.

The Redwood Highway, Route 101, leads north to the tallest, most dense stands of *Sequoia sempervirens*. At **Richardson Grove State Park** the road barrels through the very center of a magnificent grove. A short nature trail leads through this virgin timber, though the proximity of the road makes communing with nature seem a bit ludicrous.

SIGHTS

North of Garberville, follow the **Avenue of the Giants**, a 33-mile alternative route which parallels Route 101. This two-lane road winds along the Eel River south fork, tunneling through dense redwood groves. Much of the road is encompassed by **Humboldt Redwoods State Park**, a 52,000-acre preserve with some of the finest forest land found anywhere. Park headquarters contains a nice visitors center. ~ 707-946-2409.

Farther along is **Founder's Grove**, where a nature trail loops through a redwood stand. The forest is dedicated to early Save-the-Redwoods League leaders who were instrumental in preserving thousands of redwood acres, particularly in this park. Nearby **Rockefeller Forest** has another short loop trail that winds through a redwood grove. Avenue of the Giants continues through towns that are little more than way stations and then rejoins Route 101, which leads north to Eureka.

THE LOST COAST   There are alternate routes to Eureka, however, leading along the perimeter of California's **Lost Coast** re-

◀ *HIDDEN*

gion. One of the state's most remote wilderness areas, it is a tumbling region of extraordinary vistas. Here the King Range, with its sliding talus and impassable cliffs, shoots 4087 feet up from the ocean in less than three miles. No road could ever rest along its shoulder. The place has been left primitive, given over to mink, deer, river otter, and black bear; rare bald eagles and peregrine falcons work its slopes.

To get away from it all, head out along the Lost Coast, where the 4000-foot King Range has created a shoreline wilderness. Amenities are rare, but you will find a collection of clapboard cottages back up in the mountains.

The range extends about 35 miles. Along the shore is a wilderness beach from which seals, sea lions, and porpoises, as well as gray and killer whales, can be seen. There is also an abandoned lighthouse and the skeletons of ships wrecked on the rocks.

To reach this remote area, from Route 101 near Redway take Briceland–Thorne Road, which turns into Shelter Cove Road as it winds through the King Range.

Shelter Cove is a tiny bay neatly folded between sea cliffs and headlands. A point of embarkation for people exploring the Lost Coast, it has a few stores, restaurants, and hotels. Stock up here: The rest of this backcountry jaunt promises little more than a couple stores.

Outside Shelter Cove you can pick up Kings Peak Road or Ettersburg–Honeydew Road, which connect with Wilder Ridge Road and lead to the general store town of **Honeydew**. This is a prime marijuana growing region and a colony of hippies is bound to be sitting on the stoop swapping tales.

HIDDEN ►

Mattole Road heads northeast, meandering along the Mattole River, to another forest hamlet, **Petrolia**. Nestled in a river valley and marked by a white-steeple church, the town is a scene straight from a Norman Rockwell painting. Hawks glide overhead. Old men rock on their front porches.

Next, Mattole Road ascends a succession of plateaus to a ranch land of unpainted barns and broad shade trees, then noses down to the coastline and parallels the waves for perhaps five miles. Here the setting is Scottish. Hillsides are grazed by herds of sheep and covered with tenacious grasses that shake in the sea wind. The gray sand beach is covered with driftwood. Along the horizon peaks rise in jagged motions, seemingly thrust upward by the lash of the surf.

It's not far to **Cape Mendocino**, second-most westerly point in the contiguous United States. Here you'll have broad views of the ocean, including the malevolent shoals where countless ships have been slapped to timber. Next, the road curves up through forest and sheep-grazing lands before rolling down to the gentle pastureland near the unique town of Ferndale.

A Victorian-style hamlet set in the Eel River valley, **Ferndale** is so perfectly refurbished it seems unreal. Main Street and nearby thoroughfares are lined with Gothic Revival, Queen Anne, Eastlake, and Italianate-style Victorians, brightly painted and blooming with pride. Tragedy struck this picturesque town in 1992 when a 6.9-level earthquake and several powerful aftershocks rocked the entire area. Since then local residents have devotedly rebuilt the quaint Main Street district, with its boutiques and gift shops, and other affected neighborhoods. The film *Outbreak*, starring Dustin Hoffman, was shot in Ferndale.

The best way to see the town is by stopping first at the **Ferndale Museum**. Here is an ever-changing collection of antiques and memorabilia from the region, plus an old blacksmith shop. There are sometimes maps available for self-guided walking tours of this historic community. It's an architectural wonder that shouldn't be missed. Closed Monday during summer and Monday and Tuesday during winter. Admission. ~ 515 Shaw Avenue, Ferndale; 707-786-4466.

EUREKA   Eureka's 28,600 inhabitants make it the largest town on the Northern California coast. Founded in 1850, the town's first industry was mining; the name "Eureka!" came from an old gold mining exclamation meaning "I found it."

Today fishing and lumbering have replaced more romantic occupations, but much of the region's history is captured in points of interest. Stop at the **Greater Eureka Chamber of Commerce** on the way into town for maps and brochures. Closed Sunday in winter. ~ 2112 Broadway, Eureka; 707-442-3738, 800-356-6381.

Make certain to ask at the Chamber of Commerce for the **architectural tour** map. Eureka has over 100 glorious Victorian homes ranging from understated designs to the outlandish **Carson Mansion**, a multilayered confection that makes other Gothic architecture seem tame. It was built in the 1880s by William Carson, a wealthy lumber merchant with the same need for ostentation that afflicted the robber barons on San Francisco's Nob Hill. The Carson Mansion is a private club, so you can't enter, but you can drive by and view its distinctive architecture. ~ 2nd and M streets, Eureka; 707-443-5665.

Don't miss **Clarke Memorial Museum**, with its outstanding collection of California American Indian artifacts. Here are ornate baskets, feather regalia, fur quivers, beaded moccasins, war clubs, an extensive collection of woven hats, and a dugout redwood canoe. It provides a unique insight into this splendid Humboldt Bay region before the age of gold pans and axe handles. The museum's Victorian section focuses on more recent history. Closed January. Open Tuesday through Saturday from noon until 4 p.m. ~ 240 E Street, Eureka; 707-443-1947.

HIDDEN ▶

Of a more subdued nature are the **covered bridges** on the southern outskirts of town. To reach them from Route 101, take Elk River Road two miles to Berta Road or three miles to Janes Road (there is a wooden span covering both). You'll enter a picture of red barns and green pasture framed by cool, lofty forest. The bridges, crossing a small river, evoke Vermont winters and New Hampshire sleigh rides.

Fort Humboldt is stationed at this end of town. Built in the early 1850s to help settlers war against indigenous tribes of Yurok, Hoopa, Wiyot, and Mattole Indians, it has been partially restored. In addition to re-creating army life (experienced here by a hard-drinking young officer named Ulysses S. Grant), the historic park displays early logging traditions. There's a drafty logger's cabin, a small lumber industry museum, a military museum displaying army artifacts, and a couple of remarkable old steam engines. In winter, the military museum is open only on weekends. ~ 3431 Fort Avenue, Eureka; 707-445-6567.

Nearby **Sequoia Park** provides a nifty retreat from urban life. Tucked into its 52-acre preserve is a petting zoo (closed Monday), picnic area, playground, and a thick stand of redwoods. ~ W Street between Glatt and Madrone streets, Eureka.

Then head to **Old Town**, Eureka's answer to the nation's gentrification craze. This neighborhood was formerly the local bowery; the term "skid row" reputedly originated right here. It derived from the bums residing beside the nearby "skid roads," along which redwood logs were transported to the waterfront. Now the ghetto is gilded: old Victorians, woodframe warehouses, brick buildings, and clapboard houses have been rebuilt and painted striking colors. Stylish shops have sprung up and restaurants have opened.

At the foot of C Street in Old Town, where the bowery meets the bay, the **Humboldt Bay Harbor Cruise** departs. For several well-invested dollars, you'll sail past an egret rookery, oyster beds, pelican roosts, hideous pulp mills, and the town's flashy marina. The cruises are weather-dependent; always call ahead. ~ Eureka; 707-445-1910.

If you're a landlubber, however, and prefer a shoreside tour of Eureka, you can always take a horse-and-buggy ride around town. The **Old Town Carriage Company** has a turn-of-the-century reproduction carriage pulled by a massive draft horse. ~ 2nd and F streets at the gazebo, Eureka; 707-445-1610.

Heading north from Eureka there are two towns worth noting. **Arcata**, home of Humboldt State University, is a student town with an outstanding collection of old Victorians. For a self-guided architectural tour, obtain a map at the **Arcata Chamber of Commerce**. Closed Sunday. ~ 1062 G Street, Arcata; 707-822-3619.

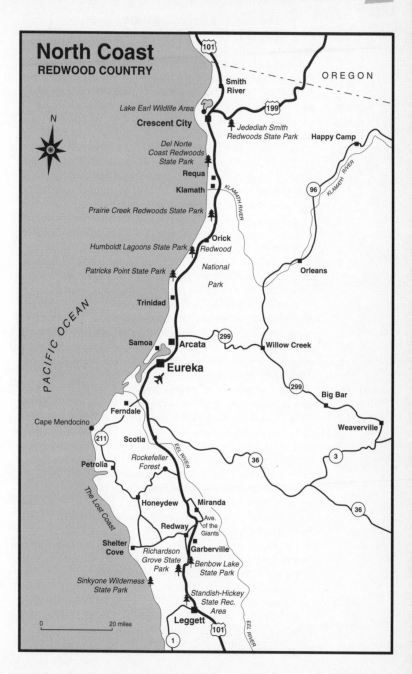

North Coast
REDWOOD COUNTRY

OREGON

Smith River

Lake Earl Wildlife Area

Crescent City

Jedediah Smith Redwoods State Park

Happy Camp

Del Norte Coast Redwoods State Park

Requa

Klamath

KLAMATH RIVER

Prairie Creek Redwoods State Park

Orleans

Orick

Redwood

National

Park

Humboldt Lagoons State Park

Patricks Point State Park

Trinidad

Willow Creek

Samoa

Arcata

Eureka

Big Bar

Ferndale

Cape Mendocino

Weaverville

Scotia

Rockefeller Forest

EEL RIVER

Petrolia

Honeydew

Miranda

The Lost Coast

Redway

Ave. of the Giants

Shelter Cove

Richardson Grove State Park

Garberville

Benbow Lake State Park

Sinkyone Wilderness State Park

Standish-Hickey State Rec. Area

EEL RIVER

0   20 miles

Leggett

PACIFIC OCEAN

Trinidad, one of the area's oldest towns, perches above a small port. Sea stacks and sailboats lie anchored offshore, watched over by a miniature lighthouse. For a tour of the pocket beaches and rocky shores lining this beautiful waterfront, take a three-mile trip south from town along Scenic Drive.

Next is **Redwood National Park**, a fitting finale to this lengthy coastal journey. Park of parks, it's a necklace strung for over 33 miles along the coast. Among its gems are secluded beaches, elk herds, and the world's tallest tree.

First link in the chain is the **Redwood Information Center**. ~ 119231 Route 101, Orick; 707-464-6101 ext. 5265. In addition to information, the center issues permits for **Tall Trees Grove**. A one- and-one-quarter-mile hike leads to a redwood stand boasting the loftiest of all California's redwoods, including a 365-foot giant—the tallest tree in the world. **Lady Bird Johnson Grove**, off Bald Hill Road on a one-mile trail, has another dense cluster of ancient trees.

Another side road, Davison Road (day-use fee), leads along remote **Gold Bluffs Beach** eight miles to Fern Canyon. Here angular walls 50 feet high are covered with rioting vegetation.

Redwood National Park encompasses three state parks—Prairie Creek Redwoods, Del Norte Redwoods, and Jedediah Smith Redwoods. Just after the main entrance to the first you'll pass **Elk Prairie**, where herds of Roosevelt elk graze across open meadows. Immediately past the entrance, Cal Barrel Road, another short detour, courses through dense redwood forest.

HIDDEN ► Also plan to turn off onto **Coastal Drive**, a gravel road paralleling Route 101. Its numerous turnouts expose extraordinary ocean vistas. The road snakes high above the coast before emptying onto the main highway near the mouth of the Klamath River.

The Del Norte section of the park reveals more startling sea views en route to Crescent City, where the **main park headquarters** is located. ~ 1111 2nd Street, Crescent City; 707-464-6101. Also try the **Crescent City—Del Norte County Chamber of Commerce** building across the street for park information. Closed Saturday and Sunday from Labor Day to Memorial Day. ~ 1001 Front Street, Crescent City; 707-464-3174.

Perched on a rocky island off Route 101 in Crescent City is **Battery Point Lighthouse**, an 1856 stone and masonry structure that is one of the best preserved original lighthouses on the Pacific Coast. At low tide from April through September visitors can walk across a spit of sand and rock to the lighthouse for tours of the lantern room and a small museum. Closed Monday and Tuesday. Closed October through March. Admission. ~ Crescent City; 707-464-3089.

Woodlands, wetlands, grasslands—you'll find them all at **Lake Earl Wildlife Area**. This preserve also offers secluded sand dunes and a sufficient number of bird species, 260 at last count, to make it look like it was created by the Audubon Society. One of the finest birdwatching spots on the North Coast, this Pacific Flyway destination is the place to see hawks, falcons, bald eagles, Canada geese, and canvasback ducks. ~ Old Mill Road, three miles north of Crescent City; 707-464-2523.

Route 101 north to Route 199 leads to the park's Jedediah Smith section with its mountain vistas and thick redwood groves. The Smith River, rich in salmon and steelhead, threads through the region. For further details on this remote area check with the **Hiouchi Information Center**. Closed from Labor Day to June 21. ~ On Route 199, 4 miles east of Route 101; 707-464-6101 ext. 5067.

One of Northern California's finest old lodges is the imposing, Tudor-style **Benbow Inn**. Located astride the Eel River, this regal retreat is bounded by lawns, gardens, and umbrella-tabled patios. The structure itself is a bold three-story manor in the English country tradition. The lobby, paneled in carved wood and adorned by ornamental molding, is a sumptuous sitting area with a grand fireplace. Jigsaw puzzles lie scattered on the clawfoot tables and rocking horses decorate the room. The dining area and lounge are equally elegant. Guest quarters offer such flourishes as quilted beds with wooden headboards, hand-painted doors, marble topped period wallprints, nightstands, and complimentary sherry. Visitors also enjoy tea and scones in the afternoon and hors d'oeuvres in the evening. The inn is closed from January 1 to mid-April. ~ 445 Lake Benbow Drive, Garberville; 707-923-2124, 800-355-3301, fax 707-923-2122. DELUXE TO ULTRA-DELUXE.

LODGING

The cheapest lodging I've found in the southern redwoods area is **Johnston's Motel**. Unlike the region's big-tag caravansaries, this 14-unit facility has rooms at budget prices. Don't expect a lot of shine. The plain rooms are small, display scarred furniture, and lack any decoration along the cinderblock walls. But they do have wall-to-wall carpeting and stall showers. ~ 839 Redwood Drive, Garberville; 707-923-3327. BUDGET.

Not that I have anything against Johnston's; it's just that Garberville is not my idea of paradise. For a few well-spent dollars more you can rent a comfortable room in any of several motels along the redwood-lined Avenue of the Giants. **Miranda Gardens Resort** is a good choice. This 16-unit resort offers guest rooms with kitchens and fully equipped cabins, as well as a heated swimming pool, a playground, and market. The facilities are tucked into a redwood grove and the rooms are partially paneled in redwood. ~ 6766 Avenue of the Giants, Miranda; 707-943-3011, fax 707-943-3584. MODERATE TO DELUXE.

The predominant business in Redwood Country is the lumber industry, which casts a lengthy shadow in surrounding towns like Scotia. Here the 1920s-era **Scotia Inn** lavishly displays the region's product in a redwood-paneled lobby. Antique furnishings decorate this sprawling hotel, which boasts a fashionable restaurant and lounge. The guest rooms are furnished in oak and adorned with armoires, brass lamps, and silk wallpaper. The bathrooms, not to be upstaged, boast brass fixtures, clawfoot tubs, and medicine cabinets of carved wood. A gem. ~ Main and Mill streets, Scotia; 707-764-5683, fax 707-764-1707. MODERATE TO ULTRA-DELUXE.

HIDDEN ► Way out in Shelter Cove, at the southern end of California's remote Lost Coast, there's the **Shelter Cove Beachcomber Inn**. A rare find, the inn rests near a bluff overlooking the ocean and consists of three houses with six units. The rooms are stylishly furnished and appointed in smart fashion. Three come with kitchens and wood-burning stoves; all seem to be lovingly cared for. All come with barbecue grills and patios. Considering that the price tag on this luxury is reasonable and that Shelter Cove is one of the coast's most secluded hideaways, the Beachcomber Inn is well worth the effort. ~ 7272 Shelter Cove Road, Shelter Cove; 707-986-7733, 800-718-4789, fax 707-986-7551. BUDGET TO MODERATE.

HIDDEN ► **Mattole River Resort** offers full-facility cottages complete with kitchenettes. Each is plain but comfortably furnished and features a sitting room and a bedroom. This rustic colony sits amid shade trees and is backdropped by thickly forested hills. ~ 42354 Mattole Road, Petrolia; 707-629-3445, 800-845-4607, fax 707-629-3494. BUDGET TO MODERATE.

The cheapest lodging of all is in the neon motels along Route 101 on the outskirts of Eureka. Many advertise room rates on highway signs along the southern entrance to town. **Sunrise Inn and Suites** is perhaps the best of these. Because it is centrally located, guests can walk to Old Town and other points of interest. The rooms are simple but very clean, with carpeting and king or queen beds. Nearly half have jacuzzi tubs. ~ 129 4th Street, Eureka; phone/fax 707-443-9751. BUDGET.

For country inn sensibility in an urban environment, **Old Town Bed & Breakfast Inn** comes highly recommended. Just a couple blocks from Eureka's fabled Carson Mansion, this six-bedroom house dates from 1871. It's a Greek Revival structure with a winding staircase and a wealth of antiques. Plushly carpeted and adorned with patterned wallpaper, the house has been beautifully redecorated. The cost includes a hot tub and a full country-style breakfast. A five percent discount is offered if you pay with cash, checks, money orders, or traveler's checks. ~ 1521 3rd Street, Eureka; 707-445-3951, 800-331-5098, fax 707-268-0231. MODERATE TO DELUXE.

Another of Eureka's spectacular bed and breakfasts is **Carter House**, one of the finest Victorians I've ever seen. This grand old four-story house is painted in light hues and decorated with contemporary artwork, lending an airy quality seldom found in vintage homes. The place is beautiful: light streams through bay windows; oriental rugs are scattered across hardwood floors; there are sumptuous sitting rooms, and oak banisters that seemingly climb forever. In the seven rooms are antique nightstands and armoires, beds with bold wooden headboards, ceramic pieces, and knickknacks. Rates include a full breakfast, complimentary wine, and cookies before bedtime. ~ 301 L Street, Eureka; 707-445-1390, 800-404-1390, fax 707-444-8067. ULTRA-DELUXE.

Mark and Christi Carter added the 23-room **Hotel Carter** to their lodging empire a few years ago. Its pale pine furniture and peach-colored walls offer a refreshing counterpoint to the Carter House across the street. Accommodations are quite spacious; some have fireplaces and whirlpool baths. Complimentary breakfast is served in the ground floor dining room, where colorful dhurrie rugs and crystal candleholders add an elegant touch. ~ 301 L Street, Eureka; 707-444-8062, 800-404-1390, fax 707-444-8067. DELUXE TO ULTRA-DELUXE.

For traditional and stylish lodging, also consider **Eureka Inn**. Set in an imposing Tudor-gabled building near Eureka's Old Town section, it provides excellent accommodations. There's a wood-beamed lobby with large fireplace and comfortable sitting area, a pool, jacuzzi and sauna, plus a café, gourmet restaurant, and piano bar. Built in 1922 and registered as a National Historic Landmark, this huge hotel has 104 guest rooms. These are well appointed and attractively decorated. ~ 7th and F streets, Eureka; 707-442-6441, 800-862-4906, fax 707-442-0637. MODERATE TO ULTRA-DELUXE.

In 1888, a Eureka newspaper reporter called the newly built mayor's home, **"Abigail's Elegant Victorian Mansion,"** now the title of the bed and breakfast that occupies this National Historic Landmark. The lavishly ornate three-room residence is one of the most photographed gingerbread-style houses in Eureka. Lush lawns and colorful flower gardens fill the surrounding property. The interior is furnished with antiques to complete the Victorian feel. A multicourse French gourmet breakfast is served to guests every morning. An architectural tour of Eureka, bicycle rentals, use of the croquet field, and occasional silent movies are gratis as well. ~ 1406 C Street, Eureka; 707-444-3144, fax 707-442-5594; www.bbchannel.com/bbc/p214341.ASP. DELUXE TO ULTRA-DELUXE.

For an extra dash of history in your nightly brew, there's the **Shaw House Bed and Breakfast** in nearby Ferndale. It's only fitting to this bed and breakfast that Ferndale is an island in time where the Victorian era still obtains. The Shaw House, built in 1854 is the oldest home in town and is on the National Historic Register. A Carpenter Gothic creation, it was modeled on Hawthorne's *House of the Seven Gables*. A library, two parlors, dining room, and balconies are available to guests, and the home is furnished throughout with precious antiques. All rooms have private baths. ~ 703 Main Street, Ferndale; mailing address: P.O. Box 1125, Ferndale, CA 95535; phone/fax 707-786-9958, 800-557-7429; e-mail shawhse@humboldt1.com. MODERATE TO DELUXE.

In a town chockablock with precious Victorians, one of the most precious of all is **The Gingerbread Mansion**. Turrets and gables, an intimate garden, interesting antiques, and a delicious homemade breakfast are among the features; but what you'll find particularly special about this bed and breakfast are the bathrooms. One has mirrored ceilings and walls; another, his-and-hers clawfoot tubs set near a tiled gas fireplace. The 11 distinct accommodations are comfortably cozy. ~ 400 Berding Street, Ferndale; 707-786-4000, 800-952-4136, fax 707-786-4381. DELUXE TO ULTRA-DELUXE.

Arcata Crew House Hostel provides lodging at inexpensive prices. One of the more commodious hostels, it has several private and double rooms; no room contains more than five sleepers. Varying from similar set-ups, the Crew House permits couples to stay together. Situated in two adjacent houses, the place features a wood-paneled living room with brick fireplace, dining room, yard, and kitchen. Open only in summer (late June to late August). ~ 1390 I Street, Arcata; 707-822-9995. BUDGET.

Set in a quiet residential neighborhood within walking distance of downtown, the **Lady Anne** has five rooms in a 1888 Queen Anne–style home. Each is appointed with antiques. One has a wood-burning stove. You can sit on the porch or in a chair in the front yard and watch the world go by, or play the grand piano and guitars in one of the inn's two parlors. ~ 902 14th Street, Arcata; 707-822-2797. DELUXE.

You will be hard pressed anywhere along the coast to find a view more alluring than that of **Trinidad Bay Bed & Breakfast**. This New England–style shingle house, set in a tiny coastal town, looks across Trinidad Bay, past fishing boats and sea rocks, seals and sandy beaches, to tree-covered headlands. The four country-style rooms are equipped with standard furnishings and painted soft colors. Two of the rooms are suites that come with a delivered breakfast. There is a fireplace and a dining room for guests to share. Closed December and January. ~ Corner of Edwards and Trinity streets, Trinidad; 707-677-0840. DELUXE TO ULTRA-DELUXE.

Redwood AYH Hostel, set in an 1890-era ranch house, provides basic accommodations for singles and couples alike. It's across the highway from a beach and features a laundry room, kitchen facilities, and a common room. ~ 14480 Route 101 at Wilson Creek Road, Klamath; 707-482-8265, fax 707-482-4665. BUDGET.

Farther north in Crescent City, along the scimitar strand that gave the town its name, is **Crescent Beach Motel.** This 27-unit motel has plate-glass views of the ocean. Rooms are small but newly decorated with oak furniture and a blue-green color scheme. They have new carpets, TVs, and most of the rooms have those oh-so-priceless sea vistas. ~ 1455 Route 101, Crescent City; 707-464-5436. MODERATE.

Personally, my favorite dining place in these parts is the **Benbow Inn.** This Tudor lodge serves meals in a glorious wood-paneled dining room that will make you feel as though you're feasting at the estate of a British baron. New hardwood floors compliment the redwood walls, and the multipane windows look out upon landscaped gardens. Every evening the bill of fare includes rack of lamb, fresh pasta, pork loin, and filet mignon. There is also salmon, duck, chicken, and trout amandine. Closed from January to mid-April. ~ 445 Lake Benbow Drive, Garberville; 707-923-2124. MODERATE TO DELUXE.

DINING

In the southern redwoods region you'll be hard pressed to find a better restaurant than **Woodrose Café.** T'aint much on looks—just a counter, a few tables and chairs, and a small patio out back. But the kitchen folk cook up some potent concoctions. That's why the place draws locals in droves. The breakfast menu offers buckwheat pancakes, lox and bagels, and spinach and feta cheese omelettes. At lunch they make homemade soups, organic salads, sandwiches, and tofu burgers; no dinner served. The Woodrose Café is a good reason to visit otherwise drab Garberville. No lunch on Saturday and Sunday. ~ 911 Redwood Drive, Garberville; 707-923-3191. BUDGET.

Proceeding north along the Avenue of the Giants, you will encounter cafés in tiny towns like Miranda, Myers Flat, Weott, and Pepperwood. Most are tourist-oriented businesses, adequate as way stations, but undistinguished and slightly overpriced.

For a touch of good taste in the heart of Redwood Country try the **Scotia Inn.** The dining room of this revered old hotel is trimly paneled in polished redwood, furnished with captain's chairs, and illuminated by brass chandeliers. It features a menu with fresh fish dishes, tenderloin of elk, pheasant, oysters, prime rib, steak, and special "ethnic theme dishes" on Sundays. No dinner on Monday and Tuesday. ~ Main and Mill streets, Scotia; 707-764-5683. MODERATE TO DELUXE.

The historic Old Town section of Eureka, a refurbished neighborhood of stately Victorians, supports several good restaurants. At **Tomaso's Tomato Pies** they serve pizzas as well as spinach pie and sausage sandwiches. That's at lunch. Come dinner they add calzone, lasagna, ravioli, cannelloni, scampi, grilled halibut, and a host of other Italian dishes. Excellent food. No lunch on Sunday. ~ 216 E Street, Eureka; 707-445-0100. MODERATE.

A meal at the **Sea Grill** is a chance to enjoy fine dining in a historic 1876 storefront. The place has an airy Victorian feel about it, with lots of peachy pastels, fabric drapes, raised wallpaper, and an antique mahogany bar. Oil paintings by local artists add to the atmosphere. Chicken, steak, and seafood dishes are the specialties here. Lunch Tuesday through Friday. Closed Sunday. ~ 316 E Street, Eureka; 707-443-7187. MODERATE.

For Asian fare there's **Samurai Restaurant**, a simple dining room appointed with Japanese antiques and folk art. The menu includes seafood, standard sukiyaki, tempura, sushi, and teriyaki dishes, plus a "Shogun's Feast" featuring marinated shrimp and beef. You can also try the "Treasure Ship," a sampler of five different entrées. Dinner only. Closed Sunday and Monday. ~ 621 5th Street, Eureka; 707-442-6802. MODERATE.

For a seafood dinner in a historic setting, one place stands above anything else. **Bracco's**, a sprawling restaurant, features shrimp and scallops prepared in a variety of ways. There's also grilled halibut and broiled salmon. The meat menu is limited to steak, lamb and chicken. Closed Monday and Tuesday. ~ 327 2nd Street, Eureka; 707-443-9717. MODERATE TO DELUXE.

HIDDEN ►

For a dining experience lumberjack-style, there's **Samoa Cookhouse** just outside Eureka. A local lumber company has opened its chow house to the public, serving three meals daily. Just join the crowd piling into this unassuming eatery, sit down at a school cafeteria–style table and dig in. You'll be served redwood-size portions of soup, salad, meat, potatoes, vegetables, and dessert—you can even ask for seconds. Ask for water and they'll plunk down a cold pitcher, order coffee and someone will bring a pot. It's noisy, hectic, crowded and great fun. Reduced rates for kids and seniors. ~ Samoa Road, Samoa; 707-442-1659. MODERATE.

The **Seascape Restaurant** is small and unassuming. There are only about three dozen tables and booths at this seafood dining room. But the walls of plate glass gaze out upon a rocky headland and expansive bay. Situated at the foot of Trinidad Pier, the local eating spot overlooks the town's tiny fishing fleet. The dishes, many drawn from surrounding waters, include halibut, rock cod, salmon, crab, and shrimp. Landlubbers can also dine on filet mignon. Lunch and breakfast menus are equally inviting. ~ Trinidad Pier, Trinidad; 707-677-3762. MODERATE TO DELUXE.

From Trinidad to the Oregon border the countryside is sparsely populated. Crescent City is the only town of real size, but you'll find nondescript cafés in such places as Orick, Klamath, and Smith River.

Crescent City—like the entire North Coast—is seafood country. Best place around is **Harbor View Grotto**, a family restaurant with an ocean view. This plate-glass eatery features a long inventory of ocean dishes—whole clams, fried prawns or oysters, scallops, red snapper, salmon, cod, halibut, and so on, not to mention the seafood salads and shrimp cocktails. There are also a few meat, chicken and pasta dishes plus an assortment of sandwiches. Worth a stop. ~ 150 Starfish Way, Crescent City; 707-464-3815. MODERATE.

SHOPPING

In Ferndale, a picturesque Victorian town south of Eureka, there's a covey of intriguing shops. The community has attracted a number of artisans, many of whom display their wares in the 19th- and early-20th-century stores lining Main Street. There are shops selling needlework, stained glass, and kinetic sculptures; others deal in ironwork, used books, and handknits. There are even stores specializing in "paper treasures," boots and saddles, dolls, and "nostalgic gifts." All are contained along a three-block section that more resembles a living museum than a downtown shopping district.

Eureka, too, has been gentrified. Most of the refurbishing has occurred in Old Town, where stately Victorians, falsefront stores, and tumbledown buildings have been transformed into sparkling shops. Window browse down 2nd and 3rd streets from C Street to H Street and you're bound to find several inviting establishments. Of particular interest is **Imperiale Square**, a quaint open-air courtyard housing several shops. ~ 320 2nd Street, Eureka. Be sure to visit **Humboldt Arts Council Gallery**, with its displays of the work of North Coast artists. ~ 636 F Street, Eureka; 707-442-0278.

NIGHTLIFE

Now don't misunderstand—California's northern coast and redwood region are wild and provocative places. It's just that the word "wild" up here is taken in the literal sense, as in wilderness and wildlife. Somehow the urban meaning of crazy nights and endless parties was never fully translated.

The **Benbow Inn** features a fine old lounge with carved walls and an ornate fireplace. A pianist plays on weekends, adding to the intimacy. Closed from January to mid-April. ~ 445 Lake Benbow Drive, Garberville; 707-923-2124.

Entertaining for almost three decades, the **Ferndale Repertory Theater** puts on a variety of plays and musicals year-round in an old movie theater. ~ 447 Main Street, Ferndale; 707-786-5483.

There's rock, blues, and reggae live at **Jambalaya**. This college town bar has a dancefloor and down-home crowd. The bands are local or national and the scene is loose. Cover. ~ 915 H Street, Arcata; 707-822-4766.

BEACHES & PARKS

HIDDEN ►

THE "LOST COAST" 🚶🚴🐎⛵🏊🎣🚤🛥⚓ California's coastal Route 1 is one of the greatest highways in America. Beginning in Southern California, it sweeps north through Big Sur, Carmel, San Francisco, and Mendocino, past ocean scenery indescribably beautiful. Then it disappears. At the foot of Redwood Country, Route 1 quits the coast and turns into Route 101.

The region it never reaches is California's fabled "Lost Coast." Most of the region is now protected as the King Range National Conservation Area. Three major trails traverse it: King Crest Trail, which climbs the main coastal ridge for 10.5 miles, with views of the ocean and Eel River Valley; the five-mile-long Chemise Mountain trail; and the 25-mile-long Lost Coast Trail along the King Range. There is also hiking along the wilderness beach.

Keep in mind that the Lost Coast is a wilderness area and not a heavily-monitored state park. Hikers and campers need to bring water or water purifiers, sturdy hiking boots, and insect repellent. If you want to hike the beach, use a tide table; hikers often get trapped for hours by the tides. Mountain bikers should stick to the area east of King Range.

The parking lot at Black Sands Beach was washed away in February 1998, making the beach inaccessible to off-highway vehicles.

One of the wettest areas along the Pacific Coast, King Range gets about 100 inches of rain a year. The precipitation is particularly heavy from October to April. Summer carries cool coastal fog and some rain. Weather permitting, it's a fascinating region to explore—wild and virgin, with the shellmounds of American Indians who inhabited the area over a century ago still scattered on the beach.

Motels, restaurants, groceries, and boat rentals are available in Shelter Cove, at the south end of the Conservation Area. ~ From Garberville on Route 101, a road leads to nearby Redway and then southwest to Shelter Cove. About 15 miles down this road, Kings Peak Road forks northwest, paralleling the Conservation Area, to Ettersberg and Honeydew. Just before Kings Peak Road, Chemise Mountain Road turns off into Nadelos and Wailaki campgrounds. For information contact the Resource Area Office, U.S. Bureau of Land Management, 1695 Heindon Road, Arcata, CA 95521; 707-825-2300.

▲ There are numerous campgrounds for tents and RVs (most sites have no hookups); Wailaki is for RVs and tents, Nadelos is for tents only. Fees range from free to $7 per night.

SINKYONE WILDERNESS STATE PARK 🚶 🐎 🛶 This 7500-acre park below the southern tip of the King Range is known for the narrow and steep winding roads leading to its interior. For this reason trailers and RVs are discouraged from entering the park—especially since there are no RV facilities. Featuring old growth redwood groves and clear-cut prairies, the park hugs the southern section of the Lost Coast. The ranch house and visitors center are a mere 200 yards from awe-inspiring bluffs. Other facilities include picnic tables and pit toilets. Day-use, $3. ~ Located 30 miles west of Redway on Briceland Road or 50 miles north of Fort Bragg on County Road 431; 707-986-7711.

▲ There are 35 drive-in sites at Usal Beach and 17 hike-in sites at Needle Rock for tents only; $11 per night. All of the north end sites are hike-in only.

STANDISH-HICKEY STATE RECREATION AREA 🚶 🏊 ✈ 🛶 Near the southern edge of Redwood Country, this 1500-acre park primarily consists of second-growth trees. The single exception is a 1200-year-old giant named after the Mayflower pilgrim, Captain Miles Standish. The forest here also has Douglas fir, oak, and maple trees. The south fork of the Eel River courses through the area, providing swimming holes and catch-and-release fishing spots. Facilities are picnic areas, restrooms, and showers. Day-use fee, $5. ~ Located along Route 101 two miles north of Leggett; 707-925-6482.

▲ There are 162 tent/RV sites (no hookups); $16 per night. For reservations call PARKNET at 800-444-7275.

RICHARDSON GROVE STATE PARK 🚶 🚴 🏊 ✈ 🛶 The first of the virgin redwood parks, this 1500-acre facility features a grove of goliaths. For some bizarre reason the highway builders chose to put the main road through the heart of the forest. This means you won't miss the redwoods, but to really appreciate them you'll have to disappear down one of the three hiking trails that loop through the grove. The south fork of the Eel River flows through the park, providing swimming and trout fishing opportunities. In summer there are nightly campfires and kids' programs. The park has an information center, a grocery, a snack bar, gift shop, picnic areas, restrooms, and showers. Day-use fee, $5. ~ Located about 18 miles north of Leggett along Route 101; 707-247-3318.

▲ There are 176 sites for tents and RVs (no hookups); $12 to $16 per night. For reservations call PARKNET at 800-444-7275.

BENBOW LAKE STATE RECREATION AREA

One of the less desirable parks in the area, this facility fronts the Eel River near the dam that creates Benbow Lake. The lake is usually full and suitable for boating from July 1 through mid-September; it's a good idea to call first. Motorized boats are not allowed. Route 101 streams through the park's center, disrupting an otherwise idyllic scene. Nevertheless, there's good swimming and fishing in the river-lake. In the summer there are nightly campfires and kids' programs. There are picnic areas, restrooms, and showers. Day-use fee, $5. ~ Located about 23 miles north of Leggett along Route 101; 707-923-3238.

▲ There are 75 sites for tents and RVs (no hookups) along the river; $12 to $16 per night. For reservations call PARKNET at 800-444-7275.

HUMBOLDT REDWOODS STATE PARK

One of the state's great parks, it is set within a 20-million-year-old forest. The park is a tribute to early conservationists who battled lumber interests in an effort to save the area's extraordinary trees. Today 100 miles of hiking trails lead through redwood groves and along the south fork of the Eel River. Within the park's 35-mile length there are also opportunities for swimming, biking, horseback riding (you must provide your own horses), fishing, or tree gazing. Facilities include an information center, picnic areas, restrooms, and showers; restaurants and groceries are in small towns within the park. Day-use fee, $5. ~ Located along the Avenue of the Giants between Miranda and Pepperwood; 707-946-2409.

▲ There are three different campgrounds (one in winter) with a total of 249 sites for tents and RVs (no hookups); $12 to $16 per night. (The best, most private sites are, appropriately enough, at Hidden Springs Campground.) For reservations call PARKNET at 800-444-7275.

CLAM BEACH COUNTY PARK

There's a broad expanse of beach here with good views of surrounding headlands, but this place is best known for its clams. Low tides and early mornings bring local people out to dig for razor clams, sweet and fleshy mollusks that can be baked, sautéed, or eaten raw. If interested, you'll need a state license. Horseback riders must provide their own horses. There's a picnic area and toilets. ~ Along Route 101 about 15 miles north of Eureka; 707-445-7652.

▲ There is a number of open ground sites here for tents and RVs (no hookups); $8 per night. No reservations accepted.

PATRICK'S POINT STATE PARK

This 650-acre park is particularly known for Agate Beach, a long crescent backdropped by wooded headlands. Here it's possible to gather not only driftwood but semiprecious agate, jasper, and black jade. There are tidepools to explore, sea lions and seals offshore, and several miles of hiking trails. Bikers enjoy tooling around on the paved roads. Leave Fido at home—dogs aren't allowed on the beach or trails. It's one-third of a mile from the main parking area. The facilities include picnic areas, restrooms, and showers. Day-use fee, $5. ~ It's off Route 101 about 25 miles north of Eureka; 707-677-3570.

▲ There are 124 sites for tents and RVs (no hookups); $12 to $16 per night. Reservations are recommended in the summer; call PARKNET at 800-444-7275.

HUMBOLDT LAGOONS STATE PARK

A 2000-acre facility, this beach park is full of surprises. The main entrance leads to a sandy beach tucked between rocky outcroppings and heaped with driftwood. Behind the beach an old lagoon has slowly transformed into a marsh of brackish water. Add the two areas together and you come up with a splendid park. Catch and release fishing at Stone Lagoon is good for cutthroat trout. Toilets and a visitors center are the only facilities. ~ Off Route 101 about 31 miles north of Eureka; 707-488-2041.

▲ There are 12 hike-in and boat-in sites; $7 per night.

REDWOOD NATIONAL AND STATE PARKS

Actually four parks in one, this 105,516-acre giant encompasses Prairie Creek Redwoods, Del Norte Coast Redwoods, Jedediah Smith Redwoods state parks and Redwood National Park. The park stretches over 33 miles along the coast from Orick to the Crescent City region. Within that span, one of California's wettest areas (69 inches of rain yearly in Del Norte), are hidden beaches, ocean cliffs, deep redwood forests, and miles of hiking trails.

Along the coast are wind-scoured bluffs and gently sloping hills. The beaches range from sandy to rocky; because of the rugged terrain in certain areas, some are inaccessible. In addition to beaches, many streams—including Prairie Creek, Redwood Creek, Klamath River, Mill Creek, and the Smith River—traverse this series of parks.

Hikers and redwood lovers will find that several spectacular groves lie adjacent to Routes 101 and 199. Others can be reached along uncrowded trails. Tan oak and madrone grow around the redwoods, while farther inland there's Jeffrey pine and Douglas fir.

Birdwatchers will encounter mallards, hawks, owl, shorebirds, quail, and great blue herons. The mammal population ranges from shrews and moles to rabbit and beaver to black-tail deer, Roosevelt elk, and an occasional bear. Along the coast live river otters and harbor seals. These and other features make the parks a natural for swimming, fishing, canoeing, and kayaking.

Facilities include information centers, picnic areas, restrooms, and showers; restaurants and groceries are in the park's small towns. Day-use fee, $5 for campsites. ~ On Route 101 between Orick and Crescent City; Jedediah Smith Redwoods State Park is along Route 199 about nine miles east of Crescent City. The park headquarters is located at 1111 2nd Street, Crescent City; 707-464-6101.

▲ In the national park, there are four hike-in primitive campgrounds: Nickel Creek, with five sites; Flint Ridge and Demartin, each with ten sites; and Little Bald Hills has four sites and one group site. All are free. The incorporated state parks offer more campgrounds: at **Prairie Creek Redwoods State Park** there are 100 sites for tents and RVs (no hookups); $14 to $16 per night. ~ 707-464-6101 ext. 5300. **Jedediah Smith State Redwoods Park** has 108 sites for tents and RVs (no hookups); $14 to $16 per night. ~ 707-464-6101 ext. 5113. **Del Norte Redwoods State Park** has 145 sites for tents and RVs (no hookups); $14 to $16 per night. ~ 707-464-6101 ext. 5101. In winter, sites are on a first come, first served basis. In summer, make reservations through PARKNET at 800-444-7275.

▼▼▼▼▼▼▼▼▼▼▼▼▼▼

Outdoor Adventures

All along the coast, charter boats depart daily to fish for salmon, Pacific snapper, or whatever else is running. Most companies leave the dock

FISHING

at 6 a.m. and return by 3:30 p.m. Please note that many fishing companies are seasonal operators.

MARIN COAST   If you hanker to try your luck for salmon, contact **Caruso's Sportfishing and Seafood**. Call 415-332-1221 for Caruso's daily fishing report. ~ Harbor Drive, Sausalito; 415-332-1015. **Loch Lomond Live Bait House** sells bait and tackle. During the summer they cruise the bay for striper and halibut. ~ Loch Lomond Marina, San Rafael; 415-456-0321.

SONOMA AND MENDOCINO COAST   Bodega Bay Sportfishing operates three boats. Besides salmon charters, they run charters for rock cod, ling cod, albacore, and crab. Whale-watching cruises run January through April, and in summer there are sunset cruises. ~ 1500 Bay Flat Road, Bodega Bay; 707-875-3344.

REDWOOD COUNTRY   For deep-sea fishing trips in search of salmon, halibut, or albacore, call **King Salmon Charters**. Bait and tackle are provided. ~ 1875 Buhne Drive, #67, Eureka; 707-442-3474.

SAILING

Nothing is more visually stunning than the sight of the sailboats on a clear, breezy San Francisco morning. Don't miss the experience of capturing the wind and drinking in endless vistas.

MARIN COUNTY   In the North Bay try **Cass' Rental Marina**. In addition to running a sailing school, they rent keel sloops. ~ 1702 Bridgeway, Sausalito; 415-332-6789. For charters on San Francisco Bay call **Ocean Voyages**, which has 26 vessels including 40-foot sailboats. ~ 1709 Bridgeway, Sausalito; 415-332-4681.

Your trip will take on a new dimension as you paddle among seals and seagulls, along the cityfronts and through the harbors of the world's largest landlocked bay. The popularity of kayaking has soared in the past few years, and the Bay Area certainly hasn't missed the boat; there are several small companies that cater to kayakers and would-be kayakers of all physical and financial abilities. While the most convenient place to paddle is on the bay itself, there are also stellar locations to the north in Marin County.

KAYAKING

MARIN COUNTY To paddle across Richardson Bay under the bright silvery moon, contact **Sea Trek Ocean Kayaking Center**. They also do trips to Angel Island. ~ Schoonmacher Point Marina, Sausalito; 415-488-1000. For kayak rentals and sales try **Boardsports Marin**. ~ 2233 Larkspur Landing Circle, Larkspur Landing; 415-925-8585.

With the Eel, Klamath, Smith, and Trinity rivers traversing many of the North Coast's parks, you're never far away from enjoying a stretch of river. In this mysterious fog-filled area, river exploration is a great way to discover natural vegetation and wildlife.

RIVER EXPLORING

All Outdoors Adventure Trips offers professionally guided rafting excursions ranging from Class III to Class V. Trips are half-day to three-day affairs, with all food and lodging included. ~ 1250 Pine Street, Suite 103, Walnut Creek; 510-932-8993.

The **Electric Rafting Company** has half-day to three-day trips on the Trinity, Smith, Klamath, Salmon, and Eel rivers for all levels. ~ P.O. Box 4418, Arcata, CA 95518; 707-826-2861.

From Marin to the Oregon border you'll find several clubs where it's relatively easy to get tee times.

GOLF

SONOMA AND MENDOCINO COAST On the Sonoma Coast, **Bodega Harbor Golf Links** is hilly and scenic. Part of this 18-hole course meanders around a freshwater marsh. ~ 21301 Heron Drive, Bodega Bay; 707-875-3538.

REDWOOD COUNTRY In the home of that lofty tree, I recommend **Eureka Municipal Golf Course**, which has an 18-hole course nestled in redwoods. There's a pro shop, a driving range, and motor carts. ~ 4750 Fairway Drive, Eureka; 707-443-4808. In Crescent City, the challenging nine-hole **Del Norte Golf Course** is set amidst redwoods. ~ 130 Club Drive; 707-458-3214.

The best bet for finding a tennis court without staying at the most expensive hotels is to call the local parks and recreation department.

TENNIS

REDWOOD COUNTRY   In Eureka, you can play at **Highland Park**. ~ Highland and Glen streets. **Hammond Park** has two courts. ~ 14th and E streets, Eureka; 707-441-4203. In Crescent City, there are three lighted courts available. ~ 301 West Washington Boulevard. For information, call 707-464-7230.

RIDING STABLES

Riding along the hauntingly beautiful North Coast is never an experience easily forgotten, and there are few prettier places to ride than Point Reyes National Seashore, where you can canter through rolling ranch country and out along sharp sea cliffs. **Five Brooks Stables** conducts mounted tours of this extraordinary area. Reservations required. ~ 8001 Route 1, Olema; 415-663-1570.

BIKING

Two-wheeling north of San Francisco is an invigorating sport. Not only is the scenery magnificent, but the accommodations aren't bad either. Many state and national parks sponsor campgrounds where cyclists and hikers can stay for a nominal fee.

   Route 1, the coast road, offers a chance to pedal past a spectacular shoreline of hidden coves, broad beaches, and sheer headlands. Unfortunately, the highway is narrow and winding, and therefore recommended for experienced cyclists only.

MARIN COAST   Point Reyes National Seashore features miles of bicycling, particularly along Bear Valley Trail.

SONOMA AND MENDOCINO COAST   Other popular areas farther north include the towns of Mendocino and where level terrain and beautiful landscape combine to create a cyclist's haven.
Bike Rentals   To rent mountain bikes, hybrids, and kids' bikes, call **Pacific Currents**. Hiking, biking, and kayak tours are also available here. ~ 10155 Route 1, Olema, in the Olema Ranch Campground. In Mendocino, **Catch a Canoe and Bicycles Too!** rents and sells state-of-the-art equipment. ~ Coast Highway 1 at Comptche-Ukiah Road; 707-937-0273. Located on the bicycle migration route between Canada and Mexico, **Fort Bragg Cyclery** does full-service repairs. Closed Sunday. ~ 579 South Franklin Street, Fort Bragg; 707-964-3509.

HIKING

To call California's North Coast a hiker's paradise is an understatement. After all, in San Francisco and north of the city is the Golden Gate National Recreation Area. Together with continuous county, state, and national parks it offers over 100,000 beautiful acres to be explored.

   Within this ambit are trails ranging from trifling nature loops to tough mountain paths. The land varies from tidal areas and seacliffs to ranch country and scenic mountains. In the far north are the giant redwood forests, located within national parks and

Whale
Watching

It is the world's longest mammal migration: 6000 miles along the Pacific coast from the Bering Sea to Baja California, then back again. The creatures making the journey measure 35 to 50 feet and weigh 40 tons. During the entire course of their incredible voyage they neither eat nor sleep.

California gray whales live to 40 or 50 years and have a world population numbering about 21,000. Their only enemies are killer whales and humans. They mate during the southern migration one year, then give birth at the end of the following year's migration. The calves, born in the warm, shallow waters of Baja, weigh a ton and measure about 16 feet. By the time they are weaned seven months later, the young are already 26 feet long.

Every year from mid-December through early February, the California gray whale cruises southward along the Northern California coast. Traveling in groups numbering three to five, these magnificent creatures hug the shore-line en route to their breeding grounds. They can be seen again from March through mid-May, though farther from shore, during their return migration north. So keep an eye sharply peeled: that rocky headland on which you are standing may be a crow's nest in disguise.

Since the whales use local coves and promontories to navigate, they are easy to spot from land. Just watch for the rolling hump, the slapping tail, or a lofty spout of spuming water. Sometimes these huge creatures will breach, leaping 30 feet above the surface, then crashing back with a thunderous splash.

The best crow's nests from which to catch this aquatic parade are Muir Beach Overlook, Chimney Rock at Point Reyes National Seashore, Bodega Head State Park, Sonoma Coast State Beach, Salt Point State Park, Mendocino Headlands State Park, Shelter Cove or Trinidad Head in Humboldt County, and Point St. George up near Crescent City. Visitors to California's Central Coast also enjoy this annual event.

Blue whales, humpback whales, dolphins, and porpoises also sometimes visit the coast.

Several outfits sponsor whale-watching cruises. During the winter and early spring, **Oceanic Society Expeditions** offers gray whale migration tours, which are led by qualified naturalists. ~ Fort Mason Center, Building E, San Francisco; 415-474-3385. For a close look at our fellow mammals from December through May, contact **New Sea Angler & Jaws**. ~ 1445 Route 1, Bodega Bay; 707-875-3495. For more intimate whale-watching groups of six or less be sure to call **King Salmon Charters**. ~ 1875 Buhne Drive, #67, Eureka; 707-442-3474.

featuring networks of hiking trails. All distances listed for hiking trails are one way unless otherwise noted.

MARIN COAST   The **Marin Headlands**, a region of bold bluffs and broad seascapes, contains a few hiking paths in its otherwise unpredictable landscape. ~ 415-331-1540.

Kirby Cove Trail (1.5 miles) leads from Conzelman Road down to a narrow beach. The views of San Francisco en route provide a lot of adventure for a short hike. Easy to moderate.

Wolf Ridge Loop (4.5 miles) begins at Rodeo Beach, follows the Coastal Trail and Wolf Ridge Trail, then returns along Miwok Trail. It ascends from a shoreline environment to heights with sweeping views of both San Francisco and Mt. Tamalpais. Moderate.

Tennessee Valley Trail (2 miles) winds along the valley floor en route to a small beach and cove. The trailhead sits off Route 1 at the end of Tennessee Valley Road. Easy.

About 45 miles of trails loop through **Mt. Tamalpais State Park** (415-388-2070). These link to a 200-mile network of hiking paths through Muir Woods National Monument and Golden Gate National Recreation Area. Explorers are amply rewarded with a diverse terrain, startling views of the entire Bay Area, and a chance to hike within commuting distance of San Francisco. Most trails begin at Pantoll Park Headquarters. Here you can pick up trail maps and descriptions from which to devise your own combination loop trails, or consult with the rangers in planning anything from an easy jaunt to a rugged trek.

Dipsea Trail (6.8 miles) is a favorite moderate path beginning in Mill Valley and heading along rolling hills, past sea vistas, then ending near Stinson Beach. The easiest way to pick up the trail is in Muir Woods, about a mile from the Mill Valley trailhead.

Matt Davis Trail (3.8 miles) descends 1200 feet from Pantoll Park Headquarters to Stinson Beach; you'll encounter deep woods, windswept knolls, and views of San Francisco and Point Reyes.

✔ CHECK THESE OUT—UNIQUE OUTDOOR ADVENTURES

- Set up a tent at Steep Ravine Environmental Camp, with its dramatic sea views. *page 119*
- Mount your steed and cantor along the rolling ranch lands or sharp sea cliffs of Marin County. *page 160*
- Pedal Route 1 past a spectacular shoreline studded with hidden coves, broad beaches, and sheer headlands. *page 160*
- Hike along the Hiouchi Trail in Del Norte Coast Redwoods State Park, with its huckleberries, trilliums, and rhododendrons. *page 165*

Steep Ravine Trail (2.8 miles), true to its name, angles sharply downward from Pantoll Park Headquarters through a redwood-studded canyon, then joins the Dipsea Trail.

Redwood Creek Trail (2.5 miles) loops through several remarkable redwood stands. A favorite with tourists, this easy trail begins near Muir Woods park headquarters and is often crowded. So it's best hiked either early or late in the day.

There are numerous other trails which combined form interesting loop hikes. For instance, from Bootjack picnic area in Mt. Tamalpais State Park, you can follow Bootjack Trail down a steep canyon of redwood and Douglas fir to Muir Woods, then take Ben Johnson Trail back up to Pantoll Park Headquarters. From there it's a half-mile walk back to Bootjack. This 4.2-mile moderate circle tour carries through relatively isolated sections of Muir Woods.

For a more challenging (9.4 miles) circular trek to the top of Mt. Tamalpais, begin at Pantoll Park Headquarters. You'll encounter an inn located along Panoramic Highway. Follow Old Railroad Grade. This will lead to West Point Inn, a cozy lodging place for hikers. From here you climb to the road leading to East Peak, one of Mt. Tamalpais' three summits. Heading down along Fern Creek Trail, you'll meet Old Railroad Grade once more. En route are flowering meadows, stands of madrone, chaparral-cloaked hillsides, and mountaintop views.

POINT REYES NATIONAL SEASHORE   Within its spectacular 72,000-acre domain, this park contains over 100 miles of hiking trails plus four hike-in campsites. The trails form a latticework across forests, ranch lands, and secluded beaches and along sea cliffs, brackish inlets, and freshwater lakes. Over 350 bird species inhabit the preserve. Black-tailed deer, Eurasian fallow deer, and spotted axis deer abound. You might also encounter raccoons, weasels, rabbits, badgers, bobcats, even a skunk or two.

Most trailheads begin near Bear Valley Visitors Center, Palomarin, Five Brooks, or Estero. For maps and information check with the rangers at the visitors center. ~ 415-663-1092.

Earthquake Trail (.6 mile) begins from the visitors center. Hikers can learn about the nearby San Andreas Fault.

Woodpecker Trail (.7 mile) is an easy self-guiding trail with markers explaining the natural environment. The annotated path leads to a horse "museum" set in a barn.

Bear Valley Trail (4.1 miles), also beginning near the visitors center, courses through range land and wooded valley to cliffs overlooking the ocean. The park's most popular trail, it is level and may unfortunately be crowded with hikers and bicyclists.

Coast Trail (16.3 miles) runs between Palomarin (near Bolinas) and Limantour Beach. Hugging the shoreline en route, this moderate, splendid trail leads past four freshwater lakes and two camping areas, then turns inland to Hostelling International's lodge.

Olema Valley Trail (5.2 miles) parallels Route 1 as it tracks a course along the infamous San Andreas Fault. Originating from Five Brooks, it alternates between glades and forest while beating a level path to Dogtown. The trail was damaged in the 1998 winter storms; check with the visitors center before heading out. Moderate.

Estero Trail (4.4 miles) shadows the shoreline of Drake's Estero and provides opportunities to view local waterfowl as well as harbor seals, sea lions, and bat rays. This trail, also, was damaged in early 1998. Check with the visitors center before walking it.

REDWOOD COUNTRY   There are more than 100 miles of hiking and riding paths within **Humboldt Redwoods State Park**. Many lead through dense redwood stands, others meander along the Eel River, and some lead to the park's hike-in camps. ~ 707-946-2409.

Founders Grove Nature Trail (.5 mile) tunnels through a virgin redwood forest that once boasted the national champion coastal redwood. Though a storm significantly shortened the 362-foot giant, it left standing a cluster of equally impressive neighbors.

Rockefeller Loop Trail (.5 mile) ducks into a magnificent grove of old growth redwoods.

There are also longer trails leading deep into the forest and to the top of 3379-foot Grasshopper Peak.

Comprising three distinct state parks and extending for miles along California's northwestern corner, **Redwood National Park**'s diverse enclave offers adventure aplenty to daytrippers and mountaineers alike. There are well over 150 miles of trails threading the parks, leading through dense redwood groves, along open beaches, and atop wind-buffeted bluffs. ~ 707-464-6101.

Yurok Loop Trail (1 mile), with its colorful berry patches and wildflowers, begins near the terminus of Coastal Trail.

Enderts Beach Trail (.5 mile), south of Crescent City, features tidepools, seaside strolling, and primitive camping. It also offers access to the moderate **Coastal Trail** (8.2 miles), an old roadway that cuts through forests of redwood, alder, and spruce and features glorious ocean views.

Within **Prairie Creek Redwoods State Park** there are numerous trails to enjoy.

Redwood Creek Trail (9 miles) leads from a trailhead two miles north of Orick to Tall Trees Grove, home of the world's tallest trees. There is backcountry camping en route; permits available at the trailhead.

Tall Trees Trail (1.6 miles) provides a shorter route to the same destination.

Lady Bird Johnson Grove Nature Loop Trail (1 mile) winds through ancient redwood country.

The moderate **Rhododendron Trail** (7.8 miles) begins at park headquarters and continues along the eastern ridge of the park, which is filled with rhododendrons.

James Irvine Trail (4.3 miles) goes from the Prairie Creek visitors center along a redwood ridge to Fern Canyon. For a longer loop (10.3 miles), hike south on Gold Bluffs Beach, then pick up Miner's Ridge Trail. This last trail follows a corduroy mining road used early in the century.

The **Fern Canyon Trail** (.8 mile) courses along a gulch dripping with vegetation.

The easy **Coastal Trail** (5 miles) begins at Fern Canyon and parallels Gold Bluffs Beach.

The moderate **West Ridge Trail** (7.1 miles) traces a sharp ridgetop through lovely virgin forest, ending at the Butler Creek backpacking camp.

The **Revelation Trail** (.3 mile), a marvelous innovation, contains handrails and a tape-recorded description of the surroundings for the blind. For those of us gifted with sight, it provides a fuller understanding of the many scents, sounds, and textures of a redwood forest.

Cathedral Trees Trail (1.4 miles) heads along streams and meadows to elk country.

Brown Creek Trail (1.2 miles), reputedly one of the park's prettiest hikes, leads along streams and through old redwood stands.

Del Norte Coast Redwoods State Park offers several areas ideal for short hikes. **Coastal Trail** (5.1 miles), located south of the state park, begins at Klamath River Overlook. In addition to ocean vistas, it offers a moderate walk through a spruce and alder forest, plus glimpses of sea lions, whales, and numerous birds.

Damnation Creek Trail (2.5 miles), a strenuous ancient Yurok Indian path, winds steeply down from Route 101 to a hidden cove and beach.

Hobbs Wall Trail (3.8 miles) leads through a former lumberjacking region.

Alder Basin Trail (1 mile) meanders along a stream through stands of willow, maple, and alder.

Farther north, **Jedediah Smith Redwoods State Park** has a number of trails to hike.

Stout Grove Trail (.5 mile) highlights several spots along its short, easy course: a 340-foot redwood tree, swimming and fishing holes, plus rhododendron regions.

Hiouchi Trail (2 miles), with its huckleberries, trilliums, and rhododendrons, is equally impressive. This moderate nature trail goes right through a burned-out redwood; it also affords scenic vistas along the Smith River.

Hatton Trail (.3 mile) tours an ancient redwood grove.

Nickerson Ranch Trail (.8 mile) leads through a corridor of ferns and redwoods.

Howland Hill Road (8 miles), a moderate to difficult trial now overgrown with salmonberries, was once a vital stagecoach route.

▼▼▼▼▼▼▼▼▼▼▼
Transportation

CAR

When traveling by car you can choose the ever-winding, spectacular coastal **Route 1**, which provides some of the prettiest scenery this side of Shangri-la. Or take **Route 101**, the faster, more direct freeway that follows an interior route.

AIR

Eureka/Arcata Airport in McKinleyville is served by United Express and Horizon Air. On a bluff above the Pacific, this is one of the most beautiful small fields in California. **Humboldt Transit System** provides hourly service (Monday through Friday) from Eureka and Arcata to the airport.

BUS

Greyhound Bus Lines travels the entire stretch of Route 101 between San Francisco and Oregon, including the main route through Redwood Country. ~ 707-442-0370, 800-231-2222.

CAR RENTALS

It's advisable to rent an auto in San Francisco rather than along the North Coast. There are more rental agencies available and prices are lower. At the Eureka/Arcata Airport you can rent from **Avis Rent A Car** (800-331-1212), **Hertz Rent A Car** (800-654-3131), and **National Interrent** (800-227-7368).

PUBLIC TRANSIT

Golden Gate Transit has bus service between San Francisco and Sausalito, then beyond to Point Reyes National Seashore (weekends only). It also covers Route 101 from San Francisco to Santa Rosa. ~ 415-923-2000.

From Santa Rosa you can pick up coastal connections on **Mendocino Transit Authority**, which travels Route 1 from Bodega Bay to Point Arena. There's only one bus a day in either direction. ~ 707-884-3723.

Public transportation from San Francisco to Marin can become a sightseeing adventure when you book passage on a **Golden Gate Transit** ferryboat. ~ 415-455-2000.

Mendocino Stage, a local line, serves Gualala, Point Arena, Mendocino, and Fort Bragg, and travels inland to Ukiah. ~ 707-964-0167.

FOUR

North Central Coast

If the North Central Coast were an oil painting, it would portray a surf-laced shoreline near the bottom of the frame. Pearly beaches and bold promontories would occupy the center, while forested peaks rose in the background. Actually, a mural would be more appropriate to the subject, since the coastline extends 150 miles from San Francisco to Big Sur. The artist would paint two mountain ranges parallel to the shore, then fill the area between with a patchwork of hills, headlands, and farmland.

Even after adding a swath of redwoods along the entire length of the mural, the painter's task would have only begun. The North Central Coast will never be captured—on canvas, in print, or in the camera's eye. It is a region of unmatched beauty and extraordinary diversity.

Due south of San Francisco is Half Moon Bay, a timeless farming and fishing community founded by Italians and Portuguese during the 1860s. The oceanside farms are so bountiful that Half Moon Bay dubs itself the pumpkin capital of the world, and Castroville, farther south, claims to be the artichoke capital. While local farmers grow prize vegetables, commercial fishing boats comb the entire coast for salmon, herring, tuna, anchovies, and cod.

In the seaside town of Santa Cruz, on the other hand, you'll encounter a quiet retirement community that has been transformed into a dynamic campus town. When the University of California opened a school here in the 1960s, it created a new role for this ever-changing place. Originally founded as a Spanish mission in 1791, Santa Cruz became a lumber port and manufacturing center when the Americans moved in around 1849. Then in the late 19th century it developed into a tourist resort filled with elaborate Victorian houses.

Like every place on the North Central Coast, Santa Cruz is reached from San Francisco along Route 1, the tortuous coast road that twists past sandy coves and granite cliffs. Paralleling it is Route 101, the inland freeway that leads through the warm, dry agricultural regions of the Salinas Valley. Between these two roadways rise the Santa Cruz Mountains, accessible along Routes 35 and 9. Unlike the low-lying coastal and inland farming areas, this range measures 3000 feet in elevation and is filled with redwood, Douglas fir, alder, and madrone.

Different still is the Monterey Peninsula, a fashionable residential area 125 miles south of San Francisco. Including the towns of Monterey, Pacific Grove, and Carmel, this wealthy enclave is a far cry from bohemian Santa Cruz. If Santa Cruz is an espresso coffeehouse, Monterey is a gourmet restaurant or designer boutique.

Farther south lies Big Sur, the most unique area of all. Extending from the Monterey Peninsula for 90 miles along the coast, and backdropped by the steep Santa Lucia Mountains, it is one of America's most magnificent natural areas. Only about 1000 residents live in this rugged region of bald crags and flower-choked canyons. None but the most adventurous occupy the nearby Ventana Wilderness, which represents the southernmost realm of the coastal redwoods. Once a nesting place for rare California condors, Ventana is still home to wild boar, black bear, and mountain lion.

The Esselen Indians, who inhabited Big Sur and its mountains, took Spanish names to avoid being slaughtered during the missionary period. In recent years they have been organizing to make the state of California and the federal government recognize their tribal status. Together with the Costanoans, who occupied the rest of the Central Coast, the Esselen may have been here for 5000 years. By the time the Europeans happened upon California, about 10,000 American Indians lived near the coast between San Francisco and Big Sur. Elk and antelope ranged the region. The American Indians also hunted sea lions, gathered seaweed, and fed on oysters, abalone, clams, and mussels.

Westerners did not settle Big Sur until after 1850, and Route 1 did not open completely until 1937. During the 1950s, novelist Henry Miller became the focus of an artists' colony here. Jack Kerouac trekked through the area, writing about it in several of his novels. Other Beat poets, lured by Big Sur's dizzying sea cliffs and otherworldly vistas, also cut a path through its hills.

Over 300 years before settlers arrived in Big Sur, Monterey was already making history. As early as 1542, Juan Rodríguez Cabrillo, a Portuguese explorer in Spanish employ, set anchor off nearby Pacific Grove. Then in 1602 Sebastian Vizcaíno came upon the peninsula again and told a whale of a fish story, grandly exaggerating the size and amenities of Monterey Bay.

His account proved so distorted that Gaspar de Portolá, leading an overland expedition in 1769, failed to recognize the harbor. When Father Junípero Serra joined him in a second journey the next year, they realized that this gentle curve was Vizcaíno's deep port. Serra established California's second mission in Monterey, then moved it a few miles in 1771 to create the Carmel Mission. Neither Serra nor Portolá explored the Big Sur coast, but the Spanish were soon building yet another mission in Santa Cruz.

In fact, they found Santa Cruz much easier to control than Monterey. By the 1820s, Yankee merchant ships were plying Monterey waters, trading for hides and tallow. This early American presence, brilliantly described in Richard Henry Dana's classic *Two Years Before the Mast*, climaxed in 1846 during the Mexican War. Commodore John Sloat seized the town for the United States. By 1849, while Big Sur was still the hunting ground of American Indians, the adobe town of Monterey had become the site of California's constitutional convention.

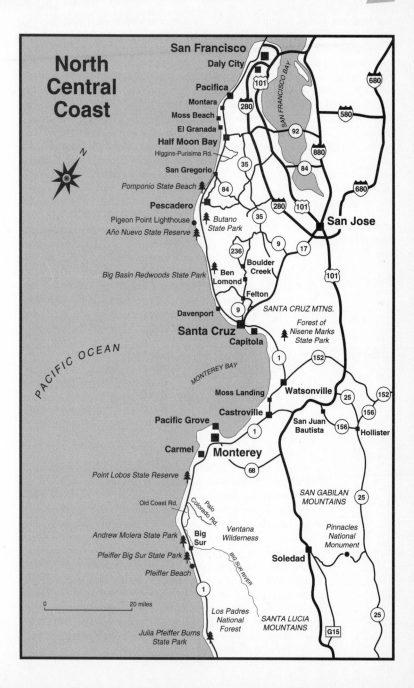

North Central Coast

San Francisco
Daly City
Pacifica
Montara
Moss Beach
El Granada
Half Moon Bay
Higgins-Purisima Rd.
San Gregorio
Pomponio State Beach
Pescadero
Pigeon Point Lighthouse
Año Nuevo State Reserve
Butano State Park
Big Basin Redwoods State Park
Ben Lomond
Boulder Creek
Felton
Davenport
Santa Cruz
Capitola
SANTA CRUZ MTNS.
Forest of Nisene Marks State Park
PACIFIC OCEAN
MONTEREY BAY
Moss Landing
Watsonville
Castroville
Pacific Grove
San Juan Bautista
Hollister
Carmel
Monterey
Point Lobos State Reserve
Old Coast Rd.
Palo Colorado Rd.
Andrew Molera State Park
Big Sur
Ventana Wilderness
Pfeiffer Big Sur State Park
Pfeiffer Beach
BIG SUR RIVER
Soledad
SAN GABILAN MOUNTAINS
Pinnacles National Monument
0   20 miles
Los Padres National Forest
SANTA LUCIA MOUNTAINS
Julia Pfeiffer Burns State Park
G15

SAN FRANCISCO BAY

San Jose

An added incentive for these early adventurers, and modern day visitors as well, was the climate along the North Central Coast. The temperature still hovers around 67° in summer and 57° during winter; Santa Cruz continues to boast 300 sunny days a year. Explorers once complained of foggy summers and rainy winters, but like today's travelers, they were rewarded with beautiful spring and fall weather.

Perhaps that's why Monterey became a tourist mecca during the 1880s. Of course the old Spanish capital also developed into a major fishing and canning region during the early 20th century. It was then that John Steinbeck, the Salinas-bred writer, added to the already rich history of Monterey with his novels and stories. Much of the landscape that became known as "Steinbeck Country" has changed drastically since the novelist's day, and the entire Central Coast is different from the days of Serra and Sloat. But the most important elements of Monterey and the North Central Coast—the foaming ocean, open sky, and wooded heights —are still here, waiting for the traveler with a bold eye and robust imagination.

▼▼▼▼▼▼▼▼▼▼▼▼▼▼▼▼▼▼

South of San Francisco

An easy drive from the city, the coast south of San Francisco is full of surprises. You might see a gray whale pod, watch the sea lions at Año Nuevo State Park, or visit one of the rural towns that dot this shoreline. The area along Route 1 between San Francisco and Santa Cruz also sports numerous beaches, bed and breakfast inns, and country roads that lead up into the Santa Cruz Mountains.

SIGHTS

Preceding the beauty, however, is the beast. The road south from San Francisco leads through one of America's ugliest towns. In fact, **Daly City** is the perfect counterpoint to the bay city: it is as hideous as San Francisco is splendid. If Tony Bennett left his heart in San Francisco, he must have discarded a gallbladder in Daly City. This town was memorialized in Malvina Reynolds' song, "Little Boxes," which describes its "ticky tacky" pastel houses and over-developed hillsides.

No matter, this suburban blight soon gives way to Route 1 which cuts through Pacifica and curls into the hills. As the road rises above a swirling coastline you'll be entering a geologic hot-spot. The **San Andreas fault**, villain of the 1906 earthquake, heads back into shore near Pacifica. As the road cuts will reveal, the sedimentary rock along this area has been twisted and warped into bizarre shapes. At **Devil's Slide**, several miles south of Pacifica, unstable hillsides periodically collapse into the sea.

Now that I have totally terrified you, I should add that this is an area not to be missed. Drive carefully and you'll be safe to enjoy the outstanding ocean vistas revealed at every hairpin turn in this winding roadway. Rocky cliffs, pocket beaches, and erupting surf open to view. There are sea stacks offshore and, in winter, gray whales cruise the coast.

At the village of **Montara,** you will pass an old lighthouse whose utility buildings have been converted to a youth hostel. As the road descends toward Moss Beach, precipitous rock faces give way to gentle slopes and placid tidepools. Then in Half Moon Bay a four-mile-long white sand beach is backdropped by new homes built on farmlands.

Half Moon Bay is what happens when the farm meets the sea. It's a hybrid town, half landlubber and half old-salt, more and more becoming a bedroom community for San Francisco. They are as likely to sell artichokes here as fresh fish. The town was named for its crescent beach, but thinks of itself as the pumpkin capital of the world. In October, it hosts the **Pumpkin Festival,** which draws over 300,000 people. At times the furrowed fields seem a geometric continuation of ocean waves, as if the sea lapped across the land and became frozen there. It is Half Moon Bay's peculiar schizophrenia, a double identity that lends an undeniable flair to the community.

From Half Moon Bay, a connecting road leads to Route 35 and Route 9, providing an alternate course to Santa Cruz; this will be covered below, in the "Santa Cruz Mountains" sightseeing section of this chapter. For now, let's stay on Route 1, which continues south, poised between the mountains and the sea.

On the southern outskirts of Half Moon Bay, watch out for the **Higgins–Purisima Road,** a country lane that curves for eight ◀ *HIDDEN* miles into the Santa Cruz Mountains, returning to Route 1. This scenic loop passes old farmhouses and sloping pastures, redwood-forested hills and mountain meadows. Immediately upon entering this bumpy road, you'll spy a stately old New England–style house set in a plowed field. That will be the **James Johnston House,** a saltbox structure with a sloping roof and white clapboard facade. Dating back to 1853 and built by an original '49er, it is the oldest house along this section of coastline. The house is rarely open to

━━

✔ CHECK THESE OUT—UNIQUE SIGHTS

- Traverse the sand dunes at **Año Nuevo State Reserve,** keeping an eye out for exotic birds, sea lions, and two-ton mating elephant seals. *page 172*
- Stroll the **Santa Cruz Beach Boardwalk** and peoplewatch or, better yet, dare to ride the ups-and-downs of the fabled roller coaster. *page 181*
- Spend the day underwater at the **Monterey Bay Aquarium,** with its outstanding marine displays, or touch the bat rays as they swim by you in an open tank. *page 203*
- Wander the trails of **Point Lobos State Reserve** where ghostly Monterey cypress trees steal against the wind. *page 214*

the public; during the summer, it occasionally opens on the third Saturday of the month.

The farming plus fishing spirit of Half Moon Bay prevails as Route 1 continues south. A short distance from the highway, you will encounter **San Gregorio**, a weather-beaten little town. Once a resort area, today it reveals a quaint collection of sagging roofs and unpainted barns. **Pescadero** represents another timeworn town hidden a short way from Route 1. It's a woodframe hamlet of front-porch rocking chairs and white-steeple churches. The name translates as "fisherman," but the Portuguese and Italian residents are farmers, planting artichokes, Brussels sprouts, beans, and lettuce in the patchwork fields surrounding the town.

> Be sure to drop by the San Gregorio General Store, a classic that's been around for over a century. ~ Stage Road and Route 84, Pescadero; 650-726-0565.

A family-owned farm open to the public, **Phipps Ranch** offers a child-friendly barnyard, a plant nursery, flower and herb gardens, and a market selling dried beans, herbs, and myriad other products grown right on the premises. During the summer visitors can pick several varieties of berries. ~ 2700 Pescadero Road, Pescadero; 650-879-0787.

The beacon several miles south is **Pigeon Point Lighthouse**, a 110-foot sentinel that's one of the nation's tallest lighthouses. The point gained a nasty reputation during the 19th century when one ship after another smashed on the rocks. The lighthouse went up in 1872, and originally contained a 1000-piece lens. Doubling as a youth hostel, it now warns sailors while welcoming travelers.

Miles of sand dunes border **Año Nuevo State Reserve**, a lovely park containing an offshore island where two-ton elephant seals breed in winter. With its tidepools, exotic bird population, sea lions, and harbor seals, the reserve is a natural playground. The Ohlone Indians highly valued the region for its abundant fish and shellfish population. It was here the Ohlone had the first contact with whites in 1769 when Juan Gaspar de Portolá trekked through en route to his discovery of San Francisco Bay. (For more information, see the "Beaches & Parks" section below.) ~ 415-879-2025.

From here to Santa Cruz, the road streams past bold headlands and magnificent seascapes. There are excellent beaches to explore and marvelous vista points along the way. You will also discover rolling farmlands where giant pumpkins grow at the edge of the sea.

About two miles north of Santa Cruz along Route 1 you'll discover **Wilder Ranch State Park**. This 6500-acre spread has 20 acres that have been designated a "cultural preserve" because of the Ohlone Indian shell mounds and historic houses dotting the property. Hiking trails allowing horses and bikes wind throughout. In addition to an 1839 adobe, the complex features a Greek Revival farmhouse dating to the 1850s and an 1890-era Queen Anne Victorian. You can also tour the outlying barns and workshops portraying life on a turn-of-the-century dairy farm, which this once was. Go on a weekend to see living history demonstrations. Open Saturday and Sunday in December; open Friday through Sunday in January and February; open Wednesday through Sunday from March through August. Admission and parking fee. ~ 831-426-0505.

If there were a hotel on the site of **Hostelling International—Point Montara Lighthouse**, it would easily charge $300 a night. Set on a bluff overlooking the ocean, on one of those dramatic points always reserved for lighthouses, the hostel charges down-to-earth prices (and requires a morning chore). The daily fee buys you a bunk in a cozy dorm-style room. Couple and family rooms are also available. There are two kitchens, a hot tub, and two common rooms in this old lightkeeper's house. Reservations are strongly recommended. ~ On Route 1 at 16th Street, Montara; 650-728-7177. BUDGET.

LODGING

The **Seal Cove Inn**, located 30 minutes south of San Francisco and six miles north of Half Moon Bay, is the perfect place to sojourn for one more night before heading farther afield. The decor is decidedly country inn, with flowers, grandfather clocks, antique furnishings, and a fireplace. But the setting is California-style, with seals, whales, long white beaches, and towering cypress trees sharing the surrounding acreage. ~ 221 Cypress Avenue, Moss Beach; 650-728-4114, 800-995-9987, fax 650-728-4116; www.sealcoveinn.com. ULTRA-DELUXE.

The Cape Cod look has become very popular with establishments in the Half Moon Bay area. One of the foremost, **Pillar Point Inn** is a fully modern bed and breakfast cloaked in 19th-century New England disguise. Overlooking the harbor, this 11-room inn combines VCRs, TVs, and refrigerators with traditional amenities like featherbeds, window seats, and fireplaces. Every guest room has a private bath, and there's a deck overlooking the waterfront. Breakfast is a full-course affair. ~ 380 Capistrano Road, Princeton-by-the-Sea; 650-728-7377, 800-400-8281, fax 650-728-8345; www.PillarPointInn.com. ULTRA-DELUXE.

One of the finest country inns along the entire Central Coast is **Mill Rose Inn**. This turn-of-the-century inn is adorned with hand-painted wallpapers, European antiques, and colorful tiles throughout. The grounds resemble an English garden and include a gazebo with hot tub and flagstone patio. Each of the six guest rooms is brilliantly appointed; even the least expensive displays an antique armoire, European featherbed, and marbletop dresser covered with old-style combs and brushes. The sitting room and spacious dining room are equally elegant. This is one of the finest country inns along the entire Central Coast. ~ 615 Mill Street, Half Moon Bay; 650-726-8750, 800-900-7673, fax 650-726-3031; www.millroseinn.com. ULTRA-DELUXE.

Sitting right above the beach a few miles north of Half Moon Bay is the 54-room **Beach House**. This contemporary facility, designed in the style of a New England summer home, features "lofts" that include kitchenettes, fireplaces and private balconies. One of the most comfortable hotels along this stretch of coastline, it creates a sense of easy elegance. There's a lobby with fireplace, a heated pool and a jacuzzi, not to mention a succession of beautiful sunsets just beyond your patio door. ~ 4100 North Cabrillo Highway, Half Moon Bay; 650-712-0220, 800-315-9366, fax 650-712-0693; www.beach-house.com. ULTRA-DELUXE.

Among lodgings on this stretch of coastline, **San Benito House** is a personal favorite. Set in a turn-of-the-century building, it's a 12-room bed-and-breakfast inn with adjoining bar and restaurant. The less expensive rooms are small but quite nice. One room I saw featured a brass light fixture, hanging plants, quilted beds, framed drawings, and wood furniture. There are both shared and private baths. Add a sauna plus a country-inn ambience and you have a bargain at the price. ~ 356 Main Street, Half Moon Bay; 650-726-3425. MODERATE.

The blue clapboard home of an early merchant in Half Moon Bay is now a bed-and-breakfast inn called the **Zaballa House**. Within the 1859 structure, the oldest in town, are 12 charming rooms, some with fireplaces and large whirlpool tubs. Eleven hotel-style rooms were recently added to another building on the property. A friendly, unpretentious atmosphere prevails throughout, with guests encouraged to put their feet up in the parlor and relax with a good book. All guests enjoy a full breakfast and afternoon wine and cheese. ~ 324 Main Street, Half Moon Bay;

▲▲

✔ CHECK THESE OUT—UNIQUE LODGING

- *Budget:* Follow the beacon of California's second-tallest lighthouse to **Hostelling International—Pigeon Point Lighthouse**, which features cottage accommodations and a clifftop hot tub. *page 175*
- *Moderate:* Unpack your bags at **Surfside Apartments** and then grab your sunscreen and head to the boardwalk two blocks away. *page 185*
- *Deluxe:* Sip a snifter of port near the cozy fireplace with a good book in the parlor at **Zaballa House**. *page 174*
- *Ultra-deluxe:* Pamper yourself in pools and saunas after a long day of Big Sur hiking at **Ventana**. *page 227*

Budget: under $60   Moderate: $60–$120   Deluxe: $120–$175   Ultra-deluxe: over $175

650-726-9123, fax 650-726-3921; www.whistler.com/zaballa. DELUXE.

The **Rancho San Gregorio**, set in the sunny valley of the same name, is a Spanish mission–style bed and breakfast not to be missed if homelike comfort and the orderliness of a five-star hotel suit you. Situated on 15 acres, the inn has four spacious rooms, decorated country fashion with exposed beam ceilings. Rooms feature wood-burning stoves, private baths, and full breakfast. ~ Route 84, five miles inland from Route 1 between the towns of San Gregorio and La Honda; 650-747-0810, fax 650-747-0814; www.scruznet.com/~prankstr/rancho/home.html. MODERATE TO DELUXE.

Comparable to the low-cost lodging at Montara is **Hostelling International—Pigeon Point Lighthouse**. It has a similarly dramatic windswept setting above the ocean. The rooms are in several shared cottages with kitchens, living rooms, and accommodations for couples. Rates, as in other American Youth Hostels, are budget, and a chore is required. Guests have access to a private, clifftop hot tub for a small fee. Set beneath California's second tallest lighthouse on a beautiful shoreline, the hostel is a charming place to stay. Reservations 48 hours in advance required; couples should call four to six months in advance. ~ Route 1, Pescadero; 650-879-0633. BUDGET.

New Davenport Store Bed & Breakfast Inn, located near the coast about ten miles north of Santa Cruz, has a singular appeal. A few rooms here are situated in a historic old house; most are upstairs from a gallery gift shop. The staff is congenial and the accommodations mighty comfortable. All rooms have private baths and are imaginatively decorated with watercolors. In fact, the owners are potters and have adorned some rooms with their handicrafts. You can also look for antique pieces, oak furniture, and wall-to-wall carpeting. Breakfast and drinks included. ~ 31 Davenport Avenue, Davenport; 831-425-1818, 800-870-1817; fax 831-423-1160; www.swanton.com/BnB/index.html. MODERATE TO DELUXE.

DINING

Nick's Restaurant has been operated by the same Greek-Italian-American family for more than seven decades and is still pulling in the Pacifica crowds. Wood sculptures of sea life decorate the walls, but the main attraction is the million-dollar view of Rockaway Beach across the street. Nick's is known for its grilled crab sandwiches, sautéed prawns, and fettuccine angelina. ~ 100 Rockaway Beach, Pacifica; 650-359-3900. MODERATE TO DELUXE.

For dinner overlooking the ocean, there's nothing quite like **Moss Beach Distillery**. The place enjoys a colorful history, dating back to Prohibition days, when this area was notorious for supplying booze to thirsty San Francisco. Today it's a bustling plate-glass restaurant with adjoining bar. The menu includes gulf shrimp, calamari sauté, cioppino, steak, and grilled pork loin medallions with wild mushroom ragoût. The bootleggers are long gone, but those splendid sea views will be here forever. Brunch served on Sunday. ~ Beach Way and Ocean Boulevard, Moss Beach; 650-728-5595. MODERATE TO DELUXE.

Speaking of seafood, **The Fishtrap** down on Half Moon Bay has some of the lowest prices around. Set in and around a small woodframe building smack on the bay, this unpretentious eatery features several fresh fish dishes daily. They're liable to be serving ling cod, halibut, and swordfish, as well as shellfish, and steak sandwiches. Calamari rings are a specialty. Friendly, inexpensive—and highly recommended. ~ 281 Capistrano Road, Princeton-by-the-Sea; 650-728-7049. BUDGET.

Or try **The Shore Bird**, set in a Cape Cod–style building overlooking the water. This expansive restaurant features a dining room, café, cocktail lounge, garden patio, and plenty of seafood. With a chef directly from Naples, Italy, the Italian flavor is authentic. ~ 390 Capistrano Road, Princeton-by-the-Sea; 650-728-5541. MODERATE.

The **Village Green** is another local snuggery. Small and cozy, it's an English-style establishment serving "farmhouse breakfasts," "ploughman's lunches," and afternoon teas. If you're in the mood for scones, English sausage, housemade Cornish pasties, or a banger and onion sandwich, this is your only chance for many many miles. Closed Wednesday and three weeks in August. ~ 89 Avenue Portola, El Granada; 650-726-3690. BUDGET.

Aficionados of Mexican food often head for **El Perico's**. With its antiqued wood paneling and exposed beam ceiling, the place is rustically fashionable. The menu includes all the south-of-the-border specialties—chile rellenos, tostadas, tacos, burritos, flautas, enchiladas, and so on. Fresh seafood is incorporated into many of these. ~ 211 San Mateo Road, Half Moon Bay; 650-726-3737. BUDGET TO MODERATE.

For contemporary California cuisine in a country inn setting, there's **San Benito House**. This gourmet restaurant with moderate-to-deluxe prices incorporates fresh seafood and produce from the surrounding ocean and farm country. On a typical night you might choose Atlantic salmon with mustard vinaigrette, homemade ravioli, or filet of beef with chanterelle mushrooms. Dinner only; closed Monday through Wednesday. The hotel also houses a budget-priced deli (open daily 11 a.m. to 3:30 p.m.) that serves homemade soup, salad, and bread. ~ 356 Main Street, Half Moon Bay; 650-726-3425. MODERATE TO DELUXE.

Once past Half Moon Bay, restaurants become mighty scarce. Practically anything will do along this lonesome stretch south; but rather than just anything, you can have **Duarte's Tavern**. Open since 1934, this restaurant and tavern has earned a reputation all down the coast for delicious food. There's a menu filled with meat and fish entrées, omelettes, and sandwiches. They also serve a variety of homemade desserts. Personally, I recommend being adventurous by trying the artichoke soup and olallieberry pie. Breakfast, lunch, and dinner daily. ~ 202 Stage Road, Pescadero; 650-879-0464. MODERATE.

Farther down the coast, the **New Davenport Cash Store Restaurant** offers a countrified atmosphere. It's adjacent to a traditional general store and decorated with colorful wall rugs, handwoven baskets, and fresh flowers. The cuisine at this eatery rambles from chorizo and eggs to tofu and vegetables to mushroom cheese-melt sandwiches to steamed clams. More ordinary fare—omelettes, hamburgers, steak, and seafood—is also on the agenda. They also feature dinner specials such as salmon, scallops, and chicken. Breakfast, lunch, and dinner daily. ~ 31 Davenport Avenue, Davenport; 831-426-4122. BUDGET TO DELUXE.

The lounge at **Nick's Restaurant** offers a full bar, TVs and a live Top-40 cover band on Friday and Saturday. ~ 100 Rockaway Beach, Pacifica; 650-359-3900.

There's jazz and classical music Sunday afternoon at the **Bach Dancing and Dynamite Society**. There's also occasional classical and jazz music on Saturday nights. Situated beachfront off Route 1 about two miles north of the Route 92 intersection, it's renowned for quality sounds. ~ Miramar Beach, off Medio Road, Half Moon Bay; 650-726-4143.

The **New Davenport Cash Store Bar** offers a mellow cafe-like setting. ~ 31 Davenport Avenue, Davenport; 831-426-4122.

NIGHTLIFE

GRAY WHALE COVE This white-sand crescent is a well-known clothing-optional beach. Tucked discreetly beneath steep cliffs, it is also a beautiful spot. The undertow is strong, so swimming is not advised. The only facilities are toilets. Day-use fee, $6.50. ~ Located along Route 1 three miles south of Pacifica. Watch for the parking lot on the east side of the highway. Cautiously cross the highway and proceed down the staircase to the beach; 650-728-5336.

MONTARA STATE BEACH Though this half-mile-long beach may be a haven to nude sunbathers, police patrols occasionally pass out tickets. Volleyball players and frisbee throwers can be found everywhere. Backdropped by a rocky bluff, it's a very pretty place. Surfers ride the small swells. The only facilities here are primitive toilets and parking is limited. ~ The beach is located along Route 1 seven miles south of Pacifica. There is a trail leading to the beach from Route 1 and 2nd Street in Montara; 650-726-8819.

BEACHES & PARKS

JAMES V. FITZGERALD MARINE RESERVE 🚶 Boasting the best facilities among the beaches in the area, this park also has a sandy beach and excellent tidepools. It's a great place to while away the hours watching crabs, sea urchins, and anemones. Since there are houses nearby, this is more of a family beach than the freewheeling areas to the immediate north and south. There are restrooms and a picnic area. ~ Located off Route 1 in Moss Beach about eight miles south of Pacifica; 650-728-3584.

HALF MOON BAY STATE BEACH (OR FRANCIS BEACH) 🚶 🚲 🐎 🛶 🚣 ⛵ Despite a four-mile-long sand beach, this park receives only a guarded recommendation. Half Moon Bay is a working harbor, so the beach lacks the seclusion and natural qualities of other strands along the coast. Of course, with civilization so near at hand, the facilities here are more complete than elsewhere. Also, Francis Beach is part of a chain of beaches that you can choose from, including Venice Beach, Roosevelt Beach, and Dunes Beach. Personally, I pick the last. Surfers head to the sandy beach break at Francis Beach and below Half Moon Bay jetty. Restrooms or toilets are available at all four beaches; picnic areas at Francis Beach. Day-use fee, $5. ~ All four park segments are located along Route 1 in Half Moon Bay; 650-726-8820.

▲ There are 56 sites for tents and RVs (no hookups) at Francis Beach; $16 per night. Hiker/biker camp available at Francis; $3 per night. First-come, first-served for all sites.

HIDDEN ▶ **SAN GREGORIO STATE BEACH** 🚶 🚣 ⛵ 🛶 There is a white sand beach here framed by sedimentary cliffs and cut by a small creek. Star of the show, though, is the nearby private nude beach (admission) north of the state beach, reputedly the first beach of its type in California. Among the nicest of the state's nude beaches, it features a narrow sand corridor shielded by high bluffs. There are picnic areas and toilets at the state beach, no facilities at the nude beach. Day-use fee, $5. ~ Located on Route 1 15 miles south of Half Moon Bay. The nude beach is several hundred yards north; 650-726-7245.

POMPONIO STATE BEACH 🚶 ⛵ 🛶 Less appealing than its neighbor to the north, this park has a white sand beach that's traversed periodically by a creek. There are headlands on either side of the beach. Facilities include picnic areas and toilets. Day-use fee, $5. ~ Located on Route 1 about 16 miles south of Half Moon Bay; 650-879-2170.

PESCADERO STATE BEACH 🚶 ⛵ 🛶 Backed by sand dunes and saltwater ponds, this lovely park also features a wide beach. There are tidepools to the south and a wildlife preserve across the highway. Steelhead run annually in the streams here, while deer, blue herons, and egrets inhabit the nearby marshland. Rangers lead guided tours. There are picnic areas and toilets. Day-use fee, $5. ~ Located on Route 1 about 19 miles south of Half Moon Bay; 650-879-2170.

BEAN HOLLOW STATE BEACH 🚶 🏊 ⛵ The small sandy beach here is bounded by rocks, so sunbathers go elsewhere while tide-pool watchers drop by. Particularly interesting is nearby Pebble Beach, a coarse-grain strand studded with jasper, serpentine, carnelians, and agates. The stones originate from a quartz reef offshore and attract rockhounds by the pack. But don't take rocks away—it's illegal. Also not to be missed is the blufftop trail between Bean Hollow and Pebble Beach, from which you can espy seals and whales in season. Facilities include a picnic area and toilets. Day-use fee, $5. ~ Located along Route 1 about 21 miles south of Half Moon Bay; Pebble Beach is about a mile north of Bean Hollow; 650-879-2170.

BUTANO STATE PARK 🚶 🚴 ⛵ This inland park, several miles from the coast, provides a welcome counterpoint to the beach parks. About 2700 acres, it features a dense redwood forest, including stands of virgin trees. Hiking trails traverse the territory. Not as well known as other nearby redwood parks, Butano suffers less human traffic. The park has picnic areas and restrooms. Day-use fee, $5. ~ Located 22 miles south of Half Moon Bay. Coming from the north on Route 1, go 20 miles south of Half Moon Bay; turn left (east) on Pescadero Road, and then right on Cloverdale Road about four miles to the park. Or, coming from the south, turn right (east) on Gazos Creek Road (two miles south of Pigeon Point Lighthouse) and then left on Cloverdale Road; 650-879-2040.

▲ There are 32 sites for tents, seven for RVs (no hookups); $16 per night. Camping by reservation only from Memorial Day to Labor Day (800-444-7275).

AÑO NUEVO STATE RESERVE 🚶 🚤 🏊 🎣 ⛵ Awesome in its beauty, abundant in wildlife, this park is one of the most spectacular on the California coast. It consists of a peninsula heaped with sand dunes. A miniature island lies just offshore. There are tidepools to search and a nature trail for exploring. Seals and sea lions inhabit the area; loons, hawks, pheasants, and albatrosses have all been spied here. But most spectacular of all the denizens are the elephant seals, those lovably grotesque creatures who come here between December 15 and March 31 to breed. Reaching two tons and 16 feet, adorned with the bulbous, trunk-like snouts for which they are named, these mammals are unique. Back in 1800, elephant seals numbered in the hundreds of thousands; by the end of the century, they were practically extinct; it's only recently that they have achieved a comeback. When breeding, the bulls stage bloody battles and collect large harems, creating a specta-cle that draws crowds every year. During breeding season, do-cents lead two-and-a-half-hour tours, which must be booked eight weeks in advance (800-444-7275). The tours cover seal-breeding areas, which otherwise are closed to the public throughout the breeding season; during the rest of the year the entire park and the seal rookery are open. Be forewarned that it's a three-mile roundtrip walk from the parking lot to the rookery. During the summer there are surf breaks off the end of beach, about ten min-utes south of the rookery. Also be aware: the elephant seal pop-ulation makes this beach attractive to sharks. The only facilities are toilets. Day-use fee, $5. ~ Located off of Route 1, about 22 miles south of Half Moon Bay; 650-879-2025.

HIDDEN ► **GREYHOUND ROCK** One of the most secluded strands around, this beach is a beauty. There are startling cliffs in the background and a gigantic boulder—Greyhound Rock—in the foreground; the area is a favorite among those who love to fish. It is also, unfortunately, a favorite for thieves. Keep your valu-ables with you and lock your car. Although the beach has good conditions for swimming, it has been known to be "sharky." Rest-rooms and picnic areas are the only facilities. The path leading to the beach was made unstable by winter storms in 1998; officially, the trail is closed. Beach enthusiasts have, however, forged another stable route from the bluff to beach. ~ Located along Route 1 about 30 miles south of Half Moon Bay. From the parking lot at the roadside follow the path down to the beach; 831-462-8333.

BONNY DOON BEACH This spot ranks among the most popular nude beaches in California. Known up and down the coast, the compact beach is protected on either flank by rugged cliffs. There are dunes at the south end of the beach, caves to the north, plus bevies of barebottomed bathers in between. Keep a close eye on your valuables. This beach has no security nor fa-cilities. ~ Located off Route 1 about eight miles north of Santa Cruz. Watch for the parking lot near the junction with Bonny Doon Road; follow the path across the railroad tracks and down to the beach.

RED, WHITE, AND BLUE BEACH There's a "clothing optional" beach here surrounded by rocky headlands. There are also more RVs than at a Fourth of July picnic. The beach is monitored for safety and no cameras or dogs are allowed. Visi-tors have to pay upon entry. The beach does provide facilities and permits camping but somehow the management takes the nature out of bathing au natural. There are picnic areas, restrooms, and hot showers. Day-use fee, $5. ~ Located off Route 1, five miles north of Santa Cruz. Watch for the red, white, and blue mailbox at Scaroni Road intersection; follow Scaroni Road a short distance west to the beach; 831-423-6332.

▲ There are 35 sites; $10 per night. Campgrounds closed November through January.

▼▼▼▼▼▼▼▼▼▼

Santa Cruz

One of California's original missions, a University of California campus, a historic railroad, and some of the finest Victorian neighborhoods on the coast are just a few of the pluses in Santa Cruz. This town of 51,000 population is in many respects one large playground. It enjoys spectacular white sand beaches, entertaining nightlife, and an old-style boardwalk amusement park. The city faces south, providing the best weather along the Central Coast. Arts and crafts flourish here, and vintage houses adorn the area.

SIGHTS

Route 1, California's magnificent coastal highway, veers slightly inland upon reaching Santa Cruz, which means it's time to find a different waterfront drive. Not to worry, the best way to begin exploring the place is at the north end of town around **Natural Bridges State Beach**. All but one of the sea arches here have collapsed, leading local wags to dub the spot "Fallen Arches." A pretty spot for a picnic, this is the place to pick up West Cliff Drive, which sweeps the Santa Cruz waterfront. The shoreline is a honeycomb of tiny coves, sea arches, and pocket beaches. From **Lighthouse Point** on a clear day, the entire 40-mile curve of Monterey Bay silhouettes the skyline. Even in foggy weather, sea lions cavort on the rocks offshore, while surfers ride the challenging "Steamer Lane" breaks.

Beach Street continues this coast-hugging route to **Santa Cruz Municipal Pier**, a half-mile-long wharf lined with bait shops, restaurants, and fishing charters. Those early morning folks with the sun-furrowed faces are either fishing or crabbing. They are here everyday with lawn chairs and tackle boxes. When reality overcomes optimism, they have been known to duck into nearby fresh fish stores for the day's catch. The pier is a perfect place to promenade, soak up sun, and seek out local color. It also provides a peaceful counterpoint to the next attraction.

Santa Cruz Beach Boardwalk is Northern California's answer to Coney Island. Pride of the city, it dates back to 1907 and sports several old-fashioned rides. The penny arcade features vintage machines as well as modernistic video games. You'll find shooting galleries and candy stalls, coin-operated fortune tellers and do-it-yourself photo machines. Shops sell everything from baubles to bikinis. Then there are the ultimate entertainments: a slow-circling Ferris wheel with chairs suspended high above the beach; the antique merry-go-round, a whirl of mirrors and flashing color; a funicular whose brightly painted cars reflect the sun; rides with names that instantaneously evoke childhood memories —tilt-a-whirl, haunted castle, bumper cars; and that soaring symbol of amusement parks everywhere, the roller coaster. Closed December and most nonsummer weekdays. ~ 400 Beach Street; 831-423-5590.

The **Cocoanut Grove Ballroom**, located on the boardwalk, has hosted Big Band greats like Benny Goodman and the Dorsey brothers, and still sponsors dancing, usually disco or salsa. ~ 400 Beach Street; 831-423-2053.

The playground for shoppers sits several blocks inland along Pacific Avenue. **Pacific Garden Mall** is a tree-lined promenade stretching from Cathcart to Water streets. The entire mall is a study in urban landscaping and planning, beautifully executed. On October 17, 1989, a 7.1 earthquake centered just a few miles from Santa Cruz sent most of the mall tumbling into the street, killing three people.

Within walking distance of the mall are several places that merit short visits. The **Museum of Art and History at the McPherson Center** features changing exhibits that focus primarily on California art. Exhibits are related to the social history of the Santa Cruz area, including photographs and artifacts. Also here is **The Octagon Gallery**, which houses a gift shop for the museums within its century-old, eight-sided structure. Closed Monday. Admission. ~ 705 Front Street; 831-429-1964.

And the **Santa Cruz Mission**, a half-scale replica of the 1791 structure, pales by comparison with the missions in Carmel and San Juan Bautista. Closed Monday. ~ Corner of Emmet and High streets; 831-426-5686.

A remarkable piece of restoration, **Santa Cruz Mission State Historic Park** provides a fascinating timeline on California's past. This 1822 adobe home was built for and by the Yokutz Indians who sold the property to Californios (children of Spanish settlers). Later it was bought by Irish immigrants. Various rooms document each of these periods with artifacts excavated on the site. Illustrating the difficulties of early-19th-century interior design, the Californio Room is decorated with mismatched wallpaper sent at different times from the East Coast. Docents lead tours every Saturday at 2 p.m. Cooking demonstrations, candlemaking, and brick-making commence on "Living History Day" (call for dates). Closed Monday through Wednesday. Admission. ~ 144 School Street near Mission Plaza; 831-425-5849.

The **Santa Cruz County Conference and Visitors Council** has information to help orient you with the area. ~ 701 Front Street; 831-425-1234, 800-833-3494.

Santa Cruz's rich history has left a legacy of elegant Victorian houses. Although there are no guided tours, if you set out on your

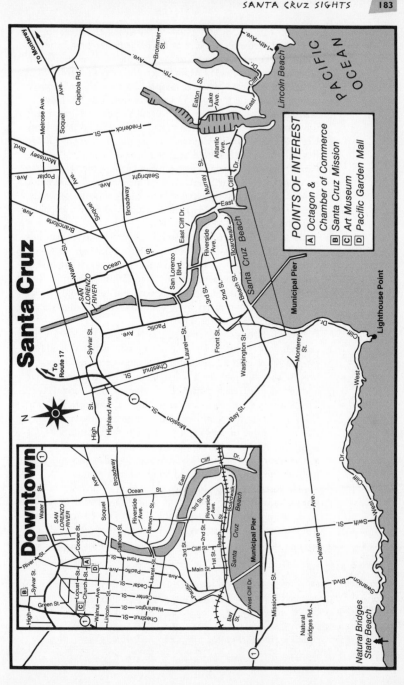

Santa Cruz

To Monterey

Brommer St.

7th Ave.

Capitola Rd.

Melrose Ave.

Soquel Ave.

Frederick St.

Eaton St.

Lake Ave.

East Cliff Dr.

Lincoln Beach

PACIFIC OCEAN

14th Ave.

Morrissey Blvd

Poplar Ave.

Branciforte Ave.

Soquel Ave.

Broadway

Seabright Ave.

Atlantic Ave.

Murray St.

Cliff Dr.

East Cliff Dr.

Water St.

Ocean St.

San Lorenzo Blvd.

SAN LORENZO RIVER

Riverside Ave.

3rd St.

2nd St.

Beach St.

Boardwalk

Santa Cruz Beach

Pacific Ave.

Sylvar St.

Front St.

Laurel St.

Washington St.

Monterey St.

Municipal Pier

West Cliff Dr.

Lighthouse Point

To Route 17

Chestnut St.

N

Highland Ave.

High St.

1

Mission St.

Bay St.

West Cliff Dr.

Swift St.

Delaware Ave.

POINTS OF INTEREST

- **A** Octagon & Chamber of Commerce
- **B** Santa Cruz Mission
- **C** Art Museum
- **D** Pacific Garden Mall

Downtown

1

Broadway

Ocean St.

Water St.

Soquel Ave.

SAN LORENZO RIVER

River St.

Sylvar St.

High St.

B

Cooper St.

Cathcart St.

Locust St.

Church St.

Walnut Ave.

Center St.

Cedar St.

Front St.

Pacific Ave.

Washington St.

Lincoln St.

Chestnut St.

Green St.

C

D

A

1

Riverside Ave.

Barson St.

3rd St.

2nd St.

Cliff St.

1st St.

Beach St.

Main St.

Boardwalk

Santa Cruz Beach

Municipal Pier

West Cliff Dr.

Bay St.

Mission St.

Natural Bridges Rd.

Swanton Blvd.

Natural Bridges State Beach

1

East Cliff Dr.

own you won't be disappointed. In the Beach Hill area, not far from the Boardwalk, be sure to see the gem-like home at **1005 Third Street**, counterpoint to the multilevel confection with Queen Anne turret at **311 Main Street**. Near Pacific Garden Mall is the Civil War–era **Calvary Episcopal Church**, with its clapboard siding and shingle roof. ~ 532 Center Street. The **200 block of Walnut Avenue** is practically wall-to-wall Victorians. Located near the Santa Cruz mission is the pretty, white-painted brick **Holy Cross Roman Catholic Church**. The steeple of this 1889 Gothic Revival beauty is a landmark for miles around. ~ 126 High Street. Nearby **Francisco Alviza House**, vintage 1850s, is the oldest home in town. ~ 109 Sylvar Street. Around the corner, the **200 block of Mission Street** displays several houses built shortly afterwards. Nearby is **W. W. Reynolds House**, which was an Episcopalian Church in 1850. ~ 123 Green Street.

From this last Victorian cluster, High Street leads to the **University of California–Santa Cruz** campus. Turn right at Glenn Coolidge Drive and you'll find an information booth dispensing maps, brochures, and words of wisdom. Those stone ruins and sunbleached buildings nearby are the remains of the old Cowell ranch and limestone quarry from which 2000 of the campus acres were drawn. ~ 831-459-0111.

No ivory tower ever enjoyed the view that UC Santa Cruz commands of Monterey Bay. Set on a hillside, with redwood forest and range land all around, the campus possesses incredible beauty. The university itself is divided into eight colleges, insular and self- defined, each marked by a different architectural style. The best way to see this campus is simply to wander: Walk the fields, trek its redwood groves, and explore the different colleges that make it one of the West's most progressive institutions. Of particular interest at UC Santa Cruz are the organic farm as well as the arboretum, with its Mediterranean garden and outstanding collection of Australian and South African plants.

The **Joseph M. Long Marine Laboratory**, a University of California research facility located off campus, has a small hands-on aquarium and museum open to the public. This 40-acre facility, overlooking marine terraces, also displays other marine life ex-

SURFER SHRINE

Testament to surfers' talent is the tiny **Santa Cruz Surfing Museum** situated in the lighthouse at Lighthouse Point. Here vintage photos and antique boards re-create the history of the Hawaiian sport that landed on the shores of Santa Cruz early in the century. Closed Tuesday. ~ West Cliff Drive and Lighthouse Point, Santa Cruz; 831-429-3429.

hibits. Closed Monday. Admission. ~ End of Delaware Avenue; 831-459-4308.

When seeking overnight accommodations in Santa Cruz, the place to look is near the beach. That is where you'll want to be and, not surprisingly, where you'll find most hotels and motels. The problem during summer months is the cost. In winter you can have a room for a song, but come June the price tags climb.

LODGING

The best bargain in town is **Surfside Apartments**. This seven-unit establishment contains several cottages and houses clustered around a flower garden and courtyard. They are truly efficiency units: no television, telephone, parking facilities, or housekeeping services. But they are comfortably furnished, possess a friendly "beach cottage" feel, and feature kitchens. Located two blocks from the Boardwalk, there are one- and two-bedroom apartments. They are only available from late June through Labor Day. ~ 311 Cliff Street; 831-423-5302. MODERATE.

Another excellent facility is **Ocean Echo Motel and Cottages**, located near a quiet neighborhood beach. This 15-unit clapboard complex sits far from the madding Boardwalk crowd, right at the beach. It represents a perfect choice for anyone seeking a studio or Cape Cod–style cottage. Some have kitchens and private patios. The catch is that the place is extremely popular and many units are rented to weekly residents. ~ 401 Johans Beach Drive; 831-462-4192, fax 831-462-0658; www.oceanecho.com. MODERATE TO DELUXE.

It's big, brash, and blocky, but the **West Coast Santa Cruz Hotel** is also right on the beach. With pool, jacuzzi, oceanfront restaurants, and lounge, this multitiered establishment extends from a hilltop perch down to a sandy strand. Long on aesthetics it isn't, and it's sometimes noisy on weekends and in the summer, but for location it can't be topped. The boardwalk and fishing pier are a short stroll away. Each of the 163 guest rooms is trimly done with fabric walls and contemporary furnishings; each sports a private balcony and ocean view. The question is whether you'll endure the plastic atmosphere for the sake of proximity to the Pacific. It's your call. (Being lazy myself, I'd book reservations in a minute.) ~ 175 West Cliff Drive; 831-426-4330, 800-426-0670, fax 831-427-2025; www.westcoasthotels.com. ULTRA-DELUXE.

There is also **Hostelling International—Santa Cruz**, located some distance from the beach. Set in restored Victorian cottages on well-located Beach Hill, it offers 40 dorm-style beds and two private family rooms. The cottages are two blocks from the beach and boardwalk. There are also hot showers, a kitchen, and a common room; bring a sleeping bag, though sheets are available. There is an 11 p.m. curfew and in summer a three-night maximum stay.

Non-members pay $3 more. ~ 321 Main Street; 831-423-8304. BUDGET.

Country inns are rare in Santa Cruz; this California custom is slowly catching on here. One exception is **Cliff Crest Bed & Breakfast Inn**, a five-bedroom establishment in a historic 1887 Victorian home. Among the features of the house are an outdoor belvedere, a yard landscaped by the designer of San Francisco's Golden Gate Park, and a solarium illuminated through stained-glass windows. Rooms vary in cost from a small room with private bath to the spacious "Rose Room," which has a fireplace. In any case, the decor you're apt to find includes patterned wall-paper and an antique bed. ~ 407 Cliff Street; 831-427-2609, 800-427-2609, fax 831-427-2710; www.virtualcities.com/ons/ ca/z/caz9801. MODERATE.

Another member of this elite club, **Château Victorian**, sits in a vintage home just one block from the Boardwalk. Guests here enjoy two sun decks and a sitting/dining room decorated with antique sideboard and wooden mantel. The entire house has been done by masterful decorators who placed plush carpeting throughout. The place is chockablock with antiques: canopied beds, oak armoires, and so on. Less expensive rooms have carpets and bay window seats and are located in the cottage. Main house rooms are more costly. All guest rooms have fireplaces and feature tile baths. ~ 118 1st Street; 831-458-9458; www.travel guides.com/bb/chateauvictorian. MODERATE TO DELUXE.

Less distinguished, but considerably cheaper, is **Harbor Inn** across town. The place sits in a two-story stucco house in a semi-residential neighborhood a couple blocks from the beach. It supports 19 bedrooms, all with refrigerators and microwaves. There are both private and shared baths. All are spacious, attractive, and inexpensively furnished. The staff is helpful and friendly, making this place a fortuitous addition to the local housing scene. ~ 645 7th Avenue; 831-479-9731, fax 831-479-1067. MODERATE.

Santa Cruz also has a string of neon motels within blocks of the Boardwalk. Count on them to provide small rooms with color television, wall-to-wall carpeting, nicked wooden tables, nauga-hyde chairs, stall showers, etc.; if they have any decorations at all you'll wish they didn't. But what the hell, for a night or two you can call them home. Their rates fluctuate wildly depending on the season and tourist flow. (Generally they charge budget prices in winter; summer prices escalate to the moderate range.) The best of the lot is **St. Charles Court**, which has a pool and is spiffier and quieter than the others. ~ 902 3rd Street; 831-423-2091. MODERATE.

Located within walking distance of the beach is **Big 6 Motel**. It sits in a two-story stucco building and contains 15 rooms with private baths. ~ 335 Riverside Avenue; 831-423-1651. BUDGET.

Right next door is the **Super 8 Motel,** which has 23 rooms decorated in a white and burgundy color scheme. Guests here enjoy lounging at the pool or soaking in the spa. ~ 321 Riverside Avenue; 831-423-9449, 800-906-9066, fax 831-425-5100. BUDGET TO MODERATE.

Most Santa Cruz restaurants can be found near the Boardwalk or in the downtown area, with a few others scattered around town. Of course, along the Boardwalk the favorite dining style is to eat while you stroll. Stop at **Hodgie's** for a corn dog, Italian sausage sandwich, or fried zucchini; try a slice from the **Big Slice Pizza Bar;** sit down to a bowl of clam chowder or crab salad at the **Fisherman's Galley;** or pause at the **Barbary Coast** for cheeseburgers, baked potatoes, or "chicken nuggets." For dessert there are caramel apples, ice cream, cotton candy, popcorn, and salt-water taffy.

DINING

If all this proves a bit much, try one of the budget restaurants on Beach Street, across from the Boardwalk. Foremost is **Beach Street Café,** an attractive little cranny with white tablecloths and potted plants. This café houses the largest U.S. collection of Maxfield Parrish limited-edition prints. Breakfast begins with guacamole omelettes, bagels, croissants, or pancakes. Matter of fact, breakfast continues until late afternoon. Try the "Eggs Sardou" (artichoke bottoms with spinach, poached eggs, and Hollandaise sauce) or the "Eggs Beach Street" (in which they cleverly replace the spinach with sautéed shrimp). The "mile high" burgers are worth trying to get your teeth around. No dinner. ~ 399 Beach Street; 831-426-7621. BUDGET.

Nearby **El Paisano Tamales** has the standard selection of tacos, tostadas, enchiladas, and burritos. Closed Monday and Tuesday in winter. ~ 605 Beach Street; 831-426-2382. BUDGET.

✔ CHECK THESE OUT—UNIQUE DINING

- *Budget:* Treat your heart to a wholesome, healthy meal at **Whole Earth Restaurant,** on the University of California–Santa Cruz campus. *page 189*
- *Moderate:* Opt for an Italian wine—or one from California's own Mediterranean climate—to enhance **Stokes Adobe's** California–Mediterranean fare. *page 205*
- *Moderate to deluxe:* Take an international gourmet journey to **India Joze,** where local artwork complements creative cuisine. *page 188*
- *Ultra-deluxe:* Feast on fabulous food and ocean views at **Sierra Mar,** where the service is as outstanding as the decor. *page 228*

Budget: under $9   Moderate: $9–$18   Deluxe: $18–$25 Ultra-deluxe: over $25

Ideal Bar and Grill is a tourist trap with tradition. It's been one since 1917. It also has decent food and a knockout view, especially from the outdoor deck right on the sand. The place is wedged in a corner between the beach and the pier, which means it looks out on everything, from boardwalk to bounding deep. The specialty is seafood—calamari, oysters, lobster, and salmon. Several pastas, plus a few meat and fowl dishes, round out the menu. ~ 106 Beach Street; 831-423-5271. MODERATE TO DELUXE.

Cozy **Casa Blanca Restaurant**, with its overhead fans and Moroccan flair, is excellent for dinner or Sunday brunch. The place has a wraparound view of the ocean, not to mention a tony decor. The menu includes such gourmet selections as grilled duck, rack of lamb, seafood linguine, and filet mignon with brandy. Casa Blanca boasts one of the largest selections of wines in Santa Cruz County. ~ 101 Main Street; 831-426-9063. MODERATE TO DELUXE.

HIDDEN ▶ Among the many places in the Pacific Garden Mall area, my personal favorite is **The Catalyst**. I don't go there so much to eat as to watch. Not that the food is bad (nor particularly good, for that matter), but simply that The Catalyst is a scene. *The* scene in Santa Cruz. At night the place transmogrifies into a club with live music and unfathomable vibrations. By day, it's just itself, a cavernous structure with a glass roof and enough plants to make it an oversized greenhouse. Indeed, some of the clientele seem to have taken root. There are two bars if you're here to people watch. Otherwise meals are cafeteria-style and include a full breakfast menu, deli sandwiches, burgers, and a few dinner selections. ~ 1011 Pacific Avenue; 831-423-1338. BUDGET.

Join the locals at their favorite Mexican restaurant, **El Palomar**, named the best Mexican restaurant by the readers of *Good Times*, a local entertainment newspaper, for several years running. This leafy Mexican cantina is housed in a beautiful 1930s hotel and sports soaring ceilings and a giant mural of an industrious Mexican woman cooking outdoors. El Palomar serves up such Mexican seafood dishes as prawn burritos and the Jose special —grilled skirt steak, snapper, and prawns. Homemade tortillas and specialty margaritas enhance the delicious fare. ~ 1336 Pacific Avenue; 831-425-7575. MODERATE.

For Japanese food there's **Benten**, a comfortable restaurant complete with a sushi bar. They serve an array of traditional dishes including *yosenabe*, sashimi, tempura, teriyaki, and a special plate called *kaki* fry (deep-fried breaded oysters). Understated and reliable. Closed Tuesday. ~ 1541 Pacific Avenue, Suite B; 831-425-7079. BUDGET TO MODERATE.

Covering the rest of the Far Eastern spectrum is **India Joze**, serving Near to Far East Asian cuisine. Stop by for lunch, dinner, or Sunday brunch and you're bound to enjoy the creative menu.

For brunch the staff recommends their *masala dolsa* (an Indian *urad dahl* crêpe filled with spiced new potatoes) served with *dahl*, Joe's yogurt, and chutney. At lunch try the dragon calamari (with tangy fresh mint, cilantro glaze, bamboo shoots, and black Asian mushrooms). The dinner menu offers up dragon chicken (boneless chicken in a mint cilantro glaze). If you are in town in August stop in for their calamari festival at lunch and dinner. Located in the Santa Cruz Arts Center, India Joze is decorated with artworks by local artisans, illuminated through skylights, and surrounded by pink pastel walls. Don't miss it. ~ 1001 Center Street; 831-427-3554. MODERATE TO DELUXE.

Aldo's Harbor Restaurant, a café with patio deck overlooking Santa Cruz Harbor, has seafood dishes, pastas, soups, salads, and sandwiches. Conveniently located near Seabright Beach, this unassuming little place serves breakfast and lunch. ~ 616 Atlantic Avenue; 831-426-3736. BUDGET.

One of the best dining deals anywhere can be found up the hillside on the University of California–Santa Cruz campus. The **Whole Earth Restaurant** not only serves tasty, nutritious meals, it does so at low prices. Limited to breakfast and lunch menus during summer, the restaurant is also open for dinner during the school year. Serving all natural foods, it features pasta and rice dishes with vegetarian sauces in addition to the regular array of sandwiches, soups, salads, and juices. On a typical night, the dinner special will be vegetarian, but occasionally there is also a chicken or a seafood dish. The restaurant itself is neatly tucked into a grove of tall trees and features outdoor dining on a wooden deck. Providing a touch of style at student prices, the facility is far removed from the bustle of busy downtown Santa Cruz. ~ Redwood Building; 831-426-8255. BUDGET.

SHOPPING

The central shopping district in Santa Cruz is along **Pacific Garden Mall**, a six-block strip of Pacific Avenue converted to a promenade. The section is neatly landscaped with flowering shrubs and potted trees and its sidewalks, widened for window browsers, overflow with people.

You can stop by **Artisans**, which deals in fine handcrafts and gift items by local artists. They feature outstanding pottery, woodwork, glassware, and jewelry. ~ 1364 Pacific Avenue; 831-423-8183. The **Bookshop Santa Cruz** is the finest among this college town's many wonderful bookstores. ~ 1520 Pacific Avenue; 831-423-0900.

Strolling along **Pacific Avenue**, you will find galleries, gift stores, plus arts-and-crafts shops run by local artists. Also, many artisans' studios are located at the center, making it a gathering place for craftspeople as well as a clearinghouse for their wares. ~ 1001 Center Street.

NIGHTLIFE   In Santa Cruz, **The Catalyst** is the common denominator. A popular restaurant and hangout by day, it becomes a favored entertainment spot at night. There's live music most weekday evenings in the Atrium, where local groups perform. But on weekends the heavyweights swing into town and The Catalyst lines up big rock performers. Some all-ages shows. Cover charge for live bands. ~ 1011 Pacific Avenue; 831-423-1336.

The unassuming **Kuumba Jazz Center** headlines top-name musicians. Folks under 21 are welcome at this club. Cover. ~ 320 Cedar Street; 831-427-2227.

The Jahva House is a funky vegetarian café in an old motor-repair shop. Relax on a couch beneath the hanging plants and soak up the (sometimes live) music while sipping a soy espresso drink. ~ 120 Union Street; 831-459-9876.

If you're in the mood to dance to disco or salsa music call the **Cocoanut Grove Ballroom**. Live bands occasionally perform here. Cover. ~ 400 Beach Street; 831-423-2053.

The Crow's Nest offers eclectic entertainment with an ocean view. On any given night they will be headlining jazz, reggae, salsa, rock, blues, or, on Sunday night, comedy. Cover. ~ 2218 East Cliff Drive; 831-476-4560.

The crowd at **Blue Lagoon** dances to taped and deejay music during the week, and watches go-go dancers on Friday and Saturday night in summer. The club draws "gay boys and girls with a few straight people thrown in for color." Cover on weekends and Tuesday ('70s disco night). ~ 923 Pacific Avenue; 831-423-7117.

BEACHES & PARKS   **NATURAL BRIDGES STATE BEACH** 🚶 🏊 🏃 🏖 🚣 ⛵ Northernmost of the Santa Cruz beaches, this is a small park with a half moon–shaped beach and tidepools. This is a popular windsurfing spot in the summer. It's quite pretty, though a row of houses flanks one side. In the winter, surfers gather on the reef break. This is also an excellent spot to watch monarch butterflies during their annual winter migration (from October through late February). During these months there are weekend guided tours of the eucalyptus groves. Facilities include picnic areas, a visitors center, a bookstore, and restrooms. No dogs are allowed. Day-use fee, $6. ~ Located at the end of West Cliff Drive near the western edge of Santa Cruz; 831-423-4609.

SANTA CRUZ BEACH 🚲 🏊 🏃 🏖 🚣 🛥 🏄 ⛵ Of the three major beaches extending along the Santa Cruz waterfront, this is the most popular, most crowded, and most famous. All for a very simple reason: the bustling Santa Cruz Boardwalk, with its gaudy amusement park and restaurants, runs the entire length of the sand, and the Santa Cruz Municipal Pier anchors one end of the beach. This, then, is the place to come for crowds and excitement. "Steamer Lane" is the Santa Cruz surfing hotspot. A series of reef breaks are located along West Cliff Drive, extending west to Lighthouse Point. Facilities at Santa Cruz Beach include restrooms, showers, seasonal lifeguard, volleyball, restaurants, and groceries. For rentals of surfboards, boogieboards, wet suits, umbrellas, and other beach equipment, you should contact Santa Cruz Beach Services at 206 Municipal Wharf; 831-429-3460. ~ Located along Beach Street; there is access from the Santa Cruz Municipal Wharf and along the Boardwalk; 831-429-5747.

SEABRIGHT BEACH Also known as Castle Beach, Seabright is second in Santa Cruz's string of beaches. This beauty extends from the San Lorenzo River mouth to the jetty at Santa Cruz Harbor. It's long, wide, and backdropped by bluffs. The views are as magnificent as from other nearby beaches, and the crowds will be lighter than along the Boardwalk. There are restrooms, fire rings, and a lifeguard. ~ Access to the beach is along East Cliff Drive at the foot of Mott and Cypress avenues, or at the end of Atlantic Avenue; 831-429-2850.

TWIN LAKES STATE BEACH Just the other side of Santa Cruz Harbor is this odd-shaped beach. Smaller than the two beaches to the north, it's also less crowded. The park is 94 acres, with a lagoon behind the beach and a jetty flanking one side. A very pretty spot. Surfing is sometimes okay in winter or after a storm. There are restrooms and seasonal lifeguards. ~ Along East Cliff Drive, south of Santa Cruz Harbor; 831-429-2850.

LINCOLN BEACH, SUNNY COVE, MORAN LAKE BEACH Located along the eastern end of Santa Cruz, these three sandy beaches are in residential areas. As a result, they draw local people, not tourists; they're also more difficult to get to, and, happily, are less crowded. All are backdropped by bluffs. If you want to buck the crowds, they're worth the trouble. There are restrooms and picnic areas at Lincoln Beach and Moran Lake Beach; otherwise amenities are scarce. Parking is a problem throughout the area (though Moran Lake Beach has a parking lot where you can park all day for a fee during summer and weekends, otherwise free). ~ All three beaches are near East Cliff Drive. Lincoln Beach (part of Twin Lakes State Beach) is at the end of 14th Avenue, Sunny Cove at the end of 17th Avenue, and Moran Lake Beach is near Lake Avenue; 831-462-8333.

Santa Cruz to Monterey

From Santa Cruz, coastal Route 1 courses south through Capitola, well known for its attractive beach and its September Begonia Festival, and through Aptos, another bedroom community with equally sparkling beaches.

SIGHTS   Aptos' most popular place these days is a foreboding forest located at latitude 37° 2' and longitude 121° 53'. That precise spot, at the end of a two-mile trail in the Forest of Nisene Marks State Park, is the **1989 earthquake epicenter.** A stake now marks ground zero of the 7.1 shaker that devastated Northern California. To reach the trailhead, follow Aptos Creek Road north from Aptos to the Nisene Marks parking lot. ~ 831-761-1795.

HIDDEN ▶   In nearby Rio del Mar, there's a **rural side trip** that carries you past miles of farmland before rejoining Route 1 near Watsonville. To take this side trip, you should follow San Andreas Road, which tunnels through forest, then opens into rich agricultural acres. Intricately tilled fields roll down to the sea and edge right up to the foot of the mountains. At the end of San Andreas Road, follow Beach Street to the ocean. The entire stretch of coastline is flanked by high sand dunes, a wild and exotic counterpoint to the furrowed fields nearby.

The Pajaro Valley area counts its wealth in strawberries, apples, flowers, and mushrooms.

Beach Street leads back into Watsonville. Central to the surrounding farm community, Watsonville is the world's strawberry-growing capital. The town is also rich in **Victorian houses,** which visitors can tour with a printed guide available from the very helpful **Chamber of Commerce.** ~ 444 Main Street, Watsonville; 831-724-3900.

Back on Route 1, you'll pass **Moss Landing,** a weather-beaten fishing harbor. With its antique stores, one-lane bridge, brightly painted boats, and unpainted fish market, the town has a warm personality. There is one eyesore, however, a huge power plant with twin smokestacks that stand out like two sentinels of an occupying army. Otherwise the place is enchanting, particularly

HIDDEN ▶   nearby **Elkhorn Slough National Estuarine Research Reserve,** a 1400-acre world of salt marshes and tidal flats managed by a federal partnership between the Department of Fish and Game and the National Oceanic and Atmospheric Administration. Within this delicate environment live some 400 species of invertebrates, 80 species of fish and 20 species of birds (among them redshouldered hawks, peregrine falcons, and acorn woodpeckers) as well as harbor seals, oysters, and clams (but don't eat the oysters or clams). Guided tours on the weekend. To get to the visitors center from Route 1, follow Dolan Road for three miles, go left on Elkhorn Road, and proceed two more miles. Closed Monday and Tuesday. Admission. ~ 1700 Elkhorn Road, Watsonville; 831-728-2822.

Next in this parade of small towns is **Castroville,** "Artichoke Center of the World." Beyond it is a cluster of towns—Marina, Sand City, and Seaside—that probably represent the sand capitals of the world. The entire area rests on a sand dune that measures up to 300 feet in depth, and extends ten miles along the coast and as much as eight miles inland. From here you can trace a course into Monterey along wind-tilled rows of sand.

Capitola Venetian Hotel is a mock Italian complex next to Capitola Beach. With its stucco and red tile veneer, ornamental molding, and carved wooden doors, it's a poor cousin to the grand villas of Venice. The 20 guest rooms come equipped with kitchens. There are few wall decorations and the furnishings lack character, but the atmosphere is pleasant. ~ 1500 Wharf Road, Capitola; 831-476-6471, 800-332-2780. DELUXE.

Harbor Lights Motel, a few steps farther uphill from the beach, is similarly laid out but in a more modern fashion. This ten-unit stucco building has rooms with completely equipped kitchens and ocean views. The accommodations have shag rugs, hokey wall paintings, and bland furniture—but remember, you're paying for what's outside, not inside. ~ 5000 Cliff Drive, Capitola; 831-476-0505, 831-476-0235. MODERATE TO DELUXE.

Does a trip around the world interest you? If so, the **Inn at Depot Hill** might save you time and money without sacrificing the feel of the trip. This 12-room bed and breakfast, fashioned from a former train station, features internationally decorated rooms with names like "Paris," "Côte d'Azur," and "Portofino." There is a fireplace in each room and most come with a patio and hot tub. Full breakfast, hors d'oeuvres with wine, and dessert are included with a night's stay. ~ 250 Monterey Avenue, Capitola; 831-462-3376, 800-572-2632, fax 831-462-3697; www.innatdepot hill.com. ULTRA-DELUXE.

Attention to cozy detail is the forte of the **Blue Spruce Inn**. The rooms come with a variety of decorations ranging from wicker furniture and gas fireplaces to carved oak beds and stained-glass murals. Indeed, this three-building bed and breakfast leaves no quaint stone unturned. In addition to a nightly pillow fluff and turn-down, guests also receive a fresh robe for a long winter's nap. Half the rooms have jacuzzi tubs; all have access to a garden-set hot tub. Full breakfast included. ~ 2815 South Main Street, Soquel; 831-464-1137, 800-559-1137, fax 831-475-0608; www. bluespruce.com. MODERATE TO DELUXE.

With two miles of beachfront, **Pajaro Dunes** is ideal for those who want to go down to the sea. Located midway between Santa Cruz and Monterey, this resort colony has 130 condominiums, townhouses, and beachhomes that range from one to five bedrooms. While decorating schemes vary from beach contemporary to brass and glass, all units offer kitchens, fireplaces, decks, and barbecues. There are 19 on-site tennis courts. The big units are a good bet for large family groups. A two-night minimum stay is required. ~ 2661 Beach Road, Watsonville; 831-722-9201, 800-675-8808; www.pajarodunes.com. ULTRA-DELUXE.

DINING   The area's foremost dining room is actually outside Santa Cruz in a nearby suburb. True to its name, the multitiered **Shadow-brook Restaurant** sits in a wooded spot through which a creek flows. Food is almost an afterthought at this elaborate affair; upon entering the grounds you descend either via a funicular or a sinuous, fern-draped path. Once inside, you'll encounter a labyrinth of dining levels and rooms, luxuriously decorated with potted plants, stone fireplaces, and candlelit tables. A mature tree grows through the floor and ceiling of one room; in others, vines climb along the walls. When you finally chart the course to a table, you'll be offered a cuisine including prime rib, salmon, and other fresh seafood dishes. Definitely a dining experience. Dinner and Sunday brunch. ~ 1750 Wharf Road, Capitola; 831-475-1511. MODERATE TO DELUXE.

Capitola Beach is wall-to-wall with seafood eateries. They line the strand, each with a different theme—but they all seem to merge into a bunch of pit stops for hungry beachgoers. If you're expecting me to recommend one you are asking more than a mortal man can do. I say, when in doubt, guess.

Put your money on the beachfront **Stockton Bridge Grille**. Seafood specialties include broiled mahimahi and grilled salmon salad. Also on the menu are smoked salmon ravioli, scallops, and scampi. The decor: modern Californian with abstract art on the walls. ~ 231 Esplanade, Capitola; 831-462-1350. MODERATE.

Maloney's Harbor Inn serves up fresh fish as well as the usual array of meat, chicken, and pasta dishes. Maloney's rests on the water overlooking a pretty harbor and an uncommonly ugly power plant. ~ Route 1, Moss Landing; 831-724-9371. MODERATE TO DELUXE.

Touted as the best Mexican restaurant in Monterey County is **The Whole Enchilada**, specializing in seafood dishes. The chef uses locally grown produce like Castroville artichokes and chiles, fresh fish, prawns and oysters. Try the "whole enchilada" entrée —fillet of red snapper wrapped in corn tortillas topped with melted cheese and chile salsa. Save room for flan! ~ 7902 Route 1 at Moss Landing Road, Moss Landing; 831-633-5398. BUDGET TO MODERATE.

SHOPPING   Located along Route 1 south of Santa Cruz, the coastal village of Moss Landing is a must for antique hounds. More than 20 shops offer a wide array of treasures from the good old days. Clustered around the intersection of Moss Landing Road and Sand Holt Road are several shops that warrant a close look.

Stepping into **Yesterday's Books** is a bit like discovering a private library filled with antiquarian treasures. Closed Tuesday. ~ 7902 Sand Holt Road, Building E, Moss Landing; 831-633-8033. **The Little Red Barn** is the biggest antique store in town. This

1400-square-foot shop sells dolls, china, art glass, furniture, and many other items. Closed Tuesday. ~ 8461 Moss Landing Station, Moss Landing; 831-633-5583.

For a relaxing evening, try **Shadowbrook Restaurant**. Its soft lighting and luxurious surroundings create a sense of well-being, like brandy and a blazing fire. They offer guitar music on Saturday nights. ~ 1750 Wharf Road, Capitola; 831-475-1511.

NIGHTLIFE

Several of the restaurant lounges lining Capitola's waterfront have nightly entertainment. Over at **Zelda's** they feature a nightly variety of live musical acts ranging from blues and jazz to rock. Cover. ~ 203 Esplanade, Capitola; 831-475-4900.

Moss Landing Inn is The Whole Enchilada's full-service bar, featuring live music nightly. ~ 7902 Route 1 at Moss Landing Road, Moss Landing; 831-633-5398.

CAPITOLA CITY BEACH Sedimentary cliffs flank a corner of this sand carpet but the rest is heavily developed. Popular with visitors for decades, Capitola is a well-known resort community. However, following a year of heavy storms the beach often disappears under the high tide, and locals claim that there was no beach to speak of in the summer of 1994 and 1995. Seafood restaurants line its shore and boutiques flourish within blocks of the beach. A great place for families because of the adjacent facilities, it trades seclusion for service. The ocean is well protected for water sports and in winter, surfers enjoy the breaks near the jetty, pier, and river mouth. There are restrooms, showers, lifeguards, a fishing pier, and volleyball. ~ Located in the center of Capitola; 831-475-7300.

BEACHES & PARKS

NEW BRIGHTON STATE BEACH This sandy crescent adjoins Seacliff Beach and enjoys a wide vista of Monterey Bay. Headlands protect the beach for swimmers and beginning surfers; clamming is also popular. Within its mere 94 acres, the park contains a forested bluff. There are picnic areas, fire pits, restrooms, and showers (for campers only). Day-use fee, $6. ~ Off Route 1 in Capitola, four miles south of Santa Cruz; 831-464-6330, 831-464-6329.

▲ There are 112 sites for tents and RVs in a wooded area inland from the beach; $14 to $19 per night. There are no RV hookups. Reservations are required; people book up to seven months in advance. Call 800-444-7275.

SEACLIFF STATE BEACH This two-mile strand is very popular. *Too* popular: during summer, RVs park along its entire length and crowds gather on the waterfront. That's because it provides the safest swimming along this section of coast. There are roving lifeguards on duty during the summer and a protective headland nearby. The visitors center offers guided walks year-round to look at fossils. The beach also sports a pier favored by anglers. It's a pretty place, but oh so busy. There are picnic areas, restrooms, and showers. Day-use fee, $6. ~ Off Route 1 in Aptos, five miles south of Santa Cruz; 831-685-6500.

▲ There are 26 sites for RVs and self-contained vehicles (full hookups); $27 per night. There are also 20 overflow sites for self-contained vehicles (no picnic tables, fireplaces, or hookups); $18 per night. Reservations are required; call 800-444-7275.

FOREST OF NISENE MARKS STATE PARK 🚶 🚲 This semi-wilderness expanse, a few miles inland, encompasses nearly 10,000 acres. Within its domain are redwood groves, meandering streams, rolling countryside, and dense forest. About 30 miles of hiking trails wind through the preserve. Along them you can explore fossil beds, deserted logger cabins, old trestles, and railroad beds; you can also hike to the epicenter of the 1989 earthquake. The park is a welcome complement to the natural features along the coast. There are picnic tables and barbeque pits. Day-use fee, $3. ~ From Route 1 southbound take the Seacliff Beach exit in Aptos, five miles south of Santa Cruz. Take an immediate left on State Park Drive, pass over the highway, and then go right on Soquel Drive. Follow this for a half-mile; then head left on Aptos Creek Road. This paved road turns to gravel as it leads into the forest; 831-763-7063.

MANRESA UPLANDS STATE BEACH 🏊 🎣 ⚓ Here you'll find a strip of white sand bookended by blufftop homes. Popular with surfers, it provides a sweeping view of Monterey Bay. A bit more removed than other nearby beaches, Manresa nevertheless can be quite popular on summer afternoons. Facilities include restrooms, lifeguards, picnic tables, fire pits, and showers. Day-use fee, $6. ~ Located 13 miles south of Santa Cruz; from Route 1, take the Larkin Valley Road and San Andreas Road exit, turn right onto San Andreas Road and follow it several miles to the park turnoff; 831-761-1795.

▲ There are 64 walk-in tent sites in Manresa Uplands Campground next to the beach; $14 to $18 per night; 831-761-1795; reservations: 800-444-7075.

SUNSET STATE BEACH 🏊 🎣 ⚓ Over three miles of beach and sand dunes create one of the area's prettiest parks. There are bluffs and meadows behind the beach as well as Monterey pines and cypress trees. This 324-acre park is a popular spot for fishing and clamming. Surfing is also done here but the break is powerful —exercise caution. But remember, there's more fog here and farther south than in the Santa Cruz area. There are picnic areas, restrooms, and showers. Day-use fee, $6. ~ Located 16 miles south of Santa Cruz; from Route 1, take the Larkin Valley and San Andreas

Road exit, turn right onto San Andreas Road and follow it several miles to the park turnoff; 831-763-7063.

▲ Permitted in 90 sites; $14 to $18 per night; no RV hookups; hiker/biker camp available ($7 per person). Reservations: 800-444-7275.

ZMUDOWSKI, MOSS LANDING, AND SALINAS RIVER STATE BEACHES These three state parks are part of a long stretch of sand dunes. They all contain broad beaches and vistas along Monterey Bay. Though relatively uncrowded, their proximity to Moss Landing's smoke-belching power plant is a severe drawback. Quite suitable anywhere else, they can't compete with their neighbors in this land of beautiful beaches. Surfing is good near the sandbar at Salinas River; great at Moss Landing, which draws locals from Santa Cruz. Each beach has toilet facilities; an equestrian concessionaire at Salinas River offers trail rides. Day-use fee at Moss Landing, $3. ~ All three are located off Route 1 within a few miles of Moss Landing; 831-384-7695.

▲ There's en route camping at Moss Landing for self-contained vehicles (no hookups); $7 per night (maximum one-night stay).

MARINA STATE BEACH The tall, fluffy sand dunes at this 170-acre park are unreal. They're part of a giant dune covering 50 square miles throughout the area. A boardwalk takes you through the sand to the beach and gives you an up-close view of the unique vegetation. There are marvelous views of Monterey here, plus a chance to fish or sunbathe. It is also the perfect place to try out hang gliding with tandem rides for first-time gliders and hang gliding rentals for the more experienced. Swimming is allowed, though rip tides occur. Regarding surfing, there's a great beach break in summer but it's dangerous in winter. The only facilities are restrooms. ~ Located along Route 1, nine miles north of Monterey; 831-384-7695.

Monterey

Over two million visitors visit the Monterey area every year. Little wonder. Its rocky coast fringed with cypress forests, its hills dotted with palatial homes—the area is unusually beautiful. The town of Monterey also serves as a gateway to the tumbling region of Big Sur.

For a tour of Monterey Peninsula, begin in Monterey itself. Here are historic homes, an old Spanish presidio, Fisherman's Wharf, and Cannery Row. Set in a natural amphitheater of forested hills, it is also home to one of the richest marine sanctuaries along the entire California coast. Little wonder that this town, with a population that numbers 32,000 people, has served as an inspiration for Robert Louis Stevenson and John Steinbeck. With a downtown district that reflects small town America and a waterfront that once supported a rich fishing and canning industry, Monterey remains one of the most vital spots on the California Coast.

SIGHTS   History in Monterey is a precious commodity that in most cases has been carefully preserved. Ancient adobe houses and Spanish-style buildings are so commonplace that some have been converted into shops and restaurants. Others are museums or points of interest that can be seen on a walking tour along the **Path of History**. This "Path," carrying through the center of Monterey, measures over two miles if walked in its entirety.

The best place to begin is the **Custom House** at #1 Custom House Plaza across from Fisherman's Wharf. California's earliest government building, the structure dates back to 1827. It was here in 1846 that Commodore Sloat raised the American flag, claiming California for the United States. Today the stone and adobe building houses displays from an 1830-era cargo ship. In Stanton Center you'll find the model ships, old nautical photographs, and a two-story-tall rotating lighthouse lens of the **Monterey Maritime Museum**. Admission. ~ 5 Custom House Plaza; 831-375-2553.

Across the plaza rises **Pacific House**, a two-story balconied adobe with a luxurious courtyard. Constructed in 1847, it was used over the years to house everything from military supplies to a tavern to a courtroom and church. The exhibits inside trace California's history from American Indian days to the advent of Spanish settlers and American pioneers and to the heyday of the canning industry in the 1930s. The house's renovation will be complete in April 1999. ~ 10 Custom House Plaza; 831-649-7118.

Just behind Pacific House sits **Casa del Oro**, a tiny white adobe that served as Monterey's general store during the 1850s. Today it houses the **Joseph Boston Store**, an old-fashioned mercantile shop selling Early American items. Closed Monday through Wednesday. ~ Olivier and Scott streets; 831-649-3364.

Diagonally across the intersection on Olivier Street sits an office complex behind which is located the **Brick House**, purportedly the first such house in California. Adjacent to this is the **Whaling Station**, an adobe with a balcony from which the early whalers spotted their migrating bounty.

California's First Theater, a block up the street, certainly qualifies as a living museum. It's a landmark building that is still used to stage theatrical performances (mostly 19th-century melodramas, complete with hisses and boos, performed by America's oldest continually operating theater troupe). Performances are held Friday and Saturday (Wednesday through Saturday during July

Monterey

MONTEREY BAY

Presidio of Monterey

To Cannery Row

Artillery St.

Seeno St.

Scott St.

California's First Theater

Casa del Oro

Pacific St.

Tunnel

Custom House

Monterey Maritime Museum

Custom House Plaza

Pacific House

Jackson St.

Van Buren St.

Casa Soberanes

PATH OF HISTORY

Lighthouse Ave.

Del Monte Ave.

Franklin St.

Casa Serrano

Visitor Information

Calle Principal

Washington St.

Adams St.

Figueroa St.

Pierce St.

Alvarado St.

Tyler St.

Bonifacio

Jefferson St.

Larkin House

Pearl St.

Alma St.

Colton Hall and Old Jail

Friendly Plaza

Casa Gutierrez

Polk St.

Cooper-Molera Adobe

Houston St.

Stevenson House

Abrego St.

Webster St.

Dutra St.

Madison St.

Monterey Peninsula Museum of Art

Church St.

Royal Presidio Chapel

Hartnell St.

Casa St.

Munras St.

Fremont St.

Fisherman's Wharf

Marina

Municipal Wharf #2

and August). Wander this clapboard and adobe building and you will encounter almost a century-and-a-half of Monterey's dramatic tradition. ~ Scott and Pacific streets; 831-375-4916.

A left on Pacific Street leads to **Casa Soberanes**, a Monterey-style house with red tile roof and second-story balcony. Completed in the 1840s, this impressive structure was built by a warden at the Custom House. Part of the Monterey State Historic Park, Casa Soberanes can be visited by a guided tour every afternoon. Admission. ~ 336 Pacific Street; 831-649-7118.

Casa Serrano, built in 1843, contains wrought-iron decorations over its narrow windows. Once home to a blind Spanish teacher, it is now open for touring only on weekends. For more information contact the Monterey History and Art Association. ~ 412 Pacific Street; 831-372-2608.

Nearby spreads **Friendly Plaza**, a tree-shaded park that serves as a focus for several important places. The **Monterey Peninsula Museum of Art** sponsors two separate museums, both featuring works and artifacts by early and contemporary California artists, as well as special exhibits. The **Civic Center** is the larger of the two and is open Wednesday through Sunday. Admission. ~ 559 Pacific Street; 831-372-7591. **La Mirada**, the other museum, is housed in an old adobe with period furnishings. Closed Monday through Wednesday. ~ 720 Mirada Avenue; 831-372-7591.

Pierce Street, running along the upper edge of the plaza, contains a string of historic 19th-century homes. **Colton Hall** is an imposing two-story stone structure with white pillars and classical portico. Site of California's 1849 constitutional convention, it displays memorabilia from that critical event. Given its unique architecture and lovely setting, it's one of Monterey's prettiest buildings. ~ Pacific Street at Jefferson and Madison streets. The squat **Old Jail** next door, fashioned from granite, with wrought-iron bars across the windows, dates back to the same era. It creates a startling contrast to its stately neighbor. **Casa Gutierrez**, located across the street, was built by a cavalryman with 15 children. That was back in 1841; its last incarnation (until late 1995) was as a Mexican restaurant.

A SACRED SPOT

The **Presidio** is also the site of an ancient Costanoan Indian village and burial ground. And a granite monument at the corner of Pacific and Artillery streets marks the spot where in 1602 the Spanish celebrated the first Catholic mass in California. In addition to historic points, the Presidio grounds enjoy marvelous views of Monterey. You can look down upon the town, then scan along the bay's curving horizon.

After exploring the plaza, turn left into Madison Street from Pacific Street, then left again along Calle Principal to one of the town's most famous homes, the **Larkin House**. Designed in 1835 by Thomas Larkin and combining New England and Spanish elements, it's a two-story adobe house with a ground floor veranda and a second-story balcony. Today the antique home is a house museum filled with period pieces. The house is especially important historically because its owner was the only United States Consul to California and a key player in the American takeover. Admission. ~ 510 Calle Principal; 831-649-7118.

A right on Jefferson Street and another quick right on Polk Street takes you past a cluster of revered houses. **Casa Amesti**, dating from 1824, is presently a private club. Call for tour information. Admission. ~ 516 Polk Street; 831-372-8173. The **Cooper-Molera Adobe**, across the road, is a sprawling affair that includes a 19th-century museum as well as a "historic garden" filled with herbs and vegetables of the Mexican era. The massive structure, over two decades in the making, housed Thomas Larkin's half-brother, a merchant who sailed the waters of South America, China, and the Pacific isles. Visit by guided tour (call for tour information). Admission. ~ 525 Polk Street; 831-649-7118. Facing each other on either side of Polk and Hartnell streets are two more vintage homes, the **Gabriel de la Torre Adobe**, 1836, and the **Stokes Adobe**, erected in the 1840s.

If you are still with me for the grand finale, backtrack along Polk Street one block to the five-way intersection, take a soft right onto Pearl Street, walk a few short blocks, then turn right on Houston Street to the **Stevenson House**. A grand two-story edifice with shuttered windows and landscaped yard, this former rooming house was Robert Louis Stevenson's residence for several months in 1879. The Scottish writer, vivacious but sickly, arrived in Monterey to visit his wife-to-be Fanny Osbourne. The fragile wanderer had sailed the Atlantic and traveled overland across the continent. Writing for local newspapers, depending in part upon the kindness of strangers for sustenance, he fell in love with Fanny and Monterey both. From the surrounding countryside he drew inspiration for some of his most famous books, including *Treasure Island*. In addition to its period furniture and early California decor, the house features numerous items from Stevenson's life. There are personal belongings, original manuscripts, and first editions, all of which can be viewed on a guided tour (call for information). Admission. ~ 530 Houston Street; 831-649-7118.

For information about guided tours of Casa Soberanes, Larkin House, Cooper-Molera Adobe, and Stevenson House contact **Monterey State Historic Park**. You can see all four buildings on a guided 90-minute walking tour that runs daily. Admission. ~ 831-649-7118.

Two additional places of historical note are located in Monterey but a significant distance from the Path of History. The **Royal Presidio Chapel** is a graceful expression of the 18th-century town. Decorative molding adorns the facade of the old adobe church while the towering belfry, rising along one side, makes the structure asymmetrical. Heavy wooden doors lead to a long, narrow chapel hung with dusty oil paintings. This was the mission that Father Junípero Serra founded in 1770, just before moving his congregation a few miles south to Carmel. ~ 550 Church Street.

The **Presidio of Monterey** sits on a hill near the northwest corner of town. Established as a fort by the Spanish in 1792, it currently serves as a foreign language institute for the military. There are cannons banked in a hillside, marking the site of Fort Mervine, built by the Americans in 1846. ~ At Pacific and Artillery streets; 831-242-5000.

Strangely, Monterey, which elsewhere demonstrates special care in preserving its heritage, has let its wharves and piers fall prey to tinsel-minded developers. **Municipal Wharf #2** is a welcome exception. It's actually all that remains from the heyday of Monterey's fishing fleet. Here broad-hulled boats still beat at their moorings, while landlubbing anglers cast from pierside. Gulls perch along the handrails, sea lions bark from beneath the pilings, and pelicans work the waterfront. On one side is the dilapidated warehouse of a long-defunct freezer company. At the end of the dock, fish companies still operate. It's a primal place of cranes and pulleys, forklifts and conveyor belts. There are ice boxes and old packing crates scattered hither-thither, exuding the romance and stench of the industry. ~ At the foot of Figueroa Street.

Then there is the parody, much better known than the original. **Fisherman's Wharf**, like its San Francisco namesake, has been transmogrified into what the travel industry thinks tourists think a fishing pier should look like. Something was lost in the translation. Few fishing boats operate from the wharf these days; several charter companies sponsor glass-bottom boat tours and whale-watching expeditions. Otherwise the waterfront haven is just one more mall, a macadam corridor lined on either side with shops. There are ersatz art galleries, shops vending candy apples and personalized mugs, plus a school of seafood restaurants. A few outdoor fish markets still sell live crabs, lobsters, and squid, but the symbol of the place is the hurdy-gurdy man with performing monkey who greets you at the entrance.

Actually this is only the most recent in the wharf's long series of changes. The dock was built in 1846 to serve cargo schooners dealing in hides. Within a decade the whaling industry took it over, followed finally by Italian fishermen catching salmon, cod, and mackerel. During the Cannery Row era of the '30s, the sardine industry played a vital part in the life of the wharf. Today all that has given way to a bizarre form of public nostalgia.

The same visionary appears responsible for the resurrection of **Cannery Row**. Made famous by John Steinbeck's feisty novels *Cannery Row* and *Sweet Thursday*, this oceanfront strip has been transformed into a neighborhood of wax museums and dainty antique shops. As Steinbeck remarked upon returning to the old sardine canning center, "They fish for tourists now."

The building that housed Doc Rickett's Marine Lab stands at 800 Cannery Row.

Cannery Row of yore was an unappealing collection of corrugated warehouses, run-down stores, seedy hotels, and gaudy whorehouses. There were about 30 canneries, 100 fishing boats, and 4000 workers populating the place. The odor was horrible, but for several decades the sardine industry breathed life into the Monterey economy. The business died when the fish ran out—just before *Cannery Row* was published in 1945.

Before the entire oceanfront strip was developed in the early 1980s, you could still capture a sense of the old Cannery Row. A few weather-beaten factories remained. Rust stained their ribbed sides, windows were punched, and roofs had settled to an inward curve. In places, the stone pilings of old loading docks still stood, haunted by sea gulls. Now only tourists and memories remain.

At the other end of the Row, Steinbeck aficionados will find a few literary settings. La Ida Café, now an ice cream parlor called **Kalisa's La Ida Café**, still retains its same tumbledown appearance. ~ 851 Cannery Row; 831-375-5328. Wing Chong Market is now **Alicia's Antiques**. Closed Monday through Wednesday. ~ 835 Cannery Row; 831-372-1423.

In the middle you'll encounter the scene of the malling of Cannery Row. Old warehouses were renovated into shopping centers, new buildings rose up, and the entire area experienced a face lift. Brightest tooth in the updated smile is the **Edgewater Packing Company**, a miniature amusement park with a hand-carved vintage-1905 carousel. ~ 640 Wave Street; 831-649-1899.

The most impressive addition is the **Monterey Bay Aquarium**, a state-of-the-art museum that re-creates the natural habitat of local sea life. Monterey Bay is one of the world's biggest submarine canyons, deeper than the Grand Canyon. At the aquarium you'll encounter about 100 display tanks representing the wealth of underwater life that inhabits this mineral-rich valley. For example, the new "Mysteries of the Deep" exhibit explores the deep sea waters of the vast Monterey submarine canyon. The Monterey Bay Habitat, a 90-foot-long glass enclosure, portrays the local submarine world complete with sharks, brilliant reef fish, and creosote-oozing pilings. The Outer Bay Galleries contains, among other delights, a million-gallon tank filled with native Californian species, including green turtles and jellyfish. Another tank contains a mature kelp forest crowded with fish. Don't forget the hands-on exhibits where you can pet bat rays and hold crabs, starfish, and sea cucumbers. Be sure to wander upstairs to where the special exhibits are housed. The many displays and exhibitions make it one of the world's great aquariums. Don't miss it. Admission. ~ Cannery Row and David Avenue; 831-648-4888, 800-756-3737; www.mbayaq.org.

LODGING   The problem with lodging on the Monterey Peninsula is the same dilemma plaguing much of the world—money. It takes a lot of it to stay here, especially when visiting one of the area's vaunted bed and breakfasts. These country inns are concentrated in Pacific Grove and Carmel, towns neighboring Monterey.

The town of Monterey features a few such inns as well as a string of moderately priced motels. Budget travelers will do well to check into the latter and also to consult several of the Carmel listings below. Monterey's motel row lies along Munras Avenue, a buzzing thoroughfare that leads from downtown to Route 1. Motels are also found along Fremont Street in the adjacent town of Seaside. These are cheaper, drabber, and not as conveniently situated as the Munras hostelries.

Since overnight facilities fill rapidly around Monterey, particularly on weekends and during summer, it's wise to reserve in advance. Contact **Resort To Me**, a free reservation agency for the Monterey Peninsula. ~ 831-642-6622, 800-757-5646, fax 831-642-6641; www.resort2me.com. Or try **Carmel's Tourist Information Room Finders**, who might prove useful in securing that elusive room. Closed weekends. ~ Mission Street between 5th and 6th streets in the Mission Patio, Carmel; 831-624-1711, 800-847-8066.

Among the moderately priced motels lining Munras Avenue, **El Adobe Inn** is closest to downtown Monterey. This 26-unit establishment offers standard motel accommodations. The rooms are clean, carpeted, and comfortable, but far from cozy. They come equipped with television, telephone, and table. There's hokey art on the walls, and the environment generally is safe but sterile. Continental breakfast and use of the motel's hot tub are included. ~ 936 Munras Avenue; 831-372-5409, 800-433-4732, fax 831-375-7236; www.placestostay.com/Mont-ElAdobe. MODERATE TO DELUXE.

Another standard, located five blocks from downtown, is the **Days Inn Monterey** features 35 rooms with private baths. ~ 1288 Munras Avenue; 831-375-2168, fax 831-375-0368. MODERATE TO DELUXE.

For good cheer and homespun atmosphere, the **Old Monterey Inn** provides a final word. Before innkeepers Ann and Gene Swett decided to open their Tudor-style house to guests, they raised six children here. Now they raise rhododendrons and camellias in the garden while hosting visitors in their ten-room bed and breakfast. The house rests on a quiet street yet is located within a few blocks of downtown Monterey. Among the trimly appointed rooms are several with feather beds, tile fireplaces, wicker furnishings, and delicate wallhangings; three have whirlpool tubs. There are spacious dining and drawing rooms downstairs and the landscaped grounds are studded with oak and redwood. An elaborate breakfast is included; they'll even serve you in bed. You'll find this friendly little inn a perfect spot for an evening fire and glass of sherry. ~ 500 Martin Street; 831-375-8284, 800-350-2344, fax 831-375-6730; www.oldmontereyinn.com. ULTRA-DELUXE.

Located in the downtown district, **Merritt House** is not only an overnight resting place but also a stopping point along Monterey's "Path of History." Part of this 25-room inn rests in a vintage 1830 adobe home. Accommodations in the old house and the adjoining modern quarters are furnished with hardwood period pieces and feature vaulted ceilings, fireplaces, and balconies. The garden abounds with magnolia, fig, pepper, and olive trees. A continental breakfast is served. ~ 386 Pacific Street; 831-646-9686, 800-541-5599, fax 831-646-5392; www.monterey.com/mc4/mh. DELUXE TO ULTRA-DELUXE.

Oceanfront on Cannery Row stands the **Spindrift Inn**, an elegant 42-room hotel. The lobby is fashionably laid out with skylight and sculptures and there is a rooftop solarium overlooking the waterfront. Guest rooms carry out the award-winning architectural motif with bay windows, hardwood floors, wood-burning fireplaces, and built-in armoires. ~ 652 Cannery Row; 831-646-8900, 800-232-4141, fax 831-646-5342; www.placestostay.com/Mont-SpindriftInn. DELUXE TO ULTRA-DELUXE.

Catering to a mixed gay and straight clientele is the **Monterey Fireside Lodge**, a 24-room hostelry. In addition to comfortable accommodations, they have a jacuzzi and patio. Continental breakfast included. ~ 1131 10th Street; 831-373-4172. MODERATE.

DINING

Few restaurants can compete with **Stokes Adobe** for ambience. Housed in an 1840 California adobe with stucco walls, artwork by local artists, and European antiques, this restaurant serves California-Mediterranean cuisine. Featuring flavors from northern Italy, southern France, and Spain, there is also an extensive wine list with French, Italian, Australian, and California vintages. ~ 500 Hartnell Street; 831-373-1110. MODERATE.

Tasty *kalbi* and *bi bim bap* are among the traditional favorites at **Won Ju Korean Restaurant**. You'll find meat dishes as well as seafood and vegetarian options. Dinner comes with a Korean potato pancake, rice, and a wide variety of side dishes such as sesame-flavored spinach and spicy *kim chee* (pickled cabbage). ~ 570 Lighthouse Avenue; 831-656-0672. MODERATE TO DELUXE.

Eating at **Gianni's Pizza** is a guaranteed good time. You can feel it when you walk in the door of this casual restaurant. The tables sport red-and-white-checked tablecloths, there are bottles of wine and pictures of Italy on the walls, and on weekends banjo and accordion players serenade diners with lively tunes. You can order fresh pastas, hand-tossed, thick-crusted pizza, or oven-baked sandwiches from various stations, and they are prepared and delivered to your table. There's also a bar, an espresso counter, and wonderful gelato for dessert. ~ 725 Lighthouse Avenue; 831-649-1500. BUDGET.

Though it's not on the water, the **Clock Garden Restaurant** features more fresh fish than Cannery Row ever dreamed of. On an average night they'll have prawn fettuccine, snapper, salmon, and shrimp salad. Not interested? How about chicken teriyaki or spare ribs? All entrées include soup, salad, and artichoke. There's a patio outside; they also serve lunch and Sunday brunch; the bar mixes potent drinks—who could ask for more? ~ 565 Abrego Street; 831-375-6100. MODERATE.

Small and personalized with an understated elegance is the most fitting way to describe **Fresh Cream**. Its light green and gray walls are decorated with French prints and leaded glass. One wall is floor-to-ceiling windows that provide a great view of the bay. Service is excellent and the menu, printed daily, numbers among the finest on the Central Coast. Only dinner is served at this gourmet retreat; entrées include a dinner salad. On a given night you might choose from beef tournedos in Madeira sauce, sautéed veal loin, blackened ahi tuna, duckling in black currant sauce, and rack of lamb. That's not even mentioning the appetizers, which are outstanding, or the desserts, which should be outlawed. Four stars. ~ Heritage Harbor, Pacific and Scott streets; 831-375-9798. ULTRA-DELUXE.

One of Monterey Bay's most abundant seafood products is squid, the inky creature that often turns up on local restaurant menus as the more palatable-sounding calamari. The best place to enjoy it is **Abalonetti**, a casual wharfside restaurant overlooking the bay. The menu presents calamari in an array of guises, including deep-fried, sautéed with wine and garlic, and baked with eggplant. Seven more fish specials round out the menu. ~ 57 Fisherman's Wharf; 831-375-5941. MODERATE TO ULTRA-DELUXE.

Enjoy a cuppa java in a coffee shop quite unlike any you've ever visited before. At **Plume's Coffee** they grind the beans for each cup and brew it individually. So that your own special cup of coffee is not mistakenly served to someone else, you pick up your order under a picture of, say, a waterfall or sunset. Plume's also serves cheesecake, fruit tarts, custard eclairs, and other sweet treats from the best bakeries in the area. ~ 400 Alvarado Street; 831-373-4526. BUDGET.

In Monterey, there are stores throughout the downtown area and malls galore over on **Cannery Row**. Every year another shopping complex seems to rise along the Row. Already the area features cheese and wine stores, clothiers, a fudge factory, and a gourmet supply store. There's also a collector's comic book store, the inevitable T-shirt shop, knickknack stores, and galleries selling artworks that are like Muzak on canvas.

SHOPPING

The classiest spot around is **McGarrett's**. Entertainment changes nightly, with two different rooms—one for deejays spinning dance tunes, the other for occasional live music. Variety is the name of the game here with special shows ranging from country music and line dancing to strip shows. Dress code. Cover. ~ 321-D Alvarado Street; 831-646-9244.

NIGHTLIFE

Viva Monterey has been called the "Cheers of Monterey" and appeals to all ages (over 21, that is). A popular afternoon hangout with three black-light pool tables, the club gets pumping with nightly music. Bands play a mix of covers and original tunes. ~ 414 Alvarado Street; 831-646-1415.

There are also several nightspots over by Cannery Row. **Kalisa's**, a funky restaurant and ice-cream parlor in a building that dates to the Steinbeck era, offers belly dancing on some weekends. This is also the home of John Steinbeck's birthday party every February 27, now a recognized town holiday. ~ 851 Cannery Row; 831-644-9316.

Doc Rickett's Lab has a mix of live and DJ music (blues, rock, funk) and dancing nightly. Occasional cover. ~ 95 Prescott Avenue; 831-649-4241.

For dancing to deejay rock Thursday through Sunday, the gay crowd heads to **After Dark**. With two bars and a high-tech design motif, the place is decorated with handsome lithographs. There's also a patio. Weekend cover. ~ 214 Lighthouse Avenue; 831-373-7828.

Kitty-corner to After Dark is the **Lighthouse Bar & Grill**, where a mixed crowd shoots pool, plays pinball, or relaxes with a drink on the patio. ~ 281 Lighthouse Avenue; 831-373-4488.

▼▼▼▼▼▼▼▼▼▼
Pacific Grove

Projecting out from the northern tip of Monterey Peninsula is the diminutive town of Pacific Grove. Covering just 1700 acres, it is reached from Monterey along Lighthouse Avenue. Better yet, pick up Ocean View Boulevard near Cannery Row and follow as it winds along Pacific Grove's surf-washed shores.

A quiet town with a lightly developed waterfront, Pacific Grove offers paths that lead for miles along a rock-crusted shore.

Costanoan Indians once dove for abalone in these waters. By the 19th century, Pacific Grove had become a religious retreat. Methodist Episcopal ministers pitched a tent city and decreed that "bathing suits shall be provided with double crotches or with skirts of ample size to cover the buttocks." The town was dry until 1969. Given the fish canneries in Monterey and teetotalers in this nearby town, local folks called the area "Carmel-by-the-Sea, Monterey-by-the-Smell, and Pacific Grove-by-God."

SIGHTS   Today Pacific Grove is a sleepy residential area decorated with Victorians, brown-shingle houses, and clapboard ocean cottages. The waterfront drive goes past rocky beaches to **Point Pinos Lighthouse**. When this beacon first flashed in 1855, it burned sperm whale oil. Little has changed except the introduction of electricity; this is the only early lighthouse along the entire California coast to be preserved in its original condition. The U.S. Coast Guard still uses it to guide ships; it is the oldest continually operating lighthouse on the West Coast. Two rooms have been restored to look as they did in Victorian times, and there's a short history of Emily Fish, the woman who ran the lighthouse in the 19th century. Open for self-guided tours from Thursday through Sunday. ~ North of Lighthouse Avenue; 831-648-3116.

Sunset Drive continues along the sea to **Asilomar State Beach**. Here sand dunes mantled with ice plant front a wave-lashed shore. There are tidepools galore, plus beaches for picnics, and trails leading through the rolling dunes.

Pacific Grove's major claim to fame lies in an area several blocks inland: around George Washington Park on Melrose Street and in a grove at 1073 Lighthouse Avenue. This otherwise unassuming municipality is known as "Butterfly Town, U.S.A." Every year in mid-October, brilliant orange-and-black **monarch butterflies** migrate here, remaining until mid-March. Some arrive from several hundred miles away to breed amid the cypress and oak trees. At night they cling to one another, curtaining the branches in clusters that sometimes number over a thousand. Then, at first light, they come to life, fluttering around the groves in a frenzy of wings and color.

Also of interest are the **Pacific Grove Museum of Natural History**, an excellent small museum with exhibits on native animals and early peoples, and a touch gallery for children. Closed Monday. ~ Central and Forest avenues; 831-648-3116.

The **ivy-cloaked cottage** at 147 11th Street is where John Steinbeck lived and wrote *Tortilla Flat*, *In Dubious Battle*, and *Of Mice and Men*. (Not open to the public.) **Gosby House Inn** is a century-old Victorian mansion decorated in period antiques. ~ 643 Lighthouse Avenue. Next door, the **Hart Mansion**, now Gernot's Victoria House Restaurant, is an elaborate old Victorian house. Closed Monday. ~ 649 Lighthouse Avenue; 831-646-1477.

17 MILE DRIVE   From Pacific Grove, 17 Mile Drive leads to Pebble Beach, one of America's most lavish communities. This place is so exclusive that the rich charge $7.25 per vehicle to anyone wishing to drive around admiring their homes. No wonder they're rich.

Galling as the gate fee might be, this is an extraordinary region that must not be missed. The road winds through pine groves down to a wind-combed beach. There are miles of rolling dunes tufted with sea vegetation. (The oceanfront can be as cool and damp as it is beautiful, so carry a sweater or jacket, or better yet, both.)

Among the first spots you'll encounter is **Spanish Bay**, where Juan Gaspar de Portolá camped during his 1769 expedition up the California coast. (The picnic area here is a choice place to spread a feast.) At **Point Joe**, converging ocean currents create a wild frothing sea that has drawn several ships to their doom.

Seal Rock and **Bird Rock**, true to their nomenclature, are carpeted with sea lions, harbor and leopard seals, cormorants, brown pelicans, and gulls. Throughout this thriving 17 Mile Drive area

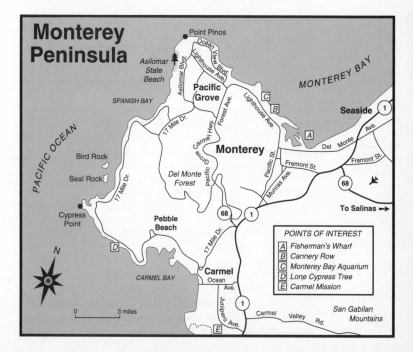

are black-tail deer, sooty shearwaters, sea otters, and, during migration periods, California gray whales.

There are crescent beaches and granite headlands as well as vista points for scanning the coast. You'll also pass the **Lone Cypress**, the solitary tree on a rocky point that has become as symbolic of Northern California as perhaps the Golden Gate Bridge.

The **private homes** en route are mansions, exquisite affairs fashioned from marble and fine hardwoods. Some appear like stone fortresses, others seem made solely of glass. They range from American Colonial to futuristic and were designed by noted architects like Bernard Maybeck, Julia Morgan, and Willis Polk.

This is also home to several of the world's most renowned **golf courses**—Pebble Beach, Spyglass Hill, and Cypress Point—where the AT&T National Pro-Am Championship takes place each year. More than the designer homes and their celebrity residents, these courses have made Pebble Beach a place fabled for wealth and beauty.

The best part of the drive lies along the coast between the Pacific Grove and Carmel gates. Along the backside of 17 Mile Drive, where it loops up into Del Monte Forest, there are marvelous views of Monterey Bay and the San Gabilan Mountains. Here also is **Huckleberry Hill**, a forest of Monterey and Bishop pine freckled with bushes.

LODGING   **Asilomar Conference Center** provides one of the area's best housing arrangements. Set in a state park, it's surrounded by 120 acres of sand dunes and pine forests. The beach is a stroll away from any of the center's 17 hotel lodges. There's a dining hall on the premises as well as meeting rooms and recreational facilities (pool and volleyball court). Breakfast is included in the price. Catering primarily to groups, Asilomar does provide accommodations (depending on availability) for independent travelers. Rooms in the "rustic buildings" are small and spartan but adequate (*and* designed by Julia Morgan). They lack carpeting on the hardwood floors and include little decoration. The "deluxe building" rooms are nicely appointed with wallhangings, study desks, and comfortable furnishings. Fireplaces are also available. Every lodge includes a spacious lounge area with stone fireplace. No doubt about it, Asilomar is a splendid place at a relaxing price. ~ 800 Asilomar Boulevard; 831-372-8016, fax 831-372-7227; www.asilomar center.com. MODERATE.

One of Monterey Peninsula's less expensive bed and breakfasts is nearby. **Gosby House Inn**, a century-old Victorian mansion, includes 22 refurbished rooms. Each is different, and all have been decorated with special attention to detail. In any one you are liable to discover an antique armoire, brass lighting fixtures, stained glass, a Tiffany lamp, or a clawfoot bathtub. The two rooms in the carriage house have jacuzzi tubs. They are all small after the Victorian fashion, which sacrifices space for coziness. The full breakfast, afternoon wine and hors d'oeuvres and nightly turn-down service add to the homey feeling. ~ 643 Lighthouse Avenue; 831-375-1287, 800-527-8828, fax 831-655-9621; www.four sisters.com. MODERATE TO DELUXE.

Green Gables Inn represents one of the region's most impressive bed and breakfasts. The house, a Queen Anne–style Victorian, dates from 1888. Adorned with step-gables, stained glass, and bay windows, it rests in a storybook setting overlooking Monterey Bay. Five bedrooms upstairs and a suite below have been fastidiously decorated with lavish antiques. Four of these share two baths, but offer the best ocean views. Set in a town filled with old Victorian homes, this oceanside residence is an ideal representation of Pacific Grove. There are also five separate units in a building adjacent to the main house. These are suites with private bath and fireplace. All rooms have king or queen beds; full breakfast, afternoon wine and cheese, and access to the main house are included. ~ 104 5th Street; 831-375-2095, 800-722-1774, fax 831-375-5437; wwwfouristers.com. MODERATE TO ULTRA-DELUXE.

Commanding a front and center view of the spectacular waterfront is the **Martine Inn**, a pastel stucco Mediterranean-style villa with 25 individually decorated rooms, many with fireplaces. Among the accommodations is the Edith Head Room, which has 1920s furnishings from the Hollywood costume designer's estate. A full sitdown breakfast and afternoon wine and hors d'oeuvres are included. There is a two-night minimum stay. ~ 255 Ocean View Boulevard; 831-373-3388, 800-852-5588, fax 831-373-3896; www.maritimeinn.com. DELUXE TO ULTRA-DELUXE.

DINING

For inexpensive snacks on the beach in Pacific Grove, try the **hot dog stand** at the bottom of the steps in Lover's Point Park. The place is something of a local institution. ~ Ocean View Boulevard at the foot of 16th Street. BUDGET.

Nearby at **The Tinnery** you'll find an American-style seafood restaurant serving breakfast, lunch, and dinner. The restaurant overlooks the water and serves some of the best clam chowder around. ~ 631 Ocean View Boulevard; 831-646-1040. MODERATE TO DELUXE.

Or step up and over to the **Old Bath House Restaurant**, a luxurious building decorated in etched glass and sporting a Victorian-style bar. The Continental-California cuisine includes duckling, lamb, lobster, steak, and seafood dishes. Dinner only. ~ 620 Ocean View Boulevard; 831-375-5195. DELUXE TO ULTRA-DELUXE.

The quaint, shingled **Red House Café** is a cozy place to join the locals for breakfast or lunch. Morning brings Belgian waffles, frittatas, and croissant sandwiches, while the noontime meal features oven-roasted chicken sandwiches and warm eggplant with fontina cheese. The freshly squeezed lemonade, which comes with free refills, is delicious. Closed Monday. ~ 662 Lighthouse Avenue; 831-643-1060. BUDGET.

Peppers Mexicali Cafe pays homage to the red chile and has attracted an incredible number of devotees, as witnessed by the sometimes lengthy wait for a table. Chile posters and pepper prints by local artists decorate the walls, and the food is Mexican and Central American seafood. Among the offerings are grilled prawns with fresh lime and cilantro dressing, grilled seafood tacos, grilled halibut, snapper Veracruz, and more mundane dishes such as tacos, burritos, and enchiladas. Closed Tuesday. Dinner only on Sunday. ~ 170 Forest Avenue; 831-373-6892. BUDGET TO MODERATE.

Conveniently located inside the American Tin Cannery Outlets, **First Awakenings** offers a shopper's respite and a hearty brunch. Their "sensational" skillets with homefries and cheese, fresh-squeezed orange juice, nine-inch plate-sized fruit pancakes, and homemade crêpes are well worth the wait on weekends. ~ 125 Ocean View Boulevard; 831-372-1125. BUDGET.

SHOPPING   The main area for window browsing in town can be found along Lighthouse Avenue. Just above this busy thoroughfare, on 17th Street, artisans have renovated a row of small beach cottages. In each is a creatively named shop. There's **Reincarnation Vintage Clothing**, which sells vintage clothing, jewelry, and accessories. Closed Sunday. ~ 214 17th Street; 831-649-0689. At **Mum's Place**, you'll find high-quality oak, maple, cherry, and pine furniture. ~ 246 Forest Avenue; 831-372-6250.

From designer fashions to gourmet cookware, the 40 shops at **American Tin Cannery Premium Outlets** are a shopper's paradise. A good place to look for luggage, books, shoes, housewares, and cosmetics, this renovated two-story complex has a variety of outlet stores. If you're looking for bargains in the Monterey area, don't miss this gem. ~ 125 Ocean View Boulevard; 831-372-1442.

NIGHTLIFE   **The Tinnery**, an attractive complex on the waterfront in Pacific Grove, spotlights local entertainers Wednesday through Saturday nights, usually a soloist playing contemporary music. The lounge kitchen serves appetizers until midnight. ~ 631 Ocean View Boulevard; 831-646-1040.

BEACHES & PARKS   **ASILOMAR STATE BEACH** 🚶 🛶   This oceanfront facility features over 100 acres of snowy white sand dunes, tidepools, and beach. It's a perfect place for daytripping and exploring. The best surfing here is just off the main sandy beach. Since northern and southern currents run together here, the waters are teeming with marine life. Swimming is not recommended. If you're into algae, you'll want to know that over 200 species congregate in the ocean here. Another species—Homo sapiens—gathers at the park's multifaceted conference center (overnight accommodations are described in "Lodging" above). ~ Along Sunset Drive in Pacific Grove; 831-648-3130.

Carmel

The first law of real estate should be this: The best land is always occupied by the military, bohemians, or the rich. Think about it. The principle holds for many of the world's prettiest spots. Generally the military arrives first, on an exploratory mission or as an occupying force. It takes strategic ground, which happens to be the beaches, headlands, and mountaintops. The bohemians select beautiful locales because they possess good taste. When the rich discover where the artists have settled, they start moving in, driving up the rents, and forcing the displaced bohemians to discover new homes, which will then be taken by another wave of the wealthy.

The Monterey Peninsula is no exception. In Carmel the military established an early beachhead when Spanish soldiers occupied a barracks in the old Catholic mission. Later the bohemians arrived in numbers. Poet George Sterling came in 1905, followed by Mary Austin, the novelist. Eventually such luminaries as Upton Sinclair, Lincoln Steffens, and Sinclair Lewis, writers all, settled for varying periods. Jack London and Ambrose Bierce also visited. Later, noted photographers Ansel Adams and Edward Weston relocated here.

> Monterey cypresses grow nowhere in the world except along Carmel Bay.

The figure most closely associated with this "seacoast of Bohemia" was Robinson Jeffers, a poet who came seeking solitude in 1914. Quarrying rock from the shoreline, he built the Tor House and Hawk Tower, where he lived and wrote haunting poems and epics about the coast.

Then like death and tax collectors, the rich inevitably moved in. As John Steinbeck noted when he later returned to this artists' colony, "If Carmel's founders should return, they could not afford to live there. . . . They would instantly be picked up as suspicious characters and deported over the city line."

It's doubtful many would want to remain anyway. Today Carmel is so cute it cloys. The tiny town is cluttered with over four dozen inns, about six dozen restaurants, and more than 300 shops. Ocean Avenue, the main street, is wall-to-wall with merchants. Shopping malls have replaced artists' garrets, and there are traffic jams where there was once solitude.

SIGHTS

Typifying the town is the **Tuck Box**, a gingerbread-style building on Dolores Street between Ocean and 7th avenues (there are no street numbers in Carmel), or the fairy tale-like **Hansel-and-Gretel cottages** on Torres Street between 5th and 6th avenues.

Still, reasons remain to visit Carmel, which is reached from Monterey via Route 1 or from the Carmel gate along the 17 Mile Drive. The window shopping is good and several galleries are outstanding. Some of the town's quaint characteristics have appeal. There are no traffic lights or parking meters, and at night few street lights. Drive around the side streets and you will encounter an architectural mixture of log cabins, adobe structures, board-and-batten cottages, and Spanish villas.

HIDDEN ▶ A secret that local residents have long withheld from visitors is **Mission Trails Park**. No signs will direct you here, so watch carefully for an entrance at the corner of Mountain View and Crespi avenues. Within this forest preserve are miles of hiking trails. They wind across footbridges, through redwood groves, and past meadows of wildflowers en route to Carmel Mission. There are ocean vistas, deer grazing the hillsides, and an arboretum seeded with native California plants.

Carmel's most alluring feature is the one which early drew the bohemians—the Pacific. At the foot of Ocean Avenue rests **Carmel Beach**, a snowy strand shadowed by cypress trees. From here, Scenic Road hugs the coast, winding above rocky outcroppings.

Just beyond stretches **Carmel River State Beach**, a sandy corridor at the foot of Carmel Bay. For additional information, see the "Beaches & Parks" section below.

Even for the non-religious, a visit to **Carmel Mission** becomes a pilgrimage. If the holiness holds no appeal, there's the aesthetic sense of the place. Dating back to 1793, its Old World beauty captivates and confounds. The courtyards are alive with flowers and birds. The adobe buildings surrounding have been dusted with time—their eaves are hunchbacked, the tile roofs coated in moss. Admission. ~ Located on Rio Road just off Route 1; 831-624-3600.

Established by Father Junípero Serra, this mission is one of California's most remarkable. The basilica is a vaulted-ceiling affair adorned with old oil paintings and wooden statues of Christ; its walls are lime plaster made from burnt seashells. The exterior is topped with a Moorish tower and 11 bells.

Junípero Serra lies buried in the sanctuary, his grave marked with a stone plaque. There are also museum rooms demonstrating early California life—a kitchen with stone hearth and rudimentary tools, the state's first library (complete with waterstained bibles), and the cell where Father Serra died, its bed a slab of wood with a single blanket and no mattress. Close by, in the cemetery beside the basilica, several thousand American Indians are also buried.

Just two miles south of Carmel lies **Point Lobos State Reserve**, an incomparable natural area of rocky headlands and placid coves. The park features hillside crow's nests from which to gaze out along Carmel Bay. Before Westerners arrived, the American Indians gathered mussels and abalone here. Later Point Lobos was a whaling station and an abalone cannery. Today it's a park intended primarily for nature hikers. You can explore pine forests and cypress groves, a jagged shoreline of granite promontories, and intriguing wave-lapped coves. Every tidepool is a miniature aquarium pulsing with color and sea life. The water is clear as sky. Offshore rise sea stacks, their rocky bases ringed with mussels, their domes crowned by sea birds. This region, also rich in wildlife and underwater life, should not be bypassed; for complete information, see the "Beaches & Parks" section below.

As if its shoreline was not enough, Carmel also boasts an extraordinary interior. Carmel Valley Road leads from Route 1 into the distant hills, paralleling the Carmel River in its circuitous course. The lower end of the Carmel Valley promises fruit orchards and fields of grazing horses before the road ascends into the wooded heights that separate Carmel from the farmlands of Salinas.

Along the way you can stop by **Château Julien Winery** for a tasting and tour (call for times; reservations required). ~ 8940 Carmel Valley Road, five miles from Route 1; 831-624-2600.

You may want to follow the trails that lead from the Carmel River through meadows to a 2000-foot peak in 5000-acre **Gar-**

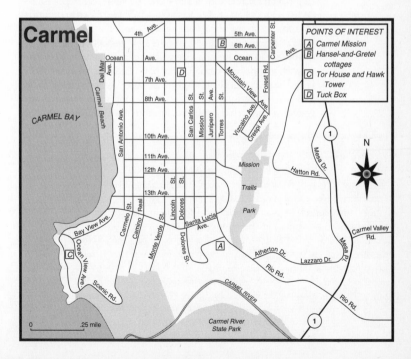

Carmel

POINTS OF INTEREST

A Carmel Mission
B Hansel-and-Gretel cottages
C Tor House and Hawk Tower
D Tuck Box

land Ranch Regional Park. Pick up a map at the visitors center for information about biking and horseback riding. ~ Carmel Valley Road, nine miles from Route 1; 831-659-4488.

LODGING   Carmel River Inn, located on the southern outskirts of town, is a 43-unit establishment with both a motel and woodframe cottages (the latter have greater appeal). The less expensive guest units are studio-size structures with wall-to-wall carpeting, televisions, refrigerators, and telephones; their interior designer was obviously a capable, if uninspired, individual. The pricier cottages vary in size and facilities, but may contain extra rooms, a fireplace, or a kitchen. ~ Route 1 at Carmel River Bridge; 831-624-1575, 800-882-8142, fax 831-624-0290; www.carmelriverinn.com. MODERATE TO DELUXE.

Carmel's most closely kept secret is a hideaway resort set on 21 acres and overlooking the ocean at a distance. Scattered about the tree-shaded grounds at the **Mission Ranch** are triplex cottages and a quadraplex unit, in addition to the older white clapboard farmhouse. There are tennis courts, trim lawns, and ancient cypress trees. With mountains in the background, the views extend across a broad lagoon and out along sandy beachfront. The ranch dining room is favored by local people. A rare find indeed with continental breakfast included. ~ 26270 Dolores Street; 831-624-6436, 800-538-8221, fax 831-626-4163. MODERATE TO ULTRA-DELUXE.

The Homestead is also one of the area's better housing arrangements. Set in a maroon house with shiplap siding, its 12 rooms each have a private bath. This is not a bed and breakfast, so it lacks the community atmosphere of other country inns, though a touch of the intimacy lingers. The rooms are carpeted and equipped with televisions; the furniture is functional more than

◆◆◆

STONE POEM

Just before the intersection with Stewart Way, gaze uphill toward those two stone edifices. Poet Robinson Jeffers' **Tor House and Hawk Tower** seem drawn from another place and time, perhaps a Scottish headland in the 19th century. In fact, the poet modeled the house after an English-style barn and built the 40-foot-high garret with walls six feet thick in the fashion of an Irish tower. Completed during the 1920s, the structures are granite and include porthole windows that Jeffers salvaged from a shipwreck. One-hour tours of the house and tower are conducted on Friday and Saturday by reservation. No children under 12 years allowed. Admission. ~ 26304 Ocean View Avenue; for information and reservations, call 831-624-1813.

fashionable. There are four studio cottages outfitted with kitch-enettes. ~ Lincoln Street and 8th Avenue; 831-624-4119, fax 831-624-7688. MODERATE.

The Pine Inn is not only Carmel's oldest hostelry, but also an-other of the town's more reasonably priced places. This 49-room hotel dates back to 1889 and still possesses the charm that has drawn visitors for decades. The lobby is a fashionable affair with red brocade settees, marbletop tables, and a brick fireplace. The less expensive accommodations are smaller but do have the an-tique reproductions, private baths, televisions, and phones com-mon to all the rooms. Each one has been designed in Edwardian style. Rather than a country inn, this is a full-service hotel with restaurant and bar downstairs as well as room service for the guests. ~ Ocean Avenue between Lincoln and Monte Verde streets; 831-624-3851, 800-228-3851, fax 831-624-3030; www.pine-inn. com. DELUXE.

Holiday House is a six-room bed and breakfast located two blocks from the beach. Set in a brown-shingle house, it features a parlor with stone fireplace and a nicely tended garden. The rooms are small, neat, and prim; though attractively furnished, they lack the lavish antiques found in more expensive country inns. The out-door decoration should adequately substitute—ask for a room with an ocean view. ~ Camino Real between Ocean and 7th ave-nues; 831-624-6267. DELUXE.

Highlands Inn is one of those raw-wood-and-polished-stone places that evoke the muted elegance of the California coast. Ultra-modern in execution, it features a stone lodge surrounded by wood shingle buildings. The lodge houses two restaurants and an ocean-view lounge while the neighboring structures contain countless guest rooms, each a warren of blond woods and pastel tiles. All the rooms have fireplaces, most have patios, and some have spas. Parked on a hillside overlooking an awesome sweep of ocean, the inn is the ultimate in Carmel chic. ~ Route 1 about four miles south of Carmel; 831-624-3801, 800-682-4811, fax 831-626-1574; www.highlands-inn.com. ULTRA-DELUXE.

In Carmel, the thing to do is drop by the **Tuck Box** for afternoon tea. The establishment sits in a dollhouselike creation with a swirl roof and curved chimney. The prim and tiny dining room also serves breakfast and lunch. During the noon meal there are omelettes, sandwiches, shrimp salad, and Welsh rarebit. Tea in-cludes scones, muffins, or homemade pie. ~ Dolores Street be-tween Ocean and 7th avenues; 831-624-6365. BUDGET.

DINING

Join the line in front of **Mondo's Trattoria** for good times and a great meal. As you step through the door you might think you're in Italy: Wine bottles, cooking utensils, and strings of garlic adorn the walls, and the staff is very friendly, often breaking into song for impromptu celebrations. If that isn't enough, the food is *motte bene*. You can't go wrong with a fresh pasta dish such as the San Remo (sun-dried tomatoes and goat cheese in cream sauce) or *la mafiosa* (calamari, prawns, and scallops in a spicy tomato sauce). Dinner specials include veal, seafood, fish, and chicken entrées, and at lunch sandwiches are added to the menu. Save room for the desserts, especially the *tiramisu*! ~ Dolores Street between Ocean and 7th avenues; 831-624-8977. MODERATE.

Then there's **Hog's Breath Inn**, a name so outrageous it begins to have appeal. If owner Clint Eastwood adds a hotel facility, he can call it The Innsomnia. Actually Carmel could use a few more doses of humor like this; the town takes itself so dreadfully seriously. Anyway, back to Hog's Breath. Quite nice, it is laid out in a courtyard arrangement with a flagstone dining patio flanked on one side by a pub and on the other by the dining room. At lunchtime, you can eat outdoors or inside next to a stone fireplace. A boar's head adorns one wall and the menu, as you may have guessed, runs heavy on meat. Dinner entrées include pork chops, filet mignon, prime rib, and chicken in whiskey; there is also a catch of the day. Lunch includes sandwiches and salads. ~ San Carlos Street between 5th and 6th avenues; 831-625-1044. MODERATE TO DELUXE.

Reasonably priced, casual, and modern. Who could ask more than what they're offering at **Rio Grill**? The cuisine at this popular dining room is American grill-style with a Southwestern touch. Smoked chicken and artichokes and calf's liver with sweet potato pancake are among the entrées. Critically acclaimed. ~ Crossroads Shopping Center, Route 1 and Rio Road; 831-625-5436. MODERATE TO DELUXE.

Dine indoors or al fresco under heat lamps and around a fire pit at the **Village Corner**. This Mediterranean bistro offers Spanish paella, fresh seafood, grilled lamb, fine wines, *tiramisu* and espresso. ~ Dolores Street at 6th Avenue; 831-624-3588. MODERATE.

The **Thunderbird Bookshop Café** combines two of the world's most pleasurable activities, eating and reading. You can browse the bookstore, then dine in the dining room or out on the patio. They serve lunch all day with entrées such as pot pies, soups, and salads. If you're just looking for a snack, they have a variety of desserts. ~ 3600 The Barnyard; 831-624-9414. BUDGET.

Patisserie Boissière belongs to that endangered species—the moderately priced French restaurant. The simple French country dining room adjoins a small bakery. In addition to outrageous pastries for breakfast, they offer full breakfast on the weekend. Entrées include coquilles St. Jacques, salmon in parchment paper, and braised rabbit. Baked brie and French onion soup are also on the bill of fare. A bargain hunter's delight in dear Carmel. Lunch daily, dinner Monday through Friday. ~ Mission Street between Ocean and 7th avenues; 831-624-5008. MODERATE.

Old time Carmel residents will tell you about the **Mission Ranch Dining Room**. How it dates back over a century to the days when it was a creamery. Today it's just a warm, homey old building with a stone fireplace plus a view of a sheep pasture and a neighboring ocean. The menu is a combination of fresh seafood and all-American fare: steak, prime rib, chicken, and pasta. Dinner, Saturday lunch, and Sunday brunch. ~ 26270 Dolores Street; 831-625-9040. MODERATE TO ULTRA-DELUXE.

Of course the ultimate dining place is **The Covey at Quail Lodge**, up in Carmel Valley. Set in one of the region's most prestigious hotels, The Covey is a contemporary European restaurant with a California influence, serving, for example, grilled salmon on prawn and artichoke hash. There's also abalone, game hen, veal, and rack of lamb. Richly decorated, it overlooks the lodge's lake and grounds. Afternoon appetizers and drinks served on the patio, accompanied by a guitarist Thursday through Sunday. Dinner jackets and reservations, please. Dinner only. ~ 8205 Valley Greens Drive; 831-624-1581. DELUXE TO ULTRA-DELUXE.

SHOPPING

In Carmel, shopping seems to be the raison d'être. If ever an entire town was dressed to look like a boutique, this is the one. Its shops are stylish and expensive.

The major shopping strip is along Ocean Avenue between Mission and Monte Verde streets, but the best stores generally are situated on the side streets. The **Doud Arcade** is a mall featuring artisan shops. Here you will find leather merchants, potters, and jewelers. ~ Ocean Avenue between San Carlos and Dolores streets.

Most of the artists who made Carmel famous have long since departed, but the city still maintains a wealth of art galleries. While many are not even worth browsing, others are outstanding. The **Carmel Bay Company** features posters by contemporary artists. ~ Lincoln Street and Ocean Avenue; 831-624-3868. The **Carmel Art Association Galleries**, owned and operated by artists, offers paintings and sculpture by local figures. ~ Dolores Street between 5th and 6th avenues; 831-624-6176. Also of note is the **Chapman Gallery**, which features local artists as well. Closed Tuesday. ~ 7th Avenue between Mission and San Carlos streets; 831-626-1766.

Carmel is recognized as an international center for photographers. Two of the nation's most famous—Ansel Adams and Edward Weston—lived here. **The Weston Gallery** displays prints by both men, as well as works by other 19th- and 20th-century photographers. Closed Tuesday. ~ 6th Avenue between Dolores and Lincoln streets; 831-624-4453. At **Photography West Gallery** Weston and Adams are represented, as are Imogen Cunningham

Text continued on page 222.

The Old Spanish Mission Town

Time permitting, there's one overland excursion that must be added to your itinerary—a visit to the **Mission at San Juan Bautista**. While this graceful mission town, located 90 miles south of San Francisco, is easily reached from Route 101, the most inspiring route is via Route 156 from the Monterey Peninsula.

Anyone who has read Frank Norris' muckraking novel about the railroads, *The Octopus*, will recognize this placid village with its thick, cool adobe church. And anyone who remembers the climax to Hitchcock's *Vertigo* will instantly picture the mission—even though the bell tower that Jimmy Stewart struggled to climb was a Hollywood addition that you won't see at the real San Juan Bautista. Founded in 1797, the mission was completed in 1812. Today it numbers among California's most enchanting locales. With its colonnade and sagging crossbeams, the mission has about it the musty scent of history. The old monastery and church consist of a low-slung building roofed in Spanish tile and topped with a belfry. ~ 831-623-4528.

My favorite spot in this most favored town is **Mission Cemetery**, a small plot bounded by a stone fence and overlooking valley and mountains. It's difficult to believe that over 4300 American Indians are buried here in unmarked graves. The few recognizable resting places are memorialized with wooden crosses and circling enclosures of stone. Shade trees cool the yard. Just below the cemetery, symbolic perhaps of change and mortality, are the old Spanish Road (*El Camino Real*) and the San Andreas Fault.

The mission rests on a grassy square facing **Plaza Hall**. Originally a dormitory for unwed American Indian women, this structure was rebuilt in 1868 and used as a meeting place and private residence. Peek inside its shuttered windows or tour the building and encounter a child's room cluttered with old dolls, a sitting room dominated by a baby grand piano, and other rooms containing period furniture.

Behind the hall sits a **blacksmith shop**, filled now with wagon wheels, oxen yokes, and the "San Juan Eagle," a hook-and-ladder wagon drawn by a ten-man firefighting crew back in 1869. Nearby **Plaza Stable** houses an impressive collection of buggies and carriages.

The **Plaza Hotel** lines another side of the square. Consisting of several adobe structures, the earliest built in 1814, the place once served as a stagecoach stop. Today its myriad rooms contain historic exhibits and 1860s-era furnishings. Admission. Similarly, the **Castro-Breen Adobe** next door is decorated with Spanish-style pieces. Owned by a Mexican general and later by Donner Party survivors, it is a window on California frontier life. Nearby are **San Juan Jail**, an oversized outhouse constructed in 1870, and the **settler's cabin**, a rough log cabin built by East Coast pioneers in the 1830s or 1840s.

All are part of the **state historic park** which comprises San Juan Bautista. Like the plaza, 3rd Street is lined with 19th-century stores and houses. Here amid porticoed haciendas and crumbling adobe are antique stores, a bakery, restaurants, and other shops. Admission. ~ 831-623-4881.

A block away is **El Teatro Campesino**, an excellent resident theater group. This Latino company originated *Zoot Suit*, an important and provocative play that was eventually filmed as a movie. With a penetrating sense of Mexi-can-American history and an unsettling awareness of contemporary Latino social roles, they are a modern expression of the vigor and spirit of this old Spanish town. From May to September summer productions are held in their theater; the Christmas show is staged in Mission San Juan Bautista. ~ 705 4th Street; 831-623-2444.

Accommodations are scarce in San Juan Bautista, but **Posada de San Juan** offers comfortable (yet somewhat sterile) rooms within walking distance of the mission and 3rd Street's shops and restaurants. The 34 rooms are equipped with wetbars, whirlpool bathtubs, and gas fireplaces. Decorated in a hacienda style, this inn reflects the distinctly Mexican flavor of San Juan Bautista. ~ 310 4th Street; 831-623-4030, fax 831-623-2378. MODERATE TO DELUXE.

Country Rose Inn is a 20-minute drive away, but well worth the effort. At the end of a country lane and surrounded by fields of garlic and marigolds, this Dutch colonial manor B&B has been on the cover of *Country Inns* magazine. Each of its five rooms is done in a rose motif, with antique furnishings and a view of the mountains or foothills in the distance. You can relax in wicker furniture on the front and back porches or in the parlor with its grand piano. A full breakfast is served. Reservations recommended. ~ 455 Fitzgerald Avenue, San Martin; 408-842-0441. DELUXE.

As for restaurants, **La Casa Rosa** sits in an 1858 house. Open for lunch only, this family-run eatery features an "old California casserole," a "new California casserole," a chicken soufflé dish, and a seafood soufflé. The first entrée is made with cheese, meat sauce, and a corn base; the second dish features green chiles. La Casa Rosa is charming and intimate. Closed Tuesday. ~ 107 3rd Street; 831-623-4563. MODERATE.

In the same block, **Jardines de San Juan** is recommended as much for its garden as its food. In addition to the usual tacos, burritos, and flautas, weekend specials get fancy: Veracruz-style red snapper served with *crema* on a bed of rice, or *pollos borrachos* cooked in sherry with ham and sausage. ~ 115 3rd Street; 831-623-4466. MODERATE.

and Brett Weston. ~ The gallery is located on Dolores Street between Ocean and 7th avenues; 831-625-1587.

The Barnyard is an innovative mall housing 47 shops and restaurants. Set amid flowering gardens is a series of raw wood structures reminiscent of old farm buildings. ~ At Route 1 and Carmel Valley Road; 831-624-8886. Browse the boutiques and gift shops, then follow those brick pathways to the **Thunderbird Bookshop & Café**. With a marvelous collection of hardbacks and paperbacks, it is one of the finest bookstores along the Central Coast. Better still, they have an adjoining café and a nearby book-and-toy store for children. ~ 3600 The Barnyard; 831-624-1803.

NIGHTLIFE   For the warm conviviality of an English pub consider **Bully III**. ~ Dolores Street and 8th Avenue; 831-625-1750. Another attractive restaurant-cum-bar is **The Forge in the Forest** with its copper walls, hand-carved bar, and open fire. ~ Junipero Street and 5th Avenue; 831-624-2233.

Possibly the prettiest place you'll ever indulge the spirits in is the **Lobos Lounge** at Highlands Inn. An entire wall of this leather-armchair-and-marble-table establishment is comprised of plate glass. And the pretty picture on the other side of those panes is classic Carmel—rocky shoreline fringed with cypress trees and lashed by passionate waves. If that's not entertainment enough, there's a piano bar featured during the week and a three-piece combo on weekends. ~ On Route 1 about four miles south of Carmel; 831-624-3801.

BEACHES   **CARMEL RIVER STATE BEACH** 🏃 🛶 This beach would be more
& PARKS   attractive were it not upstaged by Point Lobos, its remarkable neighbor to the south. Nevertheless, there's a nice sandy beach here as well as a satisfying view of the surrounding hills. The chief feature is the bird refuge along the river. The marshes offer willets, sandpipers, pelicans, hawks, and kingfishers, plus an occasional Canadian snow goose. The beach has restrooms. ~ Located at the end of Carmelo Road in Carmel (take Rio Road exit off Route 1); 831-624-4909.

POINT LOBOS STATE RESERVE 🏃 🚲 🛶 ⚓ In a region packed with uncommonly beautiful scenery, this park stands out as something special. A 1225-acre reserve, only 456 acres of which are above water, it contains over 300 species of plants and more than 250 species of animals and birds. This is a perfect place to study sea otters, harbor seals, and sea lions. During migrating season in mid-winter and mid-spring, gray whales cruise the coast. Along with Pebble Beach, Point Lobos is the only spot in the world where Monterey cypresses, those ghostly, wind-gnarled coastal trees, still survive. There are 80-foot-high kelp forests offshore, popular with avid scuba divers who know the reserve as one of the most fascinating places on the coast. Take note: reservations to dive must be made at least three weeks in advance by phone or e-mail. Facilities include picnic areas and restrooms. Day-use fee, $7. ~ Located on Route 1 about three miles south of Carmel; 831-624-4909, e-mail ptlobos@mbay.net.

PINNACLES NATIONAL MONUMENT 🚶 Set far inland amid the softly rolling San Gabilan Mountains are the sharp, dramatic volcanic peaks that centerpiece this unusual park. Sheer spires and solitary minarets vault 1200 feet from the canyon floor. Comprising the weathered remains of a 23-million-year-old volcano, these towering peaks offer a challenge to day hikers and technical rock climbers alike. Rockclimbing is a major activity here in spring and fall (it's too hot in summer). There are caves to explore, and more than 30 miles of trails leading through the remnants of the volcano. Wild boar, coyote, gray fox, and bobcat roam the region, while golden eagles and redshouldered hawks work the skies above. Since the cliffs are accessible only by trail, visitors should be prepared to hike. Bring water, durable shoes, loose clothing, and a working flashlight for cave exploring. The best time to visit the park is during the spring, when the wildflowers are in bloom, or autumn; summer brings stifling heat to the area and winter carries copious amounts of rain. The east side of the park has an information center, picnic areas, and restrooms. The west side offers a ranger station, picnic areas, and restrooms. There's a grocery on the east side, but restaurants are a good 36 miles away in Hollister. From the west side, restaurants and groceries are located about 13 miles away in Soledad. Day-use fee, $5. ~ No road traverses the park. Visitors must enter either on the east side, by following Route 25 south from Hollister for about 32 miles, then proceeding four miles west on Route 146; or on the west side along Route 146, about 13 miles east from Soledad (the town is just off Route 101); 831-389-4485. The lengthy drive to the east entrance makes for a long day trip. If you plan to hike, start early in the day.

▲ **Pinnacles Campground, Inc.,** a private facility with 128 sites (some equipped with partial RV hookups), sits astride the park's east side. Hot showers, a pool, and campfire activities are perks. Fees are $7 per person nightly or $28 for a group of up to six people. ~ 2400 Route 146, Paicines; 831-389-4462. On the west side of the park, 18 walk-in campsites are located in the park; $10 per night.

From Point Lobos, the highway hugs the coastline as it snakes south toward Big Sur. Like Route 1 north of San Francisco, this is one of America's great stretches of roadway. Situated between the Santa Lucia Mountains and the Pacific, Route 1 courses about 30 miles from Carmel to Big Sur, then spi-

▼▼▼▼▼▼▼▼▼▼
Big Sur

rals farther south along the coast toward San Luis Obispo and Los Angeles.

The Big Sur district is where the Santa Lucia Mountains encounter the Pacific. Backed by the challenging Ventana Wilderness, the region is marked by sharp coastal cliffs and unbelievable scenery. Though it's hard to conceive, Big Sur may be even more beautiful than the other sections of the Central Coast.

Along Route 1, each turnout provides another glimpse into a magic-lantern world. Here the glass pictures a beach crusted with rocks, there a wave-wracked cliff or pocket of tidepools. The canyons are narrow and precipitous, while the headlands are so close to the surf they seem like beached whales. Trees are broken and blasted before the wind. The houses, though millionaire affairs, appear inconsequential against the backdrop of ocean and stone.

SIGHTS

At **Soberanes Point**, eight miles south of Carmel, hiking trails lead out along the headlands. Here you can stand on a rock shelf directly above the ocean and gaze back at the encroaching hills.

HIDDEN ►

For an intriguing excursion into those hills, head about six miles up **Palo Colorado Road**, which intersects with Route 1 a couple of miles south of Garrapata Creek. Though paved, this country road is one lane. The corridor tunnels through an arcade of redwoods past log cabins and rustic homes. If you're feeling adventurous, follow the twisting eight-mile road to its terminus at Los Padres National Forest.

Back on Route 1 you'll traverse **Bixby Creek Bridge**, which stretches from one cliff to another across an infernal chasm. Local legend cites it incorrectly as the world's longest concrete arch span. With fluted hills in the background and a fluffy beach below, it may, however, be the world's prettiest.

For another incredible side trip, you can follow **Coast Road** for about 11 miles up into the Santa Lucia Mountains. Climbing along narrow ledges, then corkscrewing deep into overgrown canyons, the road carries you past exquisite views of forests and mountain ridges. There are hawk's-eye vistas of the Pacific, the rolling Big Sur countryside, and Pico Blanco, a 3709-foot lime-

◆◆

HENRY MILLER LITE

There's not much to the **Henry Miller Library**, but somehow the unassuming nature of the place befits its candid subject. Occupying a small woodframe house donated by Miller's friend Emil White, the museum contains volumes from the novelist's library as well as his evocative artworks. Closed Monday. ~ Route 1 about a mile south of Ventana Inn; 831-667-2574.

rich peak. This is the old coast road, the principal thoroughfare before Route 1 was completed in the 1930s. Take heed: It is so curvy it makes Route 1 seem a desert straightaway; it is also entirely unpaved, narrow, rutted, and impassable in wet weather. But oh those views!

Coast Road begins at Bixby Bridge and rejoins Route 1 at Andrew Molera State Park. If instead of detouring you stay on Route 1, it will climb along **Hurricane Point**, a promontory blessed with sweeping views and cursed by lashing winds, and descend toward **Little Sur Beach**. This sandy crescent is bounded by a shallow lagoon. There are dunes and lofty hills all around, as well as shore birds. Another lengthy beach leads to **Point Sur Light Station**, set on a volcanic headland. This solitary sentinel dates back to 1889. The only way to visit this lighthouse is by a guided tour. Tours run Saturday at 10 a.m. and 2 p.m., Sunday at 10 a.m., Monday (June through August only) at 10 a.m., and Wednesday (April through October only) at 10 a.m. and 2 p.m. Admission. ~ 831-625-4419.

Then the road enters the six-mile-long Big Sur River Valley. **Big Sur**, a rural community of about 1000 people, stretches the length of the valley. Lacking a town center, it consists of houses and a few stores dotted along the Big Sur River. The place received its name from early Spanish settlers, who called the wilderness south of Carmel *El País Grande del Sur*, "the big country to the south."

Later it became a rural retreat and an artists' colony. Henry Miller lived here from 1947 until 1964, writing *Big Sur and the Oranges of Hieronymus Bosch*, *Plexus*, and *Nexus* during his residence. Today the artists are being displaced by soaring land values, while the region is gaining increased popularity among visitors. It's not difficult to understand why as you cruise along its knife-edge cliffs and timbered mountainsides. You can drive for miles past eye-boggling vistas, then turn back on Route 1 to the Monterey Peninsula, or continue on to a strange and exotic land called Southern California.

For a variety of accommodations, consider **Big Sur Campground and Cabins**. Set in a redwood grove along the Big Sur River, this 13-acre facility has campsites, tent cabins, and A-frames. Camping out on the grounds costs $24 for two people and includes access to hot showers, a laundry, a store, a basketball and volleyball court, and a playground. The tent cabins, $45 per night, consist of woodframe skeletons with canvas roofs. They come with beds, bedding and towels and share a bath house. The tent cabins are closed during the rainy season. The "cabins" along the river are actually mobile homes, neatly furnished but rather sterile. More intimate are the A-frame cabins with Franklin stoves and sleeping

LODGING

lofts. The newer modular units include pine floors with bedrooms as well as a kitchen and a private bath. ~ Route 1; 831-667-2322. MODERATE TO DELUXE.

Ripplewood Resort has 16 cabins and a café. The least expensive cabin is a small, basic duplex unit with redwood walls, a gas heater, and carpeting. It has a bath but lacks a kitchen. The more expensive units are larger, with kitchens, sitting rooms, and decks, and are located above the river. My advice? Compromise with one of the riverfront cabins. They feature kitchens, decks, and spacious bedrooms. (No extra charge for the river tumbling past your doorstep.) ~ Route 1; 831-667-2242. MODERATE.

Located within Pfeiffer Big Sur State Park is **Big Sur Lodge**, a complex containing 20 cottages with two to six units per cottage. The "lodge" represents a full-facility establishment complete with conference center, restaurant, gift shop, grocery, laundromat, and heated pool in the summer. It's very convenient, if undistinguished. The cottages are frame houses with wood-shingle roofs. They are simple in design, yet have a kitchen and a fireplace. The interiors are pine and feature wall-to-wall carpeting and high beam ceilings; each cottage features a porch or a deck. ~ Route 1; 831-667-2171, 800-424-4787, fax 831-667-3110; www.bigsur lodge.com. MODERATE TO DELUXE.

Big Sur has long been associated with bohemian values and an easy lifestyle. Today landed gentry and wealthy speculators have taken over many of the old haunts, but a few still remain. One such is **Deetjen's Big Sur Inn**, a 20-unit slapdash affair where formality is an inconvenience. The place consists of a hodgepodge collection of clapboard buildings. The outer walls are unpainted and the doors have no locks, lending the residence a tumbledown charm. Rooms are roughhewn, poorly insulated, and funky, but some have woodburning stoves. Throw rugs are scattered about, the furniture is traditional, and local art pieces along the wall serve as decoration. No in-room phones or TVs. If all this is be-

HIDDEN ►

A ROOM WITH A VIEW

South from Big Sur about 20 miles, on the edge of an ocean cliff, sits **Lucia Lodge**. Perched 500 feet above a cobalt blue bay are ten cozy private cabins offering otherworldly views along a curving sweep of shoreline. All of the accommodations are rustic and sufficiently removed from the highway to create a sense of natural living in this extraordinary landscape. An adjacent restaurant and store make it a convenient hideaway. ~ Route 1, Lucia; 831-667-2391; www.lucia.com. MODERATE TO DELUXE.

ginning to discourage you, you're getting older than you think; after all, this offbeat hideaway does possess an enchanting quality. ~ Route 1; 831-667-2377. MODERATE TO DELUXE.

If, on the other hand, you spell Big Sur with a capital $, there are two places to consider. The first option is **Ventana**. Set along 243 mountainside acres overlooking the Pacific Ocean, this fabled resort is the *ne plus ultra* of refined rusticity. Buildings are fashioned from raw wood and most guest rooms are equipped with tile or marble fireplaces. There are cedar walls and quilt beds. With Japanese hot baths, saunas, two pools, a fitness room, a library, and a clothing-optional sun deck, the place exudes an air of languor. Guests enjoy a continental breakfast and afternoon wine and cheese, hike nearby trails, and congratulate themselves for having discovered a secluded resort where doing nothing is a way of life. Leaving the kids at home is suggested. ~ Route 1; 831-667-2331, 800-628-6500, fax 831-667-2419; www.ventanainn.com. ULTRA-DELUXE.

The second is **The Post Ranch Inn**, located just across the highway. Defying description, this cliff-edge hotel is a testimony to rustic perfection. Consisting of 30 separate units and designed to fit the surrounding landscape, the hotel features some rooms that are built into the hillside and covered by grass and others that are perched on stilts high above the forest floor. Each room is decorated by wood and stone, has a king-size bed, and, best of all, offers an open view of the Pacific Ocean or tree-covered hillside. ~ On Route 1; 831-667-2200, 800-527-2200, fax 831-667-2824; www.postranchinn.com. ULTRA-DELUXE.

The ultimate resting place in this corner of the world is the **Tassajara Zen Center**. Set deep in the Santa Lucia Mountains   ◄ HIDDEN along a meandering country road, Tassajara has been a hot springs resort since the 1880s. Before that its salubrious waters were known to American Indians and the Spanish. When the Zen Center purchased the place in 1967, they converted it into a meditation center. There are only a few telephones and electrical outlets in the entire complex, making it ideal for people seeking serenity. Every year from May until September, the Zen Center welcomes day-visitors and overnight guests to use the Japanese-style bath houses and natural steam showers. The hosts provide three vegetarian meals daily plus lodging in the private rooms and cabins dotted about the grounds. Day-visitors are charged a $14 admission, $17 on weekends (meals not available); lodging facilities with shared bath and meals included begin from $70 per person weekdays and $90 on weekends (cabins with private baths peak at $144); shuttle service into the resort is available from Jamesburg, south of the Carmel Valley. For day and overnight visits, be sure to make your reservations far in advance, since this unique place is very popular. ~ For information, contact the Zen Center, 300 Page Street, San Francisco, CA 94102; 415-863-3136; for reservations, call 415-865-1899; www.zendo.com\~sfzc.

DINING

For a gourmet dinner, **Glen Oaks Restaurant** is the prime location along Big Sur. Redwood tables, oil lamps, and lots of plants create an intimate atmosphere at this small establishment. Add to these a series of attractive local artists' paintings hung along the walls and a copper-sheathed fireplace in one corner. The cuisine has a Pacific Rim flair: there are such dishes as smoked pork loin, tofu and vegetable curry, rainbow trout with sake and lime, steak, and a selection of seafood that includes salmon, rock cod, and mahimahi. All meals include homemade bread; the wine list features central California vintages. Dinner only. Closed Tuesday. ~ Route 1; 831-667-2264. MODERATE.

Nearby **Fernwood**, a combination restaurant-bar-store, has hamburgers, sandwiches, barbecued chicken, homemade soup, and chili. The all-you-can-eat weekend barbeque features ribs and pork loin (summer only). This local gathering spot is your best bet for an inexpensive lunch or dinner. ~ Route 1; 831-667-2422. BUDGET.

Ventana Restaurant, part of the extraordinary complex that includes a prestigious inn, is one of the region's most elegant dining places. Resting on a hillside overlooking the mountains and sea, it's a perfect spot for a special meal. At lunch you'll be served salad, steak sandwiches, or fresh pasta, either inside the wood-paneled dining room, or alfresco on a sweeping veranda. For dinner you can start with oysters on the half shell or steamed artichoke, then proceed to such entrées as quail, rack of lamb, salmon, filet mignon, or fresh fish grilled over oak. ~ Route 1; 831-667-2331. DELUXE TO ULTRA-DELUXE.

Whether or not you're staying at the Post Ranch Inn, you'll hardly want to miss dinner at the resort's signature restaurant, **Sierra Mar**. The magnificent views of the ocean and surf 1100 feet below become tenfold more dramatic at dinnertime when the sun drops behind the Pacific. The menu features health-conscious California cuisine and changes daily. Among the flexible prix-fixe menu selections are lean beef, seafood, and poultry dishes seasoned and accompanied by fresh produce from the hotel's own garden. Dinner only; bar serves a light luncheon all afternoon. ~ Route 1; 831-667-2800. ULTRA-DELUXE.

Another bird's eye-view is offered at **Nepenthe**. Perched on a cliff 800 feet above the Pacific, this fabled dining spot has plenty of personality. People come across the continent to line its curving bar or dine along the open-air patio. It's a gathering place for locals, tourists, and everyone in between. There are sandwiches, quiches, and salads for lunch. At dinner the menu includes fresh fish, broiled chicken, and steak. If you're not hungry, stop in for a drink—the scene is a must. ~ Route 1; 831-667-2345. MODERATE TO DELUXE.

For breakfast or lunch, try the outdoor **Café Kevah** downstairs. Personally, I think it's a much better deal than Nepenthe. They serve standard breakfast fare—waffles, omelettes—and lunch dishes with a Mexican twist. Their homemade pastries are the perfect companions for an afternoon gazing out at the ocean. Closed in January and February and when it rains. ~ 831-667-2344. MODERATE.

SHOPPING

Set in a circular wooden structure resembling an oversized wine cask (and made from old water tanks) is one of Big Sur's best known art centers. The **Coast Gallery** is justifiably famous for its displays of arts and crafts by local artists. There are lithographs by novelist Henry Miller as well as paintings, sculptures, ceramics, woodwork, handmade candles, and blown glass by Northern California craftspeople. An adjoining shop features a wide selection of Miller's books. ~ Route 1, 33 miles south of Carmel; 831-667-2301.

NIGHTLIFE

Down in Big Sur the lights go out early. There is one place, **Big Sur River Inn**, that has a wood-paneled bar overlooking the Big Sur River and keeps a candle burning. On Sunday, Dixieland jazz livens things up. ~ Route 1; 831-667-2700.

BEACHES & PARKS

GARRAPATA STATE BEACH This broad swath of white sand is particularly favored by local people, some of whom use it as a nude beach. Easily accessible, it's nevertheless off the beaten tourist path, making an ideal hideaway for picnicking and skinny dipping. There are no facilities. A rough current and lack of lifeguards make swimming inadvisable. ~ It's along Route 1 about 12 miles south of Carmel. Watch for the curving beach from the highway; stop at the parking lot just north of the Garrapata Creek bridge. From here a trail leads down to the beach; 831-667-2315.

ANDREW MOLERA STATE PARK An adventurer's hideaway, this 4800-acre park rises from the sea to a 3455-foot elevation. It features three miles of beach and over 15 miles of hiking trails. The forests range from cottonwood to oak to redwood, while the wildlife includes mule deer, bobcat, harbor seals, and gray whales. Big Sur River rumbles through the landscape and surfers try the breaks on the beach. The only thing missing is a road: this is a hiker's oasis, its natural areas accessible only by heel and toe. The wilderness rewards are well worth the shoe leather. This is the only place in Big Sur where you can ride a horse; you can hire a horse from a concessionaire and check out Captain Cooper's Cabin, a 100-year-old pioneer log cabin. Toilets are the only facilities. Day-use fee, $4. ~ It's along Route 1 about three miles north of Big Sur; 831-667-2315.

▲ There are hike-in sites (tents only); $3 per person per night. Primitive facilities, but water is available.

PFEIFFER BIG SUR STATE PARK 🏃 🏊 🛶 One of California's southernmost redwood parks, this 800-acre facility is very popular, particularly in summer. With cottages, restaurant, grocery, gift shop, picnic areas, restrooms, showers, and laundromat on the premises, it's quite developed. However, nature still retains a toehold in these parts: the Big Sur River overflows with trout and salmon (fishing is prohibited, however), Pfeiffer Falls tumbles through a fern-banked canyon, and the park serves as the major trailhead leading to Ventana Wilderness. Day-use fee, $6. ~ Located along Route 1 in Big Sur; 831-667-2315.

▲ There are 218 sites for both tents and RVs (no hookups); $20 per night, $23 for riverside sites.

PFEIFFER BEACH 🏃 🏊 🎣 🚣 🛶 Of Big Sur's many wonders, this may be the most exotic. It's a sandy beach littered with boulders and bisected by a meandering stream. Behind the strand rise high bluffs which mark the terminus of a narrow gorge. Just offshore loom rock formations into which the sea has carved tunnels and arches. Little wonder poet Robinson Jeffers chose this haunting spot for his primal poem "Give Your Heart to the Hawks." Since we're dropping names, it's interesting to remember that Richard Burton and Elizabeth Taylor filmed *The Sandpiper* here. The only facilities are toilets. Day-use fee, $5. ~ Follow Route 1 for about a mile south past the entrance to Pfeiffer Big Sur State Park. Turn right onto Sycamore Canyon Road, which leads downhill two miles to the beach; 831-667-2423.

JULIA PFEIFFER BURNS STATE PARK 🏃 This 3580-acre extravaganza extends from the ocean to about 1500 feet elevation and is bisected by Route 1. The central park area sits in a redwood canyon with a stream that feeds through a steep defile into the ocean. Backdropped by sharp hills in a kind of natural amphitheater, it's an enchanting glade. A path leads beneath the highway to a spectacular vista point where 80-foot-high McWay Waterfall plunges into the ocean. Another path, 1.8 miles north of the park entrance, descends from the highway to an isolated beach near Partington Cove that has been declared an underwater park (permit required). There are picnic areas and restrooms. Day-use fee, $6. ~ Located on Route 1 about 11 miles south of Pfeiffer Big Sur State Park; 831-667-2315.

▲ There are two hike-in environmental campsites for tents only; $20 per night with an eight-person maximum. Reservations are required (800-444-7275).

VENTANA WILDERNESS 🏃🐎⛵🎣 Part of the Los Padres National Forest, this magnificent 216,500-acre preserve parallels Route 1 a few miles inland. It covers a broad swath of the Santa Lucia Mountains with elevations ranging from 600 feet to 5800 feet. Within its rugged confines are about 237 miles of hiking trails. Wild boars and turkeys, mountain lions, and deer roam its slopes. Bald eagles soar the skies. The only facilities are ranger stations. Parking fee, $2. ~ From Route 1 in the Big Sur area, there are two entry points. The ranger station, where maps and fire permits can be acquired, is just south of Pfeiffer Big Sur State Park. For information and permits, contact the U.S. Forest Service (Monterey District, 406 South Mildred Avenue, King City, CA 93930; 831-385-5434).

▲ There are more than 100 sites, some for self-contained RVs, others for walk-in tent camping. RV sites range from $5 to $16; hike-in is free.

The Central Coast is renowned for its open-sea fishing. Charter boats comb the waters for rock cod, salmon, and albacore. Most trips leave the dock by 6 a.m. and return by 3 p.m.

▼▼▼▼▼▼▼▼▼▼▼▼▼
Outdoor Adventures

FISHING

SOUTH OF SAN FRANCISCO If you want to test your skill or luck, contact **Captain John's Fishing Trips.** They operate four boats, ranging from 55 to 65 feet. You can go deep-sea fishing for rock cod or ling cod any day of the week. Or cruise 25 miles to the Farallon Islands on Tuesday, Friday, or Saturday. March through November there's salmon fishing and December through March there's whale watching. Bait and tackle available. ~ 21 Johnson Pier, Princeton-by-the-Sea; 650-726-2913.

SANTA CRUZ To take a charter from Santa Cruz in search of tuna, salmon or rock cod call **Shamrock Charters.** Live bait and tackle available. ~ 2210 East Cliff Drive at the Santa Cruz Yacht Harbor; 831-476-2648. For do-it-yourself adventures, **Santa Cruz Boat Rentals** has 20 boats to rent, 16-foot wooden skiffs that seat up to four adults, and fishing gear. There is also bait, tackle, and a gift shop. ~ Santa Cruz Municipal Pier; 831-423-1739.

MONTEREY **Monterey Sport Fishing & Whalewatching** has charter trips that last about eight hours. The boats explore the edges of an underwater canyon (larger than the Grand Canyon) in search of salmon, rock cod, and albacore tuna. ~ 96 Old Fisherman's Wharf #1; 831-372-2203. Or spend the day with **Randy's Fishing Trips.** They operate three boats, including two wooden boats. Advance reservations recommended. ~ 66 Old Fisherman's Wharf; 408-372-7440. **Sam's Fishing Fleet** also offers charters and day-long fishing trips for albacore, salmon, and deep-sea catches. ~ 84 Old Fisherman's Wharf; 831-372-0577.

BALLOON RIDES & HANG-GLIDING

If you want to leave terra firma behind and see the beauty of the Central Coast from on high, consider a balloon ride or a hang-gliding excursion.

SANTA CRUZ TO MONTEREY If your preference is to soar through the air, hang-gliding and paragliding lessons at Marina Beach are the way to fly. They also have ultra lights for a motor-ized hour in the air. Call **Western Hang Gliders** for more infor-mation. ~ Reservation Road and Route 1, Marina; 831-384-2622. Or, for a hot air balloon ride over the Salinas Valley, try **Balloons By the Sea** (which also offers skydiving). A four-person balloon provides views of the bay in the distance and the farmlands below. When you return to solid ground, enjoy a glass of champagne. ~ Marina Municipal Airport, Marina; 800-464-6420.

WHALE WATCHING & NATURE CRUISES

To see the whales during their annual migration, head for whale-watching lookouts at Pillar Point in Half Moon Bay, the coast around Davenport, Point Pinos in Pacific Grove, or Cypress Point in Point Lobos State Reserve. (See the "Whale Watching" feature in Chapter Three.) The summer whale watching season typically runs from mid-June through September while the winter migration is viewable from mid-December through mid-March.

MONTEREY If you'd prefer a close look at these migrating mam-mals and other marine life—sea lions, seals, otters, sea birds—catch a cruise with **Randy's Fishing Trips**. They can accommo-date up to 68 people, and the two-hour trip is fully narrated by a marine biologist. ~ 66 Old Fisherman's Wharf; 831-372-7440. To catch glimpses of blue whales, humpbacks, and dolphins, hop on board a vessel with **Monterey Sport Fishing and Whalewatch-ing**. Trips last about three hours and sonar equipment is used to help locate whales. ~ 96 Old Fisherman's Wharf #1; 831-372-2203. **Sam's Fishing Fleet** offers cruises that last anywhere from two to six hours. ~ 84 Old Fisherman's Wharf; 831-372-0577.

SEA KAYAKING

Whether you are young or old, experienced or a novice, the Cen-tral Coast awaits discovery by sea kayak.

MONTEREY Explore Monterey Bay and Elkhorn Slough, or paddle your way along the coastal waters with **Monterey Bay Kayaks** any time of the year. They also offer naturalist-led tours around the Monterey National Marine Sanctuary, where you'll see a wide variety of marine life. The six-hour tour of Elkhorn Slough goes through an inland saltwater marsh to view seals, otters, and birds. A short hike through woodlands and a lunch break at a lookout point round out the trip. There's also a shorter slough tour. Whale watching is great in the winter. Reservations required. ~ 693 Del Monte Avenue, Monterey; 831-373-5357. To experience the thrill of sea kayaking, call **Adventures by the Sea**. They have 150 double and single kayaks for rent. A two-and-a-half-hour tour is led by a marine biologist who describes the history of Cannery Row, local geology, natural history, and native lore. ~ 299 Cannery Row; 408-372-1807.

The Central Coast offers premiere diving in Northern California. Although coastal waters are quite frigid, the unique kelp forests, wide array of fish, spotted harbor seals, and other fascinating marine life make for unforgettable diving.

DIVING

SANTA CRUZ   **Adventure Sports** offers everything from one- or two-week-long dive trips taking you to hotspots to brunch dives leaving from Monastery Beach. They rent and sell all the gear, and give classes ranging from beginning to assistant instructor. ~ 303 Potrero Street #15, Santa Cruz; 831-458-3648. To explore the magical world of the deep, contact **Ocean Odyssey Dive Center**, a full-service dive shop with rentals and gear. Charter dive trips last five or six hours; they also offer night dives. Classes are available. Closed Tuesday. ~ 860 17th Avenue, Santa Cruz; 831-475-3483.

MONTEREY   **Aquarius Dive Shop** offers boat and beach dives. Boat dives are two-tank dives; the beach trips vary. They rent and sell all the gear. Classes are offered for open water, advanced rescue, and dive master. ~ 2040 Del Monte Avenue, Monterey; 831-375-1933. For morning, afternoon, or night dives, contact **Twin Otter Dive Charters**. Divers must be certified. All equipment is available to rent. ~ 225 Cannery Row; 831-656-9194.

CARMEL   **Point Lobos State Reserve** has some of the finest diving opportunities on the Pacific Coast. You'll spot sea otters, sea lions, and schools of fish. The numbers of divers per day are limited so reservations are a must. ~ Route 1; 831-624-4909, phone/fax 831-624-8413.

✔ CHECK THESE OUT—UNIQUE OUTDOOR ADVENTURES

- Paddle your way around playful sea otters and boisterous sea lions as you kayak Monterey Bay. *page 232*
- Explore the depths of 80-foot-high kelp forests and other underwater mysteries at Point Lobos State Reserve. *page 233*
- Pick and choose between world-class golf courses and tee off at Spyglass Hill or Pebble Beach Golf Course. *page 234*
- Shoot the curl at Steamer Lane, where international surfing competitions are often taking place. *page 234*

SURFING & WIND-SURFING

Catching a wave when the surf's up near Lighthouse Point north of Santa Cruz is a surfer's dream. Known as "Steamer Lane," this stretch of coastline hosts many international surfing competitions. On the east side, Pleasure Point is a popular surf spot with several reef breaks. Mavericks Break, located north of Half Moon Bay, is world-renowned among surfers for its huge—sometimes deadly—waves. Even experienced wave riders need to be careful here. Avoid surfing too far north near Año Nuevo—the waters are popular with great white sharks.

Surfboards and wet suits (the water is always cold) are available at **Arrow Surf 'n Sport**. ~ 2324 Mission Street, Santa Cruz; 831-423-8286. On the east side, long and short fiberglass boards, boogieboards, and wetsuits can be rented or purchased from **Freeline Design**. ~ 821 41st Avenue, Santa Cruz; 831-476-2950. In Capitola, try **O'Neill's Surf Shop**. A one-stop surf mecca, O'Neill's rents surf and boogieboards, wetsuits, and sells all the accessories including a few bathing suits and some clothes. ~ 1115 41st Avenue, Capitola; 831-475-4151. Or catch the wind on a windsurfing board. Rentals and lessons are available at **Club Ed Surfing and Windsurfing**, as are regular surfing lessons and equipment. Besides surfboards they also rent body boards, kayaks, wetsuits, and skinboards. ~ Look for the trailer on Cowell Beach next to the Santa Cruz wharf; 831-459-9283.

RIDING STABLES

Exploring the coast and inland trails astride a galloping horse is one way to enjoy a visit to the Central Coast.

SOUTH OF SAN FRANCISCO   With its four-mile white sand beach and surrounding farm country, Half Moon Bay is a choice region for riding. **Seahorse Ranch and Friendly Acres Ranch**, located on the coast, rents over 200 horses. They also have pony rides for kids. No reservations are necessary, and you can ride without a guide if you like. ~ 2150 Route 1, Half Moon Bay; 650-726-8550.

PACIFIC GROVE   There are escorted tours along 20 miles of trails at the **Pebble Beach Equestrian Center**. A one-and-a-half-hour ride takes you through the forest and down to the beach. Call ahead to reserve a horse. ~ Portola Road and Alva Lane, Pebble Beach; 831-624-2756.

GOLF

For golfers, visiting the Monterey Peninsula is tantamount to arriving in heaven. Pebble Beach is home to the annual AT&T National Pro-Am Golf Championship. Several courses rank among the top in the nation.

With stunning views of the rugged coastline, **Pebble Beach Golf Course** is the most noted. Three U.S. Open tournaments have been held here. Holes 7, 8, 17, 18 are world-renowned as highly difficult ocean holes. Reservations are required a day in advance for non-hotel guests. ~ 17 Mile Drive, Pebble Beach; 800-654-9300. Or you might want to tee off at **Spyglass Hill Golf Course**. Known as one of the toughest in the nation, six of the holes on this course have ocean views and the rest are set in the forest. Reservations are required. Be prepared: Green fees at these courses are steep! ~ Stevenson Road, Pebble Beach; 800-654-9300. Set on a century-old property, **Old Del Monte Golf Course** is a relatively flat course studded with ancient trees. Full-service pro shop and lessons available. ~ 1300 Sylvan Road, Monterey; 831-373-2700. **Pacific Grove Golf Course** overlooks Monterey Bay and the Pacific Ocean. It has a pro shop and driving range. ~ 77 Asilomar Boulevard, Pacific Grove; 831-648-3177.

The **Pacific Coast Bikecentennial Route** follows Route 1 through the entire Central Coast area to Big Sur and beyond. There are camping sites along the way. The awesome ocean views and miles of rolling pastures make this an ideal course to peddle, if you are experienced and careful.

BIKING

For scenic and historical bike tours of Carmel, try **Bay Bike Rentals**. They lead tours of 17 Mile Drive, the Carmel Coast down to Point Lobos, and a Big Sur downhill ride from the Old Coast Ridge through Andrew Molera State Park. They also rent hybrids, mountain bikes, tandems, and baby strollers. ~ 255 Heritage Harbor; 831-625-2453.

Both Santa Cruz and Monterey have bike paths for beginners and skilled riders alike. Especially good for touring are **17 Mile Drive**, the bike trail along the bayshore from **Seaside to Marina**, the trail from **Seaside to Lover's Point** (via Cannery Row), and the roads in **Point Lobos State Reserve**.

Bike Rentals   For hybrids, mountain bikes, tandems, and kids' bikes in Santa Cruz, go to the **Bicycle Rental Center**. ~ 131 Center Street; 831-426-8687. In Monterey, **Bay Bike Rentals** also has kids' bikes, tandems, mountain bikes, and safety equipment. ~ 640 Wave Street; 831-646-9090. For maps, brochures, sales, and rentals, contact **Freewheeling Cycles**. ~ 188 Webster Street, Monterey; 831-373-3855.

To fully capture the beauty and serenity of the region's woodlands, chaparral country, and beaches, explore its hiking trails. The Santa Cruz and Santa Lucia mountains offer several hundred miles of trails through fir, madrone, and redwood forests. Getting lost, so to speak, among these stands of ancient trees is a splendid way to vacation. Or hike the inland hills with their caves and rock spires. Down at the sea's edge you'll discover more caves, as well as tidepools, sand dunes, and a world of marine life. All distances listed are one way unless otherwise noted.

HIKING

SOUTH OF SAN FRANCISCO   If you have an urge to see elephant seals breeding, take the three-mile guided walk led by docents at **Año Nuevo State Reserve**. To protect these mammoth mammals, the preserve is open during breeding season only to those on the guided tours (December through March). The tours are popular and space is limited so make reservations well in advance; call 800-444-7275. To explore this area after mating season, you can hike on your own past sand dunes, tidepools, and sea caves. Follow **Año Nuevo Trail** (2.5 miles), beginning at the west end of the parking lot, to Año Nuevo Point.

Be careful when driving along the coast in the summer—thick fogs occasionally creep in, making for dangerous conditions.

MONTEREY AREA   One of California's most beautiful spots is the six-mile shoreline at **Point Lobos State Reserve**. The park is laced with trails leading to tidepools, sandy coves, and whale-watching vistas.

Cypress Grove Trail (.8 mile), one of the most popular (and populated) in the park, leads through a stand of Monterey cypress trees and offers cliff-top views of the ocean.

Bird Island Trail (.8 mile) takes you through coastal shrubbery to two exquisite white sand beaches—China Cove and Gibson Beach. The path also overlooks Bird Island, a refuge for cormorants and brown pelicans.

Pine Ridge Trail (.7 mile), beginning near Piney Woods, goes inland through forests of Monterey pines and Coast live oak. Deer, squirrel, and such birds as pygmy nuthatches and chestnut-backed chickadees make this a tranquil nature hike.

South Shore Trail (1 mile), an oceanside walk between Sea Lion Point and the Bird Rock parking area, allows close looks at tidepool life and shore birds. You can also play amateur geologist, examining multicolored patterns in sedimentary rocks.

For rock climbers and hikers alike, **Pinnacles National Monument** offers great sport. Because of the summer heat and winter weather, it's recommended that you come in spring or fall to explore the park's rock spires, talus caves, and covered canyons. At any time of year, bring plenty of water and a flashlight.

Hiking along the narrow ledges of **High Peaks Trail** (5.4 miles), you'll find splendid views of the entire park. The steep trail begins across from the Chalone Creek picnic area, travels up through the High Peaks and ends up at the Moses Spring parking lot. Allow at least three to four hours.

Old Pinnacles Trail (2.3 miles) begins at Chalone Creek picnic area and goes along relatively level terrain near the west fork of the creek to Balconies Caves.

Juniper Canyon Trail (1.8 miles) starts near the west end of the park at the Chaparral ranger station and climbs 760 feet to connect with the park's east side High Peaks Trail. It's the steepest trail in the monument.

BIG SUR   Over 216,500 acres of rugged mountain terrain comprise the **Ventana Wilderness** of Los Padres National Forest. About 200 miles of hiking trails make it easy to explore the Santa Lucia Mountains while escaping the trappings of civilization. Several roads off Route 1 will take you onto the preserve. Keep in mind that Big Sur Station and Bottchers Gap Station are the only staffed coastal entrances.

Bottchers Gap–Devils Peak Trail (4 miles) is a steep hike through coniferous forests to spectacular vistas overlooking the northern section of the Ventana Wilderness.

Kirk Creek–Vicente Flat Trail (5.1 miles) winds along ridgelines that afford mountain views.

Pine Ridge Trail (40.7 miles) begins at Big Sur Station and carries two miles to the park boundary before heading into the Ventana Wilderness. First stop is Ventana Camp, near the Big Sur River. Then the trail leads past several campgrounds and ends at China Camp.

▼▼▼▼▼▼▼▼▼▼▼

Transportation

From San Francisco, coastal highway **Route 1** is the most scenic way to explore the Central Coast. In the Santa Cruz Mountains, **Routes 35** and **9** lead through redwood forests and rural towns. **Route 101**, which runs inland parallel to the coast is the fastest route. Numerous side roads lead from this highway to points along the Central Coast.

CAR

Several airlines fly regular schedules to the **Monterey Airport**. America West, American Eagle Airlines, Sky West, United, and USAir service this area. ~ 831-648-7000.

AIR

Greyhound Bus Lines has service to Santa Cruz (425 Front Street; 831-423-1800) and Monterey (1042 Del Monte Avenue at the Exxon station; 831-373-4735) from San Francisco and Los Angeles. ~ 800-231-2222.

BUS

Alternatively, **Adventure Network for Travelers** provides a flexible bus service that allows you to "hop-on and hop-off" at destination points on their routes that traverse the California coast and into Arizona and Mexico. Stops include San Francisco, Santa Cruz, Monterey, Big Sur and Santa Barbara. ~ 870 Market Street, San Francisco; 800-336-6049; www.TheANT.com.

Amtrak has daily service on the "Coast Starlight." The train runs from Seattle to San Diego with stops in Oakland, San Jose, and Salinas (11 Station Place). In Salinas, passengers can transfer to a Greyhound or Monterey–Salinas Transit bus. ~ 800-872-7245.

TRAIN

CAR
RENTALS

If flying directly into Monterey, you can rent a car at the airport from **Avis Rent A Car** (800-331-1212), **Budget Rent A Car** (800-527-0700), **Hertz Rent A Car** (800-654-3131), or **National Car Rentals** (800-227-7368). Additional rental agencies are located in town. Try **American International Rent A Car** (800-392-8724).

PUBLIC
TRANSIT

Peerless Stages connects with Greyhound Bus Lines in San Jose and Oakland and travels to Santa Cruz. ~ 831-423-1800.

San Mateo County Transit, or SamTrans, leaving from the Daly City and Colma BART stations, has service to Pacifica, Moss Beach, Montara, and Half Moon Bay, and between Año Nuevo and San Mateo and Half Moon Bay during seal season (January through March). Reservations are required. ~ 800-660-4287.

From Waddell Creek in northern Santa Cruz County, the **Santa Cruz County Transit System** covers Route 1 as far south as Watsonville. ~ 831-425-8600.

From Watsonville, connections can be made to Monterey and Big Sur via the **Monterey–Salinas Transit Company**. These buses carry passengers to many points of interest including Cannery Row, Point Lobos, and Andrew Molera and Pfeiffer Big Sur State Parks. Buses from Monterey to Big Sur run twice daily from May through early September. ~ 831-899-2555; www.mst.org.

FIVE

South Central Coast

To call any one section of the California Coast the most alluring is to embark upon uncertain waters. Surely the South Central Coast, that 200-mile swath from Ventura to San Simeon, is a region of rare beauty. Stretching across Ventura, Santa Barbara, and San Luis Obispo counties, it embraces many of the West's finest beaches.

Five of California's 21 missions—in Ventura, Santa Barbara, Lompoc, San Luis Obispo, and further inland in Solvang—lie along this stretch. Chosen by the Spanish in the 1780s for their fertile pastures, natural harbors, and placid surroundings, they are a historic testimonial to the varied richness of the landscape.

The towns that grew up around these missions, evocative of old Spanish traditions, are emblems of California's singular culture. Santa Barbara, perhaps the state's prettiest town, is a warren of whitewashed buildings and red tile roofs, backdropped by rocky peaks and bounded by a five-mile palm-fringed beach.

Ventura and San Luis Obispo represent two of California's most underrated towns. In addition to a wealthy heritage, Ventura has beautiful beaches and San Luis Obispo is set amid velvet hills and rich agricultural areas. Both are less expensive than elsewhere and offer many of the same features without the pretensions.

Offshore are the Channel Islands, a 25-million-year-old chain and vital wildlife preserve. Sandblasted by fierce storms, pristine in their magnificence, they are a china shop of endangered species and unique life forms. While the nearby reefs are headstones for the many ships that have crashed here, the surrounding waters are crowded with sea life.

Together with the rest of the coast, the islands were discovered by Juan Rodríguez Cabrillo in 1542. The noted explorer found them inhabited by Chumash Indians, a collection of tribes occupying the coast from Malibu to Morro Bay. Hunters and gatherers, the Chumash were master mariners who built woodplank canoes called *tomols*, capable of carrying ten people across treacherous waters to the Channel Islands. They in turn were preceded by the Oak Grove Tribes, which inhabited the region from 7000 to 3000 B.C.

Once Gaspar de Portolá opened the coast to Spanish colonialists with his 1769 explorations, few Indians from any California tribes survived. Forced into servitude and religious conversion by the padres, the Chumash revolted at Santa Barbara Mission and Mission de la Purísima Concepción in 1824. They held Purísima for a month before troops from Monterey overwhelmed them. By 1910 the Westerners who had come to save them had so decimated the Indians that their 30,000 population dwindled to 1250.

It took Cecil B. De Mille and over 1000 workers to build the set for the epic 1923 movie *The Ten Commandments* at Nipomo Sand Dunes.

By the mid 1800s these lately arrived white men set out in pursuit of any sea mammal whose pelt would fetch a price. The South Central Coast was a prime whale-hunting ground. Harpooners by the hundreds speared leviathans, seals, and sea lions, hunting them practically to extinction. Earlier in the century American merchants, immortalized in Richard Henry Dana's *Two Years Before the Mast*, had combed the coast trading for cattle hides.

The land that bore witness to this colonial carnage endured. Today the South Central Coast and its offshore islands abound in sea lions, harbor seals, Northern fur seals, and elephant seals. Whales inhabit the deeper waters and gamefish are plentiful. The only threats remaining are those from developers and the oil industry, whose offshore drilling resulted in the disastrous 1969 Santa Barbara spill.

The South Central Coast traveler finds a Mediterranean climate, dry and hot in the summer, tempered by morning fog and winds off the ocean, then cool and rainy during winter months. Two highways, Routes 1 and 101, lead through this salubrious environment. The former hugs the coast much of the way, traveling inland to Lompoc and San Luis Obispo, and the latter, at times joining with Route 1 to form a single roadway, eventually diverges into the interior valleys.

Almost as much as the ocean, mountains play a vital part in the life of the coast. Along the southern stretches are the Santa Monica Mountains, which give way farther north to the Santa Ynez Mountains. Below them, stretching along the coastal plain, are the towns of Oxnard, Ventura, Santa Barbara, and Goleta.

Both mountain systems are part of the unique Transverse Range, which unlike most North American mountains, travels from east to west rather than north and south. They are California's Great Divide, a point of demarcation between the chic, polished regions near Santa Barbara and the rough, wild territory around San Luis Obispo.

Arriving at the ocean around Point Conception, the Transverse Range separates the curving pocket beaches of the south and the endless sand dunes to the north. Here the continent takes a sharp right turn as the beaches, facing south in Santa Barbara, wheel about to look west across the Pacific.

Amid this geologic turmoil lies Lompoc, the top flower seed producing area in the world, a region of agricultural beauty and color beyond belief, home to 40 percent of the United States' flower crop. To the north are the Nipomo Sand Dunes, extending 18 miles from Point Sal to Pismo Beach, one of the nation's largest dune systems. A habitat for the endangered California brown pelican and the California least tern, these are tremendous piles of sand, towering to 450 feet, held in place against the sea wind by a lacework of ice plant, grasses, verbena, and silver lupine.

They are also the site of an Egyptian city, complete with walls 110 feet high and a grand boulevard lined with sphinxes and pharaohs. Today, like other glorious cities of yesteryear, it lies buried beneath the sand.

In San Luis Obispo oceanfront gives way to ranch land as the landscape reveals a Western visage. Unlike Spanish-style Santa Barbara to the south and Monterey to the north, San Luis Obispo has defined its own culture, a blend of hard-riding ranch hand and easygoing college student. Its roots nonetheless are similar, deriving from the Spanish, who founded their mission here in 1772, and the 19th-century Americans who built the town's gracious Victorian homes.

Rich too in natural history, the region between San Luis Obispo and Morro Bay is dominated by nine mountain peaks, each an extinct volcano dating back 20 million years. Last in the line is Morro Rock, an imposing monolith surrounded by a fertile wetlands that represents one of the country's ten most vital bird habitats.

Farther north civilization gives way to coastal quietude. There are untracked beaches and wind-honed sea cliffs, a prelude to Big Sur further up the coast. Among the few signs of the modern world are the artist colony of Cambria and that big

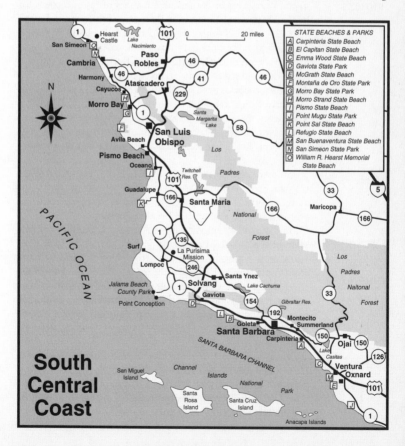

STATE BEACHES & PARKS

A Carpinteria State Beach
B El Capitan State Beach
C Emma Wood State Beach
D Gaviota State Park
E McGrath State Beach
F Montaña de Oro State Park
G Morro Bay State Park
H Morro Strand State Beach
I Pismo State Beach
J Point Mugu State Park
K Point Sal State Beach
L Refugio State Beach
M San Buenaventura State Beach
N San Simeon State Park
O William R. Hearst Memorial State Beach

South Central Coast

house on the hill, Hearst Castle, California's own eighth wonder of the world. Symbol of boundless artistry and unbridled egotism, it is also one of the coast's many wonders.

▼▼▼▼▼▼▼▼▼▼▼▼▼▼▼
Ventura–Oxnard Area

Situated 60 miles northwest of Los Angeles and 30 miles to the southeast of Santa Barbara, the 18th-century mission town of Ventura has generally been overlooked by travelers. History has not been so remiss. Long known to the Chumash Indians, who inhabited a nearby village named Shisholop, the place was revealed to Europeans in 1542 by the Portuguese explorer Juan Rodríguez Cabrillo. Father Junípero Serra founded a mission here in 1782 and the region soon became renowned for its fruit orchards. Oxnard is known chiefly as an agricultural community, contributing a large share of the area's produce.

SIGHTS   Ventura preserves its heritage in a number of historic sites. Stop by the **Visitors and Convention Bureau** for brochures and maps. ~ 89-C South California Street, Ventura; 805-648-2075.

Downtown Ventura is compact and walkable, and the highlight of a stroll through Ventura is **San Buenaventura Mission**, a whitewash and red tile church flanked by a flowering garden. The dark, deep chapel is lined with Stations of the Cross paintings and features a Romanesque altar adorned with statues and pilasters. My favorite spot is the adjacent garden with its tile fountain and stately Norfolk pines. Entrance to the mission is actually through a small gift shop a few steps to the east. ~ 211 East Main Street, Ventura; 805-643-4318.

From the mission, continuing east along the next several blocks of **Main Street** will take you past dozens of vintage, thrift, and antique stores. The avenue itself has been spruced up in the last year or two, and parking has been improved.

Just west of the mission is the **Albinger Archaeological Museum** at the site of an archaeological dig that dates back 3500 years, representing five different native cultures. The small museum displays arrowheads, shell beads, crucifixes, and pottery uncovered here. At the dig site itself you'll see the foundation of an 18th-century mission church, an ancient earth oven, and a remnant of the Spanish padres' elaborate aqueduct system. Closed Monday and Tuesday. ~ 113 East Main Street, Ventura; 805-648-5823.

Then cross Main Street to the **Ventura County Museum of History and Art**, which traces the region's secular history with displays of Chumash Indian artifacts and a farm implement collection. The art gallery features revolving exhibits of local painters and photographers. There's a collection of 32,000 photos depicting Ventura County from its origin to the present. One gallery features a permanent display of George Stuart's historical figures. The artist is exacting in his detail, right down to eyelashes and fingernails, when crafting a miniature Martin Luther King Jr. or Abraham Lincoln. Closed Monday. Admission. ~ 100 East Main Street, Ventura; 805-653-0323.

About four blocks west of the mission sits the **Ortega Adobe Historical Residence**, a small, squat home built in 1857 that eventually gave birth to Ortega Chile. With its woodplank furniture and bare interior it provides a strong example of how hard and rudimentary life was in that early era. Closed Monday and Tuesday. ~ 215 West Main Street, Ventura; 805-658-4726.

Backtrack to San Buenaventura Mission and wander down **Figueroa Plaza**, a broad promenade decorated with tile fountains and flowerbeds. This is the site of the town's old Chinatown section, long since passed into myth and memory.

Figueroa Street continues to the waterfront, where a **promenade** parallels the beach. This is a prime area for water sports, and countless surfers, with their blond hair and black wetsuits, will be waiting offshore, poised for the perfect wave. Along the far end of the esplanade, at the **Ventura Pier**, you'll encounter one more Southern California species, the surf fisherman.

If it's not too hazy, the outline of Anacapa, one of the **Channel Islands**, should be visible from the pier and other high spots in Ventura. Day trips to Anacapa, which lies about 14 miles offshore, can be arranged through Island Packers. ~ 1867 Spinnaker Drive, Ventura Harbor; 805-642-1393. For an orientation to the special habitat of the Channel Islands, visit the **Channel Islands Visitor Center** at Ventura Harbor. ~ 1901 Spinnaker Drive, Ventura Harbor; 805-658-5730. (For more information about the islands and excursions to visit them, see "The Channel Islands" in this chapter.)

✔ CHECK THESE OUT—UNIQUE SIGHTS

- Admire adobes as you stroll the 14-block **Red Tile Tour** in Santa Barbara, watching California history unfold with each step. *page 250*
- Travel back to Spanish times—roam through **La Purísma Mission**, offering the finest restoration of the state's 21 missions. *page 255*
- Pretend you're lost with Lawrence of Arabia at **Rancho Guadalupe Dunes County Park**, where you can explore the West Coast's highest sand dune, 450-foot Mussel Rock. *page 285*
- Overwhelm your senses with grandeur at **Hearst Castle**, the monumental estate of publishing magnate William Randolph Hearst. *page 289*

Another local wonder is the **Ventura County Courthouse**, a sprawling structure designed in Neo-Classical style. The place is a mélange of Doric columns, bronze fixtures, and Roman flourishes. But forget the marble entranceway and grand staircase— what makes it memorable is the row of friars' heads adorning the facade. Where else but in Southern California would a dozen baroque priests stare out at you from the hall of justice? ~ 501 Poli Street, Ventura.

The **Olivas Adobe** is a spacious hacienda surrounded by flowering gardens. This two-story gem, with balconies running the full length of the upper floor, is a study in the Monterey–style architecture of 19th-century California. The rooms are furnished in period pieces and there is a museum adjacent to the house, providing a window on the world of California's prosperous Spanish settlers. Special events such as summer concerts, a Halloween ghost story tour, and a Christmas candlelight tour are staged. Call ahead for information. Grounds open daily, museum closed weekdays. ~ 4200 Olivas Park Drive, Ventura; 805-644-4346.

It's mostly the agricultural fields of strawberries and the bustle of suburbia that you'll notice as you drive through the Oxnard area. But the city also has a seven-mile stretch of shoreline and the **Channel Islands Harbor**, a busy commercial port providing a departure point for trips to the Channel Islands. A **visitors center** supplies information. ~ 3810 West Channel Islands Boulevard; 800-994-4852. The **Harbor Hopper Water Taxi** is a fun way to see the waterfront homes, as well as a convenient mode of transport for a culinary tour of the harbor (see "Harbor-Hopping Dine Around" sidebar below). ~ 805-985-4677.

HARBOR-HOPPING DINE AROUND

Several restaurants are at Oxnard's Channel Islands Harbor, and one of the most enjoyable dining experiences in Southern California is to harbor-hop from one to another via the **Harbor Hopper Water Taxi**. Start out with a cocktail at the Lobster Trap (Casa Sirena Hotel, 3605 Peninsula Road; 805-985-6311), then move over to the popular Whale's Tail (3950 Bluefin Circle; 805-985-2511) for a starter of freshly shucked oysters. Continue to Port Royal (3900 Bluefin Circle; 805-382-7678) for poached Chilean sea bass. Make the last stop Tugs (3600 South Harbor Boulevard; 805-985-8847) for the classic New York cheesecake. The taxi costs about $1 per person per hop; operating hours vary by season and weather. And don't wait too late to get started. Oxnard is an early-to-bed sort of place—most restaurants will be closed by 10 p.m. The hotel concierge can help you make arrangements. ~ 805-985-4677.

Several of Ventura County's turn-of-the-century homes were relocated to an area called **Heritage Square** in downtown Oxnard. Most of the houses are given over to small professional offices, but there's also gift shop and a community theater. Tours are available on Saturday. ~ 715 South A Street, Oxnard; 805-483-7960.

For something spacious, plush, and formal consider the **Bella Maggiore Inn**. Set in downtown Ventura, this 28-room hostelry follows the tradition of an Italian inn. There are European appointments and antique chandeliers in the lobby and a Roman-style fountain in the courtyard. The accommodations I saw were painted in soft hues and decorated with pastel prints. The furniture was a mixture of cane, washed pine, and antiques. ~ 67 South California Street, Ventura; 805-652-0277, 800-523-8479, fax 805-648-5670. MODERATE TO DELUXE.

LODGING

Up the hill, overlooking Ventura and the ocean, sits **La Mer European Bed & Breakfast**. The flags decorating the facade of this 1890 house illustrate the inn's international theme. Each of the five guest rooms is decorated after the fashion of a European country—England, Austria, Norway, Germany, and France. All with private baths and entrances, they vary from the Norwegian "Captain's Cove," decorated nautically, to the French "Madame Pompadour," with its bay window. ~ 411 Poli Street, Ventura; 805-643-3600, fax 805-653-7329; www.vcol.net/lamer. MODERATE TO ULTRA-DELUXE.

Get into the nautical theme of the area by staying aboard a 30-foot classic sailboat that's securely docked in Ventura Harbor. **Boatel Bunk and Breakfast** offers accommodations for two on restored wooden boats. Breakfast is included, but you'll have to go topside for the toilet and shower. ~ 1567 Spinnaker Drive, Slip D-8, Ventura Harbor; 805-640-9690, fax 805-640-9694.

◄ HIDDEN

Besides being an all-suite property, **Embassy Suites Mandalay Beach** is the only full-service hotel on the beach in this area. As you might expect, the oceanfront suites are almost always sold out on weekends, so plan ahead and reserve early. A full, complimentary breakfast is included in the price. ~ 2101 Mandalay Beach Road, Oxnard; 805-984-2500, 800-362-2779, fax 805-984-8339; www.embassy-suites.com. DELUXE.

The brick-walled, flower-filled **Nona's Courtyard Café** provides a cool and charming indoor spot for lunch or dinner. Salads and sandwiches are tasty and generous, as are the pastas, risottos, chicken, and other entrées. ~ Bella Maggiore Inn, 67 South California Street, Ventura; 805-641-2783. MODERATE.

DINING

◄ HIDDEN

At **Café Voltaire**, grab a quick cappuccino and a thick slice of carrot cake and sit outside in the historic Old Town Livery. ~ 34 North Palm Street, Ventura; 805-641-1743. MODERATE.

For trendier dining, make a reservation at one of Ventura's more popular spots, **Café Zack**, a small restaurant set up in a converted cottage about five blocks east of downtown. ~ 1095 Thompson Boulevard, Ventura; 805-643-9445. MODERATE TO DELUXE.

The Santa Clara House is a 1914 Victorian decorated in a New Orleans style. The specialty here is anything off the oak barbecue. ~ 211 East Santa Clara Street, Ventura; 805-643-3264. MODERATE TO DELUXE.

Or try **Eric Ericsson's Fish Company**, a small snuggery done in casual California style with indoor and outdoor seating. At lunch they could be serving fish chowder, seafood pasta, poached shrimp, or fresh fish tacos. Then for dinner they might charbroil mahimahi, salmon, swordfish, or sea bass, depending on the season. They also have a walk-up snack shack where you can grab a smoothie, burger or breakfast sandwich while you stroll along the beach. ~ 668 Harbor Boulevard, Ventura; 805-643-4783. MODERATE TO DELUXE.

Franky's Restaurant is a trip. The place resembles a mini-art gallery, decorated with paintings, mobiles, murals, and statuary. All the artwork is for sale, so the decorative scheme is always changing. The interior is liable to be adorned with marble busts and Modernist canvases. The only fixed features are the frog murals which caricature employees and long-time customers. Moving from palette to palate, the menu contains omelettes and salads, plus pita bread sandwiches and croissants stuffed with chicken salad, shrimp, or tuna. Dinner is served Friday and Saturday only; breakfast and lunch are served daily. ~ 456 East Main Street, Ventura; 805-648-6282. BUDGET TO MODERATE.

NIGHTLIFE If it's live blues you're after, check out **The Santa Clara House** on Friday or Saturday nights. ~ 211 East Santa Clara Street, Ventura; 805-643-3264.

Bombay Bar & Grill offers live entertainment nightly with a musical medley that varies from rock to funk, ska and jazz. The room in back hosts live dance bands weekends only. Cover on weekends. ~ 143 South California Street, Ventura; 805-643-4404.

Check out the dance scene at **The Metro**. There's high-energy deejay dance music ranging from hip hop to techno. Saturday is disco night. Nightly drink and admission specials. Cover Wednesday through Sunday. ~ 317 East Main Street, Ventura; 805-653-2582.

Vallanta de Cantina draws a Spanish-speaking crowd for salsa, cumbia, and merengue dancing every day of the week. ~ 2485 East Main Street, Ventura; 805-653-9194.

BEACHES & PARKS **POINT MUGU STATE PARK** 🚶 🚴 🏇 ⛵ 🎣 This outstanding facility extends along four miles of beachfront and reaches back six miles into the Santa Monica Mountains. Much of the landscape is characterized by hilly, chaparral-cloaked terrain. Vegetation is plentiful, and the campgrounds are very open. The beaches—which include **Sycamore Cove Beach**, **Thornhill Broome**, and **Point Mugu Beach**—are wide and sandy, with rocky outcroppings and a spectacular sand dune. To the interior, the park rises to 1266-foot Mugu Peak and to Tri-Peaks, 3010 feet in elevation. There are two large canyons as well as wide, forested valleys. More than 70 miles of hiking trails lace this diverse park. Facilities include picnic areas, restrooms, and lifeguards. Swimming and bodysurfing are popular but watch for rip currents. There is good surf a few miles south of the park at **County Line Beach**. ~ On Route 1 ten miles south of Oxnard. Information center at Sycamore Cove; 818-880-0350.

▲ There are three separate park campgrounds. At Sycamore Canyon there are flush toilets, hot showers, and 45 sites for tents and RVs (no hookups); $17 to $18 per night. Thornhill Broome Beach has 63 primitive sites right on the beach for tents and RVs (no hookups); $17 to $18 per night. And La Jolla Valley has 12 sites (hike-in only) and costs $3 per person per night. Reservations are required (800-444-7275).

MCGRATH STATE BEACH 🚲 ⛺ 🏄 🚿 This long, narrow park extends for two miles along the water. The beach is broad and bounded by dunes. A lake and wildlife area attract over 200 bird species. The Santa Clara River, on the northern boundary, is home to tortoises, squirrels, muskrats, weasels, and other wildlife. Together the lake and preserve make it a great spot for camping or daytripping at the beach. There are restrooms, showers, and lifeguards. Swimming and surfing is recommended for strong swimmers only; watch for rip currents. Day-use fee, $5. ~ 2211 Harbor Boulevard, Oxnard; 805-899-1400.

▲ There are 174 sites for tents and RVs (no hookups); $17 to $18 per night. Reservations strongly recommended (800-444-7275).

SAN BUENAVENTURA STATE BEACH 🚲 ⛺ 🏄 🚿 In the world of urban parks this 114-acre facility ranks high. The broad sandy beach, bordered by dunes, extends for two miles to the Ventura pier. Since the pier is a short stroll from the city center, the beach provides a perfect escape hatch after you have toured the town. Facilities include picnic areas, restrooms, showers, dressing rooms, snack bar, lifeguards. The breakwaters here provide excellent swimming. Surfing is popular at **Surfer's Point Park**, foot of Figueroa Street; and at **Peninsula Beach**, at the north end of Spinnaker Drive. Fishing from the 1700-foot pier is good, and anglers may catch bass, shark, surf perch, corbina, and halibut. The nearby rock jetties are a haven for crabs and mussels. Day-use fee, $5. ~ Located along Harbor Boulevard southeast of the Ventura Pier in Ventura; 805-899-1400.

EMMA WOOD STATE BEACH 🏃 🚴 ⚓ 🎣 ⛵ Sandwiched between the ocean and the Southern Pacific railroad tracks, this slender park measures only 109 acres. Because of tide fluctuations, the beach can become extremely rocky, making it undesirable for swimmers and sunbathers. It is the only beach in Ventura County where dogs are allowed. There is a marsh at one end inhabited by songbirds and small mammals. Considering the fabulous beaches hereabouts, I rank this one pretty low. Restrooms are available. Cabezon, perch, bass, and corbina are caught here. Day-use fee, $5. ~ Located on the northwest boundary of Ventura just off Route 101; 805-899-1400.

▲ There's camping nearby along the small, rocky beaches north of Emma Wood State Beach at three different campgrounds. **Emma Wood–North Beach** has 61 first-come, first-served sites for tents and RVs (no hookups); $15 per night; for information, call 805-899-1400. **Faria County Park** is a bit smaller with 42 sites for tents and RVs (no hookups); $20 per night. **Hobson County Park** is smaller still with 31 sites for tents and RVs (no hookups); $20 per night. For information on the latter two parks, call 805-654-3951.

▼▼▼▼▼▼▼▼▼▼▼▼▼▼

Santa Barbara Area

From Ventura, Route 101 speeds north and west to Santa Barbara. For a slow-paced tour of the shoreline, take the Old Pacific Coast Highway instead. Paralleling the freeway and the Southern Pacific Railroad tracks, it rests on a narrow shelf between sharply rising hills and the ocean. The road glides for miles along sandy beaches and rocky shoreline, passing the woodframe communities of Solimar Beach and Seacliff Beach.

Past this last enclave the old road ends as you join Route 101 once more. With the Santa Ynez Mountains looming on one side and the Pacific extending along the other, you'll pass the resort town of Carpinteria. The temperature might be 80 with a blazing sun overhead and a soft breeze off the ocean. Certainly the furthest thing from your mind is the North Pole, but there it is, just past Carpinteria—the turnoff for Santa Claus Lane.

SIGHTS Santa Claus Lane? It's a block-long stretch of trinket shops and toy stores with a single theme. A giant rooftop Santa Claus with a waistline measuring maybe 30 feet oversees the New England–style village. It's one of those places that's so tacky you feel like you've missed something if you pass it by. If nothing else, you can mail an early Christmas card. Just drop it in the mailbox at **Toyland** and it will be postmarked (ready for this?) "Santa Claus, California." ~ 3821 Santa Claus Lane, Carpinteria; 805-684-3515.

Tucked between a curving bay and the Santa Ynez Mountains lies one of the prettiest places in all California. It's little wonder that the Spanish who settled **Santa Barbara**, establishing a presidio in 1782 and a mission several years later, called it *la tierra adorada*, the beloved land.

Discovered by a Portuguese navigator in 1542, it was an important center of Spanish culture until the Americans seized California in the 19th century. The town these Anglo interlopers built was an early-20th-century community. But a monstrous earthquake leveled the downtown area in 1925 and created a *tabula rasa* for architects and city planners.

Faced with rebuilding Santa Barbara, they returned the place to its historic roots, combining Spanish and Mission architecture to create a Mediterranean metropolis. The result is modern day Santa Barbara with its adobe walls, red tile roofs, rounded archways, and palm-lined boulevards.

Sightseeing in Santa Barbara is as simple as it is rewarding. First, you should stop at the **Santa Barbara Visitors Center**. The myriad materials here include more pamphlets, books, and booklets than you ever want to see. The most important piece is a map entitled "Santa Barbara" that outlines a "Red Tile Tour" for walk-

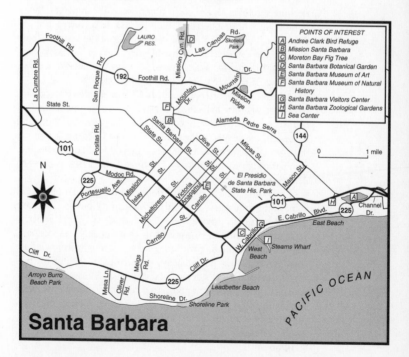

Santa Barbara

ers as well as a lengthier "Scenic Drive." Together they form two concentric circles along the perimeters of which lie nearly all the city's points of interest. ~ 1 Garden Street, Santa Barbara; 805-965-3021.

RED TILE TOUR The 14-block **Red Tile Tour** begins at the **Santa Barbara County Courthouse**, the city's grandest building. This U-shaped Spanish–Moorish "palace" covers almost three sides of a city block. The interior is a masterwork of beamed ceilings, arched corridors, and palacio tile floors. On the second floor of this 1929 courthouse are murals depicting California history. The highlight of every visit is the sweeping view of Santa Barbara at the top of the clock tower. From the Santa Ynez Mountains down to the ocean all that meets the eye are palm trees and red tile roofs. ~ 1100 block of Anacapa Street; 805-962-6464.

Two blocks down, the **Hill-Carrillo Adobe** is an 1826-vintage home built by a Massachusetts settler for his Spanish bride. The house is closed to the public but can be viewed from the street. ~ 11 East Carrillo Street.

Along State Street, the heart of Santa Barbara's shopping district, many stores occupy antique buildings. **El Paseo** represents one of the most original malls in the entire country. It is a labyrinthine shopping arcade consisting of several complexes. Incorporated into the architectural motif is **Casa de la Guerra**, a splendid house built in 1818 for the commander of the Santa Barbara presidio and described by Richard Henry Dana in his classic book *Two Years Before the Mast.* Closed Monday through Wednesday. ~ 15 East de la Guerra Street; 805-965-0093.

Across the street rests **Plaza de la Guerra**, a palm-fringed park where the first city hall stood in 1875. Nearby, another series of historic structures has been converted into a warren of shops and offices. In the center of the mall is **Presidio Gardens**, a tranquil park with a carp pond and elephant-shaped fountains that spray water through their trunks. ~ On de la Guerra Street between Anacapa and Garden streets.

The **Santiago de la Guerra Adobe** and the **Lugo Adobe**, set in a charming courtyard, are other 19th-century homes that have been converted to private use. ~ 114 East de la Guerra Street.

The **Santa Barbara Historical Museum** certainly looks its part. Set in an adobe building with tile roof and wrought-iron window bars, the facility sits behind heavy wooden doors. Within are fine art displays and a series depicting the Spanish, Mexican, and early American periods of Santa Barbara's history, including memorabilia from author Richard Henry Dana's visits. A pleasant courtyard in back with a fountain and shade trees is a perfect place for a sightseer's siesta. Closed Monday. ~ 136 East de la Guerra Street; 805-966-1601.

A right turn on Santa Barbara Street takes you to **Casa de Covarrubias.** Most places in town are a bit too neatly refurbished to provide a dusty sense of history. But this L-shaped house, and the adjacent **Historic Fremont Adobe**, are sufficiently wind-blasted to evoke the early 19th century. The former structure, dating to 1817, is said to be the site of the last Mexican assembly in 1846; the latter became headquarters for Colonel John C. Fremont after Americans captured the town later that year. ~ 715 Santa Barbara Street.

Turn back along Santa Barbara Street and pass the **Rochin Adobe**. This 1856 adobe, now covered with clapboard siding, is a private home. ~ 820 Garden Street.

It's a few steps over to **El Presidio de Santa Barbara State Historic Park,** which occupies both sides of the street and incorporates some of the city's earliest buildings. Founded in 1782, the Presidio was one of four military fortresses built by the Spanish in California. Protecting settlers and missionaries from Indians, it also served as a seat of government and center of Western culture. Today only two original buildings survive. **El Cuartel**, the guards' house, served as the soldiers' quarters. The **Cañedo Adobe**, also built as a military residence, is now the offices of the Santa Barbara Trust for Historic Preservation. Most interesting of all is the **Santa Barbara Presidio Chapel**, which re-creates an early Span-

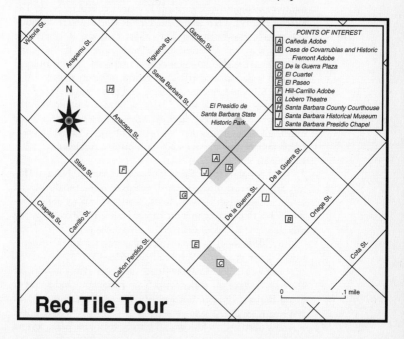

POINTS OF INTEREST

A	Cañeda Adobe
B	Casa de Covarrubias and Historic Fremont Adobe
C	De la Guerra Plaza
D	El Cuartel
E	El Paseo
F	Hill-Carrillo Adobe
G	Lobero Theatre
H	Santa Barbara County Courthouse
I	Santa Barbara Historical Museum
J	Santa Barbara Presidio Chapel

El Presidio de Santa Barbara State Historic Park

0   .1 mile

Red Tile Tour

ish church in its full array of colors. Compared to the plain exterior, the interior is a shock to the eye. Everything is done in red and yellow ochre and dark blue. The altar is painted to simulate a great cathedral. Drapes and columns, difficult to obtain during Spanish days, have been drawn onto the walls. Even the altar railing is painted to imitate colored marble. ~ 123 East Cañon Perdido Street; 805-966-9719.

The last stop on this walking tour will carry you a step closer to the present. The **Lobero Theatre** was constructed in 1924. It is a three-tiered design that ascends to a 70-foot-high stage house. The original Lobero dates back to 1872, Santa Barbara's first theater. Weekly musical performances are staged here as well as visiting dance and dramatic troupes. Call Monday through Saturday for tickets. ~ 33 East Cañon Perdido Street; 805-963-0761.

SCENIC DRIVE The **Scenic Drive** around Santa Barbara, a 21-mile circular tour, incorporates a number of the sites that are covered along the Red Tile Tour. To avoid repetition begin at the **Santa Barbara Museum of Art** with its collection of American paintings, Asian art, and classical sculpture. Closed Monday. Admission. ~ 1130 State Street; 805-963-4364.

Then head up to **Mission Santa Barbara**, which sits on a knoll overlooking the city. Founded in 1786 and restored in 1820, this twin-towered beauty, known as the "Queen of the Missions," follows a design from an ancient Roman architecture book. The interior courtyard is a colonnaded affair with a central fountain and graceful flower garden. The chapel itself is quite impressive with a row of wrought-iron chandeliers leading to a multicolored altar. There are also museum displays representing the original Indian population and early-19th-century mission artifacts. Also visit the Mission Cemetery, a placid and pretty spot where frontier families and about 4000 Chumash Indians are buried in the shade of a Moreton Bay fig tree. Mission Santa Barbara is the only California mission that has been continuously used by Franciscan fathers throughout its 200-year history. Admission. ~ 2201 Laguna Street; 805-682-4713.

Farther uphill at the **Santa Barbara Museum of Natural History** are successive rooms devoted to marine, plant, vertebrate, and insect life. Excellent for kids, it also features small exhibits of Indian tribes from throughout the United States. You'll recognize the museum by the 72-foot skeleton of a blue whale out front. There is also a lizard lounge and a planetarium with a space lab. Admission. ~ 2559 Puesta del Sol Road; 805-682-4711.

Nearby Mission Canyon Road continues into the hills for close-up views of the rocky Santa Ynez Mountains and a tour of **HIDDEN ►** **Santa Barbara Botanic Garden**. The five and one-half miles of trails here wind past a desert section carpeted with cactus and a meadow filled with wildflowers. Near the top of the park, beyond the ancient Indian trail, where the forest edges down from the mountains, is a stand of cool, lofty redwood trees. Guided tours daily. Admission. ~ 1212 Mission Canyon Road; 805-682-4726.

Backtrack to Alameda Padre Serra and cruise this elite roadway past million-dollar homes with million-dollar views. From this thoroughfare a series of side roads leads through the exclusive bedroom community of **Montecito**. Here a variety of architectural styles combine to create a luxurious neighborhood.

Montecito is where the real money is in the Santa Barbara area. A drive through this community, which flanks Santa Barbara on the south, will give you only a glimpse of the well-tended natural beauty of the place, because homes for the most part are secluded behind walls and lavish landscaping. One former resident, Madame Ganna Walska, turned her hillside estate into what is now one of the most famous private gardens in the country: **Lotusland**. By the time she arrived in Santa Barbara in 1941, Madame, a Polish-born opera singer, was on her sixth husband. He persuaded her to buy a Montecito estate in order to establish a spiritual center for Tibetan scholar-monks. When that idea, along with the marriage, failed, Madame turned to horticulture. The result was a magnificent private garden that non-members may tour on an extremely limited, reservations-only basis; call a year in advance for reservations. The gardens are open only nine months of the year from Wednesday through Saturday. Admission. ~ 805-969-9990.

After exploring the town's shady groves and manicured lawns, you can pick up **Channel Drive**, a spectacular street that skirts beaches and bluffs as it loops back toward Santa Barbara. From this curving roadway you'll spy oddly shaped structures offshore. Looking like a line of battleships ready to attack Santa Barbara, they are in fact **oil derricks**. Despite protests from environmentalists and a disastrous 1969 oil spill, these coastal waters have been the site of drilling operations for decades. Those hazy humps further out past the wells are the Channel Islands.

The **Andree Clark Bird Refuge** is a placid lagoon filled with geese and other freshwater fowl. There are three tree-tufted islands in the center and a trail around the park. ~ 1400 East Cabrillo Boulevard; 805-564-5437.

Upstaging all this is the adjacent **Santa Barbara Zoological Gardens** with its miniature train ride and population of monkeys, elephants, lions, giraffes, and exotic birds. Closed Monday. Admission. ~ 500 Niños Drive; 805-962-5339.

Cabrillo Boulevard hugs the shore as it tracks past **East Beach**, Santa Barbara's longest, prettiest strand. With its rows of palm trees, grassy acres, and sunbathing crowds, it's an enchanting spot.

Every Sunday morning, the greenbelt at East Beach next to Stearns Wharf turns into an **outdoor art show**. Dozens of local and regional artists exhibit their artwork, photography, jewelry, and crafts. Quality varies, of course, but the setting is unbeatable. ~ Cabrillo Boulevard at State Street.

For a taste of sea air and salt spray walk along **Stearns Wharf**. From the end of this wooden pier you can gaze back at Santa Barbara, realizing just how aptly author Richard Henry Dana described the place: "The town is finely situated, with a bay in front, and an amphitheater of hills behind." Favored by anglers, the wharf is also noted for the **Sea Center**, a marine museum with an aquarium, underwater photos, computerized learning center, a 37-foot replica of a gray whale and calf, and a touch tank filled with local marine life. Admission. ~ At the foot of State Street, 211 Stearns Wharf; 805-962-0885.

If you tire of walking, remember that Stearns Wharf is the departure point for the **Santa Barbara Trolley**, an old-fashioned vehicle that carries visitors along the waterfront, through the downtown area, and out to the mission. ~ 805-965-0353.

HIDDEN ▶   The **Moreton Bay Fig Tree**, another landmark, is a century-old giant with branches that spread 160 feet. This magnificent specimen stands as the largest tree of its kind in the United States. ~ Chapala and Montecito streets.

Back along the waterfront, Cabrillo Boulevard continues to the **Yacht Harbor**, where 1200 pleasure boats, some worth more than homes, lie moored. The walkway leads past yawls, ketches, sloops, and fishing boats to a breakwater. From here you can survey the fleet and take in the surrounding mountains and ocean. ~ West Cabrillo Boulevard and Castillo Street.

To continue this seafront excursion, follow Shoreline, Cliff, and Marina drives as they parallel the Pacific, past headlands and beaches, en route to **Hope Ranch**. Santa Barbara is flanked by two posh communities: Montecito in the east and this elite enclave to the west. It's a world of country clubs and cocktail parties, where money and nature meet to create forested estates.

NORTH OF SANTA BARBARA   Route 101 streams northwest past a series of suburbs, including Goleta and Isla Vista, where the **University of California–Santa Barbara** is located. Stop by the visitors center to pick up a campus map and brochures for one of the state's most beautiful universities. ~ 805-893-8000.

Cutting a swath between mountains and ocean, the road then passes a number of inviting beach parks, and turns inland toward the mountains and interior valleys.

About 35 miles from Santa Barbara Routes 101 and 1 diverge. For a rural drive past white barns and meandering creeks, follow **Route 1**. En route to Lompoc it passes farmlands, pastures, and rolling hills. About five miles south of Lompoc, you can follow

Jalama Road, a country lane that traverses through sharp canyons ◄ HIDDEN
and graceful valleys on a winding 15-mile course to the ocean,
ending at a beach park.

This journey becomes a pilgrimage when Route 1 approaches
La Purísima Mission. The best restored of all 21 California missions, this historic site has an eerie way of projecting you back
to Spanish days. There's the mayordomo's abode with the table
set and a pan on the oven, or the mission store, its barrels overflowing with corn and beans. The entire mission complex, from
the sanctified church to the tallow vats where slaughtered cattle
were rendered into soap, is re-created. Founded nearby in 1787,
the mission was re-established at this site in 1813. Today you can
tour the living quarters of priests and soldiers, the workshops
where weaving, leathermaking, and carpentry were practiced, and
the mission's original water system. You can also see animals such
as mules and goats in their period mission setting. Admission. ~
2295 Purisima Road, Lompoc; 805-733-3713.

In spring and summer the hills around **Lompoc** dazzle with
thousands of acres of cultivated flowers. The countryside is a rainbow of color throughout the season. Then in fall fields of poppies,
nasturtiums, and larkspurs bloom.

South of Santa Barbara in Carpinteria, the **Eugenia Motel** has ten   **LODGING**
rooms (four with kitchens). Each is small, carpeted, and clean.
The furniture is comfortable though nicked. The baths have stall
showers. ~ 5277 Carpinteria Avenue, Carpinteria; 805-684-4416.
BUDGET.

Because of its excellent beach, Carpinteria is very popular with
families. Many spend their entire vacation here, so most facilities
rent by the week or month. Among the less expensive spots for
overnighters is **La Casa del Sol Motel.** This complex has 23 units,
including some suites. The one I saw was paneled in knotty pine
and trimly furnished. Small pool and laundry facility. ~ 5585
Carpinteria Avenue, Carpinteria; 805-684-4307. BUDGET.

Room rates in Santa Barbara fluctuate by season and day of
the week, so it's advisable to check. To provide an idea of the full
range of accommodations available in the Santa Barbara area
there are two centralized reservation agencies. One is **Coastal Escapes Accommodations.** ~ 5320 Carpinteria Avenue, Carpinteria; 805-822-1300, 800-292-2222; www.coastalescapes.com.
The other is **Santa Barbara Hotspots.** ~ 36 State Street, Santa
Barbara; 805-564-1637, 800-793-7666; www.HotspotsUSA.com.

For modest-priced accommodations within a block or two of
the beach, check out **Cabrillo Boulevard.** This artery skirts the
shoreline for several miles. Establishments lining the boulevard
are usually a little higher in price. But along the side streets lead-

ing from Cabrillo are numerous generic motels. From these you can generally expect rooms that are small but tidy and clean. The wall-to-wall carpeting is industrial grade, the furniture consists of naugahyde chairs and formica tables, and the artworks make you appreciate minimalism. There's usually a swimming pool and surrounding terrace, plus a wall of ice machines and soda dispensers.

There are two such places located a block from Santa Barbara's best all-around beach. **Pacific Crest Motel** has 25 units renting at affordable prices. ~ 433 Corona del Mar Drive, Santa Barbara; 805-966-3103, fax 805-568-0673. MODERATE.

Next door, that generic facility, **Motel 6**, has 51 rooms. ~ 443 Corona del Mar Drive, Santa Barbara; 805-564-1392, 800-466-8356, fax 805-963-4687. MODERATE.

Over in the West Beach area, **Beach House Inn** has 12 quiet units located two blocks from the beach. Rooms here are larger than usual, most have kitchens and laundry facilities, but there's no pool. Small pets are allowed. ~ 320 West Yanonali Street, Santa Barbara; 805-966-1126. MODERATE TO DELUXE.

Montecito Del Mar Motel, a block farther away, has 22 units, including doubles and suites with kitchens and fireplaces. Ask for a room with a kitchen. There's no pool but there are on-site public jacuzzis. Continental breakfast is served. ~ 316 West Montecito Street, Santa Barbara; 805-962-0181. MODERATE TO DELUXE.

For chic surroundings there is **Villa Rosa**. Built during the 1930s in Spanish palazzo fashion, it was originally an apartment house. Today it is an 18-room inn with raw wood furnishings, pastel walls, and private baths. There's a pool and spa in the courtyard. Guests co-mingle over continental breakfast and afternoon wine and cheese, then settle into plump armchairs around a tile fireplace with port and sherry in the evening. The spacious rooms, some with fireplaces, are pleasantly understated and located half

---

✔ CHECK THESE OUT—UNIQUE LODGING

- *Budget:* Score a room with a kitchen at **La Casa del Sol Motel**, where you'll be close to Carpinteria's classic beach. *page 255*
- *Moderate to deluxe:* Hide away at the rustic **Cambria Pines Lodge**, where the lobby's stone fireplace will keep you warm on chilly nights. *page 290*
- *Deluxe:* Cozy up next to the fireplace in one of the garden cottages at the 1871 **Upham Hotel**. *page 258*.
- *Ultra-deluxe:* Stroll the 540 acres, lob a few tennis balls, or sequester yourself in one the secluded cottages at **San Ysidro Ranch**, tucked away in the hills of Montecito. *page 259*

Budget: under $60   Moderate: $60–$120   Deluxe: $120–$175   Ultra-deluxe: over $175

a block from the beach. ~ 15 Chapala Street, Santa Barbara; 805-966-0851, fax 805-962-7159; www.sbweb.com. MODERATE TO ULTRA-DELUXE.

The **California Hotel** has one thing going for it: location. It sits on the main street in Santa Barbara just a block from the beach. The hotel is in a blocky, four-story building with a restaurant and bar downstairs. Popular with Europeans; the 80 rooms are trimly appointed. If you can get an oceanside room on the fourth floor it could be worth it, otherwise keep on reading. ~ 35 State Street, Santa Barbara; 805-966-7153. MODERATE.

The **Eagle Inn** is an attractive Mediterranean-style apartment house converted into a 27-room hotel. Just two blocks from the beach, most of the rooms are studio units with kitchens. Check out the room with the cheerful sunflower theme. ~ 232 Natoma Avenue, Santa Barbara; 805-965-3586, 800-767-0030, fax 805-966-1218. DELUXE.

Small and intimate as bed and breakfasts tend to be, the **Simpson House Inn** is even more so. Close to downtown, it resides along a quiet tree-lined block secluded in an acre of English gardens complete with fountains and intimate sitting areas. The century-old Victorian inn features 14 guest rooms, restored-barn suites, and garden cottages—all decorated with antiques, fine art, and English lace. Some feature private decks or patios, fireplaces, and jacuzzis. A gourmet breakfast is served on the veranda or to private patios or rooms; beverages are served in the afternoon, and wine and hors d'oeuvres are provided in the evening. Bikes and croquet complete the package. ~ 121 East Arrellaga Street, Santa Barbara; 805-963-7067, 800-676-1280, fax 805-564-4811; www.simpsonhouseinn.com. DELUXE TO ULTRA-DELUXE.

The **Old Yacht Club Inn** is two inns in one. The main facility is a 1912 California Craftsman–style house containing five rooms. There's a cozy parlor downstairs where wine and cheese are served in the evening. Next door, in a 1927 vintage stucco, are seven guest rooms with private baths tabbed deluxe. Some have been decorated by different families and feature personal photographs and other heirlooms; other rooms feature elegant European decor. The inn is just one block from East Beach, serves a full breakfast and provides bikes, beach chairs, and towels to guests. ~ 431 Corona del Mar Drive, Santa Barbara; 805-962-1277, 800-676-1676, fax 805-962-3989; www.clia.com/members/OldYachtClub Inn. ULTRA-DELUXE.

The **Glenborough Inn** is laid out in similar fashion. The main house is a 1906 California Craftsman design with extensive wood detailing and period furniture. A suite in the main house is decorated in turn-of-the-century nouveau style with a fireplace, private entrance, garden, patio, and bath. The second house is an 1880-era cottage with rooms and suites enjoying private baths. The

theme in both abodes is romance. The rooms are beautifully fashioned with embroidered curtains, inlaid French furniture, canopied beds, crocheted coverlets, and needlepoint pieces. There's a
garden and three hot tubs at the main house and a patio beside
the cottage. Guests enjoy a gourmet breakfast brought to their
door, afternoon hors d'oeuvres, and cookies at bedtime; they also
share a cozy living room that has a tile fireplace. ~ 1327 Bath
Street, Santa Barbara; 805-966-0589, 800-962-0589, fax 805-564-
8610; www.silcom.com/~glenboro. MODERATE TO ULTRA-DELUXE.

Down the road at the **Bath Street Inn** you'll encounter a Queen
Anne Victorian constructed in 1890. It's an attractive house with
an equally charming hostess, Susan Brown. Enter along a garden
walkway into a warm living room with marble-trimmed fireplace.
The patio in back is set in another garden. Rooms on the second
floor feature the hardwood floors and patterned wallpaper which
are the hallmarks of California bed and breakfasts. The third floor
has a cozy sloped roof and a television lounge for guests. Rooms
include private baths, televisions, breakfast, and evening refresh-
ments. ~ 1720 Bath Street, Santa Barbara; 805-682-9680, 800-
341-2284, fax 805-569-1281; www.silcom.com/~bathstin. MOD-
ERATE TO DELUXE.

Personally, I prefer the **Upham Hotel**, "the oldest cosmopolitan hotel in continuous operation in Southern California." Established in 1871, it shares a sense of history with the country inns,
but enjoys the lobby and restaurant amenities of a hotel. Victorian
in style, the two-story clapboard is marked by sweeping verandas and a cupola; the accommodations here are nicely appointed
with hardwood and period furnishings. Around the landscaped
grounds are garden cottages, some with private patios and fireplaces, and a carriage house with five Victorian-style rooms. Continental breakfast, afternoon wine and cheese, and cookies at
bedtime are included. ~ 1404 de la Vina Street, Santa Barbara;
805-962-0058, 800-727-0876, fax 805-963-2825. DELUXE.

Santa Barbara's two finest hotels dominate the town's two
geographic locales, the ocean and the mountains. **Four Seasons
Biltmore Hotel** is a grand old Spanish-style hotel set on 23 acres
beside the beach. It's the kind of place where guests play croquet
or practice putting on manicured lawns, then meander over to
the hotel's Coral Casino Beach and Cabaña Club. There are several dining rooms as well as tennis courts, swimming pools, and
a complete spa. The refurbished rooms are quite large and have
an airy feel, with light wood furnishings and full marble baths.
Many are located in multiplex cottages and are spotted around
the magnificent grounds which have made the Biltmore one of
California's most famous hotels since it opened back in 1927. ~
1260 Channel Drive, Santa Barbara; 805-969-2261, 800-332-
3442, fax 805-565-8323; www.fourseasons.com. ULTRA-DELUXE.

El Encanto sits back in the Santa Barbara hills and is a favorite hideaway among Hollywood stars. The hotel's 84 rooms are set in cottages and villas that dot this ten-acre retreat. The grounds are beautifully landscaped and feature a lily pond, tennis court, and swimming pool. The ocean views are simply spectacular. Rooms are very spacious with attached sitting rooms, plus extra features like room service, refrigerator, and terrycloth bathrobes. Some have private patios. The decor is French country with a lot of brass and etched-glass fixtures. El Encanto was recently featured on PBS's *Historic Hotels of America.* ~ 1900 Lasuen Road, Santa Barbara; 805-687-5000, 800-346-7039, fax 805-687-3903; e-mail elencanto@aol. com. DELUXE TO ULTRA-DELUXE.

John and Jackie Kennedy spent part of their honeymoon at San Ysidro Ranch.

The **Miramar Hotel-Resort** is billed as "the only hotel right on the beach" in the Santa Barbara area. Indeed there is 500 feet of beautiful beachfront. It also is right on noisy Route 101. Not to worry—the Miramar is still the best bargain around. Where else will you find dining facilities, room service, two swimming pools, tennis courts, health spa, and shuffleboard at desirable prices? Granted that will place you in a plainly appointed room closer to motor city than the beach, but you can be oceanfront for a deluxe price. Wherever you choose, you'll be in a lovely 15-acre resort inhabited by blue-roofed cottages and tropical foliage. ~ 1555 South Jameson Lane, Montecito; 805-969-2203, 800-322-6983, fax 805-969-3163; www.webcrown.com/miramar. MODERATE.

In the Santa Ynez foothills above Montecito sits another retreat where the rich and powerful mix with the merely talented. **San Ysidro Ranch** sprawls across 540 acres, most of which is wilderness traversed by hiking trails. There are tennis courts, a pool, a bocce ball court and complete fitness facilities. The grounds vie with the Santa Barbara Botanic Garden in the variety of plant life: there are meadows, mountain forests, and an orange grove. The Stonehouse Restaurant serves gourmet dishes and the complex also features sitting rooms and lounges. Privacy is the password: all these features are shared by guests occupying just 37 units. The accommodations are dotted around the property in cottages and small multiplexes. Pets are welcome; 24-hour room service is available. Rooms vary in decor, but even the simplest are trimly appointed and spacious with hardwood furnishings, wood-burning fireplaces, king-size beds, and a mountain, ocean, or garden view. ~ 900 San Ysidro Lane, Montecito; 805-969-5046, 800-368-6788, fax 805-565-1995; www.sanysidroranch.com. ULTRA-DELUXE.

At **The Palms** you cook your own steak or halibut dinner, or have them prepare a shrimp, scallop, crab, lobster, or chicken meal. A family-style restaurant with oak chairs and pseudo-Tiffany lamps,

DINING

it hosts a salad bar and adjoining lounge. Dinner only. ~ 701 Linden Avenue, Carpinteria; 805-684-3811. BUDGET TO DELUXE.

For a scent of Santa Barbara salt air with your lunch or dinner, **Brophy Brothers Restaurant & Clam Bar** is the spot. Located out on the Breakwater, overlooking the marina, mountains, and open sea, it features a small dining room and patio. If you love seafood, it's heaven; if not, then fate has cast you in the wrong direction. The clam bar serves all manner of clam and oyster concoctions, and the restaurant is so committed to fresh fish they print a new menu daily to tell you what the boats brought in. When I was there the daily fare included fresh snapper, shark, scampi, salmon, sea bass, halibut, and mahimahi. ~ 119 Harbor Way, Santa Barbara; 805-966-4418. MODERATE.

One of the more romantic restaurants in Santa Barbara is the **Wine Cask**, where you can dine outside in a lovely courtyard or indoors under the colorful hand-painted ceiling mural that dates from the 1920s. Among the innovative entrées are grilled pesto-stuffed swordfish and herb-crusted Colorado lamb loin, as well as chicken, beef, and pastas. Appetizers are just as creative and tempting. Don't forget to check out the wine list, which presents more than 1400 options. ~ 813 Anacapa Street, Santa Barbara; 805-966-9463. MODERATE TO DELUXE.

HIDDEN ► Best of Santa Barbara's low-priced restaurants is **La Tolteca**. This self-order café serves delicious Mexican food. Almost everything is fresh, making it *the* place for tacos, tostadas, burritos, tamales, and enchiladas. Menu items are served à la carte, so you can mix and match to get exactly what you want. Diners have the option of sitting at one of the few tables inside or out near the sidewalk. Breakfast, lunch, and dinner. ~ 614 East Haley Street, Santa Barbara; 805-963-0847. BUDGET.

Another south-of-the-border favorite is **La Super Rica**. The menu includes tamales, *alambre de pechuga* (marinated chicken strips fried with peppers and onions on a warm tortilla), and chile rellenos. The homemade salsa is recommended. ~ 622 North Milpas Street, Santa Barbara; 805-963-4940. BUDGET.

HIDDEN ► Santa Barbara natives have been eating at **Joe's Café** for 60 years. Crowds line the coal-black bar, pile into the booths, and fill the tables. They come for a meat-and-potatoes lunch and dinner menu that stars prime rib. This is where you go for pork chops, steak, and French dip. The walls are loaded with mementos and faded photographs; softball trophies, deer antlers, and a buffalo head decorate the place; and the noise level is the same as the Indy 500. Paradise for slummers. ~ 536 State Street, Santa Barbara; 805-966-4638. MODERATE.

Santa Barbara Shellfish Company ain't fancy: just a takeout stand with a few picnic tables. But they serve fresh crab and shrimp cocktails, chowder, crab Louie, and hot seafood platters. Even better, they're located way out on Stearns Wharf where you can enjoy the open waterfront. ~ 230 Stearns Wharf, Santa Barbara; 805-963-4415. BUDGET TO MODERATE.

Downey's, a small, understated dining room, numbers among Santa Barbara's premiere restaurants. The dozen tables here are set amid peach-colored walls lined with local artwork. The food is renowned: specializing in California cuisine, Downey's has a menu that changes daily. A typical evening's entrées are salmon with forest mushrooms, lamb loin with grilled eggplant and chiles, sea bass with artichokes, duck with fresh papaya chutney, and swordfish cooked over a mesquite grill. There is a good wine list featuring California vintages. Very highly recommended. Closed Monday. ~ 1305 State Street, Santa Barbara; 805-966-5006. DELUXE.

The graphics on the wall tell a story about the cuisine at **The Palace Grill**. Portrayed are jazz musicians, catfish, redfish, and scenes from New Orleans. The message is Cajun and Creole, and this lively, informal bistro is very good at delivering it. This restaurant prepares soft-shelled crab, blackened filet mignon, crawfish *étouffée*, jambalaya, and grilled steak. For dessert, Honey, we have key lime pie and bread pudding soufflé. Dinner only. ~ 8 East Cota Street, Santa Barbara; 805-966-3133. MODERATE TO DELUXE.

If you prefer your bistros French, there's an excellent place a few doors up called **Mousse Odile**. Blue tablecloths and French art create an easy lunch ambience here. For dinner, out come the white and blue linens. Menu selections includes couscous, mushrooms on pastry shell, and veal in basil cream; lunch features *ficelles*, those foot-long Parisian sandwiches, as well as quiche and stuffed croissants. Even the breakfasts have a French flair, with a variety of pastries and coffees. Modest but well managed, Mousse Odile is quite popular with local residents. Closed Sunday. ~ 18 East Cota Street, Santa Barbara; 805-962-5393. MODERATE.

Hanging out in coffeehouses is my favorite avocation. There's no better spot in Santa Barbara than **Sojourner Coffeehouse**. Not only do they serve espresso and cappuccino, but lunch, dinner, and weekend brunch. Everybody seems to know everybody in this easygoing café. Diners come to kibitz and enjoy the tostadas, rice-and-veggie plates and stuffed baked potatoes. The accent is vegetarian so expect specials like Szechuan peanut pasta or *spanako-pita*, a Greek spinach and egg pastry. Fresh fish and chicken dishes like African-style chicken with couscous are also served. ~ 134 East Cañon Perdido, Santa Barbara; 805-965-7922. MODERATE.

For truly prodigious breakfasts, locals know that the nondescript **Esau's** is *the* place. Pancakes, omelettes, homemade hash, and scrambles are nicely prepared and served in big portions. If there's a queue (usually on weekends), try for a stool at the counter. ~ 403 State Street, Santa Barbara; 805-965-4416. BUDGET.

◄ HIDDEN

Cafe del Sol is among the very rarest of creatures, an upscale "Santa Barbara–style" eatery, where you'll find a tortilla deli/bar. Sample tapas, Mexican appetizers, and margaritas. A large bank of windows allows dining room guests a view of the Andree Clark Bird Refuge while they dine on a menu varying from lamb shanks and fish to pasta and enchiladas. ~ 30 Los Patos Way, Santa Barbara; 805-969-0448. MODERATE.

Dining at **El Encanto** is pleasurable not only for the fine California and French cuisine but for the sweeping vistas as well. The restaurant resides in a hillside resort overlooking Santa Barbara. There's a luxurious dining room and a terrace for dining outdoors. Dinner is a gourmet experience. Changing weekly according to harvest and catch, the menu could include sautéed sea bass with a tarragon crust, roast tenderloin of beef with garlic mashed potatoes, or angelhair pasta with roasted garlic and organic red and yellow tomatoes. The appetizers and desserts are equally outrageous, as are the breakfast and lunch courses. ~ 1900 Lasuen Road, Santa Barbara; 805-687-5000. DELUXE TO ULTRA-DELUXE.

At Arroyo Burro Beach Park is the **Brown Pelican**. It's a decent restaurant with great ocean views—what more need be said? Sandwiches, salads, hamburgers, and several fresh seafood and pasta dinners are served. Breakfast is available daily until 11 a.m. or later. Trimly appointed and fitted with a wall of plate glass, it looks out upon a sandy beach and tawny bluffs. ~ 2981½ Cliff Drive, Santa Barbara; 805-687-4550. MODERATE TO DELUXE.

The **Stonehouse Restaurant**, located at the legendary San Ysidro Ranch, serves breakfast, lunch, dinner, and Sunday brunch in the style of new California cuisine, with an international flavor. You can begin with fresh oysters or lobster spring rolls with a ginger glaze for dipping, then indulge in the skillet-roasted rack of lamb, salmon garlic brulée, or charred yellowfish tuna with a mango garnish. Top off the meal with something scrumptious from the ever-changing dessert selection. ~ 900 San Ysidro Lane, Montecito; 805-969-5046. DELUXE TO ULTRA-DELUXE.

◆◆

SMALL CRAFT WARNING

For over 20 years Santa Barbara County artists and craftspeople have turned out for the **Arts & Crafts Show**. Every Sunday and holiday from 10 a.m. until dusk they line East Cabrillo Boulevard. The original artwork for sale includes paintings, graphics, sculptures, and drawings. Among the crafts are macrame, stained glass, woodwork, textiles, weaving, and jewelry. If you are in town on a Sunday make it a point to stop by.

Since Santa Barbara's shops are clustered together, you can eas- **SHOPPING**
ily uncover the town's hottest items and best bargains by concen-
trating on a few key areas. The prime shopping center lies along
State Street, particularly between the 600 and 1300 blocks. **Paseo
Nuevo** is, literally, a new *paseo*—a mall, really, with department
stores, chain shops, and a few homegrown merchants lining a
tastefully designed Spanish-style pedestrian promenade. ~ 651
Paseo Nuevo, Santa Barbara; 805-963-2202.

El Paseo, a famous promenade, is one of the most imaginative malls I've ever seen. It consists of a historic adobe house and
surrounding buildings combined and converted into a succession
of stores. This is a middle- and high-ticket complex: the art galleries, jewelry stores, and designer dress stores number among
the best, but there are also curio shops and toy stores. ~ 814 State
Street, Santa Barbara; 805-965-1616.

La Arcada Court is another spiffy mall done in Spanish style.
The shops, along the upper lengths of State Street, are more chic
and contemporary than they are elsewhere. **Santa Barbara Baggage Company** (805-966-1669) sells luggage, handbags, wallets,
business bags, and gifts. ~ 1114 State Street, Santa Barbara.

Antiques in Santa Barbara are spelled Brinkerhoff Avenue.
This block-long residential street conceals a half-dozen antique
shops. My favorite, **Carl Hightower Galerie**, is crowded with jewelry, ceramics, and everything else imaginable under the sun. ~ 528
Brinkerhoff Avenue, Santa Barbara; 805-965-5687.

Near the corner of State and Cota streets is the center for vintage clothing. **Yellowstone Clothing** has Hawaiian shirts and other
old-time favorites. ~ 527 State Street, Santa Barbara; 805-963-
9609. Also try **Pure Gold**, which has everything from early exotic
to late lamented. ~ 625 State Street, Santa Barbara; 805-962-4613.

The Palms features local rock-and-roll bands every Thursday, Fri- **NIGHTLIFE**
day, and Saturday night. There's a small dancefloor here for foot-
loose revelers. ~ 701 Linden Avenue, Carpinteria; 805-684-3811.

The State Street strip in downtown Santa Barbara offers several party places. **Zelo**, a video nightclub, has dancing to a variety of DJ music including disco, hip hop, funk, and salsa. Cover.
~ 630 State Street, Santa Barbara; 805-966-5792.

Up at **Acapulco Restaurant**, in La Arcada Court, you can sip
a margarita next to an antique wooden bar or out on the patio.
Every Friday they feature live music. Cover on Friday. ~ 1114 State
Street, Santa Barbara; 805-963-3469.

If for no other reason than the view, **Harbor Restaurant** is a
prime place for the evening. A plate-glass establishment, it sits out
on a pier with the city skyline on one side and open ocean on the
other. The bar upstairs features surf videos. ~ 210 Stearns Wharf,
Santa Barbara; 805-963-3311.

For sunset views, nothing quite compares to **El Encanto Lounge**. Located in the posh El Encanto Hotel high in the Santa Barbara hills, it features a split-level terrace overlooking the city and ocean. ~ 1900 Lasuen Road, Santa Barbara; 805-687-5000.

You can also consider the **Lobero Theatre**, which presents dance, drama, concerts, and lectures. Closed Sunday. ~ 33 East Cañon Perdido Street, Santa Barbara; 805-963-0761.

La Sala is the elegant lobby lounge at the Four Seasons Biltmore where live music and dancing—the kind in which couples actually hold each other in their arms—have become very popular. The music varies nightly. ~ 1260 Channel Drive; 805-969-2261.

Or head into the mountains about 27 miles outside Santa Barbara and catch a show at the **Circle Bar B Dinner Theater**. This well-known facility offers a menu of comedies and musicals. Open weekends only from April through November. ~ 1800 Refugio Road, 27 miles north of Santa Barbara; 805-965-9652.

Part of the gay scene in Santa Barbara is represented by **Gold Coast**, which features pinball, a pool table, a small dancefloor, and occasional live entertainment. ~ 30 West Cota Street, Santa Barbara; 805-965-6701.

BEACHES & PARKS

RINCON BEACH COUNTY PARK 🚶 🏊 ⛵ Wildly popular with nudists and surfers, this is a pretty white sand beach backed by bluffs. At the bottom of the wooden stairway leading down to the beach, take a right along the strand and head over to the seawall. There will often be a bevy of nude sunbathers snuggled here between the hillside and the ocean in an area known as **Bates Beach**, or **Backside Rincon**. Be warned: nude sunbathing is illegal. Occasionally the sheriff *will* crack down on nudists. Surfers, on the other hand, turn left and paddle out to Rincon Point, one of the most popular surfing spots along the entire California coast. There are picnic areas and restrooms. ~ Located two miles southeast of Carpinteria; from Route 101 take the Bates Road exit.

CARPINTERIA STATE BEACH 🚴 🚶 🎣 ⛵ This ribbon-shaped park extends for nearly a mile along the coast. Bordered to the east by dunes and along the west by a bluff, the beach has an offshore shelf that shelters it from the surf. As a result, Carpinteria provides exceptionally good swimming and is nicknamed "the world's safest beach." Wildlife here consists of small mammals and reptiles as well as seals and many seabirds. Don't bring your pets: dogs are not allowed on the beach. It's a good spot for tidepooling; there is also a lagoon here. The Santa Ynez Mountains rise in the background. Facilities include picnic areas, restrooms, dressing rooms, showers, and lifeguards (during summer only). Swimming is excellent, and skindiving is good along the breakwater reef, a habitat for abalone and lobsters. Surfing is very good in the "tar pits" area near the east end of the park. If you are into fishing, cabezon, corbina, and barred perch are caught here. Day-use fee, $5. ~ Located at the end of Palm Avenue in Carpinteria; 805-684-2811.

▲ There are 261 sites for tents and RVs, about half have hookups and prices vary, depending on the type of site and its location, from $17 to $23 per night. Call 800-444-7275 for reservations.

SUMMERLAND BEACH 🏃 🐎 🚴 🛥 🎣 🚣 🚤 ⛵ Part of this narrow strip of white sand used to be a popular nude beach. It's backed by low-lying hills, which afford privacy from the nearby freeway and railroad tracks. The favored skinny-dipping spot is on the east end between two protective rock piles. Gay men sometimes congregate farther down the beach at Loon Point, but families are rapidly taking over. There are no facilities here, but nearby **Lookout Park** (805-969-1720) has picnic areas, restrooms, and a playground. Swimming is popular, and there is good bodysurfing here. ~ Located in Summerland six miles east of Santa Barbara. Take the Summerland exit off Route 101 and get on Wallace Avenue, the frontage road between the freeway and ocean. Follow it east for three-tenths of a mile to Finney Road and the beach.

EAST BEACH 🚴 🚣 ⛵ Everyone's favorite Santa Barbara beach, this broad beauty stretches more than a mile from Montecito to Stearns Wharf. In addition to a fluffy sand corridor there are grassy areas, palm trees, and a wealth of service facilities. Beyond the wharf the strand continues as **West Beach**. The area known as "Butterfly Beach" at the far east end is frequented by nude sunbathers. There are restrooms, showers, lifeguards, a playground, and volleyball courts. There's good fishing and swimming. **Cabrillo Pavilion Bathhouse** (1118 East Cabrillo Boulevard, Santa Barbara; 805-965-0509) provides lockers, showers, and a weight room for a small daily fee. There's a restaurant next door. Other facilities are at Stearns Wharf. ~ In Santa Barbara along East Cabrillo Boulevard between the Andree Clark Bird Refuge and Stearns Wharf. Butterfly Beach can be reached by following East Cabrillo Boulevard east past the Cabrillo Pavilion Bathhouse until the road starts to turn inland. From this juncture continue along the beach on foot. Although sunbathers use the beach as a clothing-optional area, this spot, just beyond the Clark Mansion, is sometimes patrolled by the sheriff.

LEDBETTER BEACH 🚴 🚣 🏃 🎣 🚤 A crescent of white sand, this beach rests along a shallow cove. While it is quite pretty here, with a headland bordering one end of the strand, it simply doesn't compare to nearby East Beach. There are picnic areas, restrooms, lifeguards (summer only), and a restaurant. Surfing is good,

Text continued on page 268.

The
Channel
Islands

Gaze out from the Ventura or Santa Barbara shoreline and you will spy a fleet of islands moored offshore. At times fringed with mist, on other occasions standing a hand's reach away in the crystal air, they are the Channel Islands, a group of eight volcanic islands. Situated in the Santa Barbara Channel 11 to 40 miles from the coast, they are a place apart, a wild and storm-blown region of sharp cliffs, rocky coves, and curving grasslands. Five of the islands—Anacapa, Santa Cruz, Santa Rosa, San Miguel, and Santa Barbara—comprise Channel Islands National Park while the surrounding waters are a marine sanctuary.

Nicknamed "North America's Galapagos," the chain teems with every imaginable form of life. Sea lions and harbor seals frequent the caves, blowholes, and offshore pillars. Brown pelicans and black oystercatchers roost on the sea arches and sandy beaches. There are tidepools crowded with brilliant purple hydrocorals and white-plumed sea anemones. Like the Galapagos, this isolated archipelago has given rise to many unique life forms, including 40 endemic plant species and the island fox, which grows only to the size of a house cat.

The northern islands were created about 14 million years ago by volcanic activity. Archaeological discoveries indicate that they could be among the oldest sites of human habitation in the Americas. When explorer Juan Cabrillo revealed them to the West in 1542 they were populated with thousands of Chumash Indians.

Today, long since the Chumash were removed and the islands given over to hunters, ranchers, and settlers, the Channel Islands are largely uninhabited. Several, however, are open to hikers and campers. At the mainland-based **Channel Islands National Park Visitors Center** there are contemporary museum displays, an observation deck, an indoor tidepool, and an excellent 25-minute movie to familiarize you with the park. Also on display is the skeleton of a pygmy mammoth found on Santa Rosa Island in 1997. ~ 1901 Spinnaker Drive, Ventura; 805-658-5730.

Next door at **Island Packers** you can arrange transportation to the islands. This outfit schedules regular daytrips by boat to Anacapa, Santa Barbara, Santa Cruz, Santa Rosa, and San Miguel islands. ~ 1867 Spinnaker Drive, Ventura; 805-642-1393. **Adventure Outfitters** charters six-day tours through the Channel Islands aboard a 130-foot classic schooner. Excursions incorporate a number of activities including fishing, surfing, and sea kayaking. ~ 800-430-2544. **Channel Islands Aviation** will fly you to Santa Rosa Island for a day of fishing, hiking, or overnight camping. Flights leave at 9 a.m. and return around 3:30 p.m. ~ 805-987-1301.

The Nature Conservancy leads seasonal tours of **Santa Cruz**, the largest and most diverse of the islands. Here you will find a 24-mile-long island that supports 130 types of land birds and 600 species of plants, including several unique species. There are Indian middens, earthquake faults, and two mountain ranges to explore. To the center lies a pastoral valley while the shoreline is a rugged region of cliffs, tidepools, and offshore rocks. Note: Camping is not allowed on Nature Conservancy property but *is* permitted on the eastern part on national park land. ~ 213 Stearns Wharf, Santa Barbara; 805-962-9111.

Anacapa Island, the island closest to shore, is a series of three islets parked about 11 miles southwest of Oxnard. There is a nature trail here. Like the other islands, it is a prime whale-watching spot and is surrounded by the enormous kelp forests that make the Channel Islands one of the nation's richest marine environments.

Outdoor aficionados will be glad to hear that camping is allowed in the national park. However, you must obtain a permit by calling 800-365-2267. All campgrounds have picnic tables and pit toilets, but water must be carried in—and trash must be carried out. Fires are not permitted.

Whether you are a sailor, swimmer, daytripper, hiker, archaeologist, birdwatcher, camper, tidepooler, scuba diver, seal lover, or simply an interested observer, you'll definitely find this amazing island chain to be a place of singular beauty and serenity.

particularly for beginners, west of the breakwater. ~ Located along the 800 block of Shoreline Drive in Santa Barbara.

SHORELINE PARK ⚓ The attraction here is not the park but the beach that lies below it. The park rests at the edge of a high bluff; at the bottom, secluded from view, is a narrow, curving length of white sand. It's a great spot to escape the Santa Barbara crowds while enjoying a pretty beach. Stairs from the park lead down to the shore. The beach is inaccessible at high tide. Topside in the park are picnic areas, restrooms, and a playground. ~ Located along Shoreline Drive in Santa Barbara.

HIDDEN ▶ **MESA LANE BEACH** ⚓ This is the spot Santa Barbarans head when they want to escape the crowds at the better-known beaches. It's a meandering ribbon of sand backed by steep bluffs. You can walk long distances along this secluded beach during low tide, but be careful not to get stranded when the tide comes in. No facilities; restaurants and groceries are several miles away in Santa Barbara, so pack a snack. ~ A stairway leads to the beach at the end of Mesa Lane, off Cliff Drive in Santa Barbara.

ARROYO BURRO BEACH PARK 🏃🚴🐎 ⚓ 🎣 🏊 ⛵ This 13-acre facility is a little gem on summer days. The sandy beach and surrounding hills are packed with locals, who often refer to is as "Hendry's Beach." If you can arrive at an uncrowded time you'll find beautiful scenery along this lengthy strand. There are picnic areas, restrooms, lifeguards (during summer), a restaurant, a bar, and a snack bar. Swimming and fishing here is good and surfing is excellent west of the breakwater. You can also see wildlife in the adjacent Douglas Preserve. ~ 2981 Cliff Drive, Santa Barbara; 805-687-3714.

HIDDEN ▶ **MORE MESA** ⚓ According to nude beach enthusiast Dave Patrick, this is the region's favorite bare-buns rendezvous. Thousands of sunbathers gather at this remote site on a single afternoon. "On a hot day," Patrick reports, "the beach almost takes on a carnival atmosphere, with jugglers, surfers, world-class frisbee experts, musicians, dancers, joggers, and volleyball champs." A scene that should not be missed. No facilities. ~ Located between Hope Ranch and Goleta, three miles from Route 101. Take the Turnpike Road exit from Route 101; follow it south to Hollister Avenue, then go left; from Hollister turn right on Puente Drive, right again on Vieja Drive, then left on Mockingbird Lane. At the end of Mockingbird Lane a path leads about three-quarters of a mile to the beach.

EL CAPITAN STATE BEACH 🏃 ⚓ 🎣 ⛵ 🏊 ⛵ Another one of Southern California's sparkling beaches, El Capitan stretches along three miles of oceanfront. The park is 168 acres and features a nature trail, tidepools, and wonderful opportunities for hiking along the beach. El Capitan Creek, fringed by oak and sycamore trees, traverses the area. Seals and sea lions often romp off-shore and in winter gray whales cruise by. Swimming is good. Surfing is good off El Capitan Point. This beach is also a good place to catch grunion. Facilities include picnic areas, restrooms, showers, a store, and seasonal lifeguards. Day-use fee, $5. ~ Located in Goleta off Route 101 about 20 miles north of Santa Barbara; 805-968-3294.

▲ There are 140 sites for tents and RVs (no hookups) in the park near the beach; $18 per night. Call 800-444-7275 for reservations. There is also a private campground, **El Capitan Canyon** (11560 Calle Real, Goleta; 805-685-3887), about one-half mile inland. It is a sprawling 100-acre complex with picnic areas, restrooms, showers, store, pool, playground, game areas, and outdoor theater. There are 250 sites for tents and RVs; 75 have hookups; $18 to $22 per night.

REFUGIO STATE BEACH 🏃 ⛵ 🏊 🚴 ⛺ 🛶 This is a 39-acre park with over a mile of ocean frontage. You can bask on a sandy beach, lie under palm trees on the greensward, and hike or bicycle along the two-and-a-half-mile path that connects this park with El Capitan. There are also interesting tidepools. Facilities include picnic areas, restrooms, showers, seasonal lifeguard, and a store. Fishing, swimming, and surfing are good. Day-use fee, $5. ~ On Refugio Road in Goleta, off Route 101 about 23 miles north of Santa Barbara.

▲ There are 82 sites for tents and RVs (no hookups); $18 per night. Call 800-444-7275 for reservations.

SAN ONOFRE BEACH 🏃 ⛵   ◄ *HIDDEN* This nude beach is a rare find indeed. Frequented by few people, it is a pretty white sand beach that winds along rocky headlands. There's not much here except beautiful views, shore plant life, and savvy sun bathers. Wander for miles past cliffs and coves. ~ Off Route 101, 30 miles north of Santa Barbara and two miles south of Gaviota. Driving north on Route 101 make a U-turn on Vista del Mar Road; drive south on Route 101 for seven-tenths of a mile to a dirt parking area. Cross the railroad tracks; a path next to the railroad light signal leads to the beach.

GAVIOTA STATE PARK 🏃 ⛵ 🏊 🚴 ⛺ 🛶 ⚓ This mammoth 2776-acre facility stretches along both sides of Route 101. The beach rests in a sandy cove guarded on either side by dramatic sedimentary rock formations. A railroad trestle traverses the beach and a fishing pier extends offshore. On the inland side a hiking trail leads up to **Gaviota Hot Springs** and into Los Padres National Forest. Most of the facilities here were damaged in 1998 winter storms. Expect to use pit toilets and go without showers until repairs are completed in summer 1999. Facilities include picnic areas and lifeguards. Day-use fee, $3. ~ The beach is located off Route 101 about 33 miles north of Santa Barbara. To get to the hot springs take Route 101 north from the beach park; get off at Route 1 exit; at the end of the exit ramp turn right; turn right on the frontage road and follow it a short distance to the parking lot. The trail from the parking lot leads several hundred yards to the hot springs; 805-968-3294.

▲ There are 50 sites for tents and RVs (no hookups are available); $16 per night. The vegetation is sparse from the forest fires a few years ago, and there is no drinking water, so bring your own. Sites are first-come, first-served. Note: Because of storm damage, camping will not be permitted until 1999. Call for status.

JALAMA BEACH COUNTY PARK 🏃 ♿ 🛶 This remote park sits at the far end of a 15-mile long country road. Nevertheless, in summer there are likely to be many campers here. They come because the broad sandy beach is fringed by coastal bluffs and undulating hills. Jalama Creek cuts through the park, creating a wetland frequented by the endangered California brown pelican. Point Conception lies a few miles to the south, and the area all around is undeveloped and quite pretty (though Vandenberg Air Force Base is situated north of the beach). This is a good area for beachcombing as well as rock-hounding for chert, agate, travertine, and fossils. Facilities include picnic areas, restrooms, hot showers, a store, a snack bar, and a playground. Swimming is not recommended here because of dangerous rip currents. There are no lifeguards stationed here. Surfing is good at Tarantula Point about one-half mile south of the park. You can surf-fish for perch or fish from the rocky points for cabezon and rock fish. Day-use fee, $3.50. ~ From Lompoc take Route 1 south for five miles; turn onto Jalama Beach Road and follow it 15 miles to the end; 805-736-3504.

▲ There are 110 sites for tents and RVs (28 with electrical hookups); $14 to $18 per night.

HIDDEN ▶ **POINT SAL STATE BEACH** 🛶 This is one of the most secluded and beautiful beaches along the entire Central Coast. Access is over a nine-mile country road, part of which is unpaved and impassable in wet weather. When you get to the end of this steep, serpentine monster there are no services available. The scenery, however, is magnificent. A long crescent beach curves out toward Point Sal, a bold headland with a rock island offshore. The Casmalia Hills rise sharply from the ocean, creating a natural amphitheater. Sea birds roost nearby and the beach is a habitat for harbor seals. There is surf fishing from the beach and rocks. ~ From Route 1 three miles south of Guadalupe turn west on Brown Road, then pick up Point Sal Road. Together they travel nine miles to a blufftop overlook. Steep paths lead to the beach. Note: Because of severe winter rains, the road is closed indefinitely. It's now an 18-mile hike to the beach; 805-733-7781.

Craggy volcanic peaks and rolling hills dramatically punctuate this stretch of coastline
lying about halfway between Los Angeles and

▼▼▼▼▼▼▼▼▼▼▼▼▼▼
San Luis Obispo Area

San Francisco. The towns of San Luis Obispo, Morro Bay, and
Pismo Beach are popular stopovers on the long scenic drive between northern and southern California. The county's growing
wine industry also draws visitors to tasting rooms and winery
tours (see sidebar). San Luis Obispo (don't say "San Louie"; pronounce the "s") is the region's commercial center, as well as the
site of California Polytechnic State University (Cal Poly). Home
of an old Spanish mission, pretty San Luis has enough small-city
sophistication and cultural offerings to impress even big-city cos-
mopolites, while Pismo Beach and Morro Bay retain their earthier
California beach town character.

PISMO BEACH An unattractive congeries of mobile homes and
beach rental stands, Pismo Beach is a nondescript town that has a
single saving grace—its dunes. They're sand castles in the air, curving, rolling, ever-changing hills of sand. Wave after wave of them
parallel the beach, like a crystalline continuation of the ocean.

SIGHTS

Otherwise, this town of 8000 people is a tacky tourist enclave
known for an annual clam festival and for the migrating monarch
butterflies that land just south of the town pier every year from
late-November to March. Traveling north, you reach Pismo Beach
after Route 1 completes its lengthy inland course through Lompoc
and Guadalupe, then rejoins Route 101 and returns to the coast.

Those vaunted sand piles comprise the most extensive coastal
dunes in California. From Pismo Beach the sand hills run six miles
south where they meet the 450-foot-high **Rancho Guadalupe
Dunes County Park** (see "Beaches & Parks" section below), forming a unique habitat for wildflowers and shorebirds.

Back in the 1930s and 1940s a group of bohemians, the "Dun-
ites," occupied this wild terrain. Comprised of nudists, mystics
and artists, the movement believed that the dunes were a center
of cosmic energy. Today the area is filled with beachcombers, sunbathers, and off-highway vehicles.

At the **Oceano Dunes State Vehicular Recreation Area** (see
"Beaches & Parks" section below), you may drive your car onto
the beach and operate off-highway and all-terrain vehicles in a spe-
cified area of the park.

Aside from exploring the dunes, there isn't much to see in
Pismo Beach, especially after the monarchs leave town in March.
But stop by the **Pismo Beach Chamber of Commerce & Visitors
Bureau** for brochures and maps of the San Luis Bay region. ~ 581
Dolliver Street, Pismo Beach; 805-773-2055.

An ironic twist of fate that has led to the decline of adjacent
Avila Beach may turn out to be the town's salvation. In 1989, it

was discovered that an oil pipeline leak was contaminating the ground underneath the tiny beachside enclave. As a result, property values plunged, and the town took on an increasingly run-down look. Recently, it was decided that the town's commercial core—a two-block stretch overlooking a white-sand beach and three fishing piers—would be torn down to remove tons of contaminated soil below. Eventually—it's estimated the cleanup will take 18 months—the town will be rebuilt, giving Avila Beach a much-needed facelift.

There are hot springs in the hills around Avila Beach. **Sycamore Mineral Springs Resort** has tapped these local waters and created a lovely spa with hotel units, a gift shop, and a swimming pool. The real attractions here, however, are the redwood hot tubs. Very private, they are dotted about on a hillside and shaded by oak and sycamore. Admission. ~ 1215 Avila Beach Drive, Avila Beach; 805-595-7302.

HIDDEN ►

From Pismo Beach, you can buzz into San Luis Obispo on Route 101 or take a quiet country drive into town via **See Canyon Road**. The latter begins in Avila Beach and corkscrews up into the hills past apple orchards and horse farms. Along its 13-mile length, half unpaved, you'll encounter mountain meadows and ridgetop vistas. During the fall harvest season you can pick apples at farms along the way.

SAN LUIS OBISPO   San Luis Obispo, a pretty jewel of a town, lies 12 miles from the ocean in the center of an expansive agricultural region. Backdropped by the Santa Lucia Mountains, the town focuses around an old Spanish mission. Cowboys from outlying ranches and students from the campuses of Cal Poly and Cuesta College add to the cultural mix, creating a vital atmosphere that has energized San Luis Obispo's rapid growth.

Parking on weekends and during the summer can be a nightmare, but don't let that deter you. The town is completely walkable, so once you've found a spot in one of the numerous small public lots or on the street (bring quarters), leave the car there and set out on foot. Your first stop should be the **San Luis Obispo Chamber of Commerce**. Here you can pick up brochures about the area's attractions, including a map for a self-guided walking tour. ~ 1039 Chorro Street, San Luis Obispo; 805-781-2777.

A self-guided tour of this historic town logically begins at **Mission San Luis de Tolosa**. Dating to 1772, the old Spanish outpost has been nicely reconstructed, though the complex is not as extensive as La Purísima Mission in Lompoc. There's a museum re-creating the American Indian, Spanish, and Mexican eras as well as a pretty church and a gift shop. Mission Plaza, fronting the chapel, is a well-landscaped park. ~ At Chorro and Monterey streets, San Luis Obispo; 805-543-6850.

San Luis Obispo

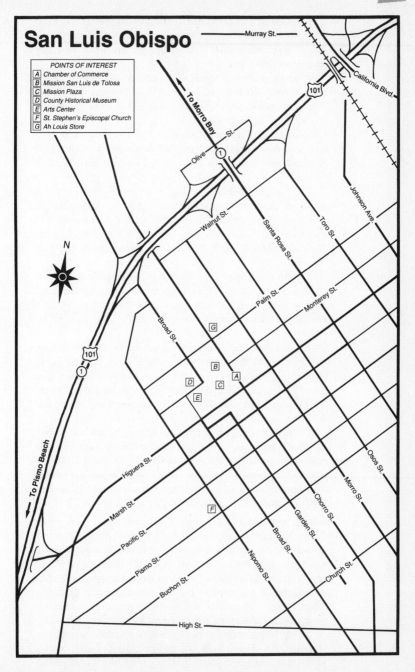

Murray St.

POINTS OF INTEREST
- A Chamber of Commerce
- B Mission San Luis de Tolosa
- C Mission Plaza
- D County Historical Museum
- E Arts Center
- F St. Stephen's Episcopal Church
- G Ah Louis Store

To Morro Bay

California Blvd.

101

Olive St.

1

N

Walnut St.

Santa Rosa St.

Toro St.

Johnson Ave.

Palm St.

Monterey St.

Broad St.

G

B

D   C   A

E

101

1

To Pismo Beach

Higuera St.

Osos St.

Marsh St.

F

Morro St.

Pacific St.

Chorro St.

Garden St.

Pismo St.

Broad St.

Buchon St.

Nipomo St.

Church St.

High St.

The **County Historical Museum** continues the historic overview with displays from the Chumash, pre-Hispanic, Spanish, and American periods. Closed Monday and Tuesday. ~ 696 Monterey Street, San Luis Obispo; 805-543-0638.

Across the street at the **San Luis Obispo Art Center** are exhibits of works by the area's artists. Closed Monday from Labor Day to Memorial Day. ~ Broad Street at Monterey Street, San Luis Obispo; 805-543-8562.

St. Stephen's Episcopal Church is a narrow, lofty, and strikingly attractive chapel. Built in 1867, it was one of California's first Episcopal churches. ~ Nipomo and Pismo streets, San Luis Obispo.

The **Dallidet Adobe**, constructed by a French vintner in 1853, is another local architectural landmark. ~ On Toro Street between Pismo and Pacific streets, San Luis Obispo. A block away and about a century later Frank Lloyd Wright designed the **Kundert Medical Building**. ~ At Pacific and Santa Rosa streets, San Luis Obispo.

The **Ah Louis Store** symbolizes the Chinese presence here. A sturdy brick building with wrought-iron shutters and balcony, it dates to 1874 and once served the 2000 Chinese coolies who worked on nearby railroad tunnels. ~ 800 Palm Street, San Luis Obispo.

Around the corner, the **Sauer-Adams Adobe**, covered in clapboard, is an 1860-era house with a second-story balcony. By the turn of the century, Victorian-style homes had become the vogue. Many of San Luis Obispo's finest Victorians are located in the blocks adjacent to where Broad Street intersects with Pismo and Buchon streets. ~ 964 Chorro Street, San Luis Obispo.

Those with young ones in tow can stop by the **San Luis Obispo Children's Museum**. In this imaginative environment kids can race to a fire engine, visit a planetarium, learn about photography, and discover a Chumash Indian cave. Closed Wednesday. (Museum hours are subject to change, so call ahead.) Admission. ~ 1010 Nipomo Street, San Luis Obispo; 805-544-5437.

MORRO BAY As Route 1 angles north and west from San Luis Obispo toward the ocean, separating again from Route 101, you'll see a series of nine volcanic peaks. Last in this geologic parade is a 576-foot plug dome called **Morro Rock**. The pride of Morro Bay, it stands like a little Gibraltar, connected to the mainland by a sand isthmus. You can drive out and inspect the brute. Years ago, before conservationists and common sense prevailed, the site was a rock quarry. Today it's a nesting area for peregrine falcons.

Morro Bay is one of those places with obscure natural treasures that are often overlooked at first glance. That's because Morro Bay is largely a working fishing town, not a pretty recreational harbor with a gleaming fleet of expensive, handsome vessels, like Newport Harbor in Orange County. Morro Bay comes with a gritty legacy, first as a busy 19th-century port for the region's cattle and dairy industry, then as a naval training base during World War II. In the 1950s, a power plant was built on the site, providing a tax base that led to the town's incorporation. The real working waterfront of Morro Bay lies to the north of Harbor Street, in the shadow of the three giant smokestacks of the power plant. A walk along the touristy waterfront stretch called the Embarcadero, which is south of Harbor Street, reveals a predictable mix of tacky tourist shops and so-called galleries, along with plenty of restaurants offering fish and chips and "harbor views." The **Morro Bay Chamber of Commerce** offers plenty of brochures and information about the area. ~ 880 Main Street, Morro Bay; 805-772-4467.

But the real pleasures of Morro Bay lie hidden behind its ugly manmade features.

The best place to learn something of the local natural environment is at the small **Morro Bay State Park Museum of Natural History**. It's located at White Point, a rocky outcropping in Morro Bay State Park, with fine views of the surrounding estuary, which is a protected habitat for migratory and resident bird species. The museum is not terribly impressive, that's true, but it is undertaking an on-going renovation to make its displays of local history and wildlife more interesting and interactive. And a docent is always on hand to answer questions. Admission. ~ Morro Bay State Park Road (from Morro Bay, follow Main Street into the park), Morro Bay; 805-772-2694.

The Morro Bay Estuary is one of the largest unspoiled coastal marshes in California. This unique environment, where salty sea meets fresh water, is a stopover for hundreds of migratory birds, including blue heron, who nest and rear their young at the **Morro Bay Heron Rookery**. When this eucalyptus grove was threatened some years ago with development, the people of California purchased it to retain it as a permanent nesting site. It is now the only remaining large rookery of great blue heron on the California coast between San Francisco and Mexico. Nesting begins in January, when the birds choose mates and build nests. Eggs are laid in February and hatch in late March. The nestlings are fed by both parents until they're able to fly away a few months later, sometime in late June or early July. ~ Morro Bay State Park Road, just south of Park View Drive, Morro Bay.

◀ HIDDEN

The Los Osos/Morro Bay chapter of the Small Wilderness Area Preservation offers monthly walks through **El Morro Elfin Forest**, an ecological preserve of pygmy oaks and other unusual flora. ~ Santa Ysabel Avenue at 15th Street, Los Osos; 805-528-4540, 805-528-2579 for more information.

◀ HIDDEN

At the mouth of Morro Bay, **Morro Rock** competes for attention, sadly, with the three concrete smokestacks of the power plant across the harbor, something that seems even to embarrass the locals. But turn your back on the travesty as they do, and gaze across the bay instead to the **sandspit** that holds back the Pacific and extends in a narrow sliver four miles and teems with bird and other wildlife.

HIDDEN ►

For a bit of underwater exploration, take a dive, so to speak, on a semi-submersible vessel with **Sub-Sea Tours** for a look at Morro Bay's giant kelp forest and the marine life that inhabits it. Otters are occasionally spotted on the tours. ~ Marina Square, 699 Embarcadero; 805-772-9463. Paddle around the bay in a rented canoe or sit-on-top kayak from **Ka'nu 2 U.** ~ Marina Square, 699 Embarcadero; 805-772-3349. **Kayaks of Morro Bay** rents kayaks and canoes. ~ 699 Embarcadero, Morro Bay; 805-772-1119. For something more formal, **Tiger Folly Too** sponsors harbor cruises in an old-fashioned paddlewheeler. ~ 1205 Embarcadero, at the Harbor Hut Restaurant, Morro Bay; 805-772-2257.

Young children might enjoy playing on the whale's tail or just watching the boats in the marina at **Tidelands Children's Park,** at the south end of Embarcadero.

Back on terra firma, visit the **Morro Bay State Park Museum** with its displays of local history and wildlife. Lots on hands-on, interactive exhibits make it enjoyable for busy children. The museum itself is relatively unimpressive, but it is located at White Point, a rock outcropping in which Indian mortar holes are still evident. From this height there are views of the sandspit, Morro Bay, and Morro Rock. The nearby estuary, a habitat for 250 migratory and resident bird species, is one of the largest salt marshes in California. Admission. ~ Morro Bay State Park Road, Morro Bay; 805-772-2694.

LODGING

Lodging in the Pismo Beach–Shell Beach area generally means finding a motel. None of these seaside towns has expanded more than a few blocks from the waterfront, so wherever you book a room will be walking distance from the beach.

Adams Pirate Cove Inn is a 20-unit hostelry (14 with kitchenettes). The furniture and decoration is standard motel, though a volleyball court and horseshoe pits distinguish this place from its peers. ~ 1000 Dolliver Street, Pismo Beach; 805-773-2065. MODERATE.

If it's panoramic Pacific Coast views you are after, try **The Best Western Shore Cliff Lodge**. Perched on the cliffs just off Route 101, the hotel offers spacious, although conventional, rooms with private balconies and expected amenities. There's a restaurant, lounge, pool, spa, sauna, and tennis courts. Rooms aren't cheap, but what a view! ~ 2555 Price Street, Pismo Beach; 805-773-4671, 800-441-8885, fax 805-773-2341. DELUXE.

The small, seven-room **Beachcomber Inn** is neat and clean and just a block from the beach. Quaintly furnished with wicker furniture and floral prints, rooms also come equipped with microwaves and coffee makers. None of the rooms, however, have a full-on ocean view. Two-night minimum during July and August. ~ 541 Cypress Street, Pismo Beach; 805-773-5505; www.pismo beach.com/beachcomberinn. DELUXE.

For your pick of typical motels in San Luis Obispo, head for the stretch of Monterey Street north of California Boulevard known as Motel Row. San Luis also offers several distinctive accommodations, including the **Adobe Inn**, a classic motel that's been transformed into a B&B with a Southwest flavor. Here the 15 rooms are simple but comfortable with double or queen-size beds and rocking chairs; some include kitchenettes. All are nonsmoking. The view is of the surrounding hills, and a night's stay includes a trip to the inn's bounteous breakfast buffet. ~ 1473 Monterey Street, San Luis Obispo; 805-549-0321, 800-676-1588, fax 805-549-0383. MODERATE.

Sycamore Mineral Springs Resort reposes on a hillside one mile inland from Avila Beach. Situated in a stand of oak and sycamore trees are 26 motel-style rooms and 24 suites. Each has a private spa and patio; there are also redwood hot tubs, open 24 hours a day, scattered about in the surrounding forest; and a swimming pool. The room decor is contemporary. ~ 1215 Avila Beach Drive, San Luis Obispo; 805-595-7302, 800-234-5831, fax 805-781-2598. DELUXE.

Heritage Inn Bed & Breakfast is a San Luis Obispo anomaly. There aren't many country inns in town and this one is not even representative of the species. It sits in a neighborhood surrounded by motels and a nearby freeway, though it's within walking distance of historic downtown. What's more, the house was moved —lock, stock, and bay windows—to this odd location. Once inside, you'll be quite pleased. There's a warm, comfortable sitting parlor and seven guest rooms, all furnished with antiques reflecting the home's 1902 birth date. Some accommodations include window seats and terraces that look out to a lovely creekside garden. Three rooms have private baths; the other four rooms share two baths. Four rooms have fireplaces. Full breakfast is included. ~ 978 Olive Street, San Luis Obispo; 805-544-7440; www.slo-online.com/HeritageInn. MODERATE.

The **Garden Street Inn**, located in the historic downtown district, is a beautifully restored, 1887 Victorian that has 13 rooms and suites. Each is individually decorated in such themes as "Walden," "Amadeus," and "Emerald Isle." Some rooms honor local history; others are filled with family mementoes. A full breakfast is served family-style in the bay-windowed morning room and the innkeeper's reception in the afternoon features hors d'oeuvres and local wines. ~ 1212 Garden Street, San Luis Obispo; 805-545-9802, 800-488-2045, fax 805-545-9403; www.fix.net/garden. MODERATE TO DELUXE.

The **Apple Farm Inn** represents another example of a classic country inn set in a neighborhood of drive-in motels. The carefully landscaped property, including a stream that runs by the old Victorian-style buildings, takes you away from the hubbub of Monterey Street and into Old America complete with apple pies fresh from the Inn's bakery and a working, water-powered mill. ~ 2015 Monterey Street, San Luis Obispo; 805-544-2040, 800-374-3705, fax 805-544-2452. ULTRA-DELUXE. The adjoining **Trellis Court** has all the advantages of the Apple Farm Inn but its 34 smaller rooms are more affordably priced. While no two rooms are the same in either accommodation, they all have working gas fireplaces. MODERATE.

Where else but the Madonna Inn does a waterfall serve as the men's room urinal?

The most outlandish place in town is a roadside confection called the **Madonna Inn**. Architecturally it's a cross between a castle and a gingerbread house, culturally it's somewhere between light opera and heavy metal. The lampposts are painted pink, and the gift shop contains the biggest, gaudiest chandeliers you've ever seen. Personally, I wouldn't be caught dead staying in the place, but I would never miss an opportunity to visit. If you prove more daring than I, there are 109 rooms on the 2000-acre ranch, each decorated in a different flamboyant style ranging from an African Safari to something out of the Flintstones. Rooms offer a wide variety of amenities including waterfall showers and seven-foot bathtubs. There are a café, a formal dining room with live music, and a fabulous bakery. ~ Located at 100 Madonna Road, San Luis Obispo; 805-543-3000, 800-543-9666, fax 805-543-1800. MODERATE TO ULTRA-DELUXE.

The countless motels to choose from in Morro Bay range across the entire spectrum in price and amenities. Information on availability can be had from the **Morro Bay Chamber of Commerce**. Closed Sunday. ~ 880 Main Street, Morro Bay; 805-772-4467, 800-231-0592.

Located next to Tidelands Park at the quieter southern portion of Embarcadero is the 32-room **Embarcadero Inn**. All rooms, which are spacious, very clean, and comfortable, face the bay; several come with gas fireplaces and balconies. Other amenities include VCRs, refrigerators, and coffee makers, as well as a continental breakfast set up in the lobby each morning. One room is disabled-friendly. ~ 456 Embarcadero, Morro Bay; 805-772-2700, 800-292-7625. DELUXE TO ULTRA-DELUXE.

The **Twin Dolphin** isn't on the waterfront, but on the rise of a hill overlooking the bay. What the 31-room motel lacks in charm it makes up in cleanliness and reasonable prices. Continental breakfast is served in the cheery breakfast room. ~ 590 Morro Avenue, Morro Bay; 805-772-4483. MODERATE TO DELUXE.

A block away, a flower-filled garden surrounds the **Marina Street Bed and Breakfast**, a yellow New England–style home with bay windows overlooking the water and Morro Rock. Operated by Vern and Claudia Foster, retired teachers from Colorado, the inn has four separately-themed rooms: the Bordeaux Room, with a tiger oak sleigh bed and bay view; the green and apricot hued Garden Room, with a willow four-poster canopy bed and bay view; the nautically-themed Dockside Room; and the romantic Battenberg Room, with delicate touches of lace throughout. The morning's full gourmet breakfast is served in the dining room and might include an apple-pecan panache or a spicy sausage casserole. ~ 305 Marina Street, Morro Bay; 805-772-4016. MODERATE TO ULTRA-DELUXE.

◄ HIDDEN

Fashionable but casual, **The Inn at Morro Bay** is a waterfront complex with the amenities of a small resort: restaurant, lounge, swimming pool, and an adjacent golf course. It sits on ten acres overlooking Morro Bay and contains 98 guest rooms. French country in decor, many have brass beds, shuttered windows, and oak armoires. ~ 60 State Park Road, Morro Bay; 805-772-5651, 800-321-9566, fax 805-772-4779; www.innatmorrobay.com. DELUXE TO ULTRA-DELUXE.

DINING

Fish-and-chip joints are everywhere on the Central Coast, but **Pismo Fish & Chips** is special—mainly because it's good, but also because it's a local institution. The fish is fresh, the portions generous, and the service friendly. Closed Monday. ~ 505 Cypress Street, Pismo Beach; 805-773-2853. BUDGET TO MODERATE.

◄ HIDDEN

If you missed the swinging doors in the saloon you'll get the idea from the moose head trophies and branding irons. "Taste the Great American West" is the motto for **F. McLintock's Saloon & Dining House**. This is the place where on Sundays you can get an 18-ounce steak for breakfast. Every evening, when the oak pit barbecue really gets going, there are a dozen kinds of steak and ribs, seafood, and grilled veal liver. If popularity means anything, this place is tops. It's always mobbed. So dust off the Stetson and prepare to chow down. ~ 750 Mattie Road, Shell Beach; 805-773-1892. MODERATE TO DELUXE.

Sick of seafood by now? Tired of saloons serving cowboy-sized steaks? Happily, San Luis Obispo has several ethnic restaurants.

Two are located in The Creamery, a turn-of-the-century dairy plant that has been transformed into a shopping mall. **Tsurugi Japanese Restaurant** features a sushi bar and dining area decorated with Oriental screens and wallhangings. At lunch and dinner there are shrimp tempura, chicken teriyaki, *nigiri*, and other Asian specialties. The atmosphere is placid and the food quite good. No lunch on Saturday and Sunday. ~ 570 Higuera Street, San Luis Obispo; 805-543-8942. MODERATE TO DELUXE.

Next door at **Tortilla Flats** they've created an attractive restaurant from the brick walls, bare ducts, and exposed rafters of the old creamery. It's lunch, dinner, and Sunday brunch at this Mexican eatery that is particularly popular with the college crowd. The bar serves pitchers of margaritas. ~ 1051 Nipomo Street, San Luis Obispo; 805-544-7575. BUDGET TO MODERATE.

If you can get past the garish red and yellow sign at **Golden China Restaurant**, there's a tempting array of standard Chinese dishes at their lunch and dinner buffets. ~ 675 Higuera Street, San Luis Obispo; 805-543-7576. BUDGET.

For casual dining on a patio overlooking San Luis Creek, try the **Creekside Café**, about a half-block from the mission. The menu includes a variety of salads, baguette sandwiches, pasta, and more elaborate entrées. Breakfast, lunch, and dinner. ~ 1040 Broad Street, San Luis Obispo; 805-541-4048. MODERATE.

Linns is famous locally for its homemade pot pies and quiches, offered daily in meat and vegetarian versions. This bustling eatery is very popular with the locals. An adjacent store sells frozen pot pies and fruit pies, as well as jams, jellies, and other food items. ~ 1141 Chorro Street, San Luis Obispo; 805-546-8444. MODERATE.

Italy enters the picture with **Cafe Roma**, a delightful restaurant decorated in country Tuscan style. Copper pots as well as portraits from the old country decorate the walls. Lunch and dinner include Italian sausage, veal marsala, steak *fiorentina*, and several daily specials. There are also assorted pasta and antipasto dishes, an extensive Italian wine list, and homemade ice cream for dessert. Run by an Italian family, it serves excellent food; highly recommended. No lunch on weekends. Closed Monday. ~ 1020 Railroad Avenue, San Luis Obispo; 805-541-6800. MODERATE.

For a low-priced meal in a white-tablecloth restaurant with views of the surrounding hills, beat a path to the California Polytechnic campus. **Vista Grande Restaurant** serves Cal Poly students as well as the public in a comfortable plate-glass dining room. Open for lunch, dinner, and Sunday brunch, it features prime rib, pasta, fish, or vegetarian dishes. There are also several different salads, a host of sandwiches, and homemade soups. Fresh bread baked daily. Closed Saturday from June through August. ~ On the Cal Poly campus, off Grand Avenue, San Luis Obispo; 805-756-1204. BUDGET TO MODERATE.

HIDDEN ►

Outside town there's a particularly good Western-style restaurant. (You didn't think I'd let you off scot-free, did you?) **This Old House** is another oak pit grill serving steak and ribs, plus lobster, sweetbreads, barbecued chicken, and fresh halibut. The decor is early Western with oxen yokes, cowboy boots, and branding irons on the wall. With its unique barbecue sauce and rib-sticking meals, This Old House merits a visit. Dinner only. ~ 740 West Foothill Boulevard, San Luis Obispo; 805-543-2690. MODERATE TO DELUXE.

You needn't cast far in Morro Bay to find a seafood restaurant. Sometimes they seem as frequent as fishing boats. One of the most venerable is **Dorn's Original Breakers Café**. It's a bright, airy place with a postcard view of the waterfront from indoor and patio tables. While they serve all three meals, in the evening you better want seafood because there are about two dozen fish dishes and only a couple of steak, chicken, pasta, and veal platters. For breakfast try their out-of-this-world blueberry pancakes with a healthy dollop of whipped cream. ~ 801 Market Street, Morro Bay; 805-772-4415. MODERATE TO DELUXE.

The **Galley Restaurant** is a bit of a surprise, as much for the unexpectedly well-prepared food—fresh fish, of course, is featured extensively on the menu—as for the friendly, but unobtrusive, and well-trained staff and the quiet classical or jazz background music. It sits on a dock over the water. ~ 899 Embarcadero, Morro Bay; 805-772-2806. MODERATE TO DELUXE.

The picturesque setting—a grove of eucalyptus trees beside a small marina in Morro Bay State Park—is enough to recommend the small, rustic **Bayside Café**, where you can sit outside on the deck and take in the scenery. Locals come here for fresh fish, of course, and California/Mexican-inspired dishes like lime and garlic chicken, shrimp pasta Vera Cruz, and chile verde. Desserts, like *tres leches* cake, are all homemade. No credit cards. ~ Morro Bay

◀ HIDDEN

✔ CHECK THESE OUT—UNIQUE DINING

- *Budget to moderate:* Linger over croissant and cappuccino at **Franky's Restaurant**, which is adorned with artwork galore. *page 246*
- *Moderate:* Savor the gastronomic delights at **Cafe del Sol**, where you can dine on lamb shanks and enchiladas. *page 262*
- *Moderate to deluxe:* Kick open the swinging saloon doors and sit down to a buffalo burger at **F. McLintock's Saloon & Dining House.** *page 279*
- *Deluxe to ultra-deluxe:* Feast your eyes on the view at **El Encanto** while dining on a gourmand's delight. *page 262*

Budget: under $9   Moderate: $9–$18   Deluxe: $18–$25   Ultra-deluxe: over $25

State Park Road (from Morro Bay, follow Main Street into the park), Morro Bay; 805-772-1465. MODERATE.

Fine California cuisine is the order of the day at **The Inn at Morro Bay**. Situated in a waterfront resort, the dining room looks out over Morro Bay. In addition to great views and commodious surroundings, it features an enticing list of both local and French entrées. All three meals are served, but the highlight is dinner. The menu might include home-smoked salmon in bouillabaisse, filet mignon, paella, fresh fish in a mustard-chive butter, and an assortment of fresh pastas. ~ 60 State Park Road, Morro Bay; 805-772-5651. MODERATE TO DELUXE.

SHOPPING   In the old Spanish town of San Luis Obispo, the best stores are located along the blocks surrounding Mission Plaza. Stroll the two blocks along Monterey Street between Osos and Chorro streets, then browse the five-block stretch on Higuera Street from Osos Street to Nipomo Street. These two arteries and the side streets between form the heart of downtown.

Notwithstanding the shopping mall resemblance that comes when national retailers like Victoria's Secret stake out space, downtown San Luis Obispo retains a historic Spanish mission-town appeal. And it's compact enough to be able to walk comfortably in an afternoon.

The unique atmosphere of **Boo Boo's Records** makes browsing as enjoyable as purchasing. The posters on the wall are as eclectic as the music playing. With a huge collection of vinyl records, new and used CDs and cassettes, you're bound to find new hits and old favorites. ~ 978 Monterey Street, San Luis Obispo; 805-541-0657.

For movie memorabilia and collectibles, **Foghorns** is the place to go. Posters, T-shirts, stuffed animals, and books herald late greats like Elvis and Marilyn Monroe, and classics like *Star Wars* and *Gone with the Wind*. They also feature a sizable Pez display. ~ 782 Higuera Street, San Luis Obispo; 805-546-0960.

FARMERS' FEAST

If you're in San Luis Obispo on a Thursday evening, be sure to stop by the **Farmers Market**. Farmers from the surrounding area turn out to sell fresh fruits and vegetables. They barbecue ribs, cook sweet corn and fresh fish, then serve them on paper plates to the throngs that turn out weekly. Puppeteers and street dancers perform as the celebration assumes a carnival atmosphere. ~ At Higuera Street between Osos and Nipomo streets, San Luis Obispo.

Decades offers a funky mix of old and new by combining vintage clothing and collectibles with new Doc Martens and Morrow footwear. They have that faux-fur jacket and polyester pantsuit you've always wanted (or always wanted to get rid of). Decades also harbors the best Hawaiian shirt collection I've seen this side of the islands. ~ 785 Higuera Street, San Luis Obispo; 805-546-0901.

The Creamery is an old dairy plant converted into an ingenious shopping center with several small restaurants and shops. **The Spin-net** carries weaving supplies and offers lessons. ~ Higuera and Nipomo streets, San Luis Obispo; 805-594-0267.

In Morro Bay, the waterfront Embarcadero offers the ubiquitous souvenir/T-shirt emporiums that predominate in such touristy enclaves. One exception is **Patronik's** bookstore; it's small, but contains a decent selection of current bestsellers and children's books. ~ 805-772-7331.

Up the hill, along Morro Bay Boulevard and Main Street, there are several antique and vintage stores that for collectors might offer an enjoyable afternoon of browsing. The Chamber of Commerce puts out a brochure and map pinpointing these shops.

San Luis Obispo's quaint downtown is home to a lively bar scene where college students and cowboys mix it up. From intimate coffeehouses and restaurants with live music to bars featuring 25-cent beers, you're likely to find something entertaining—walk around Monterey, Higuera, Marsh streets and the paths that connect them, until you find what you want. Or just head over to the 700 block of Higuera Street, where a triangle of bars offers something for everyone.

NIGHTLIFE

The **Frog and Peach Pub** is your standard sports bar. More than 70 beers on tap and a TV in every corner make it the perfect place to watch the game. The interior is dark and calm, while the back patio gets a bit more rowdy. When they host live rock or blues music, there is usually a cover. ~ 728 Higuera Street, San Luis Obispo; 805-595-3764.

Across the street at **Mother's Tavern** the mood is mellow. With live rock, blues, or disco every night, this bar serves an upscale, older clientele out for a good time. There's often a line at the door and the generous dancefloor fills quickly, but it is usually possible to grab an intimate table upstairs. Cover. ~ 725 Higuera Street, San Luis Obispo; 805-541-8733.

The mood is definitely not mellow at **The Library** next door. Despite its name's quiet, studious connotations, this is the seen-and-be-seen scene for local college students. In fact, every Cal Poly mother should be a little suspicious when her student starts spending inordinate amounts of time at "the library." The DJ music is loud, the dancefloor is packed, and nightly drink specials keep the crowd going. Cover. ~ 723 Higuera Street, San Luis Obispo; 805-542-0199.

Also popular with the college crowd is the SLO Brewing Co., a micro-brewery restaurant that offers nightly entertainment. ~ 1119 Garden Street, San Luis Obispo; 805-543-1843. Mother's Tavern, with its huge Honduran mahogany bar, is another "happening" place with a variety of music, from jazz and swing to Celtic rock and disco. ~ 725 Higuera Street, San Luis Obispo; 805-541-3853.

The $30 million Performing Arts Center of San Luis Obispo County is located on the Cal Poly campus. Seating 1350, it gives the region a year-round professional performance venue. ~ 805-756-2787 or 888-233-2787 for schedule and tickets.

Ready for a Western saloon? Stone fireplace, antlers on the wall, etc.? It's called F. McLintock's Saloon & Dining House. Unlike its rowdier counterparts, this lounge is low key. The music, seven nights a week during the summer, is by solo guitarists playing soft rock and country. ~ 750 Mattie Road, Shell Beach; 805-773-1892.

There's live entertainment on Friday and Saturday nights in the lounge at The Inn at Morro Bay. Appointed with bentwood furniture and pastel paneling, it's a beautiful bar. The most striking feature of all is the view, which extends out across the water to Morro Rock. ~ 60 State Park Road, Morro Bay; 805-772-5651.

GAY SCENE   There's no particular neighborhood in San Luis that's become the preferred turf for gay men and lesbians or that has a concentration of gay-oriented business. In fact, although there are a fair number of gays and lesbians living in the SLO area, their profile is generally conservative, quiet, and "pretty closeted," as one gay business owner put it.

Still, 1998 marked the second year for the city's gay pride parade, an event that was duly noted in the events calendar of a visitor guide. And the area is not without committed resources: the

SOUNDS OF SUMMER

The summer months bring plenty of music to SLO County. For two weeks in late July and early August, the annual Mozart Festival includes not just Mozart's music, but also the music of Vivaldi, Bach, Beethoven, and others at concerts around the county. ~ 805-781-3008.
San Luis Obispo Mission Plaza is the site for free Friday evening concerts, between 5:30 and 7:30 p.m., featuring local entertainers. ~ 805-541-0286.

Gay and Lesbian Alliance of the Central Coast (GALA) operates a community center and provides a meeting place for various groups. ~ 1306 Higuera Street, San Luis Obispo; 805-541-4252; www.slonet.org/~ipgala.

When Breezes Pub and Grill closed last year, that took care of the only gay bar in town. At press time, Breezes had not re-opened. But the gay-friendly atmosphere at **Linnea's Café**, a "hipster hangout" in downtown SLO, attracts the city's young gays and lesbians, as well as artists and other creative types. It's usually open until midnight, late for this neck of the woods. ~ 1110 Garden Street, San Luis Obispo; 805-541-5888.

◄ HIDDEN

The **Big Sky Café** is another popular and gay-friendly spot and can be recommended for its new American style cooking. ~ 1121 Broad Street, San Luis Obispo; 805-545-5401.

RANCHO GUADALUPE DUNES COUNTY PARK 🚶 🏄 ⛴ The Sahara Desert has nothing on this place. The sand dunes throughout the area are spectacular, especially 450-foot Mussel Rock, the highest dune on the West Coast. The dunes provide a habitat for California brown pelicans, California least terns, and other endangered birds and plants. The Santa Maria River, which empties here, forms a pretty wetland area. Fishing is very popular here. Primitive restrooms are on site. A discovery center, open Friday through Sunday, makes a trip to the beach educational. ~ From Route 1 in Guadalupe, follow Main Street west for five miles to the beach. Park closed to vehicles on Tuesday. Windblown sand sometimes closes the road, so call beforehand; 805-343-2455, 805-544-1767.

BEACHES & PARKS

OCEANO DUNES STATE VEHICULAR RECREATION AREA This is the only spot in California where standard and four-wheel-drive vehicles may still be driven right on the beach. An 800-acre section of dunes is open year-round to four-wheelers and all-terrain vehicles. OHVs can be driven only in designated areas and must be registered and display flags. Entry fee. ~ Off Route 1, south of downtown Pismo Beach. Enter on Pier Avenue or Grand Avenue; 805-473-7223 (recorded) or 805-473-7220.

▲ There are primitive campsites, with only chemical toilets. Reservations are necessary between May and September (call PARKNET at 800-444-7275); otherwise, it's first-come, first-served. To access the campsite, you must drive across two miles of sand and cross a creek, which can be treacherous during high tide.

PISMO STATE BEACH 🚶 🚤 🎣 🏄 ⛴ This spectacular beach runs for six miles from Pismo Beach south to the Santa Maria River. Along its oceanfront are some of the finest sand dunes in California, fluffy hills inhabited by shorebirds and tenacious plants. A freshwater lagoon abuts the campgrounds. Also home to the pismo clam, it's a wonderful place to hike and explore. Surfing is popular here, but exercise caution in the water—rip tides occur here occasionally. Lifeguards on duty. There are picnic areas here, and restrooms at one campground. Fishing for cod and red snapper is good from the Pismo Pier (at the end of Hinds Avenue in Pismo Beach). You can also dig for pismo clams along the beach (check for local restrictions). ~ The park parallels Route 1 in Pismo Beach; 805-489-1869.

▲ There are tent/RV sites (limited hookups); $18 to $24 per night. Reservations can be made by calling 800-444-7275. There is also camping at **Oceano Memorial County Park** (near Mendel Drive and Pier Avenue, Oceano; 805-781-5219) on 24 tent/RV sites (full hookups); $21 per night. Sites are first-come, first-served.

HIDDEN ▶ **PIRATE'S COVE OR MALLAGH LANDING** ⚓ This crescent-shaped nude beach is a beauty. Protected by 100-foot cliffs, it curves for a half mile along a placid cove. At one end is a rocky headland pockmarked by caves. Swimming and skindiving are very good because the beach is in a sheltered area. ~ Located ten miles south of San Luis Obispo in Avila Beach. From Route 101 take Avila Beach Drive west for two miles; turn left on Cave Landing Road (the road travels immediately uphill); go six-tenths of a mile to a dirt parking lot; crude stairs lead down to the beach.

MONTAÑA DE ORO STATE PARK 🚶 🚴 🐎 🏊 🎣 ⛵ 🚣 ⛴
This 10,000-acre facility is one of the finest parks along the entire Central Coast. It stretches over a mile along the shore, past a sandspit, tidepools, and sharp cliffs. There are remote coves for viewing seals, sea otters, and migrating whales and for sunbathing on hidden beaches. Monarch butterflies roost in the eucalyptus-filled canyons and a hiking trail leads to Valencia Peak, with views scanning almost 100 miles of coastline. Wildlife is abundant along 50 miles of hiking trails. Chaparral, Bishop pine, and coast live oak cover the hills; in spring wildflowers riot, giving the park its name, "Mountain of Gold." You can go fishing, but swimming is not recommended because of occasional rip tides and chilly water. Surfing is good around Hazard Canyon. There are picnic areas and primitive restrooms; restaurants and groceries are several miles away in Los Osos. ~ Located on Pecho Valley Road about ten miles south of Morro Bay; 805-528-0513.

▲ There are 50 tent/RV sites (no hookups); $11 per night. Reservations strongly recommended for this busy campground (800-444-7275).

MORRO BAY STATE PARK 🚶 🚴 🎣 🛶 ⛵ 🚣 ⛴ Located amid one of the biggest marshlands along the California coast, this 2435-acre domain is like an outdoor museum. The tidal basin attracts over 250 species of sea, land, and shore birds. Great blue herons roost in the eucalyptus trees. There's a marina where you can rent canoes or kayaks to explore the salt marsh and nearby sandspit, and a natural history museum with environmental displays. Camping is in an elevated area trimmed with pine and other trees. Since the park fronts the wetlands, there is no beach here, but you can reach the beach at **Montaña de Oro State Park Sand Spit** by car or private boat. Facilities include restrooms and showers. Fishing is good. Day-use fee, $6. ~ On State Park Road in Morro Bay; 805-772-7434.

▲ There are 135 tent/RV sites (limited hookups); $18 to $24 per night. Reservations required; call 800-444-7275.

MORRO STRAND STATE BEACH Another of the Central Coast's long, skinny parks, this sandy beach stretches almost two miles along Morro Bay. Private homes border one side, but in the other direction there are great views of Morro Rock. It's a good place for beachcombing, fishing, and clamming. This beach is subject to rip currents and there are no lifeguards on duty. There are restrooms and cold showers. ~ Located parallel to Route 1 north of Morro Bay; park entrance is along Yerba Buena Street; 805-772-8812.

▲ There are 23 tent sites and 81 RV sites (no hookups); $18 to $23 per night. Reservations required Memorial Day through Labor Day (800-444-7275).

LOS PADRES NATIONAL FOREST The southern section of this mammoth park parallels the coast from Ventura to San Luis Obispo. Rising from sea level to almost 9000 feet, it contains the Sierra Madre, San Rafael, Santa Ynez, and La Panza mountains. Characterized by sharp slopes and a dry climate, only one-third of the preserve is forested. But there are Coast redwoods, ancient bristlecone pines, and amazingly diverse plant life. The rare California condor, which with its nine-foot wingspan is the largest land bird in North America, has recently been reintroduced to Los Padres. Among the animals still remaining are golden eagles, quail, owls, woodpeckers, wild pig, mule deer, black bear, and desert bighorn sheep. The northern and southern sectors of the national forest contain over 1500 miles of hiking trails, almost 500 miles of streams, and a ski trail on Mt. Pinos. For information and permits contact forest headquarters at 6144 Calle Real, Goleta, CA 93117. Day-use fee is $5, but subject to change, so call ahead. ~ Route 33 cuts through the heart of Los Padres. Route 101 provides numerous access points; 805-683-6711.

▲ There are 94 tent/RV sites (no hookups); prices vary from free to $18 per night.

▼▼▼▼▼▼▼▼▼▼▼▼

Cambria and San Simeon Area

Cambria itself is a seaside town that was originally settled in the 1860s and later expanded into a major seaport and whaling center. As the railroad replaced coastal shipping Cambria fell into a decline, only to be resurrected during the past few decades as an artist colony and tourist center.

SIGHTS   If your approach to Cambria is along Route 1 from the south, you'll first pass the privately owned village of **Harmony**, which was a dairy cooperative in the early part of the century. Since the 1970s, however, it's been an artisans' colony of sorts, with the old dairy buildings converted to gift shops and glassmaking and pottery studios. In recent years, Harmony has been purchased by a new owner, the restaurant has been mostly closed, and the creative energy seems less vibrant than in the past. The post office is still in operation, however, and a Harmony Cellars winery offers daily tastings. ~ Harmony Valley Road and Route 1; 800-432-9239 (winetasting information).

A few miles north of Harmony is the turnoff for **Cambria**. The town is divided into two separate sections: the East Village and West Village. Galleries, gift shops, and antique stores abound in both villages, so it really doesn't matter where you start exploring the town. The **Chamber of Commerce** is located in the West Village. ~ 767 Main Street, Cambria; 805-927-3624.

Start wandering around and you'll find that it's a pretty place, with ridgetop homes, sandy beaches, and rocky coves. But like many of California's small creative communities, Cambria has begun peering too long in the mirror. The architecture along Main Street has assumed a cutesy mock-Tudor look and the place is taking on an air of unreality.

Still, there are many fine artists and several exceptional galleries here. It's a choice place to shop and seek out gourmet food. While you're at it, head up to **Nit Wit Ridge**. That hodgepodge house on the left, the one decorated with every type of bric-a-brac, was the home of Art Beal, a.k.a. Captain Nit Wit, who died in 1992. He worked on this folk-art estate, listed in the National Register of Historic Landmarks, from 1928 until his death. ~ Hillcrest Drive just above Cornwall Street.

Then take a ride along **Moonstone Beach Drive**, a lovely oceanfront corridor with vista points and tidepools. It's a marvelous place for beachcombers and daydreamers.

Funny thing about travel, you often end up visiting places in spite of themselves. You realize that as soon as you get back home friends are going to ask if you saw this or that, so your itinerary becomes a combination of the locales you've always longed to experience and the places everyone else says you "must see."

The world-renowned **Hearst Castle** is one of the latter. Built by newspaper magnate William Randolph Hearst and designed by architect Julia Morgan, the Hearst San Simeon State Historical Monument includes a main house that sports 37 bedrooms, three guest houses, and part of the old Hearst ranch, which once stretched 40 miles along the coast.

The entire complex took 27 years to build. In the 1930s and 1940s, when Hearst resided here and film stars like Charlie Chaplin, Mary Pickford, Clark Gable, and Cary Grant frequented the place, the grounds contained the largest private zoo in the world.

Ninety species of wild animals—including lions, tigers, yaks, and camels—roamed about Hearst Castle.

An insatiable art collector, Hearst stuffed every building with priceless works. Casa Grande, the main house, is fronted by two cathedral towers and filled with Renaissance and Gothic art. To see it is overwhelming. There is no place for the eye to rest. The main sitting room is covered everywhere with tapestries, bas-relief works, 16th-century paintings, Roman columns, and a carved wood ceiling. The walls are fashioned from 500-year-old choir pews, the French fireplace dates back 400 years; there are hand-carved tables and silver candelabra (I am still describing the same room), overstuffed furniture, and antique statuary. It is the most lavish mismatch in history.

Hearst Castle crosses the line from visual art to visual assault. The parts are exquisite, the whole a travesty. And yet, as I said, you must see the place. It's so huge that four different two-hour tours are scheduled daily to various parts of the property.

A fifth tour of "The Ranch," as Hearst called the castle, is conducted at night, on Friday and Saturday only from March through May and September through December. It begins at sunset and takes in the gardens that are illuminated by one hundred historic light fixtures. Docents dressed in 1930s fashions appear as Hearst's domestic staff and celebrated guests.

In the visitors center, which is located just off Route 1, there's a National Geographic Theater that shows the film *Building the Dream* on a huge five-story-tall movie screen. Admission. ~ 805-927-6811.

All tours of the castle, which is on the hilltop above, depart from the center. The five-mile bus ride up takes several minutes; a tour guide will greet you upon your arrival at the top. The tours involve considerable walking and include many stairs.

Since over one million people a year visit, the guided tours are often booked solid. I recommend that you reserve tickets as much as two months in advance and plan on taking Tour 1, which covers the ground floor of Casa Grande, a guest house, the pools, and the gardens. Call 800-444-4445 for reservations.

Ultimately you'll find that in spite of the pomp and grandiosity, there is a magic about the place. In the early morning, when tour shuttles begin climbing from sea level to the 1600-foot-elevation residence, fog feathers through the surrounding valleys, obscuring all but the spiked peaks of the Santa Lucia Mountains and the lofty towers of the castle. The entire complex, overbearing as it is, evokes a simpler, more glamorous era, before the Depression and World War II turned the nation's thoughts inward, when without blinking a man could build an outlandish testimonial to himself. Admission. ~ Route 1, San Simeon; 805-927-2000.

Beyond Hearst Castle, Route 1 winds north past tidepools and pocket beaches. There are pretty coves and surf-washed rocks offshore. To leeward the hills give way to mountains as the highway ascends toward the dramatic Big Sur coastline. Over two hundred miles farther north sits the city that Hearst made the center of his publishing empire, an oceanfront metropolis called San Francisco.

LODGING   In the coastal art colony of Cambria is an 1873 bed and breakfast called the **Olallieberry Inn**. The Greek Revival clapboard house contains nine guest rooms, done in Victorian style with 19th-century antiques. Most rooms have fireplaces, some have balconies, and all have private baths. The rose-colored carpet and curtains, together with the carefully selected linens, add an element of luxury to this well-appointed establishment. The sitting room is attractively furnished with oak wood. ~ 2476 Main Street, Cambria; 805-927-3222, 888-927-3222, fax 805-927-0202; www.olallieberry.com. MODERATE TO ULTRA-DELUXE.

If you would prefer a more rustic atmosphere, head up to **Cambria Pines Lodge**. Set one and a half miles from the beach, amid 25 acres of Monterey pines, are rambling split-rail lodges with additional cabins dotted about the property. The main building offers a spacious lobby with stone fireplace plus a restaurant and lounge with nightly live entertainment; other amenities include a swimming pool, sauna, jacuzzi, and beauty salon. All prices include buffet breakfast. ~ 2905 Burton Drive, Cambria; 805-927-4200, 800-445-6868, fax 805-927-4016; www.cambria-online.com/cambriapineslodge. MODERATE TO DELUXE.

North of Hearst Castle, where Route 1 becomes an isolated coastal road with few signs of civilization, are two hostelries. **Piedras Blancas Motel** has 14 standard motel-type rooms. Most of the units have ocean views. ~ Route 1, seven miles north of Hearst Castle; 805-927-4202. MODERATE.

Farther along, on a ridge poised between the highway and ocean, sits the more appealing **Ragged Point Inn**. This 20-unit facility has attractive rooms furnished with contemporary hardwood furniture. Another compelling reason to stay is the beautiful ocean view from this clifftop abode. Despite the inn's proximity to the road, it's peaceful and quiet here; a variety of wildlife wanders and flutters through the grounds and sea sounds fill the air. A steep trail leads down to a rock-and-sand beach, while other trails take you away from the ocean to see the Santa Lucia Mountains. ~ Route 1, 15 miles north of Hearst Castle; 805-927-4502, fax 805-927-8862. MODERATE TO DELUXE.

Ethnic and vegetarian food lovers will fare well at **Robin's**. Set in a 1930s Mexican-style house, it serves homemade lunches and dinners. Choices range from burritos to sweet-and-sour prawns to stir-fried tofu. It's an eclectic blend—the accent's on Italian and Asian cuisine. Patio seating is available. ~ 4095 Burton Drive, Cambria; 805-927-5007. MODERATE.

DINING

For fine California cuisine try **Ian's Restaurant**. The decor is contemporary, featuring floral prints on pastel-shaded walls, blond wood furniture, and upholstered banquettes. Ian's seasonal menu draws upon local fresh produce, herbs, and seafood. Also among the specialties are salmon, veal, lamb, and pasta. Dinner nightly. ~ 1250 Center Street, Cambria; 805-927-8649. MODERATE TO DELUXE.

Located a few miles south of Hearst Castle, the seaside enclave of Cambria has developed into an artist colony and become an important arts-and-crafts center, with numerous galleries and specialty shops. Several antique shops are also here; like the crafts stores, they cluster along Main Street and Burton Drive.

SHOPPING

Among the foremost galleries in here is **Seekers Collection & Gallery**. It's a glass menagerie inhabited by contemporary, one-of-a-kind vases, goblets, and sculptures. ~ 4090 Burton Drive, Cambria; 805-927-4352, 800-841-5250.

The Soldier Factory is a journey back to childhood. Part toy store and part aviation gallery, it serves as headquarters for thousands of hand-painted toy soldiers. Some of these antiques are deployed in battle formation, re-enacting clashes from the Civil War and other engagements. Many of the pewter pieces are made in the adjacent "factory." This unique shop has been featured in the *Wall Street Journal*. ~ 789 Main Street, Cambria; 805-927-3804.

Camozzi's Saloon is a century-old bar with longhorns over the bar, wagon wheels on the wall, and a floor that leans worse than a midnight drunk. The place is famous. Besides that, it has a rock band every Friday and Saturday and karaoke on Tuesday. ~ 2262 Main Street, Cambria; 805-927-8941.

NIGHTLIFE

SAN SIMEON STATE PARK 🚶 🚴 🎣 ⚓ ⛵ This wide sand corridor reaches for about two miles from San Simeon Creek to Santa Rosa Creek. It's a great place to wander and the streams, with their abundant wildlife, add to the enjoyment. Unfortunately,

BEACHES & PARKS

Route 1 divides the beach from the camping area and disturbs the quietude. Other parts of the park are very peaceful, especially the **Moonstone Beach** section in Cambria, known for its moonstone agates and otters. There are picnic areas, restrooms, and showers. ~ On Route 1 in Cambria; 805-927-2020.

▲ There are two campgrounds in the park with a total of 268 camp sites. The larger San Simeon Creek has spots for tents and RVs (no hookups); $18 per night. At Washburn there are 70 sites for tents and RVs (no hookups); $11 per night. Camping reservations can be made by calling 800-444-7275.

WILLIAM R. HEARST MEMORIAL STATE BEACH 🚶 🚲 🏊

🚣 🚶 🍴 ⛵ 🚿 Located directly below Hearst Castle, this is a placid crescent-shaped beach. The facility measures only two acres, including a grassy area on a rise above the beach. There's a 1000-foot-long fishing pier. Scenic San Simeon Point curves out from the shoreline, creating a pretty cove and protecting the beach from surf. Swimming and fishing is good, and there are charter boats leaving from San Simeon Landing. There are picnic areas and restrooms. Day-use fee, $4. ~ On Route 1 opposite Hearst Castle; 805-927-2020.

▼▼▼▼▼▼▼▼▼▼▼▼▼▼▼

Outdoor Adventures

SPORT-FISHING

The waters off the Central Coast and the Channel Islands provide excellent fishing. In the summer, you can fish the surface for barracuda, calico bass, and yellowtail, or the shallow waters for ling cod. Due to the relatively shallow water in the Central Coast area, winter bottom fishing is some of the best in the world. Common catches are rock cod, cabazon, red snapper, and blue bass. Most charter companies in the area sell bait and rent tackle.

If you're interested in a half-day, full-day, or overnight fishing cruise, contact **Cisco's Sportfishing**. They have a full tackle shop and rental equipment too. ~ 4151 South Victoria Avenue, Oxnard; 805-985-8511. **Sea Landing Aquatic Center** offers half-, three-quarter-, and full-day cruises. Look to catch calico bass, red snapper, barracuda, and an occasional tuna. ~ 301 West Cabrillo Boulevard, Santa Barbara; 805-963-3564. **Virg's Sportfishing** specializes in fishing trips for rock cod and albacore. They offer day trips as well as overnight trips. ~ 1215 Embarcadero, Morro Bay; 805-772-1222. **Avila Beach Sportfishing** specializes in deep sea and rock fishing, but targets salmon and albacore seasonally. ~ Pier 3, Avila Beach; 805-595-7200.

WHALE WATCHING

If you're in the mood for a whale-watching excursion, take your pick from numerous companies. You can also opt for either of two whale-watching seasons. From January through May, you'll see California gray whales on their northern migration. The second season, from June to September, brings blue and humpback whales to the Channel Islands.

Contact **Cisco's Sportfishing** for tours from January through March. ~ 4151 South Victoria Avenue, Oxnard; 805-985-8511.

For excursions in both seasons, call **Captain Don's**. From February through May, Captain Don's sails along the Santa Barbara coast on a 90-foot boat looking for gray whales around the Channel Islands. You're bound to see a sea lion, otter, or dolphin on the harbor cruise. ~ Stearns Wharf, Santa Barbara; 805-969-5217.

Sea Landing Aquatic Center will also take you on whale-watching excursions from December through April on the 88-foot *Condor*. ~ 301 West Cabrillo Boulevard, Santa Barbara; 805-963-3564. **Virg's Sportfishing** offers day trips to see gray whales from the end of December through April. ~ 1215 Embarcadero, Morro Bay; 805-772-1222. **Avila Beach Sportfishing** also operates whale-watching trips from the end of December through March. ~ Pier 3, Avila Beach; 805-595-7200.

If you're in the mood to explore the water in a semisubmersible vessel, contact Sub-Sea Tours. ~ 699 Embarcadero, Morro Bay; 805-772-9463.

Sea kayaking is excellent along the South Central Coast and out to the Channel Islands.

SEA KAYAKING

Good Clean Fun offers rentals, instructional guided tours, and lessons. ~ 136 Ocean Front, Cayucos; 805-995-1993. **Kayaks of Morro Bay** provides you the means to hobnob with seals and local birds. ~ 561 Embarcadero, Morro Bay; 805-772-1119. You can rent a kayak or arrange a one-day guided paddling trip to the sea caves of Santa Cruz Island through **Aquasports**. ~ 111 Verona Avenue, Goleta; 805-968-7231. Working in conjunction with Aquasports is **Adventours Outdoor Excursions, Inc**. Together, the companies arrange trips combining kayaking with other outdoor activities such as camping, hiking, biking, and backpacking. ~ 735 Chapala Street, Santa Barbara; 805-963-2248.

For those more interested in watching fish, several companies charter dive boats and also offer scuba diving rentals and lessons. The waters around the Channel Islands provide some of the world's best diving spots.

DIVING

Ventura Dive and Sport, a 5-star PADI facility, has one-, two-, or three-day diving excursion to the northern Channel Islands, where you will see a wide array of sea life, including harbor seals and bat rays. ~ 1559 Spinnaker Drive #108, Ventura; 805-650-6500. In Santa Barbara, call **Anacapa Dive Center** for scuba instruction, rentals, and trips to the Channel Islands. ~ 22 Anacapa Street, Santa Barbara; 805-963-8917. Dive charters to local waters and the Channel Islands are arranged by **Sea Landing Aquatic Center**. They offer one-day open-water trips as well as two-, three-, and five-day charters. ~ 301 West Cabrillo Boulevard, Santa Barbara; 805-963-3564.

SURFING   There's good surfing all along the Central Coast. In the Santa Barbara area, surfers head to Rincon, Leadbetter, Santa Claus Lane, and La Conchita.

Harbor Water Sports is a full watersport center, renting and selling surfboards, wetsuits, and boogieboards. The friendly staff also offers lessons. ~ 117-B Harbor Way, Santa Barbara; 805-962-4890. **Good Clean Fun** rents boogieboards, wetsuits, and soft longboards. Make an appointment if you want surfing lessons. ~ 136 Ocean Front, Cayucos; 805-995-1993. **Wavelengths Surf Shop** also offers wetsuits and surfboards to surfers ready to take on the waves. For a good location, try The Rock right down the street from the shop. ~ 998 Embarcadero, Morro Bay; 805-772-3904.

BOATING   The Central Coast and the Channel Islands are prime areas for boating. You can rent your own boat or go on one of the various cruises and charters offered.

To sail the Pacific, visit the Channel Islands, or take a romantic sunset champagne cruise, contact **Santa Barbara Sailing Center** for boat rentals and charters. They also offer a variety of lessons. ~ The Breakwater, Santa Barbara; 805-962-2826. **Sea Landing Aquatic Center** offers coastal cruises and charters. Many cruises are on a double-masted schooner, the *Spike Africa*. Sunset dinner trips are a specialty. ~ 301 West Cabrillo Boulevard, Santa Barbara; 805-963-3564.

GOLF   Golf enthusiasts will enjoy the weather as well as the courses along the Central Coast. Courses have 18 holes unless otherwise stated.

VENTURA–OXNARD AREA The **River Ridge Golf Club** is a links-style course with an island green on the 14th hole. ~ 2401 West Vineyard Avenue, Oxnard; 805-983-4653. A flat course, **Olivas Park** comes complete with driving range and putting green. ~ 3750 Olivas Park Drive, Ventura; 805-642-4303. The greens at **Buenaventura** are lined with eucalyptus, spruce, and pine trees. ~ 5882 Olivas Park Drive, Ventura; 805-642-2231.

SANTA BARBARA AREA Santa Barbara Golf Club's course is dotted with oaks, pines, and sycamores. ~ Las Positas Road and McCaw Avenue, Santa Barbara; 805-687-7087. The executive nine-hole **Twin Lakes Golf Course** meanders around two lakes. ~ 6034 Hollister Avenue, Goleta; 805-964-1414. Two miles north of Twin Lakes is **Sandpiper Golf Course**, a championship course right on the ocean. ~ 7925 Hollister Avenue, Goleta; 805-968-1541. A creek winds through the nine-hole **Ocean Meadows Golf Course**, which is a relatively flat playing field. ~ 6925 Whittier Drive, Goleta; 805-968-6814.

SAN LUIS OBISPO AREA A creek runs through the par-3, nine-hole **Pismo State Beach Golf Course**. Located near the beach, they also have a putting green and chipping area. ~ 25 Grand Avenue, Grover City; 805-481-5215. The nine-hole **Laguna Lake Golf Course** is a hilly green surrounded by mountains. ~ 11175 Los Osos Valley Road, San Luis Obispo; 805-781-7309. **Avila Beach Resort Golf Course** is dotted with trees and water hazards. The driving range overlooks the beach. ~ Avila Beach Road, Avila Beach; 805-595-2307. Lined with lofty pine trees, part of **Morro Bay Golf Course** overlooks the ocean. ~ 201 State Park Road, Morro Bay; 805-772-4560. **Sea Pines Golf Course** offers a nine-hole green whose gently rolling hills are speckled with mature pines. ~ 250 Howard Avenue, Los Osos; 805-528-1788.

Tennis anyone? This area offers a number of opportunities for tennis fiends. **Moranda Park Tennis Complex** has eight lighted courts situated in a beautiful park setting. Equipment rentals available. ~ 200 Moranda Parkway, Port Hueneme; 805-986-6584. **Santa Barbara Municipal Courts** has four facilities with a total of 32 courts; 14 have lighting. Bring your own equipment. Fee. ~ 805-564-5517. **Cuesta College** has eight courts that open to the public in the afternoon and evening. ~ Route 1, San Luis Obispo; 805-546-3207. **Sinsheimer Park** has six courts. ~ 900 Southwood Drive, San Luis Obispo; 805-781-7300. Additional courts are located at **French Park**, off Poinsettia Street. For night games, try the lighted courts at the high school, on the corner of San Luis Drive and California Street. There are four more courts at Shell Beach and Florin roads.

TENNIS

Horse lovers can explore the South Central Coast astride a mount with a guided tour, or venture off on their own.

RIDING STABLES

✔ CHECK THESE OUT—UNIQUE OUTDOOR ADVENTURES

- Cruise the Channel Islands with one of the local sportfishing companies in search of barracuda, bass, and other big ones. *page 292*
- Paddle a sea kayak on the protected waters of Morro Bay, where seals cavort and seabirds play. *page 293*
- Bike the beautiful seven-mile Atascadero Recreation Trail to Goleta Beach, where you can bask in the sun and play in the surf. *page 296*
- Hike past tidepools, sea caves, playful otters, and sun-tanning seals on Montaña de Oro Bluffs Trail. *page 298*

Circle Bar B Stables takes riders on a one-and-a-half-hour trip through a canyon, past waterfalls, and then up to a vista point overlooking the Channel Islands. A half-day lunch ride is also available for more experienced riders. ~ 1800 Refugio Road, Goleta; 805-968-3901. To ride right on the beach, you can go on one of The Livery Stable's guided tours during the summer; rent a horse and explore on your own in the off-season. One- to two-hour rides available for all experience levels. ~ 1207 Silverspur Place, Oceano; 805-489-8100.

BIKING

Biking the South Central Coast can be a rewarding experience. The coastal route, however, presents problems in populated areas during rush hour.

The town of **Ventura** offers an interesting bicycle tour through the historical section of town with a visit to the county historical museum and mission. Another bike tour of note, off of Harbor Boulevard, leads to the Channel Islands National Monument and Wildlife Refuge Visitors Center. A bike map of Ventura County is available at the **Ventura Visitors Bureau.** ~ 89-C South California Street, Ventura; 805-648-2075.

The Goleta Valley bikeway travels from Santa Barbara to Goleta along Cathedral Oaks Road.

Santa Barbara is chock full of beautiful bicycle paths and trails. Two notable beach excursions are the **Atascadero Recreation Trail**, which starts at the corner of Encore Drive and Modoc Road and ends over seven miles later at Goleta Beach, and **Cabrillo bikeway**, which takes you from Andree Clark Bird Refuge to Leadbetter Beach. Also, you'll find that the **University of California–Santa Barbara** has many bike paths through the campus grounds and into Isla Vista.

Up the coast, a stunning, three-mile bike path links **El Capitan** and **Refugio** state beaches.

Exploring the shores of Morro Bay is popular with cyclists. For the hardy biker a ride up **Black Mountain** leads to sweeping views of the Pacific Ocean.

Bike Rentals For bicycles in Ventura and Santa Barbara try **Beach Rentals**, which offers tandems, children's bikes, and inline skates. Helmets and locks are included. ~ Embassy Suites Mandalay Beach Resort Inn, 201 Mandalay Beach Road, Oxnard; 805-984-2500. For a larger selection of bikes try the rental shop on 22 State Street, Santa Barbara, 805-966-2282.

Despite the name, **Kites Galore** is the place to rent four-wheeled surreys in Morro Bay. ~ 1108 Front Street; 805-772-8322.

HIKING

With its endless beaches and mountain backdrop, the South Central Coast is wide open for exploration. Shoreline paths and mountain trails crisscross the entire region. All distances listed for hiking trails are one way unless otherwise noted.

First among equals in this hiker's dreamland is the **California Coastal Trail**, the 600-mile route that runs the entire length of the state. Here it begins at Point Mugu and travels along state beaches from Ventura County to Santa Barbara. In Santa Barbara the trail turns inland toward the Santa Ynez Mountains and Los Padres National Forest. It returns to the coast at Point Sal, then parallels sand dunes, passes the hot springs at Avila Beach, and continues up the coast to San Simeon.

VENTURA AREA   Bounded by the Santa Monica and Santa Ynez mountains and bordered by 43 miles of shoreline, Ventura County offers a variety of hiking opportunities. (Note, however, that some trails were damaged in the 1993 Southern California fires.) For more information on hiking trails in the area, contact the City of Ventura Community Services Department at 805-658-4733.

Ocean's Edge Trail (.6 mile) is a lovely shore hike from the Emma Wood State Beach to Seaside Wilderness Park; popular with birders.

River's Edge Trail (.3 mile) is a great hike for exploring the riparian woodlands along the Ventura River.

SANTA BARBARA AREA   What distinguishes Santa Barbara from most of California's coastal communities is the magnificent Santa Ynez mountain range, which forms a backdrop to the city and provides excellent hiking terrain.

A red steel gate marks the beginning of **Romero Canyon Trail** (5.75 miles) on Bella Vista Road in Santa Barbara. After joining a fire road at the 2350-foot elevation, the trail follows a stream shaded by oak, sycamore, and bay trees. From here you can keep climbing or return via the right fork, a fire road that offers an easier but longer return trip.

San Ysidro Trail (4.5 miles), which begins at Park Lane and Mountain Drive in Santa Barbara, follows a stream dotted with pools and falls, then climbs to the top of Camino Cielo ridge. For a different loop back, it's a short walk around to Cold Springs Trail.

Also located in the Santa Ynez Mountains is **Rattlesnake Canyon Trail** (3 miles). Beginning near Skofield Park, the trail follows Mission Creek, along which an aqueduct was built in the early 19th century. Portions of the waterway can still be seen. This pleasant trail offers shaded pools and meadows.

Cold Springs Trail, East Fork (4.5 miles) heads east from Mountain Drive in Santa Barbara. The trail takes you through a canyon covered with alder and along a creek punctuated by pools and waterfalls. It continues up into Hot Springs Canyon and crosses the flank of Montecito Peak.

Cold Springs Trail, West Fork (2 miles) leads off the better known East Fork. It climbs and descends along the left side of a lushly vegetated canyon before arriving at an open valley.

Tunnel Trail (4 miles) is named for the turn-of-the-century tunnel through the mountains which brought fresh water to Santa Barbara. The trail begins at the end of Tunnel Road in Santa Barbara and passes through various sandstone formations and crosses a creek before arriving at Mission Falls.

San Antonio Creek Trail (3.5 miles), an easy hike along a creek bed, starts from the far end of Tucker's Grove County Park in Goleta. In the morning or late afternoon you'll often catch glimpses of deer foraging in the woods.

Thirty-five miles of coastline stretches from Stearns Wharf in Santa Barbara to Gaviota State Beach. There are hiking opportunities galore along the entire span.

Summerland Trail (2.5 miles), starting at Lookout Park in Summerland, takes you along Summerland Beach, past tiny coves, then along Montecito's coast to the beach fronting the Biltmore Hotel.

Goleta Beach Trail (3.5 miles) begins at Goleta Beach County Park in Goleta and curves past tidepools and sand dunes en route to Goleta Point. Beyond the dunes is Devereux Slough, a reserve populated by egrets, herons, plovers, and sandpipers. The hike also passes the Ellwood Oil Field where a Japanese submarine fired shots at the mainland United States during World War II.

Gaviota Hot Springs and Peak Trail (2.5 miles) begins in Gaviota State Park. The first stop on this trek is the mineral pools at Gaviota Hot Springs (about a half mile from the trailhead). After a leisurely dip you can continue on a somewhat strenuous route into Los Padres National Forest, climbing to Gaviota Peak for a marvelous view of ranch land and the Pacific.

SAN LUIS OBISPO AREA The San Luis Obispo area, rich in wildlife, offers hikers everything from seaside strolls to mountain treks. Many of the trails in this area are in the Los Padres National Forest (for information, call 805-925-9538).

Guadalupe-Nipomo Dunes Preserve (2.5 miles) is especially rewarding for dune lovers. This wetland area is a habitat for many endangered birds. The boardwalk trail passes a freshwater lake, a willow community, and many dunes, ending at Pismo Beach. At Oso Flaco Lake there's an entrance kiosk with trail and hiking information. ~ 805-343-2455.

The **Point Sal Trail** (6 miles) offers an excellent opportunity to hike in a forgotten spot along the coast. (But beware, it's not for inexperienced hikers or those afraid of heights.) Alternating between cliffs and seashore, the trail takes you past tidepools, pelicans, cormorants, and basking seals. An excellent whale-watching area, the trail ends near the mouth of the Santa Maria River.

The golden mustard plants and poppies along the way give **Montaña de Oro Bluffs Trail** (2 miles) its name ("Mountain of Gold"). This coastal trail takes you past Spooner's Cove (a mooring place for bootleggers during Prohibition). You'll pass clear tidepools, sea caves, basking seals, otters, and ocean bluffs.

For an interesting hike along the sandspit that separates Morro Bay from Estero Bay, try the **Morro Bay Sandspit Trail** (4 miles). The intriguing trail leads past sand dunes and ancient Chumash shell mounds. Stay on the ocean side of the sandspit if you want to avoid the muck.

Several trails in the vicinity of **Lopez Lake Recreational Area** offer opportunities to see the region's flora and fauna. Deer, raccoon, fox, and wood-rats predominate, along with a variety of birds species (not to mention rattlesnakes and poison oak). ~ 805-489-8019.

At the entrance to the park, **Turkey Ridge Trail** (1.1 miles) is a strenuous climb through oak and chaparral and offers splendid views of the lake and the Santa Lucia Mountains.

Two Waters Trail (1.3 miles) connects the Lopez and Wittenberg arms of Lopez Lake. It is a moderate hike with marvelous views. The trailheads are located at Encinal or Miller's Cove.

Blackberry Spring Trail (.75 mile) commences at upper Squirrel campground and passes many plant species used by the Chumash Indians. This is a moderate hike with a 260-foot climb which connects with High Ridge Trail.

Little Falls Creek Trail (2.75 miles) begins along Lopez Canyon Road (High Mountain Road) and ascends 1350 feet up the canyon past a spectacular waterfall. Views of the Santa Lucia wilderness await you at the top of the mountain.

Transportation

As it proceeds north from the Los Angeles area, coastal highway **Route 1** weaves in and out from **Route 101**. The two highways join in Oxnard and continue as a single roadway until a point 30 miles north of Santa Barbara. Here they diverge, Route 1 heading toward the coast while Route 101 takes an inland route. The highways merge again near Pismo Beach and continue north to San Luis Obispo. Here Route 1 leaves Route 101 and begins its long, beautiful course up the coast past Morro Bay and San Simeon.

CAR

AIR

Santa Barbara and San Luis Obispo have small airports serving the Central Coast. Several airlines stop at the **Santa Barbara Municipal Airport**, including American Eagle, America West Express, Sky West Airlines, United Airlines, United Express, and USAir Express.

The **Santa Barbara Airbus** can be scheduled to meet arrivals at the airport; it also goes to Carpinteria, Goleta, and downtown Santa Barbara, as well as Los Angeles International Airport. ~ 805-964-7759, 800-423-1618. There are also a number of taxi companies available. For the disabled, call **Easy Lift Transportation**. ~ 805-568-5114.

San Luis Obispo Municipal Airport is serviced by United Express and Wings West Airlines. ~ 805-781-5205.

Ground transportation from San Luis Obispo Municipal Airport is provided by **Yellow Cab.** ~ 805-543-1234. Or try **Yellow Cab of Five Cities.** ~ 805-489-1155.

BUS

Greyhound Bus Lines (800-231-2222) has continual service along the Central Coast from both Los Angeles and San Francisco. The Ventura bus terminal is located at 291 East Thompson Boulevard; 805-653-0164. Santa Barbara has one at 34 West Carrillo Street; 805-965-3971. The terminal in San Luis Obispo is at 150 South Street; 805-543-2123.

TRAIN

Those who want spectacular views of the coastline, should try **Amtrak**'s "Coast Starlight." This train hugs the shoreline, providing rare views of the South Central Coast's cliffs, headlands, and untracked beaches. Amtrak stops in Oxnard, Santa Barbara, and San Luis Obispo on its way north to Oakland and Seattle. ~ 800-872-7245.

CAR RENTALS

The larger towns in the South Central Coast have car rental agencies; check the Yellow Pages to find the best bargains.

To pick up a car in the Oxnard-Ventura area, try **Avis Rent A Car** (800-331-1212), **Budget Rent A Car** (800-527-0700) or **Hertz Rent A Car** (800-654-3131).

At the airport in Santa Barbara try **Avis Rent A Car** (800-331-1212), **Budget Rent A Car** (800-527-0700), **Hertz Rent A Car** (800-654-3131), or **National Interrent** (800-227-7368). Agencies located outside the airport with free pick-up include **Dollar Rent A Car** (800-800-4000) and **Enterprise Rent A Car** (800-325-8007).

In San Luis Obispo, car-rental agencies at the airport include **Avis Rent A Car** (800-331-1212), **Budget Rent A Car** (800-527-0700), **Hertz Rent A Car** (800-654-3131) and **Thrifty Car Rental** (800-367-2277). Among those with free pickup service, try **Enterprise Rent A Car** (800-325-8007).

PUBLIC TRANSIT

Public transportation in the Central Coast is fairly limited. In the Ventura area you'll find **South Coast Area Transit,** or SCAT, which serves Oxnard, Port Hueneme, and Ventura. ~ 805-487-4222.

In the Santa Barbara area, the **Santa Barbara Metropolitan Transit** stops in Summerland, Carpinteria, Santa Barbara, Goleta, and Isla Vista. ~ Carrillo and Chapala streets; 805-683-3702.

The San Luis Obispo area has **San Luis Obispo Transit,** or SLO, which operates on weekdays during daylight hours and even less frequently on weekends. ~ 805-541-2877.

SIX

Los Angeles Coast

L.A., according to a popular song, is a great big freeway. Actually, this sprawling metropolis by the sea is a great big beach. From Long Beach north to Malibu is a 74-mile stretch of sand that attracts visitors in the tens of millions every year. Life here reflects the culture of the beach, a freewheeling, pleasure-seeking philosophy that combines hedonism with healthfulness. Perfectly fitted to this philosophy is the weather. The coastal climatic zone, called a maritime fringe, is characterized by cooler summers, warmer winters, and higher humidity than elsewhere in California. Sea breezes and salt air keep the beaches relatively free from smog. During summer months the thermometer hovers around 75° or 80° and water temperatures average 67°. Winter carries intermittent rain and brings the ocean down to a chilly 55°.

Add a broadly ranging coastal topography and Los Angeles has an urban escape valve less than an hour from downtown. The shoreline lies along the lip of the Los Angeles basin, a flat expanse interrupted by the sharp cliffs of the Palos Verdes Peninsula and the rocky heights of the Santa Monica Mountains. There are broad strands lapped by gentle waves and pocket beaches exploding with surf. Though most of the coast is built up, some sections remain raw and undeveloped.

Route 1, the Pacific Coast Highway, parallels the coast the entire length of Los Angeles County, tying its beach communities together. To the south lie Long Beach and San Pedro, industrial enclaves which form the port of Los Angeles, a world center for commerce and shipping. Embodying 50 miles of heavily developed waterfront, the port is a maze of inlets, islets, and channels protected by a six-mile breakwater. It is one of the world's largest manmade harbors; over $73 billion in cargo crosses its docks every year. Despite all this hubbub, the harbor supports over 125 fish species and over 90 types of birds, including several endangered species.

The great port dates to 1835 when a small landing was built on the shore. Following the Civil War an imaginative entrepreneur named Phineas Banning developed the area, brought in the railroad, and launched Los Angeles into the 20th-

301

century. Now Long Beach wears several hats. In addition to being a major port and manufacturing center, it is the site of a naval base and a revitalized tourist center.

Home to the retired ocean liner *Queen Mary* and the new Aquarium of the Pacific, Long Beach also contains the neighborhood of Naples, a system of islands, canals, and footbridges reminiscent of Italy's gondola cities.

Once an amusement center complete with airship, carousel, and sword swallowers, the city became one big oil field during the 1920s. That's when wildcat wells struck rich deposits and the region was transformed into a two-square-mile maze of derricks. Even today the offshore "islands" hide hundreds of oil wells.

Commercial fishing, another vital industry in Long Beach and San Pedro, supports an international collection of sailors. Mariners from Portugal, Greece, and elsewhere work the waterfront and add to the ethnic ambience.

Just a few miles north, along the Palos Verdes Peninsula, blue collar gives way to white collar and the urban surrenders to the exotic. A region of exclusive neighborhoods and striking geologic contrasts, Palos Verdes possesses Los Angeles' prettiest seascapes. A series of 13 marine terraces, interrupted by sheer cliffs, descend to a rocky shoreline. For 15 miles the roadway rides high above the surf past tidepools, rocky points, a lighthouse, and secluded coves.

This wealthy suburban environment is replaced in turn by another type of culture, typified by blond-haired surfers. Santa Monica Bay, the predominant feature of the Los Angeles Coast, is a single broad crescent of sand extending 30 miles from Redondo Beach through Venice and Santa Monica to Point Dume. South Bay—comprising the towns of Redondo Beach, Hermosa Beach, and Manhattan Beach—is the surfing center of Southern California, where the sport was first imported from Hawaii. This strip of coast is also home to Los Angeles International Airport.

Like most of the coastal communities, South Bay didn't take off as a beach resort until the turn of the century, after railroad lines were extended from the city center to the shore and several decades after downtown Los Angeles experienced its 1880s population boom.

It was well into the 20th century, 1962 to be exact, that neighboring Marina del Rey, the largest manmade small boat harbor in the world, was developed. Nearby Venice, on the other hand, was an early 1900s attempt to re-create its Italian namesake. Built around plazas and grand canals, Venice originally was a fashionable resort town with oceanfront hotels and an amusement park. Today studios and galleries have replaced canals and gondolas in this seaside artist colony. The place has become a center for thinkers at the cutting edge and street people who have stepped over it. Zany and unchartable, modern-day Venice is an open ward for artists, the place where bohemians go to the beach, where roller skating is an art form and weight lifting a way of life.

The town of Santa Monica next door was originally developed as a beachside resort in 1875. Back in 1769 explorer Gaspar de Portolá had claimed the surrounding area for the Spanish crown. Over the years this royal domain has served as a major port, retirement community, and location for silent movies; today it is a bastion of brown-shingle houses, flower-covered trellises, and left-wing politics.

Bordering it to the north are the Santa Monica Mountains, a succession of rugged peaks which are part of the Transverse Range, the only mountains in California running east and west. Extending to the very edge of the sea, the Santa Monicas create Los Angeles' most varied terrain. White sand beaches are framed by bald peaks, crystal waters and flourishing kelp beds attract abundant sea life and make for excellent fishing and skindiving, while the mountains provide a getaway for hikers and campers.

Lying along a narrow corridor between the Santa Monicas and the sea is Malibu, that quintessential symbol of California, a wealthy, glamorous community known for its movie stars and surfers. Once inhabited by Chumash Indians, a clan whose skeletal remains are still occasionally uncovered, Malibu escaped Los Angeles' coastal development until 1928, when the aging widow who controlled the region like a personal fiefdom finally succumbed to the pressures of progress and profit. Within a few years it became a haven for Hollywood. Stars like Ronald Colman and John Gilbert found their paradise on the sands of Malibu. Like figures out of *The Great Gatsby*, they lived insouciant lives in movie-set houses.

By the 1960s artists and counterculturalists, seeking to flee a town which in turn had become too commercial and crowded, left Malibu for the outlying mountains. In Topanga Canyon they established freeform communities, undermined in recent

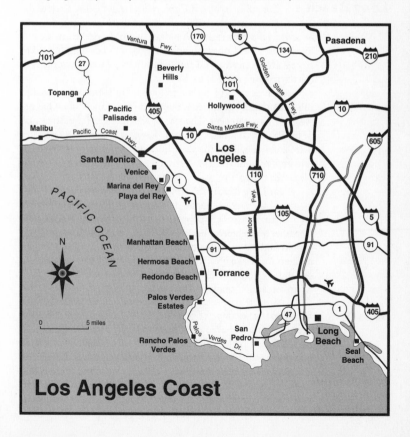

Los Angeles Coast

years by breathtaking real estate prices, but still retaining vestiges of their days as a flower children's retreat.

The most romantic locale along the Los Angeles Coast lies 22 miles offshore. Santa Catalina, highlighted by Avalon, a resort town tucked between mountains and ocean, is a 21-mile-long island almost entirely undeveloped, given over to cactus and grazing buffalo.

Through the centuries this solitary island has undergone many incarnations—habitat for Stone Age Indians; base for Russian fur hunters; center for pirates, smugglers, and gold prospectors; gathering place for the big bands of the 1930s; and strategic military base during World War II. Today it's a singular spot where visitors enjoy the amenities of Avalon and the seclusion of the island's outback. If Avalon, with its art deco waterfront, provides a picture of Los Angeles circa 1933, the rest of the island is a window on Los Angeles in its natural state, wild and alluring, long before freighters embarked from Long Beach, surfers worked the South Bay, and movie moguls uncovered Malibu.

▼▼▼▼▼▼▼▼▼▼
Long Beach

Anchoring the southern end of Los Angeles County is Long Beach, one of California's largest cities. Back in the Roaring Twenties, after oil was discovered and the area experienced a tremendous building boom, Long Beach became known as "The Coney Island of the West." Boasting five miles of beachfront and a grand amusement park, it was a favorite spot for daytripping Angelenos.

Several decades of decline followed, but recently the metropolis began a $2 billion redevelopment plan dubbed the Queensway Bay Development. The star of this facelift is the Aquarium of the Pacific, completed in 1998. Together with the *Queen Mary* and Shoreline Village, the aquarium rounds out an oceanfront triumvirate of family-oriented attractions, each of which is accessible to the others by a water taxi called the AquaBus.

Today Long Beach ranks together with neighboring San Pedro as one of the largest manmade harbors in the world and is becoming an increasingly popular tourist destination. Ignoring the Chamber of Commerce hoopla about the city's refurbishment, you should find it a revealing place, a kind of social studies lesson in modern American life. Travel Ocean Boulevard as it parallels the sea and you'll pass from quaint homes to downtown skyscrapers to fire-breathing smokestacks.

SIGHTS

For a dynamic example of what I mean, visit the enclave of **Naples** near the south end of town. Conceived early in the century, modeled on Italy's fabled canal towns, it's a tiny community of three islands separated by canals and linked with walkways. Waterfront greenswards gaze out on Alamitos Bay and its fleet of sloops and motorboats. You can wander along bayside paths past comfortable homes, contemporary condos, and humble cottages. Fountains and miniature traffic circles, alleyways and boulevards, all form an amazing labyrinth along which you undoubtedly will become lost.

Adding to the sense of old Italia is the **Gondola Getaway**, a romantic hour-long cruise through the canals of Naples. For a hefty price (less, however, than a ticket to Italy), you can climb aboard a gondola, dine on hors d'oeuvres, sip champagne and be serenaded with Italian music. ~ 5437 East Ocean Boulevard; 562-433-9595.

The **Long Beach Museum of Art** is a must. Dedicated to 20th-century art, this avant-garde museum has ever-changing exhibitions ranging from German Expressionism to contemporary Southern California work. Particularly noted for its video presentations, the museum is a window on modern culture. Closed Monday and Tuesday. Admission. ~ 2300 East Ocean Boulevard; 562-439-2119.

In 1996, in a converted skating rink, the **Museum of Latin American Art** opened officially with just two small galleries for exhibits. Then in 1998, it burst onto the cultural scene with an additional 10,000 square feet of gallery space inaugurated with a spectacular show by Oaxacan artist Laura Hernandez. The museum collects and exhibits only contemporary artists of Mexico and Central America. The museum store sells the works of local and Latin American artists. For children there are hands-on art-making workshops on Sunday. Closed Monday. Admission. ~ 628 Alamitos Avenue; 562-437-1689.

◄ HIDDEN

Across the street, the **Oceanic Art Museum Gallery** is divided between a small museum for tightly focused exhibits, such as *tapa* (barkcloth) or warrior clubs. For sale in the gallery are traditional Micronesian arts and crafts created by a guild of master artisans and apprentices on the island of Yap. Closed Monday through Wednesday. ~ 694 Alamitos Avenue; 562-432-4477.

For a touch of early Mexican culture, plan to visit the region's old adobes. Built in the 1800s with walls more than three feet

✔ CHECK THESE OUT—UNIQUE SIGHTS

- Step aboard the **Queen Mary** and explore the deco beauty of the 1000-foot-long "grand lady" from poop deck to pump room. *page 307*
- Flex your biceps at **Muscle Beach**—or just ogle others—in the roiling activity of Venice's boardwalk. *page 327*
- Get on your high horse and ride the antique carousel that was featured in the movie *The Sting* at the **Santa Monica Pier**. *page 333*
- Take a dip or drop a line at **Parson's Landing**, a remote Catalina campground situated on a brown-gray sand beach. *page 356*

thick, **Rancho Los Alamitos** is Southern California's oldest remaining house. In its gardens, which cover more than three acres, are brick walkways and majestic fig trees. You can tour old barns, a blacksmith shop, and a feed shed. There's also a chuck wagon with a coffeepot still resting on the wood-burning stove. Closed Monday and Tuesday. ~ 6400 Bixby Hill Road; 562-431-3541.

Rancho Los Cerritos, a two-story Monterey Colonial home, once served as headquarters for a 27,000-acre ranch. Surrounded by gardens, the 19th-century adobe is filled with Victorian furniture. Closed Monday and Tuesday. ~ 4600 Virginia Road; 562-570-1755.

The Pacific Ocean may be Long Beach's biggest natural attraction, but many birds in the area prefer the **El Dorado Nature Center**. Part of the 450-acre El Dorado East Regional Park, this 103-acre wildlife sanctuary offers one- and two-mile hikes past two lakes and a stream. About 150 bird species as well as numerous land animals can be sighted. Though located in a heavily urbanized area, the facility encompasses several ecological zones. There's also a quarter-mile paved, handicapped-accessible nature trail. Closed Monday. Admission. ~ 7550 East Spring Street; 562-570-1745.

Chapter Two in the Long Beach civics lesson is the steel-and-glass downtown area, where highrise hotels vie for dominance. The best way to tour this crowded commercial district is to stroll **The Promenade**, a six-block brick walkway leading from 3rd Street to the waterfront. There's a **tile mosaic** (Promenade and 3rd Street) at the near end portraying an idyllic day at the beach complete with colorful sailboats, sunbathers, and lifeguards. Midway along the landscaped thoroughfare sits the **Long Beach Area Convention & Visitors Bureau**, home to maps, brochures, and other bits of information. ~ 1 World Trade Center, #300; 562-436-3645. Then you'll arrive at a park shaded with palm trees and adjacent to **Shoreline Village**, a shopping center and marina disguised as a 19th-century fishing village. ~ 407 Shoreline Village Drive.

Long Beach Part III rises in the form of oil derricks and industrial complexes just across the water. To view the freighters, tankers, and warships lining the city's piers, gaze out from the northern fringes of Shoreline Village.

Fittingly, the climax of a Long Beach tour comes at the very end, after you have experienced the three phases of urban existence. Just across the Los Angeles River, along Harbor Scenic Drive ("scenic" in this case meaning construction cranes and cargo containers), lies one of the strangest sights I've ever encountered. The first time I saw it, peering through the steel filigree of a suspension bridge, with harbor lights emblazoning the scene, I thought something had gone colossally wrong with the world. An old-style ocean liner, gleaming eerily in the false light, appeared to be parked on the ground. Next to it an overgrown geodesic dome, a kind of giant aluminum breast, was swelling up out of the earth.

Unwittingly I had happened upon Long Beach's number one tourist attraction, the *Queen Mary*, once the world's largest ocean liner. Making her maiden voyage in 1936, the **Queen Mary** was the pride of Great Britain. Winston Churchill, the Duke and Duchess of Windsor, Greta Garbo, and Fred Astaire sailed on her, and during World War II, she was converted to military service.

Today she is the pride of Long Beach, a 1000-foot-long "city at sea" transformed into a floating museum and hotel that brilliantly re-create shipboard life. An elaborate walking tour carries you down into the engine room (a world of pumps and propellers), out along the decks, and up to each level of this multistage behemoth. There's a parking fee and admission to the boat (the admission fee is waived for hotel guests).

The *Queen Mary* is expertly refurbished and wonderfully laid out, an important addition to the Long Beach seafront and the anchor attraction for Queen Mary Seaport, which also includes The Queen's Marketplace shopping and dining area. Her neighbor is the world's largest clear-span geodesic dome. The dome, now a Warner Brothers soundstage, once housed Howard Hughes' *Spruce Goose*, the largest plane ever built. Admission. ~ 1126 Queen's Highway; 562-435-3511.

Since Marine World closed down years ago, the Los Angeles–Long Beach area has been without a major marine-themed attrac-

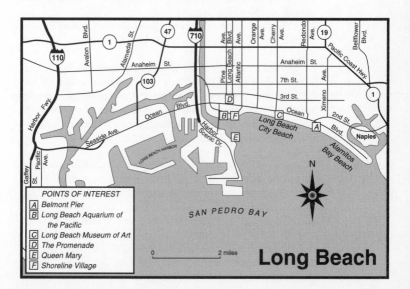

POINTS OF INTEREST
A Belmont Pier
B Long Beach Aquarium of
   the Pacific
C Long Beach Museum of Art
D The Promenade
E Queen Mary
F Shoreline Village

SAN PEDRO BAY

0 —————— 2 miles

Long Beach

tion. The opening of the **Long Beach Aquarium of the Pacific** has now filled that void. The aquarium, part of the waterfront Rainbow Harbor development in downtown Long Beach, has three major permanent galleries designed to lead visitors on a "journey of discovery" through the waters of the Pacific Ocean. The journey begins in the temperate waters of Southern California and Baja, and includes tidepools and endangered sea turtles. The Bering Sea is the focus of the exhibit representing the icy waters of the northern Pacific, which are inhabited by sea otters, a giant octopus, and spider crabs. The coral reefs and lagoons of Palau in Micronesia are spotlighted in the tropical Pacific gallery, which also features the huge Tropical Reef Tank where microphone-equipped scuba divers swim along with schools of brilliant fish and sharks, answering questions for visitors. Admission. ~ 100 Aquarium Way, Long Beach; 562-590-3100.

The *Queen Mary* carried so many troops across the Atlantic Ocean that Adolf Hitler offered $250,000 and the Iron Cross to the U-boat captain who sank her.

Long Beach's latest effort to draw tourists is the Soviet-built submarine **Scorpion**, which will be docked alongside the *Queen Mary* until 2003. Visitors enter through the forward hatch of the 300-foot Foxtrot-class Russian sub, then squeeze their way along corridors for a look through the periscope and a self-guided tour of the torpedo room, crew quarters and communications center. Admission. ~ 1126 Queen's Highway; 562-435-3511.

The **AquaBus**, a new water taxi service, links the city's main waterfront attractions—the aquarium, Shoreline Village, the *Queen Mary*, Catalina Express, and the convention center—with daily service. ~ 800-429-4601.

Long Beach is also a departure point for the **Catalina Express** shuttle boats to Santa Catalina Island. ~ 526-519-1212 or 800-897-7154.

Beyond all the shoreline hubbub, the venerable Pacific gray whales migrate along the "Whale Freeway" between late December and mid-April, and enterprises in Long Beach offer whale-watching opportunities. The Long Beach Area Convention & Visitors Bureau can put you in touch with a whale-watching operator. ~ 562-436-3645.

LODGING   Beach Terrace Manor Motel is a 43-unit complex which occupies both sides of a side street off Long Beach's main drag. Mock-Tudor in design, the facility has several units fronting the beach; most are equipped with kitchen facilities. Guest rooms are comfortable, though undistinguished. At a very reasonable price for a room with a kitchen, the Beach Terrace provides a fair bargain. ~ 1700 East Ocean Boulevard; 562-436-8204, fax 562-436-2474. MODERATE TO DELUXE.

The **Surf Motel**, with a similar layout, has 40 units, some with ocean views, many offering kitchens and all with easy access to the beach. Each room is furnished in contemporary fashion. There's also a pool and jacuzzi. ~ 2010 East Ocean Boulevard; 562-437-0771, fax 562-437-0900. MODERATE TO DELUXE.

Granted I'm a fool for gimmicks, but somehow the opportunity to stay aboard a historic ocean liner seems overwhelming. Where else but at the **Hotel Queen Mary** can you recapture the magic of British gentility before World War II? What other hotel offers guests a "sunning deck"? Staying in the original staterooms of this grand old vessel, permanently docked on the Long Beach waterfront, you are surrounded by the art deco designs for which the *Queen Mary* is famous. Some guest rooms are small (this *is* a ship!) and dimly illuminated through portholes, but the decor is classic. There are also several restaurants, lounges, and shops on board. ~ 1126 Queen's Highway; 562-432-6964. MODERATE TO ULTRA-DELUXE.

DINING

One of the first small brewery-restaurants in the Long Beach area, the **Belmont Brewing Company** brews pale and amber ales, seasonal beers, and a dark, rich porter—Long Beach Crude—which closely resembles the real stuff pumped from nearby coastal oil derricks. Gourmet pizzas, fresh seafood, and pastas are served in the dining area, at the bar, and outside on the patio. I'd opt for the patio where you can enjoy watching the sun set over the water. ~ 25 39th Place; 562-433-3891. MODERATE.

Appropriately located next door to the Museum of Latin American Art, **Viva** restaurant is only open for lunch and Sunday brunch. Dine indoors or out, selecting dishes from a menu that reflects the diversity of Latin American cooking: jicama and orange salad is a traditional Mexican ensalada; *fricase de pollo* is a *plato principale* from Cuba; the *torta* is the traditional Mexican sandwich made with marinated beef; and the *enchilada de espincaca y ajo* is inspired by a Salvadoran recipe. ~ 644 Alamitos Avenue; 562-435-4048. BUDGET.

Southern cooking at the **Shenandoah Café** is becoming a tradition among savvy shore residents. The quilts and baskets decorating this understated establishment lend a country air. Add waitresses in aprons dishing out hot apple fritters and it gets downright homey. Dinner and Sunday brunch are special events occasioned with shrimp in beer batter, "riverwalk steak" (sirloin steak in mustard caper sauce), salmon on wild-rice pancake, "granny's fried chicken," gumbo and Texas-style beef brisket. Try it! ~ 4722 East 2nd Street; 562-434-3469. MODERATE TO DELUXE.

◄ HIDDEN

In downtown Long Beach the **King's Pine Avenue Fish House** is a prime spot for seafood. The private booths and dark wood trim lend an antique atmosphere to this open-kitchen establishment. The seafood platters are too numerous to recite (besides, the menu changes daily); suffice it to say that you can have them sautéed, baked, broiled, or grilled. For those not keen on seafood, there are also pasta, pizza and chicken to choose from. ~ 100 West Broadway; 562-432-7463. MODERATE TO DELUXE.

For Italian fare, there's **L'Opera,** a plate-glass dining room with views of the Blue Line train. The chef is from Rome and the menu represents a mixture of classical and modern dishes. There's a seafood, chicken, rice, and pasta dish of the day, everyday. ~ 101 Pine Avenue; 562-491-0066. MODERATE TO DELUXE.

Back in the world of good eats and frugal budgets, **Acapulco Mexican Restaurant & Cantina** offers standard as well as innovative dishes. Tacos, burritos, and enchiladas are only the beginning; this comfortable eatery also serves Mexican-style seafood dishes. ~ 6270 East Pacific Coast Highway; 562-596-3371. BUDGET TO MODERATE.

The Reef is rambling, ramshackle, and wonderful. Built of rough-sawn cedar, it sits along the waterfront on a dizzying series of levels. The walls may be decorated with rusty signs and antique farm implements, but the cuisine includes such contemporary choices as seafood collage and beer batter shrimp. For the traditionalists, there are steaks and swordfish. ~ 880 Harbor Scenic Drive; 562-435-8013. DELUXE TO ULTRA-DELUXE.

What more elegant a setting in which to dine than aboard the *Queen Mary.* There you will find everything from snack kiosks to coffee shops to first-class dining rooms. The **Promenade Café** offers a well-priced menu of chicken, steak, seafood, and vegetarian dishes. They also have salads, sandwiches, and hamburgers. The coffee shop is a lovely art deco room featuring period lamps and wicker furnishings. ~ 1126 Queen's Highway; 562-435-3511. MODERATE.

For a true taste of regal life aboard the old ship, cast anchor at **Sir Winston's.** The Continental cuisine in this dining emporium includes rack of lamb, veal, duck, venison, châteaubriand, swordfish, and lobster. Sir Winston's is a wood-paneled dining room with copper-rimmed mirrors, white tablecloths, and upholstered armchairs. The walls are adorned with photos of the great prime minister and every window opens onto a full view of Long Beach. Men must wear a jacket and women must wear a dress or pantsuit. Reservations required. Dinner only. ~ 1126 Queen's Highway; 562-435-3511. ULTRA-DELUXE.

SHOPPING   The best street shopping in Long Beach is in Belmont Shore along **East 2nd Street.** This 15-block strip between Livingston Drive and Bayshore Avenue is a gentrified row. Either side is lined with art galleries, book shops, boutiques, jewelers, and import stores.

For **vintage-store and antiques** shoppers, Redondo Avenue, East Broadway, and East 4th Street in downtown Long Beach have nearly two dozen stores where you can find everything from Bauer pottery to antique furniture to Depression glass to beaded sweaters. Look for a copy of the Long Beach Antique and Vintage Shopping Guide to help you map out your itinerary.

Shoreline Village is one of those waterfront malls Southern California specializes in. With a marina on one side, the buildings are New England–style shingle and clapboard structures designed to re-create an Atlantic Coast port town. The village features an endangered species eco-park featuring such rainforest rarities as poison arrow frogs, pygmy hedgehogs, and giant stick insects. ~ 407 Shoreline Village Drive; 562-435-2668.

There are more than a dozen stores onboard the **Queen Mary**. There is a fee charged to board the ship. Concentrated in the Piccadilly Circus section of the old ship are several souvenir shops as well as stores specializing in artifacts and old-fashioned items. Perhaps the prettiest shopping arcade you'll ever enter, it is an art deco masterpiece complete with etched glass, dentil molding, and brass appointments. ~ 1126 Queen's Highway; 562-435-3511.

Adjacent to the *Queen Mary*, **The Queen's Marketplace** is a shopping plaza styled after a 19th-century British village and offering a variety of specialty and souvenir shops.

NIGHTLIFE

Panama Joe's cooks seven nights a week. The bands are blues ensembles, rock groups, and assorted others, which create an eclectic blend of music. Your average Tiffany-lamp-and-hanging-plant nightspot, the place is lined with sports photos and proudly displays an old oak bar. ~ 5100 East 2nd Street; 562-434-7417.

E. J. Malloy's is a small sports bar with a comfortable pub-style interior including a long wood bar, brick walls, and plenty of televisions for watching a Kings hockey game with the locals. There's also an outdoor courtyard with a fireplace, bar, and patio seating. The sports fans can get loud and rambunctious on game nights. ~ 3411 East Broadway; 562-433-3769.

Located right along the promenade in downtown Long Beach is **The Blue Café**. This tavern serves up live blues, swing, and alternative music seven nights a week and tasty dishes from the deli and grill. Hip hustlers hang out upstairs where there are plenty of billiard tables. Cover. ~ 210 Promenade North; 562-983-7111.

No matter how grand, regardless of how much money went into its design, despite the care taken to assure quality, any Long Beach nightspot is hard pressed to match the elegance of the **Observation Bar** aboard the *Queen Mary*. Once the first-class bar for this grand old ship, the room commands a 180° view across the bow and out to the Long Beach skyline. The walls are lined with fine woods, a mural decorates the bar, and art deco appointments appear everywhere. The bar features live mellow rock music as well as soft ballads on weekends. For even softer sounds you can always adjourn aft to **Sir Winston's Piano Bar**, a cozy and elegant setting decorated with memorabilia of the World War II British leader. ~ 1126 Queen's Highway; 562-435-3511.

GAY SCENE   A long-time favorite is **Ripples**, which has a dance club upstairs and a bar downstairs. There's also a game room, pool table, darts, and patio. Live entertainment on Sunday. Cover. ~ 5101 East Ocean Boulevard; 562-433-0357. **Mineshaft** has pool tables, pinball machines, and live deejay music Friday, Saturday, and Tuesday. ~ 1720 East Broadway; 562-436-2433.

The **Falcon** is a gay bar complete with pool table, CD player, pinball machines, and several dart boards. ~ 1435 East Broadway; 562-432-4146.

BEACHES & PARKS

ALAMITOS PENINSULA   The ocean side of this slender salient offers a pretty sand beach looking out on a tiny island. Paralleling the beach is an endless string of woodframe houses. The sand corridor extends all the way to the entrance of Alamitos Bay where a stone jetty provides recreation for anglers, surfers, swimmers and climbers with sturdy hiking shoes. Facilities include restrooms, lifeguards in summer, and volleyball courts; the paved bike path leading to Long Beach Aquarium begins here. ~ Located along Ocean Boulevard between 54th Place and 72nd Place; park at the end of the road.

BAYSHORE BEACH   This hook-shaped strand curves along the eastern and southern shores of a narrow inlet. Houses line the beach along most of its length. Protected from the ocean by a peninsula and breakwater, the beach faces the waterfront community of Naples. Protected from surf and tide, this is a safe, outstanding spot for swimming, and conditions are perfect for windsurfing. At the corner of Bayshore and Ocean there are basketball and volleyball courts as well as kayak and sailboat rentals. Restrooms are available at the beach. ~ Located along Bayshore Avenue and Ocean Boulevard; 562-570-3215.

LONG BEACH CITY BEACH   They don't call it Long Beach for nothing. This strand is broad and boundless, a silvery swath traveling much of the length of the town. There are several islets parked offshore. Along the miles of beachfront you'll find numerous facilities and good size crowds. Belmont Pier, a 1300-foot-long, hammerhead-shaped walkway, bisects the beach and offers boat tours and fishing services. Fishing is good from the pier, where halibut and sea bass are common catches, and the beach is protected by the harbor breakwater, making for safe swimming. A paved bike path leads to the Long Beach

Aquarium of the Pacific. Along the beach you'll find restrooms, lifeguards, a snack bar, a playground, and volleyball courts. ~ Located along Ocean Boulevard between 1st and 72nd places. Belmont Pier is at Ocean Boulevard and 39th Place; 562-570-1360.

Overlooking the busy Port of Los Angeles and scored by shipping channels, San Pedro lies at the eastern end of the rocky Palos Verdes Peninsula. In 1542 Portuguese explorer Juan Cabrillo sailed into the bay and named it "Bay of Smokes," inspired by the hillside fires of the Gabrieleño Indians; San Pedro was given its current name by Spanish navigator Sebastian Vizcaino in 1602. The city began to develop its reputation as a major port in the mid-19th century, when the railroad came to town. Almost 100 years later, during World War II, Fort MacArthur was built on the bluff to protect the bustling harbor from invasion. Now, the fort houses a small museum and a youth hostel. All manner of boats, from tankers to fishing vessels, cruise the bay in peace.

▼▼▼▼▼▼▼▼▼▼
San Pedro

The Los Angeles Harbor, a region of creosote and rust, is marked by 28 miles of busy waterfront. This landscape of oil tanks and cargo containers services thousands of ships every year.

SIGHTS

Head over to the **22nd Street Landing** and watch sportfishing boats embark on high sea adventures. Then wander the waterfront and survey this frontier of steel and oil. Here awkward, unattractive ships glide as gracefully as figure skaters and the machinery of civilization goes about the world's work with a clatter and boom. The most common shorebirds are cargo cranes. ~ At the foot of 22nd Street.

◀ HIDDEN

Ports O' Call Village, a shopping mall in the form of a 19th-century port town, houses several outfits conducting harbor cruises. ~ The entrance is at foot of 6th Street; 310-831-0287. The boats sail around the San Pedro waterfront and venture out for glimpses of the surrounding shoreline; for information, call **Spirit Cruises**. ~ Ports O' Call Village; 310-548-8080.

Moored serenely between two bustling docks is the **S.S. Lane Victory**. This World War II cargo ship, a 455-foot-long National Historic Landmark, has undergone a 2.5-million-dollar restoration and offers weekend cruises in the summer as well as daily tours. Admission. ~ Berth 94; 310-519-9545.

For more of our history on the sea, stop by the **Los Angeles Maritime Museum**. This dockside showplace displays models of ships ranging from fully rigged brigs to 19th-century steam sloops to World War II battleships. There's even an 18-foot re-creation of the ill-starred *Titanic* and the ocean liner model used to film *The Poseidon Adventure*. Closed Monday. ~ Berth 84; 310-548-7618.

HIDDEN ▶ Another piece in the port's historic puzzle is placed several miles inland at the **Phineas Banning Residence Museum**. This imposing Greek Revival house, built in 1864, was home to the man who dreamed, dredged, and developed Los Angeles Harbor. Today Phineas Banning's Mansion, complete with a cupola from which he watched ships navigate his port, is furnished in period pieces and open for guided tours. Closed Monday and Friday. ~ 401 East M Street, Wilmington; 310-548-7777.

By definition any shipping center is of strategic importance. Head up to **Fort MacArthur** and discover the batteries with which World War II generals planned to protect Los Angeles Harbor. From this cement-and-steel compound you can inspect the bunkers and a small military museum, then survey the coast. Once a site of gun turrets and grisly prospects, today it is a testimonial to the invasion that never came. ~ Angel's Gate Park, 3601 South Gaffey Street; 310-548-2631.

Another war, the Korean, will be commemorated in a monument being built nearby, but until it's completed you can visit the **Bell of Friendship**, which the people of South Korea presented to the United States during its 1976 bicentennial. Housed in a multicolor pagoda and cast with floral and symbolic images, it rests on a hilltop looking out on Los Angeles Harbor and the region's sharply profiled coastline.

Extending along 6th Street between Mesa Street and Harbor Boulevard is the Sportswalk, featuring plaques dedicated to Olympic medalists as well as great collegiate and professional athletes.

Down the hill at the **Cabrillo Marine Aquarium**, there is a modest collection of display cases with samples of shells, coral, and shorebirds. Several dozen aquariums demonstrate local fish and marine plants. Closed Monday. Admission. ~ 3720 Stephen M. White Drive; 310-548-7562. Nearby stretches 1200-foot **Cabrillo Fishing Pier**.

Of greater interest is **Point Fermin Park**, a 37-acre blufftop facility resting above spectacular tidepools and a marine preserve. The tidepools are accessible from the Cabrillo Marine Aquarium, which sponsors exploratory tours, and via steep trails from the park. Also of note (though not open to the public) is the **Point Fermin Lighthouse**, a unique 19th-century clapboard house with a beacon set in a rooftop crow's nest. From the park plateau, like lighthouse keepers of old, you'll have open vistas of the cliff-fringed coastline and a perfect perch for sighting whales during their winter migration. ~ 807 Paseo del Mar; 310-548-7756.

Then drive along Paseo del Mar, through arcades of stately palm trees and along sharp sea cliffs, until it meets 25th Street. The sedimentary rocks throughout this region have been twisted and contorted into grotesque shapes by tremendous geologic pressures.

San Pedro is also a departure point for the **Catalina Express shuttle boats** to Santa Catalina Island. ~ 800-897-7154.

Hostelling International—Los Angeles South Bay is located in the army barracks of old Fort MacArthur. Set in Angel's Gate Park on a hilltop overlooking the ocean, it's a pretty site with easy access to beaches. Men and women are housed separately in dorms but couples can be accommodated. Kitchen facilities are provided. ~ 3601 South Gaffey Street, Building 613; 310-831-2836. BUDGET.

The vintage shopping mall at **Ports O' Call Village** is Los Angeles Harbor's prime tourist center. It's situated right on the San Pedro waterfront and houses numerous restaurants. Try to avoid the high-ticket dining rooms, as they are overpriced and serve mediocre food to out-of-town hordes. But there are a number of takeout stands and ethnic eateries, priced in the budget and moderate ranges, which provide an opportunity to dine inexpensively on the water. ~ The entrance is at the foot of 6th Street; 310-831-0287.

Of course local fishermen rarely frequent Ports O' Call. The old salts are over at **Canetti's Seafood Grotto**. It ain't on the waterfront, but it is within casting distance of the fishing fleet. Which means it's just the right spot for fresh fish platters at good prices. Dinner Friday and Saturday; breakfast and lunch all week. ~ 309 East 22nd Street; 310-831-4036. MODERATE.

Trade the Pacific for the Aegean and set anchor at **Papadakis Taverna**. The menu offers moussaka, Greek-style cheese dishes, halibut baked *plaki*-style with tomatoes, wine, rosemary, garlic, and onion, and occasional specials like stuffed eggplant, fresh seafood, and regional delicacies. Dinner only. ~ 301 West 6th Street; 310-548-1186. DELUXE.

Los Angeles Harbor's answer to the theme shopping mall craze is **Ports O' Call Village**, a mock 19th-century fishing village. There are clapboard stores with shuttered windows, New England–style structures with gabled roofs, and storehouses of corrugated metal. Dozens of shops here are located right on the water, giving you a chance to view the harbor while browsing the stores. It's one of those hokey but inevitable places that I vow to avoid but always seem to end up visiting. ~ The entrance is located at the foot of 6th Street; 310-831-0287.

Landlubbers can enjoy a quiet drink on the waterfront at **Ports O' Call Restaurant**. In addition to a spiffy oak bar, they have a dockside patio. ~ Ports O' Call Village; 310-833-3553.

CABRILLO BEACH The edge of Los Angeles harbor is an unappealing locale for a beach, but here it is, a two-part strand, covered with heavy-grain sand and bisected by a fishing pier. One half faces the shipping facility; the other half looks out on the glorious Pacific and abuts on the Point Fermin Marine Life Refuge, a rocky corridor filled with outstanding tidepools and backdropped by dramatic cliffs. You'll also find restrooms, picnic areas, lifeguards, a snack bar on the pier, a museum, a playground, and volleyball courts. Fires are permitted, and restaurants and groceries are available in nearby San Pedro. Fishing can be done from the pier, and for surfing try the beachfront and near the jetty; windsurfing is great in this area as well. People do swim here, but I saw a lot of refuse from the nearby shipping harbor. After heavy rains, storm drainage increases the bacteria count; stick to the ocean side during these times. If you like tidepooling, beeline to Cabrillo—if not, there are hundreds of other beaches in the Golden State. Day-use fee, $6. ~ 3720 Stephen M. White Drive; 310-372-2166.

ROYAL PALMS BEACH 🏃 ⛱ 🐟 🏄 🛶 Situated at the base of a sedimentary cliff, this boulder-strewn beach gains its name from a grove of elegant palm trees. This was an erstwhile hub of elegant activity in the 1920s; the Royal Palms Country Club and a Japanese-owned resort presided here until a violent storm destroyed them in 1939. Today the guests of honor are surfers and tidepoolers. While the location is quite extraordinary, I prefer another beach, Point Fermin Park's **Wilder Annex**, located to the south. This little gem also lacks sand, but is built on three tiers of a cliff. The upper level is decorated with palm trees, the middle tier has a grassy plot studded with shady magnolias, and the bottom floor is a rocky beach with promising tidepools and camera-eye views of Point Fermin. Fishing is good at both parks, but for swimming you should stick with Royal Palms, since there are lifeguards. Surfing is popular at Royal Palms and off White Point, a peninsula separating the two parks. Facilities are limited to restrooms. Day-use fee, $6. ~ Both parks are located along Paseo del Mar in San Pedro. Royal Palms is near the intersection with Western Avenue and Wilder Annex is around the intersection with Meyler Street; 310-372-2166.

▼▼▼▼▼▼▼▼▼▼▼▼▼▼
Palos Verdes Peninsula

Just a few miles west of San Pedro, along the Palos Verdes Peninsula, blue collar gives way to white collar, and the urban surrenders to the exotic. A region of exclusive neighborhoods and striking geologic contrasts, Palos Verdes possesses Los Angeles' prettiest seascapes. A series of 13 marine terraces, interrupted by sheer cliffs, descend to a rocky shoreline. For 15 miles the roadway rides high above the surf past tidepools, rocky points, a lighthouse and secluded coves.

The forces of nature seem to dominate as you proceed out along the Palos Verdes Peninsula from San Pedro. Follow 25th Street, then Palos Verdes Drive South and encounter a tumbling region where terraced hills fall away to sharp coastal bluffs.

As you turn **Portuguese Bend**, the geology of this tumultuous area becomes startlingly evident when the road begins undulating through landslide zones. The earthquake faults that underlie the Los Angeles basin periodically fold and collapse the ground here. To one side you'll see the old road, fractured and useless. Even the present highway, with more patches than your favorite dungarees, is in a state of constant repair.

Of course the terrible power of nature has not dissuaded people from building here. Along the ridgetops and curving hills below are colonies of stately homes. With its rocky headlands, tidepool beaches and sun-spangled views, the place is simply so magnificent no one can resist.

Most lordly of all these structures is **The Wayfarer's Chapel**, a simple but extraordinary center designed by the son of Frank Lloyd Wright. Nestled neatly into the surrounding landscape, the sunlit chapel is built entirely of glass and commands broad views of the terrain and ocean. With its stone altar and easy repose the chapel was built to honor Emanuel Swedenborg, the 18th-century Swedish philosopher and mystic. ~ 5755 Palos Verdes Drive South, Rancho Palos Verdes; 310-377-1650.

The **Point Vicente Lighthouse** rises further down the coast, casting an antique aura upon the area. While the beacon is not

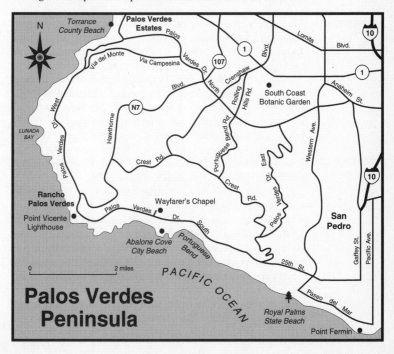

Palos Verdes Peninsula

open to the public, the nearby **Point Vicente Interpretive Center** offers a small regional museum. This is a prime whale-watching spot in the winter when onlookers gather in the adjacent park to catch glimpses of migrating gray whales. Admission. ~ 31501 Palos Verdes Drive West, Rancho Palos Verdes; 310-377-5370.

For a vision of how truly beautiful this region is, turn off Palos Verdes Drive West in Palos Verdes Estates and follow Paseo Lunado until it meets the sea at **Lunada Bay**. This half-moon inlet, backdropped by the jagged face of a rocky cliff, looks out upon an unending expanse of ocean. Steep paths lead downward to a rocky shoreline rich in tidepools.

HIDDEN ▶

The road changes names to Paseo del Mar but continues past equally extraordinary coastline. There is a series of open fields and vista points along this **shoreline preserve** where you can gaze down from the blufftop to beaches and tidepools. Below, surfers ride the curl of frothing breaks and a few hardy hikers pick their way goatlike along precipitous slopes.

The setting is decidedly more demure at the **South Coast Botanic Garden**. This 87-acre garden is planted with exotic vegetation from Africa and New Zealand as well as species from other parts of the world. Admission. ~ 26300 South Crenshaw Boulevard, Palos Verdes; 310-544-6815.

DINING

Restaurants are a rare commodity along the Palos Verdes Peninsula. You'll find a cluster of them, however, in the Golden Cove Shopping Center. Granted, a mall is not the most appetizing spot to dine, but in this case who's complaining?

The Admiral Risty is one of those nautical cliché restaurants decorated along the outside with ropes and pilings and on the interior with brass fixtures. Know the type? Normally I wouldn't mention it, but the place has a full bar, a knockout view of the ocean, and happens to be the only member of its species in the entire area. My advice is to play it safe and order fresh fish (or never leave the bar). The menu is a surf-and-turf inventory of local fish (prepared four ways), steaks, chicken dishes, and so on. Dinner and Sunday brunch. ~ 31250 Palos Verdes Drive West, Rancho Palos Verdes; 310-377-0050. DELUXE.

For genuine elegance, make lunch or dinner reservations at **La Rive Gauche**, an attractively appointed French restaurant. With its upholstered chairs, brass wall sconces, and vintage travel posters, this cozy candlelit dining room is unique to the peninsula. The three-course dinner menu is a study in classic French cooking including veal chop with *foie gras* and truffles, duck à l'orange, venison in sherry sauce, rack of lamb in garlic, and a selection of fresh seafood like Norway salmon and John Dory in saffron Pernod–flavored cream sauce. A pianist adds to the romance. The lunch offerings, while more modest, follow a similar theme. In sum, excellent gourmet cuisine, warm ambience, and a world-class wine list. No lunch on Monday. ~ 320 Tejon Place, Palos Verdes Estates; 310-378-0267. DELUXE TO ULTRA-DELUXE.

ABALONE COVE SHORELINE PARK 🏃 ⛱ 🏊 ⛵ The Palos Verdes Peninsula is so rugged and inaccessible that any beach by definition will be secluded. This gray sand hideaway is no exception. It sits in a natural amphitheater guarded by sedimentary rock formations and looks out on Catalina Island. There are tidepools to ponder and a marine ecological reserve to explore, and the fishing and swimming are good. For surfing, try the east end of the cove. There are also picnic areas, restrooms, and lifeguards on weekends, holidays, and in summer. Parking fee, $5. ~ The beach is located off Palos Verdes Drive South in Rancho Palos Verdes. From the parking lot a path leads down to the beach; 310-377-1222.

BEACHES & PARKS

TORRANCE COUNTY BEACH 🚴 ⛱ 🏃 ⛴ ⛵ This beach is a lengthy stretch of bleach-blond sand guarded on one flank by the stately Palos Verdes Peninsula and on the other by an industrial complex and colony of smokestacks. Just your average middle class beach; it's not one of my favorites, but it has the only white sand hereabouts. Also consider adjacent **Malaga Cove** (nicknamed "RAT" beach because it's "right after Torrance"), a continuation of the strand, noted for tidepools, shells, and rockhounding. Prettier than its pedestrian partner, Malaga Cove is framed by rocky bluffs. At Torrance there are restrooms, some concession stands, and lifeguards; around Malaga Cove you're on your own. Fishing for corbinas is good at both beaches, and surfing is very good at Malaga Cove with steady, rolling waves ideal for beginners. For swimming I recommend Torrance, where lifeguards are on duty year-round. Parking fee, $5. ~ Paseo de la Playa in Torrance parallels the beach. To reach Malaga Cove, walk south from Torrance toward the cliffs; 310-372-2166.

▼▼▼▼▼▼▼▼▼▼
South Bay

The birthplace of California's beach culture lies in a string of towns perched on the southern skirt of Santa Monica Bay—Redondo Beach, Hermosa Beach, and Manhattan Beach. It all began here in the South Bay with George Freeth, "the man who can walk on water." It seems that while growing up in Hawaii, Freeth resurrected the ancient Polynesian sport of surfing and transplanted it to California. Equipped with a 200-pound, solid wood board, he introduced surfing to fascinated onlookers at a 1907 event in Redondo Beach.

It wasn't until the 1950s that the surfing wave crested. That's when a group of local kids called The Beach Boys spent their days catching waves at Manhattan Beach and their nights recording classic beach songs. The surrounding towns became synonymous with the sport and a new culture was born, symbolized by blond-haired, blue-eyed surfers committed to sun, sand, and the personal freedom to ride the last wave.

Sightseeing spots are rather scarce in these beach towns. As you can imagine, the interesting places are inevitably along the waterfront. Each town sports a municipal pier, with rows of knick-knack shops, cafés, and oceanview lounges, either along the pier or on the nearby waterfront.

SIGHTS   In Redondo Beach, **Fisherman's Wharf** is home to surfcasters and hungry seagulls. Walk out past the shops, salt breeze in your face, and you can gaze along the waterfront to open ocean. Waves wash against the pilings. Beneath the wood plank walkway, sea birds dive for fish. These sights and sounds are repeated again and again on the countless piers that line the California coast.

In fact you'll find them recurring right up in Hermosa Beach at the **Municipal Pier**. Less grandiose than its neighbor, this 1320-foot concrete corridor is simply equipped with a snack bar and bait shop. From the end you'll have a sweeping view back along Hermosa Beach's low skyline. ~ Located at the foot of Pier Avenue, Hermosa Beach.

The **Manhattan Beach Pier**, which extends 900 feet from the beach, is the site of the **Roundhouse Marine Studies Lab** (310-379-8117), a community marine science center full of local organisms. A mini-reef tank, shark tank, and touch tank make this a great place to take kids. The views of the ocean and Manhattan Beach's pretty neighborhoods compliment this attraction. ~ At the foot of Manhattan Beach Boulevard, Manhattan Beach.

The other sightseeing diversion in these parts is the stroll. The stroll, that is, along the beach. **Esplanade** in Redondo Beach is a wide boulevard paralleling the waterfront. Wander its length and take in the surfers, sunbathers, and swimmers who keep this resort town on the map. Or walk down to the waterline and let the cool Pacific bathe your feet.

In Hermosa Beach you can saunter along **The Strand**. This pedestrian thoroughfare borders a broad beach and passes an endless row of bungalows, cottages, and condominiums. It's a pleasant walk with shops and restaurants along the way.

The Strand continues along Manhattan Beach but lacks the commercial storefronts of Hermosa Beach. Wide and wonderful, the beach is lined by beautiful homes with plate-glass windows that reflect the blue hues of sea and sky. Together, these oceanfront walkways link the South Bay towns in a course that bicyclists can follow for miles.

Route 1 barrels through Los Angeles' beach towns and serves as
the commercial strip for generic motels. As elsewhere, these facilities are characterized by clean, sterile rooms and comfortable,
if unimaginative surroundings. Located within walking distance
of the beach, the **Starlite Motel** offers 20 standard, motel-style
units. ~ 716 South Pacific Coast Highway, Redondo Beach; 310-
316-4314. BUDGET.

LODGING

East West Inn features 40 rooms with refrigerators, microwaves and TVs. This establishment is two blocks from the beach.
~ 435 South Pacific Coast Highway, Redondo Beach; 310-540-
5998. BUDGET.

The Portofino Hotel and Yacht Club is a big, brassy hotel set
on King Harbor. The 163 units are decorated in contemporary
fashion and look out either on the ocean or the adjoining marina. There is a decorous lobby as well as a waterside swimming
pool and a restaurant; other facilities are nearby in the marina.
~ 260 Portofino Way, Redondo Beach; 310-379-8481, 800-468-
4292, fax 310-372-7329. ULTRA-DELUXE.

The best bargain on lodging in South Bay is found at **Sea Sprite
Motel & Apartments**. Located right on Hermosa Beach, this mul-
tibuilding complex offers oceanview rooms with kitchenettes at
moderate to deluxe prices. The accommodations are tidy, well
furnished, and fairly attractive. There is a swimming pool and sundeck overlooking the beach. The central shopping district is just
two blocks away, making the location hard to match. You can
also rent suites at deluxe prices or a two-bedroom beach cottage
at an ultra-deluxe price. Be sure to ask for an oceanview room
in one of the beachfront buildings. ~ 1016 The Strand, Hermosa
Beach; 310-376-6933, fax 310-376-4107. MODERATE TO ULTRA-
DELUXE.

At the **Hi View Motel**, you're only a step away from the beach,
shopping malls, and restaurants. There are standard rooms and

* *

✔ CHECK THESE OUT—UNIQUE LODGING

- *Budget:* Curl up in the barracks of Fort MacArthur, where the price is
  right at **Hostelling International—Los Angeles South Bay.** *page 315*
- *Moderate:* Come home to a comfortable cottage and watch the surfers
  at **Topanga Ranch Motel,** near the beach in Malibu. *page 345*
- *Moderate to deluxe:* Slumber in your bunk and peek out your porthole in a stateroom aboard the historic **Queen Mary.** *page 309*
- *Ultra-deluxe:* Succumb to island magic at **The Inn on Mt. Ada,**
  overlooking the ocean on Santa Catalina island. *page 358*

Budget: under $60   Moderate: $60–$120   Deluxe: $120–$175   Ultra-deluxe: over $175

studio apartments for rent. ~ 100 South Sepulveda Boulevard, Manhattan Beach; 310-374-4608. BUDGET TO MODERATE.

The **Sea View Inn at the Beach** is an 14-unit stucco hotel a block up from the beach. There's a swimming pool and two floors of guest rooms. You'll find comfortable furniture, wall-to-wall carpeting, refrigerator, and cable television in accommodations that are tidy. In addition, it is close to the surf and lodging is rare in these parts. ~ 3400 Highland Avenue, Manhattan Beach; 310-545-1504, fax 310-545-4052. MODERATE.

Far from the South Bay beach scene, though only a mile inland, is **Barnabey's Hotel**, a sprawling 120-room Edwardian-style hostelry. Re-creating turn-of-the-century England, Barnabey's provides stylish guest rooms with antique furnishings and vintage wallpaper. The lobby is finished in dark woods and appointed with gilded clocks and crystal light fixtures. There's a restaurant and British pub, and guests also enjoy a pool and jacuzzi. ~ 3501 North Sepulveda Boulevard, Manhattan Beach; 310-545-8466, 800-552-5285. DELUXE.

DINING

In downtown Redondo Beach, a couple blocks from the water, are several small restaurants serving a diversity of cuisines. **Greens at the Beach** specializes in all-organic and vegetarian delights. ~ 247 Avenida del Norte, Redondo Beach; 310-316-9451. BUDGET.

Petit Casino, a French bakery, serves quiche, *croque monsieur*, soups, salads, and sandwiches. ~ 1767 South Elena Avenue, Redondo Beach; 310-543-5585. BUDGET.

In addition to serving good Asian food, **Thai Thani** is an extremely attractive restaurant. Black trim and pastel shades set off the blond wood furniture and etched glass. There are fresh flowers all around plus a few well-placed wall prints. The lunch and dinner selections include dozens of pork, beef, vegetable, poultry, and seafood dishes. Unusual choices like spicy shrimp coconut soup, whole pompano smothered in pork, and whole baby hen make this a dining adventure. ~ 1109 South Pacific Coast Highway, Redondo Beach; 310-316-1580. BUDGET TO MODERATE.

◆◆◆

PYNCHON'S PICK

Be sure to stop in at the **Either/Or Bookstore**. With an outstanding inventory of books and magazines, the store is also endowed with an intriguing history. It seems that years ago Thomas Pynchon—the brilliant, reclusive, rarely photographed author of *V* and *Gravity's Rainbow*—stopped in regularly to buy books and talk contemporary literature. ~ 950 Aviation Boulevard, Hermosa Beach; 310-374-2060.

The capital of "in" dining around the South Bay area is **Chez Melange**. As the name suggests, and as current trends demand, the cuisine is eclectic. You'll find a hip crowd ordering everything from Asian tacos to barbecue chicken pizza to Greek omelettes. ~ 1716 Pacific Coast Highway, Redondo Beach; 310-540-1222. MODERATE TO DELUXE.

The Strand, a pedestrian byway paralleling the waterfront in Hermosa Beach, is lined with small restaurants. Among these is **Good Stuff on the Strand,** which serves a standard breakfast; hamburgers, turkey burgers, pita-bread sandwiches, vegetarian-style Mexican favorites, and salads at lunch; and, in the evening, entrées like stuffed spuds, teriyaki chicken, seafood pasta, and linguine with green and red bell peppers served in a white wine sauce. ~ 1286 The Strand, Hermosa Beach; 310-374-2334. BUDGET.

There is excellent thin-crust pizza at **Pedone's**. Popular with the beach crowd, it's a good spot for a quick meal in a convenient locale. ~ 1501 Hermosa Avenue, Hermosa Beach; 310-376-0949. BUDGET TO MODERATE.

Café Pierre is another excellent choice for budget-minded gourmets. Black chairs and cherry wood furnishings create a contemporary but warm atmosphere. You can feast on salmon enchiladas with chipotle sauce, duck meatloaf, salad niçoise, and homemade pasta. There are daily specials at lunch and dinner, which in the evening may include stuffed swordfish or venison. Closed for lunch on Saturday and Sunday. ~ 317 Manhattan Beach Boulevard, Manhattan Beach; 310-545-5252. BUDGET TO MODERATE.

No restaurants line the strand in Manhattan Beach, so you'll have to make do with the pier's snack shop or trot a half-block uphill to **Hibachi**. Here is a take-out stand with a full bar and a patio crowded with picnic tables. Beachgoers chow down on burgers and hot dogs while table diners feast on stir-fry, seafood platters, teriyaki dishes, and other Japanese entrées. ~ 120 Manhattan Beach Boulevard, Manhattan Beach; 310-374-9493. BUDGET TO MODERATE.

SHOPPING

If they weren't famous Pacific beach communities, the South Bay enclaves of Redondo, Hermosa, and Manhattan beaches would seem like small-town America. Their central shopping districts are filled with pharmacies, supply shops, and shoe stores.

There are a few places of interest to folks from out of town. In Redondo Beach, scout out Catalina Avenue, particularly along its southern stretches. Shops in Hermosa Beach concentrate along Pier and Hermosa avenues, especially where they intersect. Likewise in Manhattan Beach, Manhattan Beach Boulevard is traversed by Highland and Manhattan avenues.

NIGHTLIFE   The Comedy & Magic Club features name acts nightly. Many of the comedians are television personalities with a regional, if not national, following. Jay Leno, for instance, frequently tests his new *Tonight Show* material on the club's Sunday night crowd. The supper club atmosphere is upscale and appealing. Reservations are required. Cover. ~ 1018 Hermosa Avenue, Hermosa Beach; 310-372-1193.

The Lighthouse Café spotlights blues, reggae, rock-and-roll, and funk bands; the different styles draw vastly different crowds. Cover on Friday and Saturday. ~ 30 Pier Avenue, Hermosa Beach; 310-372-6911.

Orville & Wilbur's Restaurant is a lush, upscale establishment with an upstairs bar that looks out over the ocean. Live music, usually in the dance and hip-hop vein, is presented nightly. ~ 401 Rosecrans Avenue, Manhattan Beach; 310-545-6639.

BEACHES & PARKS   REDONDO COUNTY BEACH 🚲 ⛵ 🏊 🚤 ⚓ Surfers know this strand and so should you. Together with neighboring Hermosa and Manhattan beaches, it symbolizes the Southern California beach scene. You'll find a long strip of white sand bordered by a hillside carpeted with ice plants. In addition to surfers, the area is populated by bicyclists and joggers, while anglers cast from the nearby piers. Not surprisingly, fishing is particularly good from nearby Fisherman's Wharf. The swimming at Redondo is good, and surfing is even better. Facilities include restrooms, lifeguards, and volleyball courts; restaurants can be found on the pier. ~ Located along the Esplanade in Redondo Beach; 310-372-2166.

HERMOSA CITY BEACH 🚲 ⛵ 🏊 ⚓ One of the great beaches of Southern California, this is a very, very wide (and very, very white) sand beach extending the entire length of Hermosa Beach. Two miles of pearly sand are only part of the attraction. There's also The Strand, a pedestrian lane that runs the length of the beach; Pier Avenue, an adjacent street lined with interesting shops; a quarter-mile fishing pier; and a local community known for its artistic creativity. Personally, if I were headed to the beach, I would head in this direction. The swimming is good and the surfing is very good around the pier and all along the beach. Lifeguards are on duty, and facilities include restrooms, volleyball courts, and a playground. Parking fee, $5. ~ At the foot of Pier Avenue in Hermosa Beach; 310-372-2166.

MANHATTAN COUNTY BEACH 🚲 ⛵ 🏊 ⚓ Back in those halcyon days when their first songs were climbing the charts, The Beach Boys were regular fixtures at this silvery strand. They came to surf, swim, and check out the scene along The Strand, the walkway that extends the length of Manhattan Beach. What can you say, the gentlemen had good taste—the surfing here is some of the best in Southern California. This sand corridor is wide as a desert, fronted by an aquamarine ocean and backed by the beautiful homes of the very lucky. If that's not enough, there's a fishing pier and an adjacent commercial area door-to-door with excellent restaurants. The swimming here is good, and the surfing is tops. Other facilities include restrooms, lifeguards, and volleyball courts. ~ Located at the foot of Manhattan Beach Boulevard in Manhattan Beach; 310-372-2166.

DOCKWEILER STATE BEACH 🚲 🏊 🎣 ⛱ ⛵ It's long, wide, and has fluffy white sand—what more could you ask? Rather, it's what less can you request. Dockweiler suffers a minor problem. It's right next to Los Angeles International Airport, one of the world's busiest terminals. Every minute planes are taking off, thundering, reverberating, right over the beach. To add insult to infamy, there is a sewage treatment plant nearby. Nevertheless, swimming and surfing are good, fires are permitted, and fishing is good from the jetties. You'll also find picnic areas and restrooms. Parking fee, $6. ~ Located at the foot of Imperial Highway, along Vista del Mar Boulevard in Playa del Rey; 310-322-4951.

▲ There is an RV park with 82 sites with full hookups and 35 without; $16 to $26 per night.

▼▼▼▼▼▼▼▼▼▼
Venice

Venice, California, was the dream of one man, a tobacco magnate named Abbot Kinney. He envisioned a "Venice of America," a Renaissance town of gondoliers and single-lane bridges, connected by 16 miles of canals.

After convincing railroad barons and city fathers, Kinney dredged swampland along Santa Monica Bay, carved a network of canals, and founded this dream city in 1905. The place was an early-20th-century answer to Disneyland with gondola rides and amusement parks. The canals were lined with vaulted arches and rococo-style hotels.

Oil spelled the doom of Kinney's dream. Once black gold was discovered beneath the sands of Venice, the region became a landscape of drilling rigs and oil derricks. Spills polluted the canals and blackened the beaches. In 1929 the city of Los Angeles filled in most of the canals and during the subsequent decades Venice more resembled a tar pit than a cultural center.

But by the 1950s latter-day visionaries—artists and bohemians—rediscovered "Kinney's Folly" and transformed it into an avant-garde community. It became a magnet for Beats in the 1950s and hippies during the next decade. Musician Jim Morrison of The Doors lived here and Venice developed a reputation as a center for the cultural renaissance that Abbot Kinney once envisioned.

Today Venice seems to represent some sort of socially ideal community where there's room for everyone—aging hippies, retirees, world-class artists, and millionaire movie stars—to call Venice home. The reality, of course, is that gentrification of beachfront districts has sent housing costs soaring and that politicians miss the point when they try to force street vendors on the boardwalk to obtain business licenses. Still, the creative energy of Venice is hard to stifle. The town is filled with galleries and covered by murals, making it one of the region's most important art centers.

SIGHTS   The revolution might have sputtered elsewhere, but in Venice artists have seized control. The old City Hall has become the **Beyond Baroque Literary Arts Center,** housing a library and bookstore devoted to small presses. ~ 681 Venice Boulevard; 310-822-3006.

Next door, the **Venice City Jail** is home to SPARC, or the Social and Public Art Resource Center. The prison is an imposing 1923 art deco-style building with a cell block converted into an art gallery. Many of the cells are intact and you'll walk through an iron door to view contemporary artwork by alternative, cutting-edge artists. The center also sponsors lectures, mural tours, and mural projects around Los Angeles. ~ 685 Venice Boulevard; 310-822-9560.

Venice, to quote Bob Dylan, represents "life and life only," but a rarefied form of life, slightly, beautifully askew.

Both the Venice City Hall and Jail are great places to learn about what's going on in the community. Also consider the **Venice Chamber of Commerce.** If you can find someone there (which is not always easy), you can obtain maps, brochures, and answers. ~ 583¾ North Venice Boulevard, Suite C; 310-396-7016.

The commercial center of Venice rests at the intersection of Windward Avenue and Main Street. Windward was the central boulevard of Kinney's dream city and the Traffic Circle, marked today by a small sculpture, was to be an equally grand lagoon. Continue along Windward Avenue to the arcades, a series of Italian-style colonnades that represent one of the few surviving elements of old Venice.

HIDDEN ►   What's left of **Kinney's canals** can be found a few blocks south of Windward between Venice and Washington boulevards. Here three small canals flanked by two larger ones comprise an enclave of charming bungalows and showy mini-mansion remodels. Strains of opera or jazz float out of open windows, as resident ducks, squawking loudly, paddle along the canals, and joggers run along the narrow walkways and over small arched wooden bridges. For a duck's-eye view of these canals, rent a canoe for an hour or two from Mark Suminski, a local entrepreneur who claims to have fought city hall to get the necessary permits to get his canoe-rental business up and going. Suminski rents his canoes seasonally, from June through October. ~ 310-822-7172.

The heart of modern-day Venice pulses along the **boardwalk**, a two-mile strip that follows Ocean Front Walk from Washington Street to Rose Avenue. **Venice Pier**, an 1100-foot fishing pier, anchors one end. The pier is renovated with excellent lighting and coin-operated telescopes for lovely views of the Strand. Between Washington Street and Windward Avenue, the promenade is bordered by a palisade of beachfront homes, two- and three-story houses with plate-glass facades. ~ Ocean Front Walk and Washington Street.

Walking north, the real action begins around 18th Avenue, at **Muscle Beach,** where rope-armed heavies work out in the world-class weight pen, smacking punching bags and flexing their pecs, while gawking onlookers dream of oiling their bodies and walking with a muscle-bound strut.

The rest of the boardwalk is a grand open-air carnival which you should try to visit on the weekend. It is a world of artists and anarchists, derelicts and dreamers, a vision of what life would be if heaven were an insane asylum. Guitarists, jugglers, conga drummers, and clowns perform for the crowds. Kids on bicycles and roller skates whiz past rickshaws and unicycles. Street hawkers and panhandlers work the unwary while singers with scratchy voices pass the hat. Vendors dispense everything from corn dogs to cotton candy, T-shirts to wind-up toys.

South of Venice and Washington Boulevard is **Marina del Rey**, the largest manmade small-boat harbor in the world. Over 6000 pleasure boats and yachts dock here. Harbor cruises are provided aboard a mock Mississippi riverboat by the **Hornblower Dining Yachts.** ~ 13755 Fiji Way; 310-301-9900.

The entire region was once a marsh inhabited by a variety of waterfowl. Personally I think they should have left it to the birds. Marina del Rey is an ersatz community, a completely fabricated place where the main shopping area, **Fisherman's Village**, resembles a New England whaling town, and everything else attempts to portray something it's not. ~ 13755 Fiji Way; 310-823-5411.

With its endless condominiums, pretentious homes, and over-priced restaurants, Marina del Rey is an artificial limb appended to the coast of Los Angeles.

Still, watching a parade of sailboats leave and enter the harbor can be a colorful spectacle. Drive or bike to the south end of **Pacific Avenue** for a good viewing spot. Across the channel in Playa del Rey is **Ballona Wetlands,** a protected wetland environment, all that remains of the fragile coastal marsh in this area. Heated debate between environmentalists and developers continues about proposals to develop more of the area surrounding the wetland.

LODGING

HIDDEN ►

There's nothing quite like **The Venice Beach House**. That may well be because there are so few bed and breakfast inns in the Los Angeles area. But it's also that this is such a charming house, an elegant and spacious California craftsman–style home built in 1911 by Abbot Kinney. The living room, with its beam ceiling, dark wood paneling, and brick fireplace, is a masterwork. Guests also enjoy a sunny alcove, patio, and garden. The stroll to the Venice boardwalk and beach is only one-half block. The nine guest rooms are beautifully appointed and furnished with antiques; each features patterned wallpaper and period artwork. I can't recommend the place highly enough. ~ 15 30th Avenue; 310-823-1966. MODERATE TO DELUXE.

Also consider the **Marina Pacific Hotel**. Located in the commercial center of Venice only 100 yards from the sand, this three-story, 92-unit hostelry has a small lobby and café downstairs. The guest rooms are spacious, nicely furnished, and well maintained; very large one-bedroom suites, complete with kitchen and fireplace, are also available. Most rooms have small patios. ~ 1697 Pacific Avenue; 310-452-1111, 800-421-8151, fax 310-452-5479. DELUXE.

For the international hostel-hopper, Venice Beach is a veritable heaven by the ocean. Among the many places offering discount lodging are two hotels run by InterClub, an international hostelry organization. The **Venice Beach Cotel** offers both private and shared rooms. ~ 25 Windward Avenue; 310-399-7649, fax 310-399-1930. BUDGET.

Hostel California features ten units with private and shared baths. Other amenities include kitchen and laundry facilities. Free airport pickup is also provided. ~ 2221 Lincoln Boulevard; 310-305-0250, fax 310-305-8590. BUDGET.

Situated a few blocks from a broad, pleasant beach, the **Inn at Playa del Rey** abuts the Ballona Wetlands, one of the last wetlands habitats in Southern California. With 21 rooms and suites, many with fireplaces and whirlpool tubs, the gray-and-white clapboard inn looks more like a New England beach house than a California B&B. Bicycles are available for guests' use, and the outdoor jacuzzi is a popular feature. In addition to a full breakfast, owner Susan Zolla provides afternoon wine and cheese. ~ 435 Culver Boulevard, Playa del Rey; 310-574-1920, fax 310-574-9920. DELUXE.

DINING

The best place for finger food and junk food in all Southern California might well be the **boardwalk** in Venice. Along Ocean Front Walk are vendor stands galore serving pizza, yogurt, hamburgers, falafel, submarine sandwiches, corn dogs, etc.

Regardless, there's really only one spot in Venice to consider for dining. It simply *is* Venice, an oceanfront café right on the

The Murals
of Venice &
Santa Monica

Nowhere is the spirit of Venice and Santa Monica more evident than in the murals adorning their walls. Both seaside cities house major art colonies and the numerous galleries and studios make them important centers for contemporary art.

Over the years, as more and more artists made their homes here, they began decorating the twin towns with their art. The product of this creative energy lives along street corners and alleyways, on storefronts and roadways. Crowded with contemporary and historic images, these murals express the inner life of the city.

Murals adorn nooks and crannies all over Venice. You'll find a cluster of them around Windward Avenue between Main Street and Ocean Front Walk. The interior of the **Post Office** is adorned with public art. There's a trompe l'oeil mural nearby on the old St. Marks Hotel that beautifully reflects the street along which you are gazing. Don't miss the woman in the upper floor window. ~ Speedway and Windward Avenue.

On the other side of the building stands a large mural facing the ocean. **Venice Reconstituted** depicts the unique culture of Venice Beach. ~ Windward Avenue and Speedway.

At last count Santa Monica boasted about two dozen outdoor murals. Route 1, or Lincoln Boulevard, is a corridor decorated with local artworks. **John Muir Woods** portrays a redwood forest. ~ Lincoln and Ocean Park boulevards. **Early Ocean Park and Venice Scenes** captures the seaside at the turn of the century. ~ Located two blocks west of Lincoln Boulevard along Kensington Road in Joslyn Park. Nearby Marine Park features **Frog's Birthday**, with a Noah's ark full of celebratory animals. ~ Marine and 16th streets.

Ocean Park Boulevard is another locus of creativity. At its intersection with the 4th Street underpass you'll encounter **Whale of a Mural**, illustrating whales and underwater life common to California waters, and **Unbridled**, which pictures a herd of horses fleeing from the Santa Monica Pier carousel. One of the area's famous murals awaits you at Ocean Park Boulevard and Main street, where **Early Ocean Park** vividly re-creates scenes from the past.

For more information or a tour of these and other murals around the city, contact the **Social and Public Art Resource Center**. ~ 685 Venice Boulevard; 310-822-9560. The **Santa Monica Cultural Affairs Division** can also help. ~ 310-458-8350. Los Angeles has earned a reputation as the mural capital of the United States, making this tour a highpoint for admirers of public art.

HIDDEN ▶ boardwalk, **The Sidewalk Café**. Skaters whiz past, drummers beat rhythms in the distance, and the sun stands like a big orange wafer above the ocean. Food is really a second thought here, but eventually they're going to want you to spend some money. So, on to the menu . . . Breakfast, lunch, and dinner are what you'd expect —omelettes, sandwiches, hamburgers, pizza, and pasta. There are also fresh fish dishes plus platters of wok-fried vegetables, steak, spicy chicken, and fried shrimp. Validated parking is a block away in the lot at Market and Speedway. ~ 1401 Ocean Front Walk at Horizon; 310-399-5547. BUDGET TO MODERATE.

Take a walk down the boardwalk to **Venice Bistro**. This beachfront establishment is a casual dining room with a tile floor and brick walls. Cozy and comfortable, it features a menu that includes hamburgers, salads, pasta, and some Mexican dishes. There's a full bar. ~ 323 Ocean Front Walk; 310-392-7472. BUDGET.

Or check out **Jody Maroni's Sausage Kingdom**, a beach stand with over a dozen types of sausage, all natural. There's sweet Italian, Yucatán chicken, Louisiana hotlinks, and, of course, Polish. All sausages are served with grilled onions and peppers on a poppyseed roll. No dinner. ~ 2011 Ocean Front Walk; 310-306-1995. BUDGET.

HIDDEN ▶ The landing ground for Venetians is a warehouse dining place called **The Rose Café**. There's a full-scale deli, bakery counter, and a restaurant offering indoor and patio service. The last serves three meals daily, including reasonably priced dinners from an everchanging menu that may include entrées like linguine with smoked salmon, sautéed chicken, and a couple of vegetarian dishes. A good spot for pasta and salad, The Rose Café, with its wall murals and paintings, is also a place to appreciate the vital culture of Venice. ~ 220 Rose Avenue; 310-399-0711. MODERATE.

In the mood for Asian cuisine? **Hama Restaurant** is a wellrespected Japanese restaurant in the center of Venice. The place features an angular sushi bar, a long, narrow dining room, and a patio out back. The crowd is young and the place is decorated to reflect Venice's vibrant culture. There are paintings on display representing many of the area's artists. In addition to scrumptious sushi, Hama offers a complete selection of Japanese dishes including tempura, teriyaki, and sashimi. ~ 213 Windward Avenue; 310-396-8783. MODERATE.

"New American club cooking"—barbecued pork ribs with ribbons of collard greens; roast chicken with a side of coffee-flavored barbecue sauce; fried calamari served with chipotle-pepper dipping sauce; calf's liver with pancetta; and iceberg lettuce with a creamy blue-cheese dressing, for example—that's what **James' Beach** is all about. Frequented by the Venice arts-and-letters crowd, this art-filled restaurant (Billy Al Bengston designed the interior) offers daily dinner specials that are well conceived and reasonably priced. Dinner and weekend brunch. ~ 60 North Venice Boulevard; 310-823-5396. MODERATE.

72 Market Street could be the last word in modern art restaurants. The place is a warren of brick, mirrors, opaque glass, and studio lights. It's adorned with striking art pieces and equipped with a sound system that seems to be vibrating from the inner ear. Moderne to the max, the restaurant serves spicy meatloaf, rack of lamb with Dijon mustard and pistachio crust, and fettuccine with chanterelles ragout. This is the place for deluxe picnic boxes to take to the Hollywood Bowl. The restaurant also hosts an oyster bar. ~ 72 Market Street; 310-392-8720. DELUXE TO ULTRA-DELUXE.

SHOPPING

To combine slumming with shopping, be sure to wander the **boardwalk** in Venice. Ocean Front Walk between Windward and Ozone avenues is lined with low-rent stalls selling beach hats, cheap jewelry, sunglasses, beach bags, and souvenirs. You'll also encounter **Small World Books and the Mystery Annex**, a marvelous beachside shop crammed with mysteries (novels, that is) and other books. ~ 1407 Ocean Front Walk; 310-399-2360.

L.A. Louver is one of Venice's many vital and original galleries. It represents David Hockney and other contemporary American and European artists. ~ 45 North Venice Boulevard; 310-822-4955.

There is also a covey of art galleries and antique shops along the 1200 to 1500 blocks of West Washington Boulevard.

The **Beyond Baroque Literary Arts Center**, a clearinghouse for local talent, has a bookstore and sponsors poetry readings, dramatic revues, lectures, and concerts. It's located in the old Venice City Hall. ~ 681 Venice Boulevard; 310-822-3006.

In the town's erstwhile jail, the **Social and Public Art Resource Center**, or SPARC, has a store offering Latin American and Southwestern folk art as well as a selection of art books, prints, and cards. ~ 685 Venice Boulevard; 310-822-9560.

PARKING POINTERS

Parking in Venice, especially on hot summer weekends, can be a pain, and an expensive one at that. Street parking close to the beach cannot be found after 10 or 11 in the morning; lots closest to the beach will charge between $8.50 and $10 per car. If you don't mind a bit of walking, try your luck in the public lots at Venice Boulevard and Pacific Avenue; a day of parking here should cost between $5 and $7. The best advice: come early and be patient.

HIDDEN ►   **Philip Garaway Native American Art** specializes in museum-quality antique American Indian art, 19th-century Navajo blankets, antique rugs, vintage kachina dolls, Western American Indian basketry, and Pueblo pottery dating from 700 A.D. to the 20th century. By appointment only. ~ Venice; 310-577-8555

NIGHTLIFE   **The Townhouse**, set in a '20s-era speakeasy, has live music sometimes as well as deejays spinning Top-40 platters. Occasional cover. ~ 52 Windward Avenue; 310-392-4040.

Across the street, **Saint Mark's** bills live rhythm-and-blues, world beat, jazz, and flamenco music Tuesday through Sunday. Cover. ~ 23 Windward Avenue; 310-452-2222.

The Venice Bistro features live rock-and-roll Thursday through Sunday. Occasional cover. ~ 323 Ocean Front Walk; 310-392-7472.

The Sidewalk Café is also a popular night spot and gathering place, more for its central location than anything else. ~ 1401 Ocean Front Walk; 310-399-5547.

A bright turquoise-colored building on the west side of the street marks **Roosterfish**, a popular gay bar with a pool table, pinball machines, and a patio out back. ~ 1302 Abbot Kinney Boulevard; 310-392-2123.

BEACHES & PARKS   **VENICE BEACH** 🚲 🏖 🏄 🛶 This broad white sand corridor runs the entire length of Venice and features Venice Pier. But the real attraction—and the reason you'll find the beach described in the "Dining," "Sightseeing," and "Shopping" sections—is the boardwalk. A center of culture, street artistry, and excitement, the boardwalk parallels Venice Beach for two miles. As far as beach facilities, you'll find picnic areas, restrooms, showers, lifeguards, playgrounds, basketball courts, weight-lifting facilities, a bike path, and paddle ball courts. If you can tear yourself away from the action on the boardwalk for a while, the swimming and surfing are good here, too. ~ Ocean Front Walk in Venice parallels the beach; 310-399-2775.

▼▼▼▼▼▼▼▼▼▼
Santa Monica

Pass from Venice into Santa Monica and you'll trade the boardwalk for a promenade. It's possible to walk for miles along Santa Monica's fluffy beach, past pastel-colored condominiums and funky woodframe houses. Roller skaters and bicyclists galore crowd the byways and chess players congregate at the picnic tables.

A middle-class answer to mod Malibu, Santa Monica started as a seaside resort in the 1870s when visitors bumped over long, dusty roads by stagecoach from Los Angeles. After flirting with the film industry in the age of silent movies, Santa Monica reverted in the 1930s to a quiet beach town that nevertheless was notorious for the gambling ships moored offshore. It was during this period that detective writer Raymond Chandler immortalized the place as "Bay City" in his brilliant Philip Marlowe novels.

Today Santa Monica is *in*. Its clean air, pretty beaches, and attractive homes have made it one of the most popular places to live in Los Angeles. As real estate prices have skyrocketed, liberal politics have ascended. Santa Monica, it seems, has become Southern California's answer to Berkeley.

SIGHTS

Highlight of the beach promenade (and perhaps all Santa Monica) is the **Santa Monica Pier**. No doubt about it, the place is a scene. Acrobats work out on the playground below, surfers catch waves offshore, and street musicians strum guitars. And I haven't even mentioned the official attractions. There's a turn-of-the-century carousel with hand-painted horses that was featured in that cinematic classic, *The Sting*. There are video parlors, pinball machines, skee ball, bumper cars, and a restaurant. ~ Located at the foot of Colorado Avenue.

At the Santa Monica Pier is **Pacific Park**, a two-acre family amusement park featuring 12 rides and a food plaza. Reaching up to 55 feet in height, the Santa Monica West Coaster cruises around the park at 35 miles per hour and makes two 360-degree turns. The nine-story-high Ferris wheel offers a bird's-eye view of the beach and coastline. Other attractions include adult and kid bumper cars and a virtual reality theater box. ~ 380 Santa Monica Pier; 310-260-8744.

From here it's a jaunt up to the **Santa Monica Visitors Center** information kiosk. Here are maps, brochures, and helpful workers. ~ 1400 Ocean Avenue; 310-393-7593.

The booth is located in **Palisades Park**, a pretty, palm-lined greensward that extends north from Colorado Avenue more than a mile along the sandstone cliffs fronting Santa Monica beach. One of the park's stranger attractions here is the **Camera Obscura**, a periscope of sorts through which you can view the pier, beach, and surrounding streets. ~ In the Senior Recreation Center, 1450 Ocean Avenue.

HELLO, DOLLY

Angels Attic is more than a great name. Contained in this 1895 Victorian is a unique museum of antique dolls and dollhouses. There's a Noah's ark worth of miniature animals plus a gallery of precious dolls. In keeping with the spirit of the museum, they serve tea on the front porch (by reservation). Closed Monday through Wednesday. Admission. ~ 516 Colorado Avenue; 310-394-8331.

For a glimpse into Santa Monica's past, take in the **California Heritage Museum**. Heirlooms and antiques are housed in a grand American Colonial Revival home. The mansion dates to 1894 and is furnished entirely in period pieces. There are photo archives, historic artifacts galore, and rotating exhibits of decorative and fine arts. Closed Monday and Tuesday. Admission. ~ 2612 Main Street; 310-392-8537.

The **Museum of Flying** is a miniature Smithsonian. Tracing the history of aviation in a single, brightly painted hangar, the museum houses everything from a 1924 Douglas World Cruiser (built in Santa Monica, it was the first plane to circle the globe) to a Douglas A-4 Skyhawk flown by the Blue Angels. Closed Monday and Tuesday. Admission. ~ 2772 Donald Douglas Loop North; 310-392-8822.

Once a stop on the old railway, Bergamot Station now houses a vast art complex with several galleries as well as the **Santa Monica Museum of Art**. The museum rotates its exhibits about every two months, and features mostly L.A. artists. ~ Bergamot Station, 2525 Michigan Avenue; 310-586-6488.

Sympathetic as it is to liberal politics, Santa Monica is nonetheless an extremely wealthy town. In fact, it's a fusion of two very different neighbors, mixing the bohemian strains of Venice with the monied elements of Malibu. For a look at the latter influence, take a drive from Ocean Avenue out along **San Vicente Boulevard**. This fashionable avenue, with its arcade of magnolias, is lined on either side with lovely homes. But they pale by comparison with the estates you will see by turning left on **La Mesa Drive**. This quiet suburban street boasts a series of marvelous Spanish Colonial, Tudor, and contemporary-style houses.

HIDDEN ▶   At first glance, the **Self Realization Fellowship Lake Shrine** in nearby Pacific Palisades is an odd amalgam of pretty things. Gathered along the shore of a placid pond are a Dutch windmill, a houseboat, and a shrine topped with something resembling a giant artichoke. In fact, the windmill is a chapel, the houseboat is a former stopping place of yogi and Self Realization Fellowship founder Paramahansa Yogananda, and the oversized artichoke is a golden lotus archway near which some of Indian leader Mahatma Gandhi's ashes are enshrined. A strange but potent collection of icons in an evocative setting. Closed Monday. ~ 17190 Sunset Boulevard, Pacific Palisades; 310-454-4114.

Several miles inland at **Will Rogers State Historic Park**, on a hillside overlooking the Pacific, you can tour the ranch and home of America's greatest cowboy philosopher. Will Rogers, who started as a trick roper in traveling rodeos, hit the big time in Hollywood during the 1920s as a kind of cerebral comedian whose humorous wisdom plucked a chord in the American psyche.

From 1928 until his tragic death in 1935, the lariat laureate occupied this 31-room home with his family. The house is deceptively large but not grand; the woodframe design is basic and unassuming, true to Will Rogers' Oklahoma roots. Similarly the interior is decorated with Indian rugs and ranch tools. Western knickknacks adorn the tables and one room is dominated by a full-sized stuffed calf which Rogers utilized for roping practice. Well worth visiting, the "house that jokes built" is a simple expression of a vital personality. Admission. ~ 1501 Will Rogers Road, Pacific Palisades; 310-454-8212.

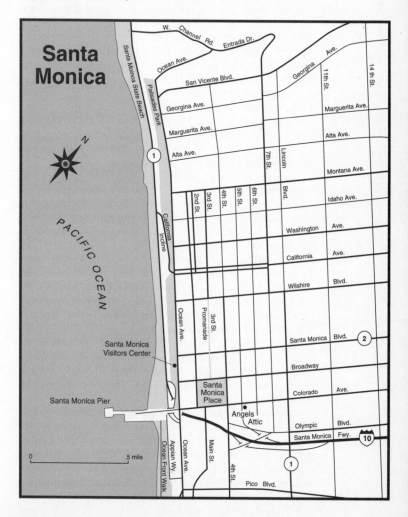

LODGING   Ocean Avenue, which runs the length of Santa Monica, parallel-ing the ocean one block above the beach, boasts the most hotels and the best location in town. Among its varied facilities are sev-eral generic motels. These are all-American type places furnished in veneer, carpeted wall-to-wall, and equipped with telephones and color televisions. If you book a room in one, ask for quiet accommodations since Ocean Avenue is a busy, noisy street.

A reasonably good bargain is the **Bayside Hotel**. Laid out in motel fashion, this two-story complex offers plusher carpets and plumper furniture than motels hereabouts. More important, it's just 50 yards from the beach across a palm-studded park. Some rooms have ocean views; no pool. ~ 2001 Ocean Avenue; 310-396-6000, 800-525-4447, fax 310-451-1111. MODERATE.

The ultimate bargain is found at **Hostelling International—Santa Monica**. This four-story, dorm-like structure boasts 30,000 square feet, room for 228 beds. There are several common rooms, a central courtyard, library, and kitchen. In addition to facilities for independent travelers, the hostel has set aside six private rooms for couples and families. ~ 1436 2nd Street; 310-393-9913, fax 310-393-1769. BUDGET.

Despite its location on a busy street, **Channel Road Inn** con-veys a cozy sense of home. Colonial Revival in style, built in 1910, this sprawling 14-room bed and breakfast offers guests a living room, library, and dining room as well as a jacuzzi and hillside garden. The guest rooms vary widely in decor—some traditional, others contemporary; some florid, others demure. ~ 219 West Channel Road; 310-459-1920, fax 310-454-9920. DELUXE TO ULTRA-DELUXE.

The **Pacific Shore Hotel** looks the part of a contemporary Southern California hotel. Across the street from the beach, this sprawling 168-room facility boasts a pool, sauna, jacuzzi, exer-cise room, and sundeck. There's a restaurant off the lobby as well as a lounge and gift shop. Guests are whisked to their rooms in a glass elevator. The accommodations are furnished with modu-lar pieces painted in brilliant enamels; the appointments are art deco and the wallpaper has been roughed to resemble raw fabric; some rooms have ocean views. Slightly plastic, but what the hell. ~ 1819 Ocean Avenue; 310-451-8711, 800-622-8711, fax 310-394-6657. ULTRA-DELUXE.

Think of sunflowers backdropped by a deep blue Mediterra-nean sky. That's what the **Hotel Oceana** evokes. From its magnifi-cent oceanfront setting to its lush courtyard planted with fragrant flowers, this exquisite hotel—reminiscent of the beauty of the Côte d'Azur—is a lesson in understated elegance. The lobby is decor-ated with a wrought-iron registration desk and floor-to-ceiling murals. Each guest suite comes with a fully equipped kitchen and is individually decorated in a French-impressionist style. The amenities include Wolfgang Puck's Cafe, a fitness center, and a swimming pool. Every morning, a basket of freshly baked breads is delivered to your door. What more can I say? ~ 849 Ocean Avenue; 310-393-0486, 800-777-0758, fax 310-458-1182. ULTRA-DELUXE.

Built in 1989, **Loews Santa Monica Beach Hotel** was the first L.A. luxury hotel with direct beach access. The peach, beige, and seafoam green "contemporary Victorian" features a mock turn-of-the-century design. Its spectacular five-story glass atrium lobby and most of the 343 rooms provide views of the famed Santa Monica Pier. Rooms are furnished in rattan and wicker and offer special amenities. Non-beachies love the ocean-view indoor/outdoor pool. ~ 1700 Ocean Avenue; 310-458-6700, 800-235-6397, fax 310-458-6761. ULTRA-DELUXE.

Randy Newman filmed his "I Love L.A." rock video at Hotel Shangri-La.

Shutters on the Beach, perched directly on Santa Monica Beach, is cozy and sedate. The lobby has two large fireplaces and the 198 green-and-white rooms are well appointed with dark walnut furniture. Most rooms have coastal views; all feature, yes, shutters, as well as marble baths complete with jacuzzis. The hotel has a lovely pool terrace, two ocean-view restaurants, and an ocean-view bar. ~ 1 Pico Boulevard; 310-458-0030, 800-334-9000, fax 310-458-4589. DELUXE TO ULTRA-DELUXE.

Now forget everything I've said. Never mind the variety and quality of accommodations here, there's only one place to stay in Santa Monica. Just ask the many Hollywood stars who have stayed at the **Hotel Shangri-La**. The place is private, stylish, and nothing short of beautiful. A 1939 art deco building with a facade like the prow of a steamship, the 55-room home-away-from-paparazzi is entirely remodeled. The art moderne–era furniture has been laminated and lacquered and each appointment is a perfect expression of the period. You get the sense that you'll see detective Philip Marlowe saunter in with liquor on his lips and a bulge beneath his jacket. Located on the palisades one block above Santa Monica Beach, many rooms sport an ocean view and have a kitchen. There's no pool or restaurant, but the hotel has a sundeck, serves continental breakfast and afternoon tea, and is close to the beach, shops, and pier. ~ 1301 Ocean Avenue; 310-394-2791, 800-345-7829, fax 310-451-3351. DELUXE TO ULTRA-DELUXE.

Santa Monica is a restaurant town. Its long tradition of seafood establishments has been expanded in recent years by a wave of ethnic and California cuisine restaurants. While some of the most fashionable and expensive dining rooms in Los Angeles are right here, there are also many excellent and inexpensive cafés. Generally you'll find everything from the sublime to the reasonable located within several commercial clusters—near the beach along

DINING

Ocean Avenue, downtown on Wilshire and Santa Monica boulevards, and in the chic, gentrified corridors of Main Street and Montana Avenue.

One of the best places in Southern California for stuffing yourself with junk food while soaking up sun and having a whale of a good time is the **Santa Monica Pier**. There are taco stands, fish-and-chips shops, hot dog vendors, oyster bars, snack shops, pizzerias, and all those good things guaranteed to leave you clutching your stomach. The prices are low to modest and the food is amusement park quality. ~ Located at the foot of Colorado Avenue.

There's a sense of the Mediterranean at the sidewalk cafés lining Santa Monica's Ocean Avenue: palm trees along the boulevard, ocean views in the distance, and (usually) a warm breeze blowing. Any of these bistros will do (since it's atmosphere we're seeking), so try **Ivy at the Shore**. It features a full bar, serves espresso, and, if you want to get serious about it, has a full lunch and dinner menu with pizza, pasta, steaks, and Cajun dishes. ~ 1541 Ocean Avenue; 310-393-3113. DELUXE TO ULTRA-DELUXE.

Every type of cuisine imaginable is found on the bottom level of **Santa Monica Place**. This multitiered shopping mall has an entire floor of take-out food stands. It's like the United Nations of dining, where everything is affordably priced. ~ On Broadway between 2nd and 4th streets. BUDGET.

Along the Third Street Promenade there is **Benita's Frites**, a Belgian french-fry stand. This diminutive entry in Santa Monica's rough-and-tumble restaurant race does not just serve plain old fries, however. They feature 20 different dips, including spicy bar-

---

✔ CHECK THESE OUT—UNIQUE DINING

- *Budget:* Take a culinary tour of Latin America at **Viva**, where traditional Mexican favorites, Salvadoran-inspired dishes, and Cuban specialties fill the menu. *page 309*
- *Budget to moderate:* Watch the world skate by as you refuel with omelettes and sandwiches at **The Sidewalk Café** on Venice's boardwalk. *page 330*
- *Deluxe to ultra-deluxe:* Feast your eyes and stomach at **Michael's**, where the walls contain original Hockneys, and the menu is filled with scrumptious masterpieces. *page 340*
- *Deluxe to ultra-deluxe:* Brighten your aura with a meal at the **Inn of the Seventh Ray**, a hippie haven in Topanga, the canyon time forgot. *page 347*

Budget: under $9   Moderate: $9–$18   Deluxe: $18–$25   Ultra-deluxe: over $25

becue, peanut sauce, and garlic mayonnaise, as well as full lunch and dinner fare. ~ 1437 3rd Street; 310-458-2889. BUDGET.

Benita's, however, is only one of many excellent eateries along Santa Monica's vaunted Third Street Promenade. This three-block-long walkway, filled with movie theaters and located in the downtown district, boasts some of the best coffeehouses and restaurants in the area.

Nearby, **Broadway Bar and Grill** features spacious booths indoors and curbside tables outside. Perfect for checking out the scene, this classic bar and grill serves steaks, fresh fish, and grilled chicken. ~ 1460 3rd Street Promenade; 310-393-4211. MODERATE.

If steak-and-kidney pie, bangers and mash, or shepherds pie sound appetizing, head over to **Ye Olde King's Head**. You won't see a king's head on the wall of this British pub, but there are several trophy animals adorning the place. You'll find them beside photographs of the celebrities who inhabit the pub. Like you, they are drawn here by the cozy ambience and the lively crowd. ~ 116 Santa Monica Boulevard; 310-451-1402. MODERATE.

Sabor Too offers an eclectic mélange of Creole and Latin cuisine. Set in a Mission-style building with whitewashed walls and Latin sculpture, this restaurant serves up such exotic fare as Salvadoran *pupusa* and Brazilian *coxinha* (a buttermilk puff pastry filled with chicken, goat cheese, and fresh herb mousse). No lunch on weekends. ~ 3221 Pico Boulevard; 310-829-3781. MODERATE.

In the world of high chic, **Chinois on Main** stands taller than most. Owned by famous restaurateur Wolfgang Puck, the fashionable dining room is done in nouveau art deco–style with track lights, pastel colors, and a central skylight. The curved bar is handpainted; contemporary artworks adorn the walls. Once you drink in the glamorous surroundings, move right on to the menu, which includes Shanghai lobster with curry sauce, whole sizzling catfish, grilled Szechuan beef, and barbecued baby pork ribs with honey-and-chile sauce. The appetizers and other entrées are equal in originality, a medley of French, Chinese, and California cuisine. This is an excellent restaurant with high standards of quality. No lunch Saturday through Tuesday. ~ 2709 Main Street; 310-392-9025, reservations 310-392-3037. DELUXE TO ULTRA- DELUXE.

The spot for breakfast in Santa Monica is **Rae's Restaurant,**   ◀ HIDDEN
a diner on the edge of town several miles from the beach. With its formica counter and naugahyde booths, Rae's is a local institution, always packed. The breakfasts are hearty American-style feasts complete with buttermilk biscuits and country-style gravy. At lunch they serve the usual selection of sandwiches and side orders. Come dinner time they have fried shrimp, pork chops, veal, liver, fried chicken, steaks, and other hot platters at prices that seem like they haven't changed since the place opened in 1958. ~ 2901 Pico Boulevard; 310-828-7937. BUDGET.

The word has spread about **Louise's**. A friendly trattoria atmosphere, creative Italian fare, and reasonable prices account for its popularity. ~ 1008 Montana Avenue; 310-394-8888. MODERATE.

There are many who believe the dining experience at **Michael's** to be the finest in all Los Angeles. Set in a restored stucco structure and decorated with original artworks by David Hockney and Jasper Johns, it is certainly one of the region's prettiest dining rooms. The menu is French-American, with original entrées such as squab on duck liver and scallops with papaya, shallots, and chervil. At lunch there is grilled salmon with a tomato-basil vinaigrette and elaborate salads. Haute cuisine is the order of the evening here. The artistry that has gone into the restaurant's cuisine and design have permanently established Michael's reputation. No lunch Saturday. Closed Sunday and Monday. ~ 1147 3rd Street; 310-451-0843. DELUXE TO ULTRA-DELUXE.

SHOPPING   Montana Avenue is Santa Monica's version of designer heaven, making it an interesting, if inflationary, strip to shop. From 7th to 17th Street chic shops and upscale establishments line either side of the thoroughfare.

For men's and women's fashion sportswear, try **Weathervane For Men**. ~ 1132 Montana Avenue; 310-395-0397.

Sara up the street is like a miniature department store with fashions, jewelry, art pieces, and distinctive gifts. ~ 1324 Montana Avenue; 310-394-2900.

The **Brenda Cain Store** features vintage jewelry, pottery, rugs, and turn-of-the-century decorative accessories. ~ 1211 Montana Avenue; 310-395-1559.

At **Federico** the merchandise ranges from textiles to jewelry to antiques in a variety of American Indian and Mexican styles. ~ 1522 Montana Avenue; 310-458-4134.

Browse **Main Street** and you'll realize that Montana Avenue is only a practice round in the gentrification of Santa Monica. Block after block of this thoroughfare has been made over in trendy fashion and filled with stylish shops. Main Street was even the focus of a civic campaign which highlighted its upscale amenities.

FOR LOVERS OF LIBERAL LANGUAGE . . .

There is one shop in particular that exemplifies Santa Monica's liberal politics. **Midnight Special Bookstore** specializes in politics and social sciences. Rather than current bestsellers, the window displays will feature books on Latin America, world hunger, Africa, or disarmament. ~ 1318 3rd Street Promenade; 310-393-2923.

The shopper's parade stretches most of the length of Main Street, but the center of action resides around the 2700 block. **Galleria Di Maio** is an art deco mall with several spiffy shops including **Suji**, which carries fun, romantic women's clothing. ~ 2525 Main Street; 310-396-7614.

Bronson Fine Arts features turn-of-the-century American and European works of art, antiquities and tribal art. They also carry contemporary sculpture and artwork on canvas and paper. Closed Saturday and Sunday. ~ 1410 2nd Street; 310-587-2577.

The last of Santa Monica's several shopping enclaves is in the center of town. Here you'll find **Santa Monica Place**, a mammoth triple-tiered complex with about 160 shops. This flashy atrium mall has everything from clothes to books to sporting goods to luggage to leather work, jewelry, toys, hats, and shoes. ~ On Broadway between 2nd and 4th streets; 310-394-5451.

Step out from this glittery gathering place and you'll immediately encounter the **Third Street Promenade**, a three-block walkway lined on either side with shops, upscale cafés, and movie theaters. ~ Located between Broadway and Wilshire Boulevard.

Muskrat Clothing specializes in vintage items like Hawaiian shirts, bowling shirts, velour jackets, and silk coats with maps of Japan embroidered on the backs. (Thought you'd never find one, eh?) ~ 1248 3rd Street Promenade; 310-394-1713.

Also consider **Na Na**, where the future is happening in the form of alternative accouterments like skull-and-crossbone earrings, big, chunky shoes, and motorcycle boots. ~ 1245 3rd Street Promenade; 310-394-9690.

For the outward bound, **California Map & Travel Center** has it all—maps, directories, and guidebooks. Or, if you're planning a little armchair traveling at home, there are globes and travelogues. ~ 3312 Pico Boulevard; 310-396-6277.

NIGHTLIFE

Ye Olde King's Head might be the most popular British pub this side of the Thames. From dart boards to dark wood walls, trophy heads to draft beer, it's a classic English watering hole. Known throughout the area, it draws crowds of local folks and expatriate Brits. ~ 116 Santa Monica Boulevard; 310-451-1402.

McCabe's Guitar Shop is a folksy spot with live entertainment on weekends. The sounds are almost all acoustic and range from Scottish folk bands to jazz to blues to country. The concert hall is a room in back lined with guitars; performances run Friday through Saturday nights. Cover. ~ 3101 Pico Boulevard; 310-828-4497.

For a raucous good time try **O'Briens**. This bar is a loud, brash place that draws hearty crowds. There are live bands nightly, ranging from Irish rock to Texas blues. The decor is what you'd expect from an Irish pub, with old pictures and beer signs adorning the walls. Cover on Friday and Saturday. ~ 2941 Main Street; 310-396-4725.

Abiding by a "casual" dress code, **The Pink** is a weekend club featuring deejay-generated hip-hop house music and speed garage on Wednesday nights. Cover. ~ 2810 Main Street; 310-392-1077.

For blues, try **Harvelle's**. Cover. ~ 1432 4th Street; 310-395-1676.

BEACHES & PARKS

SANTA MONICA CITY BEACH If the pop song is right and "L.A. is a great big freeway," then truly Santa Monica is a great big beach. Face it, the sand is very white, the water is very blue, the beach is very broad, and they all continue for miles. From Venice to Pacific Palisades, it's a sandbox gone wild. Skaters, bicyclists and strollers pass along the promenade, sunbathers lie moribund in the sand, and volleyball players perform acrobatic shots. At the center of all this stands the Santa Monica Pier with its amusement park atmosphere. If it wasn't right next door to Venice this would be the hottest beach around. Lifeguards are on duty, and facilities include picnic areas, restrooms, and snack bars. Swimming and surfing are good, and anglers usually opt for the pier. Parking fee, $7. ~ Along Route 1, at the foot of Colorado Avenue in Santa Monica; 310-458-8311.

WILL ROGERS STATE BEACH Simple and homespun he might have been, but Will Rogers was also a canny businessman with a passion for real estate. He bought up three miles of beachfront property that eventually became his namesake park. It's a wide, sandy strand with an equally expansive parking lot running the length of the beach. Route 1 parallels the parking area and beyond that rise the sharp cliffs that lend Pacific Palisades its name. Early in the morning, surf fishers try for corbina. The South Bay Bike Trail makes its northernmost appearance here. You'll find good swimming, and surfing is best in the area where Sunset Boulevard meets the ocean. Lifeguards are on duty. Facilities include restrooms, volleyball courts, and playgrounds. Day-use fees vary greatly from $3 to $10, depending on crowds expected. ~ Located south along Route 1 from Sunset Boulevard in Pacific Palisades; 310-451-2906.

WILL ROGERS STATE HISTORIC PARK The former ranch of humorist Will Rogers, this 186-acre spread sits in the hills of Pacific Palisades. The late cowboy's home is open to visitors and there are hiking trails leading around the property and out into adjacent Topanga Canyon State Park. Facilities include picnic areas, a museum, and restrooms. Day-use fee, $6. ~ 1501 Will Rogers State Park Road, Pacific Palisades; 310-454-8212.

SANTA MONICA MOUNTAINS NATIONAL RECREATION AREA   ◄ HIDDEN

🚶 🚵 🐎 One of the few mountain ranges in the United States to run transversely (from east to west), the Santa Monicas reach for 50 miles to form the northwestern boundary of the Los Angeles basin. This federal preserve, which covers part of the mountain range, encompasses about 150,000 acres between Routes 1 and 101, much of which is laced with hiking trails; in addition to high country, it includes a coastal stretch from Santa Monica to Point Mugu. Considered a "botanical island," the mountains support chaparral, coastal sage, and oak forests; mountain lions, golden eagles, and many of California's early animal species still survive here. ~ Several access roads lead into the area; Mulholland Drive and Mulholland Highway follow the crest of the Santa Monica Mountains for about 50 miles from Hollywood to Malibu. The information center is at 401 West Hillcrest Drive, Thousand Oaks; 805-370-2301.

▲ There are 23 sites for primitive camping only; $6 per night.

Malibu is a 27-mile-long ribbon lined on one side with pearly beaches and on the other by the Santa Monica Mountains. Famed as a movie star retreat and surfer's heaven, it is one of America's mythic communities.

▼▼▼▼▼▼▼▼▼▼

Malibu

It has been a favored spot among Hollywood celebrities since the 1920s when a new highway opened the region and film stars like Clara Bow and John Gilbert publicized the idyllic community. By the 1950s Malibu was rapidly developing and becoming nationally known for its rolling surf and freewheeling lifestyle. The 1959 movie *Gidget* cast Sandra Dee and James Darren as Malibu beach bums and the seaside community was on its way to surfing immortality.

Today blond-mopped surfers still line the shore and celebrities continue to congregate in beachfront bungalows. Matter of fact, the most popular sightseeing in Malibu consists of ogling the homes of the very rich. Malibu Road, which parallels the waterfront, is a prime strip. To make it as difficult as possible for common riffraff to reach the beach, the homes are built townhouse-style with no space between them. It's possible to drive for miles along the water without seeing the beach, only the backs of baronial estates. Happily there are a few accessways to the beach, so it's possible to wander along the sand enjoying views of both the ocean and the picture-window palaces. Among the accessways is one that local wags named after the "Doonesbury" character Zonker Harris.

SIGHTS

What's amazing about these beachfront colonies is not the houses, but the fact that people insist on building them so close to the ocean that every few years several are demolished by high surf and others sink into the sand.

One of Malibu's loveliest houses is open to the public. The **Adamson House**, located at Malibu Lagoon State Beach is a stately Spanish Colonial Revival–style structure adorned with ceramic tiles. With its bare-beam ceilings and inlaid floors, the house is a study in early-20th-century elegance. Outstanding as it is, the building is upstaged by the landscaped grounds, which border the beach at Malibu and overlook a lagoon alive with waterfowl and are open to the public. Though there is an admission price for the house, there is no fee to stroll the gardens. Closed Sunday, Monday, and Tuesday. Admission. ~ 23200 Pacific Coast Highway; 310-456-8432.

On weekend nights, Mulholland Drive, as it's known in town, is a rendezvous for lovers and a drag strip for daredevil drivers, but the rest of the time you'll find it a sinuous country road far from the madding mobs.

The town's most prestigious address is that of the **J. Paul Getty Museum**. Set on a hillside overlooking the sea, the building re-creates a 2000-year-old Roman villa in the most splendid manner imaginable. Reflecting the impeccable taste of founder J. Paul Getty, the museum's collection has established an awesome reputation in the art world for the fine artworks displayed. The Getty is now closed for renovation, and will reopen in 2001. Its antiquities will be displayed at this site in a lush Malibu Canyon; the rest of the Getty's holdings are now housed in the new Getty Center in Brentwood. ~ 17985 Pacific Coast Highway; 310-440-7300.

Another seafront attraction is the **Malibu Pier**. Storm damage has closed the pier, and it's ironic that in this ultra-privileged community, a lack of funding has kept the necessary repairs from being made. ~ 23000 Pacific Coast Highway.

When you tire of Malibu's sand and surf, take a drive along one of the canyon roads which lead from Route 1 up into the Santa Monica Mountains. This chaparral country is filled with oak and sycamore forests and offers sweeping views back along the coast. Topanga Canyon Boulevard, perhaps the best known of these mountain roads, curves up to the rustic town of **Topanga**. Back in the '60s it was a fabled retreat for flower children. Even today vestiges of the hip era remain in the form of health food stores, New Age shops, and natural restaurants. Many of the woodframe houses are handcrafted and the community still vibrates to a slower rhythm than coastal Malibu and cosmopolitan Los Angeles.

To reach the top of the world (while making a mountain loop of this uphill jaunt), take Old Topanga Canyon Road from town and turn left out on **Mulholland Highway**. With its panoramic views of the Los Angeles Basin and San Fernando Valley, Mulholland is justifiably famous. (To complete the entire circle follow Kanan–Dume Road back down to the ocean.)

There are several motels scattered along the coastal highway in Malibu, two of which I can recommend. **Topanga Ranch Motel** is a 30-unit complex that dates back to the 1920s. Here are cute little cottages painted white with red trim and clustered around a circular drive. Granted they're somewhat timeworn, but each is kept neat and trim with plain furnishings and little decoration. A few have kitchens. A good deal for a location right across the highway from the beach. ~ 18711 Pacific Coast Highway; 310-456-5486, 800-200-0019, fax 310-456-1447. MODERATE.

LODGING

At **Casa Malibu Inn on the Beach,** you'll be in a 21-room facility that actually overhangs the sand. Located smack in the center of Malibu, the building features a central courtyard with lawn furniture and ocean view plus a balcony dripping with flowering plants. The rooms are decorated in an attractive but casual fashion; some have private balconies, fireplaces, kitchens, and/or ocean views. ~ 22752 Pacific Coast Highway; 310-456-2219, 800-831-0858, fax 310-456-5418. MODERATE TO DELUXE.

The **Malibu Beach Inn** is posh and each of its 47 guest rooms offers spectacular ocean views from private balconies. Fireplaces and minibars round out the amenities. Some rooms feature jacuzzis. The location on the beach, one block from the Malibu Pier, makes this an ideal getaway. ~ 22878 Pacific Coast Highway; 310-456-6444, 800-462-5428, fax 310-456-1499. ULTRA-DELUXE.

At the northern Zuma Beach end of Malibu, you'll find the 15-room **Malibu Country Inn** perched atop a hillside above Pacific Coast Highway. Draped in bougainvillea, the 50-year old property has been recently upgraded with the addition of four suites and a restaurant (see "Dining"). Since the inn isn't directly on the beach, only some of the rooms have partial ocean views; but all have unobstructed mountain views, private decks, coffee makers, and a floral-wicker decor scheme. The suites include fireplace and spa tub. There's a small pool surrounded by a garden of roses and other flowers and herbs. Continental breakfast at the restaurant is included. ~ 6506 Westward Beach Road at Pacific Coast Highway; 310-457-9622, 800-386-6787. ULTRA-DELUXE.

The **Reel Inn** is my idea of heaven—a reasonably priced seafood restaurant. Located across the highway from the beach, it's an oilcloth restaurant with an outdoor patio and a flair for serving good, healthful food at low prices. Among the fresh fish lunches and dinners are salmon, snapper, lobster, and swordfish. ~ 18661 Pacific Coast Highway; 310-456-8221. MODERATE.

DINING

There's nothing fancy about **Malibu Fish & Seafood**. It's just a fish and chips stand across the highway from the beach with a few picnic tables outside, but the menu includes such tantalizing specialties as ahi tuna burgers and tender steamed lobster. The price is hard to beat when you add the ocean view. ~ 25653 Pacific Coast Highway; 310-456-3430. BUDGET.

For a possible celebrity sighting over your whole-wheat pancakes with strawberries and bananas, try **Coogie's Beach Cafe**. ~ Malibu Colony Plaza, 23700 Pacific Coast Highway; 310-317-1444. MODERATE.

Cutting-edge Continental cuisine can be found at **Granita**, where chef Wolfgang Puck's culinary cohorts whip up original creations. Watch as they prepare lavender honey–glazed Sonoma lamb with baby artichokes or big-eyed tuna grilled rare with green peppercorns. Yow! The marble terrazo tile gives an underwater effect. Dinner only; brunch on weekends. ~ Malibu Colony Plaza; 310-456-0488. DELUXE.

Beau Rivage Mediterranean Restaurant, another gourmet gathering place, located across the highway from the ocean, boasts a cozy dining room and ocean-view terrace. With exposed-beam ceiling, brick trim, and copper pots along the wall, it has the feel of a French country inn. The dinner menu, however, is strictly Mediterranean. In addition to several pasta dishes, including gnocchi al pesto and linguine with lobster, tomatoes, and garlic, there is New Zealand rack of lamb, Long Island duckling, and grilled Italian bass. Dinner only. ~ 26025 Pacific Coast Highway; 310-456-5733. DELUXE TO ULTRA-DELUXE.

The quintessential Malibu dining experience is **Geoffrey's**, a clifftop restaurant overlooking the ocean. The marble bar, whitewashed stucco walls, stone pebble tiles, and flowering plants exude wealth and elegance. The entire hillside has been landscaped and beautifully terraced, creating a Mediterranean atmosphere. The menu, a variation on California cuisine, includes grilled filet mignon with wild mushroom and sweet shallot ragoût, and salmon with angelhair pasta. The lunch and dinner menus are almost identical and on Saturday and Sunday they also serve brunch. The setting, cuisine, and high prices make Geoffrey's a prime place for celebrity gazing. ~ 27400 Pacific Coast Highway; 310-457-1519. ULTRA-DELUXE.

When you're out at the beaches around Point Dume or elsewhere in northern Malibu, there are two adjacent roadside restaurants worth checking out. **Coral Beach Cantina** is a simple Mexican restaurant with a small patio. The menu contains standard south-of-the-border fare. ~ 29350 Pacific Coast Highway; 310-457-5503. BUDGET.

HIDDEN ▶

Over at **Zuma Sushi** they have a sushi bar and table service. In addition to the house specialty there are tempura and teriyaki dishes. Like its neighbor, this is a small, unassuming café. Dinner only. ~ 29350 Pacific Coast Highway; 310-457-4131. DELUXE.

The **Hideaway Restaurant** at the Malibu Country Inn serves breakfast, lunch and dinner. Set atop a hillside at Zuma Beach, it's a pretty little place with sunny yellow chairs and a breezy outdoor deck from which you can glimpse the ocean. The menu features nothing too challenging—salads, sandwiches, pastas, fish, chicken—but the setting adds just the right ingredient. ~ 6506 Westward Beach Road at Pacific Coast Highway; 310-457-9622. MODERATE.

For a good meal near the beach there's **Neptune's Net Seafood**. Located across the highway from County Line Beach (at the Los Angeles–Ventura county border), it's a breezy café frequented by surfers. There are egg dishes for breakfast, which is served on weekends only; during the rest of the day they serve sandwiches, burgers, clam chowder, as well as shrimp, oyster, clam, and scallop baskets. Ocean views at beach bum prices. ~ 42505 Route 1; 310-457-3095. BUDGET.

Up in the Santa Monica Mountains, high above the clamor of Los Angeles, rests the **Inn of the Seventh Ray**. A throwback to the days when Topanga Canyon was a hippie enclave, this mellow dining spot serves "energized" foods to "raise your body's light vibrations." Entrées include "vegan love feast" (polenta with mushroom ragoût, eggplant with vegetarian caviar, and ginger lime soy tempeh) and "angel's delight" (roasted tofu roll stuffed with spinach, mushrooms, and pine nuts on a black bean mushroom sauce). There is also a selection of fresh seafood, duckling, and lamb dishes. Open for lunch and dinner, the restaurant features dining indoors or outside on a pretty, tree-shaded patio, where coyotes can often be seen from your table. Far out. ~ 128 Old Topanga Canyon Road, Topanga; 310-455-1311, fax 310-455-0033. DELUXE TO ULTRA-DELUXE.

SHOPPING

Somehow the name **Malibu Country Mart** doesn't quite describe this plaza shopping mall. There's not much of the "country" about the pricey boutiques and galleries here. The parking lot numbers more Porsches than pickup trucks. But these two dozen stores will provide a sense of the Malibu lifestyle and give you a chance to shop (or window shop) for quality. ~ 3835 Cross Creek Road; 310-456-2047.

Zuma Canyon Orchids features elegant and exquisite prize-winning orchids that can be shipped anywhere in the world. If you call ahead for a reservation, they will even provide a tour of the greenhouses. Closed Sunday. ~ 5949 Bonsall Drive; 310-457-9771.

Up in the secluded reaches of Topanga Canyon there are numerous artists and craftspeople who have traded the chaos of the city for the serenity of the Santa Monica Mountains. Craft shops come and go with frustrating regularity here, but it's worth a drive into the hills to see who is currently selling their wares.

NIGHTLIFE For some easy listening, check out the scene at **Beau Rivage Mediterranean Restaurant**. There's a piano player Monday, Wednesday, and Thursday; a trio performs classical and light jazz Friday. A cozy bar and fireplace add charm to the scene. ~ 26025 Pacific Coast Highway; 310-456-5733.

Malibu is largely a bedroom community; it's not known for wild nightlife, unless it's a private party at one of the beachfront homes in the colony. Lacking an invitation, look to the **Malibu Theatre**, where you might get to see one of the local residents up there on the screen. ~ 3822 Cross Creek Road; 310-456-6990. For music, theater, and dance, Pepperdine University's **Smothers Theater** offers performances by visiting artists. ~ 24255 Pacific Coast Highway; 310-456-4558.

BEACHES & PARKS **TOPANGA STATE PARK** 🚶 🚴 🐎 Not much sand here, but you will find forests of oak and fields of rye. This 11,000-plus-acre hideaway nestles in the Santa Monica Mountains above Malibu. Along the 36 miles of hiking trails and fire roads are views of the ocean, San Gabriel Mountains, and San Fernando Valley. There are meadows and a stream to explore. The park climbs from 200 to 2100 feet in elevation, providing an introduction to one of Los Angeles' few remaining natural areas. Biking is restricted to the fire trails. Facilities include an equestrian camp and trails, picnic areas, and restrooms. Parking fee, $5. ~ 20825 Entrada Road; from Route 1 in Malibu take Topanga Canyon Road up to Entrada Road; 310-455-2465.

▲ There are eight hike-in camping sites, tents only; $3 per person.

TOPANGA BEACH 🏊 🎣 🐚 This narrow sand corridor extends for over a mile. The adjacent highway breaks the quietude, but the strand is still popular with surfers and those wanting to be close to Malibu services. The swimming is good; surfing and windsurfing are excellent around Topanga Creek. Lifeguards are on duty; facilities include restrooms, showers, picnic tables, and barbecues. Parking fee, $5. ~ Located along Route 1 near Topanga Canyon Road in Malibu; 310-451-2906.

MALIBU CREEK STATE PARK 🚶 🚴 🐎 🏊 🎣 Once the location site for *M*A*S*H* and *Planet of the Apes*, this 10,000-acre facility spreads through rugged, virgin country in the Santa Monica Mountains. Among its features are 15 miles of hiking trails, four-acre Century Lake, and Malibu Creek, which is lined with willow and cottonwood. In spring the meadows explode with wildflowers; at other times of the year you'll encounter squirrels, rabbits, mule deer, coyotes and bobcats. The bird life ranges from aquatic species such as ducks and great blue herons along the lake to hawks, woodpeckers, quail and golden eagles. The lava hills, sloping grasslands, and twisted sedimentary rock formations make it an intriguing escape from the city. Facilities here include picnic areas, restrooms, and showers. Day-use fee, $5. ~ Located off Mulholland Highway at 1925 Las Vírgenes Road, Calabasas; 818-880-0367.

▲ There are 60 sites for tents and trailers or RVs (no hookups); $16 per night in season. No wood fires. Reservations, 800-444-7275.

MALIBU LAGOON STATE BEACH 🏊 ⛵ 🏄 🎣 Not only is there a pretty beach here but an estuary and wetlands area as well. You can stroll the white sands past an unending succession of lavish beachfront homes, or study a different species entirely in the park's salt marsh. Here Malibu Creek feeds into the ocean, creating a rich tidal area busy with marine life and shorebirds. The surfing is world-renowned. This is also a very popular spot for swimming; lifeguards are on duty. Facilities here include pic-

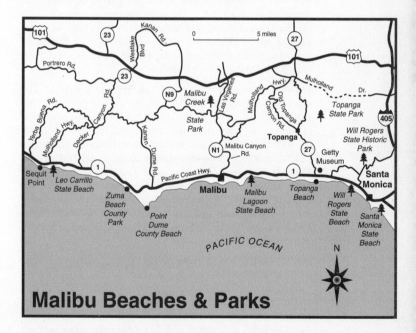

Malibu Beaches & Parks

nic areas and restrooms. Day-use fee, $6. ~ Located along Pacific Coast Highway at Cross Creek Road in Malibu; 818-880-0350.

ROBERT H. MEYER MEMORIAL STATE BEACHES 🏃 🏊 This unusual facility consists of three separate pocket beaches—**El Pescador, La Piedra,** and **El Matador.** Each is a pretty strand with sandy beach and eroded bluffs. Together they are among the nicest beaches in Malibu. My favorite is El Matador with its rock formations, sea stacks, and adjacent Malibu mansions. Use caution swimming at these beaches; there are no lifeguards. Facilities include toilets and picnic areas. Parking for all beaches is $2. ~ Located on Route 1 about 11 miles west of Malibu; 818-880-0350.

HIDDEN ▶ **WESTWARD BEACH POINT DUME STATE PARK** 🏃 🚴 🏊 🎣 🏄 This long narrow stretch is really a southerly continuation of Zuma Beach. Unlike its neighbor, it is conveniently located away from the highway and bordered by lofty sandstone cliffs. There are tidepools here and trails leading up along the bluffs. For white sand serenity this is a choice spot. Matter of fact, on the far side of Point Dume you'll encounter what was once a popular nude beach in **Pirate's Cove.** Swimming is good, but beware of dangerous currents. Surfing is good along Westward Beach and off Point Dume. Lifeguards are on duty and restrooms are available. ~ The park entrance is adjacent to the southern entrance to Zuma Beach County Park; take Westward Beach Road off Highway 1 about six miles west of Malibu. To reach the beach at Pirate's Cove, take the trail over the Point Dume Headlands; 310-457-9891.

ZUMA BEACH COUNTY PARK 🏊 🏄 🎣 🚣 🏊 🚤 This long, broad beach is a study in the territorial instincts of the species. Los Angeles County's largest beach park, it is frequented in one area by Latinos; "Vals," young residents of the San Fernando Valley, have staked claim to another section, while families and students inhabit another stretch (Zuma 3 and 4). Not quite as pretty as other Malibu beaches, Zuma offers more space and better facilities, such as restrooms, lifeguards, playgrounds, and volleyball courts. Swimming and surfing are good; for information on surf conditions, call 310-457-9701. Parking fee, $6. ~ Located along Route 1 approximately six miles west of Malibu; 310-457-9891.

LEO CARRILLO STATE PARK 🏃 🏊 🎣 🚣 🚤 Extending more than a mile, this white sand corridor rests directly below Route 1. Named after Leo Carrillo, the TV actor who played sidekick Pancho in *The Cisco Kid*, the beach offers sea caves, tidepools, interesting rock formations, and a natural tunnel. Nicer still is Leo Carrillo North Beach, a sandy swath located just beyond Sequit Point and backdropped by a sharp bluff. This entire area is a prime whale-watching site. At the south end of this 1600-acre park you can bathe in the buff—but beware, if caught you will be cited. There are picnic areas, restrooms, showers, and lifeguards. Swimming and surfing are both good; the best waves break around Sequit Point. There's excellent surfing just a few miles north at County Line Beach. Day-use fee, $6. ~ Located on Route 1, 14 miles west of Malibu. There's access to Leo Carrillo Beach North from the parking lot at 35000 Pacific Coast Highway; 818-880-0350.

▲ There are 136 sites for tents and trailers or RVs (no hookups); $14 to $17 per night. Reservations, 800-444-7275.

Twenty-six miles across the sea, (You know the song.) *Santa Catalina is a waitin' for me,* (Everyone has heard it.) *Santa Catalina, the island of Romance, romance, romance, romance.*

▼▼▼▼▼▼▼▼▼▼▼▼▼▼

Santa Catalina Island

Actually this Mediterranean hideaway is parked just 22 miles off the Los Angeles coastline. But for romance, the song portrays it perfectly. Along its 54 miles of shoreline Catalina offers sheer cliffs, pocket beaches, hidden coves, and some of the finest skin-diving anywhere. To the interior, mountains rise sharply to over 2000 feet elevation. Island fox, black antelope, and over 400 bison range the island while its waters teem with marlin, swordfish, and barracuda.

Happily, this unique habitat is preserved for posterity and adventurous travelers by an arrangement under which 86 percent of the island lies undeveloped, protected by the Santa Catalina Conservancy. Avalon, the famous coastal resort enclave, is the only town on the island. The rest is given over to mountain wilderness and pristine shoreline.

As romantic as its setting is the history of the island. Originally part of the Baja coastline, it broke off from the mainland eons ago and drifted 100 miles to the northwest. Its earliest inhabitants arrived perhaps 4000 or 5000 years ago, leaving scattered evidence of their presence before being supplanted by the Gabrieleño Indians around 500 B.C. A society of sun worshippers, the Gabrieleños constructed a sacrificial temple, fished island waters, and traded ceramics and soapstone carvings with mainland tribes, crossing the channel in canoes.

Juan Rodríguez Cabrillo discovered Catalina in 1542, but the place proved of such little interest to the Spanish that other than Sebastian Vizcaíno's exploration in 1602 they virtually ignored the island.

By the 19th century Russian fur traders, attracted by the rich colonies of sea otters, succeeded in exterminating both the otters and the indigenous people. Cattle and sheep herders took over the Gabrieleños' land while pirates and smugglers, hiding in Catalina's secluded coves, menaced the coast.

Later in the century Chinese coolies were secretly landed on the island before being illegally carried to the mainland. Even during Prohibition it proved a favorite place among rumrunners and bootleggers.

Other visionaries, seeing in Catalina a major resort area, took control. After changing hands several times the island was purchased in 1919 by William Wrigley, Jr. The Wrigley family—better known for their ownership of a chewing gum company and the Chicago Cubs baseball team—developed Avalon for tourism and left the rest of the island to nature.

SIGHTS   Attracting big-name entertainers and providing an escape from urban Los Angeles, **Avalon** soon captured the fancy of movie stars and wealthy Californians. Today Avalon is the port of entry for the island. Set in a luxurious amphitheater of green mountains, the town is like a time warp of Southern California early in the century. The architecture is a blend of Mediterranean and Victorian homes as well as vernacular structures designed by creative locals who captured both the beautiful and whimsical.

From the ferry dock you can wander **Crescent Avenue**, Avalon's oceanfront promenade. Stroll out along the **Avalon Pleasure Pier**, located at Crescent Avenue and Catalina Street, for a view of the entire town and its surrounding crescent of mountains. Located along this wood plank promenade are food stands, the harbormaster's office, and bait-and-tackle shops. The **Santa Catalina Island Chamber of Commerce and Visitors Bureau** has an information center here that will help orient you to Avalon and the island. ~ #1 Green Pier; 310-510-1520.

Among the pier kiosks are some offering **semi-submersive vessel tours** out to a nearby cove filled with colorful fish and marine plant life. Known as Catalina's "undersea gardens," the area is crowded with rich kelp beds and is a favorite haunt of brilliant red goby, golden adult Garibaldi, and leopard sharks. **Santa Catalina Island Company** features tours during the day and also at night when huge floodlights are used to attract sea life. During summer months they seek out the spectacular flying fish that seasonally inhabit these waters. They also offer coastal cruises and inland motor tours. Drop by their visitor information center. ~ 423 Crescent Avenue; 310-510-2000.

Further along the waterfront, dominating the skyline, sits the **Avalon Casino**. A massive circular building painted white and capped with a red tile roof, it was built in 1929 after a Spanish Moorish design. What can you say other than that the place is fa-

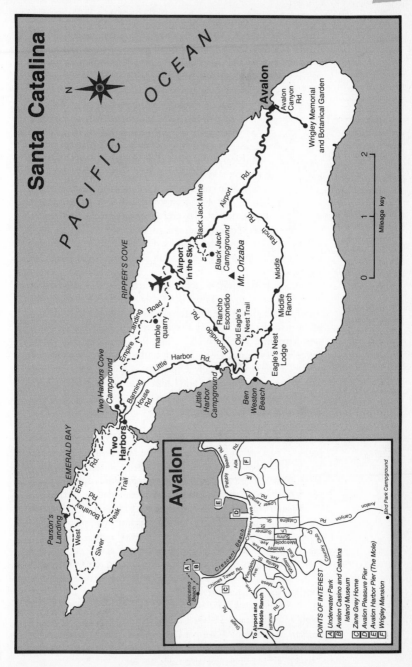

Santa Catalina

PACIFIC OCEAN

N

PACIFIC

RIPPER'S COVE

EMERALD BAY

Parson's Landing

Two Harbors Cove Campground

Two Harbors

Empire Landing Road

marble quarry

Banning House Rd.

Little Harbor Rd.

West End Rd.

Boushay Rd.

Silver Peak Trail

Little Harbor Campground

Airport in the Sky

Black Jack Mine

Black Jack Campground

▲ Mt. Orizaba

Rancho Escondido

Old Eagle's Nest Trail

Escondido Rd.

Airport Rd.

Ranch Rd.

Middle Ranch

Eagle's Nest Lodge

Ben Weston Beach

Avalon

Avalon Canyon Rd.

Wrigley Memorial and Botanical Garden

Mileage key

0   1   2

Avalon

Pebbly Beach Rd.

Mt. Ada Rd.

Descanso Beach

Crescent Beach

Chimes Tower Rd.

Sumner Ave.

Metropole Ave.

Whittley Ave.

Clarissa Ave.

Beacon St.

Marilla Ave.

La Mesa Rd.

Country Club Dr.

East Whittley Ave.

Sunny Ln.

Catalina St.

Lower Terrace Rd.

Tremont St.

To Airport and Middle Ranch

Sumner Rd.

Isthmus Rd.

Avalon Canyon Rd.

Bird Park Campground

A

B

C

D

E

F

POINTS OF INTEREST

A Underwater Park
B Avalon Casino and Catalina Island Museum
C Zane Grey Home
D Avalon Pleasure Pier
E Avalon Harbor Pier (The Mole)
F Wrigley Mansion

mous: it has appeared on countless post cards and travel posters. The ballroom has heard the big band sounds of Count Basie and Tommy Dorsey and the entire complex is a study in art deco with fabulous murals and tile paintings. ~ On Casino Way at the end of Crescent Avenue; 310-510-2000.

Downstairs is the **Catalina Island Museum** with a small collection of local artifacts. Of particular interest is the contour relief map of the island which provides an excellent perspective for anyone venturing into the interior. Admission. ~ Avalon Casino; 310-510-2414.

> Gold fever swept Santa Catalina in 1863 as miners swept onto the island, but the rush never panned out.

Another point of particular interest, located about two miles inland in Avalon Canyon, is the **Wrigley Memorial and Botanical Garden**, a tribute to William Wrigley, Jr. The monument, an imposing 130-foot structure fashioned with glazed tiles and Georgia marble, features an impressive spiral staircase in a solitary tower. The gardens, a showplace for native island plants, display an array of succulents and cactus. Admission. ~ 1400 Avalon Canyon Road; 310-510-2288.

The most exhilarating sightseeing excursion in Avalon lies in the hills around town. Head out Pebbly Beach Road along the water, turn right on Wrigley Terrace Road, and you'll be on one of the many terraces that rise above Avalon. The old Wrigley Mansion (currently The Inn on Mt. Ada, Wrigley Road), an elegant estate with sweeping views, was once the (ho hum) summer residence of the Wrigley family. Other scenic drives on the opposite side of town lie along Stage and Chimes Tower roads. Here you'll pass the **Zane Grey Hotel**, a 1926 pueblo adobe that was formerly the Western novel writer's home. ~ 199 Chimes Tower Road; 310-510-0966.

Both routes snake into the hills past rocky outcroppings and patches of cactus. The slopes are steep and unrelenting. Below you blocks of houses run in rows out to a fringe of palm trees and undergrowth. Gaze around from this precarious perch and you'll see that Avalon rests in a green bowl surrounded by mountains.

When it comes time to venture further afield, you'll find that traveling around Santa Catalina Island is more complicated than it first seems. Preserving nature is probably what the island's caretakers had in mind when they made driving cars illegal on Catalina. While golf carts are allowed in Avalon, the remainder of the island's roads must be navigated by two wheels, two feet, or a shuttle. You can hike or bicycle to most places on the island. **Brown's Bikes** rents bicycles, tandems, and mountain bikes. ~ 107 Pebbly Beach Road; 310-510-0986. In Avalon proper rent golf carts from outfits like **Cartopia Cars**. ~ 615 Crescent Avenue; 310-510-2493. Also try **Catalina Auto Rental**. ~ 301 Crescent Avenue; 310-510-0111. There are also taxis in town.

Catalina Safari Bus provides a shuttle service to Two Harbors; a bus will take you there, but if you want to return to Avalon in the afternoon, you'll be taking a boat. ~ 310-510-2800. **Santa Catalina Island Conservancy**, the agency charged with overseeing the island, shuttles visitors to the airport and provides jeep tours. ~ 125 Claressa Avenue; 310-510-2595. To hike independently outside Avalon you will need a permit from the Santa Catalina Island Conservancy. ~ 125 Claressa Avenue; 310-510-1421. Permits are also available at The Airport in the Sky. ~ 310-510-0143. You can also call the Catalina Cove and Camp Agency. ~ P.O. Box 5049, Two Harbors, CA 90704; 310-510-0303.

The other thing to remember about Catalina is that perhaps more than any other spot along the California coast, its tourism is seasonal. The season, of course, is summer, when mobs of people descend on the island. During winter everything slows down, storms wash through intermittently, and some facilities close. Spring and fall, when the crowds have subsided, the weather is good, and everything is still open, may be the best seasons of all.

Regardless of how you journey into Catalina's outback, there's only one way to get there, Airport Road. This paved thoroughfare climbs steadily from Avalon, offering views of the rugged coast and surrounding hills. Oak, pine, and eucalyptus dot the hillsides as the road follows a ridgetop with steep canyons falling away on either side. **Mt. Orizaba**, a flat-topped peak which represents the highest point on the island, rises in the distance.

A side road out to Black Jack Campground leads past **Black Jack Mine**, a silver mine closed since early in the century. Today little remains except tailing piles and a 520-foot shaft. Then the main road climbs to Catalina's **Airport in the Sky**, a small landing facility located at 1600-foot elevation.

From the airport you might want to follow a figure eight course in your route around the island, covering most of the island's roads and taking in as much of the landscape as possible (beyond the airport all the roads are dirt). Just follow Empire Landing Road, a curving, bumping track with side roads that lead down past an **old marble quarry** to **Ripper's Cove**. Characteristic of the many inlets dotting the island, the cove is framed by sharply rising hills. There's a boulder-and-sand beach here and a coastline bordered by interesting rock formations.

Two Harbors, at the intersection of the figure-eight's loops, is a half-mile wide isthmus joining the two parts of Catalina Island. A small fishing pier, a few tourist facilities, and a boat harbor make this modest enclave the only developed area outside Avalon.

From here West End Road curves and climbs, bends and descends along a rocky coast pocked with cactus and covered by scrub growth. There are Catalina cherry trees along the route and numerous coves at the bottom of steep cliffs. Not for the fainthearted, West End Road is a narrow, bumpy course that winds high above the shore.

Anchored off **Emerald Bay** are several rock islets crowded with sea birds. From **Parson's Landing**, a small inlet with a gray sand beach, dirt roads continue in a long loop out to the west end of the island, then back to Two Harbors.

Catalina possesses about 400 species of flora, some unique to the island, and is rich in wildlife. Anywhere along its slopes you are likely to spy quail, wild turkey, mountain goats, island fox, mule deer, and wild boar. Bison, placed on the island by a movie company filming a Western way back in the 1920s, graze seemingly everywhere. En route back toward Avalon, Little Harbor Road climbs into the mountains. From the hilltops around **Little Harbor** you can see a series of ridges which drop along sheer rock-faces to the frothing surf below.

Take a detour up to **Rancho Escondido**, a working ranch that boards champion Arabian horses. There's an arena here where trainers work these exquisite animals through their paces, and a "saddle and trophy room" filled with handcrafted riding gear as well as prizes from major horse shows.

Back at Little Harbor, Middle Ranch Road cuts through a mountain canyon past **Middle Ranch**, a small spread with livestock and oat fields. En route lies **Eagles' Nest Lodge**, a stagecoach stop dating to 1890. Numbered among the antique effects of this simple woodframe house are wagon wheels and a split-rail fence. Carry on to Airport Road then back to Avalon, completing this easy-eight route around an extraordinary island.

LODGING   One fact about lodging in Catalina everyone seems to agree upon is that it is overpriced. Particularly in the summer, when Avalon's population swells from under 3000 to over 10,000, hotels charge stiff rates for rooms. But what's a traveler to do? The island is both pretty and popular, so you have no recourse but to pay the piper.

It's also a fact that rates jump seasonally more than on the mainland. Summer is the most expensive period, winter the cheapest, with spring and fall somewhere in between. Weekend rates are also sometimes higher than weekday room tabs and usually require a two-night minimum.

The last fact of life for lodgers to remember is that since most of the island is a nature preserve, the hotels, with one lone exception, are located in Avalon.

Low-price lodgings are as rare as snow in Avalon. But at the **Hotel Atwater** you'll find accommodations to suit all budgets. They are renovating the hotel stage by stage; the new wing offers 26 country-style rooms in the deluxe-to-ultra-deluxe range. The older part of the hotel has less expensive plain rooms with veneer dressers, nicked night tables, soft mattresses, spotty carpets, and, if it's like the room I saw, a hole in the wall. But, hey, the place *is* clean and this *is* Catalina. Besides, it has a friendly lobby with oak trim and tasteful blue furniture, plus dozens of rooms to choose from. Good luck. ~ 125 Sumner Street; 310-510-1788, 800-322-3434, fax 310-510-7254. BUDGET TO ULTRA-DELUXE.

One of Santa Catalina's most popular hotels is the **Pavilion Lodge**, a 73-room facility on Avalon's waterfront street. Designed around a central courtyard, it offers guests a lawn and patio for sunbathing. The rooms contain modern furniture, wall-to-wall carpeting, and stall showers. If you want to be at the heart of downtown in a comfortable if undistinguished establishment, this is the place. ~ 513 Crescent Avenue; 310-510-1788, 800-322-3434, fax 310-510-2073. DELUXE TO ULTRA-DELUXE.

Plainly put, the **Hotel Vista del Mar** is a gem. Each of the 15 spacious Mediterranean-style rooms is decorated in soft pastels and features a wet bar, fireplace, and full tiled bath. All surround an open-air atrium courtyard lobby, where guests enjoy ocean breezes and views from comfortable wicker rockers. One smaller room is priced deluxe, while courtyard rooms command ultra-deluxe rates. ~ 417 Crescent Avenue; 310-510-1452, 800-601-3836, fax 310-510-2917. DELUXE TO ULTRA DELUXE.

Farther along the same street is **Hotel Villa Portofino** with 34 rooms situated around a split-level brick patio. The accommodations are small but have been stylishly decorated with modern furniture, dressing tables, and wallpaper in pastel shades. There are tile baths with stall showers. A small lobby downstairs has been finished with potted plants and marble. ~ 111 Crescent Avenue; 310-510-0555, 800-346-2326, fax 310-510-0839. MODERATE TO DELUXE.

TALLY HO. . .TEL!

Banning House Lodge, the only hotel on the island located outside Avalon, is a turn-of-the-century hunting lodge. Set in the isthmus that connects the two sections of Santa Catalina, it's a low-slung shingle building with a dining room and a mountain-lodge atmosphere. The living room boasts a brick fireplace and is adorned with a dozen trophy heads. Staring out dolefully from the wood-paneled walls are deer, bison, fox, wild turkey, boar, and mountain goats. The guest rooms are trimly decorated with throw rugs and rustic wood furniture. The lodge provides an excellent opportunity to experience the island's outback. Continental breakfast is served in the lodge's dining room. ~ Two Harbors; 310-510-0303. DELUXE TO ULTRA-DELUXE.

It's a big, bold, blue and white structure rising for five levels above the hillside. **Hotel Catalina** has been a fixture on the Avalon skyline since 1892. The 32-unit facility features a comfortable lobby complete with overhead fans, plus a sundeck and jacuzzi. The sleeping rooms are small but comfy with standard furnishings; many offer ocean views and half the rooms have small refrigerators and VCRs. There are also four trim little cottages that are warmly decorated. A bright, summer atmosphere pervades the place. ~ At 129 Whittley Avenue; 310-510-0027, 800-540-0184, fax 310-510-1495. MODERATE TO DELUXE.

> No rental cars operate on the island, and visitors are not permitted to drive.

La Paloma Cottages, a rambling complex consisting of several buildings, features a string of eight contiguous cottages. These are cozy units with original decor and comfortable furnishings. There are also six larger family units (with kitchens) available in a nearby building. Set on a terraced street in a quiet part of town, La Paloma is attractively landscaped. There are no phones or daily maid service in the rooms. However, at **Las Flores,** an addition to the original hotel, you can get pricier rooms with maid service, phones and a whirlpool bath to boot. ~ 326 Sunny Lane; 310-510-0737, 800-310-1505, fax 310-510-2424. MODERATE TO DELUXE.

Catalina Canyon Hotel Resort and Spa is a chic, modern 80-room complex complete with pool, jacuzzi, sauna, restaurant, and bar. This Mediterranean-style hotel sits on a hillside in Avalon Canyon. The grounds are nicely landscaped with banana plants and palm trees. Each guest room is furnished in white oak, adorned with art prints, and decorated in a motif of soft hues. ~ 888 Country Club Drive; 310-510-0325, 800-253-9361, fax 310-510-0900. ULTRA-DELUXE.

The romantic **Hotel St. Lauren** rises with a pink blush a block from the sand above Catalina's famed harbor. The Victorian-style hotel is a honeymoon paradise, with spacious rooms and jacuzzi tubs in minisuites. ~ Metropole and Beacon streets; 310-510-2299, fax 310-510-1369. DELUXE TO ULTRA-DELUXE.

Rare and incredible is the only way to describe **The Inn on Mt. Ada**. Nothing on the island, and few places along the California coast, compare. Perched on a hillside overlooking Avalon and its emerald shoreline, this stately hostelry resides in the old Wrigley mansion, a 7000-square-foot Georgian Colonial home built by the chewing gum baron in 1921. A masterwork of french doors and elegant columns, curved ceilings, and ornamental molding, the grande dame is beautifully appointed with antiques and plush furnishings. The entire ground floor—with rattan-furnished sitting room, oceanfront veranda, formal dining room, and spacious living room—is for the benefit of visitors. Wine and hors d'oeuvres are served in the afternoon and there's a full breakfast, deli lunch, and dinner served to guests and a limited number of visitors. The wonder of the place is that all this luxury is for just six guest rooms, guaranteeing personal service and an atmosphere of intimacy. The private rooms are stylishly furnished in period pieces and adorned with a creative selection of artwork. All meals are included. Reserve at least two months in advance. ~ 398 Wrigley Road, P.O. Box 2560, Avalon, CA 90704; 310-510-2030, 800-608-7669, fax 310-510-2237. ULTRA-DELUXE.

As with Catalina hotels, there are a few points to remember when shopping for a restaurant. Prices are higher than on the mainland. With very few exceptions the dining spots are concentrated in Avalon; services around the rest of the island are minimal. Also, business is seasonal, so restaurants may vary their schedules, serving three meals daily during summer and weekends but only dinner during winter. The wisest course is to check beforehand.

DINING

Antonio's Pizzeria is a hole-in-the-wall, but a hole-in-the-wall with panache. It's chockablock with junk—old pin-up pictures, record covers, dolls, and trophies. There's sawdust on the floor and a vague '50s theme to the place. The food—pizza, pasta, and hot sandwiches—is good, filling, and served daily at lunch and dinner. "Come on in," as the sign suggests, "and bask in the ambience of the decaying 1950s." ~ 114 Sumner Avenue; 310-510-0060. BUDGET TO MODERATE.

The Busy Bee, established in 1923, is a local gathering place located right on the beach. It's hard to match the views from the patio of this simple café. This is one place in Catalina that's open for breakfast and lunch year-round. For lunch you can dine on vegetable platters, tacos, tostadas, salads, and sandwiches while gazing out at the pier and harbor. In summer, the dinner menu offers buffalo burgers, fried shrimp, teriyaki chicken, and steak. ~ 306-B Crescent Avenue; 310-510-1983. MODERATE.

◄ HIDDEN

The other half of the vintage stucco-and-red-tile building housing the Busy Bee is the site of **Armstrong's Seafood Restaurant and Fish Market**. The interior is trimly finished in knotty pine and white tile with mounted gamefish on the walls. Since the establishment doubles as a fish market you can count on fresh seafood. The menu is the same at lunch and dinner with only the portions and prices changing. Mesquite-grilled dishes include mahimahi, scallops, swordfish, skewered shrimp, and steak. They also feature lobster, ahi, and orange roughy. You can dine indoors or on the patio along the waterfront, making Armstrong's prices a bargain. ~ 306-A Crescent Avenue; 310-510-0113. MODERATE.

Café Prego, a small Italian bistro complete with oilcloth tables and stucco arches, comes highly recommended. The specialties are seafood and pasta; you'll find a menu offering fresh swordfish, sea bass, halibut, and snapper, plus manicotti, rigatoni, lasagna, and fettuccine. There are also steak and veal dishes at this waterfront nook. It features good food and a cozy ambience. ~ 609 Crescent Avenue; 310-510-1218. MODERATE.

For a step upscale head down the street to **Ristorante Villa Portofino**. Here a baby grand piano is set off by pink stucco walls and the candlelit tables are decorated with flowers. With art deco curves and colorful art prints the place has an easy Mediterranean feel about it. The Continental cuisine includes several veal dishes, scampi, grilled filet mignon, swordfish, and a selection of pasta dishes. This is the place for a romantic dinner. Dinner only. Closed in January. ~ 111 Crescent Avenue; 310-510-0508. MODERATE TO DELUXE.

Buffalo Springs Station, situated up in the mountains at 1600 feet, is part of Catalina's Airport in the Sky complex. This facility serves egg dishes, hot cakes, buffalo burgers, and a variety of sandwiches. There's not much to the self-service restaurant itself, but it adjoins a lobby with stone fireplace and a tile patio that overlooks the surrounding mountains. No dinner. ~ 310-510-2196. BUDGET.

Catalina's remotest dining place is **Doug's Harbor Reef Restaurant**, located way out in the Two Harbors area. This rambling establishment has a dining room done in nautical motif with fish nets, shell lamps, and woven *lauhala* mats. There's also an adjoining patio for enjoying the soft breezes that blow through this isthmus area. Doug's offers such Caribbean-themed specialties as baked papaya stuffed with shrimp, scallop, crab, lobster, bananas, and curry. There are also fresh fish, steak, and pasta dishes. ~ Two Harbors; 310-510-0303. MODERATE TO DELUXE.

Next to Doug's there's an adjoining **snack bar** serving three meals daily; breakfast and lunch in winter months. It offers egg dishes, sandwiches, burgers, pizza and burritos. ~ Two Harbors. BUDGET.

SHOPPING   No one sails to Santa Catalina Island searching for bargains. Everything here has been shipped from the mainland and is that much more expensive as a result. The town of Avalon has a row of shops lining its main thoroughfare, Crescent Avenue, and other stores along the streets running up from the waterfront. Within this commercial checkerboard are also several mini-malls, one of which, **Metropole Market Place**, is a nicely designed, modern complex. ~ Crescent and Whitney avenues.

Half the stores in town are either souvenir or curio shops. I'd wait until you return to that shopping metropolis 26 miles across the sea.

Like all other Catalina amenities, nightspots are concentrated in Avalon. **NIGHTLIFE**

The **Chi Chi Club** is the hottest dance club on the island with live and deejay music (ranging from Top-40 and hip-hop to cool retro) and an enthusiastic crowd. Cover on weekends. ~ 107 Sumner Avenue; 310-510-2828.

Antonio's Cabaret hosts karaoke every Friday, Saturday, and Sunday night. ~ 230 Crescent Avenue; 310-510-0008.

Also check the schedule for the **Avalon Casino**. This fabulous vintage ballroom still hosts big bands and most of the island's major events. ~ Located at the end of Crescent Avenue; 310-510-2000.

If you are planning to camp on Catalina, there are a few things to know. First, there is a fee for camping and reservations are a must (reservation numbers are listed under the particular park). **BEACHES & PARKS**

In addition to designated beaches, camping is permitted in many of the island's coves. These are undeveloped sites with no facilities; most readily accessible by boat. Patrolling rangers collect fees here.

For information on hiking permits, camping, and transportation to campgrounds, contact the **Santa Catalina Island Conservancy** (125 Claressa Avenue, Avalon; 310-510-1421), the **Catalina Cove and Camp Agency** (P.O. Box 5049, Two Harbors; 310-510-0303), or the agent at **Two Harbors Campground** (310-510-2800) who seems to know just about everything relating to camping in the area.

CRESCENT BEACH 🏃 🚵 ⛵ 🚤 🛶 ⚓ About as relaxing as Coney Island, this beach is at the center of the action. Avalon's main drag parallels the beach and a pier divides it into two separate strips of sand. Facing Avalon Harbor, the strand is flanked on one side with a ferry dock and along the other by the famous Avalon Casino. Full service facilities (including restrooms, showers, and beach rentals) are available on the street adjacent to the beach; lifeguards are also on duty. Fishing is good from the pier, and the harbor provides protection from the surf, making it an excellent swimming area. ~ On Crescent Avenue in Avalon.

DESCANSO BEACH CLUB 🏃 ⛵ 🚤 🎣 🛶 Somehow the appeal of this private enclave escapes me. A rock-strewn beach on the far side of the Avalon Casino, it seconds as a mooring facility for sailboats. Granted, there is a rolling lawn dotted with palm trees and the complex is nicely surrounded by hills. But with all the commotion at the snack bar and volleyball courts it's more like being on an amusement pier than a beach. Besides that, you have to pay to get onto the beach. Once there, you'll find good swimming, a restaurant, horseshoes, ping-pong tables, restrooms, a playground, and showers. The beach is closed weekdays during the winter. ~ Located off Crescent Avenue past the Avalon Casino; 310-510-7410.

HERMIT GULCH CAMPGROUND 🚶 This grassy field, dotted with palm and pine trees, is the only campground serving the Avalon area. Located up in Avalon Canyon inland from the beach, it provides a convenient and inexpensive way to visit Avalon and utilize its many services. There are pretty views of the surrounding hills and hiking trails are nearby. Facilities include picnic areas, restrooms, and showers; restaurants and groceries are nearby in Avalon. ~ On Avalon Canyon Road a mile from downtown Avalon; 310-510-8368.

▲ There are extensive camping facilities, ranging from A-frames to teepee sites to equipment rentals. There are 63 tent sites, $8.50 to $10 per person per night.

HIDDEN ► **BLACK JACK CAMPGROUND** 🚶🚴🐎 Situated at 1600 feet elevation, this facility sits on a plateau below Mt. Black Jack, the island's second highest peak. It's a lovely spot shaded by pine and eucalyptus trees and affording views across the rolling hills and out along the ocean. Among backcountry facilities this is about the most popular on the island. The campground has picnic areas, toilets, and showers; restaurants and groceries are way back in Avalon. ~ Located south of The Airport in the Sky off Airport Road. Seasonal shuttle available from Avalon to Black Jack trail junction; 310-510-2800.

▲ There is a hike-in campground; $7.50 per person per night.

BEN WESTON BEACH 🚶🏊🎣 A favorite among locals, this pewter-colored beach is surrounded by rocky hills. Located at the end of a long canyon road, it is serene and secluded. Avalon residents come here to flee the tourists, so you might consider making it your hideaway. This is a day-use beach only. Fishing and swimming are good, and it is one of the island's best spots for surfing. Facilities are limited to toilets. ~ Located about two miles south of Little Harbor off Middle Ranch Road.

LITTLE HARBOR CAMPGROUND 🏊🎣 On the southwest shore of the island, this camp sits near a sandy beach between rocky headlands. It's studded with palm trees and occasionally filled with grazing bison, making it one of the island's prettiest facilities. In addition, Shark Harbor, a section of Little Harbor, is excellent for shell collecting and bodysurfing. Fishing, swimming and skindiving are good here; facilities include picnic areas, toilets, and cold showers. Restaurants and groceries are in Two Harbors. ~ Located about seven miles east of Two Harbors along Little Harbor Road; 310-510-2800.

▲ The campground has a 150-person maximum; tents only; $8.50 per person per night.

TWO HARBORS CAMPGROUND 🚶 🚲 🏊 ⛵ 🚣 🍴 Set along a series of terraces above a brown sand beach, this facility is adjacent to the services at Two Harbors. It's also a convenient base camp from which to hike out along the island's west end. Facilities include picnic areas, restrooms, showers, lockers, laundry, and volleyball; restaurants and groceries are nearby. The fishing and swimming are good, and the colorful waters here make skindiving especially rewarding. ~ Next to Two Harbors in Little Fisherman's Cove; 310-510-0303.

▲ The facilities here are extensive and include 55 tent sites, tent cabins and teepees with added amenities, a 24-hour-a-day ranger, and more. Prices vary; call for information.

PARSON'S LANDING 🚶 🚲 🏊 ⛵ 🍴 The most remote of Catalina's campgrounds, this isolated facility sits along a small brown sand beach with grass-covered hills in the background. Fishing, swimming, and skindiving are all good; facilities include picnic areas and toilets; restaurants and groceries are several miles away. ~ Located seven miles west of Two Harbors along West End Road; 310-510-2800.

▲ The campground holds a maximum of 48 people; tents only; $16.50 for the first person and $6.50 for each additional camper.

▼▼▼▼▼▼▼▼▼▼▼▼▼▼
Outdoor Adventures

Fish the waters around Los Angeles and you can try your hand at landing a barracuda, calico bass, halibut, white sea bass, white croaker, or maybe even a relative of Jaws.

SPORT-FISHING

L.A. Harbor Sportfishing offers scheduled and chartered trips for yellowtail, bass, tuna, barracuda, and bonito. ~ Berth 79, San Pedro; 310-547-9916. **Redondo Sportfishing** offers half- and three-quarter-day trips in the Santa Monica Bay near Catalina Island on three 65-foot boats. ~ 233 North Harbor Drive, Redondo Beach; 310-372-2111. For half- and full-day trips seeking yellowtail and white sea bass, contact **Marina del Rey Sportfishing**. ~ 13759 Fiji Way, Marina del Rey; 310-822-3625.

In Catalina you can contact the **Santa Catalina Island Chamber of Commerce and Visitors Bureau** for listings of private boat owners who outfit sportfishing expeditions. ~ 310-510-1520.

DIVING

If you'd rather search for starfish than stars along L.A.'s coastline, you'll find an active diving scene.

To explore Los Angeles' submerged depths, contact **Pacific Sporting Goods**, which provides lessons and equipment and organizes boat trips. ~ 11 39th Place, Long Beach; 562-434-1604. **Pacific Wilderness Ocean Sports** is a PADI training center that sells and rents equipment. ~ 1719 South Pacific Avenue, San Pedro; 310-833-2422. Lessons at **Dive 'n Surf** are also PADI-certified; dive trips to Catalina and Santa Barbara are available. ~ 504 North Broadway, Redondo Beach; 310-372-8423. For full-day trips around local islands call **Sea D Sea**. ~ 1911 South Catalina Avenue, Redondo Beach; 310-373-6355. **Blue Cheer Ocean Water Sports** runs trips from Santa Monica to Anacapa and Santa Cruz islands. ~ 1110 Wilshire Boulevard, Santa Monica; 310-828-1217. For NAUI certification classes and dive trips near the islands contact **Scuba Haus**. ~ 2501 Wilshire Boulevard, Santa Monica; 310-828-2916. **Malibu Divers** rents and sells gear and runs full-day trips to Catalina. ~ 21231 Pacific Coast Highway, Malibu; 310-456-2396.

Without doubt Santa Catalina offers some of the finest scuba diving anywhere in the world. Perfectly positioned to attract fish from both the northern and southern Pacific, it teems with sea life. Large fish ascend from the deep waters surrounding the island while small colorful species inhabit rich kelp forests along the coast. There are caves and caverns to explore as well as the wrecks of rusting ships.

Several outfits rent skindiving and scuba equipment and sponsor dive trips, including **Catalina Divers Supply**. ~ 310-510-0330. **Island Charters, Inc.** offers similar services. ~ 310-510-2616. For guided or unguided full-day chartered trips contact **Argo Diving Service**. ~ 310-510-2208. In Two Harbors, the **West End Dive Shop** offers PADI certification as well as scuba and snorkel trips. ~ 310-510-2800.

WHALE WATCHING

If you're visiting Los Angeles from winter to early spring, hop aboard a whale-watching vessel and keep your eyes peeled for plumes and tails.

During the annual whale migration several outfits offer local whale-watching trips. **Long Beach Sportfishing** also provides half-day to overnight trips to Catalina and San Clemente. ~ 555 Pico Avenue, Long Beach; 562-432-8993. For a four-hour trip call **Catalina Cruises**. ~ 320 Golden Shore, Long Beach; 562-436-5006. Out of San Pedro, **Los Angeles Harbor Cruise** takes two-and-a-half-hour trips along the coast. ~ Berth 78, San Pedro; 310-831-0996. Similar trips are available from **Spirit Cruises**. ~ Berth 77, San Pedro; 310-831-1073. **L.A. Harbor Sportfishing** offers two-and-a-half-hour trips. ~ Berth 79, San Pedro; 310-547-9916.

SURFING & WIND-SURFING

"Surfing is the only life," so when in the Southland, sample a bit of Los Angeles' seminal subculture. Redondo, Hermosa, and Manhattan beaches have come to represent the L.A. scene. Other popular spots include Royal Palms State Beach and Torrance County Beach's Malaga Cove. If you're in Malibu, check out the waves at Topanga Beach, Malibu Surfrider Beach, and Leo Carrillo State

Beach. Santa Catalina also has its share of waves: Ben Weston Beach for surfing and Shark Harbor for bodysurfing. Remember, it's more fun to hang ten than just hang out.

Rent a surfboard, bodyboard, or wetsuit from **Manhattan Beach Bike and Skate Rentals**. ~ 1116 Manhattan Avenue, Manhattan Beach; 310-372-8500. **Jeffers** offers surfboards and boogieboards. ~ 39 14th Street, Hermosa Beach; 310-372-9492. You'll find surfboard, boogieboard, and wetsuit rentals in Malibu at **Zuma Jay Surfboards**. ~ 22775 Pacific Coast Highway, Malibu; 310-456-8044.

KAYAKING

For half-day ocean kayak tours along the Malibu coast, kayaking lessons, and kayak rentals, contact **Malibu Ocean Sport**. The tours last about two and a half hours and include some basic instruction. Tours are offered only on weekends between April and October. ~ 22935 Pacific Coast Highway; 310-456-6302.

On Catalina Island, **Descanso Beach Ocean Sports** offers several different guided expeditions in the waters around Catalina, among them a short 90-minute paddle to a cove near Avalon and a full-day excursion that includes hiking and picnicking. ~ Descanso Beach, Avalon; 310-510-1226.

SKATING & SKATE-BOARDING

Los Angeles may well be the roller skating capital of California, and skateboarding, of course, is the closest thing to surfing without waves. Between the two of them, you can't get much more L.A., so find a way to put yourself on wheels.

To rent skates or a skateboard call **Manhattan Beach Bike and Skate Rentals**. ~ 1116 Manhattan Avenue, Manhattan Beach; 310-372-8500. **Rollerskates of America** has in-line skates and gear. ~ 1312 Hermosa Avenue, Hermosa Beach; 310-372-8812. **Spokes 'n Stuff** has two convenient locations and rents both inline skates

✔ **CHECK THESE OUT—UNIQUE OUTDOOR ADVENTURES**

- Take the plunge in the waters off Santa Catalina Island, where divers discover kelp forests, sunken ships, and underwater caverns. *page 364*
- Get in the middle of the most amazing commute in Southern California, the annual migration of the big grays, on a whale-watching cruise from Long Beach or San Pedro. *page 364*
- Roll past the scene on the Venice boardwalk, where skating and biking offer you a way to see the most in the shortest time. *page 365*
- Exercise your soles and your soul by hiking the California Coastal Trail, with its beautiful bluffs, basins, and beach-walks. *page 368*

and rollerskates. ~ At the parking lot on Admiralty Way at Jamaica Bay Inn Hotel, Marina del Rey, 310-306-3332; and near the Santa Monica Pier in Loews Santa Monica, 310-395-4748. Along the Santa Monica Pier **Sea Mist Skate Rentals** has inline skates, rollerskates, bikes, and anything else you might need for a day on the South Bay Trail. ~ 1619 Ocean Front Walk, at the Santa Monica Pier, Santa Monica; 310-395-7076.

GOLF

Tee off in the gentle sea breeze—L.A.'s coastal climate is ideal for spending a day on the greens. Just don't swing too hard, because those golf balls don't float! Most courses have 18 holes and rent clubs and carts.

The beautiful **El Dorado Park Municipal Golf Course** has two putting greens and a driving range. ~ 2400 Studebaker Road, Long Beach; 562-430-5411. The 18-hole **Skylink Golf Course** is a duffer's delight. ~ 4800 East Wardlow Road, Long Beach; 562-421-3388. The hilly **Recreation Park** offers both an 18-hole and a 9-hole course. ~ 5000 Deukmeijian Street, Long Beach; 562-494-5000. On the Palos Verdes Peninsula, there's **Los Verdes Golf Course**. Nicknamed the Poor Man's Pebble Beach, each hole has views of the sea and Catalina Island. ~ 7000 West Los Verdes Drive, Rancho Palos Verdes; 310-377-7370. If you can take a break from the action in Venice, head to the 9-hole **Penmar Golf Course**. ~ 1233 Rose Avenue, Venice; 310-396-6228. **Catalina Visitors Golf Club** has a hilly, narrow nine-hole course with plenty of sand traps. ~ 1 Country Club Drive, Avalon; 310-510-0530.

TENNIS

A visit to the Los Angeles coast is reason enough to re-string your racquet and start enjoying the weather. These waterfront communities sport an abundance of courts, though there's usually a fee to play; call ahead to check.

There are 15 lighted courts available at **El Dorado Park**. ~ 2800 Studebaker Road, Long Beach; 562-425-0553. The **Billie Jean King Tennis Center** offers eight lighted courts. ~ 1040 Park Avenue, Long Beach; 562-438-8509. **Alta Vista Tennis Courts** has eight lighted courts as well. Reservations required. ~ 715 Julia Avenue, Redondo Beach; 310-318-0670. Two lighted courts are available at **The Sport Center at King Harbor**. ~ 819 North Harbor Drive, Redondo Beach; 310-372-8868. **Marina Tennis Center** has ten lighted courts. ~ 13199 Mindanao Way, Marina del Rey; 310-822-2255.

In Santa Monica, it's a good idea to call for reservations at public tennis courts. **Reed Park** has six lighted courts. ~ 1133 7th Street, Santa Monica; 310-394-6011. **Memorial Park** offers four lighted courts. ~ Colorado Boulevard at 14th Street, Santa Monica; 310-394-6011. Also try one of the six courts at **Ocean View**

Park. ~ Barnard Way south of Ocean Park Boulevard, Santa Monica; 310-394-6011.

For a glimpse of the Pacific from a hilltop high above Malibu in the Santa Monica Mountains, contact **Adventures on Horseback** about one of its several horseback riding options, including guided trails rides, moonlight rides, and sunset rides. Reservations are necessary. ~ 31811 Mulholland Highway; 818-706-0888.

RIDING STABLES

Though Los Angeles might seem like one giant freeway, there are scores of shoreline bike trails and routes for scenic excursions. Whether you're up for a leisurely and level beachfront loop, or a more strenuous trek through coastal cliffside communities, the gorgeous weather and scenery make this area a beautiful place for a bike ride.

BIKING

Foremost is the **South Bay Bike Trail**, with over 22 miles of coastal vistas. The trail, an easy ride and extremely popular, runs from RAT Beach in Torrance to Will Rogers State Beach in Pacific Palisades. The path intersects the Ballona Creek Bikeway in Marina Del Rey, which extends seven miles east and passes the Venice Boardwalk, as well as piers and marinas along the way.

Naples, a Venice-like neighborhood in Long Beach, provides a charming area for freeform bike rides. There are no designated paths but you can cycle with ease past beautiful homes, parks, and canals.

Of moderate difficulty is the **Palos Verdes Peninsula** coastline trail. Offering wonderful scenery, the 14-mile round trip ride goes from Malaga Cove Plaza in Palos Verdes Estates to the Wayfarers Chapel. (Part of the trail is a bike path, the rest follows city streets.)

The **Santa Monica Loop** is an easy ride starting at San Vicente Boulevard and going up Ocean Avenue, past Palisades Park and the Santa Monica Pier. Most of the trail is on bike lanes and paths; five miles round trip.

In **Catalina,** free use of bikes is allowed only in Avalon. Elsewhere permits are required: they may be obtained from the **Catalina Conservancy.** ~ P.O. Box 2739, Avalon, CA 90704; 310-510-1421. Cross-channel carriers have special requirements for transporting bicycles and must be contacted in advance for complete details.

For maps, brochures, and additional information on bike routes in Los Angeles contact the **Department of Transportation.** ~ 205 South Broadway, Suite 400; 213-485-4277.

Bike Rentals   To rent mountain bikes, cruisers, or tandems, try **Manhattan Beach Bike and Skate Rentals.** ~ 1116 Manhattan Avenue, Manhattan Beach; 310-372-8500. In Hermosa Beach, **Jeffers** rents beach cruisers and mountain bikes. ~ 39 14th Street,

Hermosa Beach; 310-372-9492. **Spokes 'n Stuff** offers mountain bikes, tandems, and cruisers at two locations. ~ At the parking lot on Admiralty Way at Jamaica Bay Inn Hotel, Marina del Rey, 310-306-3332; and near the pier in Loews Santa Monica, 310-395-4748. Also in Santa Monica, **Sea Mist Skate Rentals** has mountain bikes and helmets. ~ 1619 Ocean Front Walk, Santa Monica; 310-395-7076. In Catalina try **Brown's Bikes**. ~ 107 Pebbly Beach Road, Avalon; 310-510-0986.

HIKING   Depending on where you go for your hike, you may want your boots, spiffy street shoes, or Tevas. The terrain of this region offers a wide array of options, from beaches and tidepools to busy boardwalks to the trails of the rugged coast range. For a unique foray, try exploring a beached shipwreck or hiking in to the familiar-looking filming location of *M*A*S*H**. The only common denominators for hiking around here are the fine weather and sweeping vistas. All distances listed are one way unless otherwise noted.

The Los Angeles portion of the **California Coastal Trail** begins on Naples Island in Long Beach. From here the trail is a varied journey across open bluffs, boat basins, rocky outcroppings accessible only at low tide, along beachwalks filled with roller skaters, jugglers, and skate boarders, and up goat trails with stunning views of the Pacific Ocean.

PALOS VERDES PENINSULA   Set beneath wave-carved bluffs, the moderate **Palos Verdes Peninsula Trail** (5 miles) takes you along a rocky beachside past coves and teeming tidepools. The trail begins at Malaga Cove and ends at Point Vicente Lighthouse.

If you're interested in exploring a shipwreck, head over to Palos Verdes Estate Shoreline Preserve, near Malaga Cove, and hike the **Seashore–Shipwreck Trail** (2.25 miles). The moderate-to-difficult trail hugs the shoreline (and requires an ability to jump boulders), skirting tidepools and coves, until it arrives at what is left of an old Greek ship, the *Dominator*. Wear sturdy hiking shoes and bring water.

SANTA MONICA MOUNTAINS   It is hard to imagine, but Los Angeles does have undeveloped mountain wilderness areas prime for trekking. The Santa Monica Mountains offer chaparral-covered landscapes, grassy knolls, mountain streams, and dark canyons.

When visiting Will Rogers State Historic Park, take a moderate hike down **Inspiration Point Trail** (1 mile) for a view overlooking the Westside.

Topanga Canyon State Park has over 36 miles of trails. The **Musch Ranch Loop Trail** (3.5 miles) passes through five different types of plant communities. Moderate. Or try the moderate **Santa Ynez Fire Road Trail** (6.6 miles), which guides you along the Palisades Highlands with views of the ocean and Santa Ynez Canyon. In spring wildflowers add to the already spectacular scenery.

Several trails trace the "backbone" of the Santa Monica Mountains. In fact, conservationists are trying to extend an unbroken trail from Will Rogers State Historic Park to Point Mugu State Park, a 70-mile stretch. The trail will be complete when National Park Service acquires the remaining six miles of private property in various patches along the backbone. They recently secured $5 million in appropriations for this purpose. Presently, you will have to be happy with routes that hop, skip, and jump through the area.

The moderate **Eagle Rock to Eagle Springs Loop Trail** (4 miles), for instance, begins in Topanga State Park and traverses oak and chaparral countryside on its way to Eagle Spring. Another section of the "Backbone Trail," **Malibu Creek State Park Loop** (12 miles roundtrip) begins near the crossroads of Pivma Road and Malibu Canyon Road. The difficult trail follows fire roads and offers choice views of the ocean and Channel Islands before it climbs up to Kanan-Dume road. **Charmlee Park** is a little-visited ◄ *HIDDEN* wildflower paradise in the hills overlooking the ocean. A 1.75-mile trail offers great coastal views. Take Encinal Canyon Road four miles into the mountains from Pacific Coast Highway. **Solstice** ◄ *HIDDEN* **Canyon Park** is another hidden beauty with trails offering hikes of up to six miles. The moderate three-mile round trip to the Roberts Ranch House ruins follows a perennial stream and ends at the burned-out remains of a terraced dream house that retains a palm-shaded charm. Take Corral Canyon Road about a quarter-mile north from Pacific Coast Highway.

For a nostalgic visit to the location of many movie and television shows, including *M*A*S*H** and *Love Is a Many Splendored Thing*, check out the **Craggs-Century Ranch Trail** (3.8 miles) in Malibu Creek State Park. The moderate trail travels along Malibu Creek to Rock Pool, the Gorge, and Century Lake. Continue over a rocky trail to view the *M*A*S*H** site.

An easy (though in spots difficult) climb up **Zuma Ridge Trail** (6.3 miles) brings you to the center of the Santa Monica Mountains and affords otherworldly views of the Pacific. The trail begins off Encinal Canyon Road, 1.5 miles from Mulholland Highway.

MALIBU Zuma-Dume Trail (3 miles) in Malibu takes you on an easy walk from Zuma Beach County Park, along Pirate's Cove (which used to be a nude beach) to the Point Dume headlands and Paradise Cove, a popular diving spot.

For a pleasant, easy hike along part of the Malibu coast dotted with coves and caves and providing terrific swimming, surfing, and skindiving, head out the **Leo Carrillo Trail** (1.5 miles), located at Leo Carrillo State Beach. Or to hike up a gently sloping hill for a view of the coastline, take the easy, nearby **Yellow Hill Trail** (2 miles).

SANTA CATALINA ISLAND For a true adventure in hiking, gather your gear and head for Santa Catalina. A network of spectacular trails crisscrosses this largely undeveloped island. Bring plenty of water and beware of rattlesnakes and poison oak. You'll also need a hiking permit (see the "Santa Catalina Island" section in this chapter).

Empire Landing Road Trail (11.5 miles) begins at Black Jack Junction and ends up at Two Harbors. The path passes a lot of interesting terrain and provides glimpses of island wildlife, especially buffalo. (You can arrange with the ferry service to ride back to the mainland from Two Harbors.)

Other routes to consider are **Sheep Chute Trail** (3.3 miles), a moderate hike between Little Harbor and Empire Landing; and **Parson's Landing to Starlight Trail** (4 miles), a strenuous trek between Silver Peak Trail and Parsons Landing.

▼▼▼▼▼▼▼▼▼▼▼
Transportation

Route 1, which parallels the coastline throughout Los Angeles County, undergoing several name changes during its course, is the main coastal route. **Route 101** shadows the coast further inland, while **Route 405** provides access to the Los Angeles basin from San Diego and **Route 10** arrives from the east.

CAR

AIR

Two airports bring visitors to the Los Angeles coast area: the small **Long Beach Airport** and the very big, very busy **Los Angeles International Airport** (LAX).

LAX is served by many domestic and foreign carriers. Currently (and this seems to change daily) the following airlines fly into LAX: Alaska Airlines, America West Airlines, American Airlines, Continental Airlines, Delta Air Lines, Hawaiian Airlines, Northwest Airlines, Southwest Airlines, United Airlines, and USAir.

International carriers are also numerous: Air Canada, Air France, Air New Zealand, All Nippon Airways, British Airways, China Airlines, Canadian Airlines International, Japan Airlines, KLM, Lufthansa German Airlines, Mexicana Airlines, Philippine Airlines, QANTAS Airways, Singapore Airlines, and TACA International Airlines. ~ 310-646-5252.

Presently, carriers into Long Beach are America West, Great America Airways, SunJet International, and United Airlines.

The Airport in the Sky, set at 1600-foot elevation in the mountains of Santa Catalina, may be the prettiest landing strip anywhere. The small terminal building conveys a mountain lodge atmosphere with a stone fireplace adorned by a trophy bison head.

~ 310-510-0143. **National Air**, also called **Catalina Vegas Airlines**, services the airport from the mainland. ~ 619-292-7311.

Another means of transportation to Catalina is **Island Express**, a helicopter service from Long Beach and San Pedro. They also offer around-the-island tours. ~ 310-510-2525.

TRAIN

Amtrak will carry you into Los Angeles via the "Coast Starlight" from the North, the "San Diegan" from San Diego, the "Southwest Chief" from Chicago, and the "Sunset Limited" from New Orleans. The downtown L.A. station, Union Station, is at 800 North Alameda Street. To get to coastal destinations, taxis and buslines are available.

BOAT

Several companies provide regular transportation to Catalina by boat. The island is just 22 miles across the sea, but it's still necessary to make advance reservations. **Catalina Express** has service to Avalon and Two Harbors from the Catalina Terminal in San Pedro; from Long Beach next to the *Queen Mary*; service to Avalon leaves. ~ 310-519-1212. **Catalina Cruises** travels from the Catalina Landing in Long Beach to Two Harbors and Avalon. ~ San Pedro; 562-436-5006. **Catalina Passenger Service** makes daily trips to Catalina from Orange County. ~ 400 Main Street, Newport Beach; 714-673-5245.

BUS

Greyhound Bus Lines (800-231-2222) has service to the Los Angeles area from around the country. The Long Beach terminal is at 464 West 3rd Street, 562-432-1842; and the Los Angeles terminal is at 1716 East 7th Street, 213-629-8400.

CAR RENTALS

Having a car in Los Angeles is practically a must. Distances are great and public transportation leaves much to be desired. It's not difficult to find a car rental agency. The challenge is to find the best deal. Be sure to request a mileage-free rental, or one with at least some free mileage. One thing is certain in the Los Angeles area, you'll be racking up mileage on the odometer.

If you arrive by air, consider renting a car at the airport. These cost a little more but eliminate the hassles of getting to the rental agency.

At LAX and the Long Beach Airport are **Avis Rent A Car** (800-331-1212), **Budget Rent A Car** (800-527-0700), **Hertz Rent A Car** (800-654-3131), and **National Interrent** (800-227-7368). **Enterprise Rent A Car** (800-325-8007) will pick you up from the airport and deliver you to their car lot. **Thrifty Car Rental** has an off-site lot at LAX and provides free pick-up service.

To save even more money, try agencies that rent used cars. In the Long Beach area this includes **Robin Hood Rent A Car**. ~ 310-518-9807, 800-743-2992.

In Catalina, golf carts are the only vehicles permitted for sight-seeing in Avalon. Check with **Catalina Auto and Bike Rental**. ~ 301 Crescent Avenue; 310-510-0111. **Island Rentals** is another option. ~ 125 Pebbly Beach Road; 310-510-1456. For further information on vehicle rentals on Catalina see the "Santa Catalina Island" section in this chapter.

PUBLIC TRANSIT

Long Beach Transit transports riders throughout the Long Beach area. Among the services is the Long Beach Runabout Shuttle Van, which carries visitors between major points of interest. ~ 1300 Gardenia Avenue, Long Beach; 562-591-2301.

MTA Bus Line serves all of Los Angeles County; disabled riders can call a hotline for information, 800-621-7828 (this number is functional only within the designated area). ~ 425 South Main Street, Los Angeles; 213-626-4455. In Santa Monica, call the **Big Blue Bus**, which hits such destinations as the new Getty Center, LAX, and downtown L.A. ~ Santa Monica Municipal Bus Lines, 1660 7th Street; 310-451-5444.

In Catalina, **Catalina Safari Bus** provides daily buses from Avalon to Two Harbors and all campgrounds. This shuttle service also takes passengers from Avalon to the Airport in the Sky. ~ 310-510-2800.

TAXIS

Long Beach Yellow Cab provides taxi service in Long Beach. ~ 562-435-6111. In Catalina you'll find the **Catalina Cab Company**. ~ 310-510-0025. Several cab companies serve Los Angeles International Airport, including **United Independent Taxi** (323-934-6700) and **L.A. Taxi** (310-412-8000, 213-627-7000).

SEVEN

Orange Coast

Places are known through their nicknames. More than official titles or proper names, sobriquets reveal the real identity of a region. "Orange Coast" can never describe the 42 miles of cobalt blue ocean and whitewashed sand from Seal Beach to San Clemente. That moniker derives from the days when Orange County was row on row with orchards of plump citrus. Today prestigious homes and marinas sprout from the shoreline. This is the "Gold Coast," habitat of beachboys, yachtsmen, and tennis buffs, the "American Riviera."

The theme that ties the territory together and gives rise to these nicknames is money. Money and the trappings that attend it—glamour, celebrity, elegance, power. Orange County is a sun-blessed realm of beautiful people, where politics is right-wing and real estate sells by the square foot.

Some half-dozen freeways crisscross the broad coastal plane where Spain's Gaspar de Portolá led the first overland expedition into present-day Orange County in 1769. Today, more than two million people live, work, and play where during the mid-19th century a few hundred Mexican ranchers tended herds of livestock on a handful of extensive land grants.

Ever since Walt Disney founded his fantasy empire here in the 1950s, Orange County has exploded with population and profits. In Disney's wake came the crowds, and as they arrived they developed housing projects and condominium complexes, mini-malls and business centers.

Along the coast progress also levied a tremendous toll but has left intact some of the natural beauty, the deep canyons and curving hills, soft sand beaches and sharp escarpments. The towns too have retained their separate styles, each projecting its own identifying image.

Seal Beach, Orange County's answer to small-town America, is a pretty community with a sense of serenity. To the south lies Huntington Beach, a place that claims the apt nickname "Surfing Capital of the World." The social capital of this beachside society is Newport Beach, a fashion-conscious center for celebrities, business mavens, and those to whom God granted little patience and a lot of money.

373

Corona del Mar is a model community with quiet streets and a placid water-front. Laguna Beach is an artist colony so *in* that real estate prices have driven the artists *out*. Dana Point represents a marina development in search of a soul. San Juan Capistrano, a small town surrounding an old mission, is closer to its roots than any place in this futuristic area. San Clemente, which served as President Nixon's Western White House, is a trim, strait-laced residential community. Linking this string of beach towns together is Route 1, the Pacific Coast Highway, which runs south from Los Angeles to Capistrano Beach.

The geography throughout Orange County is varied and unpredictable. Around Newport Beach and Huntington Beach, rugged heights give way to low-lying terrain cut by rivers and opening into estuaries. These northerly towns, together with Dana Point, are manmade harbors carved from swamps and surrounded by landfill islands and peninsulas. Huntington Harbor, the first of its kind, consists of eight islands weighted down with luxury homes and bordered by a mazework of marinas. To the south, particularly around Laguna Beach, a series of uplifted marine terraces create bold headlands, coastal bluffs, and pocket coves.

Land here is so highly prized that it's not surprising the city fathers chose to create more by dredging it from river bottoms. The Gabrieleño and Juañero Indians who originally inhabited the area considered the ground sacred, while the Spanish who conquered them divided it into two immense land grants, the San Joaquin and Niguel ranchos.

Establishing themselves at the San Juan Capistrano mission in 1776, the Spanish padres held sway until the 19th century. By the 1830s American merchants from the East Coast were sending tall-masted trading ships up from Cape Horn. Richard Henry Dana, who sailed the shoreline, giving his name to Dana Point, described the area in *Two Years Before the Mast* as "the most romantic spot along the coast."

By the 1860s, after California became a state, the Spanish ranchos were joined into the Irvine Ranch, a land parcel extending ten miles along the coast and 22 miles inland, and controlled with a steel fist by a single family.

They held in their sway all but Laguna Beach, which was settled in the 1870s by pioneers developing 160-acre government land grants. A freestyle community, Laguna developed into an artist colony filled with galleries and renowned for its cliff-rimmed beaches. Over the years artists and individualists—including the late LSD guru Timothy Leary and a retinue of hippies, who arrived during the 1960s—have been lured by the simple beauty of the place.

Just as Laguna Beach has always relied on natural beauty, Newport Beach has worked for its reputation. During the 1870s the harbor was built; channels were dredged, marshes filled, and stone jetties constructed as stern-wheelers began frequenting the "new port" between San Diego and Los Angeles. Newport Pier followed in 1888, allowing cattle hides and grain from Irvine Ranch to be loaded onto waiting ships.

While Laguna Beach developed as a resort community during the 1880s, it wasn't until 1904 that Newport Beach became a noted pleasure stop. That was the year the red trolley arrived and the town became the terminus for the Pacific Electric, Los Angeles' early streetcar line.

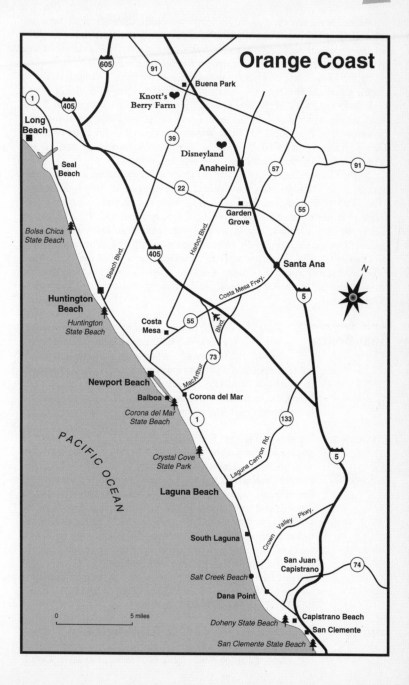

Within two years the population jumped sixfold and land values went into orbit. Balboa Pavilion was built in 1905 and soon became the center for Max Sennett–type bathing beauty contests. Years later it would be a dancehall and gambling casino, and finally a showroom for the Big Bands.

By the 1960s those brassy sounds had surrendered to the twanging strains of electric guitars as the Orange Coast earned its final nickname, "Surfer Heaven." Dick Dale, the "King of the Surf Guitar," hit the top of the charts with "Pipeline," setting off a wave which the Beach Boys and Jan and Dean rode to the crest. Down in Dana Point local boy Bruce Brown contributed to the coast culture in 1964 with a surf flick called *The Endless Summer*, which achieved cult status and earned for its director a reputation as "the Fellini of foam."

As the Orange Coast, particularly Huntington Beach, earned its surfing reputation in the 1960s, the entire county broke from the power of the Irvine Ranch. The suicide of a third-generation scion resulted in the land passing from a conservative family to an aggressive foundation. Within a few years it built Newport Center, the area's highrise district, and crowned it with the chic Fashion Island enclave. Orange County rapidly entered the modern age of multimillion-dollar development, adding a certain luster to its image (tarnished in the 1990s when risky investments forced the county temporarily into bankruptcy) and granting to its shoreline, for better or worse, an everlasting reputation as California's "Gold Coast."

▼▼▼▼▼▼▼▼▼▼
Seal Beach

Rare find indeed, this is a small town with a small-town beach tucked between Huntington Beach and Long Beach. In addition to a swath of fine-grain sand, there is a fishing pier from which you can engage in sportfishing. Oil derricks loom offshore and Long Beach rises in the misty distance. The beach, located along Ocean Avenue, features a pier and is popular with swimmers and surfers alike.

LODGING

It's only fitting that Seal Beach, Orange County's answer to a small town, houses the area's most appealing bed and breakfast. With its wrought-iron balcony, ornate fence, and garden ambience, the **Seal Beach Inn and Gardens** has garnered a reputation for style and seclusion. Its 23 rooms are furnished in hardwood antiques and appointed with period wallhangings. Guests breakfast in a cozy "tea room," then adjourn to the parlor with its upholstered armchairs and tile fireplace. The guest rooms are named for flowers, many of which grow right on the grounds. Indeed the landscaping, which includes wrought-iron lawn furniture and several early-20th-century lampposts, may be the most appealing feature of this fine old inn. ~ 212 5th Street; 562-493-2416, 800-443-3292, fax 562-799-0483. DELUXE.

HIDDEN ►

DINING

Dating back to 1930, the **Glide 'er Inn** is an unusual landmark indeed. The motif is aviation, as in model airplanes dangling from the ceiling and aeronautical pictures covering every inch of available wall space. The menu is covered with biplanes and, almost as an afterthought, includes an extensive list of seafood selections as well as European dishes like wienerschnitzel, bouillabaisse, and veal *smetana* (sautéed in light cream and mushrooms). ~ 1400 Pacific Coast Highway; 562-431-3022. MODERATE.

Walt's Wharf restaurant specializes in creative seafood dishes but there's also Walt's oyster bar with a premium well, over 40 imported beers, and over 200 wines. Start off with appetizers such as the blackened ahi sashimi or the oak-grilled artichoke. Entrées vary with the catch of the day but may include oak-grilled Chilean sea bass with roasted macadamia nut sauce or blackened Louisiana catfish with cilantro cream and fried polenta. ~ 201 Main Street; 562-598-4433. MODERATE TO DELUXE.

▼▼▼▼▼▼▼▼▼▼▼▼▼▼
Huntington Beach

In most of Orange County, a reference to "Duke" will conjure images of John Wayne, former resident and namesake of the airport here; in Huntington Beach, however, natives are more likely to assume you're talking about Duke Kahanamoku, the Hawaiian Olympic swimmer who brought the sport of surfing to the mainland in 1911. His bust stands at the foot of the Huntington Beach Pier, and his legacy continues through the international surfing competitions held here. At the surfing museum, located a few blocks from the beach, you can learn anything else you want to know about the history and culture of the sport. There are, of course, many other ways to enjoy the beautiful coastline here: you can pedal the bike paths, dig for Pismo clams, hike in a wetlands preserve, and warm up at beach bonfires in the evening. But no matter what you do, you'll encounter surfing in some shape or form, even if it's only to admire a wave rider in the distance or watch a "woody," loaded with boards, driving through the streets. While the official story is that the discovery of offshore oil made Huntington Beach the largest city in Orange County, beach bums will argue that it was the discovery of how to ride the onshore breaks.

SIGHTS

As Route 1 buzzes south from Los Angeles it is bordered on one side by broad beaches and on the other by **Bolsa Chica Ecological Reserve**. An important wetlands area dotted with islands and overgrown in cord grass and pickleweed, this 300-acre preserve features a mile-and-a-half-long loop trail. Among the hundreds of animal species inhabiting or visiting the marsh are egrets, herons, and five endangered species. There are raucous seagulls as well as rare Belding's savannah sparrows and California least terns. There is an Interpretive Center with scientific displays, educational material, and trail guides. ~ The accessways are across from the entrance to Bolsa Chica State Beach and at 3842 Warner Avenue; 714-846-1114.

Leave this natural world behind and you will enter the surf capital of California. In the mythology of surfing, Huntington Beach rides with Hawaii's Waimea Bay and the great breaks of Australia. Since the 1920s boys with boards have been as much a part of the seascape as blue skies and billowing clouds.

Synonymous with Huntington Beach is the **Huntington Beach Pier**. First built in 1904 for oil drilling purposes, the pier has been damaged by storms and extensively repaired four times. The pier's current incarnation is 1856 feet long, 38 feet above the water, and has a life expectancy of 100 years. But, as anyone who has lived by the ocean will agree, that century-long life span could be shortened dramatically by the next winter storm. ~ At the end of Main Street.

Stop in at **Your Surfing Museum** for a historic perspective on Southern California's favorite pastime. The showplace sits two blocks from the beach and features boards, boards, and more boards as well as an array of surfing paraphernalia. Closed Monday and Tuesday in the winter. Admission. ~ 411 Olive Avenue; 714-960-3483.

At the **Newland House Museum** visitors can see what life in 19th-century Huntington Beach was all about. Listed on the National Register of Historic Places and built in 1898, the grand dame is filled with furnishings and antiques from the town's early days. Closed Monday, Tuesday, and Friday. ~ 19820 Beach Boulevard; 714-962-5777.

LODGING   The **Colonial Inn Youth Hostel** is a cavernous three-story house located four blocks from the beach. Accommodating couples and families (winter only) as well as lone travelers, its many rooms each contain two to eight beds. The house is in a residential neighborhood and has a kitchen, dining room, TV room, washer, dryer, yard, and barbecue. Reservations recommended. ~ 421 8th Street; 714-536-3315, fax 714-536-9485. BUDGET.

✔ **CHECK THESE OUT—UNIQUE SIGHTS**

- Wander past the cord grass and pickleweed at the 300-acre **Bolsa Chica Ecological Reserve**, and spy egrets, herons, and rare California least terns. *page 377*
- Stroll along **Heisler Park**, where paths descend to pocket beaches and green lawns offer a place to people–gaze. *page 392*
- Follow the fabled swallows to the beautiful 1777 chapel—the state's oldest building—at **Mission San Juan Capistrano**. *page 405*
- Wax nostalgic over Watergate at **La Casa Pacífica**, the elegant Spanish-style retreat of Richard Nixon. *page 407*

Sunset Bed and Breakfast is a tiny six-room hostelry right on the highway in Huntington Beach. Decorated in bed-and-breakfast fashion, it has individual rooms as well as accommodations with bedroom-sitting room combinations. Features like overhead fans, oak armoires, and handwrought headboards add to the ambience. ~ 16401 Pacific Coast Highway; 562-592-1666. MODERATE.

DINING

At **Louise's Trattoria** you can dine on fine Italian cuisine for reasonable prices. Try one of their fresh pasta dishes, such as rigatoni with grilled vegetables tossed in olive oil, or a California-style pizza with one of their inventive salads. Daily "chef's creations" guarantee you'll never tire of the menu. The restaurant is open and airy with modern decor, plenty of windows, and a patio overlooking the ocean for open-air dining. Sunday brunch. ~ 300 Pacific Coast Highway; 714-960-0996. BUDGET TO MODERATE.

◄ HIDDEN

Harbor House Café is one of those hole-in-the-wall places packed with local folks. In this case it's "open 24 hours, 365 days a year" and has been around since 1939. Add knotty-pine walls covered with black-and-whites of your favorite movies stars and you've got a coastal classic. The menu, as you have surmised, includes burgers and sandwiches. Actually, it's pretty varied—in addition to pita bread and croissant sandwiches there are Mexican dishes, seafood platters, chicken entrées, and omelettes. ~ 16341 Pacific Coast Highway; 562-592-5404. BUDGET TO MODERATE.

Bonadonna's Shorehouse Café offers an alternative to the casual Huntington Beach scene. Their specialties come straight out of rustic Italia—*chicken marsala* (thinly sliced chicken topped with marsala wine sauce) or scampi over angelhair pasta. They also serve an extensive breakfast menu all day long. ~ 520 Main Street; 714-960-8091. MODERATE.

NIGHTLIFE

Located at the Waterfront Hilton Beach Resort, the **West Coast Club** is what one might call a gentlemen's club. Featuring live jazz Tuesday through Saturday, a fireplace, floor-to-ceiling windows, and a patio for cigar lovers, it's a perfect spot for unwinding. ~ 21100 Pacific Coast Highway; 714-960-7873.

BEACHES & PARKS

SURFSIDE BEACH 🏊 🚣 🎣 🚤 **AND SUNSET BEACH** 🏊 🎣 🚤 These contiguous strands extend over three miles along the ocean side of Huntington Harbor. Broad carpets of cushiony sand, they are lined with beach houses and lifeguard stands. Both are popular with local people. But Surfside, which fronts a private community and lacks facilities, is still a great beach to get away from the crowds. Sunset Beach has restrooms and lifeguards. Swimming and surfing are good at both beaches, although spectacular winter breaks near the jetty at the end of Surfside Beach make it the better choice during that season. For fishing, Sunset is the best bet. ~ Surfside runs north from Anderson Street, which provides the only public access to the beach; Sunset is off the Pacific Coast Highway, extending from Warner Avenue to Anderson Street in Huntington Beach; 714-834-2400.

BOLSA CHICA STATE BEACH With three miles of fluffy sand, this is another in a series of broad, beautiful beaches. There are seasonal grunion runs and rich clam beds here; the beach is backdropped by the **Bolsa Chica Ecological Reserve**, an important wetlands area. Since the summer surf is gentler here than at Huntington Beach, Bolsa Chica is ideal for swimmers and families. You'll find picnic areas, restrooms, lifeguards, outdoor showers, snack bars, and beach rentals—and all these facilities do come with a cost. The fishing is good year-round at Bolsa Chica; swimming is better in the summer. For surfing, there are small summer waves and big winter breaks. Parking fee, $6. ~ Located along Pacific Coast Highway between Warner Avenue and Huntington Pier in Huntington Beach; 714-846-3460.

▲ There are 57 sites with water and electric hookups; $24 per night. Reservations may be made by calling 800-444-7275.

HUNTINGTON CITY BEACH An urban continuation of the state beach to the south, this strand runs for several miles. This is one of the most famous surfing spots in the world. The Huntington Pier is the pride of the city. The surrounding waters are crowded with surfers in wet suits. A great place for water sports and people-watching. This surfer heaven gives way to an industrial inferno north of the pier where the oil derricks that plague offshore waters climb right up onto the beach, making it look more like the Texas coast than the blue Pacific. So stay south of the pier and make use of the fire pits, lifeguards, restrooms and outdoor showers, volleyball courts, and beach rentals. Swimming is good if you can find a time when the swells aren't too big, but the surf pumps year-round here, and international competitions are held throughout the summer months and in September. Fishing tackle shops are nearby in Huntington Beach; if you're aiming to angle, try the pier. Day-use fee, $6. ~ Located along Pacific Coast Highway in Huntington Beach with numerous accesses; 714-536-5281.

HUNTINGTON STATE BEACH One of Southern California's broadest beaches, this strand extends for three miles. In addition to a desert of soft sand, it has those curling waves that surfer dreams (and movies) are made of. Pismo clams lie buried in the sand, a bike path parallels the water, and there is a five-acre preserve for endangered least terns. Before you decide to move here permanently, take heed: these natural wonders are sandwiched between industrial plants and offshore oil derricks. Nonetheless, your visit will be made more comfortable by the restrooms, fire rings, lifeguards, outdoor showers, dressing rooms, snack bars, volleyball, and beach rentals. The fishing is good here, and the surfing is excellent. Swimming is prime when the surf is low. Day-use fee, $6. ~ Located along Pacific Coast Highway in Huntington Beach; entrances are at Beach Boulevard, Newland Street, Brookhurst Street and Magnolia Street; 714-536-1454.

▼▼▼▼▼▼▼▼▼▼

Newport Beach

Newport Beach is a mélange of manmade islands and peninsulas surrounding a small bay, and as a result, boating is the order of the day here. One of the largest pleasure harbors in the state, Newport Bay is the starting point for the famous Ensenada Race, a 125-mile sailboat race to Baja held every May. There is also an annual Christmas Festival of Lights, a nighttime procession of lighted boats. In addition to recreational boats, fishing boats are a common sight; Newport Pier, the oldest in Southern California, is where the fishing boats return every morning to sell the day's catch. If you don't buy from them directly, you can still sample local seafood at the myriad waterfront area restaurants. Although virtually the entire shoreline of the lower bay is developed, the upper bay, a narrow channel carved by a Pleistocene river, is a protected wetlands, and it offers perhaps the only escape from the constant flow of boat traffic and manmade vistas of the lower bay.

SIGHTS

For help finding your bearings around this labyrinth of waterways, contact the **Newport Harbor Area Chamber of Commerce**. ~ 1470 Jamboree Road; 949-729-4400. The **Newport Beach Conference & Visitors Bureau** can also provide information. ~ 3300 West Coast Highway; 949-722-1611, 800-942-6278.

While it certainly cannot compete with Laguna Beach as an art center, the town does offer the **Orange County Museum of Art**. Specializing in contemporary art, this facility possesses perhaps the finest collection of post–World War II California art in existence. Closed Monday. Admission. ~ 850 San Clemente Drive; 949-759-1122; 949-759-4848.

Further evidence of Newport's creativity can be found at the **Lovell Beach House**. This private residence, set on the beach, is a modern masterpiece. Designed by Rudolf Schindler in 1926, it features a Bauhaus-like design with columns and cantilevers of poured concrete creating a series of striking geometric forms. ~ 13th Street and West Ocean Front.

One of Newport Beach's prettiest neighborhoods is **Balboa Island**, composed of two manmade islets in the middle of Newport Bay. It can be reached by bridge along Marine Avenue or via a short ferry ride from Balboa Peninsula. Walk the pathways that circumnavigate both islands and you will pass clapboard cottages, Cape Cod homes, and modern block-design houses that seem made entirely of glass. While sailboats sit moored along the waterfront, streets that are little more than alleys lead into the center of the island.

Another landfill island, **Lido Isle**, sits just off Balboa Peninsula. Surrounded by Newport Bay, lined with sprawling homes and pocket beaches, it is another of Newport Beach's wealthy residential enclaves.

Nearby **Lido Peninsula** seems like yet one more upscale neighborhood. But wait a minute, doesn't that house have a corrugated roofline? And the one next to it is made entirely of metal. Far from an ordinary suburban neighborhood, Lido Peninsula is a trailer park. In Newport Beach? Granted they call them "mobile homes" here, and many are hardly mobile with their brick foundations, flower boxes, and shrubs. But a trailer park it is, probably one of the fanciest in the country, with tin homes disguised by elaborate landscape designs, awnings, and wooden additions. Surreal to say the least.

The central piece in this jigsaw puzzle of manmade plots is **Balboa Peninsula**, a long, narrow finger of land bounded by Newport Bay and the open ocean. High point of the peninsula is **Balboa Pavilion** located at the end of Main Street, a Victorian landmark that dates back to 1905, when it was a bathhouse for swimmers in ankle-length outfits. Marked by its well-known cupola, the bayfront building hosted the nation's first surfing tournament in 1932 and gave birth to its own dance sensation, the "Balboa." Today it's a mini-amusement park with carousel, Ferris wheel, photograph booths, skee ball, video games, and pinball machines.

Finding a parking space is one of the biggest challenges facing visitors to Balboa Peninsula. Be prepared to pump plenty of quarters into the metered spaces around Newport Pier, at the northern end of the peninsula, or pay $7 or more at an attendant lot near Balboa Pier, at the southern end.

Cruise ships to Catalina Island debark from the dock here and there are harbor cruises offered by **Catalina Passenger Service** aboard the *Pavilion Queen*, a mock riverboat that motors around the mazeway that is Newport Bay. Admission. ~ 400 Main Street; 949-673-5245.

This is also home to the **Balboa Island Ferry**, a kind of floating landmark that has shuttled between Balboa Peninsula and Balboa Island since 1919. A simple, single-deck ferry that carries three cars (for about $1.00 each) and sports a pilot house the size of a phone booth, it crosses the narrow waterway every few minutes. ~ 949-673-1070.

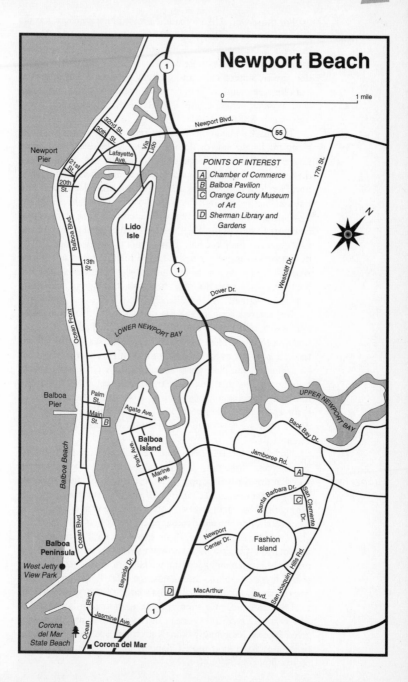

Newport Beach

0   1 mile

POINTS OF INTEREST

A Chamber of Commerce
B Balboa Pavilion
C Orange County Museum of Art
D Sherman Library and Gardens

Newport Blvd.

55

1

32nd St.
30th St.
Via Lido
Lafayette Ave.
Newport Pier
21st St.
20th St.
13th St.
Balboa Blvd.
Ocean Front

17th St.
Westcliff Dr.
Dover Dr.

Lido Isle

LOWER NEWPORT BAY

UPPER NEWPORT BAY

Balboa Pier
Palm St.
Main St. B
Agate Ave.
Balboa Island
Park Ave.
Marine Ave.

Balboa Beach

Back Bay Dr.

Jamboree Rd.

A

Santa Barbara Dr.
C
San Clemente Dr.

Newport Center Dr.

Fashion Island

San Joaquin Hills Rd.

Ocean Blvd.
Bayside Dr.

Balboa Peninsula

West Jetty View Park

D
MacArthur Blvd.

Ocean Blvd.
Jasmine Ave.
1

Corona del Mar State Beach

Corona del Mar

For those who'd like to paddle around Newport Bay, **kayaks** can be rented at the Balboa Fun Pavilion, next to the ferry launch on Balboa Peninsula (see "Outdoor Adventures"). A more romantic way to see Newport Bay is as a passenger aboard a gondola cruise, sipping cider and nibbling chocolate. **Adventures at Sea** offers one- and two-hour cruises, including an all-out three-course catered dinner cruise. ~ 3101 West Coast Highway, Newport Beach; 888-446-6365.

The beach scene in this seaside city extends for over five miles along the Pacific side of Balboa Peninsula. Here a broad white sand beach, lined with lifeguard stands and houses, reaches along the entire length. The centers of attention and amenities are **Newport Pier**, located at Balboa Boulevard and McFadden Place, and **Balboa Pier** found at Balboa Boulevard and Main Street. At Newport Pier, also known as McFadden's Pier, the skiffs of the **Newport Dory Fishing Fleet** are beached every day while local fishermen sell their catches. This flotilla of small wooden boats has been here so long it has achieved historic landmark status. At dawn the fishermen sail ten miles offshore, set trawl lines, and haul in the mackerel, flounder, rock fish, and halibut sold at the afternoon market.

To capture a sense of the beauty which still inheres in Newport Beach, take a walk out to **West Jetty View Park** at the tip of Balboa Peninsula. Here civilization meets the sea. To the left extend the rock jetties forming the mouth of Newport Harbor. Behind you are the plate-glass houses of the city. A wide beach, tufted with ice plants and palm trees, forms another border. Before you, changing its hue with the phases of the sun and clouds, is the Pacific, a single sweep of water that makes those million-dollar homes seem fragile and tenuous. ~ Ocean Boulevard at Channel Road.

Not all the wealth of Newport Beach is measured in finances. The richness of the natural environment is evident as well when

HIDDEN ▶ you venture through **Upper Newport Bay Ecological Reserve**. Whether you bike (see "Outdoor Adventures") or drive part way through the 752-acre reserve, you'll have the chance to glimpse what's left of an ancient landscape that was first carved out by glaciers some 300,000 years ago. Development has reduced the marshes to a fraction of what they used to be, but what's left is one of the last remaining coastal wetlands in California. The road passes limestone bluffs and sandstone hills. Reeds and cattails line the shore. Southern California's largest estuary, the bay is a vital stopping place for thousands of migrating birds on the Pacific Flyway. Over 200 species can be seen here; and six endangered species, including Belding's savannah sparrow, the brown pelican, and the light-footed clapper rail, live along the bay. ~ 600 Stellmaker; 949-640-6746.

Back on Route 1, head south through Corona del Mar en route to Laguna Beach. A wealthy enclave with trim lawns and spacious homes, **Corona del Mar** offers a pretty coastal drive along residential Ocean Boulevard.

Also drop by the **Sherman Library and Gardens**. Devoted to the culture and recent history of the "Pacific Southwest," this complex features a specialized library set in Early California–style buildings. Also inviting is the rose garden, tropical conservatory, and the botanical garden, a 2.3-acre desert museum alive with cacti, succulents, and other plant species. Closed weekends. Admission (free on Monday). ~ 2647 East Coast Highway, Corona del Mar; 949-673-2261.

LODGING

You'd have a hell of a time docking your boat at the **Little Inn by the Bay**. Actually it's on an island, but the island is a median strip dividing the two busiest streets on the Balboa Peninsula. Offering 17 standard motel rooms, the inn is a block from the beach and walking distance from many restaurants. ~ 2627 Newport Boulevard; 949-673-8800, 800-438-4466, fax 714-673-1057. MODERATE.

A Spanish-style hotel with cream-colored walls and a tile-roofed tower, the **Balboa Inn** is ideally situated right next to the beach at Balboa Pier. Adding to the ambience is a swimming pool that looks out on the water. The 34 rooms, some of which have ocean views, have seen better days; they are furnished in knotty pine, decorated with colorful prints, and supplied with jacuzzi tubs, brass fixtures, and fireplaces. ~ 105 Main Street; 949-675-3412, fax 949-673-4587. DELUXE.

Portofino Beach Hotel, a 15-room bed-and-breakfast inn, rests on the beach in an early-20th-century building. Richly appointed with brass beds, armoires, and antique fixtures, the Portofino has a wine bar downstairs and two oceanfront parlors over-

●●

✔ CHECK THESE OUT—UNIQUE LODGING

- *Budget:* Save your bucks for surfing lessons when you bunk at **Colonial Inn Youth Hostel**—it's only four blocks from the beach. *page 378*
- *Moderate:* Check into Balboa's only lodge, the 1925 **Balboa Island Hotel**, a quaint bed and breakfast a block from the beach. *page 386*
- *Deluxe to ultra-deluxe:* Select a suite at **The Carriage House**, a New Orleans–style B&B built around a brick courtyard. *page 394*
- *Ultra-deluxe:* Bask in the lap of luxury amid Old-World art and Pacific Ocean views at the **Ritz-Carlton Laguna-Niguel**. *page 395*

Budget: under $60   Moderate: $60–$120   Deluxe: $120–$175   Ultra-deluxe: over $175

looking Newport Pier. Each room is decorated with antiques and equipped with a private bath; many have jacuzzis, skylights, fireplaces, and ocean views. There are also five apartments with kitchenettes and two bedrooms available. ~ 2306 West Ocean Front; 949-673-7030, 800-571-8749, fax 949-723-4370. ULTRA-DELUXE.

The *only* hotel on tiny Balboa Island is the **Balboa Island Hotel**, a family-operated, three-bedroom, bed-and-breakfast affair. Set in a 1925 house, it's about one block from the water (of course on Balboa Island everything is one block from the water). Each room of this bed-and-breakfast inn has been decorated in period and furnished with antiques. The place has a small, intimate, homey feel. Guests share bathrooms and there are two porches which serve as sitting rooms. ~ 127 Agate Avenue; 949-675-3613. MODERATE.

By way of full-facility destinations, Southern California–style, few places match the **Hyatt Newporter Resort**. Situated on a hillside above Upper Newport Bay, it sprawls across 26 acres and sports three swimming pools, three jacuzzis, a nine-hole pitch-and-putt course, and a tennis club. There are restaurants, a lounge, a lavishly decorated lobby, and a series of terraced patios. Guest rooms are modern in design, comfortably furnished, and tastefully appointed. An inviting combination of elegance and amenities. ~ 1107 Jamboree Road; 949-729-1234, 800-233-1234, fax 949-644-1552. ULTRA-DELUXE.

DINING

Everything in Newport Beach was built last week. Everything, that is, except **The Cannery Restaurant and Cruises**. This 1921 fish cannery is today much as it was way back when. The conveyor belts and pulleys are still here, their gears exposed; and there are fire wagons, a fierce-looking boiler, and more tin cans than you can imagine. All part of a waterfront seafood restaurant that serves lunch, dinner, and weekend brunch. Ultra-deluxe weekend brunch cruises aboard a 58-foot boat are also offered. ~ 3010 Lafayette Avenue; 949-675-5777. MODERATE TO DELUXE.

CRUSTACEAN CELEBRATION

You won't miss **The Crab Cooker**. First, it's painted bright red; second, it's located at a busy intersection near Newport Pier; last, the place has been a local institution since the 1950s. Actually, you don't *want* to miss The Crab Cooker. This informal eatery, where lunch and dinner are served on paper plates, has fish, scallops, shrimp, crab, and oysters. There's a fish market attached to the restaurant, so freshness and quality are assured. Closed Sunday. ~ 2200 Newport Boulevard; 949-673-0100. MODERATE TO DELUXE.

21 Ocean Front is a gourmet seafood dining place known for fine cuisine. Located on the beach overlooking Newport Pier, the interior is done (or rather, overdone) in a kind of shiny Victorian style with black trim and brass chandeliers. The secret is to close your eyes and surrender to the senses of taste and smell. At dinner the chef prepares *ono* and other Hawaiian fish specials as well as abalone, Maine lobster, and bouillabaisse. For those who miss the point there's rack of lamb, pork tenderloin, and filet mignon. Live entertainment and a wine cellar room contribute to the extravagant atmosphere. Dinner only. ~ 2100 West Ocean Front; 949-673-2100. DELUXE TO ULTRA-DELUXE.

Around **Balboa Pavilion** you'll find snack bars and amusement park food stands.

A place nearby that's worth recommending is **Newport Landing**, a double-decker affair where you can have an intimate supper downstairs in a wood-paneled dining room or a casual meal upstairs on a deck overlooking the harbor and listen to the live music. Serving lunch, dinner, and weekend brunch, it specializes in fresh fish selections with a Pacific Rim flavor, but also features hickory-smoked prime rib and chicken with artichokes. ~ 503 East Edgewater Avenue; 949-675-2373. MODERATE TO DELUXE.

Who could imagine that at the end of Balboa Pier there would be a vintage 1940s-era diner complete with art deco curves and red plastic booths. **Ruby's Diner** is a classic. Plus, it provides 270° views of the ocean. Of course the menu, whether breakfast, lunch, or dinner, offers little more than omelettes, burgers, sandwiches, chili, and salads. But who's hungry anyway with all that history and scenery to savor? ~ 1 Balboa Pier; 949-675-7829. BUDGET.

What's Cooking? is a locals' favorite for reasonably priced Italian food in an informal, bistro setting. All the pastas and gnocchi are homemade, the seafood fresh, and the daily specials interesting, featuring grilled lamb chops and seafood. No lunch on weekends. ~ 2632 San Miguel Drive; 949-644-1820. MODERATE.

Because there are very few restaurants on Balboa Island, one place stands out: **Amelia's**, a family-run restaurant serving Italian dishes and seafood, is a local institution. At lunch you'll find them serving a multitude of pasta dishes, fresh fish entrées, sandwiches, and salads. Then in the evening the chef prepares calamari stuffed with crab, scallops, Icelandic cod, bouillabaisse, veal piccata, and another round of pasta platters. Sunday brunch. ~ 311 Marine Avenue; 949-673-6580. MODERATE.

◄ HIDDEN

If you were hoping to spend a little less money, **Wilma's Patio** is located just down the street. It's casual family dining at its best—open morning, noon, and night—that serves multicourse American and Mexican meals. ~ 225 Marine Avenue; 949-675-5542. MODERATE.

With a bakery on the premises, you know that the pastries at **Haute Cakes** must be fresh. Enjoy the daily waffle special in a cozy, simple setting, or have a hot scrambler out in the courtyard. If you're in the mood for lunch, the grilled-eggplant-and-vegetable salad with a sandwich hits the spot. No dinner. ~ 1807 Westcliff Drive; 949-642-4114. BUDGET TO MODERATE.

It's people-watching *par excellence* at **Bistro 201**—and the food's pretty good, too. Here the chef combines New York chic with healthy California cuisine, most notably, fresh seafood such as salmon wrapped in a crispy potato crust served with vegetable ragout and basil sauce. Locals flock here for happy hour. With views of the harbor, who could ask for more? No lunch on Saturday; Sunday brunch. ~ 3333 Pacific Coast Highway; 949-631-1551. MODERATE TO DELUXE.

For a multicourse feast, Moroccan-style, reserve a tent at **Marrakesh**. Decorated in the fashion of North Africa with tile floor and cloth drapes, this well-known dining room conveys a sense of Morocco. There are belly dancers Thursday through Sunday and any night of the week you can experience *harira* (an aromatic soup), *jine fassi* (chicken with marinated lemon rinds), couscous, and a host of rabbit, lamb, quail, duck, and chicken dishes. Dinner only. ~ 1976 Newport Boulevard; 949-645-8384. DELUXE.

Ironically enough, one of Newport Beach's top dining bargains lies at the heart of the region's priciest shopping malls. Encircling the lower level of **Fashion Island** is a collection of stands dispensing sushi, soup and sandwiches, Mexican food, pasta salads, hamburgers, and other light fare. ~ Newport Center, 401 Newport Center Drive; 949-721-2000. BUDGET TO MODERATE.

Luxury abounds in each of the six dining areas at **The Ritz** where the elegant main dining room is built in classic Georgian style with vaulted ceilings, crystal chandeliers, and multipaneled peach mirrors. Plushly padded black booths contrast against candlelit tables draped in white. Innovative Continental cuisine includes artfully prepared dinner choices such as Bavarian roast duck with red cabbage and lingonberry sauce. Lighter fare is offered at lunch. Jackets for men are required at dinner. ~ 880 Newport Center Drive; 949-640-7440. ULTRA-DELUXE.

A local favorite in Corona del Mar, the small town adjacent to Newport Beach, is **The Quiet Woman**, a small, dark, friendly place serving mesquite-grilled food. The lunch and dinner menus both feature steak and seafood. Live entertainment accompanies evening meals Wednesday through Saturday. No lunch Saturday and Sunday. ~ 3224 East Coast Highway, Corona del Mar; 949-640-7440. DELUXE.

SHOPPING   The streets radiating out from **Balboa Pavilion** (end of Main Street) are lined with beachwear stores, sundries shops, and souvenir stands. While there's little of value here, it is a good place to shop for knickknacks. The scene is much the same around **Newport Pier**, located at Balboa Avenue and McFadden Place.

For more upscale shopping, cast your anchor at **Lido Marina Village**. This well-heeled complex features a collection of shops lining a brick courtyard and adjacent boardwalk. ~ 3400 Via Oporto; 949-675-8662.

Another Newport Beach shopping enclave lies along Marine Avenue on Balboa Island. This consumer strip is door-to-door with card shops, gift shops, and sundries stores. Without exaggerating, I would estimate that more than half the outlets here are purveyors of beachwear.

After all is said and done, but hopefully before the money is all spent, the center for Newport Beach shopping is **Fashion Island**. Situated at the heart of Newport Center, the town's high-rise financial district, it is also the best place for beautiful-people watching. Every self-respecting department store is here, including Neiman Marcus, Macy's, Robinson's-May, and Bloomingdale's. ~ 501 Newport Center Drive; 949-721-2000.

There's an outdoor plaza filled with fashion outlets and an atrium displaying one floor of designer dreams. If you don't believe Newport Beach is a match for Beverly Hills in flash and cash, take a tour of the parking lot. It's a showplace for Rolls Royces, Jaguars, and Mercedes, as well as more plebeian Volvos and Audis.

NIGHTLIFE For a summer evening on Newport Bay, climb aboard the *Pavilion Queen* or *Pavilion Paddy*, two double-deck boats which depart from the Balboa Pavilion on a **harbor cruise**. ~ At the end of Main Street; 949-673-5245.

There's live blues, jazz, and rock-and-roll every night except Monday and Tuesday at the **Studio Cafe**, a waterfront watering hole near Balboa Pier. ~ 100 Main Street; 949-675-7760.

Knuckles is a lively after-hours sports bar with six televisions, pool tables, and live music Friday and Saturday. ~ Hyatt Newporter, 1107 Jamboree Road; 949-644-1700.

The Cannery Restaurant and Cruises, an old fish cannery that's been converted into a restaurant-cum-museum (and a fascinating one at that), has live contemporary music Thursday through Saturday. Closed Monday. ~ 3010 Lafayette Avenue; 949-675-5777.

BEACHES & PARKS **NEWPORT BEACH** Narrow at the northern end and widening to the south, this sandy strip extends for several miles along the base of the Balboa Peninsula. Newport Pier (also known as McFadden's Pier) and the surrounding facilities serve as the center of the strand. Here fishermen from the Newport

Dory Fishing Fleet beach their boats and sell their daily catches. A wonderful beach, with entrances along its entire length, this is an important gathering place for the crowds that pour into town. There are restrooms, lifeguards, and beach rentals; at the foot of the pier you'll find restaurants, groceries, and all amenities imaginable. The pier is also the place for fishing. Swimming and surfing are both good. If you want to ride the waves, try in the morning around Newport Pier and then in the afternoon at the 30th Street section of the beach. There are year-round breaks near the Santa Ana River mouth at the far north end of the beach. ~ The beach parallels Balboa Boulevard in Newport Beach. Newport Pier is between 20th and 21st streets; 949-675-8690.

BALBOA BEACH This broad sandy strip forms the ocean side of Balboa Peninsula and extends along its entire length. There are entrances to the beach from numerous side streets, but the center of the facility is around Balboa Pier, a wooden fishing pier. With a palm-shaded lawn and many nearby amenities, this beach, together with neighboring Newport Beach, is the most popular spot in town. Facilities include restrooms, showers, lifeguards, a playground, and beach rentals; restaurants, groceries, etc., are near the pier. Fishing is good from the pier, and swimming and surfing are good in different spots at different times. ~ The beach parallels Balboa Boulevard; Balboa Pier is at the end of Main Street; 949-675-8690.

WEST JETTY VIEW PARK Set at the very end of the Balboa Peninsula, this triangle of sand is perfectly placed. From the tip extends a rock jetty that borders Newport Harbor. You can climb the rocks and watch boats in the bay, or turn your back on these trifles and wander across the broad sand carpet that rolls down to the ocean. There are wonderful views of Newport Beach and the coast. You can stock up for your hike or fuel up afterwards at the restaurants and grocery stores about a half mile away. If you're daring enough, you can challenge the waves at **The Wedge**. Known to bodysurfers around the world, the area between the jetty and beach is one of the finest and most dangerous shore breaks anywhere, the "Mount Everest of bodysurfing." If it's any comfort, there are lifeguards. Swimming is very dangerous; the shore break here is fierce. Bodysurfing is the main sport; surfing is permitted further down the beach. But take heed, these breaks are only for veteran bodysurfers. ~ At the end of Balboa and Ocean boulevards at the tip of the Balboa Peninsula.

NEWPORT DUNES RV RESORT This resort has a broad, horseshoe-shaped beach about a half mile in length. It curves around the lake-like waters of Upper Newport Bay, one mile inland from the ocean. Very popular with families and campers, it offers a wide range of possibilities, including playground activities, volleyball, a swimming pool, jacuzzi, and boat rentals. Lifeguards are on duty in the summer. Other facilities include restrooms, a café, groceries, picnic areas, and laundry. The park is very popular, so plan to come for the attractions, not peace and quiet. Parking fee, $6. ~ 1131 Back Bay Drive, Newport Beach; 949-729-3863.

▲ There are 405 sites for freestanding tents and RVs (all with hookups, some with cable TV and phone access); $23 to $95 per night.

CORONA DEL MAR STATE BEACH Located at the mouth of Newport Harbor, this park offers an opportunity to watch sailboats tacking in and out from the bay. Bounded on one side by a jetty, on the other by homes, with a huge parking lot behind, it is less than idyllic, yet it is also inevitably crowded. Throngs congregate because of its easy access, landscaped lawn, and excellent facilities, which include restrooms, picnic areas, lifeguards, showers, concession stands, beach rentals, and volleyball courts. It's well protected for swimming and also popular for surfing and fishing—cast from the jetty bordering Newport Harbor. Skindiving is also good around the jetty. If the crowds are driving you crazy, you will find one possible escape valve: there are a pair of pocket beaches on the other side of the rocks next to the jetty. Parking fee, $6. ~ Located at Jasmine Avenue and Ocean Boulevard in Corona del Mar; 949-644-3047.

LITTLE CORONA DEL MAR STATE BEACH Another in the proud line of pocket beaches along the Orange Coast, this preserve features the **Corona del Mar Tidepool Reserve**. The bluff to the north consists of sandstone that has been contorted into a myriad of magnificent lines. There's a marsh behind the beach thick with reeds and cattails. Unfortunately you won't be the first explorer to hit the sand; Little Corona is known to a big group of local people. The beach is also popular with swimmers, surfers, snorkelers, and skindivers; for anglers, try casting from the rocks. ~ There is an entrance to the beach at Poppy Avenue and Ocean Boulevard in Corona del Mar; 949-644-3047.

Laguna Beach

Next stop on this cavalcade of coastal cities is Laguna Beach. Framed by the San Joaquin hills, the place is an intaglio of coves and bluffs, sand beaches and rock outcroppings. It conjures images of the Mediterranean with deep bays and greenery running to the sea's edge.

Little wonder that Laguna, with its wealthy residents and leisurely beachfront, has become synonymous with the chic but informal style of Southern California. Its long tradition as an artist colony adds to this sense of beauty and bounty, aesthetics and aggrandizement.

Laguna's traditional tranquility has weathered natural disasters quite well. Although hillside fires remain a threat, and winter storms sometimes leave debris on beaches, Laguna always recovers.

SIGHTS

Part of Laguna Beach's artistic tradition is the **Festival of Arts and Pageant of the Masters**, staged every year during July and August. While the festival displays the work of 160 local artists and craftspeople, the Pageant of the Masters is the high point, an event which you *absolutely must not miss*. It presents a series of *tableaux vivants* in which local residents, dressed to resemble figures from famous paintings, remain motionless against a frieze that re-creates the painting. Elaborate make-up and lighting techniques flatten the figures and create a sense of two-dimensionality. If you attend, be sure to arrange lodging, transportation and dining reservations ahead of time; check out the package deals offered by local hotels. Admission. ~ Irvine Bowl, 650 Laguna Canyon Road; 949-494-1145, 800-487-3378.

During the 1960s freelance artists, excluded from the more formal Festival of the Arts, founded the **Sawdust Festival** across the street. Over the years this fair too has become pretty established, but it still provides an opportunity to wander along sawdust-covered paths past hundreds of arts and crafts displays accompanied by musicians and jugglers from July to late August. Admission. ~ 935 Laguna Canyon Road; 949-494-3030.

Laguna Beach's artistic heritage is evident in the many studios around town. The **Laguna Beach Visitors Bureau and Chamber of Commerce**, with its maps and brochures, can help direct you. They can also assist with hotel and restaurant reservations. ~ 252 Broadway; 949-494-1018; www.lagunabeachinfo.org.

The **Laguna Art Museum** has a wonderfully chosen collection of historic and modern California paintings. Complementing the Chamber of Commerce, it will help you find your way through the local art world. Closed Monday. Admission. ~ 307 Cliff Drive; 949-494-6531.

Beauty in Laguna is not only found on canvases. The coastline too is particularly pretty and well worth exploring (see the "Beaches & Parks" section below). One of the most enchanting areas is along **Heisler Park**, a winding promenade set on the cliffs above the ocean. Here you can relax on the lawn, sit beneath a palm tree, and gaze out on the horizon. There are broad vistas out along the coast and down to the wave-whitened shoreline. Paths from the park descend to a series of coves with tidepools and sandy beaches. The surrounding rocks, twisted by geologic pressure into curving designs, rise in a series of protective bluffs. ~ Located on Cliff Drive.

Cliff Drive streams along Heisler Park and then past a series of entranceways to sparkling coves and pocket beaches. At the north end of this shoreline street take a left onto Coast Highway, then another quick left onto Crescent Bay Drive, which leads the way to **Crescent Bay Point Park**. Seated high upon a coastal cliff, this landscaped facility offers magnificent views for miles along the Laguna shore.

When you're ready to leave the beach behind and head for the hills, take Park Avenue up from the center of Laguna Beach, turn right at the end onto Alta Laguna Boulevard, and right again to head back down on Temple Hills Drive and Thalia Street. This climbing course will carry you high into the **Laguna Hills** with spectacular vistas along the coastline and into the interior valleys.

In town, in the Laguna-North section, you'll find a charming historical link with Laguna's past in this neighborhood of **1920s bungalows**. Built by year-round residents who worked or owned businesses in town to serve the seasonal visitors, the bungalows were humble interpretations of the Craftsman style popularized by Pasadena architects Charles and Henry Greene. The homeowners over the years individualized their dwellings by adding columns, changing roof styles, rebuilding entries, and making other modifications. Pick up a map at the Laguna Beach Visitors Bureau to follow a self-guided tour. ~ East of Coast Highway and north of Broadway.

◄ *HIDDEN*

South on Route 1, called the Pacific Coast Highway in these parts, you will pass through **Dana Point**. This ultramodern enclave, with its manmade port and 2500-boat marina, has a history dating back to the 1830s when Richard Henry Dana immortalized the place. Writing in *Two Years Before the Mast*, the Boston gentleman-turned-sailor described the surrounding countryside: "There was a grandeur in everything around."

Today much of the grandeur has been replaced with condominiums, leaving very little for the sightseer. There is the **Orange County Marine Institute** with a small sealife aquarium and a 130-foot replica of Dana's brig, *The Pilgrim*. They also offer evening cruises, for a fee, on weekends and selected weekdays. The Institute is closed on most major holidays, the aquarium is open only on weekends and *The Pilgrim* is shown on Sunday only. ~ 24200 Dana Point Harbor Drive; 949-496-2274.

> For a lighthouse keeper's view of the harbor and outlying coastline, take in either of the lookout points at the ends of Old Golden Lantern and Blue Lantern streets in Dana Point.

The **Nautical Heritage Society**, a facsimile of an old lighthouse, serves as a nautical museum. Here you can view a collection of model sailing ships and many other miniatures. Closed weekends. ~ 1064 Calle Negocio, Unit B, San Clemente; 949-369-6773.

LODGING Boasting 70 guest rooms, a pool, spa, and sundeck overlooking the sea, the **Inn at Laguna Beach** offers great ocean views from its blufftop perch. Rooms are small, the construction uneven, and the furnishings modern at this coastside property. ~ 211 North Coast Highway; 949-497-9722, 800-544-4479, fax 949-497-9972. ULTRA-DELUXE.

Even if you never stay there, you won't miss the **Hotel Laguna**. With its octagonal bell tower and Spanish motif, this huge whitewashed building dominates downtown Laguna Beach. The oldest hotel in Laguna, it sits in the center of town, adjacent to Main Beach. In addition to 65 guest rooms there is a restaurant, lounge, and a casual lobby terrace. The place shows signs of age and suffers some of the ills characteristic of large old hotels. But for a place on the water *and* at the center of the action, it cannot be matched. ~ 425 South Coast Highway; 949-494-1151, 800-524-2927, fax 949-497-2163. MODERATE.

The premier resting place in Laguna Beach is a sprawling 157-room establishment overhanging the sand. The **Surf & Sand Hotel** is a blocky 1950s-era complex, an architectural mélange of five buildings and a shopping mall. The accent here is on the ocean: nearly every room has a sea view and private balcony, the pool sits just above the sand, and the beach is a short step away. A full-service hotel, the Surf & Sand has a restaurant and an art deco lounge. Guest rooms are understated but attractive with raw-silk furnishings, unfinished woods, and sand-hued walls. ~ 1555 South Coast Highway; 949-497-4477, 800-524-8621, fax 949-494-2897. ULTRA-DELUXE.

HIDDEN ► **Casa Laguna Inn**, a hillside hacienda, has a dreamlike quality about it. The cottages and rooms are nestled in a garden setting complete with stone terraces and winding paths. Built in the 1930s, the Spanish-style complex features a courtyard, bell tower, and a swimming pool with an ocean view. The rooms are small, equipped with overhead fans, and furnished in antiques; many offer ocean views, though they also pick up noise from the highway. Continental breakfast and afternoon tea are served in the library. ~ 2510 South Coast Highway; 949-494-2996, 800-233-0449, fax 949-494-5009. MODERATE.

It's not just the residential neighborhood that makes **The Carriage House** unique. The colonial architecture of the "New Orleans style" B&B inn also sets it apart. Within this historic landmark structure are six suites, each with a sitting room, private bath, and separate bedroom; some have dining rooms and kitchenettes. All face a verdant brick courtyard filled with flowering plants and adorned with a tiered fountain—in case you get tired of the ocean views, that is. Certainly the Carriage House is one of the prettiest and most peaceful inns along the entire Orange Coast. ~ 1322 Catalina Street; 949-494-8945. MODERATE.

Accommodations with kitchen facilities are hard to come by in Laguna Beach. You'll find them in most of the units at **Capri Laguna**, a multilevel motel situated on the beach. This 46-unit resting place provides contemporary motel-style furnishings, plus a pool, sauna, and sundeck with barbecue facilities. Continental breakfast is included. ~ 1441 South Laguna Coast Highway; 949-494-6533, 800-225-4551, fax 949-497-6962; www.capri laguna.com. MODERATE TO DELUXE.

Holiday Inn Laguna Beach is one of those places destined to gain increasing renown. Fashioned in the style of the French Caribbean, it creates a luxurious atmosphere. The lobby is a breezy affair with provincial furnishings and hand-painted ceiling. The 54 guest rooms surround a lushly landscaped courtyard complete with swimming pool and patio. For a touch of the tropics right here in Laguna Beach, you can't go astray at this reasonably priced hotel. ~ 696 South Coast Highway; 949-494-1001, 800-228-5691, fax 949-497-7107. ULTRA-DELUXE.

Tucked into a secluded canyon is **Aliso Creek Inn and Golf** ◀ HIDDEN **Resort,** an appealing 83-acre resort complete with swimming pools, jacuzzi, Ben Brown's restaurant, lounge, and nine-hole golf course. Particularly attractive for families, every unit includes a sitting area, patio, and kitchen. Removed from the highway but within 400 yards of a beach, the resort is surrounded by steep hillsides which are populated by deer and raccoon. Tying this easy rusticity together is a small creek that tumbles through the resort. ~ 31106 South Coast Highway; 949-499-2271, 800-223-3309, fax 949-499-4601. DELUXE.

The **Ritz-Carlton Laguna Niguel**, set on a 150-foot-high cliff above the Pacific, is simply the finest resort hotel along the California coast. Built in the fashion of a Mediterranean villa, it dominates a broad sweep of coastline, a 393-room mansion replete with gourmet restaurants and dark wood lounges. An Old World interior of arched windows and Italian marble is decorated with one of the finest hotel collections of 18th- and 19th-century American and English art anywhere. The grounds are landscaped with willows, sycamores, and a spectrum of flowering plants. Tile courtyards lead to two swimming pools, a pair of jacuzzis, tennis courts, and a fitness and massage center. The rooms are equal in luxury to the rest of the resort. ~ 1 Ritz-Carlton Drive, Dana Point; 949-240-2000, 800-241-3333, fax 949-240-1061. ULTRA-DELUXE.

Most motels have a stream of traffic whizzing past outside, but the **Dana Marina Inn Motel**, situated on an island where the highway divides, manages to have traffic on both sides! The reason I'm mentioning it is not because I'm sadistic but because rooms in this 29-unit facility are inexpensive. The accommodations are roadside-motel style. ~ 34111 Coast Highway, Dana Point; 949-496-1300. BUDGET.

Four Sisters Inns, a bed-and-breakfast "chain" with several properties along the coast, has a 29-room property, **Blue Lantern Inn**, situated on an oceanside bluff in Dana Point. A contemporary building designed in classic Cape Cod–style, the bed and breakfast combines an ultramodern glass elevator with antique decor. Each room features a fireplace and jacuzzi as well as a polished hardwood armoire, and shuttered windows. The tower rooms offer spectacular ocean views and telescopes for stargazing. The sitting rooms are spacious and comfortable and the inn provides a well-done, though self-conscious, recreation of a classic era. Full breakfast and afternoon hors d'oeuvres are served. Be sure to book rooms in advance. ~ 34343 Street of the Blue Lantern, Dana Point; 949-661-1304, 800-950-1236, fax 949-496-1483; www.foursisters.com. DELUXE.

DINING

Laguna Beach is never at a loss for oceanfront restaurants. But somehow the sea seems closer and more intimate at **Laguna Village Cafe**, probably because this informal eatery was once entirely outdoors, with tables placed at the very edge of the coastal bluff (now they've added indoor seating warmed by a fireplace). The menu is simple: egg dishes in the morning, and a single menu with salads, sandwiches, and smoothies during the rest of the day. There are also house specialties like calamari, abalone, scallops amandine, teriyaki chicken, skewered shrimp, and Chinese-style chicken dumplings. ~ 577 South Coast Highway; 949-494-6344. BUDGET TO MODERATE.

The **Penguin Malt Shop** is from another era entirely. The 1950s to be exact. A tiny café featuring counter jukeboxes and swivel stools, as well as penguin memorabilia brought in by customers, it's a time capsule with a kitchen. Breakfast and lunch are all-American affairs from ham and eggs to hamburgers to pork chops.

●●

✔ CHECK THESE OUT—UNIQUE DINING

- *Budget to moderate:* Have a meal at a coastal institution, the historic **Harbor House Café**—local folks have enjoyed the varied menu items since 1939, and continue to do so 24 hours a day, every day. *page 379*
- *Moderate:* Soar in to the **Glide 'er Inn** for a taste of Europe or a smattering of seafood in a circa 1930 dining "hangar." *page 376*
- *Moderate to deluxe:* Feast on pasta and paella at **Ti Amo**, a cozy spot located on a bluff with ocean views. *page 398*
- *Ultra-deluxe:* Treat yourself to artfully prepared Continental cuisine at **The Ritz**, where all six dining rooms exude Old World elegance. *page 388*

Budget: under $9   Moderate: $9–$18   Deluxe: $18–$25   Ultra-deluxe: over $25

It's cheap, so what have you got to lose? Step on in and order a chocolate malt with a side of fries. ~ 981 South Coast Highway; 949-494-1353. BUDGET.

The White House Restaurant seems nearly as permanent a Laguna Beach fixture as the ocean. Dating to early in the century this simple wooden structure serves as bar, restaurant, and local landmark. The walls of the White House are lined with historic photos of Laguna Beach. You can drop by from early morning until late evening to partake of a menu that includes pasta, steak, chicken, and seafood dishes. ~ 340 South Coast Highway; 949-494-8088. MODERATE.

Don't get sidetracked by the extensive martini menu at **230 Forest Avenue**, because what really shines here is the inventive food. The butternut squash soup or the Oriental chicken salad pave the way for the entrées: spicy lemon caper shrimp scampi, brandy-smoked barbecued ribs, Pacific Northwest cioppino, or the restaurant's signature hazelnut-crusted halibut. Then top the savory with sweet specialties such as bread pudding and apple cake. ~ 230 Forest Avenue; 949-494-2545. MODERATE TO DELUXE.

Choose one place to symbolize the easy elegance of Laguna and it inevitably will be **Las Brisas**. Something about this white-washed Spanish building with arched windows captures the natural-living-but-class-conscious style of the Southland. Its cliffside locale on the water is part of this ambience. Then there are the beautiful people who frequent the place. Plus a dual kitchen arrangement that permits formal dining in a white-tablecloth room or bistro dining on an outdoor patio. The menu consists of Continental Mexican seafood dishes and other specialties from south of the border. Out on the patio there are sandwiches, salads, and appetizers. ~ 361 Cliff Drive; 949-497-5434. MODERATE TO DELUXE.

For people watching and swimming pool–sized cappuccinos, try **Zinc Café and Market**. Here you'll find sidewalk seating complete with the obligatory umbrellas. They serve vegetarian fare that attracts a casual-intellectual crowd. No dinner. ~ 350 Ocean Avenue; 949-494-6302. BUDGET.

Five Feet Restaurant prepares a succulent interpretation of "modern Chinese cuisine" that carries you from catfish to lamb chinoise. Also on the ever-changing and always unique bill of fare is Hawaiian swordfish with a garlic-parmesan crust and New York steak with a shallot-hoisin sauce. Applying the principles of California cuisine to Chinese cooking and adding a few French flourishes, Five Feet has gained an impressive reputation. The decor is as avant-garde as the food. Dinner only. ~ 328 Glenn-eyre Street; 949-497-4955. DELUXE TO ULTRA-DELUXE.

Dizz's As Is represents one of those singular dining spots that should not be overlooked. Funk is elevated to an art form in this woodframe house. The tiny dining room is decorated with art deco pieces and 1930s-era tunes play throughout dinner. This studied informality ends at the kitchen door where a Continental cuisine that includes veal piccata, Cornish game hen, chicken stuffed with cheese and shallots, pasta with prawns, and cioppino is prepared by talented chefs. Dinner only. ~ 2794 South Coast Highway; 949-494-5250. DELUXE.

The most remarkable aspect of the **Cottage Restaurant** is the cottage itself, an early-20th-century California bungalow. The place has been neatly decorated with turn-of-the-century antiques, oil paintings, and stained glass. Meal time in this historic house is a traditional American affair. They serve classic eggs-and-bacon breakfasts starting at 7 a.m. Lunch consists of salads and sandwiches plus specials like top sirloin, fresh fish, and steamed vegetables. For dinner there is chicken fettuccine, top sirloin, broiled lamb, fresh shrimp, and swordfish as well as daily fresh fish specials. ~ 308 North Coast Highway; 949-494-3023. BUDGET TO MODERATE.

Ti Amo is a little jewel set on a coastal bluff. Situated in a former home, it offers intimate dining indoors or outside on the patio. The restaurant has Renaissance decor with Italian-style murals and heavy draperies. In addition to ocean views, it offers daily specials. On a typical evening diners can expect such entrées as paella, fresh seafood, homemade pastas, and a variety of beef dishes. Desserts here are not to be skipped, ranging from a refreshing light berry ice cream to a decadent chocolate cake. Dinner only. ~ 31727 Coast Highway, South Laguna; 949-499-5350. MODERATE.

The **Harbor Grill**, located in spiffy Dana Point Harbor, lacks the view and polish of its splashy neighbors. But this understated restaurant serves excellent seafood dishes. The menu includes fresh swordfish and salmon with pesto sauce, but the real attraction is the list of daily specials. This might include sea bass with black bean sauce, gumbo, and other fresh fish dishes. Lunch, dinner, and Sunday brunch are served in a light, bright dining room with contemporary artwork. There is also patio dining and a full bar. ~ 34499 Golden Lantern Street, Dana Point; 949-240-1416. MODERATE TO DELUXE.

If you'd prefer to dine alfresco overlooking the harbor, there's **Proud Mary's**, a little hole in the wall where you can order sandwiches, salads, hamburgers, and a few chicken and steak platters, then dine on picnic tables outside. Breakfast is served all day. No dinner. ~ 34689 Golden Lantern Street, Dana Point; 949-493-5853. BUDGET.

SHOPPING   Given its long tradition as an artist colony, it's little wonder that Laguna Beach is crowded with galleries and studios. In addition

to painters and sculptors the town claims to support more gold-
smiths and jewelers than any place in the country. Add a few designer clothing shops plus antique stores and you have one very
promising shopping spot. The center of ◆◆◆◆◆◆◆◆◆◆◆◆◆◆◆◆◆◆◆◆◆◆◆◆
this action lies along Route 1 (Coast High-
way) between Bluebird Canyon Drive and
Laguna Canyon Road.

> At Sherwood Gallery, there is a
> colorful collection of soft sculp-
> tures portraying an odd as-
> sortment of frumpy people.
> These light-hearted exhibits
> in various media come
> from over 30 artists. ~
> 460 South Coast High-
> way; 949-497-2668.

There are several art galleries clustered together which are particularly interesting. Foremost is **Redfern Gallery**, which specializes in
early-American impressionist paintings. Closed
Monday and Tuesday. ~ 1540 South Coast Highway; 949-497-3356. The **Vladimir Sokolov Studio
Gallery** presents works by Mr. Sokolov including a
mixed media collage and other contemporary paintings. ~ 1540 South Coast Highway; 949-494-3633. **The Esther
Wells Collection** features contemporary oil paintings, watercolors,
and sculptures. ~ 1390 South Coast Highway; 949-494-2497.

Fine fashion is taken for granted at **Shebue**. This plush shop
houses beautiful designer clothing for women. *Très chic* (and *très
cher*). ~ 1555 South Coast Highway; 949-494-3148.

Chicken Little's bills itself as "The Museum of Modern
Retail." Translation: they stock New Wave knickknacks like fish
mugs and wacky greeting cards. ~ 574 South Coast Highway;
949-497-4818. Similar in spirit, though not in age, is **Tippe-
canoe's**, a vintage clothing store with a collection of antique knickknacks. ~ 648 South Coast Highway; 949-494-1200.

For imported goods there's **Khyber Pass**, dealing in rugs, statuary, and lapis lazuli pieces from Afghanistan. ~ 1970 South
Coast Highway; 949-494-5021. For contemporary paintings I
particularly recommend **Diane Nelson Fine Art**, which displays
the work of impressionist Marco Sassone and other artists. Closed
Monday. ~ 435 Ocean Avenue; 949-494-2440.

Laguna Beach's other shopping strip is Forest Avenue, a three-
block promenade wall-to-wall with specialty stores. **Laura Down-
ing** is here, a clothing store specializing in upscale sportswear and
jewelry. ~ 241 Forest Avenue; 949-494-4300.

Thee Foxes Trot has an unpredictable inventory, a kind of
cultural hodgepodge ranging from ethnic jewelry and clothing to
African art. ~ 264 Forest Avenue; 949-497-3047.

There are also two rustic, raw wood malls, **Forest Avenue Mall**
at 332 Forest Avenue (949-497-1237), and **Lumberyard Plaza** at
384 Forest Avenue, which blend neatly into the background.

An important literary center, **Up Church Brown** is a great
bookstore that hosts poetry readings every Friday night. There's
a wonderful collection of new and used books. ~ #5 384 Forest
Avenue; 949-497-8373.

NIGHTLIFE The White House Restaurant is a landmark 1917 building down-town. A wide-open dancefloor turns tradition upside down every night with live rock, reggae, blues, Motown, and funk. Cover. ~ 340 South Coast Highway; 949-494-8088.

One of Laguna Beach's hottest nightspots is also its most funky. The Sandpiper is a rundown club filled with dart boards and pinball machines. Often it is also filled with some of the finest sounds around. Rock, reggae, oldies, and other music is live nightly, sometimes preformed by well-known groups. Cover. ~ 1183 South Coast Highway; 949-494-4694.

Las Brisas, a sleek, clifftop restaurant overlooking the ocean, is a gathering place for the fast and fashionable. A wonderful place to enjoy a quiet cocktail, it features a tile bar as well as an open-air patio. Mariachis play one night each week in the sum-mer. ~ 361 Cliff Drive; 949-497-5434.

The ultimate evening destinations are located at the ultra-posh Ritz-Carlton Laguna Niguel. Here, along quiet corridors of pol-ished stone, is the Club Grill and Bar, a wood-paneled rendez-vous decorated with 19th-century paintings of equestrian scenes. Also located in the Ritz-Carlton is The Lounge, an elegant two-tiered, glass-walled lounge with sweeping ocean views. The first offers a quartet nightly and the latter features a solo pianist. ~ 1 Ritz-Carlton Drive, Dana Point; 949-240-2000.

The Wind and Sea Restaurant, on the waterfront in Dana Point Harbor, features sparkling views and musical entertain-ment nightly. ~ 34699 Golden Lantern Street, Dana Point; 949-496-6500.

GAY SCENE Laguna Beach has always been a popular weekend getaway spot for gay men and lesbians living in Los Angeles, which is about a 90-minute drive north. Not only is the natural environment attractive—so is the town's socially progressive cli-mate. Laguna Beach elected the nation's first openly gay mayor way back in 1983. Laguna's gay scene centers around the Boom Boom Room, a large, multiroom bar/dance club at the Coast Inn. This beachy discotheque one-half block from the beach boasts a dancefloor, pinball machines, pool tables, and two bars. The Wednesday night drag show, Glam-O-Rama, is always pop-ular. Cover on Friday and Saturday. ~ 1401 South Coast High-way; 949-494-7588.

Just a block from the beach, the three-tiered, rambling Coast Inn has been a legendary gay resort for about 30 years. It's es-pecially popular with young single gay men, attracted perhaps in part by the gay porn stars who have been known to stay there. ~ 1401 South Coast Highway; 949-494-7588.

There's a quieter gay scene at Main Street, which resembles *Cheers* with a predominantly male clientele. ~ 1460 South Coast Highway; 949-494-0056.

CRYSTAL COVE STATE PARK 🚶 🚴 ⚓ 🐟 🎣 🚤 This out-standing facility has a long, winding sand beach which is some-times sectioned into a series of coves by high tides. The park stretches for over three miles along the coast and extends up into the hills. Grassy terraces grace the sea cliffs and the offshore area is designated an underwater preserve. Providing long walks along an undeveloped coastline and on upland trails in El Moro Canyon, it's the perfect park when you're seeking solitude. Facilities are limited to lifeguards and restrooms; restaurants and groceries are several miles away in Laguna Beach. Onshore fishing is per-mitted, and swimming is good. For surfing, try the breaks north of Reef Point in Scotchman's Cove. Day-use fee, $6. ~ Along the Coast Highway between Corona del Mar and Laguna Beach. There are entrances at Pelican Point, Los Trancos, Reef Point, and El Moro Canyon; 949-494-3539.

BEACHES & PARKS

🅰 Environmental camping is permitted at three camp-grounds, a two- to four-mile hike inland from the parking lot; $11 per night. No open campfires allowed.

CRESCENT BAY ⚓ 🐟 🚤 This half-moon inlet is flanked by a curving cliff upon which the fortunate few have parked their palatial homes. Down on the beach, the sand is as soft and thick as the carpets in those houses. Offshore stands Seal Rock, with barking denizens whose cries echo off the surrounding cliffs. This, to say the least, is a pretty place. Visitors can swim, skin-dive, sunbathe, explore the rocks and tidepools, or venture up to the vista point that overlooks this natural setting. The beach has restrooms and summer lifeguards. Fishing and swimming are good, and there's also very good bodysurfing and excellent skin-diving. ~ Entrances to the beach are located near the intersection of Cliff Drive and Circle Way.

SHAW'S COVE, FISHERMAN'S COVE, AND DIVER'S COVE ⚓ 🐟 🚤 These three miniature inlets sit adjacent to one another, creating one of Laguna Beach's most scenic and popular sections of shoreline. Each features a white sand beach backdropped by a sharp bluff. Rock formations at either end are covered in spum-ing surf and honeycombed with tidepool pockets (particularly at the south end of Shaw's Cove). Well known to local residents, the beaches are sometimes crowded. There are lifeguards, but no other facilities. Fishing is not permitted at Diver's Cove, and swimming, while generally good, can be hazardous at Fisher-man's Cove because of rocks. Diver's Cove, in keeping with its name, is often awash with scuba divers, but skindiving is excel-lent along this entire shoreline. ~ All three coves rest along Cliff Drive. The walkway to Shaw's Cove is at the end of Fairview Street; the entrances to Fisherman's and Diver's are within 50 feet of each other in the 600 block of Cliff Drive.

HEISLER PARK, PICNIC BEACH, AND ROCK PILE BEACH ⚓

One of Laguna's prettiest stretches of shoreline lies along the clifftop in Heisler Park and below on the boulder-strewn sands of Picnic and Rock Pile beaches. The park provides a promenade with grassy areas and shade trees. You can scan the coastline from Laguna Beach south for miles, then meander down to the beach where sedimentary formations shatter the wave patterns and create marvelous tidepools. Picnic and Rock Pile form adjacent coves, both worthy of exploration. In addition to the tidepools, you'll find picnic areas, restrooms, lifeguards, and—get ready—shuffleboard. Fishing is excellent here and along most of the Laguna coast: perch, cod, bass, and halibut inhabit these waters. Swimming is permitted at Picnic Beach but not at Rock Pile Beach. Skindiving is also good at Picnic Beach, as the rocks offer great places to explore. For surfing, Rock Pile has some of the biggest waves in Laguna Beach. The best spots are at the south end. ~ Heisler Park is located along Cliff Drive. Picnic Beach lies to the north at the end of Myrtle Street; Rock Pile Beach is at the end of Jasmine Street.

MAIN BEACH ⚓ You'll have to venture north to Muscle Beach in Venice to find a scene equal to this one. It's located at the very center of Laguna Beach, with shopping streets radiating in several directions. A sinuous boardwalk winds along the waterfront, past basketball players, sunbathers, volleyball aficionados, little kids on swings, and aging kids on roller skates. Here and there an adventuresome soul has even dipped a toe in the wa-wa-water. In the midst of this humanity on holiday stands the lifeguard tower, an imposing glass-encased structure that looks more like a conning tower and has become a Laguna Beach icon. There are also restrooms, showers, picnic areas, a playground, and a grassy area. Fishing is good, and swimming is very good, as the beach is well-guarded. And because the Laguna Beach Marine Life Refuge lies just offshore, this a very popular place for diving and snorkeling. ~ Located at Coast Highway and Broadway.

STREET BEACHES ⚓ Paralleling downtown Laguna for nearly a mile is a single slender strand known to locals by the streets that intersect it. Lined with luxury homes, it provides little privacy but affords easy access to the town's amenities. There are lifeguards, and everything you want, need, or couldn't care less about is within a couple blocks. Swimming is good, and excellent peaks are created by a submerged reef off Brooks Street, making it a prime surfing and bodysurfing locale. The surf is also usually up around Thalia Street. ~ Off Coast Highway there are beach entrances at the ends of Sleepy Hollow Lane, and Cleo, St. Ann's, Thalia, Anita, Oak, and Brooks streets.

ARCH COVE 🏖️ 🏄 🏊 Stretching for more than a half mile, bordered by a palisade of luxury homes and resort hotels, this sandy swath is ideal for sunbathers. A sea arch and blowhole rise along the south end of the beach; the northern stretch is more populated and not as pretty. Lifeguards are on duty, and swimming, although not as protected as the pocket beaches, is still okay. For surfing, there are sizeable breaks around Agate Street. ~ Entrances to the beach are at the ends of Cress Street, Mountain Road, Bluebird Canyon Drive, Agate Street, and Pearl Street. As a result, you will hear sections of the strand referred to as "Agate Beach," "Pearl Beach," etc.

WOOD'S COVE 🏖️ 🏄 🤿 An S-shaped strand backed by La- ◄ *HIDDEN*
guna's ever-loving shore bluff, this is another in the town's string of hidden wonders. Three rock peninsulas give the area its topography, creating a pair of sandy pocket beaches. The sea works in, around, and over the rocks, creating a tumultuous presence in an otherwise placid scene. Swimming is well protected by rock outcroppings, and skindiving is good off the rocks; lifeguards are on duty. ~ Steps from Diamond Street and Ocean Way lead down to the water.

MOSS POINT 🏖️ 🏄 🤿 This tiny gem is little more than 50 ◄ *HIDDEN*
yards long, but for serenity and simple beauty it challenges the giant strands. Rocky points border both sides and sharp hills overlook the entire scene. The sea streams in through the mouth of a cove and debouches onto a fan-shaped beach. The cove is well protected for swimming, and there is a lifeguard; the surrounding rocks also provide interesting areas for skindiving. ~ Located at the end of Moss Street.

VICTORIA BEACH 🏖️ 🏄 🤿 Known primarily to locals, this ◄ *HIDDEN*
quarter-mile sand corridor is flanked by homes and hills. The rocks on either side of the beach make for good exploring and provide excellent tidepooling opportunities. Amenities are few, but that's the price to pay for getting away from Laguna's crowds. At least there's a lifeguard, and even volleyball. Swimming is okay, but watch out for the strong shore break and offshore rocks. Skindiving here is good. ~ From Coast Highway take Victoria Drive, then turn right on Dumond Street.

ALISO CREEK BEACH PARK 🚲 🏖️ 🏄 🏊 🤿 Set in a wide ◄ *HIDDEN*
cove and bounded by low coastal bluffs, this park is popular with local folks. The nearby highway buzzes past and the surrounding hills are adorned with houses. A sand scimitar with rocks guarding both ends, the beach is bisected by a fishing pier. To escape the crowds head over to the park's **southern cove**, a pretty ◄ *HIDDEN*
beach with fluffy sand, or check out the tidepools. Facilities include picnic areas, restrooms, showers, lifeguards, volleyball, and

a snack bar. Fishing is good from the pier. When swimming, beware of strong shore breaks. Bodysurfing is a better bet than board surfing at Aliso. ~ Along the Coast Highway in South Laguna; there's a public accessway to the southern cove along the 31300 block of Coast Highway.

HIDDEN ▶ **SOUTH LAGUNA COVES** 🚴 🏄 🏊 Hidden by the hillsides that flank South Laguna's waterfront are a series of pocket beaches. Each is a crescent of white sand bounded by sharp cliffs of conglomerate rock. These in turn are crowned with plate-glass homes. Two particularly pretty inlets can be reached via accessways called **1000 Steps** and **West Street**. Both beaches have seasonal lifeguards and restrooms. Swimming is good, and the bodysurfing is excellent in both coves. Parking fee. ~ Both accessways are on Coast Highway in South Laguna. 1000 Steps is at 9th Avenue; West Street is (surprise!) at West Street.

SALT CREEK BEACH PARK 🚲 🚴 🏄 🏊 🎣 This marvelous locale consists of two half-mile sections of beach divided by a lofty point on which the Ritz-Carlton Laguna Niguel Hotel stands. Each beach is a broad strip of white sand, backdropped by bluffs and looking out on Santa Catalina Island. The hotel above dominates the region like a palatial fortress on the Mediterranean. Though both beaches are part of Salt Creek, the strand to the south is also known as **Dana Strand**. It's possible to walk from one beach to the other. Both beaches have restrooms and seasonal lifeguards; at Salt Creek (north) there is also a snack bar. The swimming is good at either beach, but for fishing you're better off at Laguna Niguel. If you're hoping to hang ten, from Laguna Niguel you can surf "Dana Strand," located a short distance south. Salt Creek has two well-known breaks, "The Gravels," just north of the outcropping that separates the two beaches, and at "The Point" itself. Parking fee. ~ Laguna Niguel Beach Park is reached via a long stairway at the end of Selva Road. The staircase to Salt Creek is on Ritz-Carlton Drive. Both lie off Coast Highway in Laguna Niguel; 949-661-7013.

DOHENY STATE BEACH 🚲 🏊 🏄 🎣 This park wrote the book on oceanside facilities. In addition to a broad swath of sandy beach there is a five-acre lawn complete with private picnic areas, beach rentals, restrooms with changing areas, lifeguards, volleyball courts, and food concessions. The grassy area offers plenty of shade trees. Surfers work the north end of the beach and divers explore an underwater park just offshore. Dana Point Harbor, with complete marina facilities, borders the beach. For fishing, try the jetty in Dana Point Harbor. Swimming is good here, and surfing is comfortable for beginners, particularly on a south swell. Day-use fee, $5. ~ Located off Dana Point Harbor Drive in Dana Point; 949-496-6171.

▲ There are 121 sites for both tents and RVs (no hookups), including 32 beach sites. Beach sites cost $23 per night, all other sites cost $18. For reservations call 800-444-7275.

▼▼▼▼▼▼▼▼▼▼▼▼▼▼

San Juan Capistrano

When you're ready to flee Southern California's ultramodern coastline, Camino Capistrano is the perfect escape valve. At one time or another, almost everyone has heard the 1939 tune "When the Swallows Return to Capistrano." Like many other schmaltzy songs about California, it seems to remain eternally lodged in the brain whether you want it there or not. The lyrics, just to refresh your memory, describe the return of flocks of swallows every March 19. And return they still do, though in ever-decreasing numbers and not always on March 19. When you're ready to follow the swallows, head up Camino Capistrano to the mission and get out your telephoto lens—swallows are small and fast. They remain in the area until October, when winter's approach prompts them to depart for Argentina, where, blissfully, they are welcomed by no similar ditties. While you're here, take time to explore the beautiful mission and local architectural gems.

SIGHTS

Seventh in the state's chain of 21 missions, the **Mission San Juan Capistrano** was founded in 1776 by Father Junípero Serra. Considered "the jewel of the missions" it is a hauntingly beautiful site, placid and magical.

There are ponds and gardens here, ten acres of standing adobe buildings, and the ruins of the original 1797 stone church, which was destroyed by an earthquake in 1812. The museum displays American Indian crafts, early ecclesiastical artifacts, and Spanish weaponry, while an Indian cemetery memorializes the enslaved people who built this magnificent structure. There is a living-history program (admission) on the last Saturday of every month, with costumed "characters" playing the role of Father Serra and others, and craftspeople showing how old-time crafts were made. On select Saturday nights during the summer enjoy live music under the stars.

◆◆◆◆◆◆◆◆◆◆◆◆◆◆◆◆◆◆◆◆◆

The oldest continually used building in California, the chapel at San Juan Capistrano is the only remaining church used by Father Serra.

The highlight of the mission is certainly not the swallows, which are vastly outnumbered by pigeons, but the chapel, a 1777 structure adorned with Indian designs and a baroque altar. Admission. ~ Located at Camino Capistrano and Ortega Highway; 949-248-2048.

At the **O'Neill Museum**, housed in a tiny 1870s Victorian, there are walking-tour maps of the town's old adobes. Within a few blocks you'll discover about a dozen 19th-century structures. The museum is furnished with Victorian decor. Closed Monday and Saturday. ~ 31831 Los Rios Street; 949-493-8444.

The **Capistrano Depot** appeared a little later in the century but is an equally vital part of the town's history. Converted into a restaurant, the beautifully preserved 1895 depot is still operating as a train station. Built of brick in a series of Spanish-style arches, the old structure houses railroad memorabilia. An antique Pullman, a brightly colored freight car, and other vintage cars line the tracks. ~ 26701 Verdugo Street; 949-487-2322.

Jolting you back to contemporary times are two nearby buildings, both constructed in the 1980s. The **New Church of Mission San Juan Capistrano**, a towering edifice next to the town's historic chapel, is a replica of the original structure. Spanish Renaissance in design, the new church even re-creates the brilliantly painted interior of the old mission. ~ 31522 Camino Capistrano.

Just across the street rises the **San Juan Capistrano Regional Library**, an oddly eclectic building. Drawing heavily from the Moorish-style Alhambra in Spain, the architect, Michael Graves, also incorporated ideas from ancient Egypt and classical Greece. Closed Friday. ~ 31495 El Camino Real; 949-493-1752.

DINING

One of San Juan Capistrano's many historic points, a 19th-century building, **El Adobe de Capistrano** has been converted into a restaurant. The interior is a warren of white-washed rooms, supported by *vigas* and displaying the flourishes of Spanish California. Stop by for a drink next to the old jail (today a wine cellar) or tour the building. (Counterpoint to all this dusty history is a display of Richard Nixon memorabilia.) If you decide to dine, the menu includes lunch, dinner, and Sunday brunch. Naturally the cuisine is Continental Mexican, but it also includes a number of American steak and seafood entrées. ~ 31891 Camino Capistrano; 949-493-1163. MODERATE.

Who can match the combination of intimacy and French and Belgian cuisine at **L'Hirondelle**? It's quite small, and conveys a French-country atmosphere. The restaurant offers a varied menu beginning with escargots, garlic toast, and crab crêpes. Entrées include roast duckling, rabbit in wine sauce, veal cordon bleu, bouillabaisse, sautéed sweetbreads, and daily fresh fish specials. Closed Monday; dinner only on Tuesday; brunch only on Sunday. ~ 31631 Camino Capistrano; 949-661-0425. MODERATE.

Situated in a beautifully restored train depot, the **Capistrano Depot Restaurant** offers creative American cuisine at reasonable prices. Red satin and lace drapes add flourish, and guests can dine on lovely oak tables. Be sure to try the grilled black tiger shrimp with charred white corn and cilantro vinaigrette. Lovers of veggies should definitely not miss the chef's grilled vegetable Napoleon, which is served in an exquisite tomato broth. ~ 26701 Verdugo Street; 714-488-7600. MODERATE.

The mission town of San Juan Capistrano has many shops clustered along its main thoroughfare, Camino Capistrano. Not surprisingly, the most common establishment in this two-century-old town is the antique store. In line with the demands of contemporary times, there are also pocket malls featuring boutiques, jewelers, and other outlets.

Particularly noteworthy is **The Old Barn**, a warehouse-size store filled to the rafters with antiques. ~ 31792 Camino Capistrano; 949-493-9144.

Swallows Inn is a hellbent Western bar with sawdust on the floors and ranch tools tacked to the walls. Every night you can kick up your heels to live country-and-western, except when the music takes on a rock-and-roll, jazz, or blues feel. ~ 31786 Camino Capistrano; 949-493-3188.

CAPISTRANO BEACH PARK 🚲 🏊 ⛵ 🏃 This is a big rectangular sandbox facing the open ocean. Like many beaches in the area it offers ample facilities and is often quite crowded. Bounded by sedimentary cliffs and offering views of Dana Point Harbor, the beach is landscaped with palm and deciduous trees. The park is particularly popular with families and surfers, who all take advantage of the picnic areas, bonfire pits, restrooms, showers, lifeguards, volleyball and basketball courts, and inline skate rentals. Swimming is good here, but it's the surfing that's the big draw. "Killer Capo" breaks are about 400 yards offshore along the northern fringes of the beach (near Doheny State Park), and "Dody's Reef" breaks are about one-half mile to the south, but are not predictable. Parking fee. ~ Located along Coast Highway in Capistrano Beach; 949-661-7031.

▼▼▼▼▼▼▼▼▼▼

San Clemente

If any place is the capital of Republican politics, it is San Clemente, a seaside town that sets the standard for Southern California's notorious conservatism because of one man. Richard Milhous Nixon, President of the United States from 1969 until his ignominious resignation during the Watergate scandal in 1974, established the Western White House on a 25-acre site overlooking the ocean.

La Casa Pacífica, a magnificent Spanish-style home, was famous not only during Nixon's presidency, but also afterwards, when he retreated to San Clemente to lick his wounds. There are stories of Nixon, ever the brooding, socially awkward man, pacing the beach in a business suit and leather shoes.

The Nixon house is located off Avenida del Presidente in a private enclave called Cypress Shore. You can see it, a grand white stucco home with red tile roof, on the cliffs above San Clemente State Beach. Just walk south from the beach entrance about one half mile toward a point of land obscured by palms; the house is set back in the trees.

Another point of interest (quite literally) is **San Clemente Municipal Pier**, a popular fishing spot and centerpiece of the city beach. There are food concessions, bait and tackle shops, and local crowds galore. ~ Foot of Avenida del Mar.

For more information on the area, call the **San Clemente Chamber of Commerce**. ~ 1100 North El Camino Real; 949-492-1131.

LODGING

Algodon Motel is a standard 18-unit facility several blocks from the beach. Some units have kitchens. Not much to write home about, but it is clean and affordable. ~ 135 Avenida Algodon; 949-492-3382. MODERATE.

Cheaper still is the **Hostelling International—San Clemente Beach**, an AYH facility located in a stucco building on a residential street. The accommodations consist of bunk beds in dormitory rooms; one family room is also available in the summer. Visitors share a television room, kitchen, and small patio. ~ 233 Avenida Granada; 949-492-2848, 800-909-4776 ext. 42. BUDGET.

DINING

Center of the casual dining scene in San Clemente is along the beach at the foot of the municipal pier (end of Avenida del Mar). Several takeout stands and cafés are here.

The Fisherman's Restaurant and Bar, a knotty-pine-and-plate-glass establishment, sits right on the pier, affording views all along the beach. With a waterfront patio it's a good spot for seafood dishes at lunch or dinner. They offer a wide variety of fresh fish and shellfish. There is also breakfast and Sunday brunch during the summer. ~ 611 Avenida Victoria; 949-498-6390. MODERATE TO DELUXE.

SHOPPING

Sounds forbidding, but **The Mole Hole Unique Gift Gallery** is a colorful and inviting shop specializing in limited-edition collectibles from around the world. Wee Forest Folk, hand-painted Limoges boxes, and Boyds Bears are part of the unusual selection. You'll also find art glass and sculpture from nationally known artists. ~ Ocean View Plaza, 638 Camino de los Mares, Suite G140; 949-443-1670.

BEACHES & PARKS

SAN CLEMENTE CITY BEACH ⚓ 🏄 🎣 Running nearly the length of town, this silver strand is the pride of San Clemente. Landlubbers congregate near the municipal pier, anglers work its waters, and surfers blanket the beachfront. There are railroad tracks and coastal bluffs paralleling the entire beach. Eden this

ain't: San Clemente is heavily developed, but the beach is a pleasant place to spend a day. There are restaurants and other amenities at the municipal pier including picnic areas, restrooms, lifeguards, and a playground. The **Ole Hanson Beach Club** (105
Avenida Pico; 949-361-8207; admission) at the north end of the
beach is a public pool with dressing rooms. Fishing is best from
the pier, and surfing is good alongside of the pier. The beach is
also good for swimming. ~ The pier is located right at the foot
of Avenida del Mar in San Clemente.

SAN CLEMENTE STATE BEACH 🏃 🏖 🎣 🚣 Walk down the
deeply eroded cliffs guarding this coastline, and you'll discover a
long narrow strip of sand that curves north from San Diego
County up to San Clemente City Beach. There are camping areas
and picnic plots on top of the bluff. Down below a railroad track
parallels the beach and surfers paddle offshore. From here, you
can stroll north toward downtown San Clemente or south to
President Nixon's old home. Beach facilities include lifeguards,
picnic areas, and restrooms. Surf fishing is best in spring, and
surfers will find year-round breaks at the south end of the beach.
Swimmers should beware of rip currents. Day-use fee, $6. ~ Lo-
cated off Avenida Calafia in San Clemente; 949-492-3156.

▲ There are 160 sites for tents and RVs (71 with hookups);
$18 for tents; $24 for hookups.

Outdoor Adventures

Whether you want to catch or watch, the
Orange County coast offers plenty of possibilities. **Davey's Locker** offers half- and full-day
sportfishing charters for yellowtail, bass, and barracuda. ~ 400
Main Street, Balboa; 949-673-1434. For trips to Catalina and
Clemente Islands for bass, dorado, and tuna contact **Dana Wharf
Sportfishing.** ~ 34675 Golden Lantern Street, Dana Point; 949-
496-5794. For those more interested in gazing at California's big
grays, these companies also sponsor two-hour whale-watching
cruises during the migratory season (from December through
late March).

FISHING & WHALE WATCHING

The coastal waters abound in interesting kelp beds rich with sea
life; several companies are available to help you through the
kelp.

For rentals, lessons, and diving in Catalina contact **Aquatic
Center.** ~ 4537 West Coast Highway, Newport Beach; 949-650-
5440. This full-service scuba center also operates a 24-hour surf
and water condition line. ~ 714-650-5783. **Laguna Sea Sports**
rents equipment and provides lessons. ~ 925 North Coast Highway, Laguna Beach; 949-494-6965.

DIVING

SURFING & WIND- SURFING

Orange County is surfer heaven, and, as the Bee Gees once sang, "nobody gets too much heaven no more." Right on. So when you're in the area, don't miss out on Orange County's wild waves.

Practically all the beaches here are surfable; these are just a few spots to get you started. Early risers head to Newport Pier at Newport Beach. If you're in town during the winter, try the jetty at the end of Surfside Beach. World-renowned Huntington City Beach hosts international surfing competitions in the summer. The south end of San Clemente State Beach offers great breaks any time of the year. Large waves can be found at Salt Creek Beach Park and the south end of Rock Pile Beach; Capistrano Beach Park is known for its "Killer Capo" breaks. Beginners choose to learn at Doheny State Beach. If bodysurfing is your thing, the Wedge at West Jetty View Park is the place to do it.

For surfboards, boogieboards, wetsuit rentals, sales, and repairs, call **Huntington Surf and Sport**. ~ 300 Pacific Coast Highway, Huntington Beach; 714-841-4000. **Hobie Sports** also rents boards and wetsuits. ~ 24825 Del Prado, Dana Point; 949-496-2366. **Stewart's Surf Boards** sells and rents surfboards, boogieboards and wetsuits. Inquire about lessons—many of the employees offer private instruction. ~ 2102 South El Camino Real, San Clemente; 949-492-1085. For surf reports call 949-673-3371.

KAYAKING & BOATING

With elaborate marina complexes at Huntington Beach, Newport Beach, and Dana Point, this is a great area for boating. If you yearn to make some waves, call one of the outfits listed below.

Sailboats and powerboats (including fishing skiffs) are available for rent at **Davey's Locker**. ~ 400 Main Street, Balboa; 949-673-1434. Electric boats, motor boats, sailboats, kayaks, and offshore runabouts are all rented at **Balboa Boat Rentals**. ~ 510 Edgewater Avenue, Balboa; 714-673-7200. **Marina Sailing** offers lessons and six-passenger charters. ~ 300 Pacific Coast Highway, Suite F, Newport Beach; 949-548-8900. **Embarcadero Marina**, located at the public launch ramp, rents sailboats, fishing skiffs, and an electric boat. ~ 34512 Embarcadero Place, Dana Point; 949-496-6177.

GOLF

The climate and terrain of Orange County make for excellent golfing. Take a break from Southern California freeways, and do some driving on the greens instead.

Tee up in Newport at the 18-hole executive **Newport Beach Golf Course**, but expect to carry your own clubs; this course has no electric carts. ~ 3100 Irvine Avenue, Newport Beach; 949-852-8681. The enchanting nine-hole **Aliso Creek Golf Course** is set in the middle of a steep canyon with a creek winding through it. ~ 31106 Coast Highway, Laguna Beach; 949-499-1919. The coastal course at **The Golf Links at Monarch Beach** is designed by Robert Trent Jones, Jr. and has a beautiful view of the water. ~ 33033 Niguel Road, Dana Point; 949-240-8247. If you're looking for a dry course with ocean views, visit the **San Clemente Municipal Golf Course**. ~ 150 East Avenida Magdalena, San Clemente; 949-361-8384. Situated in narrow canyon, the public, par-72 **Shorecliffs Golf Course** has a driving range and putting green. The greens are small and the course is fast and in good condition. Carts are mandatory. ~ 501 Avenida Vaquero, San Clemente; 949-492-1177.

Even though public courts are hard to find in this area, who says Orange County is elitist? There are still many private clubs, and given the wonderful climate and the way you'll fit in wearing those white shorts and tennis sweaters, it's probably worth the club fee after all.

TENNIS

   In Newport Beach, you can try one of the eight lighted, plexi-paved courts at **Hotel Tennis Club**. A pro is available for lessons. Fee. ~ Marriott Hotel, 900 Newport Center Drive, Newport Beach; 714-729-3566. Laguna Beach's **Moulton Meadows Park** has two courts. ~ Del Mar and Balboa avenues, Laguna Beach; 714-497-0716. **Laguna Niguel Regional Park** features four lighted tennis courts. ~ 28241 La Paz Road, Laguna Niguel; 714-831-2791. There are eight lighted courts at **Dana Hills Tennis Center**. ~ 24911 Calle de Tenis, Dana Point; 714-240-2104. Strangely enough, San Clemente is the one Orange County town that does seem to have an abundance of public courts. **Bonito Canyon Park** offers two lighted courts. ~ 1304 Calle Valle at El Camino Real, San Clemente; 714-361-8264. There are four lighted courts at **San Luis Rey Park**. ~ 109 Avenida San Luis Rey, San Clemente;

✔ **CHECK THESE OUT—UNIQUE OUTDOOR ADVENTURES**

   • Visualize whirled peace as you ride in the curl of a wave on Huntington's legendary coastline, where a rental board and a lesson can put you on top of the world—and the whirled! *page 410*
   • Do the Newport thing by renting a sailboat and spending a day cruising on the bay. *page 410*
   • Cycle the miles of lakeways at Upper Newport Bay Ecological Reserve, one of the last coastal wetlands in California. *page 412*
   • Grab your binoculars and watch the birds fly as you trek along the Bolsa Chica Ecological Reserve Trail. *page 413*

714-361-8264. **San Gorgonio Park** has two unlit courts. ~ 2916 Via San Gorgonio, San Clemente; 714-361-8264. **Verde Park** also has two courts for day use only. ~ 301 Calle Escuela.

BIKING   Wind and wheels are a perfect blend with Southern California's weather, and you can avoid adding to the smog and sitting in traffic by tooling around on a bike rather than in a car. Whether you like road riding or mountain biking, you'll find a suitable place to cycle in Orange County. **Route 1**, the Pacific Coast Highway, gives cyclists an opportunity to explore the Orange County coastline. The problem, of course, is the traffic. Along **Bolsa Chica State Beach**, however, a special pathway runs the length of the beach. Another way to avoid traffic is to mountain-bike; Moro Canyon in Crystal Cove State Park is a favorite off-road riding area.

Skirting the **Upper Newport Bay Ecological Reserve** are about ten miles of bikeway, with some hills, but nothing too strenuous. You can park for about $6 at Newport Dunes (an RV resort) or try for one of the spots in the small Big Canyon lot in the reserve. Back Bay Drive, a multi-use paved roadway, has a double-wide bike route; it links up with a dedicated bike route around the northern perimeter of the reserve. Eventually, along the western flank, the bike route gives way to a bike lane on city-streets to complete the loop around the reserve. ~ Back Bay Drive at Jamboree Road.

Call the **Newport Beach Department of Public Works** and ask for a copy of the "Bikeways" map; it shows all the trails in Newport Beach. ~ City Hall, 3300 Newport Boulevard; 949-644-3311.

Other interesting areas to explore are **Balboa Island** and the **Balboa Peninsula** in Newport Beach. Both offer quiet residential streets and are connected by a ferry which permits bicycles. A popular inland ride is along **Santiago Canyon Road**; leaving from Orange the route skirts Irvine Lake and Cleveland National Forest. **Bike Rentals**   **Sandpiper Bicycle Repair** is a full-service shop renting hybrids, tandems, and inline skates. ~ 231 Seal Beach Boulevard, Seal Beach; 562-594-6130. **Rainbow Bicycle Company** rents, repairs, and sells mountain bikes. ~ 485 North Coast Highway, Laguna Beach; 949-494-5806. On the Balboa Peninsula, rent mountain bikes and beach cruisers at **Bob's Bikes and Skates**. ~ 118 23rd Street; 949-673-8480.

HIKING   Though heavily developed, the Orange Coast still provides several outstanding trails. All are located near the beaches and offer views of private homes and open ocean. All distances listed are one way unless otherwise noted.

The **California Coastal Trail** extends over 40 miles from the San Gabriel River in Seal Beach to San Mateo Point in San Clemente. Much of the route follows sandy beachfront and sedimentary bluffs. There are lagoons and tidepools, fishing piers, and marinas en route.

At the **Bolsa Chica Ecological Reserve Trail** (1.5 miles) you can say hello to birds traveling along the Pacific Flyway. A migratory rest stop, this lagoon features a loop trail which runs atop a levee past fields of cord grass and pickleweed.

Huntington Beach Paved Bike and Hike Trail (8.5 miles) parallels the Pacific from Bolsa Chica Lagoon to Beach Boulevard in Huntington Beach. Along the way it takes in Huntington Pier, a haven for surfers, and passes an entire army of unspeakably ugly oil derricks.

Newport Trail (2.5 miles) traces the ocean side of Balboa Peninsula from Newport Pier south to Balboa Pier, then proceeds to the peninsula's end at Jetty View Park. Private homes run the length of this pretty beach walk.

Back Bay Trail (3.5 miles) follows Back Bay Drive in Newport Beach along the shores of Upper Newport Bay. This fragile wetland, an important stop on the Pacific Flyway, is an ideal birdwatching area.

Crystal Cove Trail (3.2 miles) provides a pleasant seaside stroll. Starting from Pelican Point at the western boundary of Crystal Cove State Park, the paved path leads to the beach. The trail continues another mile to a cluster of cottages at Crystal Cove, then follows an undeveloped beach to Abalone Point, a 200-foot high promontory.

Aliso Creek Canyon Hiking Trail (1 mile) begins near the fishing pier at Aliso Beach County Park in South Laguna, leads north through a natural arch, and passes the ruins of an old boat landing.

Transportation

Several major highways crisscross Orange County. **Route 1**, known in this area as the **Pacific Coast Highway**, ends its long journey down the California Coast in Capistrano Beach. A few miles further inland, **Route 405** runs from Long Beach to Irvine, with feeder roads leading to the main coastal towns.

CAR

John Wayne International Airport, located in Santa Ana, is the main terminal in these parts. Major carriers presently serving it include Alaska Airlines, American Airlines, America West, Continental Airlines, Delta Airlines, Northwest Airlines, Reno Airlines, Southwest Airlines, Trans World Airlines, United Airlines, and USAir.

AIR

Greyhound Bus Lines (800-231-2222) serves Orange County, stopping in Anaheim, Santa Ana, Seal Beach, Huntington Beach, Newport Beach, Corona del Mar, Dana Point, Laguna Beach,

BUS

and San Clemente. Most stops are flag stops. Finally, there's the station in San Clemente. ~ 2421 South El Camino Real; 949-366-2646.

TRAIN

Amtrak's "San Diegan" train travels between Los Angeles and San Diego, with Orange County stops at the following places: Fullerton, Anaheim Stadium, Santa Ana, San Juan Capistrano, and San Clemente. ~ 800-872-7245.

CAR RENTALS

Arriving at John Wayne International Airport, you will find the following rental agencies: **Alamo Rent A Car** (800-327-9633), **Avis Rent A Car** (800-331-1212), **Budget Rent A Car** (800-527-0700), **Dollar Rent A Car** (800-800-4000), **Hertz Rent A Car** (800-654-3131), and **National Interrent** (800-227-7368). For less expensive (and also less convenient) service, try **Enterprise Rent A Car** (800-736-8222).

PUBLIC TRANSIT

Orange County Transportation Authority, or RIDE from southern Orange County, has bus service throughout Orange County, including most inland areas. Along the coast it stops at beach fronts including Seal Beach, Huntington Beach, Newport Beach, Corona del Mar, Laguna Beach, San Juan Capistrano, and San Clemente. ~ 949-636-7433.

EIGHT

San Diego Coast

 San Diego County's 4261 square miles occupy a Connecticut-sized chunk of real estate that forms the southwestern corner of the continental United States. Geographically, it is as varied a parcel of landscape as any in the world. Surely this spot is one of the few places on the planet where, in a matter of hours, you can journey from bluff-lined beaches up and over craggy mountain peaks and down again to sun-scorched desert sands.

Moving east from the Pacific to the county's interior, travelers discover lush valleys and irrigated hillsides. Planted with citrus orchards, vineyards, and rows of vegetables, this curving countryside eventually gives way to the Palomar and Laguna mountains—cool, pine-crested ranges that rise over 6500 feet.

But it is the coast—some 76 sparkling miles stretching from San Mateo Point near San Clemente to the Mexican border—that always has held the fascination of residents and visitors alike.

When Portuguese explorer Juan Rodríguez Cabrillo laid eyes on these shores in 1542, he discovered a prospering settlement of Kumeyaay Indians. For hundreds of years, these native peoples had been living in quiet contentment on lands overlooking the Pacific; they had harvested the rich estuaries and ventured only occasionally into the scrubby hills and canyons for firewood and game.

Sixty years passed before the next visitor, Spanish explorer Sebastian Vizcaíno, came seeking a hideout for royal galleons beset by pirates. It was Vizcaíno who named the bay for San Diego de Alcala.

In 1769, the Spanish came to stay. The doughty Franciscan missionary Junípero Serra marched north from Mexico with a company of other priests and soldiers and built Mission San Diego de Alcala. It was the first of a chain of 21 missions and the earliest site in California to be settled by Europeans. Father Serra's mission, relocated a few miles inland in 1774, now sits incongruously amid the shopping centers and housing developments of Mission Valley.

California's earliest civilian settlement evolved in the 1820s on a dusty mesa beneath the hilltop presidio that protected the original mission. Pueblo San Diego quickly developed into a thriving trade and cattle ranching center after the ruling Spanish colonial regime was overthrown and replaced by the Republic of Mexico.

By the end of the century, new residents, spurred partly by land speculators, had taken root and developed the harbor and downtown business district. After the rails finally reached San Diego in 1885, the city flourished. Grand Victorian buildings lined 5th Avenue all the way from the harbor to Broadway and 1400 barren acres were set aside uptown for a city park.

After its turn-of-the-century spurt of activity, the city languished until World War II, when the U.S. Navy invaded the town en masse to establish the 11th Naval District headquarters and one of the world's largest Navy bases. San Diego's reputation as "Navytown USA" persisted well after the war-weary sailors went home. Some 130,000 Navy and Marine personnel are still based in San Diego and at Camp Pendleton to the north, but civilians now outnumber service types twenty to one and military influence has diminished accordingly.

The military has not been the only force to foster San Diego's growth. In the early 1960s, construction began on an important university that was to spawn a completely new industry. Many peg the emergence of the "new" San Diego to the opening of the University of California's La Jolla campus. Not only did the influx of 15,000 students help revive a floundering economy, it tended to liberalize an otherwise insular and conservative city.

Truth is, San Diego is no longer the sleepy, semitransparent little resort city it once was. Nowhere is the fact more evident than in the downtown district, where a building boom has brought new offices, condominiums, and hotels as well as a spectacular business and entertainment complex at Horton Plaza.

But for all the city's manmade appeal, it is nature's handiwork and an ideal Mediterranean climate that most delights San Diego visitors. With bays and beaches bathed in sunshine 75 percent of the time, less than ten inches of rainfall per year and average temperatures that mirror a proverbial day in June, San Diego offers the casual outdoor lifestyle that fulfills vacation dreams. There's a beach for every taste, ranging from broad sweeps of white sand to slender scimitars beneath eroded sandstone bluffs.

Situated a smug 120 miles south of Los Angeles on Route 5, San Diego is not so much a city as a collection of communities hiding in canyons and gathered on small shoulders of land that shrug down to the sea. As a result, it hardly seems big enough (just over 1.4 million) to rank as America's sixth largest city. Total county population is 2.8 million, and nine of ten residents live within 30 miles of the coast.

The city of San Diego is divided into several geographic sections. To the south lies Coronado, nestled on a peninsula jutting into San Diego Bay and connected to the mainland by a narrow sandbar known as the Silver Strand.

Although they are within the boundaries of the city of San Diego, the seaside communities of Ocean Beach, Mission Beach, Pacific Beach, and La Jolla have developed their own identities, moods, and styles.

"OB," as the first of these is known, along with Mission and Pacific beaches, exults in the sunny, sporty Southern California lifestyle fostered by nearby Mission Bay Park. These neighboring communities are fronted by broad beaches and an almost continuous boardwalk that is jammed with joggers, skaters, and cyclists.

The beaches are saturated in the summer by local sun-seekers, but they have much to offer visitors.

Like a beautiful but slightly spoiled child, La Jolla is an enclave of wealth and stubborn independence that calls itself "The Village" and insists on having its own post office, although it's actually just another part of the extended San Diego family. Mediterranean-style mansions and small cottages shrouded by jasmine and hibiscus share million-dollar views of beaches, coves, and wild, eroded sea cliffs. Swank shops and galleries, trendy restaurants and classy little hotels combine in a Riviera-like setting that rivals even Carmel for chicness.

North County, a string of beach towns stretching from Oceanside south to Del Mar, has also been developing apace. Often stereotyped because it is the home of Camp Pendleton, the nation's largest Marine Corps base, Oceanside is struggling to shed its reputation as a rough-and-tumble military town. Its greatest strides have come along the beachfront, where a concrete pier and five-block promenade have brightened the scene.

The city of Carlsbad has pushed to the front of the North County pack in terms of sprucing up its image and attracting visitors. Along with its redeveloped down-

town area and oceanfront lodging, Carlsbad includes the community of La Costa, a labyrinth of luxury homes and parks built around the prestigious La Costa Resort & Spa.

Somnolent Leucadia remains the least developed of North County's beach communities. It's an uninspiring mix of old homes, new condominiums, and mom-and-pop commercial outlets, shaded by rows of towering eucalyptus. The place serves as a haven for artisans, musicians, vegetarians, triathletes (more of these iron types train in North County than anywhere else in the world), and others seeking lower rents and noise levels.

Encinitas, known as the "Flower Capital of the World," is home to some of the nation's largest growers. While they are slowly disappearing under pressure from housing developers, giant greenhouses and fields of flowers still dot the area.

Cardiff-by-the-Sea appears from the highway to be little more than a row of chain restaurants strung along an otherwise lovely beach.

That could also be said about Cardiff's southern neighbor, Solana Beach. There's no town center—no real focus—to this coastal community and that has always been Solana Beach's problem and charm. Visitors whiz through on Route 5 or Route 101 (the coastal highway that threads North County beaches from Oceanside to Del Mar) without even noticing the place or its excellent beaches, hidden from view by a string of condominiums and a dramatic sandstone bluff.

One gets the feeling that North County neighbor Del Mar would love to become another La Jolla. While it lacks the natural attributes of cliff and cove, it does attract the rich, famous, and hopeful to its thoroughbred racetrack.

It is safe to say that San Diego is not as eccentric and sophisticated as San Francisco, nor as glamorous and fast-paced as Los Angeles. But those who still perceive it as a laid-back mecca for beach bums—or as a lunch stop en route to Mexico— are in for a huge surprise.

▼▼▼▼▼▼▼▼▼▼▼▼▼▼▼▼▼▼▼▼
North San Diego County

Stretching along the coast above San Diego is a string of towns with a host of personalities and populations. Residents here range from the county's wealthiest folks in Rancho Santa Fe to Marine privates at Oceanside's Camp Pendleton to yogis in retreat at Encinitas. This part of the county really shines, however, in its many sparkling beaches.

The best way to see North County's fine beaches is to cruise along Old Route 101, which preceded Route 5 as the north–south coastal route. It changes names in each beach town along the way, but once you're on it you won't be easily sidetracked.

SIGHTS   Your first sightseeing opportunity in San Diego County is at **San Onofre State Beach**, about 16 miles north of Oceanside. Unique in that it's actually two beaches, North and South, this certainly is one of the county's most scenic beach parks. Its eroded sandstone bluffs hide a variety of secluded sandy coves and pocket beaches. But all this beauty is broken by an eerie and ungainly structure rising from the shoreline. Dividing the park's twin beaches is a mammoth facility, potent and ominous, the San Onofre nuclear power plant. Admission. ~ 949-492-4872.

Old Route 101 leads next into **Oceanside**, gateway to Camp Pendleton Marine Base. San Diego County's third-largest city is busy renovating its beachfront and image. The refurbished fishing pier is a lengthy one, stretching almost 2000 feet into the Pacific.

If you'd like to learn more about California's "cultural" side, stop by the **California Surfing Museum**, which features permanent exhibits on the history of the sport and its early 20th century pioneers. On display is the very first surfing trophy, named after Tom Blake, one of the first waterproof cameras that was used to capture up-close footage, and wooden boards from the pre-'60s era. A museum shop offers vintage books and videos. ~ 223 North Coast Highway, Oceanside; 760-721-6876.

From Oceanside, Mission Avenue, which merges with Route 76, will carry you to **Mission San Luis Rey**. Known as the "King of the Missions," this beautifully restored complex was originally constructed in 1789 and represents the largest California mission. Today you can visit the museum chapel and cemetery while walking these historic grounds. Admission. ~ Route 76, San Luis Rey; 760-757-3651.

Farther south, **Carlsbad** is a friendly, sunny beachfront town that has been entirely redeveloped, complete with cobblestone streets and quaint shops. Originally the place established its reputation around the similarity of its mineral waters to the springs of the original Karlsbad in Czechoslovakia. But don't waste your time looking for the fountain of youth, the spring has long since dried up. Go to the beach instead.

If you're traveling with children in the 2 to 12 range, **Legoland California** may be on their itinerary. Built by the Danish toymaker, the family theme park opened in Spring 1999. The park is divided into nine areas, each with interactive attractions, rides and enter-

◆◆

✔ CHECK THESE OUT—UNIQUE SIGHTS

- Brown your buns at **Black's Beach**, where sunbathers bask *au naturel* while hang gliders soar overhead, getting the best view. *page 433*
- Step into La Jolla's world of minimalist, pop or avant garde works at the **Museum of Contemporary Art, San Diego**, where the building itself is a striking visual masterwork. *page 432*
- Enjoy the varied offerings of **Balboa Park**, from a five-star zoo to first-class museums, not to mention the Old Globe Theater. *page 461*
- Explore old adobes on a free walking tour and shop the Bazaar del Mundo at **Old Town San Diego State Historic Park**. *page 471*

tainment, restaurants, and shops. Park designers included some 30 million Lego bricks in its decoration. Most impressive is Miniland, where miniature versions of New York City, Washington, D.C., New Orleans, the California Coast, and a New England harbor have been constructed entirely of Lego bricks. Admission. ~ One Lego Drive (exit Route 5 at Canon Road), Carlsbad; 760-918-5346, 877-534-6526.

Encinitas is popularly known as the "Flower Capital of the World" and the hillsides east of the beach are a riot of colors. A quick call to the friendly folks at the local **Chamber of Commerce** will net you information concerning the area. ~ 138 Encinitas Boulevard, Encinitas; 760-753-6041.

A self-guided walking tour at **Quail Botanical Gardens** treats visitors to 30 acres of colorful plants and flowers, including the area's natural chaparral, and gardens that display rainforest vegetation, orchids, and bamboo. A lookout tower provides a 360-degree view of the grounds. Admission. ~ 230 Quail Gardens Drive at Encinitas Boulevard, Encinitas; 760-436-3036.

Yogis, as well as those of us still residing on terra firma, might want to make a stop at Paramahansa Yogananda's **Self Realization Fellowship Center**. The gold-domed towers of this monastic retreat were built by an Indian religious sect in the 1920s and are still used as a retreat. Although the gardens inside the compound are beautifully maintained and open to the public daily, Yogananda's house is only open on Sunday. The views, overlooking the famous "Swami's" surfing beach, are spectacular. Closed Monday. ~ 215 K Street, Encinitas; 760-753-2888.

Although **Del Mar** is inundated every summer by "beautiful people" who flock here for the horse racing, the town itself has retained a casual, small-town identity. Its trim, Tudor-style village center and luxurious oceanfront homes reflect the town's subtle efforts to "keep up with the Joneses" next door (i.e., La Jolla).

On the east side of Route 5, about five miles inland on either Via de la Valle or Lomas Santa Fe Drive, is **Rancho Santa Fe**. If La Jolla is a jewel, then this stylish enclave is the crown itself. Residing in hillside mansions and horse ranches parceled out from an old Spanish land grant are some of America's wealthiest folks. Rancho Santa Fe is like Beverly Hills gone country. The area became popular as a retreat for rich industrialists and movie stars in the 1920s when Douglas Fairbanks and Mary Pickford built their sprawling **Fairbanks Ranch**. To make a looping tour of this affluent community, drive in on Via de la Valle, then return to Route 5 via Linea del Cielo and Lomas Santa Fe Drive.

LODGING   Many of San Diego's best beaches lie to the north, between Oceanside and Del Mar. Sadly, most of the good hotels do not. But don't worry, among those listed below all but a handful are either oceanfront or oceanview properties.

The **Southern California Beach Club,** a 43-suite Mediterranean-style time-share facility, is situated on the beach near Oceanside Pier. Each suite is graciously appointed with quality furnishings in contemporary hues of peach, heather, and blue. Kitchens are standard; other extras include a mini-gym, rooftop jacuzzis, and laundry facilities. ~ 121 South Pacific Highway, Oceanside; 760-722-6666, fax 760-722-8950. MODERATE TO DELUXE.

Carlsbad offers several nice oceanfront facilities, such as **Ta-marack Beach Resort,** a Mediterranean contemporary–style condominium. Finished in peach and aqua hues, the Tamarack rents standard rooms as well as one- and two-bedroom suites. Most are smashingly decorated in upbeat tones and textures and incorporate sensitive touches such as potted plants and photographic prints. Suites, though ultra-deluxe-priced, may be the best value on the North Coast. They have kitchens and private balconies. Guests can make use of the oceanfront restaurant, clubhouse, fitness center, jacuzzis, and activities program as well as enjoying the adjacent beach. ~ 3200 Carlsbad Boulevard, Carlsbad; 760-729-3500, 800-334-2199, fax 760-434-5942; www.tamarackresort. com. DELUXE TO ULTRA-DELUXE.

Advertised as "a very special bed and breakfast," the **Pelican Cove Inn** is a lovely Cape Cod–style house with eight guest rooms. Each features a fireplace and is well furnished with antique pieces, including feather beds. Some rooms have spa tubs. Visitors share a sundeck and patio with gazebo. The inn is located just two blocks from the beach. ~ 320 Walnut Avenue, Carlsbad; 760-434-5995, 888-735-2683, fax 760-434-7649; www.pelican-cove.com/pelican. MODERATE TO DELUXE.

Affordability and quiet are the order of the day at **Ocean Palms Beach Resort.** This tidy, 57-room mom-and-pop complex is so near the sea you can hear it, but a row of expensive beach houses blocks the view. Some sections of the rambling ocean manor date back to 1939, and "new" additions are 1950s vintage, so the general decor could best be described as Early-American Motel. An oldie but a goodie in this case, however. The place is clean and lovingly maintained and features a landscaped patio and pool area, complete with jacuzzi and sauna. All rooms have fully equipped kitchens. ~ 2950 Ocean Street, Carlsbad; 760-729-2493, 888-802-3224, fax 760-729-0579. MODERATE TO DELUXE.

There's not much to say about the **Best Western Beach Terrace Inn.** A 49-unit establishment with stucco facade and the feel of a motel, it is part of the Best Western chain. There's a pool, sauna, and jacuzzi, plus a single feature that differentiates the Beach Terrace from most other places hereabouts—it is located right on the beach. A broad swath of white sand borders the property, making the price for a room with kitchen a worthwhile investment. ~ 2775 Ocean Street, Carlsbad; 760-729-5951, 800-433-5415, fax 760-729-1078; www.carlsbadca.org/lodging.htm. DELUXE TO ULTRA-DELUXE.

Sporting a fresh look, the fabled **La Costa Resort & Spa** can justly claim to be one of the world's great "total" resorts. This luxurious 400-acre complex boasts 478 guest rooms, two 18-hole championship golf courses, 21 tennis courts (hard, clay, *and* grass), nine shops, four restaurants, and one of the country's largest and most respected spa and fitness centers. Simply put, the place is awesome. With rooms *starting* well up in the ethereal range, La Costa's appeal to the well-monied few is apparent. ~ 2100 Costa del Mar Road, Carlsbad; 760-438-9111, 800-854-5000, fax 760-931-7585; www.lacosta.com. ULTRA-DELUXE.

Located on a lofty knoll above the Pacific, **Best Western Encinitas Inn and Suites** is built on three levels and looks like a condominium. With a pool and jacuzzi, it has many of the same features. The 90 rooms include private balconies overlooking the ocean. Continental breakfast is served at the poolside cabaña. ~ 85 Encinitas Boulevard, Encinitas; 760-942-7455, fax 760-632-9481. MODERATE.

HIDDEN ▶

The best reasonably priced lodging around the beach in Encinitas is **Moonlight Beach Motel**. This three-story, 24-unit family-run motel is tucked away in a residential neighborhood overlooking Moonlight Beach State Park. Rooms are modern as well as clean, and contain everything you'll need, including full kitchens. Most of the accommodations command ocean views. ~ 233 2nd Street, Encinitas; 760-753-0623, 800-323-1259, fax 760-944-9827. MODERATE.

Every room is individually decorated at **Cardiff-by-the-Sea Lodge** with themes such as Old World, Southwest and Mediterranean, and many rooms have ocean views, fireplaces and in-room whirlpools. It's a bed and breakfast, but not of the converted-home variety; everyone has a private entrance and bath. Breakfast is served buffet-style in a center courtyard, but you can take it to your room or up to the rooftop garden and savor a panoramic view of the Pacific. ~ 142 Chesterfield Avenue, Cardiff; 760-944-6474, fax 760-944-6841; www.cardifflodge.com. DELUXE TO ULTRA-DELUXE.

It's all in the name when it comes to locating **Del Mar Motel on the Beach**, the only motel between Carlsbad and La Jolla on the beach. All 44 rooms in this plain stucco building are steps from the sand. That's undoubtedly where you'll spend your time because there is little about the rooms to enchant you. They are basic in design, equipped with refrigerators, color TVs, and air-conditioning. Because the hotel is at a right angle to the beach, only a few rooms have full views of the water. ~ 1702 Coast Boulevard, Del Mar; 619-755-1534, 800-223-8449, fax 619-259-5403; www.o-t-b.com/delmar.html. MODERATE TO DELUXE.

A two-story Spanish Mediterranean inn conveniently situated a few blocks from downtown Del Mar, **Les Artistes** honors several of the world's favorite artists: Diego Rivera, Georgia O'Keeffe, Erté, Claude Monet, and Paul Gauguin. The owner, who is an architect from Thailand, designed each room in the style and spirit of the artist. Other architectural delights include a pond filled with water lilies and koi, and a classical Spanish-style courtyard with a fountain. ~ 944 Camino del Mar, Del Mar; 619-755-4646, fax 619-794-7880. DELUXE.

Built on the site of a once-famous Del Mar Beach getaway, **L'Auberge Del Mar** replicates the old hotel's nostalgic past of the '20s, '30s, and '40s. The original Tudor/Craftsman inn was frequented by Hollywood greats such as Bing Crosby, Rudolph Valentino, and Jimmy Durante. Its rich lobby is dominated by a replica of the huge original brick fireplace. Along with 120 guest rooms and suites, the inn features a restaurant with patio dining, bar, full-service European spa, tennis courts, leisure and lap pools, shops, a park amphitheater, and partial ocean views. Each room has its own patio. ~ 1540 Camino del Mar, Del Mar; 619-259-1515, 800-553-1336, fax 619-755-4940; www.destinationtravel. com. ULTRA-DELUXE.

DINING

In spite of its name, **Hamburger Heaven** is a great place for breakfast. Decorated with brightly colored murals, this eatery serves up innovative omelettes, buckwheat pancakes, and delicious home fries. For lunch, try the Godfather burger topped with bell peppers, marinara sauce, and jack cheese. Patio dining is also available. No dinner. ~ 714 North Coast Highway, Oceanside; 760-722-2254. BUDGET.

◀ HIDDEN

For a downright homey café, be sure to check out **Robin's Nest**, a country-style establishment with good eats and a gregarious chef. The menu features omelettes, soups, and burgers. With a decor of soft blues and artwork by local artists, this place is quite popular with locals and has an outdoor patio that faces the harbor. ~ 280-A Harbor Drive South, Oceanside; 760-722-7837. BUDGET TO MODERATE.

La Costa Resort & Spa features four restaurants, three of which are ultra-deluxe, including **Pisces**, a gourmet seafood restaurant (that serves formal dinners only), and **Ristorante Figaro**, specializing in northern Italian and Mediterranean cuisine. Figaro only opens Thursday through Saturday. **The Brasserie** offers American and Californian cuisine as well as low-calorie, low-cholesterol meals, designed to dove-tail with La Costa's spa programs; all are superbly prepared and presented. **Center Court,** a coffee bar and pastry shop that serves breakfast and lunch, features a beautiful outdoor patio. ~ 2100 Costa del Mar Road, Carlsbad; 760-438-9111. BUDGET TO ULTRA-DELUXE.

Neiman's, an eye-catching Victorian landmark, houses both a dining room and café/bar. My favorite for lunch or dinner is the café, where LeRoy Neiman lithographs hang on the walls and the menu includes trendy dishes such as rack of lamb, chicken Dijon, and smoked chicken with cheese quesadillas. They also serve burgers, pasta, and salads. The Sunday brunch in the sprawling turn-of-the-century Sea Grill Restaurant is a definite "must," featuring a tremendous buffet assortment of breakfast and lunch items. ~ 300 South Carlsbad Village Drive, Carlsbad; 760-729-4131. MODERATE.

For light, inexpensive fare there's the **Daily News Café.** Breakfast features eggs, pancakes, French toast, and their "world famous" sticky buns, while the heartier lunch fare includes an array of soups, salads, sandwiches, and burgers. ~ 3001-A Carlsbad Boulevard, Carlsbad; 760-729-1023. BUDGET.

Pasta lovers should be sure to try the penne or fusilli in vodka-tomato sauce at **When In Rome.** The art-filled Roman decor provides the proper atmosphere, and the Italian owners certainly know their trade. All the breads and pastas are made fresh daily. Entrées include a variety of veal and seafood items. Dinner only. ~ 1108 South Coast Highway, Encinitas; 760-944-1771. MODERATE TO DELUXE.

HIDDEN ►

Most visitors to Encinitas never lay eyes on the **Potato Shack Café,** hidden away on a side street. But locals start packing its pine-paneled walls at dawn to tackle North County's best and biggest breakfast for the buck. There are three-egg omelettes, including a tasty cheese-and-tuna creation; but best of all are the homestyle taters and the old-fashioned biscuits and gravy. Lunch is also served, but the Potato Shack is really a breakfast institution, and as such serves breakfast until 2 p.m. ('til 3 p.m. on weekends). ~ 120 West I Street, Encinitas; 760-436-1282. BUDGET.

Another popular feeding spot is **Sakura Bana Sushi Bar.** The sushi here is heavenly, especially the *sakura* roll, crafted by Japanese masters from shrimp, crab, scallop, smelt egg, and avocado. The bar serves only sushi and sashimi, but table service will bring you such treats as teriyaki, tempura, and shrimp *shumai*. No lunch Saturday and Sunday; closed Monday. ~ 1031 South Coast Highway, Encinitas; 760-942-6414. BUDGET TO MODERATE.

Encinitas' contribution to the Thai food craze is an intimate café called **Siamese Basil,** set along the town's main drag. At lunch and dinner this white-washed eatery serves up about six dozen dishes. You can start with the spicy shrimp soup and satay, then graduate to an entrée menu that includes noodle, curry, seafood, and vegetable selections. House specialties include roast duck with soy bean and ginger sauce, honey-marinated spare ribs, and barbecued chicken. Closed Tuesday. ~ 527 South Coast Highway, Encinitas; 760-753-3940. BUDGET TO MODERATE.

Best of the beachfront dining spots in Cardiff is **Charlie's by the Sea**, where the surf rolls right up to the glass. Here you can choose from an innovative selection of fresh seafood items or an all-American menu of oak-smoked ribs and chicken, steak, and prime rib. Charlie's has a smartly decorated contemporary setting with a full bar, but still creates an easy and informal atmosphere. Sunday brunch. ~ 2526 South Coast Highway, Cardiff; 760-942-1300. MODERATE TO DELUXE.

For southern Mexican cuisine, try **Taco Auctioneers**, a roadside café with a deck overlooking the ocean. In addition to homemade tortillas and chips, you can feast on *arroz cabezon*, a barbecued pork dish. ~ 1951 San Elijo Avenue, Cardiff; 760-942-8226. BUDGET TO MODERATE.

Mention the words "Mexican food" in Solana Beach and the reply is sure to be **Fidel's**. This favored spot has as many rooms and patios as a rambling hacienda. Given the good food and cheap prices, all of them inevitably are crowded. Fidel's serves the best *tostada suprema* anywhere and the burritos, enchiladas, and *chimichangas* are always good. ~ 607 Valley Avenue, Solana Beach; 619-755-5292. BUDGET.

◀ HIDDEN

Mille Fleurs tops everyone's list as San Diego's best French restaurant. The à la carte menu, which changes daily, provides exquisite appetizers, soup, and such entrées as rack of veal in garlic and rosemary, Norwegian salmon in pink grapefruit sauce, and whole Dover sole. A sophisticated interior features fireside dining, Portuguese tiles, and stunning trompe l'oeil paintings. There is also a Spanish courtyard for lunch as well as a piano bar. No lunch Saturday and Sunday. ~ 6009 Paseo Delicias, Rancho Santa Fe; 619-756-3085. ULTRA-DELUXE.

Delicias, a comfortable and spacious restaurant with adjoining bar, is decorated in an intriguing mixture of antiques and wicker, accented by woven tapestries and flowers. The chefs in the open-view kitchen whip up pizza with smoked salmon, Chinese duck with ginger and orange essence, and grilled veal with a three-cheese polenta and marsala sauce. Delicious food, personable service. Open Wednesday through Saturday for lunch, Tuesday through Saturday for dinner. ~ 6106 Paseo Delicias, Rancho Santa Fe; 619-756-8000. DELUXE TO ULTRA-DELUXE.

Il Fornaio, an Italian restaurant/bakery, boasts magnificent ocean views, outside dining terraces, elegant Italian marble floors and bar, trompe l'oeil murals, and an enormous exhibition kitchen. The place is packed with eager patrons ready to sample the pastas, pizzas, rotisserie, meats, and *dolci* (desserts). There's also Sunday brunch. ~ 1555 Camino del Mar, Del Mar Plaza, Del Mar; 619-755-8876. BUDGET TO DELUXE.

Since life is lived outdoors in Southern California, **Pacifica Del Mar**, latest link in a restaurant mini-chain, features a terrace overlooking the ocean as well as a white-tablecloth dining room. The Pacific-Rim accent here is on seafood, as in sugar-spiced salmon, ahi, salad, and mustard-crusted catfish. ~ Del Mar Plaza, 1555 Camino del Mar, Del Mar; 619-792-0476. MODERATE TO DELUXE.

The place is mobbed all summer long, but **The Fish Market** remains one of my favorite Del Mar restaurants. I like the noise, nautical atmosphere, oyster bar, affordable prices, on-the-run service, and the dozen or so fresh fish items. Among the best dishes are the sea bass, yellowtail, orange roughy, and salmon, either sautéed or mesquite charbroiled. ~ 640 Via de la Valle, Del Mar; 619-755-2277. MODERATE TO DELUXE.

Scalini, housed in a classy contemporary-style building with arched windows overlooking a polo field, is strictly star-quality northern Italian fare. The place has been decorated in a mix of modern and antique furnishings and wrapped in all the latest Southern California colors. But the brightest star of all is the menu. The Caesar salad and mesquite-broiled veal chops are exceptional, as is the duck à l'orange. There are many good homemade pasta dishes including lobster fettuccine, lasagna, linguine, and tortellini. Dinner only. ~ 3790 Via de la Valle, Del Mar; 619-259-9944. DELUXE TO ULTRA-DELUXE.

SHOPPING   Carlsbad has blossomed with a variety of trendy shops. You will see many beach-and-surf type shops and a variety of gift shops. Swing by the **Village Faire Shopping Center**, a New England–style specialty mall that has Sunday afternoon concerts in the summer. ~ 300 Carlsbad Village Drive, Carlsbad; 760-752-8095.

The Lumberyard is an attractive Victorian-style woodframe shopping village with a shaded courtyard on the former site of an old lumber mill. ~ On the east side of Route 101 between I and E streets, Encinitas; 760-634-3190.

Detouring, as every sophisticated shopper must, to Rancho Santa Fe, you'll find an assortment of chic shops and galleries along Paseo Delicias. One of my favorites is **Marilyn Mulloy Estate Jewelers**, with its collection of old and new pieces. ~ 6024 Paseo Delicias, Rancho Santa Fe; 619-756-4010. There are lots of millionaires per acre here, but bargains can still be found: **Carolyn's** is a consignment shop boasting designer fashions from the closets of the community's best-dressed women. ~ 6033-J Paseo Delicias, Rancho Santa Fe; 619-756-2765.

Another place where the wealthy like to rummage is **Country Friends**, a charity-operated repository of antique furniture, silver, glass, and china priced well below local antique shops. ~ 6030 El Tordo, Rancho Santa Fe; 619-756-1192.

If little else, Solana Beach harbors an enclave of good antique stores. One of the best is the **Antique Warehouse**, with its collection of 101 small shops. ~ 212 South Cedros Avenue, Solana Beach; 619-755-5156.

A seacoast village atmosphere prevails along Del Mar's half-mile-long strip of shops. Tudor-style **Stratford Square**, the focal point, houses a number of shops in what once was a grand turn-of-the-century resort hotel. One of the most intriguing enterprises here is **Ocean Song**, a CD and cassette shop specializing in new age and international music. ~ 1438 Camino del Mar, Del Mar; 619-755-7664. Or try the adjoining **Earth Song Bookstore**, which offers traditional books as well as an eclectic selection of titles focusing on health, spirituality, and psychology. ~ 1440 Camino del Mar, Del Mar; 619-755-4254.

The stylized **Del Mar Plaza** is a welcome addition. Home to over 35 retail shops, this tri-level mall sells everything from sportswear to upscale Scandinavian fashions and has a host of eateries. ~ 1555 Camino del Mar, Del Mar; 619-792-1555.

Flower Hill Mall, a rustic mall, has the usual fashion and specialty shops. ~ 2720 Via de la Valle, Del Mar; 619-481-7131. But the real draw here is the **Bookworks** (619-755-3735) and an adjoining coffeehouse called **Pannikin Coffeehouse** (619-481-8007). Together they're perfect for a relaxed bit of book browsing and a spot of tea. ~ 2670 Via de la Valle, Del Mar.

For a harbor view, and entertainment on weekends, cast an eye toward **Monterey Bay Canners**. ~ 1325 Harbor Drive North, Oceanside; 760-722-3474.   **NIGHTLIFE**

First Street Bar is a neighborhood bar with three pool tables. It was recently voted best neighborhood bar (again) by locals. ~ 656 South Coast Highway, Encinitas; 760-944-0233.

You can hear live blues or rock Friday and Saturday nights at **Sharky's**, and sometimes on Thursday and Sunday. ~ 485 South Coast Highway, Encinitas; 760-436-7397.

◆◆

TURF AND SURF

While seasonal, the **Del Mar Race Track** and companion **Fairgrounds** are the main attractions here. The track was financed in the 1930s by such stars as Bing Crosby, Pat O'Brien, and Jimmy Durante to bring thoroughbred racing to the fairgrounds. It was no coincidence that Del Mar, "where the turf meets the surf," became a second home for these and many other top Hollywood stars. Racing season is from the end of July through mid-September. The rest of the year, you can bet on races televised via satellite. Admission. ~ Route 5 and Via de la Valle, Del Mar; racetrack 619-755-1141, fairgrounds 619-755-1161.

Solana Beach's low-profile daytime image shifts gears in the evening when the-little-town-that-could spotlights one of North County's hottest clubs. The **Belly Up Tavern** is a converted quonset hut that now houses a concert club and often draws big-name rock, reggae, jazz, and blues stars. Cover. ~ 143 South Cedros Avenue, Solana Beach; 619-481-9022.

Tucked away in the Flower Hill Mall, the **Pannikin Coffeehouse** brings a true taste of culture in the form of live jazz, classical guitarists, and poetry readings. ~ 2670 Via de la Valle, Del Mar; 619-481-8007.

BEACHES & PARKS

SAN ONOFRE STATE BEACH San Diego County's northernmost beach is about 16 miles north of Oceanside, uneasily sandwiched between Camp Pendleton and the San Onofre nuclear power plant. It's well worth a visit if you're not put off by the nearby presence of atomic energy. San Onofre has a number of sections separated by the power plant and connected via a public walkway along the seawall. On the north side of the power plant, off Cristianitos Road, is San Mateo Campground, with developed sites. Eroded bluffs rumple down to the beach creating a variety of sandy coves and pockets. South of Bluffs and not far from famous Trestles Beach is Surf Beach, a favorite with surfers and kayakers. The southern side of the plant is Bluffs Campground, a superb campground with trailer spaces and primitive tent sites, the only primitive campsite anywhere on San Diego County beaches. Gentle surf, which picks up considerably to the north, makes this a good swimming and bodysurfing spot. It is more than a rumor that some discreet nude sunbathing takes place at the end of beach path #6. You'll find restrooms, lifeguards, and trails. Parking fee, $6. ~ From Route 5, take Basilone Road exit and follow the signs to the beach; 714-492-4872 or 714-492-0802.

▲ There are 221 tent and RV sites (no hookups) at Bluffs Campground, $18 per night; and 157 tent and RV sites (hookups and showers) at San Mateo Campground, $24 per night. Call 800-444-7275 for reservations.

OCEANSIDE BEACHES Over three miles of clean, rock-free beaches front North County's largest city, stretching from Buena Vista Lagoon in the south to Oceanside Harbor in the north. Along the entire length the water is calm and shallow, ideal for swimming and bodysurfing. Lots of Marines from nearby Camp Pendleton favor this beach. The nicest section of all is around Oceanside Pier, a 1900-foot-long fishing pier. Nearby, palm trees line a grassy promenade dotted with picnickers; the sand is as clean as a pin. Added to the attractions is **Buena Vista Lagoon**, a bird sanctuary and nature reserve. Facilities include picnic areas, restrooms, lifeguards, basketball courts, and

HIDDEN ▶

volleyball courts. Kayak rentals are available at the harbor; the only boat ramp for miles is located here. Restaurants are at the end of the pier and harbor. Try fishing from the pier, rocks, or beach. Swimming is good and surfing is reliable year-round. Day-use fee, $5. ~ Located along The Strand in Oceanside; 619-722-8000.

▲ Limited to a few RV sites in a parking lot with no hookups; $15 per night.

CARLSBAD STATE BEACH 🏊 🐟 🚶 ⚓ 🚣 Conditions here are about the same as at South Carlsbad (see below), a sand and rock beach bordered by bluffs. Rock and surf fishing are quite good at this beach and even better at the adjoining Encinas Fishing Area (at the San Diego Gas and Electric power plant), where Agua Hedionda Lagoon opens to the sea. The beach extends another mile or so to the mouth of the Buena Vista Lagoon. Facilities include restrooms and lifeguards. The beach offers swimming, surfing, and skindiving. ~ The park entrance is at Tamarack Avenue, west of Carlsbad Boulevard, in Carlsbad; 619-438-3143.

SOUTH CARLSBAD STATE BEACH 🏊 🐟 🚶 ⚓ 🚣 This is a big, bustling beachfront rimmed by bluffs. The pebbles strewn everywhere put towel space at a premium, but the water is gentle and super for swimming. The beach has restrooms, lifeguards, showers, grocery, and beach rentals. Swimming, fishing, surfing, and skindiving are popular activities. ~ The beach is located west of Carlsbad Boulevard south of Palomar Airport Road, in Carlsbad; 619-438-3143.

▲ There are 226 sites for tents and RVs (no hookups), $19 per night, and a hike/bike campsite, $3 per night. For reservations, call 800-444-7275.

BEACON'S BEACH 🏊 🐟 🚶 🚴 🚣 A broad sand corridor backdropped by coastal bluffs, this beach has appeal, though it's certainly not North County's finest. The strand is widest at the north end, but the breakers are bigger at the south end, a favorite with surfers. Fishing, swimming, surfing, and skindiving are good. Facilities include restrooms, showers, a snack bar, picnic areas and firepits. Lifeguards keep watch. ~ There is a trail off the parking lot at Leucadia Boulevard and Neptune Avenue, Leucadia; 619-944-3398.

STONE STEPS BEACH 🏊 🚶 🚣 Locals go there to hide away   ◄ HIDDEN
from the tourists. It is indeed stony and narrow to boot, but secluded and hard to find. Much like Moonlight to the south, its surf conditions are good for several types of water sports. There are no facilities; a lifeguard is stationed here in summer. ~ The staircase to the beach is located at South El Portal Street, off Neptune Avenue, Leucadia.

MOONLIGHT STATE BEACH 🏊 🐟 🚶 🚴 🚣 A very popular beach, Moonlight boasts a big sandy cove flanked by sandstone bluffs. Surf is relatively tame at the center, entertaining swimmers and bodysurfers. Volleyball and badminton courts are added attractions. Surfers like the wave action to the south, particularly at the foot of D Street. Facilities are picnic areas, firepits, restrooms, showers, lifeguards, a snack bar, equipment (surfboards, boogieboards, beach gear) rentals, and places to fish. ~ Located near 3rd Street and the end of C Street, Encinitas; 619-944-3398.

SWAMI'S PARK North County's most famous surfing beach derives its name from an Indian guru who founded the Self Realization Fellowship Temple here in the 1920s. The gold-domed compound is located on the cliff-top just to the north of the park. A small, grassy picnic area gives way to stairs leading to a narrow, rocky beach favored almost exclusively by surfers, though divers and anglers like the spot as well. The reef point break here makes for spectacular waves. The stretch between this beach and D Street is a marine refuge, so don't get any ideas about taking an invertebrate. Facilities include restrooms, picnic areas, lifeguards, and a funky outdoor shower. ~ 1298 South Route 101 about one mile south of Encinitas Boulevard, Encinitas; 619-944-3398.

SAN ELIJO STATE BEACH Although the beach is wide and sandy, low tide reveals a mantle of rocks just offshore and there are reefs, too, making this one of North County's most popular surf fishing and skindiving spots. Surfers brave big breakers at "Turtles" and "Pipes" reefs at the north end of the park. Lifeguards are stationed here. There's a campground atop the bluff overlooking the beach. Most amenities are located at the campground and include restrooms, showers, beach rentals, and groceries. Day-use fee, $4. ~ Located off South Route 101 north of Chesterfield Drive, Cardiff; 619-753-5091.

▲ There are 171 sites for tents and RVs (no hookups); $18 to $23 per night. For reservations, call 800-444-7275.

CARDIFF STATE BEACH This strand begins where the cliffs of Solana Beach end and where the town's most intriguing feature, a network of tidepools, begins. Quite popular with surfers because of the interesting pitches off its reef break, this wide, sandy beach is part of a two-mile swath of state beaches. At the beach there are restrooms, cold showers, and lifeguards. Fishing, swimming, and surfing are popular activities here. Day-use fee, $4. ~ Located off South Route 101 directly west of San Elijo Lagoon, Cardiff; 619-753-5091.

FLETCHER COVE Lined by cliffs and carpeted with sand, this is a popular spot for water sports. There's a natural break in the cliffs where the beach widens and the surf eases up to allow comfortable swimming. Surfers gather to the north and the south of Plaza Street where the beach is narrow and the surf much bigger. It's also a prime area for grunion runs. Facilities include restrooms, outdoor showers, lifeguards, and basketball courts. ~ Located at the end of Plaza Street, Solana Beach; 619-755-1560.

DEL MAR BEACH Though rather narrow from Torrey Pines to about 15th Street, the beach widens further north. **Seagrove Park**, at the foot of 15th Street, is action central, with teens playing sand volleyball and frisbee while the elders read magazines beneath their umbrellas. Surfers congregate at the foot of 13th Street. Quintessential North County! There are picnic tables, a snack bar, restrooms, showers, and lifeguards. Fishing is good, and there are regular grunion runs. There is typical beach surf with smooth peaks, year-round. ~ Easiest beach access is at street ends from 15th to 29th streets off Coast Boulevard, one block below South Route 101, Del Mar; 619-755-1556.

La Jolla

A certain fascination centers around the origins of the name La Jolla. The word means "jewel" in Spanish, but according to American Indian legend it means "hole" or "caves." Both are fairly apt interpretations: this Mediterranean-style enclave perched on a bluff above the Pacific is indeed a jewel; and its dramatic coves and cliffs are pocked with sea caves. Choose your favorite interpretation but for goodness sake don't pronounce the name phonetically—it's "La Hoya."

La Jolla is a community within the city of San Diego, though it considers itself something more on the order of a principality— like Monaco. Locals call it "The Village" and boast that it's an ideal walking town, which is another way of saying La Jolla is a frustrating place to drive around. Narrow, curvy 1930-era streets are jammed with traffic and hard to follow. A parking place in The Village is truly a jewel within the jewel.

The beauty of its seven miles of cliff-lined sea coast is La Jolla's *raison d'être*. Spectacular homes, posh hotels, chic boutiques, and gourmet restaurants crowd shoulder to shoulder for a better view of the ocean. Each of the area's many beaches has its own particular character and flock of local devotees. Though most beaches are narrow, rocky, and not really suitable for swimming or sunbathing, they are the best in the county for surfing and skindiving.

SIGHTS

To get the lay of the land, wind your way up **Mount Soledad** (east on Nautilus Street from La Jolla Boulevard), where the view extends across the city skyline and out over the ocean. That large white cross at the summit is a memorial to the war dead and the setting for sunrise services every Easter Sunday.

Ah, but exploring The Village is the reason you're here, so head back down Nautilus Street, go right on La Jolla Boulevard, and continue until it leads into **Prospect Street**. This is La Jolla's hottest thoroughfare and where it intersects **Girard Avenue**, the town's traditional "main street," is the town epicenter. Here, in the heart of La Jolla, you are surrounded by the elite and elegant.

Although Girard Avenue features as wide a selection of shops as anyplace in San Diego, Prospect Street is much more interesting and stylish. By all means, walk Prospect's curving mile from the cottage shops and galleries on the north to the **Museum of Contemporary Art, San Diego** on the south. The museum, by the way, is a piece of art in itself. Its modern lines belie the fact it was designed as a private villa back in 1915, one of many striking contemporary structures in La Jolla by noted architect Irving Gill. The museum's highly regarded collection focuses on minimalist, California, pop, and other avant-garde developments in painting, sculpture, and photography. Closed Monday. Admission. ~ 700 Prospect Street; 619-454-3541.

During this stroll along Prospect Street, also visit the lovely **La Valencia Hotel**, a very pink, very prominent resting place nicknamed "La V." This pink lady is a La Jolla landmark and a local institution, serving as both village pub and town meeting hall. You can feel the charm and sense the rich tradition of the place the moment you enter. While "La V" has always been a haven for the gods and goddesses of Hollywood, the Gregory Peck and Olivia de Haviland gang of old has been replaced by a client roster of current stars like Cindy Crawford and Richard Gere. ~ 1132 Prospect Street; 619-454-0771.

Another center of interest lies at the northern end of La Jolla. The best beaches are here, stretching from the ritzy La Jolla Shores to the scientific sands at Scripps Beach.

Driving along North Torrey Pines Road you will undoubtedly cross the **University of California–San Diego** campus, a sprawling 1200 acres set on a mesa above the Pacific Ocean. Home to over 18,000 undergraduate and graduate students, the university boasts natural chaparral canyons, green lawns, and eucalyptus groves, contrasted with urban student plazas and buildings. Spread throughout this expansive campus is the **Stuart Collection of Sculpture**, featuring permanent outdoor sculptures by leading contemporary artists. ~ 619-657-7000.

Part of the university is the **Scripps Institute of Oceanography**, the oldest institution in the nation devoted to oceanography and the home of the **Birch Aquarium at Scripps**. Here you'll find 33 marine life tanks, a manmade tidepool, breathtaking exhibits of coastal underwater habitats, interactive displays for children and adults, and displays illustrating recent advances in oceanographic research. Admission. ~ 2300 Expedition Way; 619-534-3474.

Another research center, **The Salk Institute**, created by the man whose vaccine helped vanquish polio, is renowned not only for its research but its architecture as well. The surrealistic concrete structure was designed by Louis Kahn in 1960 to be an environment that would stimulate original thinking. It is a stunning site, perched on the lip of a high canyon overlooking the Pacific. ~ At the crest of North Torrey Pines Road just north of the University of California—San Diego campus; call tour information at 619-453-4100, ext. 1200.

Next to the institute is the **Torrey Pines Glider Port** where you can watch hang-gliding and paragliding masters soar over the waves from atop a 360-foot cliff. ~ 2800 Torrey Pines Scenic Drive; 619-452-9858. Trails leading down to the notorious **Black's Beach** begin here. Black's is San Diego's unofficial, illegal, ever-loving nude beach. And a beautiful strip of natural landscape it is.

◄ *HIDDEN*

Bordering Black's on the north is **Torrey Pines State Reserve and Beach**, whose 1750-acre preserve was established to protect the world's rarest pine tree, the Torrey Pine. The tree itself is a gnarled and twisted specimen. Centuries ago these pines covered the southern coast of California; today they are indigenous only to Santa Rosa Island, off the coast of Santa Barbara, and to the reserve. A network of trails through this blufftop reserve makes

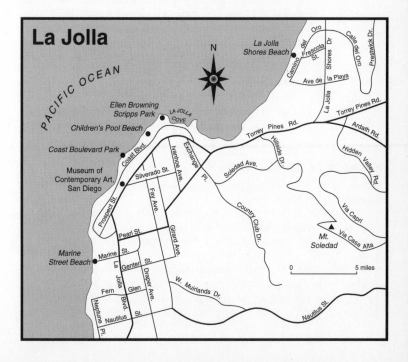

hiking sheer pleasure. Among the rewards are the views, extend-ing along the cliffs and ocean, and the chance to walk quietly among La Jolla's rare treasures. ~ Located west of North Torrey Pines Road, two miles north of Genesee Avenue.

LODGING   Like a Monopoly master, La Jolla possesses the lion's share of "Park Place" accommodations in the San Diego area. Understand-ably, there are no budget hotels in this fashionable village by the sea.

Sands of La Jolla is a small, 39-room motel on a busy thor-oughfare. Rooms are not exactly designer showcases, but they are tastefully appointed and neatly maintained. ~ 5417 La Jolla Boulevard; 619-459-3336, 800-643-0530, fax 619-454-0922. MODERATE.

Tucked away on the north fringe of the village is Andrea Villa Inn, a classy looking 49-unit motel that packs more amenities than some resorts. There is a pool, jacuzzi, concierge, and continental breakfast service. The rooms are spacious and professionally dec-orated with quality furniture. ~ 2402 Torrey Pines Road; 619-459-3311, 800-411-2141, fax 619-459-1320; e-mail marechel@cts. com. MODERATE.

Small, European-style hotels have always been popular in La Jolla, and the granddaddy of them all is the Colonial Inn. Estab-lished in 1913, the 75-room establishment features lavishly dec-orated rooms that beautifully blend colonial-style and contempo-rary furnishings. The oceanfront rooms provide matchless views. ~ 910 Prospect Street; 619-454-2181, 800-826-1278 or 800-223-0888, fax 619-454-5679; www.colonialinn.com. DELUXE TO ULTRA-DELUXE.

More than just a hotel, La Valencia is a La Jolla institution and one of the loveliest hotels in San Diego. Resplendent in pink stucco and Spanish tile, it is perched on a breezy promontory over-

━━━

✔ CHECK THESE OUT—UNIQUE LODGING

- *Budget:* Shed your armor at Hotel Churchill, a medieval manor in downtown San Diego. *page 451*
- *Moderate:* Park under the peaked roof of the Queen Anne Keating House Bed and Breakfast, an inn convenient to Balboa Park. *page 464*
- *Deluxe:* Repose in artistic splendor at Les Artistes, where each room reflects the style of a different artist. *page 423*
- *Ultra-deluxe:* Try for a turret room at the landmark Hotel del Coro-nado, hostelry to movie stars, presidents . . . and ghosts. *page 466*

Budget: under $60   Moderate: $60–$120   Deluxe: $120–$175   Ultra-deluxe: over $175

looking the coves and sea cliffs of La Jolla. From the moment guests enter via a trellis-covered tile loggia into a lobby that could pass for King Juan Carlos' living room, they are enveloped in elegance. The private rooms, however, don't always measure up to the hotel's image. Some of the 106 rooms are rather small and furnished in reproduction antiques. Ah, but out back there's a beautiful garden terrace opening onto the sea and tumbling down to a free-form swimming pool edged with lawn. Facilities include a gym, sauna, whirlpool and three distinctive restaurants. ~ 1132 Prospect Street; 619-454-0771, 800-451-0772, fax 619-456-3921; www.preferredhotels.com. ULTRA-DELUXE.

The **Sheraton Grande Torrey Pines**, adorned with marble and polished wood, is another outstanding white-glove establishment. Here, art deco visits the 21st century in a series of terraces that lead past plush dining rooms, multitiered fountains, a luxurious swimming pool and a fitness center. ~ 10950 North Torrey Pines Road; 619-558-1500, 800-762-6160, fax 619-597-6962; www. sheraton-tp.com. ULTRA-DELUXE.

Just as the village boasts San Diego's finest selection of small hotels, it can also claim a well-known bed and breakfast. **The Bed and Breakfast Inn at La Jolla,** listed as a historical site, was designed as a private home in 1913 by architect Irving Gill. The John Phillip Sousa family resided here in 1921. Faithfully restored by its present owners as a 15-room inn, it stands today as Gill's finest example of Cubist-style architecture. Ideally situated a block-and-a-half from the ocean, this inn is the essence of La Jolla. Each room features an individual decorative theme carried out in period furnishings. Some have fireplaces and ocean views. All but one tiny sleeping room have private baths. ~ 7753 Draper Avenue; 619-456-2066, 800-582-2466, fax 619-456-1510; www.innlajolla. com. MODERATE TO ULTRA-DELUXE.

La Jolla's only true beachfront hotel is **Sea Lodge on La Jolla Shores Beach**. Designed and landscaped to resemble an old California hacienda, this 128-room retreat overlooks the Pacific on a mile-long beach. With its stuccoed arches, terra-cotta roofs, ceramic tilework, fountains, and flowers, Sea Lodge offers a relaxing south-of-the-border setting. Rooms are large and fittingly appointed with Southwestern-style furnishings. All feature balconies and the usual amenities: fitness room, sauna, jacuzzi, pool, and tennis courts. ~ 8110 Camino del Oro; 619-459-8271, 800-237-5211, fax 619-456-9346; www.sealodge.com. ULTRA-DELUXE.

Just as it is blessed with many fine hotels, La Jolla is a restaurant paradise. **George's at the Cove** based its climb to success on a its knockout view of the water, a casual, contemporary environment, fine service, and a trendsetting regional menu. Daily menus incor-

DINING

porate the freshest seafood, veal, beef, lamb, poultry, and pasta available. The spicy Jamaican chicken quesadilla, which you can order in the upstairs bar, is one of my favorites. Downstairs in the fine-dining room, are selections such as ahi encrusted with nori and sesame seeds with a rosemary pappardelle pasta wrapped around brussels sprout leaves and caponata *or* the free-range veal chop with wild-mushrooms du jour in a port-flavored pan juice with foie gras salpicon. The food presentation alone is a work of art. The upstairs and downstairs have separate menus. ~ 1250 Prospect Place; 619-454-4244. DELUXE TO ULTRA-DELUXE.

Another important La Jolla dining place is **Cindy Black's**. Decorated with brightly painted murals and fresh flowers, this well-known establishment features French cuisine. You'll find provençale chicken stew, roast rack of lamb, and steamed clams with cilantro. Dinner only, closed Monday. ~ 5721 La Jolla Boulevard; 619-456-6299. MODERATE TO DELUXE.

Manhattan, which successfully replicates a New York City family-style Italian restaurant (despite the palms and pink stucco), features a singing maître d'. The most popular dishes include zesty scampi *fra diavalo* over pasta, veal marsala, and veal chops. There are wonderful Caesar salads and *cannoli* desserts offered every night. No lunch Saturday and Sunday. ~ 7766 Fay Avenue; 619-554-1444. MODERATE TO ULTRA-DELUXE.

Jose's Court Room, a noisy, down-to-earth Mexican pub, is the best place in town for quick, casual snacks. They offer all the typical taco, tostada, and enchilada plates plus tasty sautéed shrimp and chicken ranchero dinners. ~ 1037 Prospect Street; 619-454-7655. BUDGET TO MODERATE.

HIDDEN ► **John's Waffle Shop** is a traditional La Jolla stopping place for old-fashioned, counter-style breakfasts or lunches. Locals start their day here with golden waffles or eggs Benedict. The best lunches are the country-fried steak and grilled tuna melt on sourdough. Gourmet wraps and smoothies are also available. ~ 7906 Girard Avenue; 619-454-7371. BUDGET.

SHOPPING   Once a secluded seaside village, La Jolla has emerged as a world-famous resort community that offers style and substance. The shopping focuses on Girard Avenue (from Torrey Pines Road to Prospect Street) and along Prospect Street. Both are lined with designer boutiques, specialty shops, and art galleries.

In La Jolla's numerous galleries, traditional art blends with contemporary paintings, and rare Oriental antiques complement 20th-century bronze sculpture. The **Tasende Gallery** has a small display area that packs in contemporary art by big names like Henry Moore and Marino Marini. The gallery exhibits sculpture, paintings and drawings as well. ~ 820 Prospect Street; 619-454-3691.

Housed as it is in a landmark 1903 cottage covered with wisteria, **John Cole's Book Shop** provides a refuge from these slick, chic La Jolla shops. Its nooks and crannies are lined with books ranging from bestsellers to rare editions. ~ 780 Prospect Street; 619-454-4766.

Located some distance south of the village center, **Capriccio** has made its mark in the world of women's fashions, having been numbered by *Women's Wear Daily* among the top three fashion stores in America. ~ 6919 La Jolla Boulevard; 619-459-4189.

NIGHTLIFE

The dark-paneled **Whaling Bar** attracts lots of La Jolla's big fish. A fine place to relax and nibble gourmet hors d'oeuvres. ~ La Valencia Hotel, 1132 Prospect Street; 619-454-0771.

Among the most romantic restaurants in town, **Top O' The Cove** features an equally romantic piano bar, open Friday and Saturday. ~ 1216 Prospect Street; 619-454-7779. A panoramic view of the ocean makes **Crescent Shores Grill** the perfect place to enjoy entertainment Thursday through Saturday. ~ Hotel La Jolla, 7955 La Jolla Shores Drive; 619-459-0541.

The Comedy Store features comedians exclusively, many with national reputations. Cover, open Wednesday through Sunday. ~ 916 Pearl Street; 619-454-9176.

The San Diego area finally got its own **Hard Rock Cafe**, where crowds line the streets just to get in. The main attraction here is the varied collection of rock-and-roll memorabilia. ~ 909 Prospect Street; 619-454-5101.

◄ *HIDDEN*

D. G. Wills Books is a tiny literary haven featuring lectures and poetry readings, as well as an occasional jazz night. ~ 7461 Girard Avenue; 619-456-1800.

The **La Jolla Chamber Music Society** hosts year-round performances by such notables as Isaac Stern, Yo-Yo Ma, and the Stuttgart Chamber Orchestra. ~ 619-459-3728.

The very prestigious **La Jolla Playhouse**, located on the University of California's San Diego campus, produces innovative dramas and musicals and spotlights famous actors, during the summer and fall. ~ 619-550-1070.

WHERE THE FISH SHOP FOR SCALES

One of the oldest and most unusual shops in La Jolla guards the entrance to a sea cave. Dating to 1903, the **La Jolla Cave and Shell Shop** displays every kind of shell imaginable along with a variety of nautical gifts and tourist baubles. From inside the shop, 145 steps lead down a tunnel to the main chamber of Sunny Jim Cave. Admission. ~ 1325 Coast Boulevard; 619-454-6080.

BEACHES & PARKS

TORREY PINES STATE RESERVE AND BEACH 🚶 🏊 🚣 A long, wide, sandy stretch adjacent to Los Peñasquitos Lagoon and Torrey Pines State Reserve, this beach is highly visible from the highway and therefore heavily used. It is popular for sunning, swimming, surf fishing, volleyball, and sunset barbecues. Nearby trails lead through the reserves with their lagoons, rare trees, and abundant birdlife. The beach is patrolled only in summer so exercise caution in and out of the surf. Restrooms are available. Surfers might want to steer clear of this beach because there are powerful peaks. Day-use fee, $4 per car. ~ Located just south of Carmel Valley Road, Del Mar; 619-755-2063.

HIDDEN ▶ **BLACK'S BEACH** 🏄 One of the world's most famous nude beaches, on hot summer days it attracts bathers by the thousands, many in the buff. The sand is lovely and soft and the 300-foot cliffs rising up behind make for a spectacular setting. Hang-gliders and paragliders soar from the glider port above to add even more enchantment. Swimming is dangerous; beware of the currents and exercise caution as the beach is infrequently patrolled. Surfing is excellent; one of the most awesome beach breaks in California. Lifeguards are here in the summer. ~ From Route 5 in La Jolla follow Genesee Avenue west; turn left on North Torrey Pines Road, then right at Torrey Pines Scenic Drive. There's a parking lot at the Torrey Pines Glider Port, but trails to the beach from here are very steep and often dangerous. If you're in doubt just park at the Torrey Pines State Reserve lot one mile north and walk back along the shore to Black's during low tide.

SCRIPPS BEACH 🚶 With coastal bluffs above, narrow sand beach below, and rich tidepools offshore, this is a great strand for beachcombers. Two **underwater reserves** as well as museum displays at the Scripps Institute of Oceanography are among the attractions. There are museum facilities at Scripps Institute. ~ Scripps Institute is located at the 8600 block of La Jolla Shores Drive in La Jolla. You can park at Kellogg Park–La Jolla Shores Beach and walk north to Scripps.

KELLOGG PARK–LA JOLLA SHORES BEACH 🏊 🏄 The sand is wide and the swimming is easy at La Jolla Shores; so, naturally, the beach is covered with bodies whenever the sun appears. Just to the east is Kellogg Park, an ideal place for a picnic, swimming, and surfing. There are restrooms, a playground, and lifeguards. ~ Off Camino del Oro and Costa Boulevard in La Jolla.

ELLEN BROWNING SCRIPPS PARK AND LA JOLLA COVE 🏊 🏄 This grassy park sits on a bluff overlooking the cove and is the scenic focal point of La Jolla. The naturally formed cove is almost always free of breakers, has a small but sandy beach, and is a popular spot for swimmers and divers. It's also the site of the **La Jolla Ecological Reserve,** an underwater park and diving reserve. There are picnic areas, restrooms, shuffleboard, and lifeguards. La Jolla's big wave action lies outside the cove so surfers should exercise caution. ~ Near Coast Boulevard and Girard Avenue in La Jolla.

CHILDREN'S POOL BEACH At the north end of Coast Boulevard Beach (see below) a concrete breakwater loops around a small lagoon. Despite its name, the beach's strong rip currents can make swimming hazardous. There are lifeguards and restrooms. Fishing is good from the surf. Seasonal rip tides can be hazardous to swimmers, so check with lifeguards. ~ Located off Coast Boulevard in La Jolla.

COAST BOULEVARD PARK After about a half-mile of wide sandy beach, the bluffs and tiny pocket beaches that characterize Windansea (see below) reappear at what locals call "Coast Beach." The pounding waves make watersports unsafe, but savvy locals find the smooth sandstone boulders and sandy coves perfect for reading, sunbathing, and picnicking. ~ Paths lead to the beach at several points along Coast Boulevard in La Jolla.

MARINE STREET BEACH Separated from Windansea to the south by towering sandstone bluffs, this is a much wider and more sandy strand, favored by sunbathers, swimmers, skindivers, and frisbee-tossing youths. The rock-free shoreline is ideal for walking or jogging. The beach is good for board and body-surfing; watch for rip currents and high surf. ~ Turn west off La Jolla Boulevard on Marine Street.

WINDANSEA BEACH This is surely one of the most picturesque beaches in the country. It has been portrayed in the movies and was immortalized in Tom Wolfe's 1968 nonfiction classic, *The Pumphouse Gang*, about the surfers who still hang around the old pumphouse (part of the city's sewer system), zealously protecting their famous surf from outsiders. Windansea is rated by experts as one of the best surfing locales on the West Coast. In the evenings, crowds line the Neptune Place sidewalk, which runs along the top of the cliffs, to watch the sunset. North of the pumphouse are several sandy nooks sandwiched between sandstone outcroppings. Romantic spot! There are lifeguards on duty in the summer. ~ Located at the end of Nautilus Street in La Jolla.

HERMOSA TERRACE PARK This beach is said to be "seasonally sandy," which is another way of saying it's rocky at times. Best chance for sand is in the summer when this is a pretty good sunning beach. The surfing is good. There are no facilities. ~ Located off Winamar Avenue in La Jolla; a paved path leads to the beach.

BIRD ROCK 🏃 Named for a large sandstone boulder about 50 yards off the coast, this beach is rocky and thus favored by divers. The surf rarely breaks here, but when it does this spot is primo for surfing; exercise caution. Fishing is also good. Facilities are nonexistent. ~ Located at the end of Bird Rock Avenue in La Jolla.

SOUTH BIRD ROCK 🏃 Tidepools are the attractions along this rocky, cliff-lined beach. Surfing is best in the summer. ~ From Midway or Forward streets in La Jolla follow paths down to the beach.

TOURMALINE SURFING PARK 🏊 🏃 A year-round reef break and consistently big waves make La Jolla one of the best surfing areas on the West Coast. Tourmaline is popular with surfers. Skindiving is permitted, as is swimming. You'll find picnic areas and restrooms. ~ Located at the end of Tourmaline Street in La Jolla.

▼▼▼▼▼▼▼▼▼▼▼▼▼▼▼
Mission Bay Park Area

Dredged from a shallow, mosquito-infested tidal bay, 4600-acre Mission Bay Park is the largest municipal aquatic park in the world. For San Diego's athletic set it is Mecca, a recreational paradise dotted with islands and lagoons and ringed by 27 miles of sandy beaches.

Here, visitors join with residents to enjoy swimming, sailing, windsurfing, waterskiing, fishing, jogging, cycling, golf, and tennis. Or perhaps a relaxing day of kite flying and sunbathing.

SIGHTS

More than just a playground, Mission Bay Park features a shopping complex, resort hotels, restaurants, and the popular marine park, **SeaWorld Adventure Park**. This 150-acre park-within-a-park is the world's largest oceanarium. Admission. ~ Sea World Drive; 619-226-3901.

Among the attractions are performing killer whales; the largest penguin colony north of Antarctica; a "Forbidden Reef" inhabited by bat rays and over 100 moray eels; and "Rocky Point Preserve," an exhibit boasting a wave pool, pettable dolphins, and a colony of Alaskan sea otters (rescued from the 1989 *Exxon Valdez* oil spill). "Manatee Rescue," the only U.S. manatee exhibit outside of Florida, is a venture designed to relieve the Florida Sea-World of its overflowing supply of rehabilitating manatees. The exhibit provides over 800 feet of underwater viewing. The only ride in the park, Wild Arctic takes visitors on a helicopter ride to an Arctic research station to explore two capsized sailing ships from a century-old wreck, and to see native Arctic mammals.

One of the best bargains at SeaWorld is the 90-minute guided tour of the park (fee). It's the only way to get a behind-the-scenes look at the Animal Care Facility, where holding pools house an-

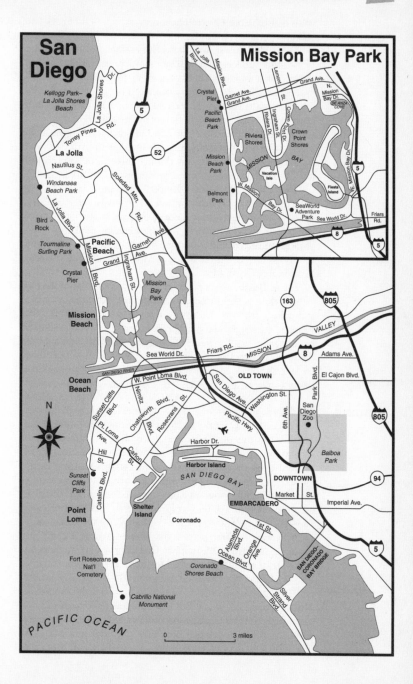

imals that have been placed under observation. In the Shark Lab, you also get to pet a tiny bamboo shark.

The park also hosts world-class water-skiers, a Sky Tower that lifts visitors 320 feet above Mission Bay. I prefer simply to watch the penguins waddling about on a simulated iceberg and zipping around after fish in their glass-contained ocean, or to peer in at the fearsome makos at "Shark Encounter." The park's magnificent marine creatures are all the entertainment I need.

Down along the oceanfront, **Mission Beach** is strung out along a narrow jetty of sand protecting Mission Bay from the sea. Mission Boulevard threads its way through this eclectic, wall-to-wall mix of shingled beach shanties, condominiums, and luxury homes.

The historic 1925 "Giant Dipper" has come back to life after years of neglect at the **Belmont Park**. One of only two West Coast seaside coasters, this beauty is not all the park has to offer. There's also a carousel, video arcade, indoor swimming pool, and a host of shops and eateries along the beach and boardwalk. ~ 3146 Mission Boulevard or on the beach at Mission Boulevard and West Mission Bay Drive; 619-488-0668.

Pacific Beach, which picks up at the northern edge of the bay, is the liveliest of the city beaches, an area packed with high school and college students. Designer shorts, a garish Hawaiian shirt, strapped-on sunglasses, and a skate board are all you need to fit in perfectly along the frenetic boardwalk at "PB." Stop and see the 1920s **Crystal Pier** with its tiny hotel built out over the waves. Or take a stroll along the boardwalk, checking out the sunbathers, skaters, joggers, and cyclists. ~ At the end of Garnet Avenue.

LODGING   Pacific Beach boasts the San Diego County lodging with the most character of all. **Crystal Pier Hotel** is a throwback to the 1930s. That's when this quaint-looking assemblage of 29 cottages on Crystal Pier was built. This blue-and-white woodframe complex, perched over the waves, features little cottages that are hardly more than huts. Each comes with a kitchen and patio-over-the-sea, not to mention your own parking place on the pier. A unique discovery indeed. ~ 4500 Ocean Boulevard, Pacific Beach; 619-483-6983, 800-748-5894, fax 619-483-6811. ULTRA-DELUXE.

A bargain in these parts is the **Western Shores**, located just across the street from Mission Bay Golf Course. This is a quiet 40-unit court that can't be matched for value anywhere in the area. ~ 4345 Mission Bay Drive, Pacific Beach; 619-273-1121. BUDGET.

There aren't many beachfront facilities along Pacific Beach, Mission Beach, and Ocean Beach, except for condominiums. One particularly pretty four-unit condominium, **Ventanas al Mar**, overlooks the ocean in Mission Beach. Its contemporary two- and three-bedroom units feature fireplaces, jacuzzis, kitchens, and washer-dryers. They sleep as many as eight people. In the summer, these rent by the week only. ~ 3631 Ocean Front Walk, Mission Beach; 619-488-1580, 800-869-7858, fax 619-488-1584; www.billluther.com. ULTRA-DELUXE.

Just a few doors away is the family-oriented **Far Horizons**, a two-story gray-frame fourplex. The apartment at 705 Ormond Court, for instance, features a full kitchen, living and dining areas, a TV, washer and dryer, and other feel-at-home furnishings. The one-bedroom apartments have ocean views and in summer rent by the week only. ~ 3643-45 Ocean Front Walk, Mission Beach; 619-488-9178. DELUXE.

Most of the hotels within sprawling Mission Bay Park are upscale resorts in the deluxe to ultra-deluxe price range. But there's budget-priced relief at **Banana Bungalow**, a privately run hostel right on Mission Beach. The accommodations are of the co-ed bunk-bed variety for the backpacking set who don't mind sharing rooms with strangers. You must be a student with a student ID. U.S. citizens are lodged in the off-season. A complimentary breakfast is served every morning. Accommodations are on a first-come, first-served basis. ~ 707 Reed Avenue, Mission Beach; 619-273-3060, 800-546-7835, fax 619-273-1440; www.banana bungalow.com. BUDGET.

Only one Mission Bay resort stands out as unique—the **San Diego Paradise Point Resort**. Over 40 acres of lush gardens, lagoons, and white sand beach surround the bungalows of this 462-room resort. Except for some fancy suites, room decor is motel-modern, with quality furnishings. But guests don't spend much time in their rooms anyway. At the Princess there's more than a mile of beach, catamaran rentals, a fitness center, six tennis courts, six pools, three restaurants, two lounges, and an 18-hole putting course. A self-contained island paradise. ~ 1404 West Vacation Road, Mission Beach; 619-274-4630, 800-344-2626, fax 619-581-5929; www.paradisepoint.com. DELUXE.

DINING

Critic's choice for the area's best omelettes is **Broken Yoke Café**. Choose from nearly 30 of these eggy creations or invent your own. If you can eat it all within an hour, the ironman/woman special—including a dozen eggs, mushrooms, onions, cheese, etc.—it costs only $1.98. Faint or fail and you pay much more. They make soups, sandwiches, and salads, too. Breakfast and lunch only. ~ 1851 Garnet Avenue, Pacific Beach; 619-270-0045. BUDGET.

The most creative restaurant in Pacific Beach is **Château Orleans**, one of the city's finest Cajun-Creole restaurants. Tasty appetizers fresh from the bayous include Louisiana crabcakes and Southern-fried 'gator bites. Yes, indeed, they eat alligators down in Cajun country, and you should be brave enough to find out why. Mardi Gras Gumbo (chocked with crawfish), the "Bourbon Street Stripper" steak, chicken sauce piquant, and colorful jambalaya are typical menu choices. Everything is authentic except the decor, which thankfully shuns board floors and bare bulbs in favor of carpets, original New Orleans artwork, and patio seating in a New Orleans–style garden. Live jazz and blues Thursday through Saturday. Dinner only. Closed Sunday. ~ 926 Turquoise Street, Pacific Beach; 619-488-6744. MODERATE TO DELUXE.

The Mission is a casual neighborhood restaurant where folks are likely to chat with whoever is dining next to them. The ambience is funky, the furniture eclectic, and the walls are enlivened with local art. Blending Asian and Latin influences, the cuisine emphasizes food that is healthy, tasty, and original. There are breakfast standards with a twist such as French toast served with berries and blueberry purée. If you're in the mood for something more Mexican, order the *plata verde con huevos* (slightly sweet tamales with eggs, roasted chile verde, and cheese). For lunch there are such creations as the ginger-sesame chicken roll-up or Baja shrimp wrap. No dinner. ~ 3795 Mission Boulevard, Mission Beach; 619-488-9060. BUDGET.

HIDDEN ▶

Hidden away in Ocean Beach is a quaint cottage restaurant called The Belgian Lion. Nobody in San Diego provides lustier, tastier European provincial fare than the folks here, who prepare French onion soup, braised rabbit, crispy confit of duck, turnip soufflé, and steaming cassoulets in the classic manner. Homegrown herbs and spices delight both the sauces and the senses. But go easy when you order; the portions are meant to satisfy a Flemish farmer. Service here is especially personalized. Dinner is served only on Thursday, Friday, and Saturday. ~ 2265 Bacon Street, Ocean Beach; 619-223-2700. DELUXE.

✔ CHECK THESE OUT—UNIQUE DINING

- *Budget:* Satisfy your ironman-size appetite with the **Broken Yoke Café's** hearty homestyle omelettes. *page 443*
- *Budget to moderate:* Sample spicy shrimp soup at **Siamese Basil,** an intimate Thai eatery with curries and spareribs that will make your mouth water. *page 424*
- *Moderate to deluxe:* Hum bars of "Bad Leroy Brown" to yourself as you peruse the international menu at **Croce's Restaurant,** a bar/restaurant run by Jim Croce's widow, Ingrid. *page 454*
- *Ultra-deluxe:* Saunter into San Diego's best French restaurant, **Mille Fleurs,** where the à la carte menu changes daily. *page 425*

Budget: under $9   Moderate: $9–$18   Deluxe: $18–$25   Ultra-deluxe: over $25

Commercial enterprises in the beach communities cater primarily to sun worshipers. Beachie boutiques and rental shops are everywhere. A shopping center on the beach, **Belmont Park** has a host of shops and restaurants. ~ 3146 Mission Boulevard, Mission Bay Park; 619-488-0668.

SHOPPING

The **Promenade at Pacific Beach**, a modern, Mediterranean-style shopping complex, houses around 12 smartly decorated specialty shops. ~ Located on Mission Boulevard between Pacific Beach Drive and Reed Street, Pacific Beach; 619-490-9097.

Blind Melons, beside the Crystal Pier, is best described as a Chicago beach bar featuring live blues on Tuesday (a national blues act twice a month) and local acts the other nights of the week. Cover. ~ 710 Garnet Avenue, Pacific Beach; 619-483-7844.

NIGHTLIFE

The **Cannibal Bar** features a variety of live music Wednesday through Sunday. Bands may play blues, ska, rock or even jazz. Cover. ~ Catamaran Hotel, 3999 Mission Boulevard, Pacific Beach; 619-488-1081.

Moose McGillycuddy's is a popular nightclub where recorded music keeps the crowd active on Wednesday, Friday, Saturday and Sunday. Cover. ~ 1165 Garnet Avenue, Pacific Beach; 619-274-2323.

The **Pennent** is a Mission Beach landmark where local beachies congregate en masse on the deck to get rowdy and watch the sunset. The entertainment here is the clientele. ~ 2893 Mission Boulevard, Mission Beach; 619-488-1671.

Delta Six is frequented by a mostly twentysomething crowd that enjoys occasional live jazz and blues. If you're lucky, you'll get to hear Tom "Cat" Courtney, a real-life legend who has strummed guitar with the likes of T-Bone Walker, Lightnin' Hopkins, and Freddie King. Cover for live acts. ~ 4970 Voltaire Street, Ocean Beach; 619-222-6895.

PACIFIC BEACH PARK At its south end, "PB" is a major gathering place, its boardwalk crowded with teens and assorted rowdies, but a few blocks north, just before Crystal Pier, the boardwalk becomes a quieter concrete promenade that follows scenic, sloping cliffs. The beach widens here and the crowd becomes more family oriented. The surf is moderate and fine for swimming and bodysurfing. Pier and surf fishing are great for corbina and surf perch. South of the pier Ocean Boulevard becomes a pedestrian-only mall with a bike path, benches, and picnic tables. Facilities include restrooms, lifeguards, and restaurants. ~ Located near Grand Avenue and Pacific Beach Drive.

BEACHES & PARKS

◄ *HIDDEN*

MISSION BAY PARK One of the nation's largest and most diverse city-owned aquatic parks, Mission Bay has something to suit just about everyone's recreational interest. Key areas and facilities are as follows: **Dana Landing** and **Quivira Basin** make up the southwest portion of this 4600-acre park. Most boating activities begin here, where port headquarters and a large marina are located. Adjacent is **Bonita Cove,** used for swimming, picnicking and volleyball. There is a softball field at **Marina's Point.** Mission Boulevard shops, restaurants, and recreational equipment rentals are within easy walking distance. **Ventura Cove** houses a large hotel complex but its sandy beach is open to the public. Calm waters make it a popular swimming spot for small children.

Vacation Isle and **Ski Beach** are easily reached via the bridge on Ingram Street, which bisects the island. The west side contains public swimming areas, boat rentals, and a model yacht basin. Ski Beach is on the east side and is the favorite spot in the bay for waterskiing. **Fiesta Island** is situated on the southwest side of the park. It's ringed with soft sand swimming beaches and laced with jogging, cycling, and skating paths. A favorite spot for fishing from the quieter coves and for kite flying. On the south side of Fiesta Island sits South Shores, a large boat-launching area.

Over on the **East Shore,** you'll find landscaped picnic areas, playgrounds, a physical fitness course, a sandy beach for swimming, and the park information center. **De Anza Cove,** at the extreme northeast corner of the park, has a sandy beach for swimming plus a sizable private campground. **Crown Point Shores** provides a sandy beach, picnic area, nature study area, physical fitness course, and a waterski landing.

Sail Bay and **Riviera Shores** make up the northwest portion of Mission Bay and back up against the apartments and condominiums of Pacific Beach. Sail Bay's beaches aren't the best in the park and are usually submerged during high tides. Riviera Shores has a better beach with waterski areas.

Santa Clara and **El Carmel Points** jut out into the westernmost side of Mission Bay. They are perfect for water sports: swimming, snorkeling, surfing, waterskiing, windsurfing, and boating. Santa Clara Point is of interest to the visitor with its recreation center, tennis courts, and softball field. A sandy beach fronts San Juan Cove between the two points.

Just about every facility imaginable can be found somewhere in the park. There are also catamaran and windsurfer rentals, playgrounds and parks, frisbee and golf, and restaurants and groceries. ~ Located along Mission Boulevard between West Mission Bay Drive and East Mission Bay Drive; 619-221-8900.

▲ The finest and largest of San Diego's commercial campgrounds is **Campland On The Bay** (2211 Pacific Beach Drive; 800-422-9386; www.campland.com), featuring 600 hookup sites for RVs, vans, tents, and boats; $22 to $150 per night.

MISSION BEACH PARK 🚲 🌊 🏊 The wide, sandy beach at the southern end of the park is a favorite haunt of both high schoolers and college students. The hot spot appears to be at the foot of Capistrano Court. A paved boardwalk runs parallel to the beach and is always bustling with a crowd of bicyclists, joggers, and roller skaters. Farther north, up around the old Belmont Park roller coaster, the beach grows narrower and the surf quite a bit rougher. The crowd tends to get that way, too, with teenage heavy-metal enthusiasts, sailors, and bikers hanging out along the sea wall, ogling and sometimes harassing the bikini set. This is the closest San Diego comes to Los Angeles' colorful but funky Venice Beach. The facilities include restrooms, lifeguards, and a boardwalk lined with restaurants and beach rentals. Surfing is popular along the jetty. ~ Located along Mission Boulevard north of West Mission Bay Drive.

San Diego's beautiful harbor is a notable exception to the rule that big-city waterfronts lack appeal. Here, the city embraces its bay and presents its finest profile along the water.

▼▼▼▼▼▼▼▼▼▼▼▼

San Diego Harbor

The best way to see it all is on a harbor tour. A variety of vessels dock near Harbor Drive at the foot of Broadway. **San Diego Harbor Excursion** provides leisurely trips around the 22-square-mile harbor, which is colorfully backdropped by commercial and naval vessels as well as the dramatic cityscape. A ferry to Coronado Island from downtown is also operated by Harbor Excursion. Admission. ~ 1050 North Harbor Drive; 619-234-4111. My favorite sunset harbor cruises are aboard the 151-foot yacht *Lord Hornblower*. Admission. ~ 1066 North Harbor Drive; 619-234-8687.

SIGHTS

All along the cityside of the harbor from the Coast Guard Station opposite Lindbergh Field to Seaport Village is a lovely landscaped boardwalk called the **Embarcadero**. It offers parks where you can stroll and play, a floating maritime museum, and a thriving assortment of waterfront diversions.

The **Maritime Museum of San Diego** is composed of three vintage ships: most familiar is the 1863 *Star of India*, the nation's oldest iron-hulled merchant ship still afloat. Visitors go aboard for a hint of what life was like on the high seas more than a century ago. You can also visit the 1898 ferry *Berkeley*, which helped in the evacuation of San Francisco during the 1906 earthquake, and the 1904 steam yacht *Medea*. Admission. ~ 1306 North Harbor Drive; 619-234-9153.

Nautical buffs or anyone concerned about American naval power will be interested in the **U.S. Navy** presence in San Diego harbor. As headquarters of the Commander Naval Base, San

Diego hosts one of the world's largest fleets of fighting ships—from aircraft carriers to nuclear submarines. Naval docks and yards are off-limits but you'll see the sprawling facilities and plenty of those distinctive gray-hulled ships during a harbor cruise. Naval vessels moored at the Broadway Pier hold open house on weekends. ~ 619-532-3130.

The Marine Center presents colorful **military reviews** most Fridays. Marching ceremonies begin at exactly 10 a.m. at the Marine Corps Recruiting Depot (619-524-1772). ~ The center may be reached from downtown by going north on Pacific Highway to Barnett Avenue, then left to Gate 1.

Near the south end of the Embarcadero sits the popular shopping and entertainment complex known as **Seaport Village**. Designed to replicate an Early California seaport, it comprises 14 acres of bayfront parks and promenades, shops, and galleries. ~ Pacific Highway and Harbor Drive; 619-235-4013.

On the south side, overlooking the water, is the 45-foot-high **Mukilteo Lighthouse**, official symbol of the village, a recreation of a famous lighthouse located in Washington state. Nearby is the **Broadway Flying Horses Carousel**, a hand-carved, turn-of-the-century model that originally whirled around on Coney Island.

Nearby, the **San Diego Convention Center** looks like an erector set gone mad. An uncontained congeries of flying buttresses, giant tents, and curved glass, it is fashioned in the form of a ship, seemingly poised to set sail across San Diego Harbor. This architectural exclamation mark is certainly worth a drive by or a quick tour. ~ 111 West Harbor Drive; 619-525-5000.

▼▼▼▼▼▼▼▼▼▼▼▼▼▼▼▼
Downtown San Diego

At one time downtown San Diego was a collection of porn shops, tattoo parlors, and strip-tease bars. Billions of dollars invested in a stunning array of new buildings and in the restoration of many old ones have changed all that.

Within the compact city center there's Horton Plaza, an exciting example of avant-garde urban architecture, and the adjacent Gaslamp Quarter, which reveals how San Diego looked at the peak of its Victorian-era boom in the 1880s.

SIGHTS   Horton Plaza is totally unlike any other shopping center or urban redevelopment project. It has transcended its genre in whimsical, rambling paths, bridges, towers, piazzas, sculptures, fountains, and live greenery. Mimes, minstrels, and fortune tellers meander about the six-block complex performing for patrons. The success of this structure sparked downtown's renewal by revamping local businesses and attracting more tourists.

Horton Plaza was inspired by European shopping streets and districts such as the Plaka of Athens, the Ramblas of Barcelona, and Portobello Road in London. ~ The Plaza is bounded by Broadway and G Street and 1st and 4th avenues.

The **Gaslamp Quarter** is one of America's largest national historic districts, covering a 16-block strip along 4th, 5th, and 6th avenues from Broadway to the waterfront. Architecturally, the Quarter reveals some of the very finest Victorian-style commercial buildings constructed in San Diego during the 50 years between the Civil War and World War I. It was this area, along 5th Avenue, that became San Diego's first main street. The city's core began on the bay where Alonzo Horton first built a wharf in 1869.

It was this same area that later fell into disrepute as the heart of the business district moved north beyond Broadway. By the 1890s, prostitution and gambling were rampant. Offices above the street level were converted into bordellos and opium dens. The area south of Market Street became known as the "Stingaree," an unflattering reference coined by the many who were stung by card sharks, con men, and of course, con ladies.

Rescued by the city and a dedicated group of preservationists, the area not only survived but played a major role in the massive redevelopment of downtown San Diego. The city added wide brick sidewalks, period street lamps, trees, and benches. In all, more than 100 grand old Victorian buildings were restored to their original splendor.

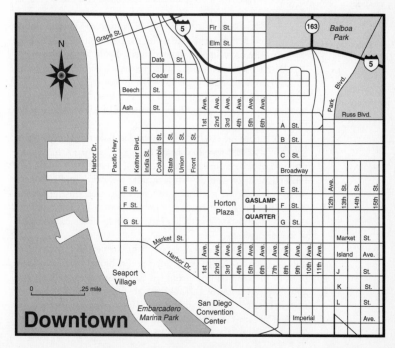

History buffs and lovers of antique buildings should promptly don their walking shoes for a tour of the Gaslamp Quarter. One way to do this is to join a walking tour (see the "Transportation" section in this chapter). Or head out on your own, accompanied by a map often available at the **William Heath Davis House Museum**. Call for museum hours. ~ 410 Island Avenue; 619-233-4692.

HIDDEN ▶

Located in the basement of what used to be a mortuary and casket-making company, the **Museum of Death** presents several mortality-related exhibits, such as a collection of body bags (the different colors of the bags indicate a different use), antique coffins, antique mortuary instruments, animal and human skulls, and crime- and accident-scene photos. Letters and artwork by serial killers are also displayed (the museum's founders, Cathee Shultz and James Healy, correspond with several convicted murderers).

Upstairs is the newly opened **Freak Farm U.S.A.**, which corrals live and stuffed freak animals. The live ones include two-headed turtles, "Chick," the hen with the double derriere, and an "albino swamp" with albino critters—most notably the albino cannibalistic horned frog. "He's evil," the woman at the museum told me. You can pay separate admission for either museum or get a reduced price for a double-ticket. ~ 548 5th Avenue; 619-338-8153.

Fourteen different styles, ranging from Renaissance to Post Modern, are employed in the design of Horton Plaza.

The Quarter includes 153 buildings so I couldn't hope to describe them all, but let me take you on a mini-tour of the most important structures. Begin at the aforementioned William Heath Davis House, a well-preserved example of a prefabricated "salt box" family home, dating to about 1850. Framed on the East Coast, it was shipped to San Diego by boat around Cape Horn and represents the oldest structure in the Quarter.

Just across the street is the **Royal Pie Bakery**. Almost unbelievably, a bakery was on this site from 1871 until 1996. Around the turn of the century the bakery found itself in the middle of a red-light district. It didn't stop turning out cakes and pies until recently, though a notorious bordello operated on the second floor. Such durability doesn't count now, however. The building, outfitted for restaurants, bears little reminder of its bakery past. ~ 554 4th Avenue.

Go back down Island Avenue to 5th Avenue and turn left. Not only was this block part of the Stingaree, as hinted by the old 1887 hotel by the same name on your left, at 542 5th Avenue, but it was San Diego's Chinatown. **Nanking Café** was built in 1912 and is now a Thai restaurant called Royal Thai. ~ 467 5th Avenue.

The nearby **Timken Building**, notable for its fancy arched brick facade, was erected in 1894. ~ Located at 5th Avenue and

Market Street. Across the street is another historical site, the **Backesto Building**, a beautifully restored late-19th-century structure.

The tall, Romanesque Revival **Keating Building** was one of the most prestigious office buildings in San Diego during the 1890s, complete with such modern conveniences as steam heat and a wire-cage elevator. ~ 5th Avenue and F Street. Next door is the **Ingersoll Tutton Building**. When this 90-foot-long structure was built in 1894 for $20,000 it was the most expensive building on the block! ~ 832 5th Avenue.

Most of the block on the other side of 5th Avenue, from F up to E streets, represents the most architecturally significant row in the Gaslamp Quarter. From south to north, there's the **Marston Building** on the corner of F Street. Built in 1881, it was downtown San Diego's leading department store. Next is the 1887 **Hubbell Building**, originally a dry goods establishment. The **Nesmith-Greeley Building** next door is another example of the then fashionable Romanesque Revival style with its ornamental brick coursing. With twin towers and intricate Baroque Revival architecture, the 1888 **Louis Bank of Commerce** is probably the most beautiful building in the Quarter. It originally housed a ground-floor oyster bar that was a favorite haunt of Wyatt Earp. The famous Western lawman-cum-real-estate speculator resided in San Diego from 1886 to 1893. Be sure to go to the fourth floor to see the beautiful skylight.

Though it's situated a few blocks east of the Gaslamp Quarter, make a point to visit the **Villa Montezuma–Jesse Shepard House**. This ornate, Queen Anne–style Victorian mansion, magnificently restored, was constructed by a wealthy group of San Diegans in 1887 as a gift to a visiting musician. Culture-hungry civic leaders actually "imported" world-famous troubadour Jesse Shepard to live in the opulent dwelling as something of a court musician to the city's upper crust. Shepard stayed only two years but decorated his villa to the hilt with dozens of stained-glass windows and elaborate hand-carved wood trim and decorations. Open weekends. Admission. ~ 1925 K Street; 619-239-2211.

Providing contrast to all this preserved history is the **Museum of Contemporary Art**, adjacent to the American Plaza Trolley Transfer Station. Two floors and four galleries showcase an internationally renowned collection and temporary exhibits featuring cutting-edge modern art. Educational tours and a well-stocked bookstore complement the exhibits. Closed Monday. Admission. ~ 1001 Kettner Boulevard at Broadway; 619-234-1001.

LODGING

Among the very few decent downtown budget overnight spots, **Hotel Churchill** is about the cleanest and most livable. Billed as "small, quaint, and unique," this venerable seven-story, 92-room hotel is mostly quaint. Built in 1915, it was somewhat tastelessly remodeled to "depict an authentic medieval English castle." In an equally kitschy decorative scheme, 30 of the Churchill's better rooms are done up in different thematic motifs such as "Hawaiian Sunset" and "American Indian." Bedspreads and wall murals are the only difference. To really save money during a downtown stay, ask for one of the rooms with a shared bathroom. ~ 827 C Street; 619-234-5186, fax 619-231-9012. BUDGET.

Treat yourself to a nice dinner with the money you save staying at **Hostelling International–San Diego the Metropolitan,** centrally located in the Gaslamp Quarter. Featuring a blue-and-yellow trompe l'oeil mural on the outside, this Mediterranean-style hostelry has 20 sex-segregated dorm facilities and 5 private rooms, as well as a fully equipped kitchen and common area. Unlike other hostels, there is no curfew. Reservations recommended. ~ 521 Market Street, 619-525-1531, 800-909-4776, fax 619-338-0129; www.hostelweb.com/sandiego/metro.htm. BUDGET.

Chain hotels are normally not included in these listings, but because of the lack of good, low-cost lodgings downtown, I'm compelled to tell you about **Super 8 Bayview**. This 98-room property offers pleasant, affordable rooms downtown. Queen-sized beds complement a bright, functional, and contemporary environment; you'll also find a pool and jacuzzi. ~ 1835 Columbia Street; 619-544-0164, 800-537-9902, fax 619-237-9940. MODERATE.

A recommended midtown hotel is the **Best Western Bayside Inn**. Small enough (122 rooms) to offer some degree of personalized service, this modern highrise promises nearly all the niceties you would pay extra for at more prestigious downtown hotels, including a harbor view. Furnishings and amenities are virtually on a par with those found in the typical Hilton or Sheraton. There is a pool and spa, plus a restaurant and cocktail lounge. ~ 555 West Ash Street; 619-233-7500, 800-528-1234, fax 619-239-8060; www.baysideinn.com. MODERATE.

On the more charming side are San Diego's guesthouses, bed and breakfasts, and historic hotels. **Harbor Hill Guest House** overlooks the harbor in a centrally located area known as "Banker's Hill." This elegant 1920 home once belonged to the city's mayor. Six smartly decorated rooms with private entrances and baths are arranged on three levels. Each level offers a kitchen-dining area and sitting room. There is also a lovely garden and redwood deck. ~ 2330 Albatross Street; 619-233-0638. MODERATE.

No downtown hotel has a more colorful past than the **Horton Grand Hotel**. This 132-room Victorian gem is actually two old hotels that were disassembled piece by piece and resurrected a few blocks away. The two were lavishly reconstructed and linked by an atrium-lobby and courtyard. The 1880s theme is faithfully executed, from the hotel's antique-furnished rooms (each with a fireplace) to its period-costumed staff. Such amenities as a concierge and afternoon tea (served Thursday through Saturday) combine with friendly service and perfect location to make it one of the city's best hotel values. ~ 311 Island Avenue; 619-544-1886, 800-542-1886, fax 619-239-3823. DELUXE TO ULTRA-DELUXE.

Built in 1910 in honor of the 18th president by his son Ulysses S. Grant, Jr., the **U.S. Grant Hotel** reigned as downtown San Diego's premier hotel for decades. The U.S. Grant is a showcase boasting 280 rooms, a restaurant, and a lounge. It is quite possibly the most elegant and certainly the most beautifully restored historic building in the city. There's a marble-floored lobby with cathedral-height ceilings and enormous crystal chandeliers. Rooms are richly furnished with mahogany poster beds, Queen Anne–style armoires, and wing-back chairs. ~ 326 Broadway; 619-232-3121, 800-237-5029, fax 619-236-3626; www.grantheritage.com. ULTRA-DELUXE.

DINING

A couple of San Diego's better restaurant finds lie "uptown" just east of Route 5. **Fifth and Hawthorn** is a neighborhood sensation, but not many tourists find their way to this chic little dining room. The owners present an array of tasty dishes, specializing in fresh seafood ranging from sea bass with ginger to fresh salmon baked in shredded potato. Usually available is filet mignon with green peppers and cabernet sauce. Lunch served weekdays only; dinner nightly. ~ 515 Hawthorn Street at 5th Avenue; 619-544-0940. MODERATE TO DELUXE.

As its name suggests, **Liaison** is an intimate bistro with beautiful French doors, a wood-burning fireplace, and a patio with a waterfall. Add candlelight and superb French cuisine, and you're talking about the perfect place for a rendezvous. The five- or six-course, prix-fixe dinner varies and may include lamb curry served with rice, medallions of filet mignon with béarnaise sauce, and salmon served in a crayfish butter sauce. Or select dishes à la carte. For a romantic dinner, this place comes highly praised. Reservations are recommended. Dinner only. Closed Monday. ~ 2202 4th Avenue; 619-234-5540. DELUXE TO ULTRA-DELUXE.

History, atmosphere, and great cooking combine to make dining at **Ida Bailey's Restaurant** a memorable experience. Located in the Horton Grand Hotel, Ida's was once a brothel, operated back in the 1890s by a madam of the same name. Things are tamer now, but the rich Victorian furnishings serve as a reminder of San Diego's opulent past. The chef serves a varied menu highlighted by old-fashioned American fare, including Victorian pot roast, rack of lamb, and tenderloin. Breakfast, lunch, and dinner are served. ~ 311 Island Avenue; 619-544-1886. MODERATE TO DELUXE.

Visitors to Horton Plaza are bombarded with dining opportunities. But for those who can resist the temptation to chow down on pizza, french fries, and enchiladas at nearby fast-food shops, there is a special culinary reward. On the plaza's top level sits **Panda Inn**. Here the plush, contemporary design alludes only subtly to Asia with a scattering of classic artwork. But the menu is all-Chinese. Three dishes in particular stand out: the orange-flavored beef with asparagus, tangy lemon scallops, and chicken with garlic sauce. Lunch and dinner menus together present more than 100 dishes. Dine on the glassed-in veranda for a excellent view of the harbor. ~ 506 Horton Plaza; 619-233-7800. MODERATE.

HIDDEN ▶   For Mexican food head to **El Indio** in the Gaslamp Quarter. Dressed in a pink-and-white color scheme, this self-service café has chimichangas, shredded beef burritos, and a host of other south-of-the-border dishes. ~ 409 F Street; 619-239-8151. BUDGET.

Fans of the late Jim Croce ("Bad Leroy Brown," "Time in a Bottle") will surely enjoy a visit to **Croce's Restaurant**. This bar and restaurant in the heart of the Gaslamp Quarter is managed enthusiastically by Jim's widow, Ingrid Croce, and features an eclectic mix of dishes served in a friendly cabaret setting. Daily dinner specials vary and are best described as American home-style ranging from salads to pasta, beef, chicken, and fresh fish dishes. Dinner only. ~ 802 5th Avenue; 619-233-4355. MODERATE TO DELUXE.

Next door **Croce's West** serves up Southwest cuisine Santa Fe–style: painted desert pasta, grilled mahimahi, and chile rellenos. Breakfast, lunch, and dinner are served, as well as Sunday brunch. ~ 619-233-3660. MODERATE TO DELUXE.

You'd be remiss to visit San Diego without enjoying a fresh seafood feast at a spot overlooking the harbor. Why not go first class at **Anthony's Star of the Sea**? This place wears more awards than a Navy admiral. Dramatically set over the water and elegantly decorated, Anthony's presents a remarkable seasonal-seafood menu. Reservations are recommended. Dinner only. ~ 1360 North Harbor Drive; 619-232-7408. DELUXE TO ULTRA-DELUXE.

If your can't afford the "Star," check out the other Anthony's next door—the **Fish Grotto**. ~ 619-232-5103. MODERATE.

HIDDEN ▶   For decades, San Diegans have enjoyed the authentic Mexican dishes at **Chuey's**. Nestled in the shadow of Coronado Bridge, it draws crowds with great tacos made the authentic way, crammed with juicy string beef and heaped with grated Mexican cheese. You can also get American fare such as chicken-fried steak and liver and onions. ~ 1894 Main Street; 619-234-6937. BUDGET.

SHOPPING   No other shopping center in the county is quite like **Horton Plaza**. More than 140 specialty stores are situated here. Anchored by three department stores, a flood of specialty and one-of-a-kind shops complete the picture. Along the tiled boulevard are shops and vendors offering whimsical items—everything from saltwater taffy to psychic readings. ~ Between Broadway and G Street, 1st and 4th avenues; 619-239-8180.

Clever designs distinguish many of the shops, such as **Adventure 16** on the fourth floor, where a split-log cabin facade invites you in to shop for outdoor and adventure travel apparel, books, and accessories. ~ 619-234-1751. There are men's apparel shops, shoe stores, jewelry shops, and women's haute couture boutiques, dozens of stores in all.

The **Gaslamp Quarter**, along 5th Avenue, is a charming 16-square-block assemblage of shops, galleries, and sidewalk cafés in the downtown center. Faithfully replicated in the quarter are Victorian-era street lamps, red-brick sidewalks, and window displays thematic of turn-of-the-century San Diego. Stroll down the **G Street Arts Corridor** to the **International Gallery**, where you'll find a dazzling collection of American contemporary crafts combined with primitive and folk art. Wander this wood-and-brick warehouse and let your eyes feast on the brilliant array of Kilim rugs from North Africa, the Middle East, and Central Asia. ~ 643 G Street; 619-235-8255.

A favorite spot for antique lovers is **The Olde Cracker Factory**, which offers a more than 20-store selection in the nicely restored 1913 Bishop Cracker Factory. Legend has it that a resident ghost by the name of "Crunch" shuffles through mounds of broken crackers here searching for a small brass cookie cutter. ~ 448 West Market Street; 619-233-1669.

A perfect place to stock up on supplies for a picnic is at the **Farmers Bazaar**, a down-to-earth produce market. ~ 245 7th Avenue; 619-239-7615.

Seaport Village was designed to capture the look and feel of an Early California waterfront setting. Its 65 shops dot a 14-acre village and include the usual mix of boutiques, galleries, clothing stores, and gift shops. ~ Foot of Pacific Highway and Harbor Drive; 619-235-4013.

From Thursday through Sunday, **Kobey's Swap Meet** converts the parking lot of the San Diego Sports Arena into a giant flea market where over 1000 sellers hawk new and used wares. ~ Sports Arena Boulevard; 619-226-0650.

The sun is certainly the main attraction in San Diego, but the city also features a rich and varied nightlife, offering the night owl everything from traditional folk music to high-energy discos. There are piano bars, singles bars, and a growing number of jazz clubs. **NIGHTLIFE**

Call the **San Diego Performing Arts League** for its monthly arts calendar and information about inexpensive events. Or check out the website at www.sandiego-online.com/sdpal. ~ 619-238-

0700. KIFM Radio (98.1 FM) hosts **Jazz Hotline**, a 24-hour information line, that provides the latest in jazz happenings. ~ 619-454-4981.

THE BEST BARS An elegant Old World setting of marble, brass, and leather makes **Grant Grill Lounge** *the* place for the elite to meet. Live jazz keeps the wingtips tapping on the weekend. ~ U. S. Grant Hotel, 326 Broadway; 619-232-3121.

For a good-time bar try **Kenny's Steak Pub**. This beautifully appointed mahogany-and-glass bar is accented by shamrock green carpets. Kenny's draws the after-work crowd and is enlivened on weekend nights with live music. ~ 939 4th Avenue; 619-231-8500.

Fans of the immortal Jim Croce will love **The Jazz Bar** at Croce's, built as a memorial to the late singer-songwriter by his wife, Ingrid. Family mementos line the walls in tribute to a talented recording artist. ~ 802 5th Avenue; 619-233-4355. Just next door, **Croce's Top Hat Bar and Grill** is a snazzy New Orleans–style club featuring live rhythm-and-blues. Cover. ~ 818 5th Avenue; 619-233-6945.

Karl Strass Brewery and Grill Downtown may well have the best beer in town—San Diego's original microbrew. ~ 1157 Columbia Street; 619-234-2739.

It's easy to spot the shocking pink, neon-lit facade of **Fat City**. Art deco styling marks the exterior, but the bar features an authentic Victorian decor. It's not a meat market, but Fat City is a favorite among friendly young singles. ~ 2137 Pacific Highway; 619-232-0686.

If you're a culture vulture with a limited pocketbook, try ArtTix, a 24-hour recording listing half-priced theater, music, and dance tickets. ~ 619-497-5000.

Plaza Bar, at the distinctive Westgate Hotel, is a graceful period French lounge where prominent locals and visitors enjoy classy piano entertainment nightly. ~ 1055 2nd Avenue; 619-238-1818.

Mr. A's is the critics' choice for "best drinking with a view." The atmosphere at this elegant restaurant and piano bar is one of monied luxury, and gentlemen are expected to wear jackets. ~ 2550 5th Avenue, 12th floor; 619-239-1377.

There's a wonderful view of San Diego Bay from the Seaport Village restaurant, **Edgewater Grill**, where an ocean setting creates a relaxed atmosphere. ~ 861 West Harbor Drive; 619-232-7581.

THEATER In addition to performances of the San Diego Opera, the **San Diego Civic Theater** presents a variety of entertainment ranging from pop artists to plays to dance performances. ~ 202 C Street; 619-236-6510.

The **San Diego Repertory Theatre** performs dramas, comedies, and musicals. ~ 79 Horton Plaza; 619-235-8025.

OPERA, SYMPHONY, AND DANCE With performances at the San Diego Civic Theater, the **San Diego Opera** presents such international stars as Richard Leech, Jane Eaglen, and Deborah Riedel. The season runs from January through May, with some additional recitals in spring and fall. ~ 202 C Street; 619-232-7636.

California Ballet Company and School presents a diverse repertoire of contemporary and traditional ballets at area theaters. ~ 8276 Ronson Road; 619-560-5676.

EMBARCADERO MARINA PARKS The center city's only real waterfront park is a breezy promenade situated on the bay and divided into two sections. The northern part has a nicely landscaped lawn and garden, picnic tables, and benches. The southern half features a fishing pier, basketball courts, and an athletic course. Restrooms are available. ~ Enter at the southern end at Harbor Drive and 8th Street; at the northern end, from Seaport Village Shopping Center; 619-686-6200.

BEACHES & PARKS

SPANISH LANDING PARK This is a slender sandy beach with walkways and a grassy picnic area that's situated close to San Diego International Airport. The park overlooks Harbor Island Marina and offers lovely views of the bay and city. Restrooms are available. ~ Located just west of the airport on North Harbor Drive; 619-686-6200.

Ironically, it's thanks to the strong 50-year presence of the U.S. Navy that San Diego has such a significant gay scene. After World War

San Diego Gay Scene

II, thousands of newly discharged men and women who had discovered their sexual identities during their military service opted to remain in places like San Diego and San Francisco instead of returning home. The long-time military presence contributed to the fairly conservative personality of San Diego's gay community, but a more liberalizing effect began to take place in the 1960s with the arrival of the University of California in La Jolla. Today, San Diego's gay and lesbian community is more out than it's ever been, and the center of attention is the section of town just to the north of Balboa Park called Hillcrest.

The '50s architecture and neon also give the area a campy feel (a neon sign, which works intermittently, hangs across University Avenue and signals entrance into Hillcrest). Bookstores, trendy boutiques, and coffeeshops line University Avenue, 5th Avenue, and Robinson Street—all within easy walking distance of one another. And because Hillcrest boasts some of the best movie houses and restaurants in San Diego, you'll see everyone there: gay yuppies, leather-clad lesbians, and Ozzie and Harriet lookalikes.

LODGING   Since over 30 percent of its guests hail from outside the U.S., the **Hillcrest Inn Hotel** considers itself an international hotel. Right in the hub of Hillcrest activity, the 45 modestly furnished rooms, outfitted with microwaves and refrigerators, provide its gay guests with a comfortable stay. Fatigued wayfarers will appreciate the sun patio and spa after long days (and nights) of sightseeing. ~ 3754 5th Avenue; 619-293-7078, 800-258-2280, fax 619-298-3861; e-mail hillcrestinn@juno.com. BUDGET.

The **Balboa Park Inn** is a very popular caravansary with gays. Like Balboa Park nearby, the four-building inn was built in 1915 for the Panama–California Exposition. Its 26 rooms are decorated in different themes; you can choose to luxuriate in *Gone With the Wind's* "Tara," get sentimental in 1930s Paris, or go wild in Greystoke. Some suites boast jacuzzis, kitchens, and fireplaces, and *everyone* can request a continental breakfast served in bed. A courtyard and sun terrace round out the facilities of this winsome getaway. Reservations recommended. ~ 3402 Park Boulevard; 619-298-0823, 800-938-8181, fax 619-294-8070; www.balboa parkinn.com. MODERATE TO ULTRA-DELUXE.

Not located in Hillcrest but catering to an exclusively gay clientele, **Dmitri's Guesthouse** offers five rooms close to Horton Plaza. Each suite comes with a ceiling fan and a refrigerator (one includes a full kitchen). Feel free to shed your clothing on the sundeck and immerse yourself in the hot tub or swimming pool. Ensconced in a century-old house, Dmitri's serves a continental breakfast by the poolside every morning. Reservations recommended. ~ 931 21st Street; 619-238-5547. BUDGET TO MODERATE.

DINING   If you're looking for a really hot time in Hillcrest, there is nothing better than a plate of *poo ja* followed by a spicy serving of *gang ped*. Enjoy these and other wonderful Thai favorites at **Celedon**. Mild or spicy, Celedon's curried and stir-fried specialties are delicious. The stylish art nouveau surroundings, which are nicely appointed with original Thai brassworks and tapestries, add to the graceful flair of this eatery. No lunch on Saturday. Closed Sunday. ~ 3628 5th Avenue; 619-295-8800. BUDGET TO MODERATE.

Judging by the name itself, you'd think **Hamburger Mary's** was a typical burger joint. It peddles burgers, yes, but with washboards, surfboards, and murals decorating the walls, it definitely ain't typical. Besides hamburgers, you'll find steak and halibut dinners, vegetarian plates, and salads, which can be eaten outdoors on the patio. Afterward, you'll want to join the festivities at Kickers, the gay country-western bar in the same building. Sunday brunch is also served. ~ 308 University Avenue; 619-491-0400. BUDGET.

Bread lovers will think they have landed in paradise when they enter **Bread & Cie**. The aroma of fig, jalapeño, cheese, and rosemary breads lingers in this amazing bakery, which also serves lunch and cappuccinos. Open 7 a.m. to 7 p.m. ~ 350 University Avenue; 619-683-9322. BUDGET.   ◄ *HIDDEN*

Attracting attention has never been a problem for the **Corvette Diner**. Although it's usually crammed full of families and high school kids, the decor is not to be missed. Cool 1950s music, a soda fountain (complete with resident jerks), rock-and-roll memorabilia, dancing waitresses, and a classy Corvette have proven a magnetic formula for this Hillcrest haven. The place is jammed for lunch and dinner. The simple "blue-plate" diner fare includes meatloaf, chicken-fried steak, and generous-sized burgers affectionately named for familiar 1950s notables like Annette, Eddie, and Kookie. ~ 3946 5th Avenue; 619-542-1001. BUDGET.

Located in the middle of the Rainbow Block, **California Cuisine** offers sumptuous dishes for your discriminating palate. Beef tenderloin and New Zealand lamb loin are among the many items on their ever-changing menu, as are pasta, salads, and vegetarian fare. You also get a taste of promising local artists whose original work adorns the walls. No lunch Saturday or Sunday. Closed Monday. ~ 1027 University Avenue; 619-543-0790. DELUXE.

Obelisk carries gay, lesbian, and bisexual reading material, as well as gift items to tickle your fancy—jewelry, shirts, and cards—to name a few. ~ 1029 University Avenue; 619-297-4171.   **SHOPPING**

Searching high and low for that Betty Page calendar? How about some sweater-girl paper dolls? **Babbette Schwartz**, the local drag queen, has a store that carries an array of novelty items, including lava lamps and Barbie dolls. ~ 421 University Avenue; 619-220-7048.

Enter the **Blue Door Bookstore** and browse through the extensive collection of gay and lesbian fiction, poetry, and philosophy. It stocks contemporary, classical, and modern literature, too. ~ 3823 5th Avenue; 619-298-8610.

California Man is a modern-day haberdashery, catering to the needs of an active '90s man. You'll find some casual wear for shopping in, beach wear to sunbathe and swim in, and dressy wear for more formal affairs. ~ 3930 5th Avenue; 619-294-9108.

Unlike other antique stores in the area, **Circa a.d.** offers anything but the usual American antiques. It proudly displays a vast assortment of Asian, Spanish, African, and European artwork, textiles, and pottery, specializing in goods from around the Pacific Rim. It even carries bonsai trees. ~ 3867 4th Avenue; 619-293-3328.

NIGHTLIFE The **Brass Rail**, which opened in 1958, is San Diego's oldest gay bar. The bartenders' famed congeniality keeps the primarily male clientele coming back year after year for more—more drinks and more dancing (which is in full swing Wednesday through Saturday). Thursday is Latino night. ~ 3796 5th Avenue; 619-298-2233.

A few doors down from the Brass Rail and next to the Hillcrest Inn Hotel is **David's Place**. Designed to look like a living room with a couch and antique furniture, this popular coffeehouse is a home away from home for travelers and locals alike; pets are also welcome. Aside from knocking back espresso and admiring the passing scenery, you might engage your neighbor with a board game. David's Place is a nonprofit establishment that donates its proceeds to local AIDS organizations. ~ 3766 5th Avenue; 619-294-8908.

Also in this same stretch of 5th Avenue, **The Loft** is a gay bar offering jukebox music and pool playing. ~ 3610 5th Avenue; 619-296-6407.

The short trek up to University Avenue brings you to Hamburger Mary's restaurant, home of **Kickers**. This lively country-and-western bar keeps gay, lesbian, and straight folks kickin' with free line dancing and two-step lessons Monday through Friday. On Saturday and Sunday patrons are left to fend for themselves on the dancefloor. Earlier on Sunday, disco is the soundtrack for the tea dance. Cover for tea dance. ~ 308 University Avenue; 619-491-0400.

The real action on University Avenue is over at the Rainbow Block. First there's **Flicks**, a video bar that flashes visual stimuli on its four big screens while playing dance and progressive music. Depending on the evening, comedians or male dancers might be performing, or you could pop in for a Monday night round of the dating game. Pool, pinball, and darts are also on the menu for the young gay men who frequent this joint. ~ 1017 University Avenue; 619-297-2056.

At the far end of the block, **Rich's** heats up Thursday through Sunday with high energy dancing until 2 a.m. The DJ-mixed music sets the beat: groove, techno, deep house, and tribal rhythms. The music isn't the only thing to stimulate your senses; your eyes will no doubt be dazzled by the specially created visual effects. Each night has a different theme. Thursday is Club Hedonism (enough said). On Friday nights Rich's go-go boys "work it." On Saturday the go-go boys give way to enthusiastically received erotic dancers. To finish off the weekend, there is The Tea on Sunday with the doors opening at 7 p.m., two hours earlier than on other nights. Cover. ~ 1051 University Avenue; 619-295-2195.

Perfectly situated between the hotspots Rich's and Flicks, **Euphoria** is *the* place to take a breather from dancing and barhopping. Their espresso drinks and sugar-enriched pastries are a sure way to re-energize. Euphoria, which displays local artistic talent on its walls, maintains a cozy, mellow atmosphere from early morning until late in the evening. ~ 1045 University Avenue; 619-295-1769.

Beyond the Rainbow Block you can take a pleasant stroll along the north side of Balboa Park to **The Flame**. Touted as "San Diego's hottest women's nightclub," this postmodern apocalypse features a dancefloor, pool tables, and a smoking bar. Although men are always welcome here, Tuesday is officially "Boys' Night." Dancing runs seven nights a week with deejays spinning everything from salsa rhythms to disco delights. No cover Thursday. ~ 3780 Park Boulevard; 619-295-4163.

While the vast majority of the gay bars are located in the Hillcrest neighborhood, there is a place near the beach. **Matador**, only one block from Mission Beach, features taped music, a pool table, and video games. ~ 4633 Mission Boulevard; 619-483-6943.

There's an older, yuppie, mostly-woman crowd that enjoys an endless line-up of activities at **Club Bombay**. The Bombay—which is friendly to all patrons—has Internet access and "national trivia" machines. Along with weekday happy hour and Sunday barbecue, customers enjoy Monday pool tournaments, Tuesday dart contests, and Wednesday karaoke. On Friday, the deejay takes a spin at roiling up the dancefloor. Saturday there are usually live acts. Cover on weekends. ~ 3175 India Street; 619-296-6789.

Other gay bars around town include **Bourbon Street**, a comfortable piano bar that features an outdoor patio, with entertainment every night and a primarily male clientele. ~ 4612 Park Boulevard; 619-291-0173. The action at the **Chee Chee Club**, a local cruise bar, revolves around shooting pool and playing pinball. Occasionally performers present shows for the mostly male crowd. ~ 929 Broadway; 619-234-4404. **Shooter's**, a popular sports bar, boasts two large-screen TVs, six pool tables, pinball, and video games. The **Odyssey Club**, located inside, is a dance club frequented by men. ~ 3815 30th Street; 619-574-0744.

▼▼▼▼▼▼▼▼▼▼▼▼

Balboa Park & the San Diego Zoo

History is unclear as to whether it was intelligent foresight or unbridled optimism that led to the creation of Balboa Park. Certain that a fine neighborhood would flourish around it, city fathers in 1868 set aside 1400 acres of rattlesnake-infested hillside above "New Town" as a public park. The park's later development, and most of its lovely Spanish Baroque buildings, came as the result of two world's fairs—The Panama–California Exposition of 1915–16 and the California–Pacific International Exposition of 1935–36.

Today Balboa Park ranks among the largest and finest of America's city parks. Wide avenues and walkways curve through luxurious subtropical foliage leading to nine major museums, three art galleries, four theaters, picnic groves, the world's largest zoo, a golf course, and countless other recreation facilities. Its verdant grounds teem with cyclists, joggers, skaters, picnickers, weekend artists, and museum mavens.

SIGHTS

The main entrance is from 6th Avenue onto Laurel Street, which becomes El Prado as you cross Cabrillo Bridge. Begin your visit at the **Balboa Park Visitors Center**, located on the northeast corner of Plaza de Panama. They provide plenty of free pamphlets and maps on the park. Balboa Park's museums charge an admission fee but every Tuesday select museums can be visited free. ~ House of Hospitality, 1549 El Prado; 619-239-0512.

From here you can stroll about, taking in Balboa Park's main attractions. To the right, as you head east on the pedestrian-only section of El Prado, is the **Casa de Balboa**. This building houses several worthwhile exhibits, including the **San Diego Model Railroad Museum** (619-696-0199), which features the largest collection of mini-gauge trains in the world. Closed Monday. Here, too, is the San Diego Historical Society's extensive collection of documents and photographs spanning the urban history of San Diego. Closed Monday and Tuesday. Just upstairs, the **Museum of Photographic Arts** (619-238-7559) has exhibits of internationally known photographers. The museum will be closed until spring of 2000 for renovations. Exhibits from its collections can be seen at the Museum of Contemporary Art downtown (619-234-1001). Sports fans will want to take in the **Hall of Champions Sports Museum** (619-234-2544). It houses a Hall of Fame and exhibits featuring world-class San Diego athletes from more than 40 sports. Admission. ~ 1649 El Prado.

Continuing east to the fountain, you'll see the **Reuben H. Fleet Science Center** on your right. Among the park's finest attractions, it features one of the largest planetariums and most impressive multimedia theaters in the country. The galleries offer various hands-on exhibits and displays dealing with modern phenomena. Admission. ~ 619-238-1233.

Across the courtyard is the **Natural History Museum** with displays devoted mostly to the environment of Southern California. There are also fossils (whales, dinosaurs, land mammals) galore. Admission. ~ 619-232-3821.

Going back along El Prado, take a moment to admire your reflection in the Lily Pond. With the old, latticed **Botanical Building** in the background, the scene is a favorite among photographers. The fern collection inside is equally striking.

Next is the **Timken Museum of Art**, considered to have one of the West Coast's finest collections of European and Early American paintings. The displays include works by Rembrandt and

Copley, as well as an amazing collection of Russian icons. Closed Monday. ~ 619-239-5548.

Right next door on the plaza is the **San Diego Museum of Art**, with an entrance facade patterned after the University of Salamanca in Spain. The museum treasures a permanent collection of Italian Renaissance, Dutch, and Spanish Baroque paintings and sculpture, a display of Asian art, a gallery of Impressionist paintings, contemporary California art, and a contemporary American collection. Closed Monday. Admission. ~ 619-232-7931.

Across El Prado from the Museum of Art is the **Mingei International Museum of Folk Art**. The Mingei (pronounced *min-gay*), with its superb collection of world folk art, finally outgrew its storefront location in a shopping center and moved into the House of Charm in 1996. Closed Monday. Admission. ~ 1489 El Prado; 619-239-0003.

◄ HIDDEN

The grandest of all Balboa Park structures, built as the centerpiece for the 1915 Panama–California Exposition, is the 200-foot Spanish Renaissance **California Tower**. The **Museum of Man**, at the base of the tower, is a must for anthropology buffs and those with an interest in Egyptian mummies and American Indian cultures. Admission. ~ 619-239-2001.

Another museum not to be missed is the **San Diego Aerospace Museum**, several blocks south of the plaza. It contains over 65 aircraft including a replica of Charles Lindbergh's famous *Spirit of St. Louis*, the original of which was built in San Diego. Admission. ~ 619-234-8291.

En route you'll pass the **Spreckels Organ Pavilion**. Those 4416 pipes make it the world's largest outdoor instrument of its kind.

On display at the Aerospace Museum is Black Bird, the world's fastest plane.

You'll want to attend a play at the **Old Globe Theatre** to absorb the full greatness of this Tony Award-winning stage, but for starters you can stroll around the 581-seat theater, famed for its Shakespearean presentations. Located in a grove on the north side of California Tower, the Old Globe is part of the trio of theaters that includes the **Cassius Carter Centre Stage** and the outdoor **Lowell Davies Festival Theatre**. Admission. ~ 619-239-2255.

North of the Balboa Park museum and theater complex is the **San Diego Zoo**, which needs no introduction. It quite simply is the world's top-rated zoo. The numbers alone are mind-boggling: 3900 animals, representing 800 species, spread out over 100 acres. Most of these wild animals live in surroundings as natural as man can make them. Rather than cages there are many moated enclosures where lions roam free on grassy islands and multihued birds fly through tropical rainforests. All around is a manmade jungle forest overgrown with countless species of rare and exotic plants.

Of particular merit is "Polar Bear Plunge." Here you can watch the polar bears as they gracefully swim underwater in their deep saltwater bay. At "Hippo Beach," Funani and Jabba delight all with their infamous underwater hippo ballet. The zoo's state-of-the-art primate exhibit, the "Gorilla Tropics," is a two-and-a-half acre African rainforest that is home to seven lowland gorillas and hundreds of jungle birds. Within this area is "Pygmy Chimps at Bonobo Road," home to frolicsome troupes of pygmy chimps and Angolan colobus monkeys. At the nearby "Sun Bear Forest," an equatorial rainforest, you'll encounter sun bears and lion-tailed macaques. The only pandas in the western hemisphere can be seen at the "Panda Research Station." For a bird's-eye view of the entire zoo, you can take the "Skyfari" aerial tramway. At the **Children's Zoo,** where there are just as many adults as kids, you can watch baby chicks peck out of their shells in the hatchery. Don't miss the pygmy marmosets. They are the world's smallest monkeys, weighing in at only four ounces when full grown. Admission. ~ Located off Park Boulevard; 619-234-3153.

LODGING

The best value for your dollar among reasonably priced hotels in the area is the 67-room **Comfort Inn**. They feature wood furniture, designer color schemes, and high-grade carpeting. The inn has a pool-sized jacuzzi and serves a continental breakfast. Conveniently located next to Balboa Park just a few blocks from the city center. ~ 719 Ash Street; 619-232-2525, 800-228-5150, fax 619-687-3024. MODERATE.

My vote for the prettiest and most hospitable of San Diego's bed and breakfasts goes to the **Keating House Bed and Breakfast**. This historically designated 1888 Victorian home in a sunny hillside residential area between Balboa Park and downtown offers eight comfy rooms—six in the main house and two in the cottage out back. The cottage rooms feature private baths. With its gabled roof, octagonal window turret, and conical peak, this beautifully restored Queen Anne is every bit as nice inside. A garden completes the homey scene. ~ 2331 2nd Avenue; 619-239-8585, 800-995-8644, fax 619-239-5774; www.caliburnus.com/keating. MODERATE.

Situated on Florida Canyon on the edge of Balboa Park, **Katy's Herbs & Things** is a true bed and breakfast. There is a one-bedroom suite with kitchenette and private patio overlooking the herb garden. The other room has a queen-sized bed and private bath overlooking the front court fountain. Every morning, the owner will treat you to a lovely full breakfast. The proprietress is also an enthusiastic storyteller. This place comes highly praised. ~ 2818 Juniper Street; 619-544-0375, 800-544-0568, fax 619-696-6877; e-mail katysherbs@aol.com. MODERATE.

When you're visiting the San Diego Zoo, consider **Albert's Restaurant**. Named for the gorilla who once occupied the area, this sit-down eatery offers a variety of salads, sandwiches, fresh pastas, and fish and meat entrées. Dinner only in summer. ~ 2920 Zoo Drive, the San Diego Zoo; 619-685-3200. MODERATE.

DINING

The **Simon Edison Theatre Centre for the Performing Arts** presents classic and contemporary plays in three Balboa Park theatres. ~ Balboa Park; 619-239-2255.

NIGHTLIFE

An isolated and exclusive community in San Diego Bay, Coronado is almost an island, connected to the mainland only by the graceful San Diego–Coronado Bay Bridge and by a long, narrow sandspit called the Silver Strand. Long a playground of the rich and famous, the city's hotels reflect this ritzy heritage.

▼▼▼▼▼▼▼▼▼▼
Coronado

Once known as the "Nickel Snatcher," the Coronado Ferry for years crossed the waters of San Diego Harbor between the Embarcadero and Coronado. All for five cents each way. That's history, of course, but the 1940-vintage, double-deck *Silvergate* still plies the waters. The **San Diego Bay Ferry** leaves from the Bay Café on North Harbor Drive at the foot of Broadway on the hour and docks 15 minutes later at the Ferry Marketplace Landing on the Coronado side. ~ 619-234-4111.

SIGHTS

The town's main attraction is the **Hotel del Coronado**, a red-roofed, Victorian-style, wooden wonder, a century-old National Historic Landmark. Explore the old palace and its manicured grounds, discovering the intricate corridors and cavernous public rooms. It was Elisha Babcock's dream, when he purchased 4100 acres of barren, wind-blown peninsula in 1888, to build a hotel that would be the "talk of the Western world." Realizing Babcock's dream from the beginning, it attracted such famous guests as Thomas Edison, Robert Todd Lincoln, and Henry Ford. ~ 1500 Orange Avenue; 619-435-6611.

Although shadowed by its noted neighbor, the **Glorietta Bay Inn** is a worthy landmark in its own right. It was built in 1908 as the private mansion of sugar scion John D. Spreckels. From here you can cruise the quiet neighborhood streets that radiate off Orange Avenue between the bay and the ocean, enjoying the town's handsome blend of cottages and historic homes. ~ 1630 Glorietta Boulevard; 619-435-3101.

El Cordova Hotel is in the heart of Coronado. Originally built as a private mansion in 1902, El Cordova's moderate size (40 rooms) and lovely Spanish-hacienda architecture make it a relaxing get-

LODGING

away spot. A pool and patio restaurant are added niceties. ~ 1351 Orange Avenue; 619-435-4131, 800-229-2032, fax 619-435-0632. MODERATE TO ULTRA-DELUXE.

Nothing can detract from the glamour of the **Hotel del Coronado**. With its turrets, cupolas, and gingerbread facade, it is one of the great hotels of California. The last in a proud line of extravagant seaside resorts, the Hotel del Coronado has long been the relaxing place of United States presidents and Hollywood stars. Remember, however, this celebrated Victorian landmark is a major tourist attraction, so in addition to the guests, who usually fill its 692 rooms to capacity, thousands of visitors crowd the lobby, grounds, and shops every day. Be aware, too, that many rooms are in two structures adjacent to the original building and though more comfortable are not the real thing. "Hotel Del" has two pools, a long stretch of beach, nine eating areas, five tennis courts, a first-class health club, and a gallery of shops. Reservations recommended. ~ 1500 Orange Avenue; 619-522-8000, 800-468-3533, fax 619-522-8262; www.hoteldel.com. ULTRA-DELUXE.

> At least a dozen United States presidents have bedded down at the "Hotel Del."

Across the street rises the **Glorietta Bay Inn**, the 1908 Edwardian mansion of sugar king John D. Spreckels which has been transformed into an elegant 100-room hotel. Suites here reflect the grandeur of Spreckels' time, but ordinary rooms are, in fact, rather ordinary. Continental breakfast, ladies and gentlemen, is served on the mansion terrace. ~ 1630 Glorietta Boulevard; 619-435-3101, 800-283-9383, fax 619-435-6182; www.gloriettabayinn.com. DELUXE TO ULTRA-DELUXE.

The **Coronado Victorian House** is quite possibly the only hotel anywhere to offer dance, exercise, and gourmet cooking classes with a night's stay. Located in a century-old historic-designated building near the beach and downtown Coronado, the decor of this seven-room bed and breakfast includes Persian rugs, stained-glass windows, private baths with claw-foot tubs, and jacuzzis; rooms are named after artists and dancers. Those guests not interested in the extracurricular activities are invited to relax and enjoy such healthy and home-cooked specialties as baklava, stuffed grape leaves and homemade yogurt. Two-night minimum. ~ 1000 8th Street; 619-435-2200, 888-299-2822, fax 619-435-4760. ULTRA-DELUXE.

DINING

Visitors crossing over to Coronado invariably tour the famous Hotel del Coronado, and many are lured into the **Crown-Coronet Room**. Its grand Victorian architecture and enormous domed ceiling set a tone of elegance and style unmatched anywhere on the Pacific Coast. The place is so magnificent the food seems unimportant. Most critics, in fact, assert that dinner in the hotel's deluxe- to ultra-deluxe-priced **Prince of Wales Room** is better, but the moderate- to deluxe-priced breakfast, lunch, dinner, or Sunday brunch at the Crown Room will never disappoint. Reservations recommended for the Prince of Wales Room. ~ 1500 Orange Avenue; 619-435-6611. DELUXE TO ULTRA-DELUXE.

Locals looking to avoid the crowds at "Hotel Del" usually head for **Chez Loma**. Set in a charming 1889 Victorian house, it serves a lovely Continental/French dinner—excellent *canard roti façon Chez Loma* (traditional roast duckling with Montorency cherry port wine sauce and lingonberries)—plus Sunday brunch. Dine inside or out. ~ 1132 Loma Avenue; 619-435-0661. DELUXE TO ULTRA-DELUXE.

Peohe's, located at the Ferry Landing Marketplace, is primarily praised for its panoramic views of San Diego Bay and for its tropical decor. The aqua-accented dining room features green palms and rushing cascades of water flowing into ponds of live fish. The dinner menu is mostly fresh fish plus lobster, shrimp, and a daily featured "catch." There are also prime rib, chicken, and lamb. I prefer the lunch, with a tasty soup/salad/sandwich combo at an affordable price. Sunday brunch is an option. ~ 1201 1st Street; 619-437-4474. MODERATE TO DELUXE.

SHOPPING

Coronado's fancy Orange Avenue in the village center harbors an assortment of unusual shops in the **El Cordova Hotel**. ~ 1351 Orange Avenue; 619-435-4131.

The **Ferry Landing Marketplace** is a modern shopping area complete with boutiques, specialty shops, galleries, and eateries. ~ 1201 1st Street; 619-435-8895.

The **Hotel del Coronado** is a city within a city and home to many intriguing specialty shops, such as **Victorian Corner**, which has an interesting selection of pins, hats, and other Victorian accessories. ~ 1500 Orange Avenue; 619-435-9131.

NIGHTLIFE

If you're out Coronado way, stop for a cocktail in the famed Hotel del Coronado's **Ocean Terrace Lounge**. Live music after nine every night. The Del's **Palm Court** offers live piano music in a palm-studded lounge. Every Sunday evening from 5 to 9:30 is a dinner-dance in the Crown-Coronet Room. ~ 1550 Orange Avenue; 619-435-6611.

Check out the boisterous Irish scene at **McP's**, a full swinging bar and grill with shamrock-plastered walls and a bartender with the gift of gab. McP's is a Navy SEAL hang-out, so as one glib bartender noted, it's the most likely place in town to pet a seal. Entertainment includes live rock and jazz bands on a nightly basis. ~ 1107 Orange Avenue; 619-435-5280.

The historic Spreckels Building in Coronado is a vintage-1917 opera house that has been restored to a 347-seat venue, the **Lamb's Players Theatre**. ~ 1142 Orange Avenue; 619-437-0600.

BEACHES & PARKS

CORONADO SHORES BEACH 🏊 ⛱ 🚻 It's the widest beach in the county but hardly atmospheric, backed up as it is by a row of towering condominiums. Still, crowds flock to this roomy expanse of clean, soft sand where gentle waves make for good swimming and surfing. The younger crowd gathers at the north end, just south of the Hotel del Coronado. There are lifeguards. ~ Located off Ocean Boulevard in Coronado.

CORONADO CITY BEACH 🏊 ⛱ 🚻 That same wide sandy beach prevails to the north. Here the city has a large, grassy picnic area known as **Sunset Park** where frisbees and the aroma of fried chicken fill the air. There are firepits, restrooms, and lifeguards. The beach offers good fishing and swimming. Surfing is restricted to the north end during the busy summer months; it's generally safe, but be wary of unpredictable breaks. ~ On Ocean Boulevard north of Avenue G in Coronado.

▼▼▼▼▼▼▼▼▼▼▼▼▼
Point Loma Area

The Point Loma peninsula forms a high promontory that shelters San Diego Bay from the Pacific. It also provided Juan Rodríguez Cabrillo an excellent place from which to contemplate his 16th-century discovery of California. For those of us today interested in contemplating life —or just zoning out on a view—Point Loma peninsula presents the perfect opportunity.

SIGHTS

Naturally, **Cabrillo National Monument**, featuring a statue of the navigator, stands facing his landing site at Ballast Point. The sculpture itself, a gift from Cabrillo's native Portugal, isn't very impressive but the view is outstanding. With the bay and city spread below, you can often see all the way from Mexico to the La Jolla mesa. The visitors center includes a small museum. The nearby **Old Point Loma Lighthouse** guided shipping from 1855 to 1891. Admission. ~ 1800 Cabrillo Memorial Drive, Point Loma; 619-557-5450.

On the ocean side of the peninsula is **Whale Watch Lookout Point** where, during winter months, you can observe the southward migration of California gray whales. Close by is a superb network of tidepools.

To reach Point Loma from San Diego, go southwest on Rosecrans Street and follow the signs. You'll enter the monument through the U.S. Navy's Fort Rosecrans, home to a variety of sophisticated military facilities and the haunting **Fort Rosecrans National Cemetery**. Here, thousands of trim, white markers march down a grassy hillside in mute testimony to San Diego's fallen troops and deep military roots.

When you leave the monument, follow Catalina Boulevard to Hill Street and go left. At water's edge turn right onto Sunset Cliffs Boulevard and enjoy one of San Diego County's most dramatic coastlines. Continue north a bit to **Ocean Beach,** whose reputation as a haven for hippie hold-outs is not entirely undeserved.

Ensconced in a plain vanilla, two-story former church building, the **Hostelling International–Point Loma** is filled with 60 economy-minded guests almost every night during the summer. Comfortable bunk beds are grouped in 13 rooms housing from two to eight persons in youth-hostel fashion. Family rooms and private rooms are also available, and there is a common kitchen and dining area. The courtyard has Ping-Pong and other recreational activities. ~ 3790 Udall Street, Point Loma; 619-223-4778, 800-909-4776, fax 619-223-1883; www.hiayh.org. BUDGET.

LODGING

A rare beachfront find in residential Point Loma is the **Ocean Manor Apartment Hotel.** This trim, white, two-story, 25-room apartment hotel sits right on the seaside cliffs. Rooms are neat and clean but very basic. You can play Ping-Pong or shuffleboard, or lounge by the pool. There are also bachelor and studio apartments (with kitchenettes) available for rent overnight, otherwise there's a three-night minimum. ~ 1370 Sunset Cliffs Boulevard, Point Loma; 619-222-7901. MODERATE.

Manmade Shelter and Harbor Islands jut out into San Diego Bay, providing space for several large resorts. For a relaxing, off-beat alternative to these mammoth hotels try **Humphrey's Half Moon Inn.** Surrounded by subtropical plants, this nautical 182-room complex overlooks the yacht harbor and gives the feeling of staying on an island. The rooms are tastefully decorated with a Polynesian theme. There is a pool, spa, putting green, and restaurant. ~ 2303 Shelter Island Drive, Point Loma; 619-224-3411, 800-345-9995, fax 619-224-3478; www.halfmooninn.com. DELUXE TO ULTRA-DELUXE.

A marine view and whirling ceiling fans at **Humphrey's** suggest Casablanca. California coastal cuisine is the fare, with lots of fresh seafood. Breakfast, lunch, and dinner are served. ~ Adjacent to the Half Moon Inn, 2241 Shelter Island Drive, Point Loma; 619-224-3577. MODERATE TO ULTRA-DELUXE.

DINING

At Fisherman's Village in Point Loma you'll find **The Blue Crab Restaurant.** Appealing Cape Cod decor and terrific bay views set the mood for fresh seafood, including Maryland blue and soft-shell crabs. There's great mesquite-broiled swordfish. Prime rib and steak satisfy the landlubbers. ~ 4922 North Harbor Drive, Point Loma; 619-224-3000. DELUXE TO ULTRA-DELUXE.

San Diego's best soup-and-salad bar and my personal favorite for healthy budget dining is **Souplantation,** featuring two bars loaded with the prettiest produce this side of the farmer's market. Included are over 60 items to heap on your plate. Six tasty soups are made from scratch daily, and a variety of muffins are served hot from the oven. Fresh fruit rounds out this wholesome fare. It's a comfortable wood-paneled environment. ~ 3960 West Point Loma Boulevard, Point Loma; 619-222-7404. BUDGET.

NIGHTLIFE For the mellow crowd interested in enjoying cocktails, yummy appetizers, and conversation while overlooking a picturesque marina, there's **Doc Masters**. ~ 2051 Shelter Island Drive, Point Loma; 619-223-2572.

Even musicians head outdoors during San Diego summers. **Humphrey's** hosts the city's most ambitious series of jazz, comedy and mellow rock shows, which include an impressive lineup of name artists in a beautiful bayside lawn setting. ~ 2241 Shelter Island Drive, Point Loma; 619-224-3577.

Aside from being a popular restaurant and lounge, **Tom Ham's Lighthouse** is a real lighthouse and the official Coast Guard–sanctioned beacon of Harbor Island. This scrimshaw-filled nautical lounge is a piano bar Wednesday through Friday, then a karaoke bar later in the evening, Thursday through Saturday. ~ 2150 Harbor Island Drive, Point Loma; 619-291-9110.

BEACHES & PARKS **HARBOR ISLAND** There are no sandy beaches on this man-made island, but there is a walkway bordered by lawn and benches along its entire length. You'll get fabulous views of the city, and there's great fishing here. Facilities here include restrooms and restaurants. ~ Located south of San Diego International Airport on Harbor Island Drive; 619-686-6200.

SHELTER ISLAND Like Harbor Island, its neighbor to the northeast, Shelter Island functions primarily as a boating center, but there's a beach facing the bay that is popular for swimming, fishing, and picnicking. A landscaped walkway runs the length of the island. There are picnic areas, restrooms, a fishing pier, and restaurants. ~ Located on Shelter Island Drive near Rosecrans Street; 619-686-6200.

SUNSET CLIFFS PARK The jagged cliffs and sandstone bluffs along Point Loma peninsula give this park a spectacular setting. High-cresting waves make it popular with expert surfers, who favor the rocky beach at the foot of Ladera Avenue. Tidepools evidence the rich marine life that attracts many divers. Winding staircases (at Bermuda and Santa Cruz avenues) and steep trails lead down to some nice pocket beaches. ~ Off of Sunset Cliffs Boulevard south of Ocean Beach; 619-531-1527.

OCEAN BEACH Where you toss down your towel at "OB" will probably depend as much on your age as your interests. Surfers, sailors, and what's left of the hippie crowd hang out around the pier; farther north, where the surf is milder and the beach wider, families and retired folks can be found sunbathing and strolling. There are picnic areas, restrooms, and restaurants. Fishing is good from the surf or the fishing pier. Swimming and surfing is very popular here. ~ Take Ocean Beach Freeway (Route 8) west until it ends; turn left onto Sunset Cliffs Boulevard, then right on Voltaire Street; 619-531-1527.

▼▼▼▼▼▼▼▼▼▼

Old Town Area

Back in 1769, Spanish explorer Gaspar de Portolá selected a hilltop site overlooking the bay for a mission that would begin the European settlement of California. A town soon spread out at the foot of the hill, complete with plaza, a church, a school, and the tile-roofed adobe casas of California's first families. Throughout the years, Spanish, Mexican, and American settlements thrived until a devastating 1872 fire destroyed much of the town, prompting developers to relocate the commercial district nearer the bay.

SIGHTS

Some of the buildings and relics of the early era survived and have been brought back to life at **Old Town San Diego State Historic Park**. Lined with adobe restorations and brightened with colorful shops, the six blocks of Old Town provide a lively and interesting opportunity for visitors to stroll, shop, and sightsee. ~ Park headquarters, 4002 Wallace Street; 619-220-5422.

The park sponsors a free walking tour at 10:30 a.m. and 2 p.m. daily, or you can easily do it on your own by picking up a copy of the *Old San Diego Gazette*. The paper, which comes out once a month and includes a map of the area, is free at local stores. You can also hop aboard the **Old Town Trolley** for a delightful two-hour narrated tour of Old Town and a variety of other highlights in San Diego and Coronado. It makes nine stops, and you're allowed to get on and off all day long. Admission. ~ 4040 Twiggs Street, 619-298-8687.

As it has for over a century, everything focuses on **Old Town Plaza**. Before 1872 this was the social and recreational center of the town: political meetings, barbecues, dances, shootouts, and bullfights all happened here. ~ Couts and San Diego avenues.

Casa de Estudillo is the finest of the original adobe buildings. It was a mansion in its time, built in 1827 for the commander of the Mexican Presidio. Admission. ~ Located at the Mason Street corner of the plaza.

Casa de Bandini was built in 1829 as a one-story adobe but gained a second level when it became the Cosmopolitan Hotel in the late 1860s. **Seeley Stables** next door is a replica of the barns and stables of Albert Seeley, who operated the stage line. Nowadays it houses a collection of horse-drawn vehicles and Western memorabilia, and has a slide show. ~ Mason and Calhoun streets.

The San Diego Union building was Old Town's first frame building and the site where the *San Diego Union* was first printed in 1868. It has been restored as a 19th-century printing office. ~ Located at San Diego Avenue and Twiggs Street. Adjacent to the old newspaper office is **Dodson's Corner**, a collection of shops finished with Old West–style falsefronts.

Shoppers seem to gravitate in large numbers toward the north side of the plaza to browse the unusual shops comprising **Bazaar del Mundo**. Built in circular fashion around a tropical courtyard, this complex also houses several restaurants.

The original mission and Spanish Presidio once stood high on a hill behind Old Town. This site of California's birthplace now houses **Junipero Serra Museum**, a handsome Spanish Colonial structure containing an excellent collection of American Indian and Spanish artifacts from California's pioneer days and relics from the Royal Presidio dig sites. Closed Monday. Admission. ~ Presidio Drive; 619-297-3258.

Within five years after Father Serra dedicated the first of California's 21 missions, the site had become much too small for the growing numbers it served. So **Mission San Diego de Alcala** was moved from Presidio Hill six miles east into Mission Valley. Surrounded now by shopping centers and suburban homes, the "Mother of Missions" retains its simple but striking white adobe facade topped by a graceful campanile. There's a museum containing mission records in Junípero Serra's handwriting and a lovely courtyard with gnarled pepper trees. Admission. ~ 10818 San Diego Mission Road; 619-281-8449.

LODGING   For a choice of several motels ranging from budget to deluxe, try looking for accommodations along **Hotel Circle**, on the north side of Presidio Park. The road loops under a portion of Route 8.

A good bet in the lower price categories is the appropriately named **Old Town Inn**. Strolling distance from Old Town, and across from the Old Town Transit Center (the transportation hub), this spiffy little 84-room family-owned motel has two types of rooms: the economy units and the handicapped-accessible deluxe rooms, which have full kitchens. A guest laundry, a pool, and a jacuzzi round things out. A deluxe continental breakfast is served in the breakfast room. ~ 4444 Pacific Highway; 619-260-8024, 800-643-3025, fax 619-296-0524. BUDGET TO MODERATE.

OLD TOWN VICTORIANA

About one and a half blocks east of Old Town lies **Heritage Park**, an area dedicated to the preservation of the city's Victorian past. Seven historic 1880-era houses and an old Jewish temple have been moved to the hillside site and beautifully restored. ~ Juan and Harney streets.

For the romantic, **Heritage Park Inn**, a storybook 1889 Queen Anne mansion with a striking turret, is an enchanting bed and breakfast. Set on a grassy hillside, it provides a tranquil escape. Choose from 12 distinctive chambers (all with private baths), each furnished with museum-quality antiques. Most feature ornate brass or four-poster canopy beds and old-fashioned quilts. ~ 2470 Heritage Park Row; 619-299-6832, 800-995-2470, fax 619-299-9465; e-mail innkeeper@heritageparkinn.com. MODERATE TO ULTRA-DELUXE.

Mexican food and atmosphere abound in Old Town, especially in the popular Bazaar del Mundo. Here two restaurants lure a steady stream of diners into festive, flowered courtyards. **Casa de Pico** is a great place to sit and munch cheese nachos and sip margaritas. Mexican entrées are served outside or in one of the hacienda-style dining rooms. ~ 2754 Calhoun Street; 619-296-3267. BUDGET TO MODERATE.

Next door, in a magnificent 1829 hacienda, **Casa de Bandini**, you will find the cuisine a bit more refined. Seafood is good here, especially the crab enchiladas, and the health-conscious will like the low-fat menu. Mariachis often play at both restaurants. ~ Mason and Juan streets; 619-297-8211. BUDGET TO MODERATE.

Two Old Town charmers provide satisfying diversions from a Mexican diet. **Berta's** specializes in Latin American cuisine. *Vatapa* (coconut sauce over mahimahi, scallops, and shrimp) and *cansado* (a plate of pinto beans, rice, salsa, plantain, and green salad) are wonderfully prepared. Closed Monday. ~ 3928 Twigg Street; 619-295-2343. MODERATE.

Café Pacífica rates equally high marks for a creative menu of fresh fish specialties including Hawaiian ahi tuna with shiitake mushrooms in a ginger butter sauce. Stylish but comfortable environs include a patio under a removable roof and a friendly bar. Dinner only. ~ 2414 San Diego Avenue; 619-291-6666. MODERATE TO DELUXE.

Less than a mile from Old Town lies a pair of excellent ethnic take-out shops that few visitors ever find. **El Indio** opened in 1940 as a family-operated *tortillería*, then added an informal restaurant serving quesadillas, enchiladas, tostadas, burritos, tacos, and taquitos (or "little tacos"). Quality homemade Mexican food at Taco Bell prices; you can sit indoors, out on the patio, or order to go. Open for breakfast, lunch, and dinner. ~ 3695 India Street; 619-299-0333. BUDGET.

Another one-of-a-kind fast-food operation with an equally fervent following, **Saffron Chicken** cooks up some zesty Thai grilled chicken on a special rotisserie. The aroma is positively exquisite and so is the chicken served with jasmine rice, Cambodian salad, and the five tangy sauces. Eat on an adjacent patio or take a picnic to the beach. Also, next door is **Saffron Noodles**, owned by the same restauranteurs. ~ 3731-B India Street; 619-574-0177. BUDGET TO MODERATE.

SHOPPING   Historic Old Town is blessed with several exciting bazaars and shopping squares. By far the grandest is the **Bazaar del Mundo**, Old Town's version of the famous marketplaces of Spain and Mexico. Adobe casitas house a variety of international shops. Here **Fabrics and Finery** (619-296-3161) unfurls cloth, beads, and craft accessories from all around the world, and **Ariana** (619-296-4989) features wearable art. ~ Calhoun Street between Twigg and Juan streets.

A haven for art lovers is **Spanish Village Center**. Over 35 studios are staffed by artists displaying their work. For sale are original paintings, sculpture, photographs, ceramics, jewelry, and gems. ~ 1770 Village Place, near the San Diego Zoo entrance; 619-233-9050.

NIGHTLIFE   The prevailing culture in Old Town is Mexican, as in mariachis and margaritas. The **Old Town Mexican Café y Cantina**, a festive, friendly establishment, has a patio bar. ~ 2489 San Diego Avenue; 619-297-4330.

O'Hungry's, a nearby restaurant, features a classic-rock guitarist nightly. ~ 2547 San Diego Avenue; 619-298-0133.

For country-and-western dancing, try **In Cahoots**, which has free dance lessons every night but Wednesday. There are also occasional live acts. Cover Wednesday through Sunday. ~ 5373 Mission Center Road; 619-291-8635.

▼▼▼▼▼▼▼▼▼▼▼▼▼▼▼▼▼
South San Diego County

Linking downtown with the Mexican border city of Tijuana, 20 miles south, a string of seaside cities straddle Route 5. While thriving as manufacturing, commercial, and residential communities, Imperial Beach, Chula Vista, and National City are beginning to develop as tourist industries.

SIGHTS   The **Chula Vista Nature Center** is located in the Sweetwater National Wildlife Refuge on San Diego Bay and, through interactive exhibits especially appealing to children, offers a close-up look at the history and geology of Southern California wetlands. Admission. ~ 1000 Gunpowder Point Drive; Chula Vista; 619-422-2473.

Visitors to Chula Vista also have an opportunity to glimpse Olympic athletes in training at the ARCO **Olympic Training Center**. Guided tours are conducted from the visitors center hourly, Monday through Saturday, from 9 a.m. to 3:30 p.m., and on Sunday, from noon to 3:30 p.m. ~ 2800 Olympic Parkway, Chula Vista; 619-656-1500.

Along this southern coastline is the **Tijuana River National Estuary Research Reserve**, which comprises the county's largest and most pristine estuarine sanctuary (Tijuana Slough National Wildlife Refuge) and a three-mile stretch of sandy beach (Border Field State Park). For nature lovers, this haven of salt marsh and sand dunes is a must-see diversion: more than 370 species of birds are found there. The visitors center features exhibits and a library. Trails lead to the beach and wildlife refuge at this fascinating wetland (see the "Beaches & Parks" and "Hiking" sections for more information). Visitors center is closed Monday and Tuesday; Border Field State Park is closed Monday through Wednesday. ~ Visitors center: 301 Caspian Way, Imperial Beach; see "South San Diego County Beaches & Parks" for directions to the state park; 619-575-3613.

LODGING

Among all those identical motels grouped around the freeway exits in Chula Vista, **The Traveler Inn Suites** is your best bet. Conveniently located just a block from the highway, this family-owned 85-unit motel is early Holiday Inn throughout, but its rates hark back to 1960s. Not that you would really expect them, but extras include two pools, laundry facilities, and color cable TV. Continental breakfast is served. ~ 235 Woodlawn Avenue, Chula Vista; 619-427-9170, fax 619-427-5247. MODERATE.

The **Seacoast Inn** is the only hostelry located directly on the sands of Imperial Beach. Decked out with a heated outdoor pool and hot tub, this 38-room complex looks good inside and out. Beachside units are especially nice and have full kitchens. It helps to make summer reservations well in advance. ~ 800 Seacoast Drive, Imperial Beach; 619-424-5183, 800-732-2627, fax 619-424-3090; www.pacificahost.com. MODERATE TO DELUXE.

DINING

La Bella Pizza Garden is like an annex to Chula Vista's town hall, and owner Kitty Raso is known as the "Mayor of Third Avenue." But the food will interest you far more than the latest political gossip. Besides pizza, there's great lasagna, rigatoni, and ravioli. La Bella features tender veal dishes, too, from a menu that amazingly rarely strays beyond budget prices. It's the best Italian food for the money in the San Diego area, and it's open from 7 a.m. to 1 a.m. every day. ~ 373 3rd Avenue, Chula Vista; 619-426-8820. BUDGET.

Another good bet for low-cost dining with an international twist lies just up the *strasse* at **House of Munich**. Here the traditional German dishes include wienerschnitzel, potato pancakes, sauerbraten, potato dill soup, and bratwurst. For dessert, try the traditional apple strudel! With its lace tablecloths and European feel, this eatery is wonderfully authentic. Brunch on Sunday, no

Text continued on page 478.

South of the Border

Tijuana, a favorite day-trip destination for San Diego visitors, has been amazingly transformed in recent years from a bawdy bordertown to a modern, bustling city of more than two million people. Gone, or very well hidden, are the borderline attractions that once lured sailors and marines. In their place is a colorful center of tourism suitable for the entire family.

A major revitalization effort brought highrise buildings, broad boulevards, huge shopping centers, and classy shops and restaurants. But don't get the idea Tijuana has become completely Americanized. It still retains much of its traditional Mexican flavor and offers visitors an exciting outing and some surprising cultural experiences.

Perhaps the most impressive attraction, ideal for learning about Mexico, is the **Centro Cultural Tijuana**. Here the striking 85-foot-high Omnimax Space Theater is a silvery sphere held up by a stylized hand that symbolizes the earth housing a world of culture. Inside, the giant 180° screen carries viewers on a journey through various films pertaining to Mexico. The complex, designed by Pedro Ramírez Váquez, architect of Mexico City's famous Anthropological Museum, houses four exhibit halls and a multilevel cultural and historical museum. Admission. ~ Paseo de los Héroes at Calle Mina; 52-66-84-11-11.

Three blocks away from Avenida Revolución, on a rooftop above a parking garage (look for a giant glass piñata), is **Mexitlán**, an outdoor museum of Mexico in miniature. There's a breathtaking display of more than 200 scale models of the country's greatest architectural achievements, including temples, churches, and monuments. Admission. ~ Avenida Ocampo at Calle 2; 52-66-38-41-01.

No doubt a major reason to visit "TJ" is to shop. The central shopping district is downtown, along Avenida Revolución, where arcades, stalls, and hawkers line the boulevard promoting the usual selection of tourist trinkets, piñatas, colorful flowers, serapes, pottery, and lace. There are numerous shops featuring quality merchandise such as leather goods, designer clothes, perfumes, artwork, and jewelry at incredible savings. **Sara's Imports** has ladies designer fashions and perfumes. ~ Avenida Revolución No. 635 at Calle 4a; 52-66-85-76-85. **Tolan-Arte de México** offers authentic Mexican folk art and fashions. ~ Avenida Revolución between Calles 7 and 8; 52-66-88-36-37.

American currency is accepted everywhere but small bills are recommended since getting change can sometimes be a problem. U.S. residents receive a duty and federal tax exemption on the first $400 in personal goods purchased in Mexico. One liter of alcoholic beverage is allowed for those 21 years and older.

Spectator sports are an exciting and popular pastime for Tijuana visitors, including video horse racing and greyhound racing at **Caliente Race Track**. ~ Boulevard Agua Caliente, 52-66-81-78-11 in Tijuana; 619-231-1919 from San Diego. Catch a colorful bullfight at **Toreo de Tijuana**. ~ Boulevard Agua Caliente. Or try **Plaza Monumental**. ~ Located six miles west via Highway 1D. Call **Five Star Tours** for tickets and information. ~ 619-232-5049.

Call the **Baja Visitors Information** for information about all events. You can also visit their office in Mission Valley and pick up helpful literature. ~ 7860 Mission Center Court, Suite 202; 619-298-4105.

Tijuana has some exceptional restaurants. **La Costa** serves succulent seafood in a quiet, comfortable atmosphere. ~ Calle 7a between Avenida Revolución and Avenida Constitución; 52-66-85-84-94. Try dinner at the restaurant that invented the Caesar salad: **Caesar's**. Made according to the original recipe. ~ Avenida Revolución 827; 52-66-88-27-94. The **Tijuana Chamber of Commerce Tourism Information** will provide visitors with a wealth of information on the city's shops and restaurants. ~ Corner of Avenida Primera and Avenida Revolución; 52-66-85-84-72.

Should you decide to stay longer than a day, enjoy Tijuana's stylish hotel, **The Grand Hotel Tijuana**. This 422-room luxury complex boasts dramatic city views from its 25-story glass towers and offers four restaurants, three bars, a disco, a gallery of shops, tennis courts, swimming pool, and a health club. ~ Boulevard Agua Caliente No. 4500, 52-66-81-70-00, 706-681-7000 in Tijuana; 800-472-6385 in San Diego. MODERATE.

Just a little farther south of Tijuana, located right along the coast, the small towns of Rosarito Beach and Ensenada provide a less commercial glimpse of Mexico. A modern highway makes the trip easy and comfortable.

If you venture down south, remember to bring your valid passport or identification for return to the U.S. and a copy of *Hidden Baja* (Ulysses Press, 1998). If you do not want to drive across the border, you can take a trolley to the border, walk on a pedestrian overpass across the International border, and then take a taxi into town for about $5 per person.

lunch Saturday; closed Monday. ~ 230 3rd Avenue, Chula Vista; 619-426-5172. MODERATE.

SHOPPING

Plaza Bonita in National City is a modern mall with four department stores and a range of smaller outlets. ~ 3030 Plaza Bonita Road, National City; 619-267-2851.

Chula Vista's newly renovated downtown is highlighted by **Park Plaza at the Village Shopping Plaza.** Here 20 stores, including fashion and specialty shops, cluster around a central court. In addition, the shopping district on 3rd Avenue between E and H streets is a charming mix of long-standing family businesses and quality shops. ~ 310 3rd Avenue, Chula Vista; 619-282-6814.

NIGHTLIFE

If you're looking for nighttime entertainment in these areas, you'll probably want to consider a trip to the city. Otherwise be content with scattered restaurant bars and local pubs. There's a notable exception: **Marisol's Million Dollar Club.** A sports bar by day, this nightclub heats up the dancefloor with salsa and other Latin styles. Cover. ~ 1680 Broadway, Suites A–C, Chula Vista; 619-429-8045.

BEACHES & PARKS

SILVER STRAND STATE BEACH 🏊 🏄 ⛵ This two-mile strip of fluffy white sand fronts a narrow isthmus separating the Pacific Ocean and San Diego Bay. It was named for tiny silver sea shells found in abundance along the shore. The water here is shallow and fairly calm on the ocean side, making it a good swimming beach. Things are even calmer and the water much warmer on the bay shore. Silver Strand State Beach is also popular for surf fishing and shell hunting. Facilities include picnic areas, restrooms, lifeguards, showers, food concessions, and equipment rentals. Day-use fee, $4. ~ Located on Route 75 (Silver Strand Boulevard) and Coronado Caves Boulevard between Imperial Beach and Coronado; 619-435-5184.

▲ There are 138 sites for RVs and trailers (no hookups); $16 per night.

IMPERIAL BEACH 🏊 🏄 🎣 ⛵ A wide, sandy beach, popular at the south end with surfers; boogie-boarders and swimmers ply the waters between the two jetties farther north, just past the renovated fishing pier. The crowd is mostly young with many military personnel. Each July Imperial Beach hosts the annual U.S. Open Sandcastle Competition, attracting huge crowds. There are restrooms and lifeguards. There is also a deli nearby. Surfing is very popular on both sides of the pier and rock jetties. ~ Take Palm Avenue exit west off Route 5 all the way to the water.

BORDER FIELD STATE PARK 🚶 🚴 🐎 🏊 ⛵ True to its name, this oceanfront park within the Tijuana River National Estuarine

Research Reserve actually borders on Mexico. It features a three-mile-long stretch of sandy beach, backed by dunes and salt marshes studded with daisies and chaparral. Equestrian and hiking trails crisscross this unsullied wetlands area which adjoins a federal wildlife refuge at the mouth of the Tijuana River. Sounds idyllic except for the constant racket from Border Patrol helicopters and the ever-present threat of untreated sewage drifting north from Mexico. Restrooms and picnic areas are available, and a visitors center houses exhibits and a library. Fishing and swimming are not recommended because of pollution. Closed Monday through Wednesday. ~ Take the Dairy Mart Road exit off Route 5 and go west. The name changes to Monument Road about a mile before reaching the park entrance. The visitors center is at 301 Caspian Way, Imperial Beach; 619-575-3613.

The lure of sport and bottom fishing attracts thousands of enthusiasts to San Diego every year. Yellowtail, barracuda, bonita, and sea bass are the close-in favorites, with marlin, dorado and tuna the prime objectives for longer charters. Most outfitters provide bait and tackle.

▼▼▼▼▼▼▼▼▼▼▼▼▼

Outdoor Adventures

SPORT-FISHING

For deep-sea and local sportfishing, contact **Helgren's Sportfishing**; five-day excursions lead down into Mexico. ~ 315 Harbor Drive South, Oceanside; 760-722-2133. **Seaforth Sportfishing** uses 36- to 85-foot boats for their runs. Longer trips head out to Mexican waters for albacore. ~ 1717 Quivira Road, Mission Bay; 619-224-3383. **Islandia Sportfishing** offers trips for albacore, mackerel, and skipjack. ~ 1551 West Mission Bay Drive, Mission Bay; 619-222-1164. **Coronado Boat Rentals** provides half- and full-day charters on a 38-foot Uniflight. Maximum group of six. ~ 1715 Strand Way, Coronado; 619-437-1514. **H & M Landing** arranges half-day jaunts to local kelp beds or 18-day expeditions past the tip of Baja for giant yellowfin tuna. ~ 2803 Emerson Street, Point Loma; 619-222-1144. Call **Fish 'N Cruise** for custom-designed charters. ~ 1231 Shafter Street, San Diego; 619-224-2464. **Point Loma Sportfishing** has a fleet of 10 boats. Their day trip goes down to Mexico for tuna. ~ 1403 Scott Street, Point Loma; 619-223-1627. Also in Point Loma is **Fisherman's Landing**, which takes groups of 6 to 35 on fishing excursions. The 23-day charter winds up in Cabo San Lucas. ~ 2838 Garrison Street, Point Loma; 619-222-0391.

Spearfishing is very popular off La Jolla beaches, especially south of La Jolla Cove. Contact **San Diego Divers Supply** for supplies, tours, and information. They also offer Coronado Island dive trips. ~ 4004 Sports Arena Boulevard, San Diego; 619-224-3439. *Note:* Spearfishing is not allowed in protected reserves from La Jolla Cove north.

WHALE-
WATCHING
The stately progress of our fellow mammalian creatures in migration is a wonderful sight to behold. A free whale-watching station at Cabrillo National Monument on Point Loma features a glassed-in observatory. To get an even closer look at these mammoth cetaceans, book a charter with one of the many whale-watching companies; most outfitters guarantee marine sightings. The season runs from late December through late February (mid-January is the best time).

Helgren's Sportfishing sets sail from mid-December through March—that's when you'll see California gray whales. ~ 315 Harbor Drive South, Oceanside; 760-722-2133. **Islandia Sportfishing** serves the Mission Bay area, accommodating up to 147 guests. ~ 1551 West Mission Bay Drive, Mission Bay; 619-222-1164. In Point Loma, **H & M Landing** takes you out on 60- to 85-foot boats in search of whales. ~ 2803 Emerson Street, Point Loma; 619-222-1144. **Point Loma Sportfishing** offers three-hour trips through local waters. ~ 1403 Scott Street, Point Loma; 619-223-1627. **San Diego Harbor Excursion** provides three-hour whale-watching tours during winter. ~ 1050 North Harbor Drive; 619-234-4111.

DIVING
San Diego offers countless spots for skindiving. The rocky La Jolla coves boast the clearest water on the California coast. Bird Rock, La Jolla Underwater Park, and the underwater Scripp's Canyon are ideal havens for scuba and skindivers. In Point Loma try the colorful tidepools at Cabrillo Underwater Reserve; at "No Surf Beach" (Sunset Cliff Boulevard) pools and reefs are for experienced divers only.

For diving rentals, sales, instruction, and tips, contact **Underwater Schools of America**. ~ 707 Oceanside Boulevard, Oceanside; 760-722-7826. **San Diego Shark Diving Expeditions** offers three-day trips to San Clemente Island to dive within the safety of a shark cage and observe (or film) free-swimming blue and mako sharks. For the less adventurous, there are two-tank trips to kelp beds or Wreck Alley and three-tank trips to the Coronado Islands. Reservations are a must. ~ 6747 Friar's Road #112, San Diego. **Ocean Enterprises** teaches a variety of diving classes. They also have dive trips and rent and sell gear. ~ 7710 Balboa Avenue, San Diego; 619-565-6054. **Diving Locker** offers open-water certification, full-dive trips, and night dives, as well as rentals and sales. ~ 405 North Highway 101, Solana Beach; 619-755-6822. You can arrange dives with **San Diego Diver's Supply**. They also have instruction, sell gear, and do repairs. ~ 4004 Sports Arena Boulevard, San Diego, 619-224-3439. In Pacific Beach, the **Diving Locker** offers open-water certification along with a variety of dive trips. Dives at local kelp beds use two tanks; longer-range and overnight dives include spots such as Los Coronados and San

Clemente islands. They also do night dives and rent and sell gear.
~ 1020 Grand Avenue, Pacific Beach; 619-272-1120.

Surf's up in the San Diego area. Pacific, Mission, and Ocean   **SURFING**
beaches, Tourmaline Surfing Park, and Windansea, La Jolla
Shores, Swami, and Moonlight beaches are well-known hangouts for surfers. Sailboarding is concentrated within Mission Bay.
Oceanside is home to annual world-class boogie-board and surfing competitions.

For surfboard, bodyboard, wetsuit, and snorkel rentals and
sales, try **Mitch's**. ~ 631 Pearl Street, La Jolla; 619-459-5933.
Surfrider rents and sells surfboards, boogieboards, bodyboards,
fins, and wetsuits. ~ 1909 South Coast Highway 101, Oceanside;
760-433-4020. **Hanson's** offers lessons on softboards (surfboards
for beginners) and rents recreational gear such as kayaks, snorkel
equipment, surfboards, and bodyboards, as well as wetsuits. ~
1105 South Coast Highway 101, Encinitas; 760-753-6595. **C. P.
Water Sports** has rentals and lessons for "every watersport imaginable." ~ 1775 East Mission Bay Drive, Mission Bay; 619-275-
8945. Surfboards, boogieboards, and sailboards are available at
Mission Bay Sportscenter. They have wetsuits and surfing instruction as well. ~ 1010 Santa Clara Place, Mission Bay; 619-488-
1004.

You can sail under the Coronado Bridge, skirt the gorgeous   **BOATING
downtown skyline, and even get a taste of open ocean in this   & SAILING**
Southern California sailing mecca.

Several sailing companies operate out of Harbor Island West
in San Diego, including **Harbor Sailboats**. They offer instruction
as well as sailboat rentals. ~ 2040 Harbor Island Drive, Suite
104, San Diego; 619-291-9568. For sailboat rentals and party
yacht charters, try **San Diego Yacht Charters**. ~ 1880 Harbor

---

✔ CHECK THESE OUT—UNIQUE OUTDOOR ADVENTURES

- Peer into the clearest water on the California coast when you dive in the
  La Jolla coves, where world-class oceanographers train. *page 480*
- Soar out over the ocean from a bluff at Torrey Pines, where the buf-
  feting breezes make conditions prime for hang gliding pros. *page 482*
- Lift a glass of champagne over the Del Mar Valley in a hot-air balloon as the sun sinks into the Pacific. *page 482*
- Hike the beautiful Bayside Trail in Cabrillo National Monument,
  which leads from the restored Old Point Loma Lighthouse
  through rolling coastal terrain with sweeping vistas. *page 485*

Island Drive, San Diego; 619-297-4555. You can also charter, rent, or learn from the **San Diego Sailing Club and School**. ~ 1880 Harbor Island Drive, San Diego; 619-298-6623.

Kayak, motorboat, and sailboat rentals can be found at **C. P. Water Sports**, where they also teach sailing. ~ 1775 East Mission Bay Drive, Mission Bay; 619-276-4010. **Mission Bay Sportscenter** has the same options, as well as waterski instruction. ~ 1010 Santa Clara Place, Mission Bay; 619-488-1004. **Seaforth Mission Bay Boat Rental** rents motorboats, sailboats, paddleboats, canoes, and kayaks. ~ Located at 1641 Quivira Road, Mission Bay; 619-223-1681. **Coronado Boat Rentals** has motorboats and sailboats. ~ 1715 Strand Way, Coronado; 619-437-1514.

Yacht charters are available through **Hornblower Dining Yachts**. ~ 1066 North Harbor, San Diego; 619-234-8687.

HANG GLIDING

Torrey Pines Glider Port is an expert-rated hang gliding site, located atop a towering sandstone bluff overlooking Black's Beach. Lesson packages and half-hour tandem flights are available. If you're not yet an expert, there is a great vantage point to watch from. ~ 2800 Torrey Pines Scenic Drive, La Jolla; 619-452-9858.

BALLOON RIDES

Hot-air ballooning is a romantic pursuit that has soared in popularity in the Del Mar area. A growing number of ballooning companies provide spectacular dawn and sunset flights.

Contact **A Skysurfer Balloon Company** for daily, one-hour sunset flights over the coastal valley area. The three-and-a-half-hour affair includes on-board champagne and soft drinks, and concludes with an after-flight hors d'oeuvres celebration. Choose between 6- and 12-person balloons. ~ 1221 Camino Del Mar, Del Mar; 619-481-6800.

GOLF

You don't have to look far for a green to practice your swing. Most courses in San Diego rent clubs and carts so you're in luck if you didn't plan ahead.

The 18-hole **Emerald Isle Golf Course** is a public executive green. ~ 660 El Camino Real, Oceanside; 760-721-4700. Tee off at **Oceanside Golf Course**, a public, 18-hole course. At the 13th hole, take a minute to admire the view of rolling hills and majestic mountains. ~ 825 Douglas Drive, Oceanside; 760-433-1360. You'll have to caddy your clubs by pull cart at the executive, public **Rancho Carlsbad Golf Course**, a par-56, 18-hole green. ~ 5200 El Camino Real, Carlsbad; 760-438-1772. In Rancho Sante Fe, try the semiprivate **Morgan Run Golf Course**, where there are three nine-hole greens. ~ 5690 Cancha de Golf, Rancho Santa Fe; 619-756-2471.

Beautiful **Torrey Pines Municipal Golf Course** is famous for its two 18-hole, par-72 championship courses. ~ 11480 North Torrey Pines Road, La Jolla; 619-570-1234.

A duffer's delight, the 18-hole **Balboa Park Municipal Golf Course** is a par-72 championship course. It also features a nine-hole intermediate course. ~ Golf Course Drive, Balboa Park; 619-235-1184.

Mission Bay Golf Resort is a public, 18-hole course. ~ 2702 North Mission Bay Drive, Mission Bay; 619-490-3370.

The **Coronado Municipal Golf Course**, an 18-hole green, runs along Glorietta Bay. ~ 2000 Visalia Row, Coronado; 619-435-3121.

San Diego has many private and public courts open to traveling tennis buffs. Some of the nine outdoor courts at the **La Jolla Recreation Center** are lighted. ~ 615 Prospect Street, La Jolla; 619-552-1658. In Ocean Beach, try the 12 courts at **Peninsula Tennis Club**, which are outdoor and lighted. ~ 2525 Bacon Street, Ocean Beach; 619-226-3407. The **Balboa Tennis Club** has 25 outdoor courts, 19 of which are lighted. ~ 2221 Morley Field Drive, San Diego; 619-295-9278. The **Coronado Tennis Center** has eight outdoor courts, three of which are lighted. ~ 1501 Glorietta Boulevard; 619-435-1616. You'll find two unlighted courts at the **Cabrillo Recreation Center**. ~ 3051 Cañon Street, Point Loma; 619-531-1534. Three outdoor, lighted courts are found at **Mission Valley YMCA**. ~ 5505 Friars Road, Mission Valley; 619-298-3576.

TENNIS

An area just outside Imperial Beach is one of the few places in the county where you can ride on the beach. **Hilltop Stable** rents mounts for rides at Border Field State Beach. ~ 2181 Hollister Street, San Diego; 619-428-5441.

RIDING STABLES

North County's **Old Route 101** provides almost 40 miles of scintillating cycling along the coast from Oceanside to La Jolla. Traffic is heavy but bikes are almost as numerous as autos along this stretch. Bike lanes are designated along most of the route.

BIKING

Cycling has skyrocketed in popularity throughout San Diego County, especially in coastal areas. The **Mission Bay Bike Path** (18 miles) starts at the San Diego Convention Center, winds along the harbor, crosses Mission Bay, and heads up the coast to La Jolla. **Balboa Park** and **Mission Bay Park** both have excellent bike routes (see the "Balboa Park and the San Diego Zoo" and "Mission Bay Park Area" sections of this chapter).

Check with Regional Transit about their special "biker" passes.

Bike Rentals To rent a bike (mountain, road, kid's) in downtown San Diego, contact **Pennyfarthings Bicycle Store**. ~ 314 G Street; 619-233-7696. If you're near the San Diego Convention Center, go to **The Original Bike Cab Company** for beach cruisers, three-speeds, mountain bikes, and children's bikes. All rentals include helmets, locks, and maps, as well as helpful suggestions from the friendly staff. ~ 523 Island Avenue, San Diego; 619-595-0211. **Holland's Bicycles** sells, rents, and repairs cruisers, mountain bikes, and tandems. Rentals come with helmets and locks. ~ 977 Orange Avenue at 10th Street, Coronado; 619-435-3153.

HIKING   Most of the San Diego County coastline is developed for either residential or commercial purposes, limiting the hiking possibilities. There are some protected areas set aside to preserve remnants of the county's unique coastal chaparral communities and tidelands. These reserves offer short hiking trails. Inland San Diego County, particularly in the Palomar and Laguna mountains, also provides backpacking opportunities. All distances listed are one way unless otherwise noted.

Serious hikers might also consider taking on the San Diego section of the **California Coastal Trail**. It follows the shoreline, as much as possible, from the Mexican border all the way to San Onofre State Beach.

NORTH SAN DIEGO COUNTY   Three Lagoons Trail (5 miles) originates on the beach in Leucadia and heads north along the sand past three saltwater lagoons, ending in Carlsbad. Best place to begin is at the beach parking lot at Grandview Street in Leucadia.

LA JOLLA   La Jolla Coastal Walk (1 mile), a dirt path atop La Jolla Bluffs, affords some of the most spectacular views anywhere on the San Diego County coastline. It begins on Coast Boulevard just up the hill from La Jolla Cove and continues past a sea cave accessible from the trail.

Without a doubt, the 1750-acre **Torrey Pines State Park and Reserve** offers the county's best hiking. The park was named for the world's rarest pine tree *(Pinus torreyana)* which the reserve was established to protect. An estimated 6000 of the gnarled and twisted trees cling to rugged cliffs and ravines, some growing as tall as 60 feet.

Several major trails offer hikers a variety of challenges and natural attractions. Most are easily walked loops through groves of pines, such as **Guy Fleming Trail** (.6-mile loop), which scans the coast at South and North overlooks, and **Parry Grove Trail** (.4-mile loop), which passes stands of manzanita, yucca, and other shrubs. There are more strenuous treks such as the **Razor Point Trail** (.6 mile), which follows the Canyon of the Swifts, then links up with the **Beach Trail** (.8 mile); and the south fork of **Broken Hill Trail** (1.3 miles), which zigzags to the coast past chamiso and scrub oak (the north fork is 1.2 miles).

Del Mar Beach Trail (3 miles) leads from the Del Mar Amtrak Station along the beach past flatrock tidepools and up to the bluffs of Torrey Pines State Reserve.

POINT LOMA AREA Cabrillo National Monument offers the Bayside Trail (1 mile). It begins at the Old Point Loma Lighthouse, beautifully restored to its original 1855 condition, and meanders through the heart of a scenic coastal chaparral community. A wide variety of native plants including prickly pear cactus, yucca, buckwheat, and Indian paintbrush grow along the path. In addition to stunning views of San Diego, there are some remnants of the coastal defense system built here during World Wars I and II. ~ 619-557-5450.

SOUTH SAN DIEGO COUNTY Four miles of hiking trails crisscross the dunes and marshes of the largely undeveloped **Tijuana River National Estuarine Research Reserve**, which forms the coastal border between the United States and Mexico. Trails lead through dunes anchored by salt grass, pickleweed, and sand verbena. The marshy areas, especially those in the wildlife refuge around the Tijuana River estuary, provide feeding and nesting grounds for several hundred species of native and migratory birds, including hawks, pelicans, plovers, terns, and ducks.

Border Field to Tijuana River Trail (1.5 miles) is a level beach walk past sand dunes and the Tijuana River Estuary.

Transportation

Even though it is located in California's extreme southwest corner, San Diego is the hub of an elaborate highway network. The city is easily reached from north or south via **Route 5**; **Route 8** serves drivers from the east; and **Route 15** is the major inland freeway for travelers arriving from the mountain west.

CAR

San Diego International Airport (Lindbergh Field) lies just three miles northwest of downtown San Diego and is easily accessible from either Route 5 or Route 8. The airport is served by most major airlines, including America West Airlines, American Airlines, Continental Airlines, Delta Airlines, Northwest Airlines, Reno Air, Skywest, Southwest Airlines, TWA, United Airlines, and USAir.

AIR

Taxis, limousines, and buses provide service from the airport. **San Diego Transit System** bus #992 carries passengers to downtown. ~ 619-233-3004. Or try the **Southwest Shuttle** which travels to major points in the city as well as to Orange County and Los Angeles. ~ 619-231-1123.

Greyhound Bus Lines (800-231-2222) services San Diego from around the country. The terminal is downtown at 120 West Broadway and 1st Avenue; 619-239-3266. There's also an Oceanside station at 205 South Tremont Street; 760-722-1587.

BUS

Chugging to a stop at historic Santa Fe Depot, at Kettner Boulevard and Broadway downtown, is a nice and convenient way to

TRAIN

arrive in San Diego. **Amtrak** offers several coast-hugging round-trips daily between Los Angeles and San Diego, with stops at Oceanside and Solano Beach. ~ 800-872-7245.

CAR RENTALS

Much like the rest of Southern California, San Diego is spread out over a wide area and is best seen by car. Car rental companies abound. Most major rental agencies have franchises at the airport. These include **Avis Rent A Car** (800-831-2847), **Dollar Rent A Car** (800-800-4000), **Hertz Rent A Car** (800-654-3131), and **National Interrent** (800-227-7368).

For better rates (but less convenient service) try agencies located near the airport that provide pick-up service: **Aztec Rent A Car** (800-231-0400), **Thrifty Car Rental** (800-367-2277), **Rent A Wreck** (800-535-1391) or (619-280-7244), and **Budget Rent A Car** (800-527-0700).

PUBLIC TRANSIT

North County Transit District, or NCTD, covers the general area from Camp Pendleton to Del Mar along the coast. NCTD operates numerous North County bus routes that service the communities of Oceanside, Carlsbad, Encinitas, Leucadia, Cardiff, Rancho Santa Fe, Solana Beach, and Del Mar. ~ 760-722-6283 or 619-233-3004.

Several modern and efficient public transportation systems operate throughout San Diego. Information and schedules are available for all systems by calling **Regional Transit**. ~ 619-233-3004.

The Regional Transit bus system is the city's largest public transportation network, with lines linking all major points. All Regional Transit stops are marked with a blue rectangle.

The city's most venturesome mode of public transportation is the **San Diego Trolley**. The light rail system's line operates daily from the Santa Fe Depot to the Mexican border. Understandably, this line is known as the "Tijuana Trolley," or the "blue line." It also serves the south bay cities of National City, Chula Vista, and Imperial Beach. The East Line, also departing from the Santa Fe Depot, serves southeastern San Diego and inland communities to El Cajon. The Mission Valley Line runs from Santa Fe Depot to the Fashion Vallet Transit Center in Mission Valley, stopping at points in between. ~ 619-233-3004.

National City Transit serves National City. ~ 619-233-3004. **Chula Vista Transit** serves Bonita and the city of Chula Vista. ~ 619-233-3004. ATC/Vancom runs from downtown San Diego to National City and Chula Vista and on to the San Ysidro international border. In addition, ATC/Vancom runs from Coronado along the Silver Strand to Imperial Beach. ~ 619-233-3004.

TAXIS

In North County (Del Mar to Carlsbad), you can call **Bill's Cab** (619-755-6737) or **Oceanside Yellow Cab** 760-722-4217).

San Diego is not a taxi town in the usual big-city sense, but there's a cab if you need it—just a phone call away. Leading companies include **Silver Cabs** (619-280-5555), **Yellow Cab** (619-234-6161), **Orange Cab** (619-291-3333), and **USA Cab** (619-231-1144).

Several San Diego organizations and tour operators offer organized walks: **Gaslamp Quarter Historical Foundation** conducts two-hour, docent-led walking tours of the restored downtown historic district. ~ 410 Island Avenue, corner of 4th and Island; 619-233-4692.

WALKING TOURS

Walking tours of **Old Town State Historic Park** are offered daily at 2 p.m. through park headquarters. ~ 4002 Wallace Street; 619-220-5423.

Join **Coronado Touring** for a one-and-a-half-hour leisurely guided stroll through quaint Coronado. Tours leave from the Glorietta Bay Inn (1630 Glorietta Boulevard) at 11 a.m. on Tuesday, Thursday, and Saturday. ~ 1110 Isabella Avenue, Coronado 92118; 619-435-5993, 619-435-5444.

Index

Lodging Index

Dining Index

HIDDEN GUIDES

Adventure travel or a relaxing vacation?—"Hidden" guidebooks are the only travel books in the business to provide detailed information on both. Aimed at environmentally aware travelers, our motto is "Adventure Travel Plus." These books combine details on unique hotels, restaurants and sightseeing with information on camping, sports and hiking for the outdoor enthusiast.

THE NEW KEY GUIDES

Based on the concept of ecotourism, The New Key Guides are dedicated to the preservation of Central America's rare and endangered species, architecture and archaeology. Filled with helpful tips, they give travelers everything they need to know about these exotic destinations.

ULTIMATE FAMILY GUIDES

These innovative guides present the best and most unique features of a family destination. Quality is the keynote. In addition to thoroughly covering each destination, they feature short articles and one-line "teasers" that are both fun and informative.

Ulysses Press books are available at bookstores everywhere. If any of the following titles are unavailable at your local bookstore, ask the bookseller to order them.

You can also order books directly from Ulysses Press
P.O. Box 3440, Berkeley, CA 94703
800-377-2542 or 510-601-8301
fax: 510-601-8307
e-mail: ulysses@ulyssespress.com

Order Form

HIDDEN GUIDEBOOKS

____ Hidden Arizona, $14.95

____ Hidden Bahamas, $12.95

____ Hidden Baja, $14.95

____ Hidden Boston and Cape Cod, $13.95

____ Hidden Cancún & the Yucatán, $16.95

____ Hidden Carolinas, $17.95

____ Hidden Coast of California, $17.95

____ Hidden Colorado, $13.95

____ Hidden Florida, $17.95

____ Hidden Florida Keys & Everglades, $11.95

____ Hidden Georgia, $14.95

____ Hidden Hawaii, $17.95

____ Hidden Idaho, $13.95

____ Hidden Maui, $12.95

____ Hidden Montana, $14.95

____ Hidden New England, $17.95

____ Hidden New Mexico, $14.95

____ Hidden Oahu, $12.95

____ Hidden Oregon, $14.95

____ Hidden Pacific Northwest, $17.95

____ Hidden Rockies, $16.95

____ Hidden San Francisco and Northern California, $17.95

____ Hidden Southern California, $17.95

____ Hidden Southwest, $17.95

____ Hidden Tahiti, $17.95

____ Hidden Tennessee, $15.95

____ Hidden Washington, $14.95

____ Hidden Wyoming, $14.95

THE NEW KEY GUIDEBOOKS

____ The New Key to Belize, $14.95

____ The New Key to Costa Rica, $17.95

____ The New Key to Guatemala, $14.95

____ The New Key to Ecuador and the Galápagos, $16.95

ULTIMATE FAMILY GUIDEBOOKS

____ Disneyland and Beyond, $12.95

____ Disney World and Beyond, $13.95

Mark the book(s) you're ordering and enter the total cost here ⇨ [   ]

California residents add 8% sales tax here ⇨ [   ]

Shipping, check box for your preferred method and enter cost here ⇨ [   ]

☐ BOOK RATE   **FREE! FREE! FREE!**

☐ PRIORITY MAIL $3.00 First book, $1.00/each additional book

☐ UPS 2-DAY AIR $7.00 First book, $1.00/each additional book   [   ]

Billing, enter total amount due here and check method of payment ⇨ [   ]

☐ CHECK   ☐ MONEY ORDER

☐ VISA/MASTERCARD_____EXP. DATE _____

NAME _____PHONE _____

ADDRESS_____

_____

CITY_____ STATE _____ ZIP_____

MONEY-BACK GUARANTEE ON DIRECT ORDERS PLACED THROUGH ULYSSES PRESS.

ABOUT THE AUTHOR

RAY RIEGERT is the author of seven travel books, including *Hidden Southern California*. His most popular work, *Hidden Hawaii*, won the coveted Lowell Thomas Travel Journalism Award for Best Guidebook. In addition to his role as publisher of Ulysses Press, he has written for the *Chicago Tribune*, *Saturday Evening Post*, *San Francisco Examiner and Chronicle*, and *Travel & Leisure*. A member of the Society of American Travel Writers, he lives in the San Francisco Bay area with his wife, co-publisher Leslie Henriques, and their son Keith and daughter Alice.

ABOUT THE UPDATE AUTHOR

STEPHEN DOLAINSKI, former editor-in-chief of *Guest Informant* and a regular contributor to *Westways* and *Avenues*, is a freelance travel editor and writer living in Southern California. He has written about travel, culture, the arts, entertainment and business for magazines, and has contributed to several travel guidebooks, including *Hidden Southern California* and *Disneyland and Beyond*.

ABOUT THE ILLUSTRATOR

VICTOR ICHIOKA, son of Japanese parents who immigrated to California, holds a master's degree in painting from the University of California. He has illustrated a book of Jamaican short stories as well as books on fly-fishing and restaurants. Spending his spare time painting and combing the coast, Victor lives in Berkeley, California, with his wife Marilyn and their children, Sarah and Michael.